AF183707

Lecture Notes in Computer Science

Lecture Notes in Bioinformatics 16690

The series Lecture Notes in Bioinformatics (LNBI) was established in 2003 as a topical subseries of LNCS devoted to bioinformatics and computational biology.

The series publishes state-of-the-art research results at a high level. As with the LNCS mother series, the mission of the series is to serve the international R & D community by providing an invaluable service, mainly focused on the publication of conference and workshop proceedings and postproceedings.

Xuefeng Cui · Xiujuan Lei · Yuri Porozov
Editors

Bioinformatics Research and Applications

22nd International Symposium, ISBRA 2026
Macao, China, July 22–24, 2026
Proceedings, Part I

Springer

Editors
Xuefeng Cui
Shandong University
Jinan, China

Xiujuan Lei
Shaanxi Normal University
Xi'an, China

Yuri Porozov
HSE University
Moscow, Russia

ISSN 0302-9743 ISSN 1611-3349 (electronic)
Lecture Notes in Bioinformatics
ISBN 978-981-92-3715-9 ISBN 978-981-92-3716-6 (eBook)
https://doi.org/10.1007/978-981-92-3716-6

LNCS Sublibrary: SL8 – Bioinformatics

This Springer imprint is published by the registered company Springer Nature Singapore Pte Ltd.
The registered company address is: 152 Beach Road, #21-01/04 Gateway East, Singapore 189721, Singapore

Preface

On behalf of the Program Committee, it is our great pleasure to welcome you to the 22nd International Symposium on Bioinformatics Research and Applications (ISBRA 2026), held in the vibrant city of Macau, China, July 22–24, 2026. This year's symposium brought together leading researchers, scientists, and industry professionals from around the world to share cutting-edge advancements, foster collaboration, and explore the future of bioinformatics and computational biology.

We received 168 submissions presenting original research articles across all areas of bioinformatics and computational biology. Each submission was single-blindly reviewed by at least two independent reviewers, with an average of nearly four reviewers per paper. The Program Committee selected 61 papers for full publication in the symposium proceedings.

We would like to express our sincere gratitude to all the Program Committee members and reviewers for their contributions. We also extend our special thanks to the steering committee and general chairs for their leadership and guidance throughout the organization of ISBRA 2026. We are grateful to the Macao Association of Convention, Exhibition & Tourism Sectors for their generous support in providing student travel grants to 30 students. We hope you enjoyed an exciting and inspiring symposium.

May 2026

Xuefeng Cui
Xiujuan Lei
Yuri Porozov

Organization

Organization Committee

Steering Committee

Dan Gusfield	University of California, Davis, USA
Ion Mandoiu	University of Connecticut, USA
Yi Pan (Chair)	Shenzhen University of Advanced Technology, China
Marie-France Sagot	INRIA, France
Zhirong Sun	Tsinghua University, China
Ying Xu	University of Georgia, USA
Aidong Zhang	University of Virginia, USA
Zhipeng Cai	Georgia State University, USA

General Chairs

Zhiguo Gong	University of Macau, China
Sanguthevar Rajasekaran	University of Connecticut, USA

General Vice Chairs

Le Zhang	Sichuan University, China
Yanjie Wei	Shenzhen Institutes of Advanced Technology, CAS, China

Program Co-chairs

Xuefeng Cui	Shandong University, China
Xiujuan Lei	Shaanxi Normal University, China
Yuri Porozov	HSE University, Russia

Publicity Co-chairs

Xiaowen Liu	Tulane University, USA
Jin Gu	Tsinghua University, China
Hebing Chen	Academy of Military Medical Sciences, China
Yulian Ding	Shenzhen Institutes of Advanced Technology, CAS, China

Publication Co-chairs

Wei Peng	Kunming University of Science and Technology, China
Yi Xiong	Shanghai Jiao Tong University, China
Qiao Liu	Yale University, USA

Workshop Chair

Zheng Hu	Shenzhen Institutes of Advanced Technology, CAS, China

Program Committee

Dongmei Ai	University of Science and Technology Beijing, China
Tatsuya Akutsu	Kyoto University, Japan
Max Alekseyev	George Washington University, USA
Ying An	Central South University, China
Mahua Bhattacharya	IIITM, Gwalior, India
Xuehua Bi	Xinjiang Medical University, China
Zhipeng Cai	Georgia State University, USA
Yunpeng Cai	Shenzhen Institutes of Advanced Technology, CAS, Chna
Rita Casadio	University of Bologna, Italy
Bolin Chen	Northwestern Polytechnical University, China
Hebing Chen	Academy of Military Medical Sciences, China
Hailin Chen	East China Jiaotong University, China
Xiang Chen	Central South University, China
Cheng Chen	Shandong University, China
Xing Chen	Jiangnan University, China

Jianhong Cheng	Central South University, China
Xuefeng Cui	Shandong University, China
Yingbo Cui	National University of Defense Technology, China
Alexandre G. de Brevern	INSERM - Université Paris Cité, France
Chao Deng	Central South University, China
Yulian Ding	Shenzhen Institutes of Advanced Technology, CAS, China
Pufeng Du	Tianjin University, China
Lei Du	Northwestern Polytechnical University, China
Oliver Eulenstein	Iowa State University, USA
Yongxian Fan	Guilin University of Electronic Technology, China
Jin Gu	Tsinghua University, China
Xuan Guo	University of North Texas, USA
Fei Guo	Tianjin University, China
Jincheng Guo	Beijing University of Chinese Medicine, China
Steffen Heber	North Carolina State University, USA
Kai Hu	Xiangtan University, China
Wei Jiang	Fujian Medical University, China
Jintao Meng	Shenzhen Institutes of Advanced Technology, CAS, China
Zhen Ju	University of Chinese Academy of Sciences, China
Danny Krizanc	Wesleyan University, USA
Hulin Kuang	Central South University, China
Pavel Kuksa	Rutgers University, USA
Manuel Lafond	Université de Sherbrooke, Canada
Xin Lai	Tampere University, Finland
Wei Lan	Guangxi University, China
Xiujuan Lei	Shaanxi Normal University, China
Hongdong Li	Central South University, China
Xingyi Li	Northwestern Polytechnical University, China
Xiangtao Li	Jilin University, China
Yaqiao Li	Shenzhen University, China
Yaohang Li	Old Dominion University, USA
Xingyu Liao	Northwestern Polytechnical University, China
Weiguo Liu	Shandong University, China
Jin Liu	Central South University, China
Yajun Liu	Xi'an University of Technology, China
Zhi-Ping Liu	Shandong University, China
Chengqian Lu	Xiangtan University, China
Zhilong Lv	Xidian University, China

Ion Mandoiu	University of Connecticut, USA
Serghei Mangul	University of California, Los Angeles, USA
Qiaozhen Meng	Xiangtan University, China
Xiangmao Meng	Xiangtan University, China
Wenwen Min	Yunnan University, China
Le Ou-Yang	Shenzhen MSU-BIT University, China
Murray Patterson	Georgia State University, USA
Andrei Paun	University of Bucharest, Romania
Wei Peng	Kunming University of Science and Technology, China
Xiaoqing Peng	Central South University, China
Yuri Porozov	I.M. Sechenov First Moscow State Medical University, Russia
Lianrong Pu	University of California, San Diego, USA
Russell Schwartz	Carnegie Mellon University, USA
Joao Setubal	University of São Paulo, Brazil
Junliang Shang	Qufu Normal University, China
Dan Shao	Jilin University, China
Jian-Yu Shi	Northwestern Polytechnical University, China
Mindy Shi	Temple University, USA
Chao Song	University of South China, China
Joe Song	New Mexico State University, USA
Emily Chia-Yu Su	National Yang Ming Chiao Tung University, Taiwan
Lingtao Su	Jilin University, China
Shiwei Sun	Institute of Computing Technology, CAS, China
Sing-Hoi Sze	Texas A & M University, USA
Jing Tang	University of Helsinki, Finland
Weitian Tong	Georgia Southern University, USA
Xiaohua Wan	Beijing Institute of Technology, China
Shaokai Wang	Hong Kong University of Science and Technology, China
Kaili Wang	Donghua University, China
Xinyue Wang	Renmin University of China, China
Han Wang	Northeast Normal University, China
Hongqiang Wang	Hefei Institutes of Physical Science, CAS, China
Jianxin Wang	Central South University, China
Jiayin Wang	Xi'an Jiaotong University, China
Yaojun Wang	China Agricultural University, China
Yanjie Wei	Shenzhen Institutes of Advanced Technology, CAS, China
Ka-Chun Wong	City University of Hong Kong, China

Fangxiang Wu	University of Saskatchewan, Canada
Jingli Wu	Guangxi Normal University, China
Ju Xiang	Changsha University of Science and Technology, China
Linxia Xiao	Shenzhen Institutes of Advanced Technology, CAS, China
Yuying Xie	Michigan State University, USA
Yungang Xu	Xi'an Jiaotong University, China
Shankai Yan	Hainan University, China
Cheng Yan	Hunan University of Chinese Medicine, China
Lulu Yan	Northwest A&F University, China
Yang Yang	Shanghai Jiao Tong University, China
Yaning Yang	Xiangtan University, China
Yusen Ye	Xidian University, China
Min Zeng	Central South University, China
Dongxu Zhang	Xiamen University, China
Fa Zhang	Beijing Institute of Technology, China
Fuhao Zhang	Northwest A&F University, China
Jingjing Zhang	Shenzhen Institutes of Advanced Technology, CAS, China
Wen Zhang	Huazhong Agricultural University, China
Lu Zhang	Hong Kong Baptist University, China
Le Zhang	Sichuan University, China
Shihua Zhang	Academy of Mathematics and Systems Science, CAS, China
Xiaoqing Zhang	Shenzhen Institutes of Advanced Technology, CAS, China
Yiming Zhang	University of Connecticut, USA
Yongqing Zhang	Chengdu University of Information Technology, China
Yuchen Zhang	Northwest A & F University, China
Haochen Zhao	Central South University, China
Qichang Zhao	Central South University, China
Ruiqing Zheng	Central South University, China
Xubin Zheng	Great Bay University, China
Jiancheng Zhong	Central South University, China
Binhai Zhu	Montana State University, USA
Shanfeng Zhu	Fudan University, China
Xiaoshu Zhu	Guilin University of Electronic Technology, China

Contents

MCAF: Improving Mortality Risk Prediction Using Multimodal Learning with Balanced Pre-training and Correlation-Aware Fusion

Abdulrahman Al-badwi[1,2], Chengchao Shen[1(✉)], Abdulrahman Al-Dailami[1,2], Raeed Al-Sabri[1], Hulin Kuang[1], and Jianxin Wang[1]

[1] Hunan Provincial Key Lab on Bioinformatics, School of Computer Science and Engineering, Central South University, Changsha 410083, Hunan, China
scc.cs@csu.edu.cn

[2] Faculty of Computers and Information Technology, Sana'a University, Sana'a, Yemen

Abstract. The growing availability of multimodal Electronic Health Records (EHRs) data provides promising research on multimodal representation learning. Leveraging multimodal EHRs data and extracting inter-modality correlation among them has achieved acceptable performance for the mortality risk prediction task. However, the existing methods do not address the problem of the imbalanced convergence for each modality encoder. Furthermore, the inter-modality correlation fusion among different modalities is limited. This work proposes multimodal representation learning with pre-training and inter-modality correlation-aware fusion to address the imbalanced training convergence and capture the inter-modality correlation among all modalities' representations. Specifically, the proposed method comprises two main stages. In the first stage, we pre-train the time series and demographic information modalities' encoders separately and fine-tune the pre-trained Biomedical Bidirectional Encoder Representations Transformer (BioClinicalBERT) to provide a balanced training convergence. In the second stage, the pre-trained encoders from the first proposed stage are utilized to encode the time series, demographic, and clinical notes modalities. Then, we fuse their representations to extract the intercorrelation utilizing the low-rank multimodal fusion and the concatenation operation to provide the final patient representation. We evaluate the proposed framework on the MIMIC-III dataset. The experimental results demonstrate that the proposed framework outperforms the state-of-the-art models for mortality risk prediction.

Keywords: Mortality risk prediction · Electronic health records · Model Pre-training · Correlation-aware multimodal fusion

X. Cui et al. (Eds.): ISBRA 2026, LNBI 16690, pp. 1–13, 2027.
https://doi.org/10.1007/978-981-92-3716-6_1

1 Introduction

Hospitals generate vast amounts of multimodal medical data. The rise of Electronic Health Records (EHRs) and deep learning has driven significant interest in medical outcome prediction. While traditional studies often focused on single modalities [5], clinical practice relies on integrating diverse information. Consequently, multimodal learning approaches have emerged, showing improved predictive performance by fusing data types like static demographics, time-series, and unstructured clinical notes [2,7,10,14,15]. These methods use modality-specific encoders, such as Fully Connected networks for tabular data, sequence models for time-series, and Transformer-based models like BERT for clinical text [7,10,14]. Despite this progress, two key challenges still need to be addressed:
A) Imbalanced training convergence for each modality encoder: State-of-the-art models leverage the BioBERT and its fine-tuned BioClinicalBERT (BCB) [3], which have exhibited superior performance in encoding clinical note for outcome prediction [7,14]. However, a pertinent issue arises in multimodal learning settings when training other companion EHRs modalities' encoders from scratch, as the clinical notes modality encoder convergence occurs rapidly. This imbalance in the training is biased towards the clinical notes modality encoder, which hinders the overall prediction performance. Figure 1 explains the imbalance training convergence across different modalities. For example, in the work [14], the model reaches its peak performance AUROC of 0.877 in the early epochs, which occurs because the pre-trained encoder of the clinical notes alone achieves an AUROC of 0.85, whereas the time series encoder starts training from scratch. Consequently, both the time series and the demographic encoders perform poorly. In the later epochs, we note that their performance increases, while the clinical notes encoder's performance slightly improves. We aim to solve this imbalanced representation learning problem by providing balanced training convergence for each modality encoder.
B) Inter-modality correlation-aware fusion: In the multimodality learning area, various fusion methods are proposed to fuse multiple modalities, providing a unified patient representation. The typical fusion methods, such as concatenation, multiplication, and average functions, are used in the majority of research [7,14,16,19]. However, they do not capture the full interaction among all modalities. To address this limitation, tensor fusion networks (TFN) and low-rank multimodal fusion (LMF) [13] are effective for extracting the interaction among all modalities. We aim to find an effective fusion method to capture inter-modality correlation among different modalities.

To address the above-mentioned challenges, this study proposes a multimodal representation learning framework with pre-training and inter-modality correlation-aware fusion (MCAF) to improve the mortality risk prediction task. To conquer the first challenge, the pre-training stage provides pre-trained encoders with a balanced representation learning for each modality. The second stage utilizes the well-trained encoders from the first stage to encode each modality. To address the second challenge, the proposed inter-modality correlation-aware fusion method extracts the interdependencies between modalities repre-

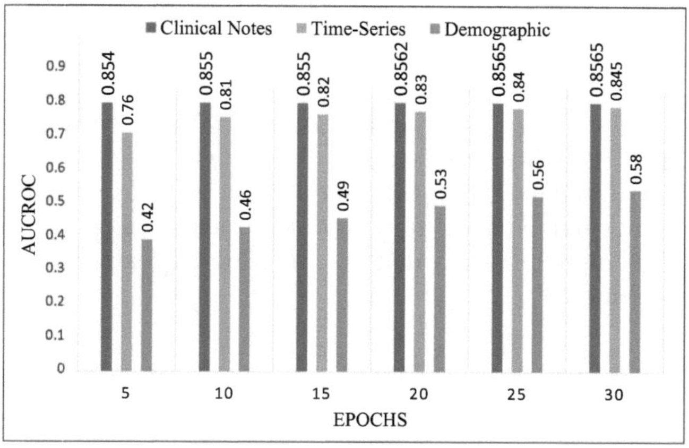

Fig. 1. The imbalanced training convergence across the time series, demographics, and clinical notes modalities encoders.

sentations to produce a unified intercorrelation representation. Furthermore, this study incorporates an interpretation study to provide clinicians with transparent, actionable insights into how the MCAF framework determines mortality risk.

2 Materials and Methods

2.1 Data Preparation and Preliminary Information

The experiments of this study are conducted on the MIMIC-III dataset [9]. First, we extract the cohort from the MIMIC-III dataset [9] following the pipeline benchmark study in [8]. This cohort provides 21139 samples for adult patients (18+ years) with the time series and demographic modalities during the first 48 h of the admission. After that, we followed the studies [7,14] to extract the clinical notes. Furthermore, we followed the work [15] to select the personalized demographic features (age, gender, height, weight, and ethnicity). To ensure all samples have all modalities, we filtered out the samples without clinical notes during the first 48 h, ending with 20261 samples for 17456 patients.

2.2 Problem Definition and Data Notations

The aim of this study is to predict the mortality risk based on data observed within the first 48 h (T = 48) of an Intensive Care Unit (ICU) stay. The label of mortality is made after 48 h, whether the patient has passed (positive) or has been discharged from the hospital (negative). For each patient (P), each visit (or stay) is characterized by three modalities, denoted as $P_v = \{X^T, S, N^K\}$ representing the time series, demographic, and clinical notes modalities, respectively where K is the total number of clinical notes. In this work, we split the extracted cohort into two parts: Part 1 and Part 2, where each part has 50%. Our modalities can be denoted as follows: $D_{Pre} = [X^T_{Pre}, S_{Pre}, N^K_{Pre}]$ is the first part of the dataset (Part 1) that is used for the pre-training purposes, and $D_{MM} = [X^T_{MM}, S_{MM}, N^K_{MM}]$ is the second part of the dataset (Part 2) that is used for the multimodality representation learning purpose. Besides, each part of the data is separated into 70%, 15%, and 15% as training, validation, and testing for pre-training and multimodality representation learning, respectively. This separation of the inputs ensures that the multimodal representation is learned from the unseen data.

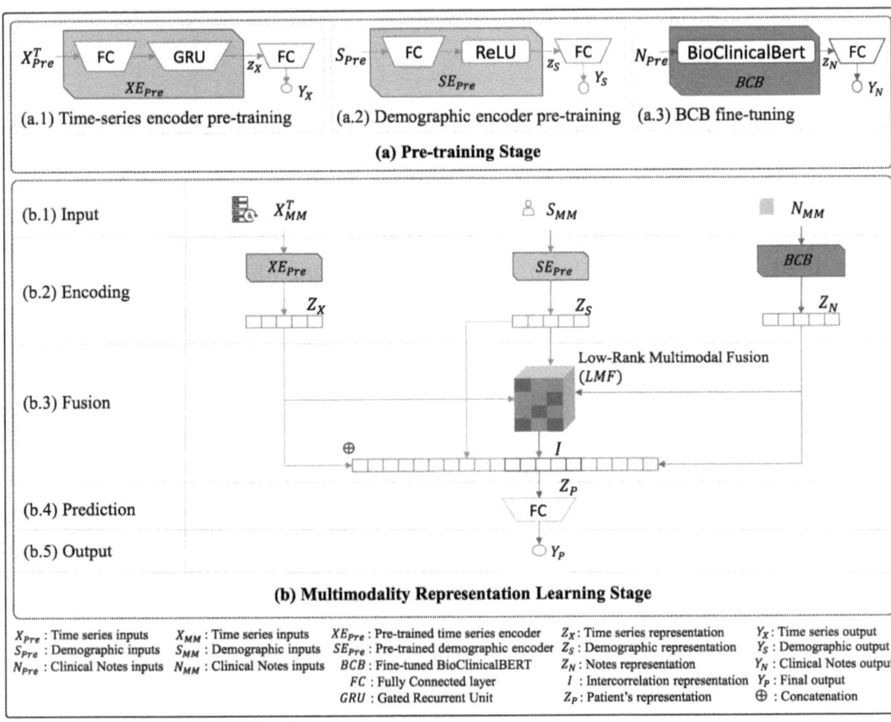

Fig. 2. The proposed framework MCAF. (a) The pre-training stage (b) The multimodality representation learning stage.

2.3 Method Overview

In this study, the proposed framework, MCAF, improves the mortality risk prediction task by solving the imbalanced training challenge and extracting intercorrelation among multimodality. As shown in Fig. 2, the proposed MCAF framework comprises two stages. The first stage, the pre-training, produces balanced training convergence for the time series and demographic encoders alongside fine-tuning the clinical notes encoder. The second stage, the multimodality representation learning, encodes all modalities leveraging the well-pretrained encoders and then fuses their representations using the proposed inter-modality correlation-aware method. Specifically, as shown in Fig. 2, the proposed framework MCAF starts the first stage by pre-training the encoders X^T_{Pre} and S_{Pre}, then saving their weights in XE_{Pre} and SE_{Pre} for time series and demographic encoders, respectively. In addition, it fine-tunes the BioClinicalBERT encoder of the clinical note for the mortality risk prediction task. In the second stage, it loads the pre-trained encoders XE_{Pre},SE_{Pre}, and BCB to encode the time series data X_{MM}, the demographic data S_{MM}, and the clinical notes N_{MM}, respectively. After that, it fuses the representation of all encoders using LMF [13] and the concatenation fusion. Finally, it applies an FC to predict the mortality risk.

2.4 Pre-training Stage

The proposed framework improves the multimodality representation learning by providing balanced training convergence. In the first stage, we pre-train and fine-tune the time series and demographic encoders separately, as well as fine-tune the BioClinicalBERT model for the mortality risk prediction task.

Pre-training the Time Series Modality Encoder. Time series data is sequential, multivariate data collected over time. To provide a pre-trained time series encoder, in the pre-training stage, we feed the first part of the time series data X^T_{Pre} into the time series encoder XE_{Pre} that contains an FC followed by a Gated Recurrent Units (*GRU*) [11] as:

$$Z_X = GRU(FC(X^T_{Pre})), \tag{1}$$

where $T = 48$ is the number of hours during the stay, and Z_X is the final hidden state of the time series encoder. After that, the last hidden state representation Z_X is fed into an FC to predict the patient mortality risk as follows:

$$O_X = \sigma(FC(Z_X)), \tag{2}$$

where σ is the sigmoid function and O_X is the final prediction output of the time series encoder.

Pre-training the Demographic Modality Encoder. The demographic features are the static personalized information of the patients. In the pre-training stage, we feed the first part of the demographic data S_{Pre} into the demographic encoder SE_{Pre} that contains an FC followed by *ReLU* activation function as:

$$Z_S = ReLU(FC(S_{Pre})), \tag{3}$$

where Z_S is the demographic representation, which is then fed into an FC to predict the patient mortality as follows:

$$O_S = \sigma(FC(Z_S)), \tag{4}$$

where O_S is the final prediction output of the demographic encoder.

Fine-Tuning the Clinical Notes Encoder. BERT-based models, powerful natural language processing (NLP) models, are widely used in various domains, including healthcare [6,7,12,14,18]. BioClinicalBERT is a domain-specific variant of BERT that has been pre-trained on biomedical text. It is particularly well-suited for healthcare applications, leading to more informative representations of clinical note [3]. Inspired by [7,14], we follow [3] by fine-tuning the BioBERT model for the mortality risk prediction task. Then, we feed each clinical note of N_{Pre} into the BioClinicalBERT [3] model as follows:

$$Z_N = BioClinicalBERT(N_{Pre}), \tag{5}$$

where Z_N is the classification token (CLS) output used to represent the clinical note model. After that, the Z_N is fed into an FC to predict the patient mortality risk as follows:

$$O_N = \sigma(FC(Z_N)), \tag{6}$$

where σ is the sigmoid function and O_N is the final prediction output of the clinical notes modality encoder. During the evaluation step, we save the best weights of XE_{Pre}, SE_{Pre}, and BCB encoders produced by Eqs. (1), (3), and (5) as the pre-trained encoders for the time series, the demographic, and clinical notes modalities, respectively.

2.5 Multimodality Representation Learning Stage

After getting all pre-trained models, in the second stage, we encode each modality using the corresponding pre-trained model produced in the first stage. In this sub-section, we describe each modality encoding as follows:

Time Series Modality Encoding. In this stage, the pre-trained encoder XE_{Pre} produced in the first stage is engaged to encode the time series modality. We feed the second part of the data X_{MM} into the pre-trained encoder XE_{Pre}. This process can be expressed as:

$$Z_X = XE_{Pre}(X_{MM}), \tag{7}$$

where Z_X is the final representation of the time series encoder.

Demographic Modality Encoding. Similarly, the pre-trained encoder SE_{Pre} is engaged to encode the demographic modality. We feed the second part of the data S_{MM} into the pre-trained encoder SE_{Pre}. This process can be represented as:

$$Z_S = SE_{Pre}(S_{MM}), \tag{8}$$

where Z_S is the final representation of the demographic encoder.

Clinical Note Modality Encoding. Furthermore, we encode the clinical notes to get the final clinical notes representation as:

$$Z_N = \frac{1}{K}\sum_{i=1}^{K} BCB(n_i) \tag{9}$$

where Z_N is the final representation of the clinical notes modality, and n_i is the ith note.

2.6 Inter-modality Correlation-Aware Fusion

Simple concatenation of modality representations fails to capture complex inter-modality interactions. To address this, we use LMF [13], which efficiently models these interactions by decomposing high-dimensional tensors into low-rank factors, avoiding the computational complexity of earlier methods like Tensor Fusion Networks (TFN). We leverage LMF to compute the inter-modal correlation:

$$I = (\sum_{i=1}^{r} w_X^{(i)}.Z_X) \circ (\sum_{i=1}^{r} w_S^{(i)}.Z_S) \circ (\sum_{i=1}^{r} w_N^{(i)}.Z_N), \tag{10}$$

where I is the inter-modality interaction representation, r is the rank of the LMF model, w_X, w_S, and w_N are the LMF parameters for time series, demographic, and clinical notes representations, respectively.

To provide a complementary representation for the patient, the original modalities' representations are fused alongside the output of the inter-modality interaction representation I using the concatenation operation as follows:

$$Z_P = I \oplus Z_X \oplus Z_S \oplus Z_N, \tag{11}$$

where is Z_P final patient's representation and $\oplus$ is the concatenation operation.

2.7 Mortality Risk Prediction

Finally, we feed the final patient representation Z_P into an FC followed by the sigmoid activation function to predict the mortality risk O_P as:

$$O_P = \sigma(FC(Z_P)), \tag{12}$$

where σ is the sigmoid function. Furthermore, the binary cross-entropy loss function $\mathcal{L}$ is calculated by passing the predicted probabilities and true labels. The loss function is outlined below:

$$\mathcal{L} = -[y * log(O_P) + (1 - y) * log(1 - O_P)], \quad (13)$$

where y represents the ground truth of the sample indicating the mortality outcome (0 or 1), and O_P represents the predicted probability of mortality.

3 Results

3.1 Comparison with Baselines

We compare the proposed framework *MCAF* with the baselines ConCare [15], MM-1DCNN [10], MM-BCB-LSTM [7], MM-Transformer [14], ARMOUR [12], Wang et al. [18], and EMF [1]. Table 1 demonstrates that *MCAF* outperforms all baselines on the MIMIC-III sub-dataset D_{MM}. Specifically, *MCAF* achieves 0.8808 AUROC and 0.5358 AUPRC, outperforming EMF [1] by 0.76% ($p=0.043$) and 1.0% ($p=0.027$) respectively (Welch's t-test). Improvements over AMFA [4] are also highly significant ($p<0.01$ for both metrics). These results indicate that the proposed framework *MCAF* improves the multimodality representation learning by pre-training each modality encoder and the inter-modality correlation-aware fusion method.

Table 1. The comparison of the proposed framework MCAF and the baselines on the MIMIC-III dataset.

Model	*AUROC*	*AUPRC*
ConCare [15]	0.8186±0.002	0.3942±0.006
MM-1DCNN [10]	0.8453±0.004	0.4552±0.014
MM-BCB-LSTM [7]	0.8666±0.002	0.5177±0.003
MM-Transformer [14]	0.8587±0.002	0.4945±0.004
ARMOUR [12]	0.8622±0.002	0.5125±0.008
Wang et al. [18]	0.8563±0.003	0.5101±0.005
AMFA [4]	0.8713±0.003	0.5211±0.002
EMF [1]	0.8732±0.005	0.5258±0.005
MCAF	**0.8808±0.002**	**0.5358±0.004**

3.2 Ablation Study

This section conducts ablation studies for each component on the MIMIC-III dataset to assess the efficacy of each component in the proposed framework *MCAF*. These studies explore the benefits of our pre-training approach for solving the imbalanced training convergence and demonstrate the benefits of the correlation-aware fusion method.

Effectiveness of the Pre-training Approach: To measure the effectiveness of the proposed pre-training approach, we apply experiments with/without the pre-training stage for the time series and the demographic modalities encoders. We denote the variant of the proposed model without the pre-training stage as $MCAF_{Pre-}$. Table 2 demonstrates that pre-training the time series and the demographic encoders using one part of the dataset D_{Pre}, and further training them using the other split D_{MM}, enhances the framework's performance. The $MCAF_{Pre-}$ framework is improved in the AUROC and AUPRC by 1.16% and 1.09%, respectively. These experimental results demonstrate the necessity and effectiveness of the pre-training step that provides an imbalanced model convergence for each modality encoder.

Table 2. The effectiveness of the pre-training stage in the proposed framework $MCAF$ on the split D_{MM} of the MIMIC-III dataset.

Model	$AUROC$	$AUPRC$
$MCAF_{Pre-}$	0.8692±0.002	0.5249±0.005
$MCAF$	**0.8808±0.002**	**0.5358±0.004**

Table 3. The effectiveness of the proposed correlation-aware fusion in the proposed framework $MCAF$ on the MIMIC-III dataset.

Model	$AUROC$	$AUPRC$
$MCAF_{Concat}$	0.8733±0.003	0.5267±0.005
$MCAF_{LMF}$	0.8655±0.005	0.5183±0.006
$MCAF$	**0.8808±0.002**	**0.5358±0.004**

Effectiveness of the Inter-modality Correlation-Aware Fusion: To investigate the effectiveness of the proposed correlation-aware fusion method, we conduct two ablation studies by utilizing only one method individually. The concatenation method is applied in the first study to fuse the three modalities' representations ($MCAF_{Concat}$). Additionally, in the second study, the LMF method is utilized to fuse the three modalities' representations ($MCAF_{LMF}$). We compare these fusion methods against the proposed correlation-aware fusion method in $MCAF$, as shown in Table 3.

Table 3 demonstrates that the proposed $MCAF$ based on the correlation-aware fusion achieves better than the $MCAF_{Concat}$ and $MCAF_{LMF}$. We notice that by fusing the three modalities using either the concatenation method or the low-rank multimodal fusion method, the performance is decreased. The proposed fusion of $MCAF$ improves the performance compared to the concatenation method $MCAF_{Concat}$ by an AUROC and an AUPRC by 0.71% and 0.63%, respectively, as well as to the LMF method $MCAF_{LMF}$ by an AUROC and an AUPRC by 1.53% and 1.75%, respectively. While LMF effectively models complex non-linear cross-modal interactions, concatenation acts as a skip-connection that preserves the uncompressed, modality-specific features. Integrating them allows the final classifier to leverage both the learned inter-modal dynamics and the complete original representations.

4 Discussion

The findings demonstrate that MCAF outperforms all baselines for mortality risk prediction on MIMIC-III, while ablation studies validate its pre-training and correlation-aware fusion components. To further contextualize these successes, this section explores the framework's generalization capabilities by substituting the pre-training and evaluation data splits against baselines. Subsequently, we present an interpretation study to provide transparency into how the proposed method arrives at its predictions.

Performance of the MCAF When Switching Two Data-Split Parts: In Sect. 3.1, we have conducted the experiments using Part 2 as D_{MM} and Part 1 as D_{Pre}. To explore the generality of the proposed $MCAF$, we switch the two data-split parts as follows: Part 2 of the MIMIC-III dataset is used as D_{Pre} for the pre-training, whereas Part 1 is used as D_{MM} for the multimodal representation learning.

Table 4. The comparison of the proposed framework $MCAF$ and the baselines on Part 1 of the MIMIC-III dataset.

Model	*AUROC*	*AUPRC*
ConCare [15]	0.8254±0.001	0.4070±0.003
MM-1DCNN [10]	0.8562±0.003	0.5044±0.005
MM-BCB-LSTM [7]	0.9080±0.001	0.6199±0.002
MM-Transformer [14]	0.8923±0.002	0.5874±0.005
ARMOUR [12]	0.9032±0.001	0.6188±0.004
Wang et al. [18]	0.9020±0.001	0.6167±0.005
AMFA [4]	0.9028±0.001	0.6030±0.005
EMF [1]	0.9055±0.001	0.6265±0.004
MCAF	**0.9098±0.002**	**0.6346±0.003**

Table 4 shows that the proposed framework $MCAF$ outperforms the baseline models in terms of all evaluation metrics when using Part 1 for multimodal representation learning. These results indicate that the proposed framework can be

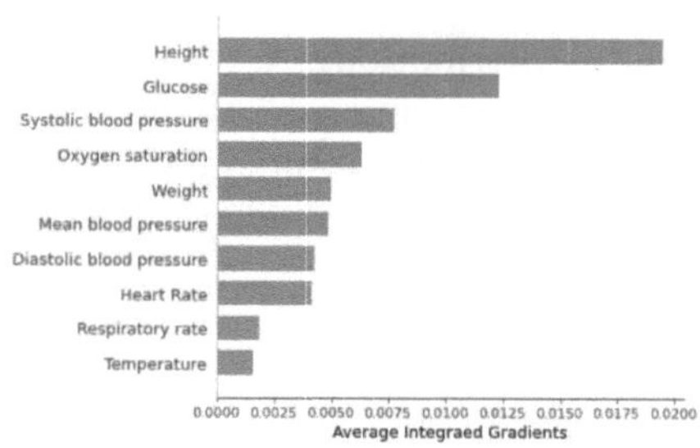

(a) Top 10 time-series features.

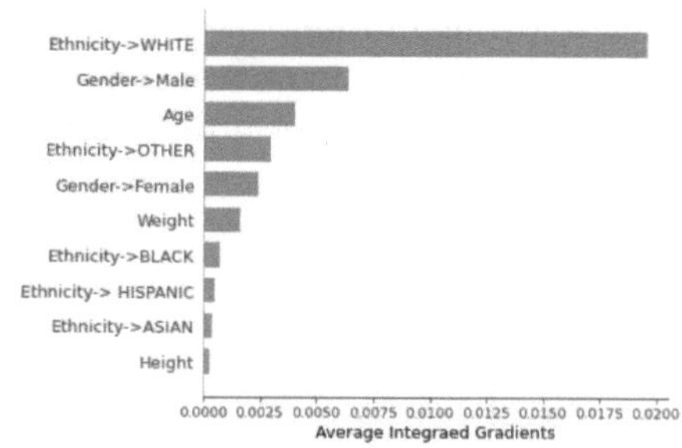

(b) Important demographic features.

Fig. 3. Importance of tabular features for the MCAF framework based on average Integrated Gradients. (a) shows the top 10 time-series features. (b) shows the important demographic features.

generalized to pre-train the encoders on any part of the dataset and then utilize the pre-trained encoder to encode the modalities of the other part effectively.

Model Interpretation: To provide clinical insights into our model's predictions, we employed the Integrated Gradients (IG) algorithm [17], a widely used Explainable AI (XAI) technique. This analysis was performed on the complete, trained MCAF model after fusion, ensuring that the calculated importance for any feature or word reflects its contribution within the context of all input modalities. We used average IG to rank the importance of time-series and demographic features (Fig. 3a and Fig. 3b). The analysis revealed that static patient attributes like Height, Weight, Ethnicity, Gender, and Age were highly influential. Among dynamic time-series variables, Glucose, Blood Pressure (SBP/DBP), and Heart Rate (HR) also showed significant importance, aligning with their known roles as critical indicators of patient acuity.

For the clinical notes, Layer Integrated Gradients (LIG) [17] is used to assess the word-level importance in clinical notes (Fig. 4). Words highlighted in green

Legend: ■Negative □Neutral ■Positive

True Label	Predicted Label	Word Importance
Mortality	Survive	… impression : new multi ##fo ##cal al ##ve ##olar op ##ac ##ities with in the right lung , which could be due to di ##ff ##use pneumonia , as ## piration …
Mortality	Mortality	… she was read ##mit ##ted post - op w increasing sob . no report of fev er , but worse ##ning a ##b ##g and increased t ##rac ##hia ##l secret ##i ons …
Mortality	Survive	…no e ##ct ##opy . b ##p = 110 / 50s. skin :co ##cc ##yx red , appears t o have healed wound. r g ##lut w/ 2 friction tears and l g ##lut intact , but red - duo ##der ##m applied to all areas …
Mortality	Mortality	… at that time was made a d ##n ##r . at the start of shift p ##t had been on prop ##of ##ol but during this she was changed to a f ##ent ##any ##l / verse ##d g ##tt combination …

Fig. 4. Example of word importance based on Layer Integrated Gradients (LIG) values on the MIMIC-III Dataset.

indicate a contribution towards mortality risk (positive attribution), while red indicates a contribution towards survival (negative attribution). As shown, terms directly describing clinical deterioration such as "increasing sob" (Shortness of Breath), "worsening a b g" (Arterial Blood Gas), and "pneumonia" showed strong positive attribution, confirming the model's ability to identify critical textual indicators of high mortality risk.

5 Conclusion

The proposed MCAF framework advances multimodal mortality risk prediction by resolving two critical challenges. Its two-stage pre-training approach provides balanced learning representations for diverse encoders (time-series, demographic, notes), overcoming imbalanced convergence. Secondly, its correlation-aware fusion method effectively extracts interdependencies among all modalities. By integrating these solutions, MCAF offers a robust contribution to multimodal learning that can assist clinicians in making prompt and informed decisions for patient care.

Acknowledgments. This work is supported by the National Natural Science Foundation of China (No. U25A20449). This work was carried out in part using computing resources at the High-Performance Computing Center of Central South University

References

1. Al-badwi, A., Kuang, H., Al-Dailami, A., Wang, J.: EMF: enhancing mortality risk prediction via evidential multimodal fusion. In: International Symposium on Bioinformatics Research and Applications, pp. 337–348. Springer, Heidelberg (2025). DOI: https://doi.org/10.1007/978-981-95-0698-9_28
2. Al-Dailami, A., Kuang, H., Wang, J.: Predicting length of stay in ICU and mortality with temporal dilated separable convolution and context-aware feature fusion. Comput. Biol. Med. **151**, 106278 (2022)
3. Alsentzer, E., et al.: Publicly available clinical BERT embeddings. In: Proceedings of the 2nd Clinical Natural Language Processing Workshop, pp. 72–78 (2019)
4. An, Y., Qiu, R., Guo, L., Chen, X.: Attention-based multimodal fusion with adversarial network for in-hospital mortality prediction. In: 2024 IEEE International Conference on Bioinformatics and Biomedicine (BIBM), pp. 1789–1795 (2024)
5. Bajor, J.M., Lasko, T.A.: Predicting medications from diagnostic codes with recurrent neural networks. In: 5th International Conference on Learning Representations, ICLR, pp. 1–12 (2017)
6. Devlin, J., Chang, M., Lee, K., Toutanova, K.: BERT: pre-training of deep bidirectional transformers for language understanding. In: Proceedings of the 2019 Conference of the North American Chapter of the Association for Computational Linguistics: Human Language Technologies, vol. 1, pp. 4171–4186 (2019)
7. Deznabi, I., Iyyer, M., Fiterau, M.: Predicting in-hospital mortality by combining clinical notes with time-series data. In: Findings of the Association for Computational Linguistics: ACL-IJCNLP 2021, pp. 4026–4031 (2021)

8. Harutyunyan, H., et al.: Multitask learning and benchmarking with clinical time series data. Sci. Data **6**, 96 (2019)
9. Johnson, A.E., et al.: Mimic-III, a freely accessible critical care database. Sci. Data **3**(1), 1–9 (2016)
10. Khadanga, S.A.: Using clinical notes with time series data for ICU management. In: 9th International Joint Conference on Natural Language Processing (EMNLP-IJCNLP), pp. 6432–6437 (2019)
11. Kyunghyun Cho, B.V.M., et al.: Learning phrase representations using rnn encoder–decoder for statistical machine translation. In: Conference on Empirical Methods in Natural Language Processing (2014)
12. Liu, J., Capurro, D., Nguyen, A.N., Verspoor, K.: Attention-based multimodal fusion with contrast for robust clinical prediction in the face of missing modalities. J. Biomed. Inf. **145**, 104466 (2023)
13. Liu, Z., Shen, Y., Lakshminarasimhan, V.B., Liang, P.P., Zadeh, A., Morency, L.: Efficient low-rank multimodal fusion with modality-specific factors. In: Gurevych, I., Miyao, Y. (eds.) Proceedings of the 56th Annual Meeting of the Association for Computational Linguistics, ACL, pp. 2247–2256 (2018)
14. Lyu, W., et al.: A multimodal transformer: fusing clinical notes with structured EHR data for interpretable in-hospital mortality prediction. In: AMIA 2022, American Medical Informatics Association Annual Symposium, p. 719 (2022)
15. Ma, L., Zhang, C.: Concare: personalized clinical feature embedding via capturing the healthcare context. In: Proceedings of the AAAI Conference on Artificial Intelligence, vol. 34, pp. 833–840 (2020)
16. Stahlschmidt, S.R., Ulfenborg, B., Synnergren, J.: Multimodal deep learning for biomedical data fusion: a review. Brief. Bioinf. **23**(2), bbab569 (2022)
17. Sundararajan, M., Taly, A., Yan, Q.: Axiomatic attribution for deep networks. In: Proceedings of the 34th International Conference on Machine Learning (2017)
18. Wang, Y., Yin, C., Zhang, P.: Multimodal risk prediction with physiological signals, medical images and clinical notes. Heliyon **10**(5), e26772 (2024)
19. Zhu, L., Zhu, Z., Zhang, C., et al.: Multimodal sentiment analysis based on fusion methods: a survey. Inf. Fusion **95**, 306–325 (2023)

AttentionNABP: Attention-Based Deep Learning Framework for Nucleic Acid-Binding Proteins Classification and Identification

Md. Sifat Ali[1], Haochen Zhao[2(✉)], Muhammad Habibulla Alamin[1], Qichang Zhao[1], and Jianxin Wang[1]

[1] Hunan Provincial Key Lab on Bioinformatics, School of Computer Science and Engineering, Changsha 410083, China
[2] Big Data Institute, Central South University, Changsha 410083, China
zhaohaochen@csu.edu.cn

Abstract. Nucleic acid-binding proteins (NABPs), including single-stranded DNA-binding proteins (SSBs), double-stranded DNA-binding proteins (DSBs), and RNA-binding proteins (RBPs), play pivotal roles in essential biological processes. Many computational approaches have been developed for the classification and identification of these NABP subtypes through machine learning and deep learning techniques. However, these methods exhibit limitations in accurately classifying NABP types, particularly in cross-prediction scenarios such as misclassifying SSBs as RBPs and vice versa. To address these challenges and improve the prediction accuracy of different types of NABPs, we proposed AttentionNABP, a deep learning framework that integrates convolutional neural networks, a multi-head self-attention mechanism, and long short-term memory networks. Our method offers two complementary prediction strategies: a hierarchical cascaded classifier and a simultaneous multi-class classifier. The hierarchical approach achieves prediction accuracies of up to 96.39 ± 0.44% with area under the receiver operating characteristic curve (AUC) scores of 96.20 ± 1.65% at each classification stage, while the multi-class model attains an overall accuracy of 85.25 ± 1.78% (AUC = 95.72 ± 0.48%). These results demonstrate that AttentionNABP significantly reduces cross-prediction errors and enables precise discrimination among non-NABPs, RBPs, DSBs, and SSBs. By leveraging pre-trained protein language model embeddings and a logit-adjusted loss function to handle class imbalance, our framework provides a robust computational tool for classification and identification of nucleic acid-binding proteins.

Keywords: Nucleic acid-binding proteins · Single-stranded DNA-binding proteins · Multi-head self-attention mechanism · Hierarchical framework

X. Cui et al. (Eds.): ISBRA 2026, LNBI 16690, pp. 14–26, 2027.
https://doi.org/10.1007/978-981-92-3716-6_2

1 Introduction

Nucleic acid-binding proteins (NABPs), encompassing DNA-binding proteins (DBPs) and RNA-binding proteins (RBPs), involved in key cellular processes such as replication, transcription, and gene regulation [1,2]. DBPs can be categorized into single-stranded DNA-binding proteins (SSBs) and double-stranded DNA-binding proteins (DSBs). SSBs are mainly involved in DNA recombination, replication, and repair, serving as critical factors in maintaining genomic stability, whereas DSBs are involved in transcriptional regulation, DNA cleavage, and chromosomal organization [3]. These biological processes are involved in various diseases, particularly cancer, myeloid leukaemia, human genetic disorders, and also related to viral infections [4–6]. Therefore, the accurate classification and identification of NABPs are vital for understanding their biological roles and potential therapeutic applications. Experimental methods such as electrophoretic mobility shift assays, chromatin immunoprecipitation, and crosslinking immunoprecipitation are traditionally employed to identify NABPs; however, these techniques are often time-consuming and expensive [7–9]. Consequently, computational approaches have gained prominence as efficient alternatives for classification and identification of proteins within large-scale databases. Several machine learning-based models, including support vector machines (SVM), random forests (RF), and gradient boosting classifiers (such as XGBoost and LightGBM) have been employed to predict NABPs based on sequence-derived features [8–11]. Recently, deep learning architectures such as convolutional neural networks (CNNs) have been employed to enhance predictive accuracy [12,13]. While these predictors predominantly employ CNN architectures that effectively capture local sequence patterns, but they fail to model global sequence context and long-range dependencies. Zhang et al. developed two-level predictor using CNN and long short-term memory (LSTM) to predict DBPs/RBPs [14]. Conversely, Manavi et al. employed CNN-based model with evolution-based features to classify DSBs and SSBs, although, this model assumes each input protein is a known DBPs [15]. However, these predictors mainly target one type of NABPs, either DBPs/RBPs, or SSBs/DSBs which limits their application in predicting the types of NABPs for proteins with unknown functions. Recent studies attempt to address these limitations; such as, Wu et al. proposed a hierarchical and multi-class framework for NABPs prediction; however, their model exhibited a lower performance up to 40% in SSB prediction, additionally, the hierarchical approach did not include an SSB/DSB classifier, and the multi-class approach failed to classify SSBs and DSBs categories [16]. A major challenge in these methods is the misclassification of SSBs as RBPs and vice versa, which impedes reliable prediction of NABPs types.

To overcome these limitations and improve the accuracy of NABPs classification and identification, we developed AttentionNABP, a novel hierarchical and multi-class deep learning framework that integrates evolutionary-scale protein language models with advanced neural architectures. Specifically, the proposed framework (i) combines hierarchical cascaded classification and multi-class prediction strategies for comprehensive NABP identification, (ii) leverages ESM2 embeddings together with CNN, multi-head self-attention, and LSTM modules to capture both local motifs and global sequence dependencies, and (iii) employs a logit-adjusted loss function to effectively address class imbalance. The hierarchical approach follows a cascaded classification system (non-NABPs/NABPs → DBPs/RBPs → SSBs/DSBs), while the multi-class model simultaneously predicts four categories: non-NABPs, RBPs, DSBs, and SSBs.

2 Materials and Methods

2.1 Datasets

In this study, we used non-redundant datasets recently introduced by Wu et al. [16] for model training, validation, and testing. After applying redundancy removal using CD-HIT with a sequence identity threshold of 40%, the datasets comprised the following: 347 SSBs, 4211 DSBs, 5627 RBPs, and 12899 non-NABPs. For the hierarchical classification approach, the first step involved, classifying between non-NABPs and NABPs. The NABP dataset (10185 proteins) formed by combining all SSBs, DSBs, and RBPs. The second step focused on differentiating DBPs from RBPs. Here, all SSBs and DSBs were pooled to form the DBP dataset (4558 proteins). The third step distinguishing SSBs from DSBs. For the multi-class classification approach, we used non-NABP, RBP, DSB, and SSB datasets simultaneously as separate classes. The hierarchical framework consists of sequential binary classifiers, which can collectively produce multi-class predictions through cascaded decision paths. In contrast, the multi-class model performs simultaneous classification. To ensure robust performance evaluation, a standardized data partitioning strategy was employed across all experiments. For each prediction task, the corresponding dataset was randomly divided into training (70%) and independent test (30%) subsets, while preserving the original class distribution through stratified sampling. Within the training set, a five-fold cross-validation scheme was implemented for hyperparameter optimization and model selection. To mitigate potential bias arising from a single random partition and to assess performance stability, we conducted five independent prediction runs. In each run, the dataset was re-partitioned into 70% training and 30% testing subsets, followed by complete model training, validation, and evaluation cycles. Final performance metrics were reported as the mean ± standard deviation (SD) calculated across these five independent runs.

2.2 Neural Network Architecture and Implementation

The proposed AttentionNABP architecture is designed to capture complementary aspects of protein sequences through a coordinated processing pipeline. Protein sequences are first encoded into contextual embeddings using ESM2, which provide rich evolutionary and structural information. These embeddings are then passed through CNN layers to extract local sequence motifs. The resulting feature maps are further processed by a multi-head self-attention mechanism to capture long-range dependencies and non-local interactions between distant amino acids. Subsequently, an LSTM layer models sequential dependencies and aggregates the learned features into a global representation of the protein sequence. This hierarchical information flow enables effective feature learning, and the entire framework is trained end-to-end. The architectural details are presented in Fig. 1.

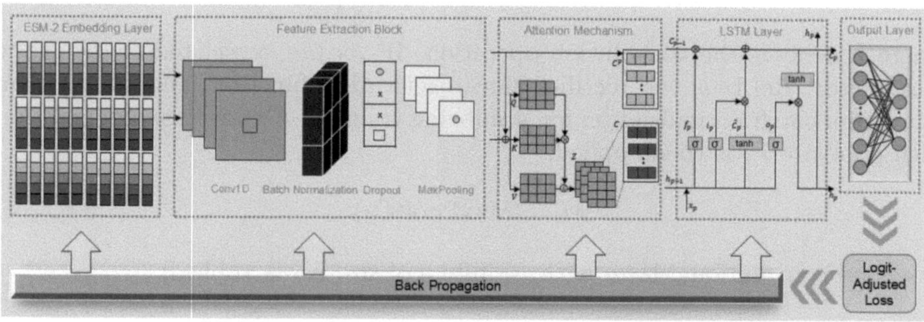

Fig. 1. Architecture of the AttentionNABP framework for nucleic acid-binding protein classification.

Protein Sequence Representation Using ESM2 Embeddings. In this study, we employed the evolutionary scale modeling version 2 (ESM2) [17], specifically the esm2_t33_650M_UR50D variant with 650 million parameters. ESM2 was trained on the UniRef50 database using a masked language modeling objective, enabling it to learn evolutionary and structural constraints directly from protein sequences. Compared with conventional handcrafted features, ESM2 embeddings provide context-aware representations learned from large-scale protein data, capturing evolutionary and structural patterns. This enables improved discrimination of closely related NABP subtypes [18]. Each protein sequence S was processed through the pre-trained ESM2 model to generate a fixed-dimensional embedding vector:

$$E = \text{ESM2}(S) \in R^{1280} \tag{1}$$

These 1280 dimensional embeddings capture contextual information about each amino acid and the overall protein sequence, encoding patterns of evolutionary conservation, secondary structure propensity, and functional constraints. To prepare these embeddings for subsequent convolutional processing, we applied a reshape operation:

$$X = \text{Reshape}(E) \in R^{1280\times 1} \tag{2}$$

The resulting matrix X serves as the input to the convolutional feature extraction layers.

Feature Extraction with Convolutional Neural Networks. The ESM2 embeddings X are passed through two successive one-dimensional convolutional layers to extract local patterns and motifs characteristic of nucleic acid-binding proteins. The first convolutional layer employs N_1 filters with kernel size K_1, producing a feature map:

$$C_1 = \text{ReLU}(\text{BatchNorm}(X * W_1 + b_1)) \tag{3}$$

where $*$ denotes the convolution operation, W_1 is the kernel tensor, b_1 is the bias vector, ReLU is the rectified linear activation function, and BatchNorm represents batch normalization for stabilizing training. A max-pooling operation with pool size P_1 is then applied:

$$M_1 = \text{MaxPool}(C_1) \tag{4}$$

A second convolutional layer with N_2 filters of size K_2 is applied:

$$C_2 = \text{ReLU}(\text{BatchNorm}(M_1 * W_2 + b_2)) \tag{5}$$

followed by another max-pooling layer with pool size P_2 to yield the final CNN output $M_2 \in R^{L' \times N_2}$, where L' is the reduced sequence length. Dropout regularization is applied after each convolutional layer to prevent overfitting.

Modeling Long-Range Dependencies with Multi-Head Self-Attention. To capture long-range dependencies and non-local interactions between distal amino acids, M_2 is processed through a multi-head self-attention mechanism. For each head $i \in \{1, \ldots, h\}$, learnable projections generate query, key, and value matrices: $Q_i = M_2 W_i^Q$, $K_i = M_2 W_i^K$, and $V_i = M_2 W_i^V$ respectively. The scaled dot-product attention for each head is computed as:

$$\text{head}_i = \text{softmax}\left(\frac{Q_i K_i^T}{\sqrt{d_k}}\right) V_i \tag{6}$$

where d_k is the dimension of the key vectors. The outputs of all h heads are concatenated and linearly projected as $A = \text{Concat}(\text{head}_1, \ldots, \text{head}_h) W^o$ where W^o is a trainable weight matrix. Layer normalization with $\epsilon = 10^{-6}$ is applied to stabilize training as $A' = \text{LayerNorm}(A)$.

Sequential Processing with LSTM. The normalized feature map A' is fed into a long short-term memory layer to model sequential dependencies and temporal relationships within the protein sequence. The LSTM unit at each position p processes the input vector x_p and the previous hidden state h_{p-1} to compute a new hidden state h_p. The internal operations are governed by the forget gate, input gate, candidate memory, cell state update, output gate, and hidden state update, as described in Eqs. 7–12, respectively.

$$f_p = \sigma(W_f \cdot [h_{p-1}, x_p] + b_f) \tag{7}$$

$$i_p = \sigma(W_i \cdot [h_{p-1}, x_p] + b_i) \tag{8}$$

$$\tilde{C}_p = \tanh(W_c \cdot [h_{p-1}, x_p] + b_c) \tag{9}$$

$$C_p = f_p \odot C_{p-1} + i_p \odot \tilde{C}_p \tag{10}$$

$$o_p = \sigma(W_o \cdot [h_{p-1}, x_p] + b_o) \tag{11}$$

$$h_p = o_p \odot \tanh(C_p) \tag{12}$$

where σ and $\odot$ denote the sigmoid activation function and Hadamard product, respectively. The LSTM layer contains U units and returns only the final hidden state h_L, which serves as a comprehensive feature vector summarizing the entire sequence. Dropout regularization is applied to the LSTM output to mitigate overfitting.

Handling Class Imbalance with Logit-Adjusted Loss. To address inherent class imbalances in nucleic acid-binding protein datasets, we employed a logit-adjusted loss function. This strategy is particularly suitable for scenarios where class distributions are highly imbalanced. By adjusting logits based on class priors, the model reduces bias toward majority classes and improves recognition of underrepresented categories [19]. Given class priors π_c calculated from the training data for each classifier, the logit adjustment modifies the model's output logits z before computing the cross-entropy loss:

$$z_{\text{adj}} = z - \tau \cdot \log(\pi + \epsilon) \tag{13}$$

where $\tau = 1.0$ is the adjustment temperature parameter, π is the vector of class priors, and $\epsilon = 10^{-8}$ is a small constant for numerical stability. The final hidden state from the LSTM layer is passed through fully connected layers:

$$d_1 = \text{ReLU}(W_1 h_L + b_1) \tag{14}$$

$$d_1' = \text{Dropout}(d_1) \tag{15}$$

$$z = W_2 d_1' + b_2 \tag{16}$$

During training, the logit-adjusted loss is computed as:

$$L = -\frac{1}{N} \sum_{i=1}^{N} \sum_{c=1}^{C} y_{i,c} \log \left(\frac{\exp(z_{\text{adj},i,c})}{\sum_{j=1}^{C} \exp(z_{\text{adj},i,j})} \right) \tag{17}$$

where C is the number of classes (2 for binary classifiers, 4 for the multi-class classifier). During inference, standard softmax activation is applied to obtain class probabilities as $\hat{y} = \text{softmax}(z)$.

Model optimization was performed using the Adam optimizer with a learning rate of 0.001. All models were trained for 100 epochs with early stopping (patience = 15, monitoring the validation loss) and a batch size of 32. The complete set of hyperparameters for each hierarchical and multi-class classifier is presented in Table 1.

Table 1. Optimized hyperparameters for each classifier in the hierarchical and multi-class framework

Hyperparameter	Value in Models			
	non-NABP/NABP	DBP/RBP	SSB/DSB	Multi-class
Filters (N_1, N_2)	128, 64	128, 64	128, 64	128, 64
Kernel Size (K_1, K_2)	15, 11	11, 7	11, 7	11, 9
Dropout Rate	0.2, 0.2, 0.3, 0.2	0.2, 0.2, 0.3, 0.2	0.2, 0.2, 0.3, 0.2	0.2, 0.2, 0.3, 0.2
Pool Size (P_1, P_2)	4, 6	4, 6	4, 6	4, 6
Attention Heads (h)	12	12	12	8
LSTM Unit (U)	50	50	50	50

3 Results and Discussion

3.1 Performance of Our Models

The proposed AttentionNABP framework demonstrated strong performance across all nucleic acid-binding protein classification tasks, as detailed in Table 2. The hierarchical classifier achieved accuracies of $89.55 \pm 2.77\%$ for non-NABP/NABP discrimination, $90.79 \pm 1.25\%$ for DBP/RBP classification, and $96.39 \pm 0.44\%$ for SSB/DSB distinction. High AUC values ($95.96 \pm 1.74\%$, $96.68 \pm 0.60\%$, and $96.20 \pm 1.65\%$, respectively) confirmed robust discriminative ability. While the AUPRC for SSB/DSB classifier ($81.92 \pm 4.74\%$) is relatively lower compared to other metrics, the high AUC ($96.20 \pm 1.65\%$) value confirm strong discriminative power and model reliability. The multi-class classifier maintained competitive performance with $85.25 \pm 1.78\%$ accuracy and an AUC of $95.72 \pm 0.48\%$, demonstrating that simultaneous four-class discrimination remains feasible without substantial performance degradation. Although slightly less accurate than the hierarchical approach, its high AUC ($95.72 \pm 0.48\%$) indicates that it retains strong discriminative ability, offering a potentially more efficient alternative for applications where a single-step classification is preferred. The superior performance of the hierarchical model can be attributed to its staged decision process, which simplifies complex classification tasks and reduces ambiguity between closely related classes. In contrast, the multi-class model requires simultaneous discrimination among all classes, making it inherently more challenging. Notably, all classifiers maintain stable performance due to rich ESM2 representations that generalize across protein families, complementary modules capturing various sequence scales, and a logit-adjusted loss that reduces variance on minority classes.

These results demonstrate that AttentionNABP effectively captures distinguishing features that overcome persistent classification ambiguities in the field.

3.2 Comparative Performance Analysis

A comprehensive performance comparison was conducted to evaluate AttentionNABP against state-of-the-art methods across all hierarchical classification

Table 2. Performance evaluation of proposed hierarchical and multi-class frameworks

Classifiers	ACC ± SD (%)	REC ± SD (%)	PRE ± SD (%)	F1 ± SD (%)	AUC ± SD (%)	AUPRC ± SD (%)
non-NABP/NABP	89.55 ± 2.77	89.55 ± 2.77	89.61 ± 2.75	89.56 ± 2.77	95.96 ± 1.74	96.66 ± 1.35
DBP/RBP	90.79 ± 1.25	90.79 ± 1.25	90.84 ± 1.18	90.79 ± 1.24	96.68 ± 0.60	96.93 ± 0.52
SSB/DSB	96.39 ± 0.44	96.39 ± 0.44	96.24 ± 0.56	96.17 ± 0.63	96.20 ± 1.65	81.92 ± 4.74
Multi-class	85.25 ± 1.78	85.25 ± 1.78	85.71 ± 1.05	85.29 ± 1.66	95.72 ± 0.48	92.96 ± 0.64

tasks. To ensure fair comparison, we followed the original experimental settings of baseline methods where available. For methods without publicly available implementations, results were obtained from corresponding web servers. The results (see Table 3) demonstrate that AttentionNABP consistently outperformed existing methods across all tasks. For non-NABP/NABP classification, our model (89.55 ± 2.77% accuracy) exceeded DRBP-EDP (86.24 ± 3.02%) and hierarchical CNN-LSTM (80.42 ± 1.40%). For DBP/RBP discrimination, our approach (90.79 ± 1.25% accuracy, 96.68 ± 0.60% AUC) surpassed all existing predictors, including DRBP-EDP (85.52 ± 3.37%) and DeepDRBP-2L (78.73 ± 3.60%). The SSB/DSB classifier set new standards with exceptional accuracy (96.39 ± 0.44%) and F1-score (96.17 ± 0.63%), significantly outperforming CNN-Pred (90.44 ± 3.80%) and traditional machine learning approaches (71–76% accuracy).

These results demonstrate that AttentionNABP establishes new performance standards across all NABP classification tasks, particularly in reducing cross-prediction errors, improving discrimination between SSBs and DSBs, and maintaining balanced performance metrics.

Table 3. Performance comparison of each hierarchical classifier with existing methods

Models	Prediction Types	ACC ± SD (%)	REC ± SD (%)	PRE ± SD (%)	F1 ± SD (%)	AUC ± SD (%)	AUPRC ± SD (%)
DRBP-EDP (stage 1) [7]	non-NABP/NABP	86.24 ± 3.02	86.66 ± 3.77	83.80 ± 3.21	85.24 ± 3.81	92.03 ± 2.47	92.12 ± 1.63
Hierarchical non-NABP/NABP [16]	non-NABP/NABP	80.42 ± 1.40	80.30 ± 1.31	76.50 ± 2.82	78.21 ± 1.71	88.01 ± 1.77	83.02 ± 1.87
AttentionNABP (ours)	non-NABP/NABP	**89.55 ± 2.77**	**89.55 ± 2.77**	**89.61 ± 2.75**	**89.56 ± 2.77**	**95.96 ± 1.74**	**96.66 ± 1.35**
DPP-PseAAC [8]	DBP	77.60 ± 3.67	78.10 ± 3.85	49.30 ± 8.62	57.40 ± 3.17	82.32 ± 3.19	62.87 ± 4.73
Qu YH et al. [13]	DBP	87.82 ± 1.83	90.00 ± 1.50	88.01 ± 1.51	88.99 ± 1.48	92.11 ± 2.02	91.02 ± 2.10
DeepRBPPred (balance) [12]	RBP	69.04 ± 7.76	79.51 ± 7.70	64.94 ± 9.64	66.14 ± 8.54	73.29 ± 4.91	69.12 ± 4.88
DeepRBPPred (unbalance) [12]	RBP	68.88 ± 8.13	74.61 ± 13.90	65.19 ± 8.11	64.87 ± 8.29	71.01 ± 5.11	67.87 ± 5.79
RNAPred [10]*	RBP	62.93 ± 4.81	74.20 ± 3.66	56.60 ± 3.61	60.20 ± 3.73	–	–
DeepDRBP-2L [14]*	DBP/RBP	78.73 ± 3.60	78.92 ± 3.46	74.84 ± 3.97	77.20 ± 3.65	–	–
DRBP-EDP (stage 2) [7]	DBP/RBP	85.52 ± 3.37	85.50 ± 2.20	82.81 ± 3.81	82.10 ± 3.89	93.73 ± 2.60	93.32 ± 2.71
Hierarchical DBP/RBP [16]	DBP/RBP	80.52 ± 1.47	80.62 ± 2.04	76.72 ± 0.87	78.56 ± 1.07	84.87 ± 2.13	87.19 ± 1.93
AttentionNABP (ours)	DBP/RBP	**90.79 ± 1.25**	**90.79 ± 1.25**	**90.84 ± 1.18**	**90.79 ± 1.24**	**96.68 ± 0.60**	**96.93 ± 0.52**
Wang et al. (SVM) [20]	SSB/DSB	71.86 ± 3.37	71.20 ± 3.61	94.80 ± 0.40	82.01 ± 2.61	81.01 ± 4.01	72.03 ± 3.30
Wang et al. (RF) [20]	SSB/DSB	72.70 ± 3.28	71.01 ± 2.10	93.11 ± 0.43	84.23 ± 2.19	76.17 ± 2.37	67.83 ± 4.21
Sharma et al. [21]	SSB/DSB	76.35 ± 5.07	76.35 ± 5.07	83.97 ± 3.02	85.57 ± 3.31	86.03 ± 2.13	80.27 ± 4.02
CNN-Pred [15]	SSB/DSB	90.44 ± 3.80	90.55 ± 3.88	94.99 ± 0.39	92.69 ± 2.97	92.88 ± 2.33	**82.39 ± 3.56**
AttentionNABP (ours)	SSB/DSB	**96.39 ± 0.44**	**96.39 ± 0.44**	**96.24 ± 0.56**	**96.17 ± 0.63**	**96.20 ± 1.65**	81.92 ± 4.74

*These results were obtained by using the webserver of these predictors, since the source code for these predictors are not available.
Bold font indicates the higher performance

3.3 Ablation Study

To systematically evaluate the contributions of our model's design, we conducted an extensive ablation study on all NABP classification tasks. We compared variations in seven key areas: core architectures, class imbalance handling strategies, convolutional kernel sizes, number of attention heads, network depth, dropout rates, and the number of LSTM units. The final model was configured with the optimal hyperparameters identified from this analysis. For architectural components, we compared CNN-only, CNN-LSTM, CNN-Attention, and CNN-Multi-Head Self-Attention-LSTM, with the latter yielding optimal performance. Given the inherent class imbalance in our datasets, we evaluated several mitigation strategies: training on the original unbalanced data, down-sampling the majority class, class-balanced loss ($\beta = 0.999$), and logit-adjusted loss ($\tau = 1.0$), with logit-adjusted loss providing superior performance. For convolutional kernel sizes, we tested $\{15, 11\}$, $\{25, 15\}$, $\{37, 29\}$, $\{50, 30\}$, $\{15, 9\}$, $\{11, 7\}$, and $\{11, 9\}$, where $\{11, 7\}$ and $\{11, 9\}$ proved optimal. The number of attention heads examined included 0, 4, 8, 12, and 16 heads, with 12 heads performing best. Network depth variation spanned 1, 2, 3, and 4 CNN layers, establishing two layers as optimal. Dropout rates evaluated were $\{0.1, 0.1, 0.3, 0.2\}$, $\{0.2, 0.2, 0.3, 0.2\}$, and $\{0.3, 0.3, 0.3, 0.2\}$, with the $\{0.2, 0.2, 0.3, 0.2\}$ configuration yielding best results. Finally, LSTM units tested were 32, 50, and 64 units, where 50 units proved optimal across all tasks. This systematic optimization not only defines the optimal configuration for our model but also provides valuable insights into the architectural constraints for effectively processing biological sequence data.

3.4 Case Study

Hierarchical Attention Analysis of a Newly Released Protein. We analyzed a newly released protein (PDB ID: 8RAU_1, June 2025) excluded from training data. Our hierarchical pipeline classified it sequentially as nucleic acid-binding, DNA-binding, and finally single-stranded DNA-binding protein. Attention maps (see Fig. 2a–c) provided residue-level rationale for these predictions. Across all three levels, attention consistently highlighted basic residues (K, R) essential for electrostatic interactions with the DNA backbone, aromatic residues (F, Y, W) critical for base-stacking, and polar residues (N, Q, T, S) involved in hydrogen bonding [22,23]. Attention adaptively shifted across classification levels: histidine and proline at the first level suggested recognition of metal-coordination and flexible loop regions; glutamine and serine at the second level reflected hydrogen-bonding for sequence-specific recognition; and lysine with tyrosine at the final SSB level indicated enhanced electrostatic and stacking interactions characteristic of single-stranded DNA binding [23]. The mechanism captured context-dependent residue evaluation and long-range dependencies by assigning high scores to non-contiguous residues, reflecting the spatial proximity of binding interfaces despite sequence distance.

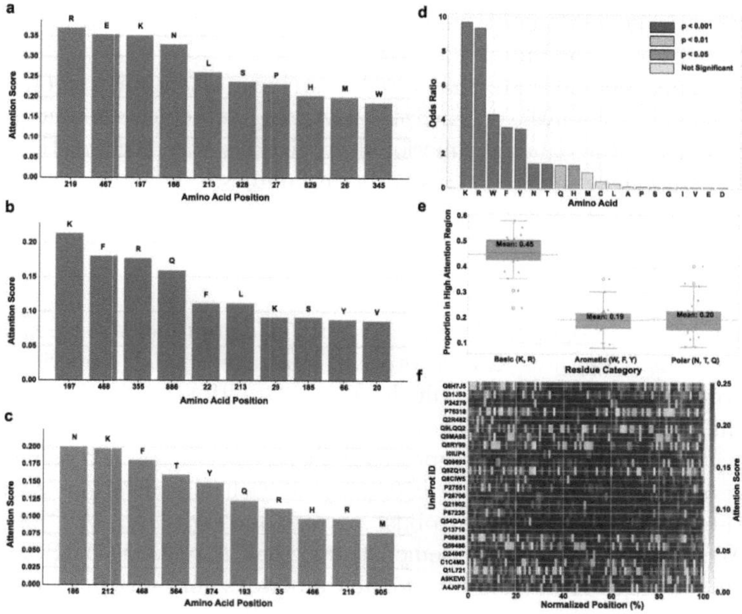

Fig. 2. Hierarchical attention analysis of protein 8RAU_1 and statistical validation of attention patterns across 25 single-stranded DNA-binding proteins. (a-c) The top ten amino acid positions with the highest attention weights for non-NABP/NABP, DBP/RBP, and SSB/DSB classification step respectively. Residue labels above each bar indicate the amino acid at the corresponding position. (d) Odds ratios from Fisher's exact test showing significant enrichment of residues in high attention regions. Amino acids are ranked by odds ratio and significance levels are denoted by color. (e) Box plots showing prevalence of key residue categories in high attention regions across all proteins. (f) Heatmap of attention scores for each protein (rows) plotted against normalized sequence position (columns). Color scale indicates attention intensity.

Statistical Validation Across 25 SSB Proteins. To validate generalizability, we analyzed 25 single-stranded DNA-binding proteins from the test set, extracting the top 15% of residues by attention score. Fisher's exact test revealed significant enrichment patterns (see Fig. 2d): basic residues showed the strongest enrichment (K: OR = 9.70, R: OR = 9.35; $p<0.001$), followed by aromatic residues (W: OR = 4.30, F: OR = 3.55, Y: OR = 3.46; $p<0.001$) and polar residues (N, Q, T; OR = 1.34–1.42; $p<0.01$). Hydrophobic and small residues showed no significant enrichment (odds ratios < 1.0, $p > 0.05$). Key residue categories maintained consistent prevalence across all proteins (see Fig. 2e): basic residues constituted $44.8 \pm 7.6\%$, aromatic residues $19.3 \pm 5.8\%$, and polar residues $19.6 \pm 7.8\%$, collectively accounting for 83.7% of high-attention positions. The heatmap visualization (see Fig. 2f) confirmed consistent biochemical principles across diverse sequences. Population-level analysis refined observations from the 8RAU_1 case: tryptophan emerged as more consistently enriched than phenylalanine, and methionine showed no significant class-wide enrichment despite appearing in the individual protein.

These results demonstrate that our hierarchical attention framework identifies fundamental biophysical principles governing protein-nucleic acid interactions, providing both confident functional predictions and mechanistically interpretable insights generalizable across protein families.

4 Conclusion

In this study, we developed AttentionNABP, a comprehensive deep learning framework that integrates ESM2 protein language model embeddings with convolutional neural networks, multi-head self-attention mechanisms, and long short-term memory networks for accurate classification and identification of nucleic acid-binding protein subtypes. Our hierarchical approach achieved high predictive accuracy (up to $96.39 \pm 0.44\%$) at each classification stage, while the multi-class model maintains robust performance with an AUC of $95.72 \pm 0.48\%$. Attention score analysis demonstrates that AttentionNABP provides a reliable and interpretable computational framework for NABPs classification. The framework is particularly suitable for large-scale bioinformatics applications requiring accurate subtype discrimination. In future work, we plan to incorporate structural information (predicted 3D structures), post-translational modification features, and hybrid sequence-structure representations to further enhance predictive performance and biological interpretability.

Acknowledgments. This work was supported in part by the National Natural Science Foundation of China (Grant Nos. 62472202 and 62502541). This work was also carried out in part using computing resources at the High Performance Computing Center of Central South University.

Data Availability. The source code and datasets are available at https://github.com/Sifato5/Attention-Based-NABPs-Classification

References

1. William, H.H., Ortlund, E.A.: The structure, function and evolution of proteins that bind dna and rna. Nat. Rev. Mol. Cell Biol. **15**(11), 749–760 (2014)
2. Guo, F., et al.: Foundation models in bioinformatics. Natl. Sci. Rev. **12**(4), nwaf028 (2025)
3. Lin, M., Malik, F.K., Guo, J.: A comparative study of protein-ssdna interactions. NAR Genom. Bioinf. **3**(1), lqab006 (2021)

4. Cui, F., et al.: Deepmc-inabp: deep learning for multiclass identification and classification of nucleic acid-binding proteins. Comput. Struct. Biotechnol. J. **20**, 2020–2028 (2022)
5. Zhao, H., et al.: Identifying the serious clinical outcomes of adverse reactions to drugs by a multi-task deep learning framework. Commun. Biol. **6**(1), 870 (2023)
6. Gebauer, F., Schwarzl, T., Valcárcel, J., Hentze, M.W.: Rna-binding proteins in human genetic disease. Nat. Rev. Genet. **22**(3), 185–198 (2021)
7. Mu, Q., Yu, G., Zhou, G., He, Y., Zhang, J.: DRBP-EDP: classification of DNA-binding proteins and RNA-binding proteins using ESM-2 and dual-path neural network. NAR Genom. Bioinf. **7**(2), lqaf058 (2025)
8. Rahman, M.S., Shatabda, S., Saha, S., Kaykobad, M., Rahman, M.S.: DPP-PSEAAC: a dna-binding protein prediction model using chou's general pseaac. J. Theor. Biol. **452**, 22–34 (2018)
9. Zhang, X., Liu, S.: RBPPRED: predicting RNA-binding proteins from sequence using SVM. Bioinformatics **33**(6), 854–862 (2017)
10. Kumar, M., Gromiha, M.M., Raghava, G.P.S.: SVM based prediction of RNA-binding proteins using binding residues and evolutionary information. J. Mol. Recognit. **24**(2), 303–313 (2011)
11. Ali, F., Kumar, H., Patil, S., Kotecha, K., Banjar, A., Daud, A.: Target-dbppred: an intelligent model for prediction of DNA-binding proteins using discrete wavelet transform based compression and light extreme gradient boosting. Comput. Biol. Med. **145**, 105533 (2022)
12. Zheng, J., et al.: Deep-rbppred: predicting RNA binding proteins in the proteome scale based on deep learning. Sci. Rep. **8**(1), 15264 (2018)
13. Qu, Y.H., Yu, H., Gong, X.J., Xu, J.H., Lee, H.S.: On the prediction of DNA-binding proteins only from primary sequences: a deep learning approach. PLoS ONE **12**(12), e0188129 (2017)
14. Zhang, J., Chen, Q., Liu, B.: Deepdrbp-2l: a new genome annotation predictor for identifying DNA-binding proteins and RNA-binding proteins using convolutional neural network and long short-term memory. IEEE/ACM Trans. Comput. Biol. Bioinf. **18**(4), 1451–1463 (2019)
15. Manavi, F., Sharma, A., Sharma, R., Tsunoda, T., Shatabda, S., Dehzangi, I.: CNN-PRED: prediction of single-stranded and double-stranded DNA-binding protein using convolutional neural networks. Gene **853**, 147045 (2023)
16. Wu, S., Guo, J.: Improved prediction of DNA and RNA binding proteins with deep learning models. Brief. Bioinf. **25**(4), bbae285 (2024)
17. Lin, Z., et al.: Evolutionary-scale prediction of atomic-level protein structure with a language model. Science **379**(6637), 1123–1130 (2023)
18. Zeng, W., Dou, Y., Pan, L., Liwen, X., Peng, S.: Improving prediction performance of general protein language model by domain-adaptive pretraining on DNA-binding protein. Nat. Commun. **15**(1), 7838 (2024)
19. Lee, H., Park, T., Kim, H.: Learnable logit adjustment for imbalanced semi-supervised learning under class distribution mismatch. In: Proceedings of the IEEE/CVF International Conference on Computer Vision, pp. 2664–2674 (2025)
20. Wang, W., et al.: Analysis and prediction of single-stranded and double-stranded DNA binding proteins based on protein sequences. BMC Bioinf. **18**(1), 300 (2017)
21. Sharma, R., Kumar, S., Tsunoda, T., Kumarevel, T., Sharma, A.: Single-stranded and double-stranded DNA-binding protein prediction using hmm profiles. Anal. Biochem. **612**, 113954 (2021)

22. Schiopu, I., Dragomir, I., Asandei, A.: Single molecule technique unveils the role of electrostatic interactions in SSDNA-gp32 molecular complex stability. RSC Adv. **14**(8), 5449–5460 (2024)
23. Khamis, M.I., Casas-Finet, J.R., Maki, A.H.: Stacking interactions of tryptophan residues and nucleotide bases in complexes formed between escherichia coli single-stranded DNA binding protein and heavy atom-modified poly (uridylic) acid: a study by optically detected magnetic resonance spectroscopy. J. Biol. Chem. **262**(4), 1725–1733 (1987)

scMMGC: A Generative Multi-omics Integration Method Based on Dual-Mask Contrastive Fusion of Co-expression Graph

Xiang Chen(✉), Zihan Yang, Yongkang Ma, and Xiaoyu Liu

Hunan University of Science and Technology, Xiangtan, Hunan, China
chenxofhit@gmail.com

Abstract. Integrating single-cell multi-omics data is crucial for analyzing cellular heterogeneity and explaining biological mechanisms. Through techniques such as scRNA-seq and scATAC-seq, complex interactions between factors such as gene expression and chromatin accessibility can be revealed at cell resolution. Despite growing interest in multi-omics integration, sparsity, noise, and batch effects still hinder robust alignment and downstream analysis, and many existing methods do not fully leverage cross-modal co-expression or model cross-modal feature interactions. To address these challenges, we propose scMMGC, which combines co-expression graphs with a masked autoencoder and cross-modal fusion to learn high-quality joint cell embeddings. scMMGC constructs co-expression graphs to capture shared topology across modalities and applies bilateral contrastive learning within and between modalities to encourage consistent representations and mitigate batch effects. It further uses dual masked autoencoding to randomly mask and reconstruct expression features, reducing sensitivity to modality-specific noise, sparsity, and rare global signals. Finally, a cross-fusion module promotes feature interaction between modalities to drive integration. Across benchmark datasets, scMMGC achieves strong alignment and consistently improves or matches mainstream methods on label transfer and clustering, while reducing batch effects and preserving biological structure. The learned embeddings also support trajectory inference, enabling accurate reconstruction of differentiation paths and providing a practical foundation for multi-omics downstream analyses such as cell-type annotation and developmental mapping.

Keywords: single-cell multi-omics · data integration · co-expression graph · contrastive learning · masked autoencoder · cross-modal fusion

1 Introduction

With the rapid development of single-cell sequencing technology, especially the wide application of single-cell transcriptome sequencing (scRNA-seq) [20] and

X. Cui et al. (Eds.): ISBRA 2026, LNBI 16690, pp. 27–41, 2027.
https://doi.org/10.1007/978-981-92-3716-6_3

single-cell chromatin accessibility sequencing (scATAC-seq) [10], the cross-modal interactions between gene expression and epigenetic regulation can now be studied at single-cell resolution [28]. By capturing multi-layered features of the same cell, these technologies have helped reveal developmental dynamics, regulatory networks, and pathological mechanisms of complex diseases [1,2,9]. Although multi-omics integration shows great potential, researchers still face challenges in handling these data due to the complexity of biological samples and the limitations of sequencing technology [14,24]. Single-cell omics data generally exhibit high-dimensional sparsity, strong noise, and batch effects, which increase the difficulty of integration and downstream analysis [3,26].

As a result, many integration algorithms have emerged, which can be roughly divided into four computational paradigms: manifold alignment and geometric matching, topological preservation and graph-based architectures, joint decomposition and optimal transport, and contrastive learning with masked coding. Methods based on manifold alignment and geometric matching, including UnionCom [4], JointMDS [6], and Seurat v5 [11], project cells onto a shared low-dimensional manifold via global distance matrices but ignore cross-omics topological associations. Methods such as scTopoGAN [18], Pamona [5], and scMGCL [7] emphasize the stability of local structures and use graph autoencoders or GANs to bridge modality-specific features. However, they are prone to introducing artifacts and are sensitive to hyperparameters. SCOT [8] and Mowgli [13] minimize integration cost through joint decomposition and optimal transport, but their computational cost can be high. In addition, scPairing [17] and scDRMAE [27] adopt contrastive learning and masked coding architectures. Although they can learn cross-modal relationships, the variational assumption is prone to discarding fine-grained variation. With the accumulation of single-cell multi-omics datasets, existing methods still show limitations in handling extreme sparsity, noise interference, and insufficient cross-modal representation [16].

To address these issues, we propose scMMGC, a generative integration method that combines a co-expression graph with a masked autoencoder framework and is driven by cross-modal fusion. The core contributions of scMMGC are: (i) topological consistency enhancement: a cross-modal shared co-expression graph is constructed to capture the common topological structure of each modality, strengthen consistency constraints, and implicitly reduce batch effects through bilateral contrastive learning within and between modalities [15]; (ii) mask-based robust representation: by using dual-mask views to randomly mask and reconstruct the data, the model reduces its reliance on global features, thereby alleviating the interference of modality-specific noise and sparsity; (iii) cross-modal feature interaction: through a cross-fusion module, feature interaction between modalities is promoted to achieve alignment and generate high-quality joint cell embeddings.

We conducted extensive benchmarking of scMMGC on publicly available paired datasets. The results show that scMMGC achieves strong cross-modal alignment on all test data and consistently improves upon or matches mainstream methods in label transfer, clustering, and biological preservation. Further analysis indicates that the learned embeddings can reconstruct differentiation pathways, reveal cell type-specific regulatory logic, and provide a practical tool for downstream single-cell multi-omics analysis.

2 Materials and Methods

scMMGC is a generative integration method based on co-expression graphs and dual-mask autoencoders, designed to integrate scRNA-seq and scATAC-seq data into high-quality joint cell embeddings. It consists of three modules: the cross-modal co-expression graph module, the dual-mask autoencoder module, and the cross-fusion module. The model architecture is shown in Fig. 1.

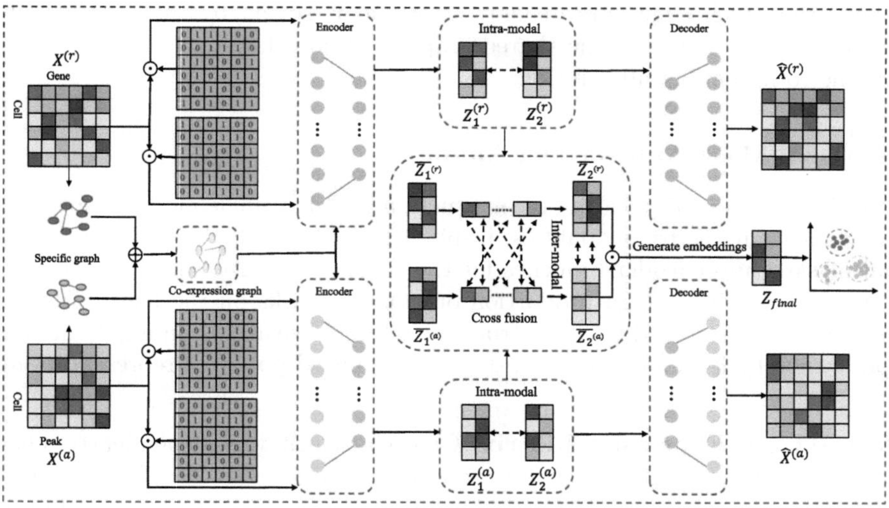

Fig. 1. The architecture of scMMGC.

2.1 Cross-Modality Co-expression Graph Module

To effectively capture structural similarities in single-cell multi-omics data and overcome data sparsity, scMMGC adopts a graph construction strategy based on local topological enhancement. This module integrates the KNN graphs constructed by each of the two modalities to generate a shared adjacency structure, enabling the graph neural network to simultaneously propagate the features of RNA and ATAC under a consistent neighborhood relationship, thereby enhancing the collaborative expression of cross-modal information.

Specifically, this module first takes the RNA expression matrix $\mathbf{X}^{(r)} \in \mathbb{R}^{N \times G}$ and the ATAC accessibility matrix $\mathbf{X}^{(a)} \in \mathbb{R}^{N \times P}$, and constructs their respective k-nearest neighbor graphs to obtain edge indexes $\mathcal{E}^{(r)}$ and $\mathcal{E}^{(a)}$:

$$\mathcal{E}^{(r)} = \text{KNN}(\text{PCA}(\mathbf{X}^{(r)}), k), \mathcal{E}^{(a)} = \text{KNN}(\text{PCA}(\mathbf{X}^{(a)}), k) \tag{1}$$

where PCA(·) denotes principal component analysis for dimensionality reduction of the original high-dimensional features (50 components), and KNN$(\cdot, k)$ constructs k-nearest neighbor connections based on Euclidean distance. Subsequently, the edge sets of the two modalities are fused by union:

$$\mathcal{E}_{\text{shared}} = \mathcal{E}^{(r)} \cup \mathcal{E}^{(a)} \tag{2}$$

To eliminate duplicate edges, we perform de-duplication and sorting operations on the merged edge set:

$$(\mathcal{E}_{\text{shared}}, \emptyset) \leftarrow \text{coalesce}(\mathcal{E}^{(r)} \oplus \mathcal{E}^{(a)}, \text{num\_nodes} = N) \tag{3}$$

Here, $\oplus$ represents the edge-dimension concatenation operation, and coalesce(·) ensures that each edge appears only once and is sorted by the source node. Finally, the edge index of the shared graph is obtained, $\mathcal{E}_{\text{shared}} \in \mathbb{Z}^{2\times E}$, where E is the total number after fusion.

2.2 Dual-Mask Autoencoder Module

To achieve high-quality feature reconstruction within a single modality and contrastive learning across modalities, inspired by MAE [12], this module designs dual masked autoencoder branches for the RNA and ATAC modalities respectively. By applying a high proportion of random masks on the feature dimension, the model is forced to reconstruct the original features from highly missing inputs, thereby learning more robust and generalized potential representations.

Masked Gene Expression Matrix. On each branch, we independently generate a double random mask view for the input feature matrix $\mathbf{X} \in \mathbb{R}^{N\times F}$ (where N is the number of cells and F is the feature dimension). For each forward propagation, generate a mask matrix $\mathbf{M} \in \{0,1\}^{N\times F}$ of a Bernoulli distribution:

$$M_{i,j} \sim \text{Bernoulli}(p = 1 - r_m) \tag{4}$$

where r_m represents the mask ratio, meaning that the probability of each feature position having r_m is masked (set to 0).

$$\tilde{\mathbf{X}}_1 = \mathbf{X} \odot \mathbf{M}_1, \tilde{\mathbf{X}}_2 = \mathbf{X} \odot \mathbf{M}_2 \tag{5}$$

where $\odot$ represents Hadamard product. Each modality generates two highly masked but distinct views per iteration for contrastive learning and reconstruction.

Masked Graph Encoder. We designed a masked graph encoder based on GraphSAGE to extract latent representations from the masked input features $\tilde{\mathbf{X}} \in \mathbb{R}^{N\times F}$, using multi-layer GraphSAGE convolution:

$$\mathbf{H}^{(l+1)} = \text{SAGEConv}^{(l)}\left(\mathbf{H}^{(l)}, \mathcal{E}_{\text{shared}}\right) \tag{6}$$

Here, $\mathcal{E}_{\text{shared}}$ is the edge index of the cross-modal co-expression graph, and SAGEConv is the GraphSAGE aggregation layer. The final output is a low-dimensional embedding:

$$\mathbf{Z} = \text{SAGEConv}_{\text{last}}\left(\mathbf{H}^{(L-1)}, \mathcal{E}_{\text{shared}}\right) \in \mathbb{R}^{N\times d_z} \tag{7}$$

Here, d_z represents the latent dimension. This encoder performs message passing on a shared graph structure, enabling the masked features to be effectively inferred through the complete information of neighboring cells.

MLP as Decoder. To effectively reproduce the original high-dimensional features, we adopt a lightweight multi-layer perceptron (MLP) decoder and optimize the self-supervised reconstruction loss through nonlinear mapping. Let $\hat{Z}$ denote an aligned latent embedding, the first-layer hidden representation $H \in \mathbb{R}^{N\times h}$ (h is the hidden dimension) is computed as:

$$f(\hat{Z}) = W_2 \cdot \text{Dropout}(\sigma(W_1\hat{Z} + b_1)) + b_2 \tag{8}$$

where $W_1 \in \mathbb{R}^{h\times d_z}$, $W_2 \in \mathbb{R}^{F\times h}$, $b_1 \in \mathbb{R}^h$ and $b_2 \in \mathbb{R}^F$, σ = ReLU, with parameters initialized from a normal distribution to stabilize training dynamics.

The Overall Forward Flow of the Module. In each training iteration, the RNA and ATAC branches independently run the dual-mask autoencoders:

$$(\mathbf{Z}_1^{(r)}, \hat{\mathbf{X}}_1^{(r)}, \mathbf{M}_1^{(r)}), (\mathbf{Z}_2^{(r)}, \hat{\mathbf{X}}_2^{(r)}, \mathbf{M}_2^{(r)}) = \text{RNA-Branch}(\mathbf{X}^{(r)}, \mathcal{E}_{\text{shared}}) \tag{9}$$

$$(\mathbf{Z}_1^{(a)}, \hat{\mathbf{X}}_1^{(a)}, \mathbf{M}_1^{(a)}), (\mathbf{Z}_2^{(a)}, \hat{\mathbf{X}}_2^{(a)}, \mathbf{M}_2^{(a)}) = \text{ATAC-Branch}(\mathbf{X}^{(a)}, \mathcal{E}_{\text{shared}}) \tag{10}$$

Through the dual-mask autoencoder module, the model can learn robust single-modality representations at high mask rates and provide diverse views for subsequent contrastive learning and cross-modal fusion.

2.3 Cross-Fusion Module

To integrate the latent representations of the RNA and ATAC modalities, inspired by the Transformer [22], we propose a fusion module based on bidirectional cross-attention. This module enables each modality to independently query features from the other, achieving dynamic interaction and complementary enhancement of cross-modal information, and ultimately generating a unified joint cell representation. Given the pre-fusion representations of the RNA modality $\mathbf{Z}^{(r)} \in \mathbb{R}^{N\times d_z}$ and the ATAC modality $\mathbf{Z}^{(a)} \in \mathbb{R}^{N\times d_z}$, for the ATAC-to-RNA direction, the attention output $\mathbf{A}_h^{(a\to r)} \in \mathbb{R}^{N\times d_h}$ ($d_h = d_z/H$, where H is the number of heads) for head h is computed as:

$$A_h^{(a\to r)} = \text{softmax}\left(\frac{Q_h^{(a)}(K_h^{(r)})^T}{\sqrt{d_h}}\right)V_h^{(r)} \tag{11}$$

where query $Q_h^{(a)} = W_Q^{(h)} Z^{(a)}$, key $K_h^{(r)} = W_K^{(h)} Z^{(r)}$, and value $V_h^{(r)} = W_V^{(h)} Z^{(r)}$ ($W_Q^{(h)}, W_K^{(h)}, W_V^{(h)}$ are learnable projection matrices), and softmax is temperature-scaled ($\sqrt{d_h}$) to stabilize gradients. After multi-head concatenation, $A^{(a\to r)} = [A_1^{(a\to r)}; \ldots; A_H^{(a\to r)}]W_O$ (W_O is the output projection). Updated by residual Layernorm and FFN as:

$$\hat{\mathbf{Z}}^{(a)} = \text{LayerNorm}(\text{LayerNorm}(Z^{(a)} + A^{(a\to r)}) + \text{FFN}(\text{LayerNorm}(Z^{(a)} + A^{(a\to r)}))) \quad (12)$$

Similarly, the RNA-to-ATAC direction computes $A^{(r\to a)}$, generating $\hat{\mathbf{Z}}^{(r)}$. The entire process can be expressed as:

$$(\hat{\mathbf{Z}}^{(r)}, \hat{\mathbf{Z}}^{(a)}) = \text{CrossAttentionFusion}(\mathbf{Z}^{(r)}, \mathbf{Z}^{(a)}) \quad (13)$$

Ultimately, a unified joint representation $\mathbf{Z}_{\text{final}}$ is generated through adjustable weighted linear fusion:

$$\mathbf{Z}_{\text{final}} = w \cdot \hat{\mathbf{Z}}^{(r)} + (1 - w) \cdot \hat{\mathbf{Z}}^{(a)} \quad (14)$$

Here, the weight $w \in [0, 1]$ controls the relative contributions of the two modalities in the joint representation.

2.4 Overall Loss Function

The overall loss function $\mathcal{L}_{\text{total}}$ consists of three parts:

$$\mathcal{L}_{\text{total}} = \mathcal{L}_{\text{rna}} + \mathcal{L}_{\text{atac}} + \delta \cdot \mathcal{L}_{\text{cross\_contra}} \quad (15)$$

where $\mathcal{L}_{\text{rna}}$ and $\mathcal{L}_{\text{atac}}$ are the total single-modality losses of the RNA and ATAC modalities, respectively, $\mathcal{L}_{\text{cross\_contra}}$ is the cross-modal contrastive loss, and δ is the cross-modal loss weight.

Single-Modality Total Loss. For each modality (using RNA as an example), the single-modality loss $\mathcal{L}_{\text{rna}}$ consists of three terms:

$$\mathcal{L}_{\text{rna}} = \alpha \cdot \mathcal{L}_{\text{rec}} + \beta \cdot \mathcal{L}_{\text{intra\_cont}} + \gamma \cdot \mathcal{L}_{\text{mask}} \quad (16)$$

$\mathcal{L}_{\text{rec}}$: The mean square error (MSE) is used to measure the reconstruction quality of two mask views and is averaged across all positions.

$$\mathcal{L}_{\text{rec}} = \frac{1}{2}\left(\text{MSE}(\hat{\mathbf{X}}_1^{(r)}, \mathbf{X}^{(r)}) + \text{MSE}(\hat{\mathbf{X}}_2^{(r)}, \mathbf{X}^{(r)})\right) \quad (17)$$

$\mathcal{L}_{\text{intra\_contra}}$: Based on the InfoNCE form, contrastive learning is performed on the two mask views of the same modality to bring the positive pair (two views of the same cell) closer and push negative samples away:

$$\mathcal{L}_{\text{intra\_contra}} = -\frac{1}{2N}\sum_{i=1}^{2N} \log \frac{\exp(\text{sim}(z_i, z_i^+)/\tau)}{\sum_{j=1}^{2N} \exp(\text{sim}(z_i, z_j)/\tau)} \quad (18)$$

where z_i^+ denotes the positive sample (corresponding view), τ is the temperature parameter, and $\text{sim}(\cdot,\cdot)$ is cosine similarity.
$\mathcal{L}_{\text{mask}}$: Use binary cross-entropy (BCE with logits) to supervise the predictive ability of the mask predictor for the real mask, and encourage the model to learn the features that provide information for restoring the original data distribution:

$$\mathcal{L}_{\text{mask}} = \text{BCE}(\hat{\mathbf{M}}_r, \mathbf{M}_r \| \mathbf{M}_r) \tag{19}$$

The RNA and ATAC modalities adopt the same loss form, where $\alpha, \beta, \gamma \in [0,1]$ and $\alpha + \beta + \gamma = 1$.

Cross-Modal Loss. $\mathcal{L}_{\text{cross\_contra}}$: Given the fused embeddings $\hat{\mathbf{Z}}^{(r)}, \hat{\mathbf{Z}}^{(a)} \in \mathbb{R}^{N \times L}$, this loss maximizes positive-pair similarity:

$$\mathcal{L}_{\text{cross\_contra}} = -\frac{1}{N}\sum_{i=1}^{N} \log \frac{\exp(\text{sim}(\hat{\mathbf{Z}}_i^{(r)}, \hat{\mathbf{Z}}_i^{(a)})/\tau)}{\sum_{j=1}^{N} \exp(\text{sim}(\hat{\mathbf{Z}}_i^{(r)}, \hat{\mathbf{Z}}_j^{(a)})/\tau)} \tag{20}$$

3 Experiments

This study selected four multi-omics datasets from different platforms covering single-cell transcriptome and chromatin accessibility, as shown in Table 1. We transformed the non-RNA modalities in each dataset into representations that share the feature space with scRNA-seq, using Signac [21] for the transformation. Separate preprocessing pipelines were applied to the scRNA-seq and transformed scATAC-seq data respectively.

In the benchmark test, we selected seven recent integration methods for systematic comparison: UnionCom [4], JointMDS [6], scTopoGAN [18], Pamona [5], scMGCL [7], SCOT [8], and scPairing [17]. These methods represent the mainstream technical paradigms in multi-omics integration. The experimental procedures and parameter settings of each method follow their original publications.

Following previous studies [19] and benchmark evaluations [25], we adopted FOSCTTM and LAT as the core metrics for evaluating cell-matching accuracy in the integration task; ARI, NMI, and AMI are used to quantify clustering performance of the generated embeddings. Furthermore, we evaluated the ability to mitigate batch effects and preserve cell type specificity through ASW and cLISI.

4 Results

4.1 Strong and Robust Alignment

We conducted integration tests on the BMMC data, performing 10 independent experiments on each of the eight methods: scMMGC, JointMDS, Pamona, SCOT, UnionCom, scTopoGAN, scMGCL, and scPairing. We recorded the performance of each method across all metrics after each run. To ensure the stability

Table 1. The summary of datasets.

Dataset	Cells	Genes	Peaks	Cell Types	Protocol
BMMC	6,224	13,381	116,490	21	10x Genomics
CITE_PBMC	9,631	20,955	107,194	19	CITE-seq
TEA_PBMC	5,041	9,955	14,732	11	TEA-seq
P0BraCor	5,081	19,322	229,439	19	SNARE-seq

and validity of the experimental results, we report the average over the 10 runs as the final score for each method.

Figure 2A shows the visualization results of the integrated embeddings from the top three methods of the core indicator FOSCTTM. Compared with scPairing and UnionCom, the embeddings generated by scMMGC show tighter aggregation of cells of the same type and clearer boundaries between different types, indicating stronger qualitative integration. To evaluate whether each method can learn modality-specific features, we predict cell types during the ATAC-to-RNA label transfer process, as shown in Fig. 2B, which presents the confusion matrices of the two top-performing methods on LAT. Both methods show a clear diagonal pattern, indicating that they capture most cell types. Notably, scMMGC more accurately predicts T cell subtypes (CD4+T activated, CD4+T naive, and CD8+ T) compared with scPairing. Contrastive learning and autoencoder models (such as scPairing) usually rely on global features to classify subtypes, which is vulnerable to noise. However, scMMGC partially masks the input data and reconstructs the data to capture the structure of local features, reducing the impact of noise on the model through data augmentation strategies.

Figure 2C quantitatively presents the scores of each method on FOSCTTM and LAT. scMMGC achieves the best scores on both metrics. Compared with single-modality graph input models (such as scMGCL), the co-expression graph captures the shared topology across modalities more effectively, confirming the value of co-expression graphs and data augmentation for autoencoder models. Overall, scMMGC demonstrates strong and robust integration performance across all comparisons.

4.2 Clustering Performance

To further demonstrate the applicability of scMMGC, we conducted clustering experiments on the CITE_PBMC dataset. To ensure fairness and repeatability, we applied the K-Means algorithm to the embeddings generated by each method, with the number of clusters set to the actual number of cell types in the dataset for all methods.

Figure 3A shows the UMAP clustering visualization of the three methods with the highest ARI results. It can be observed that compared with the clustering results of the Pamona and scTopoGAN methods, the cell clusters embedded in scMMGC are not only compactly distributed internally, but also have high

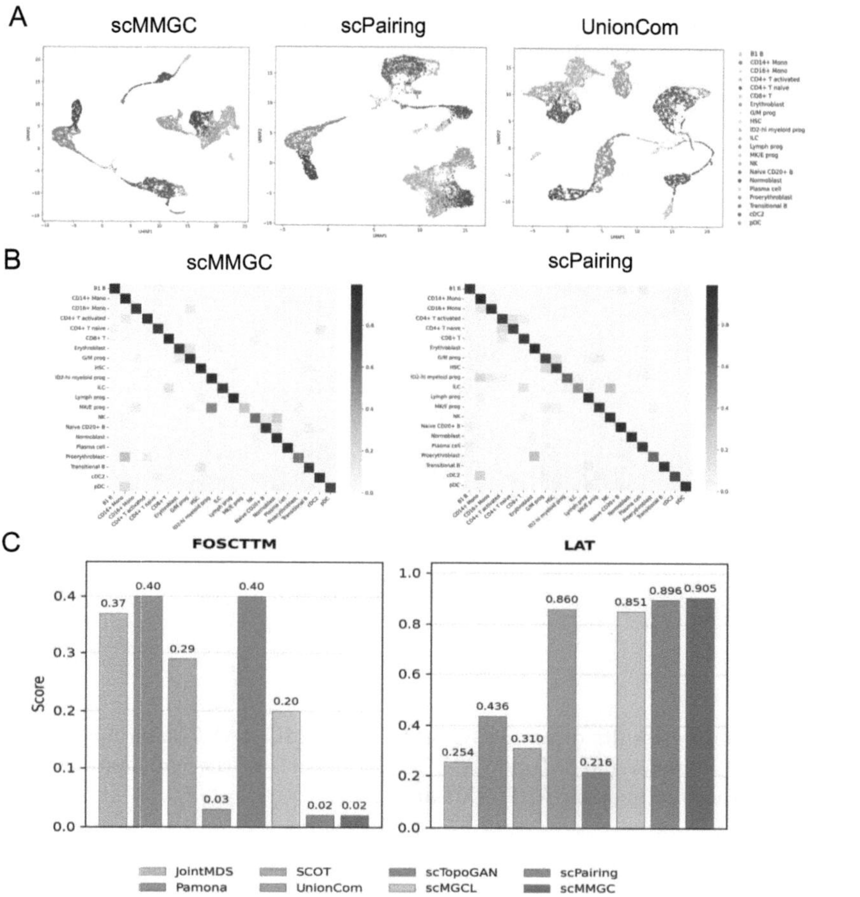

Fig. 2. Integration performance of scMMGC on the BMMC. (A) Embedding visualization of scMMGC, scPairing and UnionCom. (B) Confusion matrix of LAT results of scMMGC and scPairing. (C) Bar charts of the indicators of scMMGC and seven other methods on FOSCTTM and LAT.

boundary discrimination of key subtypes and relatively clear boundaries. The boundaries of the other two methods are blurred and the intra-cluster structures are fragmented, indicating that they have lost the inherent heterogeneity of cells to a certain extent.

The quantitative results (Fig. 3B) show that scMMGC achieves ARI, NMI, and AMI of 0.586, 0.795, and 0.791 respectively, outperforming comparison methods such as Pamona and consistent with the qualitative observations in the UMAP visualization. In contrast, scMGCL lags behind the other representative methods across all metrics. Compared with the graph encoder model Pamona, scMMGC further integrates bilateral contrastive learning on top of the dual-mask graph encoder, enhancing clustering by learning cross-omics sample similarity and providing clearer boundaries for the identified cell populations. Both visualization and quantitative analysis on CITE_PBMC confirm the strong clustering performance of scMMGC.

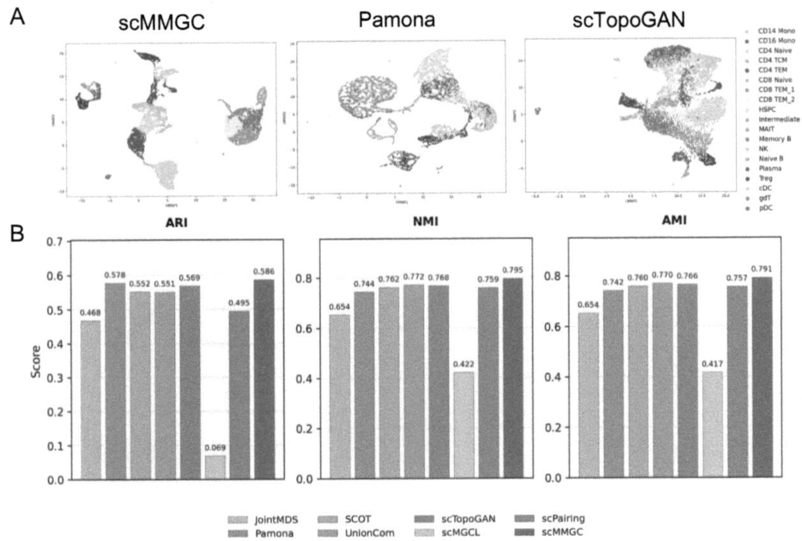

Fig. 3. Clustering results of scMMGC on CITE_PBMC. (A) Clustering Visualization of scMMGC, Pamona and scTopoGAN. (B) Bar charts of the indicators of scMMGC and seven other methods on ARI, NMI and AMI.

4.3 Achieving Batch Correction and Biological Preservation

Batch effects are usually caused by factors such as experimental conditions, sequencing techniques, and processing time, often introducing systematic biases and masking the true biological characteristics, thereby affecting the reliability and interpretability of the data. It is a widespread and challenging problem in multi-omics integration, which may lead to limited omics integration, incorrect cell clustering and distorted gene expression in downstream analysis.

Therefore, developing methods that can effectively mitigate batch effects while preserving biology is of vital importance for single-cell multi-omics analysis. We conducted the corresponding batch correction and biological retention experiments on the TEA_PBMC dataset. Beyond integration and clustering, scMMGC also mitigates batch effects while preserving biological signals. scMMGC achieved the best results on both batch-corrected ASW and biological retention cLISI (Fig. 4), with an ASW of 0.572 and a cLISI of 1.1315, outperforming all seven comparison methods.

Compared with the graph encoder Pamona and the contrastive learning-based scPairing, the cross-fusion module and bilateral contrastive learning adopted by scMMGC enhance cross-modal feature interaction, mitigating batch effects while retaining biological features.

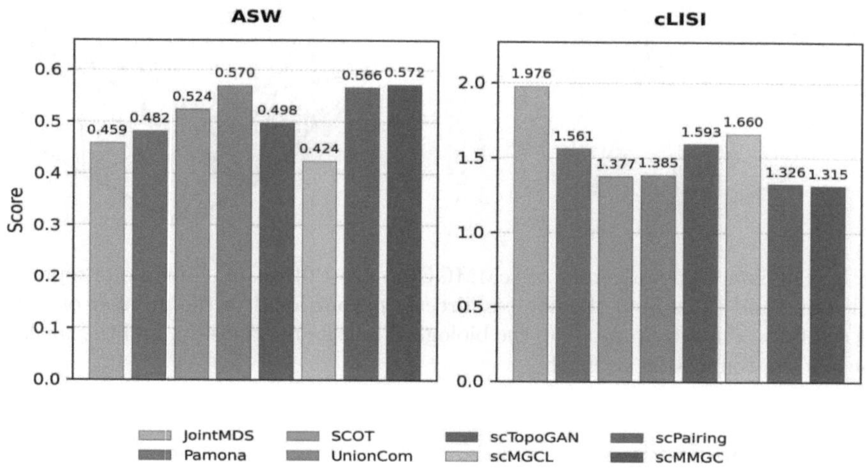

Fig. 4. Bar charts of ASW and cLISI indicators of scMMGC on TEA_PBMC.

4.4 Revealing Underlying Developmental Trajectory

Trajectory inference helps integrate transcriptome features and developmental positions to organize the sequence of cells, which is crucial for understanding how cells differentiate under different conditions. In this study, we conducted PAGA analysis on P0BraCor based on the integrated embeddings [23] to obtain the differentiation trajectories of the cell topologies of each lineage over time.

As shown in Fig. 5, this process captures the transitional states between lineage cells and reveals the continuum of cell differentiation. The cell state connections in the PAGA graph displayed by scMGCL are rather complex, and the key transition nodes are concealed by redundant edges. The PAGA map presented by scMMGC clearly restores the developmental differentiation path starting from RG (radial glial cells), mirroring the cortical structure and pseudo-temporal dynamics of mice after birth, which is crucial for the analysis of the brain after birth.

Notably, even between highly heterogeneous neuronal subtypes (such as Ex56_Epha6 and Ex345_Foxp1), the model maintains a reasonable topological distance, identifying weak developmental signals while avoiding false connections caused by batch effects. This indicates that scMMGC can reliably distinguish cell lineages and reveal biologically plausible developmental trajectories.

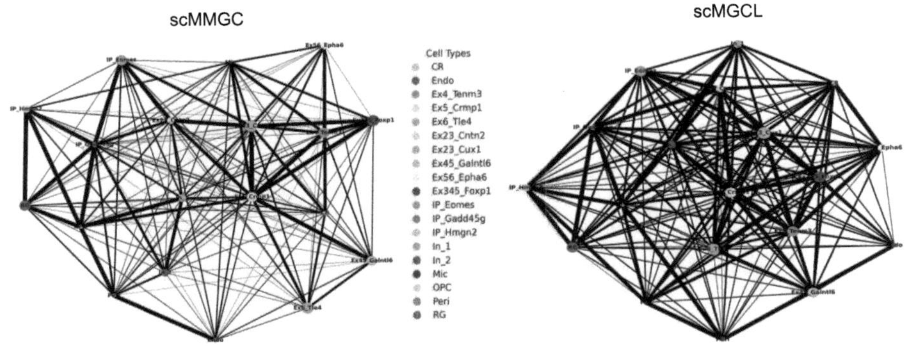

Fig. 5. The inference trajectory of scMMGC on the P0BraCor. Each node represents a cell type, and the size of the node is directly proportional to the number of cells of that cell type. The edge represents the biological lineage relationship, and the thickness indicates the connection strength.

4.5 Ablation Study

scMMGC consists of three modules: the cross-modal co-expression graph module (C-EGM), the dual-mask autoencoder module (D-MEM), and the cross-fusion module (C-FM). C-EGM extracts shared topological information across modalities, D-MEM reduces redundant feature dependence under high-noise conditions, and C-FM facilitates feature interaction to achieve alignment. We conducted ablation studies on the BMMC, TEA_PBMC, and P0BraCor datasets, systematically removing functional modules while maintaining the integrity of the remaining architecture to demonstrate the effectiveness of each module, as shown in Table 2.

By removing the C-EGM module, our results showed that LAT, ARI and ASW decreased by 66.19%, 7.72% and 16.04% respectively on BMMC, and decreased by 46.56%, 5.93% and 12.41% respectively on TEA_PBMC. It decreased by 38.14%, 31.70% and 12.07% on P0BraCor. This indicates that the cross-modal nearest neighbor co-expression graph captures shared topological features across modalities and overcomes data sparsity, enhancing cross-modal alignment. Secondly, removing the D-MEM module led to a notable decline on all three datasets. Specifically, among the positive metrics on BMMC, LAT showed the largest drop of 53.81%, and TEA_PBMC and P0BraCor also exhibited clear performance losses. This confirms that random masking enables the model to learn key features while suppressing modality-specific noise in single-cell data. Finally, after removing the C-FM module, the positive metrics decreased by an average of 12.62%, 39.95%, and 7.52% on the three datasets. This quantitatively confirms the role of the C-FM module in achieving alignment through cross-modal feature interaction.

After the removal of each module, the negative metrics all increased to varying degrees. Notably, FOSCTTM rose sharply after the removal of D-MEM, indicating that the masking mechanism substantially improves integration quality. In conclusion, this ablation study confirms that the three modules jointly contribute to the performance of scMMGC in multi-omics integration.

Table 2. Ablation study results on different datasets.

Dataset	C-EGM	D-MEM	C-FM	FOSCTTM	LAT	ARI	ASW	cLISI
BMMC		✓	✓	0.31	0.306	0.574	0.513	1.277
	✓		✓	0.20	0.418	0.566	0.490	1.320
	✓	✓		0.07	0.774	0.453	0.545	1.172
	✓	✓	✓	0.02	0.905	0.622	0.611	1.167
TEA_PBMC		✓	✓	0.34	0.458	0.444	0.501	1.376
	✓		✓	0.16	0.675	0.451	0.488	1.474
	✓	✓		0.08	0.747	0.247	0.547	1.322
	✓	✓	✓	0.01	0.857	0.472	0.572	1.315
P0BraCor		✓	✓	0.23	0.446	0.278	0.488	2.008
	✓		✓	0.15	0.563	0.321	0.492	2.341
	✓	✓		0.05	0.645	0.278	0.514	1.974
	✓	✓	✓	0.01	0.721	0.407	0.555	1.901

5 Discussion

In this study, we propose scMMGC, a generative integration method that combines co-expression graphs with a masked autoencoder framework and is driven by cross-modal fusion, to generate high-quality joint cell embeddings. We capture cross-modal shared information through co-expression graphs, implicitly reduce batch effects through bilateral contrastive learning, use masked autoencoders to reduce the model's dependence on redundant features, and promote feature interaction through the cross-fusion module. Experimental results show that scMMGC consistently matches or outperforms mainstream methods in core integration tasks. The generated embeddings differentiate cell subtypes and support clustering, while mitigating batch effects and retaining cell type specificity. In trajectory inference, scMMGC recovers clear neuronal lineage structure, enabling reconstruction of differentiation paths. These results provide a practical tool for studying cellular heterogeneity, development, and immune regulation.

In future work, this framework can be extended to other omics modalities (such as spatial transcriptomics) and may benefit from adversarial models or spatio-temporal priors to further improve embedding quality, scalability, and applicability.

Acknowledgments. This work was supported by the National Natural Science Foundation of China under Grants (No.62202162).

Data Availability Statement. All datasets used in this study are publicly available. The BMMC dataset (GSE194122), and P0BraCor (GSE126074) were obtained from the GEO database. The CITE_PBMC dataset is from the 10x Genomics platform https://www.10xgenomics.com/datasets/pbmc-from-a-healthy-donor-granulocytes-removed-through-cell-sorting-3-k-1-standard-2-0-0. The TEA_PBMC dataset is from https://github.com/PYangLab/Matilda/tree/main/data/TEAseq.

Competing Interests. The authors declare no competing interests.

References

1. Baysoy, A., Bai, Z., Satija, R., Fan, R.: The technological landscape and applications of single-cell multi-omics. Nat. Rev. Mol. Cell Biol. **24**(10), 695–713 (2023)
2. Buenrostro, J.D., et al.: Single-cell chromatin accessibility reveals principles of regulatory variation. Nature **523**(7561), 486–490 (2015)
3. Butler, A., Hoffman, P., Smibert, P., Papalexi, E., Satija, R.: Integrating single-cell transcriptomic data across different conditions, technologies, and species. Nat. Biotechnol. **36**(5), 411–420 (2018)
4. Cao, K., Bai, X., Hong, Y., Wan, L.: Unsupervised topological alignment for single-cell multi-omics integration. Bioinformatics **36**(Supplement_1), i48–i56 (2020)
5. Cao, K., Hong, Y., Wan, L.: Manifold alignment for heterogeneous single-cell multi-omics data integration using pamona. Bioinformatics **38**(1), 211–219 (2021)
6. Chen, D., Fan, B., Oliver, C., Borgwardt, K.: Unsupervised manifold alignment with joint multidimensional scaling. In: Proceedings of the Eleventh International Conference on Learning Representations. OpenReview.net, Kigali, Rwanda, accepted at ICLR 2023 (2023)
7. Cheng, Z., Lu, R., Zhang, S.: scmgcl: accurate and efficient integration representation of single-cell multi-omics data. Bioinformatics **41**(7), btaf392 (2025)
8. Demetci, P., Santorella, R., Sandstede, B., Noble, W.S., Singh, R.: Scot: single-cell multi-omics alignment with optimal transport. J. Comput. Biol. **29**(1), 3–18 (2022)
9. Goltsev, Y., et al.: Deep profiling of mouse splenic architecture with codex multiplexed imaging. Cell **174**(4), 968–981 (2018)
10. Hao, Y., et al.: Integrated analysis of multimodal single-cell data. Cell **184**(13), 3573-3587.e29 (2021)
11. Hao, Y., Stuart, T., Kowalski, M.H., Choudhary, S., Satija, R., et al.: Dictionary learning for integrative, multimodal and scalable single-cell analysis. Nat. Biotechnol. **42**(2), 293–304 (2024)
12. He, K., Chen, X., Xie, S., Li, Y., Dollár, P., Girshick, R.B.: Masked autoencoders are scalable vision learners. In: 2022 IEEE/CVF Conference on Computer Vision and Pattern Recognition (CVPR), pp. 15979–15988. IEEE, New Orleans (2022)
13. Huizing, G.J., Deutschmann, I.M., Peyré, G., Cantini, L.: Paired single-cell multi-omics data integration with mowgli. Nat. Commun. **14**(1), 7711 (2023)
14. Kaya-Okur, H.S., Liu, H., Henikoff, J.G., Charte, J., Henikoff, S.: CUT&Tag for efficient epigenomic profiling of small samples and single cells. Nat. Methods **16**(10), 1101–1103 (2019)
15. Li, W., et al.: A versatile deep graph contrastive learning framework for single-cell proteomics embedding. In: bioRxiv, pp. 2022–12 (2022)
16. Ma, A., McDermaid, A., Xu, J., Chang, Y., Ma, Q.: Integrative methods and practical challenges for single-cell multi-omics. Trends Biotechnol. **38**(9), 1007–1022 (2020)

17. Niu, J., Vasquez-Rios, C., Ding, J.: Single-cell multiomics data integration and generation with scpairing. Cell Rep. Methods (2025)
18. Singh, A., Biharie, K., Reinders, M.J., Mahfouz, A., Abdelaal, T.: sctopogan: unsupervised manifold alignment of single-cell data. Bioinf. Adv. **3**(1), vbad171 (2023)
19. Singh, R., et al.: Unsupervised manifold alignment for single-cell multi-omics data. In: Proceedings of the 11th ACM International Conference on Bioinformatics, Computational Biology and Health Informatics, pp. 1–10 (2020)
20. Stoeckius, M., et al.: Simultaneous epitope and transcriptome measurement in single cells. Nat. Methods **14**(9), 865–868 (2017)
21. Stuart, T., Srivastava, A., Madad, S., Lareau, C.A., Satija, R.: Single-cell chromatin state analysis with signac. Nat. Methods **18**(11), 1333–1341 (2021)
22. Vaswani, A., et al.: Attention is all you need. Adv. Neural Inf. Process. Syst. **30** (2017)
23. Wolf, F.A., et al.: Paga: graph abstraction reconciles clustering with trajectory inference through a topology preserving map of single cells. Genome Biol. **20**(1), 59 (2019)
24. Xu, Y., McCord, R.P.: Diagonal integration of multimodal single-cell data: potential pitfalls and paths forward. Nat. Commun. **13**, 3505 (2022)
25. Yáñez, A., et al.: Granulocyte-monocyte progenitors and monocyte-dendritic cell progenitors independently produce functionally distinct monocytes. Immunity **47**(5), 890–902 (2017)
26. Zhang, K., Zemke, N.R., Armand, E.J., et al.: A fast, scalable and versatile tool for analysis of single-cell omics data. Nat. Methods **21**, 217–227 (2024)
27. Zhang, T., Zhang, H., Ren, J., Wu, Z., Zhao, Z., Wang, G.: scdrmae: integrating masked autoencoder with residual attention networks to leverage omics feature dependencies for accurate cell clustering. Bioinformatics **40**(10), btae599 (2024)
28. Zheng, G.X., et al.: Massively parallel digital transcriptional profiling of single cells. Nat. Commun. **8**(1), 14049 (2017)

A Dependency-Aware Generative Model with Bi-decoders for Super-Resolving Spatial Transcriptome Data from Histology Images

Yuqi Chen[1,2], Peng Jiang[1,2], Tian Tian[1,2], and Juan Liu[1,2(✉)]

[1] School of Artificial Intelligence, Wuhan University, Wuhan 430072, China
{chenyuqi,pelenjiang,tiantian87,liujuan}@whu.edu.cn
[2] School of Computer Science, Wuhan University, Wuhan 430072, China

Abstract. Due to the high cost of sequencing, there is a scarcity of high-resolved spatial transcriptome (ST) data available for downstream analysis. In this paper, we propose a deep generative model based on a dependency-aware Variational AutoEncoder (VAE) with bi-decoders, called HistoSST, to infer super-resolved ST data from histology images. HistoSST combines a Gaussian Process prior and a Gaussian prior to dynamically capture the spatial dependency and global information in histology images. And then, it establishes the close correlation between the image patch and gene expression via dual decoders. Depending on the size of the image patch, HistoSST can generate ST data of any resolution. If the patch is smaller than a spot of existing ST data, HistoSST can generate its super-resolved data. The source code is available at https://github.com/PelenJiang/HistoSST.

Keywords: Spatial transcriptome · Histology image · Variational Autoencoder · Super Resolution · Gene expression prediction

1 Introduction

The spatial transcriptome (ST) sequencing technologies can simultaneously obtain the gene expression and spatial location of spots in tissues, effectively overcoming the limitations of traditional bulk and single-cell sequencing technologies in capturing spatial information. Since emerging, such technologies have played increasingly important roles in fields such as biological science research, disease diagnosis, drug development, and precision medicine. However, due to high cost and the need for specialized equipment and conditions in sample preparation and sequencing processes, the ST technologies are currently unable to be widely applied in many research institutions and laboratories, resulting in a scarcity of available ST data. At the same time, the existing ST technologies either have high resolution but cannot cover the entire transcriptome, or can cover the entire transcriptome but have low resolution. Neither of which can

X. Cui et al. (Eds.): ISBRA 2026, LNBI 16690, pp. 42–53, 2027.
https://doi.org/10.1007/978-981-92-3716-6_4

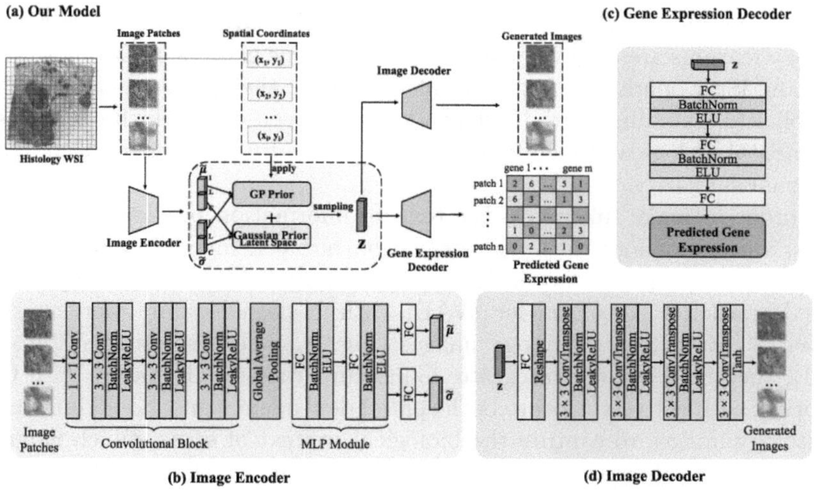

Fig. 1. Our Model and Its Key Components. (a) Architecture of HistoSST. (b) Image Encoder. (c) Gene Expression Decoder. (d) Image Decoder.

achieve high resolution and high gene multiplexing capabilities simultaneously, which limits the application of ST data in research fields such as disease mechanisms and biological developmental processes.

Machine learning techniques have been used to predict spatial gene expression values from histology images, such as ST-Net [4], BLEEP [13], Hist2ST [14], THItoGene [6], and HistoGene [9]. However, above mentioned models are limited to inferring ST data with the same resolution as the ST data used to train them, we called spot-level resolution hereinafter. Though the dense image patch sampling strategy proposed in [9] can be used to enable these methods to predict super-resolved ST data with 4, 9, 25, or even higher times of the original spot-level resolution, the models themselves do not directly learn the fine-grained correlation between image super-pixels (patches) and gene expression during construction, resulting in low prediction performance.

Recently, several researches focus on predicting super-resolved gene expression from low-resolution ST data. Bergenstråhle *et al.* proposed a deep generative model called XFuse for inferring super-resolved gene expression by integrating low-resolution ISC data with high-resolution histology image data from the same tissue section [3]. Since XFuse uses Gaussian distribution to characterize the image data, the rich texture information in the image is underutilized. In order to fully utilize the rich information provided by histology images, Zhang *et al.* proposed the iStar method based on hierarchical image feature extraction for integrating ST data and high-resolution histology images to predict super-resolved gene expression [15]. They conducted comparative experiments to show that the performance of iStar is superior to that of XFuse, both in-sample and out-of-sample predictions [15]. Nevertheless, the training process of the histology feature extractor in iStar is independent of that of the super-resolved gene expression predictor, which makes it impossible to guarantee that the extracted histology features are highly correlated with the gene expression. Moreover, both Xfuse and iStar operate on a significant limitation: they predict gene expression by implicitly assuming spatial independence between cells, which overlooks the fundamental biological principle that spatial proximity is strongly linked to transcriptional similarity.

In order to make full use of the texture information provided by histology images, and to explore the close correlation between image features and gene expression, we propose a novel deep generative model based on a dependency-aware Variational AutoEncoder (VAE) with bi-decoders for inferring super-resolved ST data from histology images (Fig. 1), called as HistoSST. Inspired by [11], HistoSST adeptly integrates Gaussian Process (GP) priors with Gaussian priors to effectively capture both spatial dependency and global information in histology images to capture the biological context of spots, which is ignored by current state-of-the-art (SOTA). The experimental results on three publicly available datasets show that the HistoSST achieves SOTA performance in both spot-level and super-resolved gene expression prediction.

2 Methods

2.1 Overview of HistoSST

As shown in Fig. 1(a), each histology whole slide image (WSI) is firstly cropped into a set of image patches with fixed size. Then HistoSST incorporates image patches together with their spatial context as input and applies a VAE-based generative framework to generate the associated gene expression data. Specifically, HistoSST is comprised of an encoder and two decoders including an image decoder and a gene expression decoder, facilitating collaborative feature learning. Using variational inference, the encoder maps each image patch to a latent space and then the dual decoders reconstruct the image patch and predict gene expression, respectively, enabling joint learning from both modalities. To better model spatial correlations and global patterns, HistoSST utilizes hybrid latent embeddings sampled from both GP and standard Gaussian priors.

2.2 Image Encoder

The image encoder consists of a convolutional block for image feature extraction, a multilayer perceptron (MLP) module for further feature integration and compression to map the image features into the latent space, and two fully connected (FC) layers for learning the parameters of the latent distribution, μ and σ^2, as illustrated in Fig. 1(b). The convolutional block contains four convolutional layers, each followed by Batch Normalization and a nonlinear activation function, to extract multi-scale spatial features from histological images. The resulting feature maps are flattened by a global average pooling (GAP) layer and fed into the MLP. The MLP module comprises two fully connected layers, each followed by Batch Normalization and a nonlinear activation function.

Finally, the encoded features are passed through two separate FC layers to infer the mean and variance of the latent variables.

2.3 Dual Decoders

To enhance the accuracy of gene expression prediction, we design a dual-decoder architecture comprising a gene expression decoder and a histological image decoder. As shown in Fig. 1(c) and (d), the gene expression decoder has a structure similar to the MLP in the encoder, ending with a fully connected (FC) layer to model the mean of the predicted gene distribution. The histological image decoder first uses a fully connected layer to increase the feature dimensionality, then reshapes the tensor into a 3D feature map, and finally reconstructs the image through four transposed convolutional layers with a kernel size of 3.

2.4 Variational Inference with GP and Gaussian Priors

The ultimate objective of this generative model is to maximize the joint conditional log-likelihood of observing image $\mathbf{x}$ and gene expression $\mathbf{g}$ given the spatial coordinates $\mathbf{y}$, $\log p(\mathbf{x}, \mathbf{g} \mid \mathbf{y})$, which is equivalent to maximize the evidence lower bound (ELBO). Let $\mathbf{z}$ be a C-dimensional latent embedding obtained via the image encoder, we can derive the ELBO by introducing a variational posterior $q(\mathbf{z} \mid \mathbf{x}, \mathbf{y})$, where $KL(.)$ represents the KullbackLeibler (KL) divergence:

$$ELBO = \underbrace{\mathbb{E}_{q(\mathbf{z}|\mathbf{x},\mathbf{y})}\left[\log p\left(\mathbf{g} \mid \mathbf{z}\right)\right]}_{\text{Gene Prediction}} + \underbrace{\mathbb{E}_{q(\mathbf{z}|\mathbf{x},\mathbf{y})}\left[\log p\left(\mathbf{x} \mid \mathbf{z}\right)\right]}_{\text{Image Reconstruciton}} - \underbrace{\mathrm{KL}\left(q\left(\mathbf{z} \mid \mathbf{x}, \mathbf{y}\right) \| p(\mathbf{z} \mid \mathbf{y})\right)}_{\text{Spatial Regularization}}. \tag{1}$$

We believe that the spatial location information of image patches in WSI essentially serves as a bridge connecting local details with global structure - it not only carries the natural spatial orderliness of biological tissues but also provides contextual constraints for model learning. Therefore, we have introduced an additional GP prior in addition to the original Gaussian prior of VAE. They work together to model the potential embedding $\mathbf{z}$. Specifically, the first L dimensions of the latent embedding $\mathbf{z}$ are modeled with a GP prior, while the remaining $C-L$ dimensions follow a standard Gaussian prior. Consequently, the KL divergence in Eq. (1) can be decomposed into GP prior and Gaussian prior terms:

$$KL(.) = \underbrace{\mathrm{KL}\left(q\left(\mathbf{z}^{1:L} \mid \mathbf{x}, \mathbf{y}\right) \| p(\mathbf{z}^{1:L} \mid \mathbf{y})\right)}_{\text{Spatial Regularization}} + \underbrace{\mathrm{KL}\left(q\left(\mathbf{z}^{L+1:C} \mid \mathbf{x}\right) \| p(\mathbf{z}^{L+1:C})\right)}_{\text{Other Regularization}}. \tag{2}$$

2.5 Overall Loss Function

Based in ELBO, wen can obtain the overall loss function L_{Total} of HistoSST as the sum of three components: the generation loss of gene expression, the reconstruction loss of histological images, and the KL divergence loss:

$$L_{Total} = -ELBO = L_{gene} + L_{image} + L_{KL}. \tag{3}$$

Gene expression data are fundamentally count-based, exhibiting discrete, non-negative, and discontinuous characteristics. Therefore, the gene likelihood is usually modeled by the NB distribution. As a result, we can define the generation loss of gene expression using the negative log-likelihood of the NB distribution:

$$L_{\text{gene}} = -\mathbb{E}_{q(\mathbf{z}|\mathbf{x},\mathbf{y})}\left[\log p(\mathbf{g} \mid \mathbf{z})\right] = -\log\big(\text{NB}(\mathbf{g} \mid \mathbf{r}, \theta)\big), \tag{4}$$

where θ is a trainable parameter set in NB representing the dispersion of genes.

The reconstruction loss for histological images is typically calculated using mean squared error (MSE):

$$L_{image} = -\mathbb{E}_{q(\mathbf{z}|\mathbf{x},\mathbf{y})}\left[\log p(\mathbf{x} \mid \mathbf{z})\right] = \sum_i \|x_i - \hat{x}_i\|^2 \tag{5}$$

where x_i, $\hat{x}_i$ denote the original and reconstructed image patches, respectively.

The KL loss includes both KL divergence of Gaussian and GP priors, as Eq. (2). The specific calculation process can be referred to [10,11].

3 Experiments and Results

3.1 Datasets and Preprocessing

We used three public ST datasets for the evaluation experiments: HER2+ [2], cSCC [5], and HD mouse kidney datasets. The resolution of ST data in HER2+ and cSCC datasets is relatively low, with each spot containing multiple cells and gaps between spots, while HD mouse kidney dataset provides high-resolved ST data at the cellular and subcellular levels, with no gaps between spots. Each histological whole slide image (WSI) paired with the ST data has been preprocessed into a set of image patches. we set the patch size as the default (32).

In the evaluation experiments, we chose the spatially variable genes (SVGs) as the evaluation genes in all experiments. This is because that SVGs refer to genes with significantly altered expression patterns within a specific spatial domain, which are often associated with changes in tissue structure. To this end, we chose 314 SVGs for HER2+ dataset, 448 SVGs for cSCC dataset and 1,152 SVGs for HD mouse kidney dataset. Furthermore, we used SSIM, PCC, RMSE and JSD as the measurements of the prediction performance.

3.2 Experiment Settings

Our model was implemented in Python language based on PyTorch framework. All models were trained on a server running 64 bit Ubuntu 18.04.6 with 2 Nvidia RTX 3090 GPUs. We set number of inducing points as 361, batch size as 32, learning rate as 0.001, and maximum iteration number as 1000 for our method. For other methods, we used their default parameter settings.

3.3 Prediction of Spot-Level Gene Expression

In this experiment, we compared our method with four representative methods for predicting spot-level gene expression from histology images using the H1 and H2 samples from the HER2+ dataset, together with the P9_rep2 and P9_rep3 samples from the cSCC dataset. The current experimental setup focuses on samples with relatively consistent tissue morphology and biological context, providing a controlled evaluation setting for method validation. This design mitigates confounding effects introduced by substantial tissue heterogeneity and enables a more reliable assessment of the imagegene expression mapping. For the Her2+ dataset, H1 and H2 were utilized for training and testing, respectively. For cSCC dataset, P9_rep2 and P9_rep3 were employed for training and testing, respectively. Since our method generated the super-resolved gene expression, we took the sum of the predicted sub-region gene expression inside each spot as the gene expression at that spot. The comparison results are presented in Table 1. From which we can see that our method performs the best in all four indicators on both datasets, demonstrating its good predictive ability and strong generalizability.

Table 1. Comparison of Different Methods in Predicting Spot-Level Gene Expression

Dataset	Methods	SSIM (↑)	PCC (↑)	RMSE (↓)	JSD (↓)
HER2+	ST-Net [4]	0.0125	0.0790	0.0374	0.5568
	HistoGene [9]	0.0834	0.0996	0.6805	0.5302
	Hist2ST [14]	0.1905	0.2818	0.6392	0.4990
	THItoGene [6]	0.2026	0.2734	0.6367	0.4966
	HistoSST	**0.4268**	**0.5298**	**0.0049**	**0.4755**
cSCC	ST-Net [4]	0.1485	0.0715	0.4606	0.6973
	HistoGene [9]	0.0459	0.1103	0.4549	0.6824
	Hist2ST [14]	0.0797	0.1610	0.4874	0.6711
	THItoGene [6]	0.0772	0.1688	0.4987	0.6644
	HistoSST	**0.3405**	**0.4115**	**0.0032**	**0.5981**

3.4 Prediction of Super-Resolved Gene Expression

As we know, XFuse and iStar are two existing SOTA methods for predicting super-resolved gene expression from histology images. Now that Zhang *et al.* have showed that iStar outperformed XFuse in their recent work [15], we evaluated the predictive ability of our method for super resolved gene expression by comparing it with iStar. Since the HD mouse kidney dataset provides gene expression data at three resolutions for the same tissue section, we used ST data at two resolutions in this experiment. Specifically, we used the data at 16 μm resolution as input to make the super-resolved gene expression prediction. As we set the patch size to 32 in this paper, each spot with 16 μm resolution has been equally divided into four subspots, each corresponding to an image patch. Therefore, the predicted gene expression for each patch can exactly correspond to the gene expression of the corresponding spot with 8 μm resolution. As a result, we used the data at 8 μm resolution as the ground-truth to evaluate the prediction results of the models.

In this experiment, we randomly divided the image patches into training and test sets in a 9:1 ratio. We trained the iStar and our models on the training set, respectively. In the test stage, the predicted super-resolved gene expression of patches in the test set were evaluated against the corresponding ground-truth gene expression at 8 μm resolution.

From the results presented in Table 2, we can see that our model achieved higher PCC and SSIM values than iStar on the test set, indicating the good performance of our method on super-resolved gene expression prediction.

Table 2. Comparing with iStar in Predicting Super Resolution Gene Expression

Methods	SSIM (↑)	PCC (↑)	RMSE (↓)	JSD (↓)
iStar [15]	0.0442	0.1931	0.4577	0.6980
HistoSST	**0.1252**	**0.2648**	**0.0020**	**0.6913**

In order to present the comparative results more intuitively, we showed the predicted results of seven most significant marker genes in seven tissue functional regions [12] in Fig. 2. From the figure we can see that the prediction results of both methods are highly consistent with the distribution of the ground-truth illustrated in the histology images, indicating that they can accurately predict the spatial pattern of gene expression. However, the spatial gene expression predicted by our method are more consistent with the ground-truth than those predicted by iStar. Moreover, from the last two rows, it can be seen that the spatial pattern of the predicted values outside the sequencing region are coherent with those inside the sequencing region, indicating that our method can smoothly supplement the gene expression values in non sequencing region thus has good ability to reconstruct different tissue functional regions in the WSI.

3.5 Ablation Experiments

We performed ablation experiments on GP prior, image decoder and NB loss to assess their contribution to prediction performance of the HistoSST, respectively. In the ablation experiment on NB loss, we replaced it with three commonly used loss functions and then trained and tested the resulted models: Mean Squared Error (MSE) loss, Poisson loss and Gaussian loss. All experiments were conducted on HER2+ dataset, where H1 and H2 were used to train and test the models respectively. The results are listed in Table 3, in which "w/o GP" and "w/o ImageDecoder" stand for the models obtained by excluding the GP prior

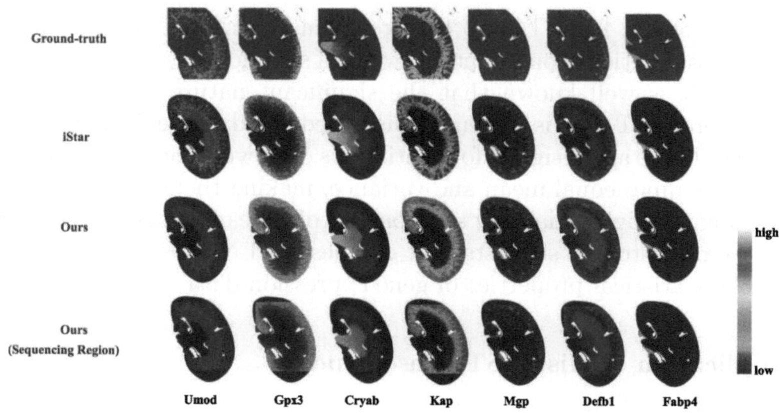

Fig. 2. Prediction results in the HD mouse kidney dataset. The first row shows the ground-truth of the seven genes at a resolution of 8 μm; the second and third rows show the prediction results of two methods in the WSI; and the last row shows the prediction results of our method in the actual ST sequencing region.

and the image decoder, respectively, from the original HistoSST; "r/ MSE", "r/ Poisson" and "r/ Gaussian" stand for the corresponding models that were obtained by replacing the NB loss function in the original model with MSE, Poisson and Gaussian loss functions, respectively.

Table 3. Results of the Ablation Study

Methods	SSIM (↑)	PCC (↑)	RMSE (↓)	JSD (↓)
HistoSST	**0.4268**	**0.5298**	**0.0049**	**0.4755**
w/o GP	0.4142	0.4816	0.0050	0.4780
w/o ImageDecoder	0.4131	0.4902	0.1572	0.4825
r/ MSE	0.2091	0.4742	0.0677	0.5316
r/ Poisson	0.3858	0.5009	0.0050	0.4816
r/ Gaussian	0.0548	0.2728	0.3908	0.5583

From Table 3 we can see that excluding the GP prior from HistoSST leads to a significant decrease in the values of SSIM and PCC, which highlights the effectiveness of GP prior in capturing spatial dependencies and enhancing predictive accuracy. We can also see that the design of bi-decoder by adding the image decoder can significantly improve the performance of gene expression prediction, which confirms that adding the image decoder can better capture the correlation between image features and gene expression, help to obtain the latent representation that are more beneficial for improving the performance of gene expression prediction.

It is also notable from Table 3 that replacing the NB loss with any of the other three loss functions consistently leads to a significant decrease in predictive performance. It is well known that the significant nature of gene expression (count number) in ST data is extremely dispersed and discrete. However the MSE and Gaussian losses are designed for continuous data with constant variance, and Poisson loss assumes equal mean and variance, making them all less suitable for characterizing the high variability and sparsity of gene expression data. The best performance of HistoSST suggests that our designed NB loss function is better suited to the statistical properties of gene expression data.

3.6 Application of HistoSST: Case Study

Denoising of ST Data. Due to various technical factors such as sequencing depth, capture efficiency, staining process, and batch effects, spatial transcriptome data commonly contains noise, which can interfere with downstream tasks and reduce the reliability of research results. The HistoSST model proposed in this article is a probability generation model based on VAE. By introducing probability distribution constraints and KL divergence regularization term, it can effectively map noise to smaller disturbance areas in the latent space during encoding, and generate smoother and more realistic gene expression data during decoding. Therefore, it is evident that HistoSST can be used for preprocessing existing ST data to reduce data noise and help improve the reliability of results in downstream analysis tasks. To assess its denoising capability, we selected the H1 sample from the Her2+ dataset, which includes labeled histological regions, for quantitative evaluation. Although predictions can be compared with observed data, the latter also contains noise. Consequently, we applied the Leiden clustering algorithm to both the original and predicted expression data, utilizing 7 clusters corresponding to the annotated tissue types.

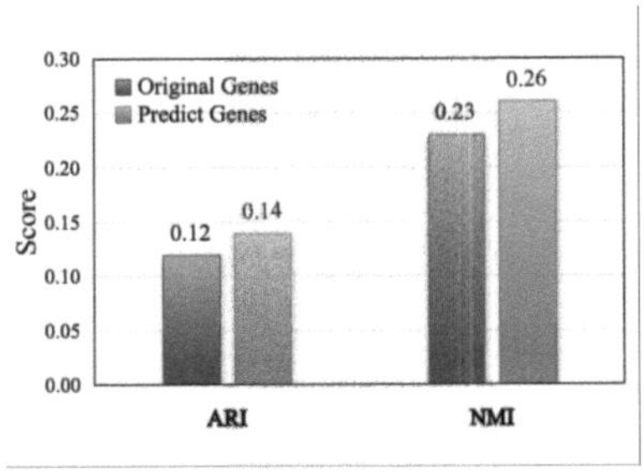

Fig. 3. ARI and NMI Scores of Clustering Original and Predicted Gene Expression.

As shown in Fig. 3, clustering the predicted gene expression data yielded an ARI score of 0.14 and a NMI score of 0.26, both surpassing the scores obtained from clustering the original expression data. These findings suggest that HistoSST effectively preserves the intrinsic tissue architecture while demonstrating robust denoising capabilities. By reducing technical noise present in the original data, the model enhances the reliability of downstream tasks.

Resolution Enhancement of ST Data. Since our HistoSST can predict super-resolved gene expression, it can not only enrich the gene expression within the original spots, but also fill in the missing gene expression between spots, thus generating a more fine-grained gene expression map. We performed the case study to demonstrate that the super-resolved data is helpful for deeper analysis of tissue spatial structure and detailed gene functions. We applied HistoSST trained with the H1 sample in the HER2+ dataset to predict the super-resolved gene expression from the histology image of H2 sample in this experiment.

ERBB2 (HER2) and ITGB6 (Integrin beta-6 subunit) have been confirmed to be gene markers of HER2+ breast cancer. And patients who have high ITGB6 gene expression have statistically significantly reduced survival [8]. Moreover, B2M is considered a tumor marker and its over-expression in breast cancer is often a sign of malignancy, potential for invasion, and poor prognosis [1,7]. Therefore, we chose ITGB6, ERBB2 and B2M as example to showcase the super-resolved gene expression maps can better depict corresponding tissue regions.

By referring to the second column of Fig. 4(a) and Fig. 4(b), it is obvious that the predicted super-resolved results can more clearly depict the subtle differences of gene expression patterns at different positions within the spot, thereby obtaining more accurate gene expression maps. By comparing the first and third columns in Fig. 4(a), it can be seen that the predicted spatial gene expression are more spatially coherent, and the corresponding tissue functional regions represented by them exhibit clearer boundaries, which is helpful to further analyze the spatial heterogeneity of tissues and reveal the complex gene expression patterns in different regions.

Referring to the annotation in Fig. 4(c), it can be seen that, the highly expressed regions of the marker genes match the annotations of the cancer-related regions of the sample. Specifically, ITGB5 is highly expressed in cancer in situ region and partial invasive cancer region; ERBB2 is highly expressed in cancer in situ region and most of the invasive cancer region; and B2M is highly expressed in immune infiltrate region, most of the cancer in situ region, and minority of the invasive cancer region. That is to say, by using HistoSST to predict the super-resolved gene expression from the histology image, detailed spatial gene expression patterns of the tissue that cannot be obtained solely from the histology image or low-resolution ST data can be revealed, which helps to achieve accurate tumor diagnosis, treatment and prognosis evaluation.

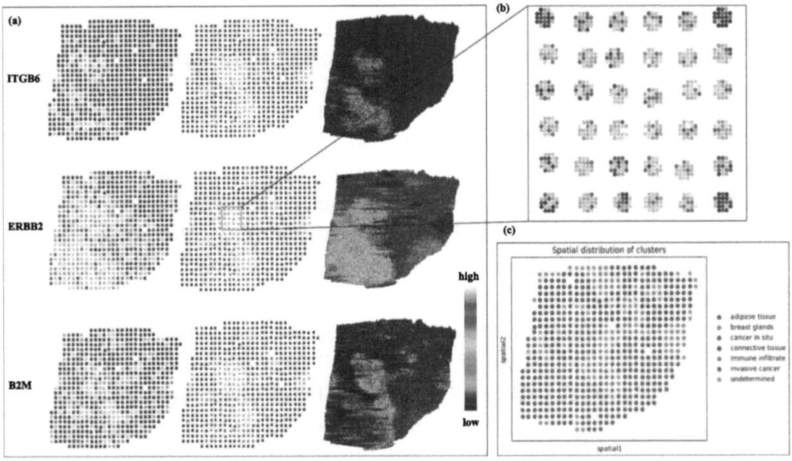

Fig. 4. Illustration of resolution enhancement results of three marker genes. (a) Original and super-resolution gene expression. The first column shows the expression maps in the original ST data, the second and third columns show the predicted super-resolved expression in the intra-spot regions and the WSI region (including intra- and inter- spot regions), respectively. (b) Taking the gene ERBB2 as example to enlarge and display the super-resolved prediction results of several intra-spot regions in the second column of (a). (c) Ground-truth annotations of the tissue and spots provided in the dataset.

4 Conclusion

In this paper, we presented a dependency-aware variational autoencoder with bi-decoders based deep generative model, HistoSST, to predict gene expression from histology images. This model incorporates GP and standard Gaussian priors to effectively capture spatial dependency and global features in the images. In order to capture the close association between image features and gene expression, we designed dual encoders to reconstruct images and to generate gene expression, respectively. In the meanwhile, we employed a NB distribution to approximate the dispersed and discrete gene expression data, thereby enhancing the prediction accuracy of gene expression. Experiments on three public ST datasets have shown the SOTA performance of HistoSST on both spot-level and super-resolved gene expression prediction. HistoSST cannot only enhance the resolution of existing ST data and reduce data noise, but also generate super-resolved ST data when only histology images are available. In fact, by setting the appropriate image patch size, the model can generate ST data of any desired resolution from the histology images. In the near future, we will evaluate the generalizability of HistoSST on broader datasets.

Acknowledgments. This study was funded by the National Key Research and Development Program of China (grant 2019YFA0904303).

Disclosure of Interests. The authors have no competing interests to declare that are relevant to the content of this article.

References

1. Achim, R., et al.: T-cell metagene predicts a favorable prognosis in estrogen receptor-negative and her2-positive breast cancers. Breast Cancer Res. **11**(R15) (2009)
2. Andersson, A., et al.: Spatial deconvolution of her2-positive breast cancer delineates tumor-associated cell type interactions. Nat. Commun. **12**(1), 6012 (2021)
3. Bergenstråhle, L., et al.: Super-resolved spatial transcriptomics by deep data fusion. Nat. Biotechnol. **40**(4), 476–479 (2022)
4. He, B., et al.: Integrating spatial gene expression and breast tumour morphology via deep learning. Nat. Biomed. Eng. **4**(8), 827–834 (2020)
5. Ji, A.L., et al.: Multimodal analysis of composition and spatial architecture in human squamous cell carcinoma. Cell **182**(2), 497–514 (2020)
6. Jia, Y., Liu, J., Chen, L., Zhao, T., Wang, Y.: Thitogene: a deep learning method for predicting spatial transcriptomics from histological images. Brief. Bioinf. **25**(1), bbad464 (2024)
7. Kesheng, L., et al.: Characterization of β2-microglobulin expression in different types of breast cancer. BMC Cancer **14**(750) (2014)
8. Moore, K., et al..: Therapeutic targeting of integrin αvβ6 in breast cancer. J. Natl. Cancer Inst. **106**(8) (2014)
9. Pang, M., Su, K., Li, M.: Leveraging information in spatial transcriptomics to predict super-resolution gene expression from histology images in tumors. BioRxiv (2021). https://doi.org/10.1101/2021.11.28.470212
10. Pearce, M.: The Gaussian process prior vae for interpretable latent dynamics from pixels. In: Symposium on Advances in Approximate Bayesian Inference, pp. 1–12. PMLR (2020)
11. Tian, T., Zhang, J., Lin, X., Wei, Z., Hakonarson, H.: Dependency-aware deep generative models for multitasking analysis of spatial omics data. Nat. Methods **21**(8), 1501–1513 (2024)
12. Vargas, C.S., Struelens, L., D'Huyvetter, M., Caveliers, V., Covens, P.: A realistic multiregion mouse kidney dosimetry model to support the preclinical evaluation of potential nephrotoxicity of radiopharmaceutical therapy. J. Nucl. Med. **64**(3), 493–499 (2023)
13. Xie, R., Pang, K., Chung, S., Perciani, C., MacParland, S., Wang, B., Bader, G.: Spatially resolved gene expression prediction from histology images via bi-modal contrastive learning. Adv. Neural Inf. Process. Syst. **36** (2024)
14. Zeng, Y., et al.: Spatial transcriptomics prediction from histology jointly through transformer and graph neural networks. Brief. Bioinf. **23**(5), bbac297 (2022)
15. Zhang, D., et al.: Inferring super-resolution tissue architecture by integrating spatial transcriptomics with histology. Nat. Biotechnol. 1–6 (2024)

Dual-Axis Message Passing on Molecular Graphs: Layerwise Multi-hop Convolution Meets Depthwise Dense Mixing

Xuefeng Cui[1](✉) and Shiwei Sun[2]

[1] School of Computer Science and Technology, Shandong University, Qingdao, China
xfcui@email.sdu.edu.cn

[2] Key Lab of Intelligent Information Processing, Institute of Computing Technology, Chinese Academy of Sciences, Beijing, China
dwsun@ict.ac.cn

Abstract. Accurate prediction of quantum chemical properties from molecular graphs is a fundamental challenge in computational chemistry and drug discovery. Standard message-passing neural networks propagate information along bonds one hop at a time and one layer at a time, limiting their ability to capture long-range interactions and causing over-smoothing when stacked deeply. We propose DuAxMPNN, a dual-axis message-passing architecture that addresses both limitations simultaneously. Along the *layer axis*, explicit multi-hop edges (2-hop through 4-hop, derived from acyclic path counts) allow each convolution step to aggregate information across distant atoms directly. Along the *depth axis*, a cross-layer dense mixing mechanism gates and combines representations from all preceding layers, preserving fine-grained local chemistry alongside coarse global topology. These two axes are supported by a chemistry-aware molecular graph construction—selectively retaining active hydrogens and encoding tetrahedral chirality via directional neighbor ranking—and a Mixture-of-Activations (MoAct) embedding that maps continuous electronic descriptors (electronegativity, Gasteiger charges) through learnable, bounded, monotone basis functions. As an initial study, we evaluate DuAxMPNN on the PCQM4Mv2 benchmark (~3.8M molecules, HOMO–LUMO gap prediction), demonstrating competitive MAE with strict parameter and computational efficiency, and providing ablation evidence that each proposed component contributes meaningful gains. Code is available at https://github.com/xfcui/DuAxMPNN.

Keywords: Graph Neural Networks · Multi-Hop Message Passing · Dense Cross-Layer Mixing · Molecular Property Prediction · Quantum Chemistry

1 Introduction

Predicting quantum chemical properties from molecular graphs is central to computational chemistry and drug discovery [9,28]. Message Passing Neural Net-

X. Cui et al. (Eds.): ISBRA 2026, LNBI 16690, pp. 54–68, 2027.
https://doi.org/10.1007/978-981-92-3716-6_5

works (MPNNs) are the dominant paradigm: they treat atoms as nodes, bonds as edges, and update each atom by aggregating information from its bonded neighbors [17,29,33]. This locality is chemically meaningful, but it also creates a tension. Global electronic properties such as the HOMO–LUMO gap depend on interactions that may span several bonds, while a standard MPNN reaches those atoms only by stacking more layers [4].

Several strategies address this receptive-field problem. Graph transformers apply global attention to expand the receptive field beyond local neighborhoods [2,26,34], while k-hop message passing and topology-augmented features aggregate information from extended neighborhoods [7,10,24]. Self-supervised pretraining and contrastive learning improve representations from large unlabeled corpora [11,19,27]. More recently, hybrid convolution–transformer architectures [25], Kolmogorov–Arnold basis functions [20], geometry-enhanced representations [6,30], and fractional denoising pretraining [23] have further advanced the field.

Despite these advances—including our own prior work on convolution–attention hybrids [35], graph-based reaction representation [31], MetaFormer multi-hop convolutions [36], and fragment-based pretraining [22]—two practical challenges persist. First, deep GNNs suffer from over-smoothing, where node representations converge and local chemical detail is lost [18,21]. Second, full graph attention scales quadratically with atom count and weakens the sparse molecular-topology bias that makes message passing efficient. The design goal, therefore, is not simply to look farther, but to look farther without forcing the model to become deeper or fully dense.

We propose the **Dual-Axis Message Passing Neural Network (DuAxMPNN)**, which decouples the spatial receptive field from network depth through two complementary axes:

- **Layerwise Axis (Multi-Hop Convolution):** Each layer processes 1-hop through 4-hop edges (derived from acyclic path counts) in parallel, giving every convolution step direct access to distant atoms without additional depth.
- **Depthwise Axis (Cross-Layer Dense Mixing):** A gated dense mixing mechanism combines representations from all preceding layers, preserving early-layer local chemistry alongside later-layer global topology and preventing over-smoothing.

The two-axis architecture depends on a graph representation that carries the relevant chemical signals before message passing begins. DuAxMPNN therefore incorporates two representational enhancements. A *chemistry-aware graph construction* selectively retains active hydrogens, collapses non-active ones, and encodes tetrahedral chirality via directional neighbor ranking. A *Mixture-of-Activations (MoAct)* embedding maps continuous electronic descriptors (electronegativity, Gasteiger charges) through learnable, bounded, monotone basis functions—better suited to saturating electronic signals than standard MLPs or sinusoidal encodings.

2 Methods

We describe DuAxMPNN in the same order that data flows through the model: molecular graph construction, continuous feature embedding, and dual-axis message passing. This ordering is important because later modules assume the earlier ones have already separated discrete topology, continuous electronic descriptors, and directional stereochemical information.

2.1 Chemistry-Aware Graph Construction

Standard molecular graphs treat atoms as nodes and bonds as edges. Our construction keeps that familiar representation, but adjusts it for the electronic-property task: it selectively retains active hydrogens, enriches node and edge descriptors, and encodes tetrahedral chirality via a directional edge feature. These choices provide the local chemical detail that the depthwise mixer is designed to preserve later.

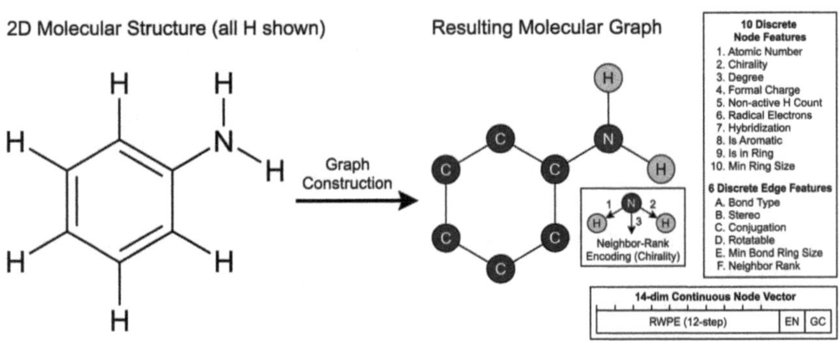

Fig. 1. Chemistry-aware graph construction. An input molecule (left) is converted to a molecular graph (right) in which only active hydrogens (bonded to N, O, or S) are retained as explicit nodes; non-active hydrogens are collapsed into a count feature on the parent heavy atom. Each node carries ten discrete chemical descriptors and a 14-dimensional continuous vector (12-step RWPE plus carbon-centred electronegativity and Gasteiger partial charge); each directed edge carries six bond features. At tetrahedral chiral centers, a directed neighbor-rank arrow records the position of the source atom in the chiral atom's sorted neighbor list.

Selective Hydrogen Handling. A hydrogen is *active* if it is terminally bonded to N, O, or S—the standard H-bond donor elements. Active hydrogens are retained as explicit graph nodes to preserve donor geometry; all others are collapsed into a count feature on their parent heavy atom. This compromise keeps chemically informative donor positions available without making every C–H bond a separate message-passing site. Retaining only active hydrogens adds $\sim$1.3 nodes per molecule on average, whereas keeping all hydrogens would add $\sim$15—roughly doubling graph size for negligible predictive benefit.

Node Features. Each node carries discrete and continuous features (Fig. 1). Ten categorical properties—atomic number, chirality tag, degree, formal charge, non-active hydrogen count, radical electrons, hybridization, aromaticity, ring membership, and minimum ring size—are embedded via learned lookup tables. The continuous features form a 14-dimensional vector: a 12-step Random Walk Positional Encoding (RWPE) [5] computed on the lazy walk ($A+I$) to suppress odd-step oscillation, plus two absolute electronic scalars—carbon-centred Pauling electronegativity and Gasteiger partial charge [8]. Absolute per-atom values are stored rather than per-bond differences because they are strictly information-dominant: any pairwise function (difference, sum, product) is derivable in a single message-passing step.

Edge Features and Chirality. Six categorical bond features characterize each directed edge: bond type, stereo, conjugation, rotatable flag (strict definition, excluding bonds with partial double-bond character), minimum ring size, and neighbor rank. The first five are symmetric across bond directions. Neighbor rank is inherently *asymmetric*: for edge ($u \to v$), it records the position of u in v's sorted neighbor list, but only when v carries a tetrahedral chiral tag (`CW`/`CCW`); otherwise a default value is assigned. This restores order information to the otherwise permutation-invariant aggregation, enabling the model to distinguish enantiomeric configurations (Fig. 1). The later chirality case study uses this feature as a physical sanity check: it should matter for stereosensitive targets, but not necessarily for the HOMO–LUMO gap.

2.2 Mixture of Activations (MoAct) for Continuous Feature Embedding

Motivation. The graph construction above supplies two kinds of information: categorical chemistry, handled naturally by lookup embeddings, and continuous electronic scalars, which require a different treatment. Continuous chemical scalars used in edge modulation—such as electronegativity and charge differences—are bounded and monotonically informative. Standard ReLU/GELU MLPs lack built-in boundedness, naive binning destroys ordering, and sinusoidal encodings impose spurious periodicity.

MoAct Layer. MoAct maps a scalar input x through a learned mixture of basis functions:

$$f(x) = \sum_{i=1}^{K} w_i \cdot \sigma(s_i \cdot x) \tag{1}$$

where σ is a user-chosen basis (e.g., tanh). The mixing weights are normalized and the scales are positive:

$$w_i = \frac{\text{softplus}(\hat{w}_i)}{\sum_j \text{softplus}(\hat{w}_j) + \epsilon}, \qquad s_i = \text{softplus}(\hat{s}_i). \tag{2}$$

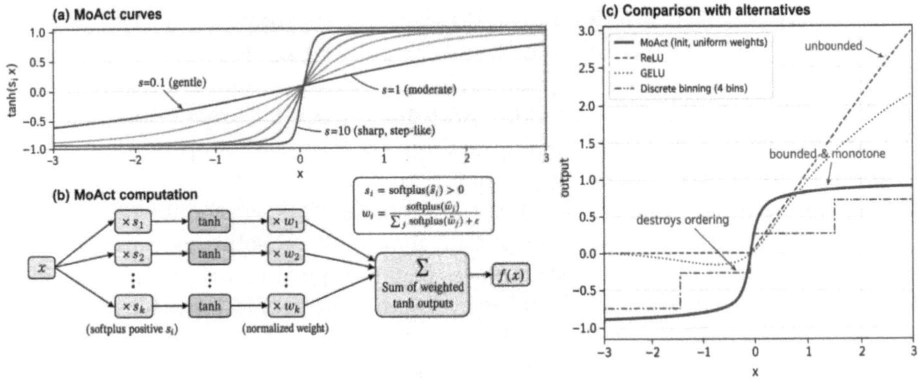

Fig. 2. Mixture of Activations (MoAct). **(a)** Default initialisation of the $K = 8$ basis curves $\sigma(s_i x) = \tanh(s_i x)$, with scales s_i log-spaced in [0.1, 10] to give shallow-to-steep responses. **(b)** Block diagram of $f(x) = \sum_i w_i \, \sigma(s_i x)$ with softplus-positive scales and softplus-normalised mixing weights w_i. **(c)** Resulting fitted curve compared with ReLU, GELU, and a 4-bin discrete lookup on the same input range.

Here, ϵ is a small numerical stabilizer. The scales are initialized by interpolating in inverse-softplus space so that s_i spans $[0.1, 10]$, giving the mixture both shallow and steep response curves at initialization.

Properties and Integration. With a tanh or sigmoid basis, MoAct is bounded, monotone per channel, and has learnable curvature—well-suited for saturating electronic signals. It is used in the `DiffEmbedLayer` for per-edge electronegativity and charge embedding; the RWPE is projected separately via a *gated linear block* (GLB) with softplus activations. A GLB extends the gated linear unit [3] with an optional additive bias b: $\mathrm{GLB}(x, b) = W_1 x \odot \sigma(W_2 x + b)$, where σ is a sigmoid gate. This same gated form reappears in the convolution and depth-mixing modules, so MoAct and GLB together provide the continuous and gated transformations used throughout the architecture. Figure 2 compares MoAct with alternative activations.

2.3 Dual-Axis Message Passing

With the graph and feature embeddings defined, the model can address the two limitations identified in the Introduction. The core of DuAxMPNN expands the spatial receptive field within each layer and preserves representational depth across layers (Fig. 3).

Layerwise Axis: Multi-hop Convolution. The layerwise axis answers the question "how far can a single update look?" Directed 2-, 3-, and 4-hop edges are precomputed from acyclic path counts; each k-hop edge carries a k-dimensional

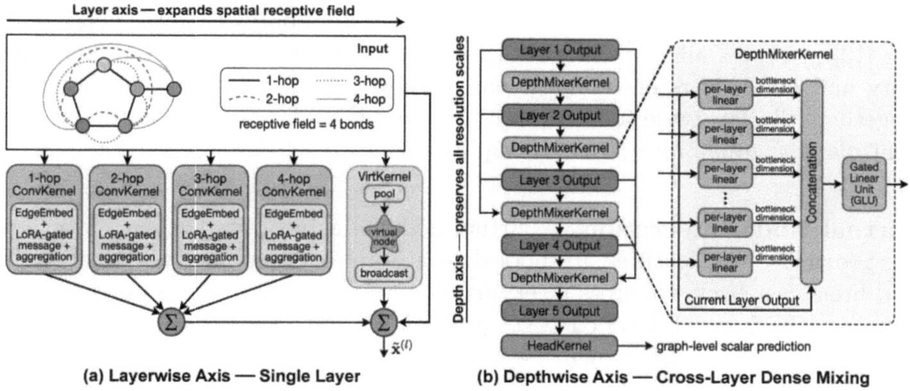

Fig. 3. Dual-axis message-passing architecture. **(a)** Layerwise axis (single layer): parallel 1- to 4-hop `ConvKernel` streams with low-rank edge modulation are summed and combined with a `VirtKernel` virtual-node update, giving an effective receptive field of 4 bonds per layer. **(b)** Depthwise axis: across L stacked layers, a `DepthMixerKernel` after each layer gates and combines outputs from all preceding layers (dense connectivity); a final graph-level readout pools the depth-mixed representation to the prediction.

feature encoding the number of acyclic paths at each intermediate length. Per layer, separate `ConvKernel` instances process the 1-hop (bond), 2-hop, 3-hop, and 4-hop streams in parallel and sum their outputs, giving an effective receptive field of 4 bonds per layer without requiring four sequential layers.

Each `ConvKernel` applies low-rank edge modulation: discrete bond features and MoAct-embedded electronegativity differences multiplicatively gate a low-rank projection of neighbor messages. The message from node j to node i is:

$$m_{ij} = W_{\text{pre}}(x_i + x_j) + ((x_i + x_j)W_{\text{down}} \odot e_{ij})\, W_{\text{up}} \tag{3}$$

where e_{ij} is the combined edge embedding. The convolution output applies a GLB with a degree-dependent bias:

$$x_i^{(\text{out})} = \text{GLB}\left(\sum_{j \in \mathcal{N}(i)} m_{ji},\ \text{EmbedDeg}(d_i)\right) \tag{4}$$

The degree bias lets the gate adapt to local coordination number, linking the aggregation strength to the atom's immediate chemical environment.

Depthwise Axis: Cross-Layer Dense Mixing. The depthwise axis answers the complementary question "which resolution of representation should be kept?" After layer ℓ, the `DepthMixerKernel` projects each prior output $x^{(k)}$ ($k < \ell$) through a per-layer transform W_k to a bottleneck dimension, concatenates the projections with $x^{(\ell)}$, and combines them via a GLB (with $b = 0$):

$$h^{(\ell)} = \text{GLB}\Big(\Big[x^{(\ell)} \parallel x^{(1)}W_1 \parallel \cdots \parallel x^{(\ell-1)}W_{\ell-1}\Big]\Big) \tag{5}$$

Unlike standard residual connections [1] that shortcut only one layer, dense mixing [13] preserves all resolution scales—early layers encoding local bond chemistry and later layers encoding global topology—with learned gating weights. Together, the layerwise axis controls *how far to look* and the depthwise axis controls *how deeply to process*, decoupling spatial reach from network depth.

Virtual Node Integration. A virtual node [9] is integrated at each layer via `VirtKernel`: node features are pooled to a graph-level summary, transformed, and broadcast back. No cross-layer virtual state is accumulated, so this module supplies a fresh graph-level context at each layer while the dense mixer remains responsible for cross-layer memory.

3 Experiments

3.1 Experimental Setup

Dataset. We evaluate DuAxMPNN on PCQM4Mv2 from the Open Graph Benchmark Large-Scale Challenge [12], containing ~3.8M molecules with DFT-computed HOMO–LUMO gaps (eV) as regression targets. The standard split provides ~3.38M training and ~73.5K validation molecules; we report mean absolute error (MAE) on the validation set.

Model Configuration. The default DuAxMPNN uses $L = 5$ message-passing layers with hidden dimension $d = 256$ and $H = 16$ attention heads of dimension $d_h = 16$. Each layer processes 1- through 4-hop edges in parallel via separate `ConvKernel` instances with low-rank edge modulation; cross-layer dense mixing is applied after every layer. The MoAct embedding uses $K = 8$ tanh basis functions for continuous electronic scalars. Neighbor-rank chirality encoding and absolute per-atom electronegativity/charge features are enabled. Only active hydrogens (bonded to N, O, or S) are retained as explicit nodes. The model totals ~10.0M trainable parameters.

Training. We train with the Adan optimizer [32]; its peak learning rate is $\eta = 2\times10^{-3}$ and base weight decay is $\lambda = 1\times10^{-2}$. Per-parameter learning-rate multipliers are 0.5× for atom embeddings and readout scalars, 4× for convolution edge embeddings and low-rank factors, and 1× elsewhere. Weight decay applies at 1× to linear kernels, 0.5× to embedding tables, and 0× to biases and normalization scalars; low-rank factors receive separate product-norm regularization. The learning rate follows a periodic geometric schedule with period k epochs: linear warmup (period 0), constant peak (period 1), and cosine decay (periods $\geq$2) whose endpoints shrink by $1/\varphi$ ($\varphi = (1+\sqrt{5})/2$) per period. We use two training regimes, both with batch size 512 and dropout 0.1: a long-training regime ($k = 12$, $k^2 = 144$ epochs, 9 seeds) for the headline preliminary number, and a shorter regime ($k = 8$, $k^2 = 64$ epochs, 5 seeds) for the ablation study. We select the checkpoint with the lowest validation MAE.

Implementation. DuAxMPNN is implemented in JAX with Equinox [15] for module abstractions and Optax for optimisation. Molecular graphs are preprocessed from SMILES via RDKit: lazy-walk ($A+I$) positional encodings [5] at 12 steps, Gasteiger partial charges [8], and multi-hop edge sets with acyclic path counts are precomputed and stored in HDF5 for efficient batched loading.

3.2 Preliminary Performance

We first ask whether the complete architecture is competitive at the benchmark level before isolating individual components. We compare DuAxMPNN on the PCQM4Mv2 validation set against representative baselines from the OGB Large-Scale Challenge leaderboard [12] and our previous architectures [35,36]. As summarized in Table 1, after training for 144 epochs across 9 independent seeds, DuAxMPNN achieves a median validation MAE of 0.0900 ± 0.0003 eV with approximately 10.0M parameters.

Table 1. Preliminary performance comparison on the PCQM4Mv2 validation set. Baseline results are sourced from the OGB Large-Scale Challenge leaderboard and our prior works.

Method	# Parameters	Validation MAE ↓
Standard Message-Passing Networks		
GCN-virtual [12]	4.9M	0.1153
GIN-virtual [12]	6.7M	0.1083
Graph Transformers & Hybrid Models		
EGT [14]	89.3M	0.0857
TokenGT [16]	48.5M	0.0910
CoAtGIN [35]	6.4M	0.0901
MetaGIN [36]	8.9M	0.0851
DuAxMPNN (Ours)	**10.0M**	$\mathbf{0.0900 \pm 0.0003}$

Standard 1-hop MPNNs such as GCN-virtual and GIN-virtual achieve validation MAEs of 0.1153 eV and 0.1083 eV, respectively. DuAxMPNN reduces the error by 16.9% relative to GIN-virtual (0.1083 → 0.0900 eV). This comparison is the first callback to the Introduction's core claim: adding controlled spatial reach and cross-layer memory improves a sparse message-passing model without abandoning molecular topology.

Against graph transformers, DuAxMPNN matches TokenGT [16] (0.0910 eV) with ~5× fewer parameters (10.0M vs 48.5M) and trails EGT [14] (0.0857 eV) by 0.0043 eV with ~9× fewer parameters (10.0M vs 89.3M). Among our own architectures, DuAxMPNN matches CoAtGIN (0.0901 eV) [35] and narrows the gap to MetaGIN (0.0851 eV) [36] to 0.0049 eV—all while retaining the linear complexity of sparse message passing. Self-supervised pretraining strategies such as fragment-based augmentation [22] offer a natural avenue for closing this remaining gap.

3.3 Component Analysis

To understand whether the benchmark result follows from the intended design rather than incidental capacity, we conduct an ablation study on the validation set. All model variants are trained under the shorter 64-epoch regime (8 periods of 8 epochs) across 5 independent seeds; we report median MAE ± standard deviation. The analysis mirrors the Methods section: spatial reach and depth mixing test the dual-axis mechanism, continuous feature embedding tests MoAct, and graph representation tests the chemistry-aware input design. The results are summarized in Table 2.

Table 2. Ablation study of DuAxMPNN components on the PCQM4Mv2 validation set (median ± std over 5 seeds, 64 training epochs). Default settings are marked with an asterisk (*).

Model Variant	# Params	Validation MAE (eV)
Spatial Reach & Depth Mixing		
1-hop ResNet	3.9M	0.1013 ± 0.0013
1-hop Dense	6.2M	0.0982 ± 0.0003
1- to 2-hop ResNet	5.2M	0.0967 ± 0.0007
1- to 3-hop ResNet	6.4M	0.0935 ± 0.0004
1- to 4-hop ResNet	7.7M	0.0934 ± 0.0004
1- to 4-hop Dense (Default)*	10.0M	0.0926 ± 0.0004
Continuous Feature Embedding		
Discrete Binning	10.1M	0.0930 ± 0.0006
Linear Projection	10.0M	0.0925 ± 0.0004
MoAct ($K = 1$)	10.0M	0.0930 ± 0.0006
MoAct ($K = 2$)	10.0M	0.0925 ± 0.0006
MoAct ($K = 4$)	10.0M	0.0924 ± 0.0003
MoAct ($K = 8$)*	10.0M	0.0926 ± 0.0004
MoAct ($K = 16$)	10.0M	0.0926 ± 0.0002
Graph Representation		
All Hydrogens	10.0M	0.0934 ± 0.0005
Heavy Atoms Only	10.0M	0.0926 ± 0.0004
Active Hydrogens*	10.0M	0.0926 ± 0.0004
No Neighbor Rank	10.0M	0.0924 ± 0.0002
Per-bond Edge Mod. (No Low-Rank)	10.0M	0.0928 ± 0.0006

Spatial Reach and Depth Mixing. A 1-hop ResNet baseline achieves a median MAE of 0.1013 eV; replacing residual connections with dense cross-layer mixing (1-hop Dense) improves it to 0.0982 eV—a 3.1% relative reduction at the same single-hop receptive field. Progressively extending the spatial reach yields consistent gains: 2-hop ResNet 0.0967 eV, 3-hop 0.0935 eV, and 4-hop 0.0934 eV. The default DuAxMPNN (4-hop Dense) reaches 0.0926 ± 0.0004 eV, edging out 4-hop ResNet (0.0934 ± 0.0004 eV) by 0.0008 eV (twice the per-seed std). The pattern matches the intended division of labor: the layerwise axis supplies most of the missing spatial reach (1-hop→4-hop ResNet: 0.1013 → 0.0934, −7.8%), while the depthwise axis preserves useful intermediate representations. Its gain is largest when the receptive field is narrow (0.1013 → 0.0982, −3.1%) and smaller but still positive on top of 4-hop convolution (0.0934 → 0.0926, ~0.9%), which is consistent with the layer-level gating patterns explored in the case studies.

Continuous Feature Embedding. The default MoAct ($K = 8$) achieves a median MAE of 0.0926 ± 0.0004 eV, outperforming discrete binning (0.0930 ± 0.0006 eV). Linear projection (0.0925 eV) and the wider MoAct variants ($K = 2$: 0.0925 eV; $K = 4$: 0.0924 eV; $K = 16$: 0.0926 eV) all perform comparably within one standard deviation. The single-basis variant ($K = 1$: 0.0930 ± 0.0006 eV) is the only continuous embedding that matches discrete binning rather than the other continuous variants, confirming that a single saturating tanh is too rigid to fit the bounded electronic scalars; the curve flexibility provided by $K \geq 2$ recovers the gap. Thus, the main empirical requirement is not a particular basis family, but a continuous treatment that preserves ordering, avoids quantization artifacts, and carries at least two learnable response curves. We retain MoAct as the default because its bounded, monotone inductive bias matches the electronic scalars described in the Methods; consistent with this, the long-training headline number (Table 1) was obtained with the wider $K = 16$ variant of the same family.

Graph Representation. Hydrogen handling produces a clear ordering. Including all hydrogens degrades the median MAE to 0.0934 ± 0.0005 eV—a 0.9% regression from added topological noise—while stripping all hydrogens matches the default (0.0926 ± 0.0004 eV) on this target. The default active-hydrogen strategy (0.0926 ± 0.0004 eV) therefore retains accuracy while preserving donor-group geometry needed for downstream tasks beyond the HOMO–LUMO gap. Disabling neighbor-rank chirality encoding (0.0924 ± 0.0002 eV) or replacing low-rank edge modulation with per-bond parameters (0.0928 ± 0.0006 eV) produces differences within one standard deviation on this regression target. The neighbor-rank null does *not* mean that chirality is unimportant—the chirality case study below shows that stereoisomers can differ by up to ~1.5 eV in HOMO–LUMO gap, so the chirality issue is electronically critical but remains open under 2D message passing, including ours. The headline gains therefore arise primarily from dual-axis message passing, while the auxiliary graph encodings keep the representation chemically complete for downstream tasks beyond the HOMO–LUMO gap.

3.4 Case Studies

The ablation table establishes average effects; the case studies check whether those effects appear in the molecular situations where the design predicts they should. We probe three design choices with targeted validation-set analyses (Fig. 4(a–d)), with all per-subset MAE values reported as in-figure annotations. Panels (e) and (f) provide dataset-level context via graph diameter and ring-size distributions ($N = 10{,}000$ random PCQM4Mv2 molecules).

Long-Range Substituent Effects. This case study targets the layerwise axis on a chemically homogeneous subset. We isolate 419 para-substituted biphenyl molecules (SMARTS: `c1ccc(-c2ccc(*)cc2)cc1`) in which the para-substituent and the opposite ring lie ≥4 bonds apart across the biaryl backbone (Fig. 4(a)). DuAxMPNN (4-hop Dense, 0.0386 eV) reduces the 1-hop ResNet error (0.0537 eV) by 28.0%. The four-variant decomposition isolates each axis: extending the receptive field captures most of the gain under either backbone—−26.2% from 1-hop ResNet to 4-hop ResNet (0.0396 eV), and −22.0% from 1-hop Dense (0.0495 eV) to 4-hop Dense—while depthwise dense mixing contributes the remainder, recovering about a quarter of the total gap at 1-hop reach and adding a further 2.5% on top of 4-hop ResNet. The layerwise axis therefore dominates on this long-range subset, with the depthwise axis providing a smaller but consistent additional gain at every reach. Mean graph diameter on the chemistry-aware topology is ∼8.4 (Fig. 4(e)), so long-range electronic effects routinely exceed single-hop neighborhoods, and 4-hop edges let a single layer bridge the biaryl backbone directly rather than relying on four sequential 1-hop updates.

Chirality Representation via Neighbor Rank. On 24,835 chiral-center molecules (Fig. 4(b), bottom), the full model and the no-rank ablation produce essentially identical per-molecule MAEs (0.1201 vs. 0.1200 eV) with near-congruent distributions, ruling out cancellation in the average. To probe sensitivity directly, we extract 2,194 stereoisomeric pairs—identical heavy-atom connectivity but different chirality, including both enantiomers and diastereomers—and compare ground-truth $|\Delta\text{label}|$ with predicted $|\Delta\text{pred}|$ gap differences. The top gray violin confirms that stereochemistry is chemically critical: $|\Delta\text{label}|$ averages 0.153 eV and reaches ∼1.5 eV. Both models, however, predict pair differences nearly an order of magnitude smaller (mean ∼0.015 eV), and the rank encoding nudges sensitivity only marginally (0.0152 vs. 0.0141 eV)—vanishing relative to the ∼0.15 eV signal it should match. We read this as direct evidence that chirality remains a critical but open problem for 2D message passing: directional graph features can flag stereocenters, but recovering the electronic consequences of tetrahedral geometry appears to require explicit 3D information that geometry-free message passing does not supply.

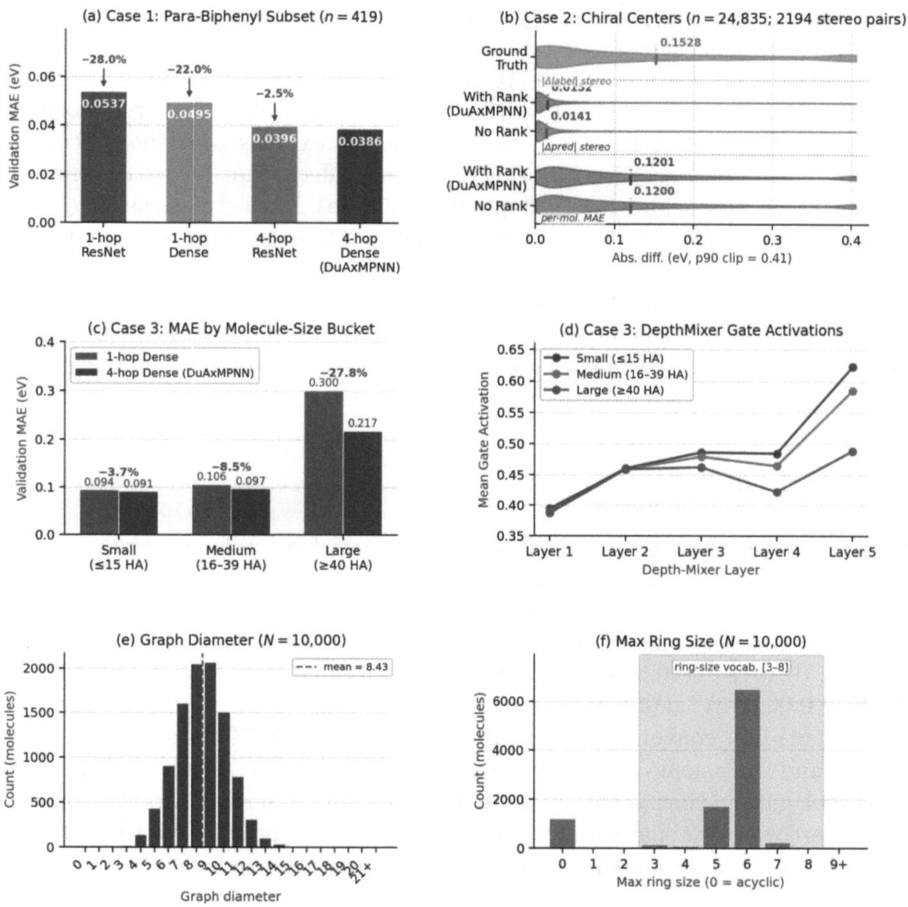

Fig. 4. Case study analyses; per-subset MAE values are annotated directly on the bars. **(a)** Para-biphenyl subset ($n = 419$): four ablation variants with Δ annotations relative to each baseline, isolating the layerwise and depthwise axes. **(b)** Chirality analysis on 24,835 chiral molecules and 2,194 stereoisomeric pairs (90th-pct-clipped violin KDEs; dashed line = mean). Bottom: per-molecule MAE for the default (with neighbor rank) vs. no-rank ablation. Middle: predicted gap difference $|\Delta\text{pred}|$ between paired stereoisomers (same heavy-atom topology, different chirality). Top (gray): ground-truth $|\Delta\text{label}|$ for the same pairs (mean 0.153, up to ~1.5 eV). **(c)** MAE by heavy-atom (HA) bucket, 4-hop Dense vs. 1-hop Dense: small ($\leq$15 HA, n = 46,708), medium (16–39 HA, n = 26,806), large ($\geq$40 HA, n = 31). **(d)** Per-layer `DepthMixerKernel` gate activations across the same three size buckets, probing how the depth mixer reweights resolutions. **(e)** Graph diameter distribution on N = 10,000 random PCQM4Mv2 molecules (dashed line marks the mean 8.43), motivating multi-hop reach. **(f)** Maximum SSSR ring-size distribution on the same N,000 sample; the shaded band marks the discrete ring-size vocabulary [3–8] used by the node encoder.

Depth Mixing Under Molecular Size Variation. Across three heavy-atom (HA) buckets (Fig. 4(c)), multi-hop dense mixing improves over the 1-hop dense ablation in every bucket: −3.7% on small molecules (≤15 HA, $n = 46{,}708$; 0.0908 vs. 0.0943 eV), −8.5% on medium (16–39 HA, $n = 26{,}806$; 0.0970 vs. 0.1060 eV), and −27.8% on large (≥40 HA, $n = 31$; 0.2168 vs. 0.3002 eV). The large-molecule gain echoes the biphenyl finding: once a molecule exceeds the 1-hop receptive horizon, multi-hop edges directly bridge electronic effects that 1-hop convolutions can only reach by stacking layers. `DepthMixerKernel` gate activations (Fig. 4(d)) rise with depth from ~ 0.39 at layer 1 to 0.49–0.62 at layer 5; small molecules show the highest layer-5 value (0.62) and large molecules the lowest (0.49), indicating that the depth mixer leans more heavily on accumulated multi-resolution representations when the molecule is compact and information saturates earlier. Figure 4(f) confirms that maximum SSSR ring sizes concentrate in the drug-like range [3–8], validating the discrete ring-size vocabulary used in the node encoder.

4 Conclusion

We presented DuAxMPNN, which decouples spatial reach from network depth via layerwise multi-hop convolution and depthwise dense mixing, retaining the linear cost of sparse message passing. On PCQM4Mv2, the two axes are complementary: extending the receptive field from 1- to 4-hop cuts 64-epoch MAE by 7.8% (0.1013 → 0.0934 eV), and dense cross-layer mixing adds 0.9% to 0.0926 ± 0.0004 eV at 4-hop (versus 3.1% at 1-hop). Case studies confirm the scope: multi-hop convolution improves MAE by 3.7–28.0% across heavy-atom buckets and on a long-range para-biphenyl subset, while dense mixing yields layer-level gating that scales with molecular compactness. Chirality remains open: stereoisomeric pairs differ by up to ~1.5 eV in HOMO–LUMO gap, yet both the default model and the no-rank ablation predict pair differences of only ~0.015 eV, indicating that 2D topology cannot recover the electronic effect of tetrahedral geometry. Trained for 144 epochs, DuAxMPNN reaches 0.0900 ± 0.0003 eV (9 seeds) with 10.0M parameters, matching TokenGT with ~5× fewer parameters and our prior CoAtGIN. Future work will explore self-supervised pretraining [22], adaptive hop selection, and 3D conformer-aware message passing.

Acknowledgments. This work was supported by the National Key R&D Program of China (Grant No. 2025YFA0923200), the National Natural Science Foundation of China (NSFC; Grant Nos. 62533015 and 62072283), and the National Science and Technology Major Project on Prevention and Control of Emerging and Major Infectious Diseases (Grant No. 2025ZD01901001).

Disclosure of Interests. The authors have no competing interests to declare that are relevant to the content of this article.

References

1. Bachlechner, T., Majumder, B.P., Mao, H., Cottrell, G., McAuley, J.: Rezero is all you need: Fast convergence at large depth. In: Proceedings of the 37th Conference on Uncertainty in Artificial Intelligence, pp. 1352–1361. PMLR (2021)
2. Buterez, D., Janet, J.P., Oglic, D., Liò, P.: An end-to-end attention-based approach for learning on graphs. Nat. Commun. **16**(1), 5244 (2025)
3. Dauphin, Y.N., Fan, A., Auli, M., Grangier, D.: Language modeling with gated convolutional networks. In: International Conference on Machine Learning, pp. 933–941. PMLR (2017)
4. Dwivedi, V.P., Luu, A.T., Laurent, T., Bengio, Y., Bresson, X.: Graph neural networks with learnable structural and positional representations. In: Proceedings of the 10th International Conference on Learning Representations (2022)
5. Dwivedi, V.P., et al.: Long range graph benchmark. Adv. Neural. Inf. Process. Syst. **35**, 22326–22340 (2022)
6. Fang, X., et al.: Geometry-enhanced molecular representation learning for property prediction. Na. Mach. Intell. **4**(2), 127–134 (2022)
7. Feng, J., Chen, Y., Li, F., Sarkar, A., Zhang, M.: How powerful are k-hop message passing graph neural networks. In: Proceedings of the 36th International Conference on Neural Information Processing Systems, pp. 4776–4790 (2022)
8. Gasteiger, J., Marsili, M.: Iterative partial equalization of orbital electronegativity–a rapid access to atomic charges. Tetrahedron **36**(22), 3219–3228 (1980)
9. Gilmer, J., Schoenholz, S.S., Riley, P.F., Vinyals, O., Dahl, G.E.: Neural message passing for quantum chemistry. In: International Conference on Machine Learning, pp. 1263–1272. PMLR (2017)
10. He, W., et al.: TGF-M: topology-augmented geometric features enhance molecular property prediction. PLoS Comput. Biol. **21**(4), e1013004 (2025)
11. Hu, W., et al.: Strategies for pre-training graph neural networks. In: International Conference on Learning Representations, pp. 1024–1034 (2020)
12. Hu, W., Fey, M., Ren, H., Nakata, M., Dong, Y., Leskovec, J.: OGB-LSC: a large-scale challenge for machine learning on graphs. In: Proceedings of the Neural Information Processing Systems Track on Datasets and Benchmarks (2021)
13. Huang, G., Liu, Z., Van Der Maaten, L., Weinberger, K.Q.: Densely connected convolutional networks. In: Proceedings of the IEEE Conference on Computer Vision and Pattern Recognition, pp. 4700–4708 (2017)
14. Hussain, M.S., Zaki, M.J., Subramanian, D.: Global self-attention as a replacement for graph convolution. In: Proceedings of the 28th ACM SIGKDD Conference on Knowledge Discovery and Data Mining, pp. 655–665 (2022)
15. Kidger, P., Garcia, C.: Equinox: neural networks in JAX via callable PyTrees and filtered transformations. In: NeurIPS 2021 Workshop on Differentiable Programming (2021)
16. Kim, J., et al.: Pure transformers are powerful graph learners. Adv. Neural. Inf. Process. Syst. **35**, 14582–14595 (2022)
17. Kipf, T.N., Welling, M.: Semi-supervised classification with graph convolutional networks. In: International Conference on Learning Representations (2017)
18. Li, G., Xiong, C., Qian, G., Thabet, A., Ghanem, B.: Deepergcn: training deeper GCNs with generalized aggregation functions. IEEE Trans. Pattern Anal. Mach. Intell. **45**(11), 13024–13034 (2023)
19. Li, H., Zhang, R., Min, Y., Ma, D., Zhao, D., Zeng, J.: A knowledge-guided pre-training framework for improving molecular representation learning. Nat. Commun. **14**(1), 7568 (2023)

20. Li, L., Zhang, Y., Wang, G., Xia, K.: Kolmogorov-Arnold graph neural networks for molecular property prediction. Nat. Mach. Intell. **7**(8), 1346–1354 (2025)
21. Liu, L., et al.: Gem-2: next generation molecular property prediction network by modeling full-range many-body interactions. arXiv preprint arXiv:2208.05863 (2022)
22. Meng, Z., Chen, C., Zhang, X., Zhao, W., Cui, X.: Exploring fragment adding strategies to enhance molecule pretraining in ai-driven drug discovery. Big Data Mining Anal. **7**(3), 565–576 (2024)
23. Ni, Y., et al.: Pre-training with fractional denoising to enhance molecular property prediction. Nat. Mach. Intell. **6**(10), 1169–1178 (2024)
24. Nikolentzos, G., Dasoulas, G., Vazirgiannis, M.: k-hop graph neural networks. Neural Netw. **130**, 195–205 (2020)
25. Qin, M., Sun, Z., Feng, L., Han, C., Xia, J., Han, L.: Moleculeformer is a GCN-transformer architecture for molecular property prediction. Commun. Biol. **8**(1), 1668 (2025)
26. Rampášek, L., Galkin, M., Dwivedi, V.P., Luu, A.T., Wolf, G., Beaini, D.: Recipe for a general, powerful, scalable graph transformer. In: Proceedings of the 36th International Conference on Neural Information Processing Systems, p. 1054 (2022)
27. Rong, Y., et al.: Self-supervised graph transformer on large-scale molecular data. In: Proceedings of the 34th International Conference on Neural Information Processing Systems, pp. 12559–12571 (2020)
28. Schütt, K.T., Kindermans, P.J., Sauceda, H.E., Chmiela, S., Tkatchenko, A., Müller, K.R.: Schnet: a continuous-filter convolutional neural network for modeling quantum interactions. In: Proceedings of the 31st International Conference on Neural Information Processing Systems, pp. 992–1002 (2017)
29. Veličković, P., Cucurull, G., Casanova, A., Romero, A., Lio, P., Bengio, Y.: Graph attention networks. In: International Conference on Learning Representations (2018)
30. Wang, Y., et al.: Enhancing geometric representations for molecules with equivariant vector-scalar interactive message passing. Nat. Commun. **15**(1), 313 (2024)
31. Wang, Z., et al.: Graph-based reaction classification by contrasting between precursors and products. In: Proceedings of the IEEE International Conference on Bioinformatics and Biomedicine (BIBM), Las Vegas, NV, USA, pp. 354–359 (2022)
32. Xie, X., Zhou, P., Li, H., Lin, Z., Yan, S.: Adan: adaptive Nesterov momentum algorithm for faster optimizing deep models. IEEE Trans. Pattern Anal. Mach. Intell. **46**(12), 9508–9520 (2024)
33. Xu, K., Hu, W., Leskovec, J., Jegelka, S.: How powerful are graph neural networks? In: International Conference on Learning Representations (2019)
34. Ying, C., et al.: Do transformers really perform badly for graph representation? Adv. Neural. Inf. Process. Syst. **34**, 28877–28888 (2021)
35. Zhang, X., Chen, C., Meng, Z., Yang, Z., Jiang, H., Cui, X.: Coatgin: marrying convolution and attention for graph-based molecule property prediction. In: Proceedings of the IEEE International Conference on Bioinformatics and Biomedicine (BIBM), Las Vegas, NV, USA, pp. 374–379 (2022)
36. Zhang, X., Chen, C., Wang, X., Jiang, H., Zhao, W., Cui, X.: Metagin: a lightweight framework for molecular property prediction. Front. Comp. Sci. **19**(5), 195912 (2025)

Construction and Practice of a 5C3S Collaborative Innovation Model for Graduate Education Reform: A Case Study Based on a Biomedical Imaging Analysis Project

Yang Gao, Hongdong Li, Senzhang Wang, and Min Li(✉)

School of Computer Science and Engineering, Central South University, Changsha, China
limin@mail.csu.edu.cn

Abstract. As postgraduate education enters the artificial intelligence (AI) era, traditional knowledge-transmission models struggle to cultivate interdisciplinary talent capable of solving complex problems at the intersection of computer science, bioinformatics, and medicine. To address this urgent need for a competency-based educational paradigm, we propose the "5C3S" Collaborative Innovation Model. This systematic framework focuses on cultivating five core competencies (5C: cross disciplinary capability, creativity, complex-problem solving, collaboration, and critical thinking) supported by a three-pillar infrastructure (3S: student-centered philosophy, self-directed learning, and AI skill integration). We demonstrate the practical implementation of this model through a comprehensive interdisciplinary case study: a multi-modal brain tumor segmentation and prognostic prediction project using the BraTS dataset. By guiding mixed-background cohorts through progressive engineering challenges—from unstructured MRI data preprocessing to deep learning architecture optimization and survival analysis—the curriculum effectively bridges the gap between algorithmic theory and clinical application. Dual-track evaluations indicate that the 5C3S model significantly dismantles disciplinary boundaries, enabling computer science and medical students to collaboratively innovate. This structured pedagogical approach provides a scalable and highly effective framework for cultivating outstanding interdisciplinary talent in medical AI.

Keywords: Biomedical Imaging Analysis · Postgraduate Education Reform · Artificial Intelligence · Interdisciplinary Talent Cultivation

1 Introduction

As China's postgraduate education enters a new development stage, it is transitioning from quantitative expansion to high-quality advancement. This shift demands new competency structures for high-level talent to systematically address complex engineering and interdisciplinary scientific problems, preparing

X. Cui et al. (Eds.): ISBRA 2026, LNBI 16690, pp. 69–83, 2027.
https://doi.org/10.1007/978-981-92-3716-6_6

them for diverse career paths spanning industry, academia, and clinical research. Graduate students must now evolve from possessing singular academic abilities to integrated innovation capabilities, expand from individual research capacity to collaborative innovation proficiency, and deepen their focus from knowledge acquisition to complex problem-solving skills [1,2]. Traditional knowledge transmission models, which overemphasize disciplinary boundaries and theoretical completeness, no longer meet the competency development needs of innovative talent in the AI era. This paradigm shift in competency requirements is driving a systemic reconstruction of graduate education from a "knowledge-based" to a "competency-based" paradigm.

However, several practical challenges have become increasingly evident. Key issues include the systemic disconnect between educational objectives and implementation pathways, the gap between curriculum design and research practice, inefficient collaborative education mechanisms, and the absence of structured frameworks for competency development, all of which constrain effective talent cultivation [3,13]. More specifically, weakened interdisciplinary integration mechanisms fail to meet complex industry knowledge demands; diminished emphasis on practical innovation creates disconnects from authentic industry scenarios; and poorly coordinated supervisory teams limit interdisciplinary education depth [4,14]. Although universities have explored AI and interdisciplinary fields, most reforms remain isolated, single-dimensional attempts. Educational objectives and support systems often operate separately, failing to form systematic, multi-layered collaborative structures [5,6].

In response, scholars and institutions have initiated various reforms. Competency oriented models emphasize curricula restructuring around student competency development. Collaborative education models focus on multi-stakeholder participation and resource sharing. Industry-education integration strengthens engineering practice through university-industry partnerships. Project-driven approaches use authentic problems to foster innovation [7]. Leading international universities, such as MIT's New Engineering Education Transformation (NEET) and Carnegie Mellon University's Master of Science in Artificial Intelligence and Innovation, have accumulated valuable experience in interdisciplinary curriculum integration and university-industry-research collaboration [8,15,16]. Meanwhile, numerous Chinese universities have established AI colleges and are exploring "AI+X" interdisciplinary talent cultivation [9–12]. While these initiatives have achieved positive outcomes in specific areas, most reforms exhibit limitations: some focus narrowly on curriculum optimization while neglecting research practice support; others emphasize industry-education synergy but lack structured competency development design. This results in a persistent disconnect between educational goals and support frameworks [4,6]. Thus, a systematic, structured collaborative innovation framework is needed—one that integrates educational objectives, curriculum systems, research training, engineering practice, and evaluation mechanisms to forge a new paradigm with clear goals, comprehensive support, and well-defined implementation pathways.

To address this need, this paper proposes the "5C3S" Collaborative Innovation Graduate Training Model, developed by leveraging Central South University's strengths in computer science, pharmacy, medicine, and public health, while drawing on successful experiences from premier research universities worldwide. This student-centred model cultivates five core competencies: cross disciplinary capability, creativity, complex-problem solving capability, collaboration, and critical thinking. These "5C" competencies are supported by a "3S" framework centered on skills integration using AI tools. Through systematic implementation across four dimensions, curriculum reconfiguration, research innovation capacity building, engineering practice development, and whole-process evaluation, the "5C3S" model provides an actionable and scalable framework for cultivating interdisciplinary innovative talent in the new AI era.

2 Methodology

2.1 The 5C3S Framework

The 5C3S model responds to the demand for competency-based graduate education in the AI era. It builds on three theoretical foundations: competency-based education theory with its emphasis on outcome-oriented training, collaborative education theory focusing on multi-stakeholder integration, and systems theory requiring alignment across objectives, processes, and support structures. The model also draws on international practices such as MIT's NEET program and Carnegie Mellon's MS in Artificial Intelligence and Innovation, while leveraging Central South University's strengths in computer science, medicine, and pharmacy. Furthermore, the 5C3S model builds upon established academic frameworks, such as the ISCB (International Society for Computational Biology) core competencies for bioinformatics [16] and the ACM/IEEE guidelines for AI curricula. While prior literature largely focuses on domain-specific knowledge acquisition (e.g., statistical proficiency or biological data literacy), the 5C3S model extends these works by explicitly defining and operationalizing interpersonal and cognitive competencies—specifically, structured collaboration and critical thinking—which are critical for resolving the 'black-box' nature of AI in clinical settings.

The framework consists of two interconnected layers. The 5C layer defines five core competencies: cross disciplinary capability, creativity, complex-problem solving capability, collaboration, and critical thinking. These serve as the ultimate goals of graduate training. The 3S layer provides the supporting infrastructure: student-centred education as the guiding philosophy, self-directed and lifelong learning mechanisms as the institutional backbone, and skills integration using AI as the technological platform. The model operates through a three-level coupling logic where objectives define what to cultivate, support structures provide the means for cultivation, and implementation components specify how cultivation occurs. These levels form an integrated system where objectives guide support structures, supports enable implementation, and evaluation results feed back to optimize both objectives and supports (Fig. 1).

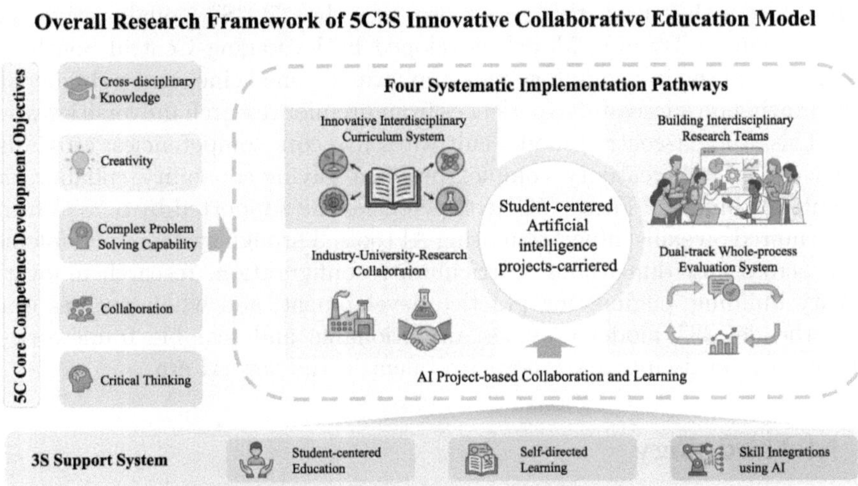

Fig. 1. Overall framework of the proposed 5C3S innovative collaborative education model.

2.2 The 5C Competency System

The five competencies represent concrete targets that can be cultivated through specific practices and assessed through observable behaviors. cross disciplinary capability means integrating knowledge, methods, and thinking across disciplinary boundaries. At the graduate level, this requires not only mastering core concepts from at least two disciplines but also synthesizing them to generate special interdisciplinary knowledge—such as domain-specific feature engineering in computational biology—that is not traditionally covered in either standalone discipline. Creativity involves generating novel ideas or methods that lead to original contributions, requiring students to identify research gaps and translate creative ideas into executable tasks. Complex-problem solving capability means systematically analyzing ill-structured, multi-factor problems, which demands skills in problem decomposition and optimization under uncertainty. Collaboration refers to effective communication and task coordination in multidisciplinary teams, requiring team skills and the ability to contribute disciplinary expertise. Critical thinking involves rationally examining arguments and methods, identifying hidden assumptions, and forming independent judgments.

These five competencies are mutually reinforcing. cross disciplinary capability provides the knowledge base for creativity. Complex-problem solving tests the validity of creative solutions. Collaboration enables team-based innovation. Critical thinking ensures continuous reflection and refinement. Together they form an integrated competency structure for the AI era.

2.3 The 3S Support Infrastructure

The 3S layer provides institutional and technological foundations for competency development. Student-centred education serves as the philosophical foundation, manifested through individualized training plans, mutual selection between students and supervisors, and research rotation mechanisms. Its core function is to activate intrinsic motivation, shifting students from passive recipients to active constructors of knowledge. Self-directed and lifelong learning mechanisms address rapid technological change through learning resource platforms, pathway planning tools, and self-assessment systems. By enabling students to select courses based on research needs and track frontier developments, these mechanisms help students continuously update their knowledge structures. Crucially, this self-directed mechanism is designed to prevent students from merely mastering short-term 'hot' technologies. By focusing on fundamental problem-solving methodologies and continuous knowledge updating, the framework equips students with the long-term adaptability required to remain productive as AI technologies and scientific paradigms evolve over their entire careers.

Skills integration using AI provides the technological infrastructure, integrating AI teaching tools, virtual simulation environments, and collaborative research spaces. AI enables personalized learning recommendations, intelligent tutoring, and research assistance. By aggregating multidisciplinary resources, the platform supports cross disciplinary modeling and analysis. These three supports work together: student-centred philosophy grants learning autonomy, self-directed mechanisms provide developmental pathways, and AI platforms enable competency integration.

2.4 Operational Mechanism

The 5C3S model operates through a closed loop. First, the 5C competencies are translated into operational indicators. These indicators guide curriculum design, project selection, and evaluation criteria. The 3S infrastructure then allocates resources and tools based on these indicators. Next, the four implementation components translate objectives and supports into concrete educational activities. The evaluation system collects data on student development and identifies strengths and gaps. Finally, assessment results drive adjustments to objectives, refinements to support structures, and improvements to implementation strategies. This closed-loop mechanism is grounded in Biggs' theory of Constructive Alignment, ensuring that intended learning outcomes, teaching activities, and assessment tasks are mutually supportive. The evaluation system employs both formative and summative assessments. Formative learning experiences—such as weekly peer code reviews and interim milestone presentations—provide continuous feedback to guide student development during the process. Summative assessments, including the final defense and quantitative model metrics (e.g., C-index for prognostic models), evaluate the ultimate attainment of the 5C competencies.

2.5 Implementation Through Four Research Components

The four research components operationalize the 5C3S framework. Each component starts with a reform objective, specifies core tasks, identifies which competencies it strengthens, indicates which supports it relies on, and clarifies its role in the overall model.

Component one focuses on interdisciplinary curriculum development. Its objective is to build an AI-era curriculum that transcends disciplinary boundaries. Core tasks include integrating knowledge from computer science, medicine, and pharmacy, developing modular interdisciplinary courses, using AI tools to enhance teaching, and implementing project-driven learning. This component strengthens cross disciplinary capability and creativity. It relies on the AI platform for intelligent course delivery and the student-centred philosophy for personalized learning pathways. Its role is to provide the knowledge foundation for competency development.

Component two addresses interdisciplinary supervision and research innovation. Its objective is to establish effective cross disciplinary supervisory teams and strengthen research capabilities at the AI-medicine-pharmacy interface. Core tasks include forming multi-disciplinary supervisory teams with clear coordination mechanisms, enhancing literature review and problem identification skills through academic interest cultivation and frontier seminars. This component strengthens creativity, complex-problem solving, and critical thinking. It relies on self-directed learning mechanisms for student exploration and the student-centred philosophy for respecting research interests. Its role is to transform knowledge into innovative outcomes through competency internalization.

Component three targets engineering practice and university-industry collaboration. Its objective is to build an engineering innovation system based on training projects and industry partnerships. Core tasks include designing progressive engineering projects, utilizing on-campus software bases and engineering research centers, and engaging students in real-world industry projects to enhance hands-on skills. This component strengthens complex-problem solving and collaboration. It relies on the AI platform for technical support and self-directed mechanisms for encouraging students to tackle engineering challenges. Its role is to bridge theory and practice by developing integrated capabilities for solving real-world problems.

Component four develops a two-pathway whole-process evaluation system (research-oriented vs. engineering-oriented). Its objective is to establish an intelligent evaluation system that accommodates both research-oriented and engineering-oriented pathways. Core tasks include designing separate evaluation tracks for research and engineering capabilities, collecting multi-source data from classroom performance, mid-term assessments, and thesis defense, and constructing dynamic evaluation models with feedback mechanisms. This component assesses all five competencies. It relies on the AI platform for data collection and intelligent analysis and self-directed mechanisms for supporting adaptive learning based on evaluation results. Its role is to close the feedback loop and ensure continuous quality improvement.

These four components form a logical progression. Curriculum provides the knowledge foundation. Research training enables competency internalization. Engineering practice facilitates knowledge transfer. Evaluation ensures continuous optimization. This structured implementation pathway translates the 5C3S framework from theory into practice.

3 Case Study: Multi-modal Brain Tumor Analysis Project Under the 5C3S Framework

To demonstrate the practical efficacy of the 5C3S model, we present a case study based on a fully implemented graduate course project. This mechanism was tested during the Fall 2023 semester as an eight-week core module within the 'Advanced Medical Artificial Intelligence' course. The primary goal was to train students to transition from theoretical algorithm design to solving open-ended clinical challenges. multi-modal brain tumor segmentation and prognostic prediction represents a highly complex interdisciplinary challenge, requiring the seamless integration of computer vision, radiology, and biostatistics. Traditional instructional models often struggle in this context, as computer science students typically lack clinical intuition, while medical students face steep learning curves in algorithmic implementation. To address this educational gap, we selected the comprehensive analysis of the Brain Tumor Segmentation (BraTS) dataset as the practical showcase for the proposed 5C3S collaborative innovation model.

Student Cohort and Prior Knowledge

The pilot involved 32 first-year master's students (18 from Computer Science; 14 from Medical Imaging/Bioinformatics). No PhD students participated. CS students had completed at least one graduate-level deep learning course and were proficient in Python, but had no medical training. Conversely, medical students had completed coursework in radiology and neuroanatomy, but possessed only introductory Python skills and no formal AI training. This mixed starting point was intentional, requiring active bridging through the framework's collaborative supports.

3.1 Reconstructing the Knowledge Base: Fostering Cross Disciplinary Capability

Pedagogically, this phase was driven by three specific learning objectives: (1) Cognitive: students must map abstract imaging physics to tensor representations; (2) Interpersonal: students must develop a shared interdisciplinary vocabulary; (3) Evaluative: students must independently critique the clinical validity of AI-generated segmentations. The educational experience was structured around 'reciprocal teaching,' where the foundation of the collaborative educational model relies on dismantling rigid boundaries between disciplines to foster cross disciplinary capability. Rather than passively feeding students isolated medical or mathematical theories, this phase leverages self-directed learning mechanisms and a student-centered philosophy to help learners construct a shared knowledge base.

To build intrinsic motivation, the course begins by guiding students to explore the historical trajectory of brain tumor analysis. Instead of relying on traditional lectures, students conduct self-directed literature reviews to trace the evolution of magnetic resonance imaging. By independently investigating the progression from early single-modal imaging to the modern standard combining T1, contrast-enhanced T1, T2, and fluid-attenuated inversion recovery sequences, computer science students grasp the clinical necessity of multi-modal data fusion for distinguishing active tumors from peritumoral edema (the swelling caused by fluid accumulation around the tumor). Simultaneously, medical students review the paradigm shift from handcrafted radiomic features to modern deep learning architectures. This historical exposition helps both cohorts appreciate how the convergence of clinical needs and computational power drives scientific discovery.

Understanding the theoretical foundations of multi-modal MRI physics and deep learning segmentation requires overcoming significant cognitive hurdles. To bridge this gap, the instructional team implements a reciprocal teaching strategy supported by artificial intelligence tools. During the theoretical modules, students from different academic backgrounds are deliberately paired. When studying multi-modal MRI principles, medical students use interactive visualization software and AI-generated anatomical models. These tools help them demonstrate to their engineering peers how specific imaging sequences highlight blood-brain barrier disruptions.

Conversely, when delving into deep learning segmentation models, computer science students use AI-assisted coding platforms and intelligent tutoring systems. These resources help demystify the encoder-decoder architecture of the U-Net. They visually explain how convolutional layers capture spatial context and how skip connections enable precise localization. In this way, the computational black box becomes transparent to the medical cohort.

This pedagogical shift successfully translates abstract theories, such as image preprocessing and bias field correction, into a shared, actionable language. Students acquire fundamental cross disciplinary capabilities, transitioning from asking isolated technical questions to forming holistic inquiries about how specific architectural modifications might better capture the heterogeneity of a necrotic core (the dead tissue at the center of advanced tumors). This cognitive shift establishes the essential theoretical groundwork required for tackling the complex engineering practices in the subsequent project phase.

3.2 Project-Driven Implementation: Cultivating Core Competencies

Building upon the theoretical foundation, the curriculum transitions into an eight-week hands-on project. Students work in interdisciplinary groups to develop a complete system that segments brain tumor subregions from multi-modal MRI and predicts patient survival. This phase is meticulously designed to operationalize the remaining core competencies of the 5C3S framework through progressive engineering challenges, effectively transforming the traditional coding assignment into an authentic collaborative research experience.

The eight-week project is structured as follows. Weeks 1–2 focus on data preprocessing, including resampling, N4 bias field correction, and intensity normalization using SimpleITK; this phase is intentionally allocated two weeks because raw BraTS data contain real-world artifacts that require iterative tuning. Weeks 3–5 are dedicated to model construction and optimization, where teams implement a 3D U-Net in PyTorch, experiment with hyperparameters, and use AI tools for debugging; three weeks allow for multiple design iterations (e.g., adding attention gates or deep supervision). Week 6 emphasizes evaluation and critical reflection, requiring teams to analyze segmentation errors and critique loss function choices. Week 7 moves to prognostic modeling, where students extract radiomic features and build Cox proportional hazards models. Finally, week 8 is reserved for integration, scientific report writing, and oral defense.

Data Preprocessing: Tackling Unstructured Complexity. In the initial phase, students are tasked with handling the raw BraTS dataset. Rather than providing pre-cleaned and aligned data, the instructional team exposes students to real-world technical noise, requiring them to implement resampling, N4 bias field correction (an algorithm to remove low-frequency intensity variations caused by the magnetic field), and intensity normalization using Python libraries such as SimpleITK. This purposeful exposure to unstructured data cultivates complex-problem solving capabilities. Medical students are required to guide the preprocessing logic based on tissue properties—ensuring, for instance, that z-score normalization does not inadvertently erase crucial hyperintense edema signals on FLAIR sequences (an MRI technique that suppresses fluid signals to make lesions more visible)—while computer science students handle the programmatic execution.

Model Construction and Optimization: Integrating AI Assistance. Following preprocessing, teams construct a 3D U-Net architecture using PyTorch. The implementation requires configuring input layers for four-channel data and softmax outputs for multi-class segmentation (enhancing tumor, edema, and necrosis). Throughout this rigorous process, students are actively encouraged to utilize AI platforms and large language models as intelligent tutors to assist with syntax errors, tensor dimension mismatches, and hyperparameter tuning. By integrating AI tools into their workflow, students can bypass repetitive coding hurdles and focus their cognitive efforts on architectural optimization and problem decomposition, directly experiencing the skill integration mechanism of the 3S support system. While AI tools (e.g., ChatGPT-4, Copilot) provided valuable assistance in syntax correction and hyperparameter tuning, we also observed potential downsides. Some students began to rely heavily on AI for debugging, losing the ability to trace tensor dimension mismatches manually. Others accepted AI-proposed architectural changes (e.g., adding attention modules) without understanding the rationale. To mitigate over-reliance, we implemented two strategies. First, students were required to annotate any AI-generated code with line-by-line explanations in their own words. Second, we held weekly 'no-AI' debugging sessions where teams diagnosed errors using only documentation and peer discussion. These practices helped preserve conceptual understanding while still leveraging AI for efficiency.

Training, Evaluation, and Critical Reflection. Once the architecture is established, students split the data for training and validation, utilizing Dice loss and optimization algorithms such as Adam. However, the evaluation extends far beyond standard computational metrics. Instructors foster critical thinking by requiring students to analyze discrepancies between their predicted contours and the expert ground truth annotations. When a model achieves a high overall Dice similarity coefficient but systematically fails to identify the necrotic core boundary, students must rationally examine their methods. They are challenged to identify hidden assumptions in their loss function design, form independent judgments, and implement targeted auxiliary losses or spatial attention mechanisms to refine the model's focus on clinically relevant regions.

Prognostic Modeling: Stimulating Creative Integration. The project then advances to prognostic modeling, where creativity and cross disciplinary knowledge are heavily tested. Using their generated segmentation masks, students extract high-dimensional radiomic features via PyRadiomics, capturing shape, texture, and first-order statistics. These imaging phenotypes are combined with clinical variables such as patient age. Teams are challenged to perform feature selection using LASSO regression and build Cox proportional hazards models to estimate survival risks. This integration of pure image segmentation with survival analysis forces students to generate novel ideas regarding which textural features might serve as the most robust biomarkers for tumor progression. This step effectively translates creative hypotheses into executable research tasks, moving beyond pure image quantification toward clinically actionable insights.

Team Organization and Scientific Communication. The entire project lifecycle is underpinned by a robust collaborative framework. A total of 32 students participated (18 computer science, 14 medical/bioinformatics). They were divided into eight interdisciplinary teams of exactly 4 members. Teams were intentionally structured to ensure heterogeneous expertise: six teams had a strict 2 CS + 2 medical ratio, while two teams were composed of 3 CS + 1 medical student. This enforced heterogeneity was crucial for facilitating the reciprocal teaching strategy. Teams assign rotating roles, conduct weekly progress meetings, and maintain a shared code repository. To prevent students from retreating into their disciplinary comfort zones, the instructional team mandated weekly role rotations among four positions: (1) Data Curator (responsible for preprocessing and quality control), (2) Model Architect (responsible for network coding and debugging), (3) Clinical Advisor (responsible for biological interpretation and feature selection), and (4) Project Manager (responsible for GitHub merges and meeting minutes). This structured rotation ensured that, for example, a medical student would act as the Model Architect (supported by CS peers and AI tools), while a CS student would be forced to serve as the Clinical Advisor, ensuring equal contribution and genuine cross-disciplinary engagement.

This structure simulates key aspects of authentic research and industry environments (e.g., raw data, multidisciplinary teamwork, open-ended questions) while incorporating pedagogical scaffolding (e.g., fixed timeline, staged workflow, AI assistance) to manage cognitive load. Collaboration is structurally required; a successful pipeline cannot be built without iterative communication between the medical domain experts interpreting the tumor morphology and the algorithmic developers optimizing the network gradient flow. To clarify the degree of authenticity, we explicitly distinguish between authentic elements and pedagogical simplifications. Authentic elements include: (a) use of real BraTS clinical MRI data with raw artifacts; (b) requirement to handle unstructured preprocessing steps (resampling, bias correction, normalization); (c) interdisciplinary team composition with rotating roles; (d) an open-ended prognostic question requiring independent feature selection; and (e) the need to justify clinical interpretations of segmentation and survival results. Pedagogical simplifications include: (a) an eight-week fixed duration; (b) a predefined milestone structure that stages the workflow; (c) availability of AI coding tutors as scaffolding; (d) a curated dataset without missing modalities or hardware constraints; and (e) a provided computing environment. This balance allows students to experience core complexities without being overwhelmed.

Despite the benefits of reciprocal teaching, early team interactions were often hindered by cognitive and communicative barriers. Medical students struggled to articulate imaging findings in tensor operations, while CS students found it difficult to interpret clinical descriptions of tumor morphology. To address these issues, we introduced structured 'translation sessions' where each team member explained one core concept (e.g., 'edema' or 'skip connection') without discipline-specific jargon. Additionally, teams co-constructed a shared glossary of key terms. These strategies gradually reduced miscommunication, though some tensions persisted throughout the project—an honest reflection that interdisciplinary fluency takes sustained practice. In the final week, students integrate all components into a comprehensive scientific report and deliver a structured oral presentation. They must justify their preprocessing decisions, explain the rationale behind their network architecture variations, and provide clinical interpretations of their prognostic risk stratification. This team-based culmination ensures that students not only internalize complex technical knowledge but also master the ability to coordinate tasks, communicate effectively, and innovate collaboratively within an interdisciplinary setting.

3.3 Dual-Track Evaluation and Teaching Outcomes

To comprehensively assess the effectiveness of the 5C3S collaborative innovation model, we implemented a formative and summative evaluation framework (distinct from the two-pathway outcome system described in Sect. 2.5).[1] This approach moves beyond traditional summative examinations (e.g., final paper tests) to capture the dynamic development of the five core competencies throughout the multi-modal brain tumor analysis project.

Process Evaluation: Monitoring Competency Growth. During the eight-week project, instructors and teaching assistants continuously monitored student progress through weekly code repository reviews (e.g., GitHub commits), team meeting minutes, and interim milestone presentations. This formative assessment focused on *Collaboration (C4)* and *Complex-Problem Solving (C3)*. Early observations indicated that interdisciplinary teams frequently encountered communication barriers, often struggling to reconcile the CS students' focus on algorithmic optimization (e.g., minimizing Dice loss) with the medical students' emphasis on clinical validity (e.g., distinguishing true tumor progression from pseudo-progression).

However, guided by the student-centered philosophy and AI-assisted learning tools, these barriers were significantly mitigated by the mid-term. Medical students demonstrated an increased capacity to understand basic Python data structures and neural network data flows, while CS students began incorporating clinical terminology (such as necrosis, edema, and enhancing core) into their architectural justifications. This qualitative shift evidenced a successful internalization of *cross disciplinary Capability (C1)*.

Summative Outcomes and Academic Achievements. The final evaluation track assessed the project deliverables: the accuracy of the multi-class segmentation model, the concordance index (C-index) of the prognostic survival model, and the quality of the final scientific report and oral defense. The defense panel, comprising experts from both the computer science and medical faculties, evaluated the teams on their *Critical Thinking (C5)* and *Creativity (C2)*. Students were required to not only present their highest-performing models but also critically analyze their failure cases, such as boundaries where the fluid-attenuated inversion recovery (FLAIR) signals were ambiguous.[2]

The outcomes of this pilot implementation were highly encouraging. Teaching feedback indicated that students profoundly appreciated the project-driven, AI-integrated learning experience, noting that it bridged the gap between theoretical algorithms and real-world clinical applications. More importantly, the

[1] The two-pathway system differentiates research vs. engineering outcome expectations; the formative+summative approach differentiates process vs. final assessment. Both are integrated in our implementation.

[2] The defense explicitly included questions probing conceptual understanding of AI-assisted components to evaluate if students bypassed fundamental learning.

5C3S model catalyzed tangible academic and engineering innovations. To provide a precise quantitative assessment, pre- and post-course surveys (using a 5-point Likert scale) were administered to the 32 students. The results demonstrated significant growth across all competencies. Notably, self-rated 'Cross-disciplinary Capability' increased from a baseline of 2.1 to 4.3, and 'Collaboration' improved from 3.0 to 4.6. Furthermore, the objective academic evaluations were strong: the average final project grade, assessed independently by a blind panel of three professors using a standardized rubric, was 88.5/100, with all eight teams successfully completing the prognostic pipeline (either via Cox regression or logistic classification). Several student teams successfully extended their course projects into competitive submissions for international medical image computing challenges (such as the BraTS challenge), and refined their prognostic modeling pipelines into co-authored interdisciplinary research papers. These hard outcomes validate that the 5C3S framework effectively transforms graduate students from passive knowledge recipients into proactive, collaborative innovators equipped for the AI era.

3.4 Challenges and Limitations Observed

Despite overall positive outcomes, several difficulties emerged. First, critical thinking proved the most challenging competency. Most teams initially accepted the standard Dice loss without questioning its suitability for imbalanced tumor subregions; only after targeted prompts did some teams experiment with auxiliary loss functions. Second, the prognostic modeling phase caused unexpected difficulty. Two out of eight teams were unable to complete the Cox proportional hazards model within the timeline and reverted to a simpler logistic regression for survival risk classification. This revealed gaps in students' statistical background. Third, time management was a recurring issue: teams consistently underestimated preprocessing time, leaving insufficient room for model architecture tuning. Finally, while four teams submitted their work to the BraTS challenge, none achieved top-tier performance—a realistic reminder that educational projects prioritize learning over competition. These observations are reported to help other educators anticipate similar challenges when adopting the 5C3S model.

4 Conclusion

As graduate education transitions toward a competency-based paradigm, developing structured frameworks for interdisciplinary talent cultivation is paramount. This paper proposes the 5C3S Collaborative Innovation Model, which integrates five core competencies (cross disciplinary capability, creativity, complex-problem solving, collaboration, and critical thinking) with a three-pillar support system (student-centered philosophy, self-directed learning, and AI skill integration).

By detailing the implementation of a multi-modal brain tumor analysis project, we demonstrated how this model translates abstract educational objectives into actionable, project-driven pathways. The case study illustrates that when students are immersed in authentic, complex industry scenarios—supported by AI tools and interdisciplinary mentorship—they can successfully navigate the cognitive leaps required to integrate computer vision, radiology, and biostatistics. The observed improvements in students' collaborative communication, critical analysis of algorithms, and subsequent academic outputs confirm the efficacy of the model.

In the future, we plan to refine the 5C3S framework by introducing automated, data-driven evaluation platforms and expanding the curriculum to include broader multi-omics data integration. Furthermore, by strengthening partnerships with biopharmaceutical companies and clinical research centers, we aim to continually align this educational model with the frontier demands of artificial intelligence and healthcare innovation.

Acknowledgments. This work is supported by Hunan Provincial Project for Graduate Education and Teaching Reform under Grant No. 2025JGA002.

References

1. Lu, J.F., Wu, T.S., Wu, S.G., et al.: Research on the cultivation of innovative postgraduates in interdisciplinary disciplines. China High. Educ. Res. **1**, 46–48 (2006)
2. He, G., Chen, X.Y.: Understanding and reflection on the cultivation of interdisciplinary graduate students. Acad. Degrees Graduate Educ. **12**, 20–23 (2005)
3. Ren, J., Wang, F., Li, M.: Dynamics and characteristics of interdisciplinary research in scientific breakthroughs: case studies of Nobel-winning research in the past 120 years. Scientometrics **128**, 4383–4419 (2023)
4. Tao, J.G., Xie, L.X.: Research on improving college students' scientific research innovation ability under the background of interdisciplinary integration. China Univ. Teach. **10**, 20–27 (2022)
5. Shi, Y.Y., Pei, R.M., Chen, G., et al.: Foreign artificial intelligence talent training policies and their implications for China. Jinri Keyuan **5**, 22–28 (2021)
6. Han, S.Y., Chen, Y.H., Wu, P., et al.: Research and practice on multidisciplinary interdisciplinary training of graduate students in the field of artificial intelligence. Softw. Guide **20**(12), 247–252 (2021)
7. Lu, G.D., Li, T.Y.: Reflections on the path of emerging engineering education construction and development. Res. High. Educ. Eng. **3**, 20–26 (2017)
8. Liu, J., Wang, L.Y.: MIT's new engineering education transformation: origins, framework and implications. Res. High. Educ. Eng. **6**, 162–171 (2019)
9. Qie, H.X., Zhao, Z.Z.: Exploring paths to improve the quality of emerging engineering talent training in the age of artificial intelligence: taking Stanford University's computer science program as an example. Kejiao Fazhan Pinglun **8**, 13–25 (2020)
10. Liang, X.B., Tu, W., Wu, X.J.: Characteristics and implications of Harvard University's artificial intelligence curriculum. Chin. J. ICT Educ. **14**, 34–40 (2021)

11. Zhu, J., Deng, X.Q., Li, X.L., et al.: Research on the cultivation mode of graduate students' innovation ability under the background of "artificial intelligence + emerging engineering education". J. Higher Educ. **21**, 35–37 (2019)
12. Jiang, S., Su, F., Xiao, B.: Research on the construction of interdisciplinary graduate training mechanism empowered by artificial intelligence. Ind. Inf. Technol. Educ. (9), 36–40, 47 (2022)
13. Işık, E.B., Brazas, M.D., Schwartz, R., et al.: Grand challenges in bioinformatics education and training. Nat. Biotechnol. **41**(8), 1171–1174 (2023)
14. Orlova, N.G., Orlov, Y.L.: Challenges in bioinformatics education courses organization. Biophys. Rev. 1–9 (2025)
15. Shue, E., Liu, L., Li, B., et al.: Empowering beginners in bioinformatics with ChatGPT. Quant. Biol. **11**(2), 105–108 (2023)
16. Mulder, N., Schwartz, R., Brazas, M.D., et al.: The development and application of bioinformatics core competencies to improve bioinformatics training and education. PLoS Comput. Biol. **14**(2), e1005772 (2018)

BioFC-GAT: Biomarker-Oriented GAT for ASD Diagnosis from rs-fMRI Data

Hongyu Guo[1] and Fang-Xiang Wu[2(✉)]

[1] School of Computing and Digital Innovation, Saskatchewan Polytechnic, 1130 Idylwyld Dr N, Saskatoon S7K 3R5, Canada
[2] Department of Mechanical Engineering, Department of Computer Science, and Division of Biomedical Engineering, University of Saskatchewan, Campus Dr. 57, Saskatoon S7N 5A9, Canada
fangxiang.wu@usask.ca

Abstract. Autism spectrum disorder (ASD) is a heterogeneous neurodevelopmental disorder for which decisive neuroimaging biomarkers remain limited. Resting-state fMRI (rs-fMRI) enables whole-brain functional connectivity (FC) analysis, yet many existing models emphasize predictive accuracy over biological interpretability. In this study, we present BioFC-GAT, a biomarker-oriented graph attention framework for rs-fMRI-based ASD diagnosis. Each subject is represented as an FC graph, where regions of interest (ROIs) are modeled as nodes with connectivity-profile features. A sparse multi-head graph attention mechanism captures discriminative interactions by focusing on the strongest connections while suppressing noisy edges. To enhance interpretability, attention weights are integrated with gradient-based attribution to identify salient ROIs and functional connections. Experiments on ABIDE I demonstrate stable classification performance (AUC 0.823 ± 0.041) and reveal consistent multi-scale biomarkers. The identified patterns show a clear concentration in somatomotor and visual systems, with additional involvement of default mode, attention, salience, and subcortical networks. At the connectivity level, both strong within-network interactions and structured cross-network connections are observed, supporting the network dysconnectivity hypothesis of ASD. Cross-atlas analysis further indicates that these biomarkers exhibit stable spatial and network-level consistency. These results highlight BioFC-GAT as an interpretable and robust framework for connectome-based biomarker discovery in ASD.

Keywords: Autism spectrum disorder · Biomarker discovery · Resting-state fMRI · Graph attention network · Explainable AI · Functional connectivity

1 Introduction

Autism spectrum disorder (ASD) is a heterogeneous neurodevelopmental condition characterized by social communication deficits and restricted behaviors.

X. Cui et al. (Eds.): ISBRA 2026, LNBI 16690, pp. 84–96, 2027.
https://doi.org/10.1007/978-981-92-3716-6_7

Its prevalence has reached approximately 0.77% worldwide [10], yet diagnosis remains largely behavior-based, motivating the study of objective neuroimaging biomarkers.

Resting-state fMRI (rs-fMRI) enables non-invasive analysis of functional connectivity (FC) across brain regions [18]. Large-scale datasets such as ABIDE I [4] have supported connectome-based ASD studies, where brain interactions are modeled as graphs. While machine learning methods achieve promising classification performance [5,9,14,29], many lack interpretability.

Graph neural networks, particularly graph attention networks (GATs) [23], provide flexible modeling of connectivity patterns via adaptive edge weighting. However, attention alone is not a reliable explanation [11,27], motivating integration with complementary attribution methods [20]. Existing GNN-based ASD studies primarily focus on classification, with limited emphasis on explicit biomarker discovery or multi-scale interpretation [28].

In this study, we propose *BioFC-GAT*, a biomarker-oriented graph attention framework for rs-fMRI analysis. Each subject is represented as a FC graph, where sparse multi-head attention emphasizes discriminative interactions while suppressing noise. By integrating attention with gradient-based attribution, the model identifies ROI- and edge-level biomarkers and supports multi-scale interpretation across functional systems. BioFC-GAT achieves stable performance on ABIDE I and generalizes across sites and atlases while preserving biologically meaningful representations. The main contributions are summarized as follows:

- We propose *BioFC-GAT*, a graph attention framework that constructs top-k connectivity graphs to suppress noisy edges.
- We introduce a hybrid explainability strategy that integrates attention and gradient-based sensitivity to identify ROI- and edge-level biomarkers, enabling multi-scale characterization of ASD with dominant somatomotor and visual patterns and cross-network dysconnectivity.
- We demonstrate stable performance and generalization across sites and atlases while maintaining interpretable representations.

2 Methods

2.1 Overview of the Proposed Framework

BioFC-GAT is a graph-based framework for interpretable biomarker discovery from rs-fMRI-derived FC networks (Fig. 1). Each subject is represented as an FC graph, where ROIs are nodes with connectivity-profile features derived from Pearson correlation (PCC) of blood-oxygen-level-dependent (BOLD) signals.

Sparse multi-head graph attention retains only the top-k strongest connections per node, reducing noise while capturing discriminative interactions. Attention is computed via query, key, and value projections, followed by neighborhood aggregation and attention-based pooling to produce subject-level representations. Interpretability is achieved by integrating attention weights with gradient-based attribution, enabling identification of salient ROIs and connectivity patterns associated with ASD.

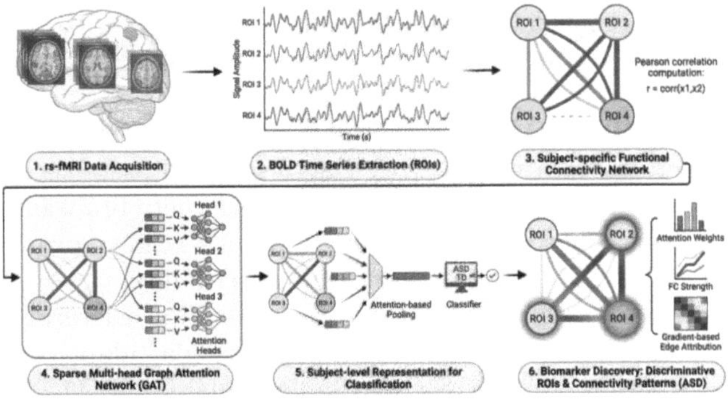

Fig. 1. Overview of the BioFC-GAT framework.

2.2 Functional Connectivity Network Construction

For each subject, rs-fMRI data are represented as $X \in \mathbb{R}^{N \times T}$ with $N = 264$. Missing values are imputed (median), outliers are suppressed via IQR winsorization, and signals are z-score normalized. Functional connectivity is computed using PCC, yielding $R \in \mathbb{R}^{N \times N}$. Values are clipped and transformed using Fisher z-transformation, with diagonal entries set to zero. The resulting matrix $Z \in \mathbb{R}^{N \times N}$ defines a weighted graph, where nodes represent ROIs and edge weights encode FC strength, serving as input to the model.

2.3 BioFC-GAT Connectome Learning Model

Node Feature Encoding. Given the FC matrix $Z \in \mathbb{R}^{N \times N}$, ROI i is represented by its connectivity profile, $\mathbf{x}_i = Z_{i,:} \in \mathbb{R}^N$, which captures interactions between ROI i and all other regions.

Node features are projected into a latent space as $\mathbf{h}_i = f_\theta(\mathbf{x}_i)$, where f_θ is a two-layer neural encoder consisting of linear transformations, layer normalization, GELU activation, and dropout. This encoding enhances representation capacity while improving training stability and robustness to noise.

Sparse Multi-head Graph Attention. To reduce noise, we construct a sparse graph by retaining the top-k strongest connections per ROI, $\mathcal{N}_i = \mathrm{TopK}(|Z_{i,:}|, k)$, excluding self-connections and masking invalid nodes.

On this graph, multi-head attention is applied. For node i and neighbor $j \in \mathcal{N}_i$, $Q_i = W_Q h_i$, $K_j = W_K h_j$, $V_j = W_V h_j$, with logits $\alpha_{ij}^{(h)} = \frac{Q_i^{(h)\top} K_j^{(h)}}{\sqrt{d_h}}$.

Connectivity-aware bias is incorporated as

$$\tilde{\alpha}_{ij}^{(h)} = \alpha_{ij}^{(h)} + \gamma \cdot \frac{\log(1 + |Z_{ij}|)}{\frac{1}{k} \sum_{j' \in \mathcal{N}_i} \log(1 + |Z_{ij'}|) + \epsilon}, \tag{1}$$

where $\gamma = \sigma(\theta)$. Attention weights are $a_{ij}^{(h)} = \mathrm{softmax}_j(\tilde{\alpha}_{ij}^{(h)})$.

Values are further modulated as $\tilde{V}_j^{(h)} = V_j^{(h)}(1 + \gamma\hat{w}_{ij})$. Node updates are:

$$h'_i = W_O \left(\|_{h=1}^{H} \sum_{j \in \mathcal{N}_i} a_{ij}^{(h)} \tilde{V}_j^{(h)} \right), \tag{2}$$

where $\|$ denotes concatenation across attention heads. The final representation is $h_i^{new} = \text{GELU}(h_i + h'_i)$, with masking applied to invalid nodes.

Graph-Level Representation and Classification. A subject-level representation is obtained via attention-based pooling:

$$w_i = \frac{\exp(g(h_i))}{\sum_j \exp(g(h_j))}, \quad \mathbf{g} = \sum_i w_i h_i, \tag{3}$$

where $g(\cdot)$ is a learnable scoring function. The pooled representation $\mathbf{g}$ is fed to an MLP for binary classification. The model is trained with binary cross-entropy loss to learn discriminative connectome patterns while maintaining interpretability for biomarker discovery.

2.4 Biomarker Discovery

To identify interpretable neurobiological signatures associated with ASD, we employ a multi-scale framework that extracts both ROI- and edge-level importance from the trained model.

Edge importance is estimated by combining attention weights with gradient-based attribution. Let $\mathbf{Z} \in \mathbb{R}^{N \times N}$ denote the FC matrix, $\mathbf{A} \in \mathbb{R}^{N \times N}$ the attention-based importance (aggregated from top-k neighbors and multi-heads), and $\mathbf{G} \in \mathbb{R}^{N \times N}$ the gradients of the model output with respect to $\mathbf{Z}$. Let $\hat{\mathbf{G}}$ denote the normalized gradient matrix. The unified importance is defined as

$$\mathbf{S} = \alpha\hat{\mathbf{G}} + (1 - \alpha)(\hat{\mathbf{G}} \odot \mathbf{A}), \tag{4}$$

where $\odot$ denotes the element-wise product and $\alpha \in [0, 1]$ balances gradient-based sensitivity and attention-modulated importance. In this study, we set $\alpha = 0.7$.

ROI-level importance is obtained by aggregating edge importance as $r_i = \frac{1}{N}\sum_j |S_{ij}|$. ROIs are selected using a percentile-based threshold (top 10%), and robustness is ensured by aggregating results across repeated cross-validation runs, retaining consistently selected regions.

Edge biomarkers are extracted from the subgraph induced by the selected ROI set $\mathcal{R}$, i.e., $\mathbf{S}_{\mathcal{R}} = \mathbf{S}[\mathcal{R}, \mathcal{R}]$. The strongest connections are selected as $\mathcal{E} = \text{TopK}(|\mathbf{S}_{\mathcal{R}}|)$, corresponding to approximately the top 10% of edges. Self-connections are removed and symmetric pairs are merged to produce an undirected, interpretable edge set.

For neurobiological interpretation, biomarkers are mapped to large-scale functional systems using the Power atlas [16]. The distribution of edge biomarkers across network pairs is computed as $C_{uv} = |\{(i, j) \in \mathcal{E} \mid i \in u,\ j \in v\}|$, capturing both within- and cross-network interactions. This framework enables consistent identification of region- and connection-level biomarkers, providing a systems-level characterization of ASD-related dysconnectivity [1].

3 Results and Discussion

3.1 Dataset and Preprocessing

We use rs-fMRI data from ABIDE I [4], comprising 1112 subjects (539 ASD, 573 controls). Standard preprocessing includes slice-timing and motion correction, nuisance regression, spatial normalization (MNI152), smoothing, and band-pass filtering (0.01–0.1 Hz), improving signal quality and cross-site consistency. The brain is parcellated using the Power atlas [16] into 264 ROIs, from which mean BOLD time series are extracted. Additional details are in [14,21].

3.2 Model Training, Evaluation, and Ablation Analysis

BioFC-GAT is evaluated on ABIDE I using repeated stratified 10-fold cross-validation ($R = 3$, 30 runs) with PCC-based FC networks. The model is trained for up to 50 epochs (batch size 16)(lr 5×10^{-4}, weight decay 5×10^{-5}) with early stopping on validation AUC (patience 12). The best checkpoint per fold is used for evaluation and biomarker analysis. The model achieves AUC 0.823 ± 0.041 and accuracy 0.770 ± 0.037, with AUC ranging from 0.729 to 0.910. The interquartile range (0.803–0.850) indicates stable generalization across sites.

We analyze graph sparsity by varying $k \in \{5, 8, 10, 15, 20\}$. Smaller k yields higher peaks but greater variance, while larger k introduces weaker edges without consistent gains. We find $k = 10$ provides the best trade-off between performance and stability. We also compare single- and multi-layer GATs [23]. While deeper models slightly improve accuracy, a single-layer design yields more interpretable attention patterns and is adopted.

As shown in Table 1, BioFC-GAT achieves competitive performance among rs-fMRI-only methods. Higher-performing approaches typically rely on multi-modal or phenotypic inputs, whereas our model attains strong results using FC alone, highlighting a favorable trade-off between diagnosis performance and interpretability.

Table 1. Comparison with recent ASD classification methods on ABIDE I.

Method	Year	Input	Results
GAT [24]	2025	FC graph	ACC 74.07%
SWNet [31]	2024	rs-fMRI	AUC 0.81; ACC 76.52%
RGTNet [26]	2024	rs-fMRI GTrans	ACC 73.40%
MHNet [12]	2025	rs-fMRI	AUC 0.78; ACC 76.29%
MADE [13]	2024	rs-fMRI, demo., atlas	ACC 75.20%
GraphNet [30]	2025	rs-fMRI, atlas	ACC 75.25%
MTGWNN [17]	2025	fMRI, pheno	AUC 0.92; ACC 87.25%
DAGMNet [25]	2025	sMRI, fMRI, pheno	AUC 0.96; ACC 91.59%
BioFC-GAT	–	FC graph	AUC 0.82; ACC 77.0%

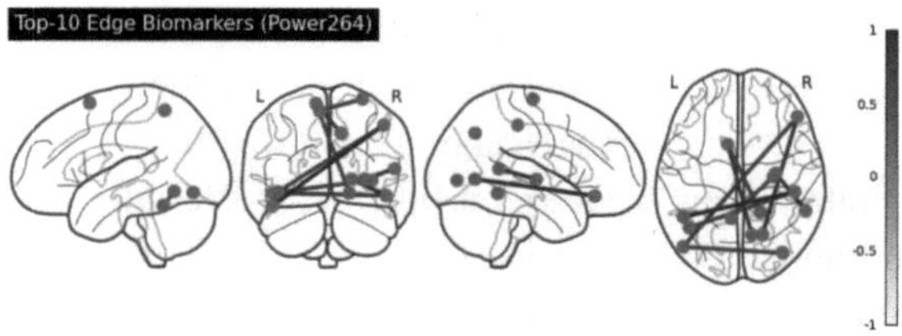

Fig. 2. Visualization of top edge-level biomarkers.

3.3 Biomarker Discovery

ROI-Level Biomarkers. We integrate gradient- and attention-based saliency through weighted fusion to obtain a unified importance measure. ROIs are selected using a data-driven percentile strategy combined with cross-model stability. Specifically, for each model, ROIs whose importance scores fall within the top 10% of the empirical distribution are retained, and only those consistently selected in at least 90% of models are considered stable biomarkers. Using this criterion, we identify 24 ROIs as key biomarkers shown in Table 2.

The identified ROI-level biomarkers are primarily concentrated in the somatomotor network (SMN), including the precentral and postcentral gyri and the precuneus, highlighting strong involvement of sensorimotor systems [19,22]. Visual regions (e.g., occipital and lingual) are also prominent, indicating altered perceptual processing [8,22]. Default mode network (DMN) regions, including medial and inferior frontal areas, suggest disruptions in higher-order cognitive functions [19]. Additional contributions from attention networks and subcortical structures (e.g., superior temporal gyrus, supplementary motor area, thalamus and putamen) indicate widespread involvement across functional systems. Overall, these results support distributed, multi-system alterations in ASD.

Edge-Level Biomarkers. Edge-level biomarkers are extracted by integrating attention weights with gradient-based attribution, restricting to the ROI-induced

Table 2. Top ROI-level biomarkers with network annotations and MNI coordinates.

ROI	Region	AAL	Net	X	Y	Z
262	Sub-Gyral	Temporal_Inf_L	DAN	−42	−60	−9
255	Postcentral Gyrus	Postcentral_R	SMN	47	−30	49
240	Sup. Temporal Gyrus	Temporal_Sup_R	VAN	56	−46	11
21	Precentral Gyrus	Precentral_R	SMN	29	−17	71
138	Sup. Frontal Gyrus	Supp_Motor_Area_L	VAN	−10	11	67
173	Mid. Occipital Gyrus	Occipital_Mid_R	Visual	37	−81	1
224	Thalamus	Thalamus_L	Subcortical	−10	−18	7
217	Anterior Cingulate	Cingulum_Ant_R	Salience	10	22	27
13	Precuneus	Precuneus_L	SMN	−7	−52	61
76	Medial Frontal Gyrus	Rectus_R	DMN	8	48	−15
253	Fusiform Gyrus	Temporal_Inf_L	Unc.	−47	−51	−21
139	Inf. Frontal Gyrus	Frontal_Inf_Orb_R	DMN	49	35	−12
183	Declive	Cerebellum_Crus1_L	Unc.	−18	−76	−24
154	Mid. Occipital Gyrus	Occipital_Inf_L	Visual	−47	−76	−10
143	Parahippocampal Gyrus	Lingual_R	Visual	18	−47	−10
210	Inf. Frontal Gyrus	Frontal_Inf_Orb_R	Salience	37	32	−2
229	Extra-Nuclear	Putamen_R	Subcortical	31	−14	2
135	Precuneus	Precuneus_R	Memory	11	−66	42
148	Lingual Gyrus	Lingual_R	Visual	20	−66	2
115	Medial Frontal Gyrus	Frontal_Sup_Medial_L	DMN	−8	48	23
23	Postcentral Gyrus	Postcentral_L	SMN	−23	−30	72
30	Postcentral Gyrus	Postcentral_L	SMN	−29	−43	61
22	Postcentral Gyrus	Postcentral_R	SMN	10	−46	73
17	Medial Frontal Gyrus	Frontal_Sup_Medial_L	SMN	−7	−21	65

FPN: Frontoparietal; DMN: Default Mode; SMN: Somatomotor;
DAN: Dorsal Attention; VAN: Ventral Attention; Unc.: Uncertain.

subgraph, and selecting the top ∼10% strongest connections, capturing the most discriminative interactions in the connectome (Table 3).

As shown in Table 3 and Fig. 2, the selected edges exhibit a structured, non-uniform distribution, with clear concentration in sensorimotor, visual, and frontal regions. A dominant pattern is the prevalence of within-network connectivity in the somatomotor network (SMN), with repeated links among precentral and postcentral gyri, indicating strong sensorimotor contributions to ASD discrimination [19,22].

The model also captures structured cross-network interactions, including links between default mode (DMN) and visual regions, as well as between sensorimotor and attention networks (DAN/VAN), reflecting disrupted coordination

Table 3. Top edge-level biomarkers with region pairs and network assignments (network abbreviations as in Table 2).

Edge	Edge Name	Net Pair
254–255	Fusiform Gyrus – Postcentral Gyrus	Uncertain – SMN
139–148	Inferior Frontal Gyrus – Lingual Gyrus	DMN – Visual
229–240	Extra-Nuclear – Sup. Temporal Gyrus	Subcortical – VAN
135–138	Precuneus – Sup. Frontal Gyrus	Memory – VAN
139–154	Inferior Frontal Gyrus – Mid. Occipital Gyrus	DMN – Visual
255–262	Postcentral Gyrus – Sub-Gyral	SMN – DAN
253–262	Fusiform Gyrus – Sub-Gyral	Uncertain – DAN
13–21	Precuneus – Precentral Gyrus	SMN – SMN
154–173	Mid. Occipital Gyrus – Mid. Occipital Gyrus	Visual – Visual
138–143	Sup. Frontal Gyrus – Parahippocampal Gyrus	VAN – Visual
13–22	Precuneus – Postcentral Gyrus	SMN – SMN
148–173	Lingual Gyrus – Mid. Occipital Gyrus	Visual – Visual
148–154	Lingual Gyrus – Mid. Occipital Gyrus	Visual – Visual
21–22	Precentral Gyrus – Postcentral Gyrus	SMN – SMN
17–23	Medial Frontal Gyrus – Postcentral Gyrus	SMN – SMN
13–30	Precuneus – Postcentral Gyrus	SMN – SMN
173–183	Mid. Occipital Gyrus – Declive	Visual – Uncertain
21–30	Precentral Gyrus – Postcentral Gyrus	SMN – SMN
22–23	Postcentral Gyrus – Postcentral Gyrus	SMN – SMN
183–210	Declive – Inferior Frontal Gyrus	Uncertain – Salience
183–217	Declive – Anterior Cingulate	Uncertain – Salience
135–143	Precuneus – Parahippocampal Gyrus	Memory – Visual
224–240	Thalamus – Sup. Temporal Gyrus	Subcortical – VAN
240–262	Sup. Temporal Gyrus – Sub-Gyral	VAN – DAN
224–255	Thalamus – Postcentral Gyrus	Subcortical – SMN
139–173	Inferior Frontal Gyrus – Mid. Occipital Gyrus	DMN – Visual
210–217	Inferior Frontal Gyrus – Anterior Cingulate	Salience – Salience

across sensory, cognitive, and attentional systems [2]. Subcortical regions (e.g., thalamus) further act as integrative hubs.

Overall, the biomarkers reveal a dual pattern of strong within-network concentration—particularly in SMN and visual systems—and cross-network dysconnectivity, supporting both localized alterations and impaired large-scale integration in ASD.

Functional Network Interaction Analysis. At the network level, edge biomarkers are dominated by within-network SMN connectivity, which accounts for the largest proportion of edges. Additional prominent patterns include DMN–Visual and Visual–Visual interactions, indicating altered coupling between perceptual and higher-order cognitive systems.

Edges involving attention-related networks (DAN/VAN, salience) and subcortical regions further suggest widespread disruptions across large-scale brain systems. Overall, the coexistence of strong within-network connectivity (e.g., SMN–SMN) and cross-network interactions (e.g., DMN–Visual) supports the network dysconnectivity hypothesis of ASD, reflecting both localized abnormalities and impaired inter-network integration [8,22].

Cross-Atlas Biomarker Consistency. Cross-atlas generalization is evaluated using the CC200 atlas [3] under a leave-one-site-out protocol, yielding a mean AUC of 0.61 ± 0.13(median 0.62, weighted 0.624), indicating stable performance across sites. Strong results on Olin (0.79), USM (0.78), Yale (0.77), and NYU (0.75) further indicate robustness to inter-site variability despite domain shifts.

Spatial comparison with Power264 shows 64.3% overlap within 30 mm and a Jaccard similarity of 0.23, indicating moderate agreement. Consistent patterns are observed at the network level, with biomarkers concentrated in temporal, visual, limbic, and subcortical systems. Both hypo- and hyper-connectivity patterns are identified, reflecting characteristic ASD dysconnectivity. These results suggest that the learned representations capture stable, biologically meaningful structures beyond specific atlas definitions.

3.4 Comparison with Prior ASD Biomarker Studies

To validate the proposed biomarkers, we compare our results with prior ASD studies from spatial, anatomical, and functional perspectives. Using the Power atlas, spatial consistency with [7] is evaluated in MNI space. Under a 20 mm threshold, 66% of ROIs overlap (Jaccard: 0.42), while a stricter 10 mm threshold yields 50.0% overlap (Jaccard: 0.25), indicating moderate agreement at a fine anatomical scale. The identified biomarkers are primarily concentrated in the somatomotor (SMN) and visual (VIS) networks, with additional contributions from the default mode (DMN), attention networks (DAN, VAN), and subcortical regions. This distribution supports ASD as involving both sensory abnormalities and large-scale network dysconnectivity (Fig. 3).

Our findings are consistent with previous studies reporting the involvement of postcentral, occipital, frontal, and temporal visual regions in ASD [5]. At the ROI level, highly stable regions—including the precentral and postcentral gyri (SMN), middle occipital and lingual gyri (VIS), and superior temporal gyrus (VAN)—indicate strong involvement of sensory and perceptual systems. The presence of the anterior cingulate cortex and thalamus further suggests interaction between salience processing and sensory pathways, consistent with prior evidence linking increased salience network connectivity to enhanced sensoryattention coupling in ASD [6].

Comparison with recent graph-based methods shows substantial agreement. Visual regions such as the fusiform and inferior temporal gyri reported in [24]

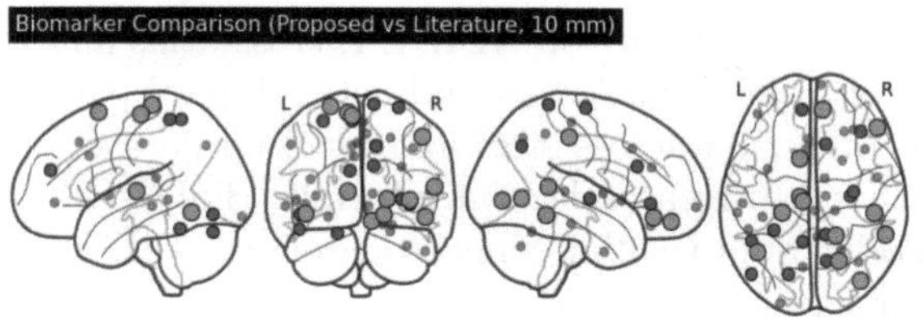

Fig. 3. Spatial distribution of proposed biomarkers (red), literature-reported regions (blue), and overlapping regions (green). Overlapping regions demonstrate consistency with prior findings, while non-overlapping regions suggest potential novel biomarkers across large-scale brain networks in ASD.

correspond closely to our findings, while the thalamus and motor cortices align with our subcortical and somatomotor results. Frontal and cingulate regions also overlap, indicating consistent involvement of higher-order cognitive systems. Compared to DAGMNet [25], our results show partial agreement, with shared regions including the fusiform gyrus, superior temporal gyrus, anterior cingulate cortex, medial frontal gyrus, and precuneus. However, our model places greater emphasis on somatomotor, visual, and subcortical regions, suggesting a stronger role of sensoryattention interactions.

Finally, our findings strongly align with prior work on motor system abnormalities in ASD. The consistent identification of the precentral and postcentral gyri with high importance supports their critical role in ASD-related alterations, consistent with evidence of atypical connectivity and reduced motor segregation in the precentral gyrus [15].

4 Conclusion

We present *BioFC-GAT*, a graph-based framework for interpretable biomarker discovery in ASD from resting-state functional connectivity. By leveraging sparse multi-head graph attention, the model captures ROI- and edge-level importance, enabling multi-scale characterization of brain network alterations with stable performance.

The identified biomarkers are concentrated in somatomotor and visual systems, with additional involvement of default mode, attention, salience, and subcortical networks. Connectivity patterns reveal strong within-network interactions (e.g., SMN–SMN, Visual–Visual) alongside structured cross-network links, supporting a network-level dysconnectivity view of ASD [19,22].

BioFC-GAT provides interpretable representations linking learned attention to anatomically meaningful regions and connections. However, multi-site variability, cohort heterogeneity, and preprocessing choices may affect performance and attribution stability. Moreover, attention- and gradient-based attributions reflect model reliance rather than causality and should be interpreted as hypothesis-generating [11].

Although evaluated primarily on ABIDE I, cross-atlas analysis (e.g., CC200 vs. Power264) shows consistent spatial and network-level patterns. Future work will evaluate generalization across sites and external datasets (e.g., ABIDE II) and assess sensitivity to atlas selection. Overall, BioFC-GAT offers an effective and interpretable approach for connectome-based ASD analysis, supporting multi-scale network dysconnectivity.

Acknowledgments. This work is partially supported by the Natural Sciences and Engineering Research Council of Canada (NSERC).

References

1. Bullmore, E., Sporns, O.: Complex brain networks: graph theoretical analysis of structural and functional systems. Nat. Rev. Neurosci. **10**(3), 186–198 (2009)
2. Cole, M.W., Reynolds, J.R., Power, J.D., Repovs, G., Anticevic, A., Braver, T.S.: Multi-task connectivity reveals flexible hubs for adaptive task control. Nat. Neurosci. **16**(9), 1348–1355 (2013)
3. Craddock, R.C., James, G.A., Holtzheimer, P.E., III., Hu, X.P., Mayberg, H.S.: A whole brain fMRI atlas generated via spatially constrained spectral clustering. Hum. Brain Mapp. **33**(8), 1914–1928 (2012)
4. Di Martino, A., et al.: The autism brain imaging data exchange: towards a large-scale evaluation of the intrinsic brain architecture in autism. Mol. Psychiatry **19**(6), 659–667 (2014)
5. Dvornek, N.C., Ventola, P., Pelphrey, K.A., Duncan, J.S.: Identifying autism from resting-state fMRI using long short-term memory networks. Mach. Learn. Med. Imaging 362–370 (2017)
6. Green, S.A., Hernandez, L., Tottenham, N., Krasileva, K., Bookheimer, S.Y., Dapretto, M.: Salience network connectivity in autism is related to brain and behavioral markers of sensory overresponsivity. J. Am. Acad. Child Adolesc. Psychiatry **55**(7), 618–626 (2016)
7. Guo, H., Yin, W., Mostafa, S., Wu, F.X.: Diagnosis of ASD from rs-fMRI images based on brain dynamic networks. In: International Symposium on Bioinformatics Research and Applications, pp. 166–177. Springer (2020)
8. Hahamy, A., Behrmann, M., Malach, R.: The idiosyncratic brain: distortion of spontaneous connectivity patterns in autism spectrum disorder. Nat. Neurosci. **18**(2), 302–309 (2015)
9. Heinsfeld, A.S., Franco, A.R., Craddock, R.C., Buchweitz, A., Meneguzzi, F.: Identification of autism spectrum disorder using deep learning and the abide dataset. NeuroImage Clin. **17**, 16–23 (2018)
10. Issac, A., et al.: The global prevalence of autism spectrum disorder in children: a systematic review and meta-analysis. Osong Public Health Res. Perspect. **16**(1), 3 (2025)
11. Jain, S., Wallace, B.C.: Attention is not explanation. In: Proceedings of the 2019 Conference of the North American Chapter of the Association for Computational Linguistics: Human Language Technologies, Volume 1 (Long and Short Papers), pp. 3543–3556 (2019)
12. Li, Y., et al.: Mhnet: multi-view high-order network for diagnosing neurodevelopmental disorders using resting-state fMRI. J. Imaging Inform. Med. 1–21 (2025)

13. Liu, X., Hasan, M.R., Gedeon, T., Hossain, M.Z.: MADE-for-ASD: a multi-atlas deep ensemble network for diagnosing autism spectrum disorder. Comput. Biol. Med. **182**, 109083 (2024)
14. Mostafa, S., Wu, F.X.: Diagnosis of autism spectrum disorder with convolutional autoencoder and structural MRI images. In: Neural Engineering Techniques for Autism Spectrum Disorder, pp. 23–38. Elsevier (2021)
15. Nebel, M.B., Eloyan, A., Barber, A.D., Mostofsky, S.H.: Precentral gyrus functional connectivity signatures of autism. Front. Syst. Neurosci. **8**, 80 (2014)
16. Power, J.D., et al.: Functional network organization of the human brain. Neuron **72**(4), 665–678 (2011)
17. Shan, S., Ren, Y., Jiao, Z., Li, X.: Mtgwnn: a multi-template graph wavelet neural network identification model for autism spectrum disorder. Int. J. Imaging Syst. Technol. **35**(1), e70010 (2025)
18. Smith, S.M., et al.: Functional connectomics from resting-state fMRI. Trends Cogn. Sci. **17**(12), 666–682 (2013)
19. Song, Y., Epalle, T.M., Lu, H.: Characterizing and predicting autism spectrum disorder by performing resting-state functional network community pattern analysis. Front. Hum. Neurosci. **13**, 203 (2019)
20. Sundararajan, M., Taly, A., Yan, Q.: Axiomatic attribution for deep networks. In: Precup, D., Teh, Y.W. (eds.) Proceedings of the 34th International Conference on Machine Learning. Proceedings of Machine Learning Research, vol. 70, pp. 3319–3328. PMLR (2017)
21. Tang, L., Mostafa, S., Liao, B., Wu, F.X.: A network clustering based feature selection strategy for classifying autism spectrum disorder. BMC Med. Genomics **12**(Suppl 7), 153 (2019)
22. Uddin, L.Q., et al.: Salience network-based classification and prediction of symptom severity in children with autism. JAMA Psychiat. **70**(8) (2013)
23. Veličković, P., et al.: Graph attention networks. In: International Conference on Learning Representations, vol. 6, p. 2. Ithaca (2018)
24. Wang, C., Xiao, Z., Xu, Y., Zhang, Q., Chen, J.: A novel approach for ASD recognition based on graph attention networks. Front. Comput. Neurosci. **18**, 1388083 (2024)
25. Wang, L., Li, X., Yuan, J., Chen, Y.: Dagmnet: dual-branch attention-pruned graph neural network for multimodal sMRI and fMRI fusion in autism prediction. Biomedicines **13**(9), 2168 (2025)
26. Wang, Y., Long, H., Bo, T., Zheng, J.: Residual graph transformer for autism spectrum disorder prediction. Comput. Methods Programs Biomed. **247**, 108065 (2024)
27. Wiegreffe, S., Pinter, Y.: Attention is not not explanation. In: Proceedings of the 2019 Conference on Empirical Methods in Natural Language Processing and the 9th International Joint Conference on Natural Language Processing (EMNLP-IJCNLP), pp. 11–20 (2019)
28. Yin, W., Li, L., Wu, F.X.: A graph attention neural network for diagnosing ASD with fMRI data. In: 2021 IEEE International Conference on Bioinformatics and Biomedicine (BIBM), pp. 1131–1136. IEEE (2021)
29. Yin, W., Li, L., Wu, F.X.: A semi-supervised autoencoder for autism disease diagnosis. Neurocomputing **483**, 140–147 (2022)
30. Zeraati, M., Davoodi, A.: ASD-Graphnet: a novel graph learning approach for autism spectrum disorder diagnosis using fMRI data. Comput. Biol. Med. **196**, 110723 (2025)

31. Zhang, J., Guo, J., Lu, D., Cao, Y.: ASD-SWNet: a novel shared-weight feature extraction and classification network for autism spectrum disorder diagnosis. Sci. Rep. **14**(1), 13696 (2024)

circ-EGAT: Enhanced Graph Attention Network with Multi-information Integration for circRNA-RBP Binding Sites Prediction

Yajing Guo and Xiujuan Lei(✉)

School of Artificial Intelligence and Computer Science, Shaanxi Normal University, Xi'an 710119, China
xjlei@snnu.edu.cn

Abstract. Accurate identification of circular RNA (circRNA)-RNA binding protein (RBP) binding sites at nucleotide resolution is crucial. To capture interactions between non-adjacent but functionally related nucleotides, we propose circ-EGAT. circRNA sequences are first one-hot encoded and processed through two parallel pathways. A Bi-directional Gated Recurrent Unit (BiGRU) captures contextual edge features, while a multi-scale convolutional neural network (CNN) combined with a position-aware attention module extracts refined node features. A dynamic graph structure learner subsequently generates an adaptive adjacency matrix from the attention-enhanced features. By integrating node features, edge features, and the adjacency matrix within an enhanced multi-head graph attention network (GAT), circ-EGAT effectively captures complex, non-local interactions. The GAT output is fused with the attention-based node features via a gated mechanism, followed by three fully connected layers for final nucleotide-level predictions. Experimental results demonstrate that circ-EGAT achieves superior performance in identifying binding site positions, with ablation studies confirming the significant contributions of multi-scale CNN and gating components.

Keywords: Graph structure learning · Enhanced GAT · Gated fusion

1 Introduction

Unlike traditional linear RNAs, circular RNA (circRNA) features a covalently closed circular structure without a 5' end cap or a 3' end poly(A) tail [1]. This makes it resistant to RNA exonucleases, resulting in more stable expression and reduced degradation [2]. circRNA is involved in regulating the occurrence and development of many diseases [3–6]. The structural stability of intron-derived circRNA confers lower immunogenicity compared to other RNA species, positioning it as promising candidates for the development of RNA-based therapeutics [7, 8] and vaccine research [9, 10]. RNA binding protein (RBP) participates in nearly all stages of circRNA lifecycle and has been implicated in promoting circRNA biogenesis in the context of cancer biology [11]. circRNA-RBP interactions play a critical role in tumorigenesis and progression [12]. These interactions can modulate oncogenic pathways and influence key cancer hallmarks [13]. Thus,

X. Cui et al. (Eds.): ISBRA 2026, LNBI 16690, pp. 97–108, 2027.
https://doi.org/10.1007/978-981-92-3716-6_8

accurate prediction of circRNA-RBP binding sites is essential to uncover how circRNA recruit RBP for gene regulation, providing a crucial basis for therapeutic target discovery and disease intervention strategies.

Traditional biological experiments are time-consuming, labor-intensive, and costly. The powerful feature learning capabilities of deep learning have provided new methodologies for bioinformatics and have been widely adopted [14, 15]. Existing methods for predicting binding sites of circRNA-RBP based on deep learning can be classified into two categories: sequence-level prediction and nucleotide-level prediction. Sequence-level methods treat the entire circRNA sequence as a single sample to predict RBP binding. Most existing methods follow this approach. For example, CRIP employs a stack encoding scheme based on codons and a hybrid deep learning architecture [16]. CRPBsites employs Long Short-Term Memory (LSTM)-based encoding-decoding framework and attention mechanism for predictions [17]. circ-pSBLA constructs a pseudo-Siamese network comprising CNN and BiLSTM, then averages the predictions from both branches to produce the final result [18]. DMSK is based on multi-view deep learning, subspace learning and multi-view classifier [19]. ASCRB employs five encoding methods to obtain multi-view features, and then uses CNN, Squeeze Excitation Network (SE-net) and BiLSTM to filter and fuse these features [20]. CRMSS utilizes the features of circRNA and RBP, then employs multi-scale residual blocks, BiLSTM, and attention mechanism to make predictions [21]. circ-CNNED first performs preprocessing using CNN, then uses the time convolutional network (TCN) and CNN to respectively construct the encoding and decoding modules [22]. CR-deal integrates sequence and structural features via graph attention network (GAT), effectively leveraging structural information to improve accuracy [23].

Nucleotide-level methods treat each nucleotide as a sample to predict RBP binding, yet such methods remain relatively scarce. CircSLNN employs a CNN-LSTM-conditional random field (CRF) hybrid network for sequence labeling [24]. CPBFCN employs a fully CNN framework [25]. CircSite combines Bi-directional Gated Recurrent Unit (BiGRU)-Transformer for nucleotide-resolution prediction [26]. circdpb constructs a feature pyramid architecture based on TCN, and combines it with BiGRU for nucleotide-level prediction [27].

Given the scarcity of nucleotide-level prediction methods and the limitations of existing approaches that treat sequences as linear chains, which fail to capture the interactions between non-adjacent but functionally related nucleotides, we propose circ-EGAT, a dynamic graph structure learning approach with enhanced multi-head GAT. The architecture is illustrated in Fig. 1. The main contributions are: (i) A position-aware attention module is combined with multi-scale CNN to capture node features. (ii) A dynamic graph structure learner is employed to capture the relationships between non-adjacent nucleotides. (iii) The node features, edge features and an adjacency matrix are integrated to multi-head GAT. (iiii) The output of multi-head GAT and node features are merged through gated fusion to make prediction.

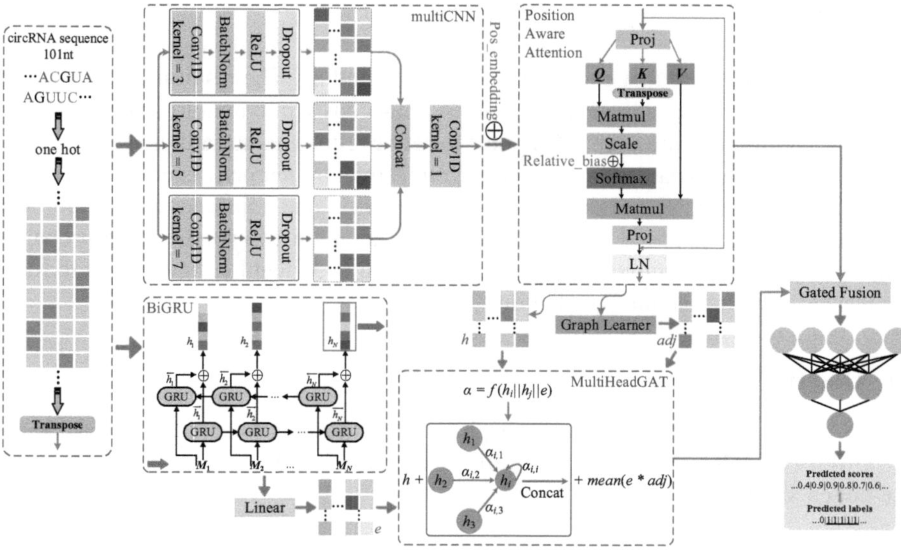

Fig. 1. The architecture of circ-EGAT.

2 Datasets

37 benchmark datasets are constructed, each containing RBP-specific circRNA sequences from the CircInteractome database [28]. For each circRNA, a 101-nucleotide (nt) sequence is extracted by extending 50nt both upstream and downstream from the center of the binding region. Sequences are deduplicated using CD-HIT Suite [29] with a threshold 0.8. The sequence numbers of 37 datasets are shown in Table 1. Following CircInteractome, nucleotides within binding regions are labeled '1' and others '0', yielding a 101-bit binary vector per sequence.

Table 1. The sequence numbers of 37 datasets.

RBP		RBP		RBP		RBP	
AGO1	17318	EIF4A3	20000	IGF2BP1	20000	QKI	1033
AGO2	20000	EWSR1	4695	IGF2BP2	10000	SFRS1	8595
AGO3	3124	FMRP	20000	IGF2BP3	20000	TAF15	1467
ALKBH5	770	FOX2	605	LIN28A	18277	TDP43	5484
AUF1	2896	FUS	20000	LIN28B	7888	TIA1	2202
C17ORF85	1016	FXR1	927	METTL3	2666	TIAL1	5456
C22ORF28	5292	FXR2	5635	MOV10	5889	TNRC6	1101
CAPRIN1	5298	HNRNPC	14224	PTB	20000	U2AF65	8224
DGCR8	20000	HUR	20000	PUM2	2829	WTAP	496
						ZC3H7B	13119

3 Method

circRNA sequences are first encoded by one-hot encoding. The resulting matrix is fed into a BiGRU to extract edge features and simultaneously into a multi-scale CNN followed by a position-aware attention module to derive refined node features. The attention module output is also passed to a dynamic graph structure learner to generate an adaptive adjacency matrix. The node features, edge features, and adjacency matrix are then integrated into an enhanced multi-head GAT for attention computation and propagation. Finally, the GAT output is gated-fused with the node features and passed to fully connected layers for the final prediction.

3.1 One-Hot Encoding

circRNA sequences are represented through one-hot encoding to capture positional identity. Given a circRNA sequence $S = \{s_0, s_1, \ldots, s_n\}, n = 100$. $M_{101\times4}$ is obtained through one-hot encoding:

$$M_{i,j} = \begin{cases} 1, \text{ if} s_i = j\text{–thmemberof}\{\text{A, C, G, U}\} \\ 0, \text{ else} \end{cases} \tag{1}$$

where $i = 0, 1, \ldots, 100$. $j = 0, 1, 2, 3$.

3.2 Node Feature Extraction

To capture multi-scale contextual patterns, the encoding matrix M is fed into three parallel 1D convolution layers with distinct kernel sizes (3, 5, 7). The resulting feature maps are concatenated along the channel dimension and subsequently integrated by a 1D convolution layer to produce the final multi-scale representation. The calculation process is as follows:

$$O_c = Conv_1(concat(multiCNN_3(M), multiCNN_5(M), multiCNN_7(M))) \tag{2}$$

$$multiCNN(M) = Dropout(ReLU(BN(Conv(M)))) \tag{3}$$

where O_c is the output of multi-scale CNN, *Conv* represents the 1D convolution, *BN* represents the batch normalization, and the subscript indicates the size of the convolution kernel.

Then O_c is input to position-aware attention module. Firstly, a learnable absolute positional encoding is added to the input, and the resulting representation is projected to obtain query(Q), key(K), and value(V) matrices:

$$O_c = O_c + pos\_embedding \tag{4}$$

$$Q, K, V = proj(O_c) \tag{5}$$

where *pos_embedding* is the learnable absolute positional encoding matrix, randomly initialized from a normal distribution with a mean of 0 and a standard deviation of

0.1. *Proj* is linear projection. When calculating the attention score, a learnable relative position bias is introduced. The calculation process is as follows:

$$attn\_score = \frac{Q \cdot K^T}{\sqrt{d_k}} \tag{6}$$

$$attn\_score = attn\_score + relative\_bias \tag{7}$$

where *relative_bias* is the relative position bias which is randomly initialized. The attention scores are normalized and the final output is calculated as follows:

$$attn\_weight = softmax(attn\_score) \tag{8}$$

$$h = LN(O_c + proj(attn\_weight \odot V)) \tag{9}$$

where *LN* is layer normalization and h is the node features.

3.3 Graph Structure Learner

To capture spatial relationships between non-adjacent yet functionally proximal nucleotides in circRNA three-dimensional conformations, we introduce Graph structure learner. Given the node feature h, the module first constructs pairwise representations by concatenating the features of each node pair, resulting in $P_{ij} = [h_i; h_j]$. These pairwise vectors are then fed into multi-layer perceptron (MLP) to compute a relation score $R_{ij} \in [0,1]$, indicating the strength of their potential connection.

To ensure graph sparsity and focus on the most salient interactions, we retain only the top-k strongest connections for each node via a masking strategy. Additionally, a learnable threshold τ (0.5) is applied to filter out weak or spurious relations. The resulting adjacency matrix *adj* is then symmetrized to enforce an undirected graph structure, which is more biologically plausible for modeling interactions between nucleotides. This dynamic, input-dependent graph construction allows to adaptively uncover meaningful dependencies that transcend linear sequence proximity.

3.4 Edge Feature Extraction

BiGRU is composed of two GRUs in opposite directions. GRU incorporates a gating mechanism that effectively captures long-term dependencies while suppressing superfluous noise. GRU primarily includes an update gate, a reset gate, and a candidate state. Take the forward GRU as an example, the calculation formulas are as follows:

$$\overrightarrow{z_t} = \sigma(W_z \odot [\overrightarrow{h_{t-1}}, M_t] + b_z) \tag{10}$$

$$\overrightarrow{r_t} = \sigma(W_r \odot [\overrightarrow{h_{t-1}}, M_t] + b_r) \tag{11}$$

$$\widetilde{h_t} = \tanh(W_h \odot [\overrightarrow{r_t} \odot \overrightarrow{h_{t-1}}, M_t] + b_h) \tag{12}$$

where $\overrightarrow{z_t}$, $\overrightarrow{r_t}$, $\widetilde{h_t}$ are respectively update gate, reset gate, new candidate state at time t. σ is Sigmoid activation function. $\odot$ denotes element-by-element multiplication. W_z, W_r, W_h are weight matrices and b_z, b_r, b_h are biases. $\overrightarrow{h_{t-1}}$ is hidden state at time t-1. A_t is the input at time t. The new hidden state $\overrightarrow{h_t}$ at time t is calculated as:

$$\overrightarrow{h_t} = (1 - \overrightarrow{z_t}) \odot \overrightarrow{h_{t-1}} + \overrightarrow{z_t} \odot \widetilde{h_t} \tag{13}$$

Utilizing the identical computational mechanism, the reverse hidden state $\overleftarrow{h_t}$ at time t can be obtained. BiGRU produces the ultimate output h by amalgamating the hidden states at time N in both forward and backward directions:

$$e = \text{concat}(\overrightarrow{h_N}, \overleftarrow{h_N}) \tag{14}$$

where concat() represents the concatenation operation. $\overrightarrow{h_N}$, $\overleftarrow{h_N}$ represent the hidden states of the forward and backward GRU at time step N, respectively. e is the output of BiGRU which is used as edge features.

3.5 Enhanced Multi-Head GAT

To effectively model the complex interactions between nucleotides in circRNA sequences, an enhanced multi-head GAT is used which jointly leverages node features, edge features, and the adjacency matrix *adj*. Firstly, apply separate linear transformations to project them into a common latent space:

$$H_i = W_{node} \cdot h_i,\ E_{ij} = W_{edge} \cdot e_{ij} \tag{15}$$

where W_{node}, W_{edge} are learnable weight matrices. Unlike standard GAT which computes attention coefficients solely based on node features, the enhanced GAT incorporates edge features into the attention computation. For each node pair (i, j), the attention coefficient is calculated as:

$$\alpha_{ij} = LeakyReLU(a^T [H_i \| H_j \| E_{ij}) \tag{16}$$

where || denotes concatenation, and a is a learnable attention vector initialized via Xavier uniform initialization. To leverage the biologically meaningful relationships captured by the dynamic graph structure learner, we apply the learned adjacency matrix *adj* as a mask to the attention coefficients:

$$\alpha_{ij} = \alpha_{ij} \cdot adj_{ij} \tag{17}$$

This ensures that only functionally relevant node pairs participate in the message passing process. The masked coefficients are then normalized across all neighbors using the softmax function:

$$\hat{\alpha}_{ij} = softmax(\alpha_{ij}) \tag{18}$$

The aggregated node representation is computed as a weighted sum of the transformed neighbor features:

$$H_{i'} = \sum_{j \in N_i} \hat{\alpha}_{ij} H_j \tag{19}$$

To preserve both the original node information and the edge-based relational information, we introduce a residual connection and an edge feature contribution term:

$$H_i^{out} = H_{i'} + H_i + \frac{1}{N_i} \sum_{j \in N_i} E_{ij} adj_{ij} \tag{20}$$

This design enables each node to aggregate information from its neighbors' features, its own features, and the features of its incident edges. To capture diverse aspects of node interactions, multiple independent attention heads are applied in parallel, and their outputs are concatenated:

$$H^{gat} = LN(W_{out}(||_{k=1}^{K} H_k^{out}) + H) \tag{21}$$

where W_{out} projects the concatenated multi-head outputs back to the original hidden dimension. K is the number of heads. The enhanced GAT comprehensively captures the intricate relationships within circRNA sequences, integrating both sequential and structural information for more accurate binding sites prediction.

To integrate the complementary information captured by the position-aware attention module and the enhanced GAT, a gated feature fusion module is employed:

$$F_{out} = \Phi(G \odot W_1 h + (1 - G) \odot W_2 H^{gat}) \tag{22}$$

$$G = \sigma(W[W_1 h || W_2 H^{gat}] + b) \tag{23}$$

where Φ represents linear transformation, layer normalization, ReLU and Dropout. σ is sigmoid function. $\odot$ is multiplication of each element. Finally, F_{out} is input to three fully connected layers to predict.

4 Results

4.1 Comparison with Other Methods

circ-EGAT is evaluated using five-fold cross-validation on 37 datasets with sequence-level partitioning, ensuring that all nucleotides from a same circRNA are kept together and never split across training and testing sets. Each fold adopts an 80/20 split for training and testing. The batch size is 32, the maximum epoch is 150, and the early stopping strategy is adopted during the training process. The Receiver Operating Characteristic (ROC) Curve and the Precision/Recall curve of circ-EGAT are shown in Fig. 2. It can be seen that circ-EGAT achieved good performance.

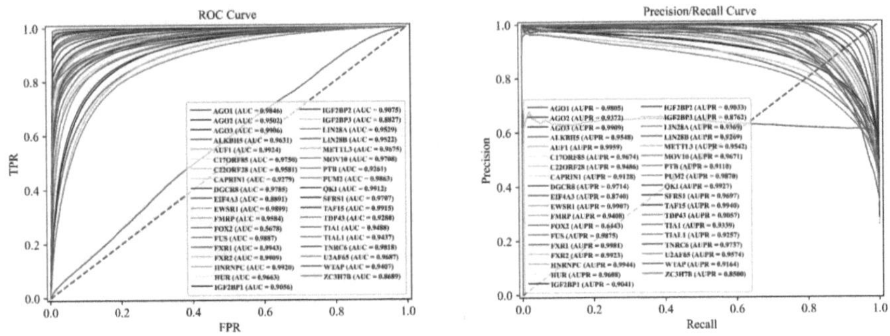

Fig. 2. The ROC curve and Precision/Recall curve of circ-EGAT.

circ-EGAT is also compared with three nucleotide-level prediction methods: CircSLNN, CircSite and CPBFCN. Six evaluation metrics are used including the Area Under the Receiver Operating Characteristic curve (*AUC*), Area Under the Precision-Recall curve (*AUPR*), Accuracy (*Acc*), Precision (*Prec*), Recall (*Rec*), and *F*1-*Score*. The calculation formulas are as follows:

$$Acc = \frac{TP + TN}{TP + TN + FP + FN} \tag{24}$$

$$Prec = \frac{TP}{TP + FP} \tag{25}$$

$$Rec = \frac{TP}{TP + FN} \tag{26}$$

$$F1{-}Score = \frac{2 \times Precision \times Recall}{Precision + Recall} \tag{27}$$

The results are shown in Table 2 and the highest performance metric is indicated in bold. Given the class imbalance between positive and negative samples, *AUPR* serves as a more robust performance indicator. Consequently, kernel smoothing is employed to fit the *AUPR* distribution across the four methods in Fig. 3. As evidenced by the experimental results, circ-EGAT exhibits superior performance and substantially outperforms the three competing approaches.

Table 2. The average of different methods on each metrics.

	AUC	*AUPR*	*Acc*	*Prec*	*Rec*	*F1-Score*
CircSLNN	0.5184	0.3930	0.7819	0.5213	0.6645	0.5287
CircSite	0.7895	0.7474	0.7446	0.7479	0.5499	0.6244
CPBFCN	0.8732	0.8122	0.8616	0.8252	0.7586	0.7718
circ-EGAT	**0.9471**	**0.9413**	**0.9048**	**0.8983**	**0.8671**	**0.8820**

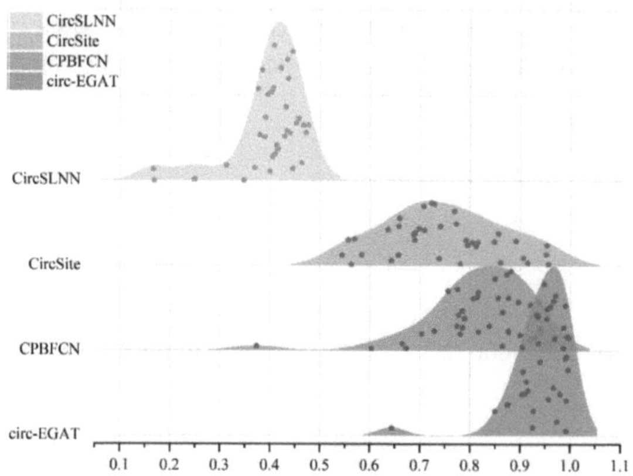

Fig. 3. The *AUPR* distribution across four methods.

4.2 Ablation Experiment

The following variants are constructed for ablation experiments:

no_fusion: Instead of using gated fusion, simple concatenation is employed.

single_CNN: Instead of using multi-scale CNN, a single-kernel CNN is employed.

The result is shown in Fig. 4 and the purple-red line indicates the mean value. The result indicates that both the gated fusion and the multi-scale CNN contribute to the model's performance, with the multi-scale CNN making a particularly greater contribution.

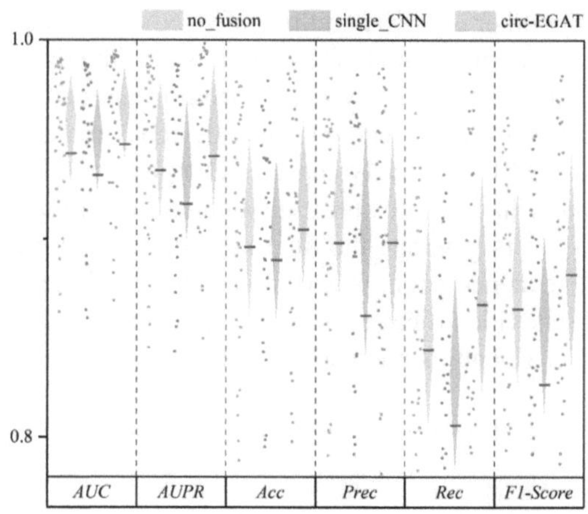

Fig. 4. The comparison of different variants.

4.3 Visual Analysis

A visual comparison of real and predicted binding sites is performed using RNAfold server [30]. The comparison results are shown in Fig. 5. Using four circRNA-RBP pairs as examples, the red color in the left image represents the real binding sites, while the green color in the right represents the predicted binding sites by circ-EGAT. The visualization results show that circ-EGAT can accurately predict the location of binding sites.

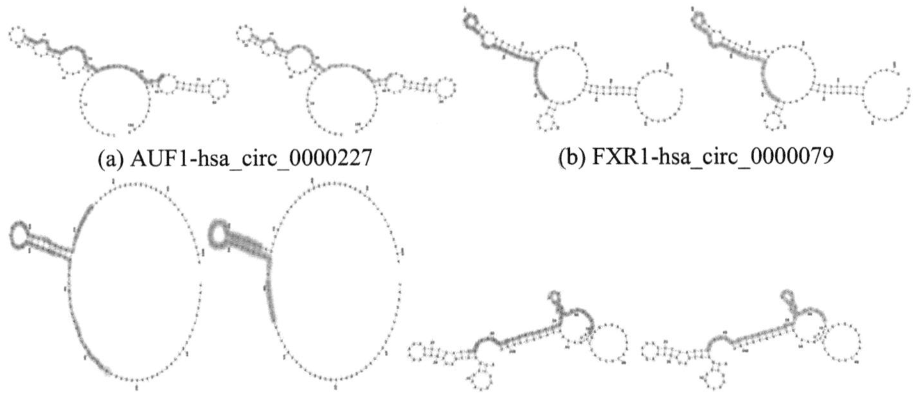

(a) AUF1-hsa_circ_0000227 (b) FXR1-hsa_circ_0000079

(c) MOV10-hsa_circ_0000005 (d) TDP43-hsa_circ_0000005

Fig. 5. The comparison of real and predicted binding sites.

5 Conclusion

We propose circ-EGAT for circRNA-RBP binding sites prediction at nucleotide-level. circRNA sequences are represented by one-hot encoding, which are then processed through two parallel pathways. One pathway leverages BiGRU to capture contextual edge features, while the other utilizes a multi-scale CNN followed by a position-aware attention module to derive refined node features. Besides, the dynamic graph structure learner generates an adaptive adjacency matrix from the attention-enhanced features. By integrating node features, edge features, and adjacency matrix within an enhanced multi-head GAT, circ-EGAT effectively captures complex, non-local interactions. The output of GAT is fused with node features via a gated fusion mechanism, after which three fully connected layers generate the final nucleotide-level prediction. circ-EGAT can model both local sequence patterns and global structural dependencies, leading to more accurate binding sites identification. Experimental results validate both the superior performance of circ-EGAT and its precision in identifying binding site positions.

Acknowledgments. This work was supported by the National Natural Science Foundation of China (62272288).

Disclosure of Interests. The authors have no competing interests to declare that are relevant to the content of this article.

References

1. Feng, X.-Y., Zhu, S.-X., Pu, K.-J., Huang, H.-J., Chen, Y.-Q., Wang, W.-T.: New insight into circRNAs: characterization, strategies, and biomedical applications. Exp. Hematol. Oncol. **12**(1), 91 (2023)

2. Zhou, W.-Y., Cai, Z.-R., Liu, J., Wang, D.-S., Ju, H.-Q., Xu, R.-H.: Circular RNA: metabolism, functions and interactions with proteins. Mol. Cancer **19**(1), 172 (2020)
3. Zhang, F., Jiang, J., Qian, H., Yan, Y., Xu, W.: Exosomal circRNA: emerging insights into cancer progression and clinical application potential. J. Hematol. Oncol. **16**(1), 67 (2023)
4. Conn, V.M., Chinnaiyan, A.M., Conn, S.J.: Circular RNA in cancer. Nat. Rev. Cancer **24**(9), 597–613 (2024)
5. Yang, J., Lei, X., Pan, Y.: Predicting circRNA-disease associations by using multi-biomolecular networks based on variational graph auto-encoder with attention mechanism. Chin. J. Electron. **33**(6), 1526–1537 (2024)
6. Wang, X., Yu, L., Qian, X., Yu, Z.: A ESRP1/circPHGDH/miR-149/RAP1B positive feedback loop promotes the malignant behaviors and glycolysis of prostate cancer cell. Exp. Mol. Med. (2026). https://doi.org/10.1038/s12276-026-01646-x
7. Wang, Y., Lei, X., Chen, Y., Guo, L., Wu, F.-X.: Circular RNA-drug association prediction based on multi-scale convolutional neural networks and adversarial autoencoders. Int. J. Int. J. Mol. Sci. **26**(4), 1509 (2025)
8. Lin, Y., et al.: Circular RNA-based therapy targeting metabolic vulnerability of fatty acid synthesis overcomes castration-resistant prostate cancer. Proc. Natl. Acad. Sci. U.S.A. **123**(1), e2504904123 (2026)
9. Xie, J., et al.: Circular RNA: a promising new star of vaccine. J. Transl. Intern. Med. **11**(4), 372–381 (2023)
10. Zhou, R., et al.: Circular RNA-based HPV16 therapeutic vaccine elicits potent and durable antitumor immunity. J. Exp. Clin. Cancer Res. **45**(1), 33 (2026)
11. Huang, A., Zheng, H., Wu, Z., Chen, M., Huang, Y.: Circular RNA-protein interactions: functions, mechanisms, and identification. Theranostics **10**(8), 3503–3517 (2020)
12. Li, L., et al.: Expanded insights into the mechanisms of RNA-binding protein regulation of circRNA generation and function in cancer biology and therapy. Genes Dis. **12**(4), 101383 (2024)
13. Zhang, N., et al.: Mechanisms and therapeutic implications of gene expression regulation by circRNA-protein interactions in cancer. Commun. Biol. **8**(1), 77 (2025)
14. Ma, M., Lei, X.: BiAtt-GVAE: molecular design for specific target via graph variational autoencoder based on bi-channel interactive attention network. IEEE Trans. Comput. Biol. Bioinform. **22**(5), 1967–1978 (2025)
15. Jiang, J., et al.: Artificial intelligence in bioinformatics: a survey. Briefings Bioinform. **26**(6), bbaf576 (2025)
16. Zhang, K., Pan, X., Yang, Y., Shen, H.-B.: CRIP: predicting circRNA-RBP-binding sites using a codon-based encoding and hybrid deep neural networks. RNA **25**(12), 1604–1615 (2019)
17. Wang, Z., Lei, X.: Prediction of RBP binding sites on circRNAs using an LSTM-based deep sequence learning architecture. Briefings Bioinform. **22**(6), bbab342 (2021)
18. Guo, Y., Lei, X.: A pseudo-Siamese framework for circRNA-RBP binding sites prediction integrating BiLSTM and soft attention mechanism. Methods **207**, 57–64 (2022)
19. Li, H., et al.: circRNA-binding protein site prediction based on multi-view deep learning, subspace learning and multi-view classifier. Briefings Bioinform. **23**(1), bbab394 (2022)
20. Li, L., Xue, Z., Du, X.: ASCRB: Multi-view based attentional feature selection for CircRNA-binding site prediction. Comput. Biol. Med. **162**, 107077 (2023)
21. Zhang, L., Lu, C., Zeng, M., Li, Y., Wang, J.: CRMSS: predicting circRNA-RBP binding sites based on multi-scale characterizing sequence and structure features. Briefings Bioinform. **24**(1) (2023)
22. Guo, Y., Lei, X., Pan, Y.: An encoding-decoding framework based on CNN for circRNA-RBP binding sites prediction. Chin. J. Electron. **33**(1), 256–263 (2024)

23. Wei, Y., Tan, Z., Liu, L.: CR-deal: explainable neural network for circRNA-RBP binding site recognition and interpretation. Interdisc. Sci.-Comput. Life Sci. **17**(2), 463–476 (2025)
24. Ju, Y., Yuan, L., Yang, Y., Zhao, H.: CircSLNN: identifying RBP-binding sites on circRNAs via sequence labeling neural networks. Front. Genet. **10**, 1184 (2019)
25. Shen, Z., Liu, W., Zhao, S., Zhang, Q., Wang, S., Yuan, L.: Nucleotide-level prediction of CircRNA-protein binding based on fully convolutional neural network. Front. Genet. **14**, 1283404 (2023)
26. Wu, H., et al.: Decoding protein binding landscape on circular RNAs with base-resolution transformer models. Comput. Biol. Med. **171**, 108175 (2024)
27. Guo, Y., Lei, X., Wang, Z., Guo, L., Wu, F.-X., Pan, Y.: Nucleotide-level circRNA-RBP binding sites prediction based on hybrid encoding scheme and enhanced feature extraction. Neural Netw. **192**, 107923 (2025)
28. Dudekulay, D.B., Panda, A.C., Grammatikakis, I., De, S., Abdelmohsen, K., Gorospe, M.: CircInteractome: a web tool for exploring circular RNAs and their interacting proteins and microRNAs. RNA Biol. **13**(1), 34–42 (2016)
29. Huang, Y., Niu, B., Gao, Y., Fu, L., Li, W.: CD-HIT Suite: a web server for clustering and comparing biological sequences. Bioinformatics **26**(5), 680–682 (2010)
30. Gruber, A.R., Lorenz, R., Bernhart, S.H., Neuboeck, R., Hofacker, I.L.: The vienna RNA websuite. Nucleic Acids Res. **36**, W70–W74 (2008)

BioMOE-CDG: Pretrained Biological Sequence Embedding-Guided MoE for Cancer Driver Gene Prediction

Yang Hu, Wei Dai(✉), Xinyue Xu, Wei Peng(✉), Xiaodong Fu, Li Liu, and Lijun Liu

Faculty of Information Engineering and Automation, Kunming University of Science and Technology, Kunming 650050, China
daiwei@kust.edu.cn, weipeng@kust.edu.cn

Abstract. Identifying cancer driver genes is a fundamental prerequisite for deciphering tumorigenesis mechanisms, discovering therapeutic targets, and advancing precision oncology. Existing identification methods predominantly focus on multi-omics phenotypes and biological network topology, yet they rarely exploit the deep functional semantics embedded within endogenous gene sequences. Furthermore, reliance on uniform, single-model frameworks often fails to account for cancer heterogeneity and gene-specific functional roles, leading to suboptimal predictive performance. In this paper, we propose BioMOE-CDG, a novel framework that integrates pre-trained biological model embeddings with a sparse mixture-of-experts (MoE) architecture for high-accuracy driver gene prediction. Our method first extracts gene sequence features from the pre-trained DNAGPT2 model, which are then compressed via a variational autoencoder (VAE) to obtain functional semantic embeddings. These embeddings are fused with multi-omics phenotypes and Protein-Protein Interaction (PPI) network attributes to construct comprehensive initial gene representations. The core innovation of BioMOE-CDG is its feature-guided sparse MoE architecture, which utilizes an expert pool of independently parameterized dual-view Chebyshev graph convolutional modules. Each module is constructed on dual-view graphs—the original PPI network and a diffusion-enhanced counterpart—to capture high-order biological associations through two Chebyshev graph convolutional networks. Guided by the sequence-informed initial features, a gating network dynamically assigns the most relevant expert to each gene for specialized feature learning. Extensive experiments across pan-cancer and 15 specific cancer types demonstrate that BioMOE-CDG significantly outperforms state-of-the-art methods. The code and data are available at: https://github.com/weiba/BioMOE-CDG.

Keywords: Cancer driver gene prediction · Large pretrained biological model · Mixture of expert · Gene representation · Cancer heterogeneity

X. Cui et al. (Eds.): ISBRA 2026, LNBI 16690, pp. 109–124, 2027.
https://doi.org/10.1007/978-981-92-3716-6_9

1 Introduction

Cancer is a complex genetic disease characterized by the progressive evolution of normal cells into a malignant state. Genes regulating cellular growth generally fall into two functional categories: oncogenes (growth-promoting) and tumor suppressors (growth-inhibiting). Among these, cancer driver genes [1,2] are defined by mutations that confer a selective fitness advantage to tumor cells, facilitating uncontrolled division and immune evasion. In contrast, passenger genes accumulate mutations that do not directly contribute to oncogenesis. Distinguishing drivers from passengers is essential for deciphering cancer mechanisms and developing precision therapies; however, identifying these critical genes amidst genomic "noise" remains a formidable challenge. The advent of high-throughput sequencing has catalyzed large-scale genomic initiatives such as TCGA [3], ICGC [4], and COSMIC [5], and the public availability of these vast datasets has significantly accelerated the development of sophisticated computational frameworks.

Currently, identification methods for cancer driver genes are primarily categorized into omics-based and network-based approaches. Omics-based methods rely on genomic sequences, structural variations, and transcriptomic profiles to distinguish driver genes from passenger genes by analyzing intrinsic molecular properties and abnormal mutation patterns without requiring interaction data. Among these, mutation frequency and pattern-based approaches are the most prevalent, utilizing criteria such as mutation rates or non-synonymous to synonymous ratios (dN/dS). For example, MutSigCV [6] and OncodriveCLUST [7] quantify the significance of genomic mutations for initial screening, while others focus on sequence architecture and functional elements, such as gene length, exon count, and conserved regions. Tools like PolyPhen-2 [8] and SIFT [9] predict the impact of amino acid substitutions on protein structure and function, whereas integrated models like IDriver [10] and Moonlight [11] combine mutations, expression changes, and DNA methylation to enhance predictive comprehensiveness.

Network-based methods transcend the limitations of individual gene features by leveraging biological networks, such as protein-protein interaction (PPI) and co-expression networks, to integrate connectivity patterns and interaction data with multi-omics features. Early iterations of these methods focused on topological attributes like degree and centrality, operating on the premise that driver genes occupy core regulatory positions, as seen in models like DriverNet [12], MUFFINN [13], and HotNet2 [14]. To reduce network noise, subsequent approaches like LNDriver [15], Subdyquency [16], and EntroRank [17] fused topological features with multi-omics data (e.g., mutations, differential expression, subcellular localization, and GO/Pathway annotations). Recently, the field has recently shifted toward deep learning, specifically utilizing Graph Convolutional Networks (GCN) to treat omics data as node features and biological networks as the underlying graph structure. Models such as EMOGI [18] apply GCN to single PPI networks, while MTGCN [19] employs Chebyshev graph convolution within a multi-task framework, and ECD-CDGI [20] utilizes energy-constrained diffusion mechanisms to extract gene features. More advanced multi-graph neural networks now construct multi-view environments by combining PPI, co-expression, and pathway graphs. Techniques like DGCL_DWA [21] use personalized PageRank to generate diffusion views, while MNGCL [22] and MODIG [23] utilize contrastive learning or attention modules (GAT) to fuse shared and specific feature patterns across multiple gene networks. This multi-view approach provides a holistic technical framework that learns robust gene representations for driver gene identification.

Despite the success achieved, existing methods still face two fundamental limitations. First, existing models often lack sufficient feature representation due to a deficit in sequence-level semantic information. While current approaches focus on genomic variation, transcriptomic profiles, and network topology, they frequently overlook the rich biological knowledge encoded within endogenous gene sequences. These sequences contain critical indicators of evolutionary conservation, functional motifs, and regulatory elements that dictate a gene's role in cellular pathways. By failing to incorporate these functional semantics, current methods may miss subtle but significant driver mutations that do not manifest through high mutation frequencies or large-scale expression shifts. Second, current graph neural network methods typically employ a uniform architecture with identical parameters to process all genes regardless of their functional roles or cancer types. This "one-size-fits-all" approach ignores both gene functional diversity and cancer heterogeneity, where the same gene may exhibit context-dependent oncogenic or tumor-suppressive functions across different cancer types. The main contributions of this work are summarized as follows:

1. Innovatively introduce gene sequence features pretrained by large biological models and form gene prediction features after VAE denoising, providing a new approach for using knowledge from large biological models to assist in cancer driver gene prediction.
2. Proposed a feature-guided MoE framework effectively captures both cancer-type-specific and gene-function-specific feature patterns, thereby significantly enhancing identification precision.
3. Comprehensive evaluations across pan-cancer and 15 specific cancer types demonstrate that BioMOE-CDG consistently outperforms state-of-the-art methods. Furthermore, ablation studies validate the framework's ability to effectively capture gene-function-specific features within diverse cancer contexts.

2 Method

The BioMOE-CDG framework (Fig. 1) follows a four-stage pipeline for cancer driver gene prediction. First, the model extracts deep functional semantic embeddings from gene sequences using the pre-trained DNAGPT2 model. Second, these sequence-based embeddings are integrated with multi-omics phenotypic data, including genomic variations, transcriptomic expression, and DNA methylation, alongside PPI network topological attributes to form a comprehensive initial representation. Third, a pre-training feature-guided sparse Mixture-of-Experts

(MoE) architecture is employed for adaptive gene representation learning; here, a gating network, informed by the initial sequence features, dynamically assigns each gene to the top-k most relevant experts; the expert pool consists of several independently parameterized, multi-view Chebyshev graph convolutional modules. Finally, the specialized features from the selected experts are weighted and fused within each network view, and these view-specific representations are processed through a final ChebConv layer and combined via a classifier to yield driver gene predictions.

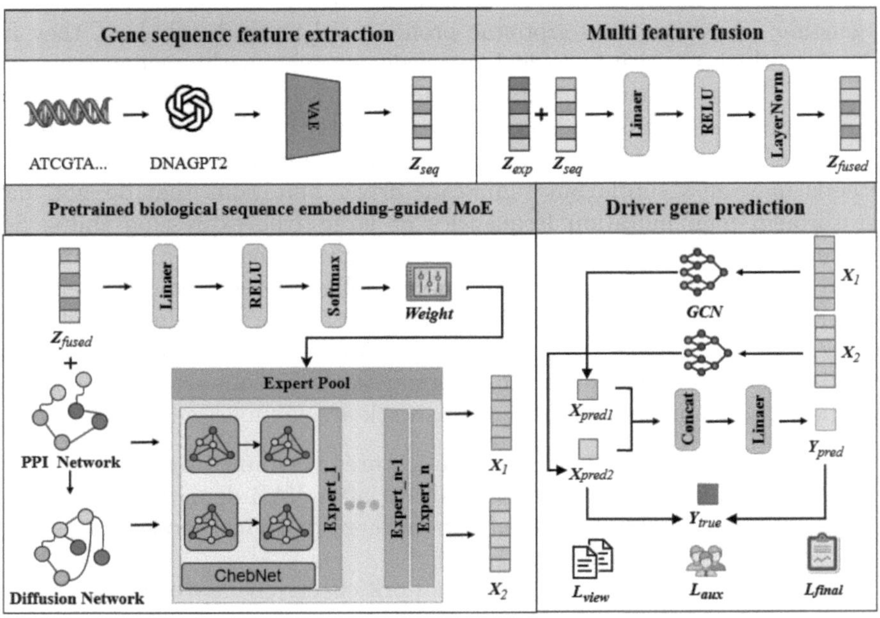

Fig. 1. Overall Framework of BioMOE-CDG.

2.1 Gene Sequence Feature Extraction

To capture the intrinsic biological characteristics of genes, we extract gene sequence embeddings using DNAGPT2 [24], a foundational model pretrained on large-scale genomic sequences. Gene sequences were retrieved from the Ensembl [27] database using the pyensembl Python package and uniformly truncate or pad it to a fixed length of $L = 3000$ nucleotides. The processed sequence of each gene is formally represented as: The processed sequence of each gene is formally represented as $\mathbf{s}_i = [s_i^{(1)}, s_i^{(2)}, \ldots, s_i^{(L)}] \in \mathcal{A}^L$, where $\mathcal{A} = \{\mathrm{A}, \mathrm{T}, \mathrm{C}, \mathrm{G}\}$. represents the four types of nucleotide bases (adenine A, thymine T, cytosine C, and guanine G), and $s_i^{(j)} \in \mathcal{A}$ indicates the base type at the jth position of the ith gene. The preprocessed sequence $\mathbf{s}_i$ is input into DNAGPT2 [24] to obtain the original sequence embedding:

$$\mathbf{h}_i = \text{DNAGPT2}(\mathbf{s}_i) \tag{1}$$

$$\mathbf{z}_{\text{seq}_i} = f_{\text{VAE}}(\mathbf{h}_i) \tag{2}$$

$$\mathbf{Z}_{\text{seq}} = \left(\mathbf{z}_{\text{seq}_1}, \cdots, \mathbf{z}_{\text{seq}_n}\right)^{\mathsf{T}} \in \mathbb{R}^{n\times 64} \tag{3}$$

where $\mathbf{h}_i$ is the 768-dimensional embedding of the i-th gene, $f_{\text{VAE}}(\cdot)$ represents the encoder network of the variational autoencoder [25], which compresses the high-dimensional input $\mathbf{s}_i$ into a low-dimensional latent representation $\mathbf{z}_{\text{seq}_i} \in \mathbb{R}^{64}$.

The VAE is trained by minimizing the reconstruction error and KL divergence:

$$\mathcal{L}_{\text{VAE}} = -\mathbb{E}_{q_\phi(\mathbf{z}_{\text{seq}_i}|\mathbf{h}_i)}\left[\log p_\theta(\mathbf{h}_i|\mathbf{z}_{\text{seq}_i})\right] + \text{KL}\left(q_\phi(\mathbf{z}_{\text{seq}_i}|\mathbf{h}_i) \parallel p(\mathbf{z}_{\text{seq}_i})\right) \tag{4}$$

2.2 Multifeature Fusion

Following established paradigms [18,19], cancer driver genes are characterized by distinct clinical alterations, including gene expression dysregulation, somatic mutations, and epigenetic methylation shifts, as well as their strategic topological positioning within biological networks. Consequently, we integrated multi-modal genomic features (Z_{omics}), encompassing differential expression levels, mutation frequencies, and methylation alteration rates derived from large-scale cohorts such as TCGA [18,19]. To complement these phenotypic data, we extracted network topological features ($Z_{topo} \in \mathbb{R}^{n\times 16}$) from the PPI network using the Node2Vec algorithm. These components were concatenated with the previously extracted gene sequence features and processed through a normalized linear layer to produce the comprehensive initial gene representations (Z_{fused}), defined as follows:

$$\mathbf{Z}_{\text{joint}} = [\mathbf{Z}_{\text{exp}} \parallel \mathbf{Z}_{\text{seq}}]$$

$$\mathbf{Z}_{\text{fused}} = \text{LayerNorm}\left(\text{ReLU}\left(\mathbf{Z}_{\text{joint}}\mathbf{W}_1 + \mathbf{b}_1\right)\right) \tag{5}$$

2.3 Pretrained Biological Sequence Embedding-Guided MoE

We developed a sparse Mixture-of-Experts (MoE) architecture, guided by pretrained biological sequence embeddings, to learn robust gene representations for driver gene prediction. The framework consists of two primary components: a gating network and an expert pool comprising independently parameterized dual-view Chebyshev graph convolutional modules.

1. Dual-view Chebyshev graph convolutional module To capture higher-order relationships between genes, we construct two complementary graph views. The first view is the original PPI network, which captures direct physical interactions between proteins. The second view is derived via Personalized

PageRank (PPR) graph diffusion to capture higher-order topological relationships and provides complementary information to the original PPI network.

Let the original PPI network be $G = (V, E, \mathbf{A}_{\text{ori}})$, where V is the set of n gene nodes, E is the set of interactions, and $\mathbf{A}_{\text{ori}} \in \{0,1\}^{n \times n}$ is the adjacency matrix. The PPR diffusion matrix is computed as:

$$\mathbf{\Pi}_{\text{PPR}} = \alpha \left(\mathbf{I} - (1-\alpha)\tilde{\mathbf{A}}_{\text{ori}} \right)^{-1} \tag{6}$$

where $\alpha = 0.9$ is the teleport probability, $\mathbf{I}$ is the identity matrix, and $\tilde{\mathbf{A}}_{\text{ori}} = \mathbf{D}^{-1/2}\mathbf{A}_{\text{ori}}\mathbf{D}^{-1/2}$ is the symmetrically normalized adjacency matrix with degree matrix $\mathbf{D}$.

To obtain a sparse graph structure suitable for graph neural networks, we apply top-m sparsification to the PPR diffusion matrix with $m = 30$, retaining only the m largest values per row. The resulting edge set and adjacency matrix for the second view are:

$$E_{\text{PPR}} = \{(i,j) \mid \mathbf{\Pi}^{(m)}_{\text{PPR}}[i,j] > 0,\ i \neq j\} \tag{7}$$

$$\mathbf{A}_{\text{PPR}}[i,j] = \begin{cases} 1, \text{ if } (i,j) \in E_{\text{PPR}} \\ 0, \text{ otherwise} \end{cases} \tag{8}$$

Following the PPR diffusion process, we obtain two distinct graph structures: $G_1 = (V, E, \mathbf{A}_{\text{ori}})$, $G_2 = (V, E_{\text{PPR}}, \mathbf{A}_{\text{PPR}})$. The second view G_2 captures higher-order and indirect gene interactions, complementing the direct interactions in G_1. Then we employ a dual-view graph neural network with parallel streams for feature extraction. To enhance model robustness, we apply feature and edge dropout to both views:

$$\mathbf{Z}_1 = \text{Dropout}(\mathbf{Z}_{\text{fused}}, p_{f1}), \quad \mathbf{A}_1 = \text{DropoutEdge}(\mathbf{A}_{\text{ori}}, p_{e1}) \tag{9}$$

$$\mathbf{Z}_2 = \text{Dropout}(\mathbf{Z}_{\text{fused}}, p_{f2}), \quad \mathbf{A}_2 = \text{DropoutEdge}(\mathbf{A}_{\text{PPR}}, p_{e2}) \tag{10}$$

where the feature dropout rates are set to $p_{f1} = 0.5$, $p_{f2} = 0.3$, and edge dropout rates are $p_{e1} = p_{e2} = 0.5$. Hence, we implement two Chebyshev graph convolutional on the graphs to get gene representations $\text{R}_1, R_2, p_{f1} = 0.5$. view $v \in \{1,2\}$ means original graph and diffusion graph.

$$\mathbf{R}_1 = \text{ReLU}\left(\text{ChebConv}_1(\mathbf{Z}_v, \mathbf{A}_v)\right) \tag{11}$$

$$\mathbf{R}_2 = \text{ReLU}\left(\text{ChebConv}_2\left(\mathbf{R}_1, \mathbf{A}_v\right)\right) \tag{12}$$

2. Gating network The gating network serves as the decision center in the MOE, dynamically selecting the most appropriate expert based on input gene features. It computes the weight distribution across the expert pool as follows:

$$\mathbf{g}_i = \text{Gate}(\mathbf{z}_{\text{fused}_i}) = \text{Softmax}\left(\frac{\text{ReLU}(\mathbf{W}_g \mathbf{z}_{\text{fused}_i} + \mathbf{b}_g)}{\tau} \right) \tag{13}$$

where $\mathbf{W}_g$ is a learnable weight matrix, $\mathbf{b}_g$ is a bias term, $\tau = 1.0$ is a temperature parameter controlling the smoothness of the weight distribution, and the Softmax function ensures $\sum_{j=1}^{N} g_i^{(j)} = 1$ with $g_i^{(j)} > 0$, denotes the weight assigned to the j-th expert for gene i.

Let $\mathbf{E} = \{\text{Expert}_1, \text{Expert}_2, \ldots, \text{Expert}_N\}$ be the expert pool with N experts, where each expert is a two-layer dual-view Chebyshev graph convolutional module that captures two gene representations from both views independently. Let $\text{Expert}_j(\mathbf{Z}_v, \mathbf{A}_v)$ denote the output gene representation for view $v \in \{1, 2\}$ calculated by Eq. 11, 12.

To reduce computational complexity and improve model efficiency, we employ a top-k expert selection strategy, activating only the most relevant k experts for each gene:

$$\mathbf{E}_{\text{selected}}^{(i)} = \text{TopK}(\mathbf{g}_i, k) \tag{14}$$

After identifying the top-k experts with the highest gating weights, we renormalizing these weights to sum to one. The final representation for each gene in each view is obtained by weighted summation of the selected expert outputs:

$$\mathbf{X}_v = \sum_{j \in \mathbf{O}_{\text{selected}}^{(i)}} \frac{g_i^{(j)}}{\sum_{m \in \mathbf{O}_{\text{selected}}^{(i)}} g_i^{(m)}} \cdot \text{Expert}_j(\mathbf{Z}_v, \mathbf{A}_v) \tag{15}$$

where $\mathbf{E}_{\text{selected}}^{(i)}$ denotes the set of top-k experts selected for gene i, $\mathbf{X}_v \in \mathbb{R}^{n \times 50}$ is the fused feature vector in view v. This process is applied independently to both views, yielding two representation matrices $\mathbf{X}_1$ (from the PPI view) and $\mathbf{X}_2$ (from the diffusion view) that capture complementary aspects of gene interactions.

2.4 Driver Gene Prediction

Using the node representations $\mathbf{X}_1$ and $\mathbf{X}_2$, each view independently generates predictions via a Chebyshev convolutional(ChebConv) layer:

$$\mathbf{X}_{\text{pred1}} = \sigma\left(\text{ChebConv}_{\text{pred}}^{(1)}(\mathbf{X}_1, \mathbf{A}_1)\right) \tag{16}$$

$$\mathbf{X}_{\text{pred2}} = \sigma\left(\text{ChebConv}_{\text{pred}}^{(2)}(\mathbf{X}_2, \mathbf{A}_2)\right) \tag{17}$$

Here, each ChebConv layer maps the 50-dimensional node representations to a 1-dimensional prediction, followed by a sigmoid activation function (σ) to constrain the values. To integrate complementary information captured by both views, we concatenate the prediction vectors:

$$\mathbf{X}_{\text{pred}} = [\mathbf{X}_{\text{pred1}} \| \mathbf{X}_{\text{pred2}}]$$

The final prediction is obtained via a learnable linear layer:

$$\mathbf{Y}_{\text{pred}} = \sigma(\mathbf{X}_{\text{pred}} \mathbf{W}_{\text{pred}} + \mathbf{b}_{\text{pred}}) \tag{18}$$

2.5 Model Optimization

The overall training objective combines supervised loss and load balancing loss. Given the training set mask $\mathcal{T}$, the supervised loss consists of a final prediction loss and two view-specific auxiliary losses:

$$\mathcal{L}_{\text{final}} = -\frac{1}{|\mathcal{T}|}\sum_{i\in\mathcal{T}} [y_i \log(\sigma(\mathbf{y}_{\text{pred}}[i])) + (1-y_i)\log(1-\sigma(\mathbf{y}_{\text{pred}}[i]))] \quad (19)$$

For each view $v \in \{1, 2\}$, the view-specific supervised loss is defined similarly to ensure robust representation learning within each network perspective:

$$\mathcal{L}_{\text{view}_v} = -\frac{1}{|\mathcal{T}|}\sum_{i\in\mathcal{T}} [y_i \log(\sigma(\mathbf{x}_{\text{pred}_v}[i])) + (1-y_i)\log(1-\sigma(\mathbf{x}_{\text{pred}_v}[i]))] \quad (20)$$

To encourage balanced expert utilization across the MoE architecture, we introduce a load balancing loss:

$$\mathcal{L}_{\text{aux}} = \sum_{j=1}^{N} f_j \cdot P_j, \quad f_j = \frac{1}{|\mathcal{B}|}\sum_{i\in\mathcal{B}} [j \in \mathbf{E}^{(i)}_{\text{selected}}], \quad P_j = \frac{1}{|\mathcal{B}|}\sum_{i\in\mathcal{B}} g_i^{(j)} \quad (21)$$

where N is the number of experts, $\mathcal{B}$ is the training batch, $\mathbf{O}^{(i)}_{\text{selected}}$ is the set of top-k experts selected for gene i, and $g_i^{(j)}$ is the corresponding gating weight. The overall training objective is a weighted combination:

$$\mathcal{L}_{\text{total}} = \mathcal{L}_{\text{final}} + 0.3 \cdot \frac{\mathcal{L}_{\text{view1}} + \mathcal{L}_{\text{view2}}}{2} + 0.01 \cdot \mathcal{L}_{\text{aux}} \quad (22)$$

This composite loss enables BioMOE-CDG to learn accurate predictions from the fused representation while maintaining view-specific prediction capability and balanced expert utilization.

3 Results

3.1 Datasets and Materials

This study utilized two PPI networks from the Consensus Pathway Database (CPDB) [31] and STRING Database [32]. The CPDB network comprises 13,627 genes and 504,378 edges, the STRING network comprises 13,179 genes and 673,099 edges after filtering interactions with a score below 0.5.

We analyzed multi-omics data for 16 cancer types from The Cancer Genome Atlas (TCGA), including BRCA, LUAD, BLCA, LIHC, CESC, COAD, ESCA, HNSC, KIRC, KIRP, LUSC, PRAD, STAD, THCA, UCEC, and READ. These datasets contain more than 8,000 samples. We retained only samples with gene expression and DNA methylation data available in both tumor and normal tissues.

Validated cancer driver genes were retrieved from NCG 6.0 [33], and negative samples were obtained by removing NCG, OMIM [34], COSMIC [5], and KEGG [35] genes from the gene network. This yielded 2,187 negative samples. As READ lacked qualifying positive samples, data from 15 cancer types were retained. For pan-cancer gene prediction, the final dataset in CPDB network comprises 796 positive and 2,187 negative samples, in STRING network comprises 792 positive and 2,055 negative samples, 15 cancer types share all the 2187 negative samples. There are 201, 179, 95, 82, 16, 141, 71, 143, 43, 22, 26, 50, 73, 64, 68 cancer genes for BRCA, LUAD, BLCA, LIHC, CESC, COAD, ESCA, HNSC, KIRC, KIRP, LUSC, PRAD, STAD, THCA, UCEC, respectively.

3.2 Experimental Setup

To comprehensively evaluate BioMOE-CDG, we benchmarked its performance against two foundational Graph Neural Network (GNN) architectures and six state-of-the-art cancer driver gene identification frameworks. The GNN baselines, Chebyshev Graph Convolutional Networks (ChebNet), were implemented using initial gene omics features on the PPI network to quantify the relative gains provided by our specialized architectural components. Among the state-of-the-art frameworks, we included EMOGI [18] and MTGCN [19], which integrates multi-omics data with PPI networks via GCN or ChebNet. DGCL_DWA [21] and MNGCL [22], which employs a multi-view contrastive learning strategy to fuse PPI network with diffustion PPI network or GO similarity network, and ECD-CDGI [20], which introduces an energy-constrained diffusion mechanism. Finally, we included the most recent advancements in the field: DISHyper [36] and DISFusion [37], both of which leverage multi-omics data and functional annotations. To ensure a rigorous and fair comparison, all baseline models were implemented using the optimal hyperparameters recommended in their original publications, ensuring each method performed at its full reported capacity.

Our model was implemented in Python 3.8 using PyTorch 2.4.0 and PyTorch Geometric 2.6.1. The Adam optimizer was employed for training. Hyperparameter optimization was performed using grid search on the CPDB, STRING and 15 cancer types dataset, learning rate set to 0.001, EPOCH set to 300, total experts number set to 6, activated experts number set to 3. To ensure robustness and prevent overfitting, five-fold cross-validation with ten repetitions was conducted on the training set for each hyperparameter combination.

The method adopts a transductive setting. For specific cancers, positive and negative samples are independently divided. Positive and negative samples are randomly shuffled and divided into 5 parts, taking turns as the test set to ensure the proportion of positive and negative samples remains consistent and in line with the actual situation (there are far more nondriver genes than driver genes). Each fold's positive and negative samples are independently divided. There will be no cross-over between positive and negative samples in each fold. The partitioning of the pan cancer training validation set depends on pre-defined k_sets.

3.3 Performance on Pan-Cancer Driver Gene Prediction

We compared BioMOE-CDG against several baseline methods for pan-cancer driver gene prediction using both the CPDB and STRING datasets. As shown in Table 1, BioMOE-CDG achieves an AUC of 0.943 and an AUPRC of 0.926 on the CPDB dataset, outperforming the second-best method, DISFusion, by 2.1% and 9.7%, respectively. Similarly, on the STRING dataset, our framework achieves an AUC of 0.930 and an AUPRC of 0.838. We particularly note the substantial improvement in AUPRC, a metric that is highly sensitive to the class imbalance present in our data (796 positive vs. 2,187 negative samples). This elevation in AUPRC indicates that our method is exceptionally effective at identifying true driver genes while maintaining a low false-positive rate.

Such superior performance demonstrates that the integration of DNAGPT2-derived sequence embeddings provides critical, complementary biological information beyond traditional expression and network features. Furthermore, the MoE architecture allows the model to capture functionally specific gene features that are highly predictive of oncogenic potential.

Table 1. Performance in Pan-Cancer Driver Gene Prediction

Method	CPDB		STRING	
	AUC	AUPRC	AUC	AUPRC
GCN	$0.901_{\pm 0.0003}$	$0.814_{\pm 0.0007}$	$0.909_{\pm 0.0002}$	$0.804_{\pm 0.0007}$
GAT	$0.814_{\pm 0.0004}$	$0.580_{\pm 0.0020}$	$0.844_{\pm 0.0003}$	$0.588_{\pm 0.0019}$
ChebNet	$0.902_{\pm 0.0003}$	$0.815_{\pm 0.0007}$	$0.908_{\pm 0.0001}$	$0.807_{\pm 0.0005}$
EMOGI	$0.899_{\pm 0.0002}$	$0.815_{\pm 0.0006}$	$0.905_{\pm 0.0001}$	$0.801_{\pm 0.0002}$
ECD-CDGI	$0.896_{\pm 0.0002}$	$0.808_{\pm 0.0006}$	$0.892_{\pm 0.0002}$	$0.762_{\pm 0.0008}$
MTGCN	$0.910_{\pm 0.0002}$	$0.833_{\pm 0.0006}$	$0.917_{\pm 0.0002}$	$0.819_{\pm 0.0002}$
MNGCL	$0.918_{\pm 0.0004}$	$0.840_{\pm 0.0005}$	$0.919_{\pm 0.0000}$	$0.816_{\pm 0.0002}$
DISHyper	$0.889_{\pm 0.0002}$	$0.802_{\pm 0.0008}$	$0.893_{\pm 0.0002}$	$0.781_{\pm 0.0005}$
DISFusion	$0.924_{\pm 0.0002}$	$0.844_{\pm 0.0005}$	$0.926_{\pm 0.0001}$	$0.830_{\pm 0.0004}$
DGCL_DWA	$0.914_{\pm 0.0009}$	$0.837_{\pm 0.0022}$	$0.918_{\pm 0.0014}$	$0.823_{\pm 0.0022}$
BioMOE-CDG	$\mathbf{0.943_{\pm 0.0003}}$	$\mathbf{0.926_{\pm 0.0036}}$	$\mathbf{0.930_{\pm 0.0031}}$	$\mathbf{0.838_{\pm 0.0250}}$

3.4 Performance on Cancer-Sepcific Driver Gene Prediction

We also applied BioMOE-CDG and baselines to predict cancer driver genes for 15 cancer types. For each cancer type, the initial gene representations consist of a 19-dimensional feature vector: three cancer-specific biological attributes (mutation rate, differential DNA methylation, and differential gene expression) and 16-dimensional structural features derived from the gene network. Tables 2 and 3 summarize the performance across 15 specific cancer types. In terms of AUC,

BioMOE-CDG achieves the highest performance in 11 out of 15 cancer types, with particularly notable gains in ESCA (0.947 vs. MTGCN's 0.911), COAD (0.900 vs. MNGCL's 0.834), and HNSC (0.923 vs. MTGCN's 0.852).

Regarding AUPRC, our framework outperforms all baseline methods across every cancer type, demonstrating its exceptional robustness to class imbalance across diverse oncological contexts. BioMOE-CDG achieves significant AUPRC improvements in challenging datasets—such as CESC (0.740 vs. MTGCN's 0.527), COAD (0.693 vs. MTGCN's 0.417), and PRAD (0.740 vs. MTGCN's 0.649). Furthermore, in well-characterized cohorts like BRCA and LUAD, BioMOE-CDG surpasses the second-best method (MTGCN) by 12.6% (0.800 vs. 0.674) and 18.0% (0.815 vs. 0.635) in AUPRC, respectively. These results indicate that the synergy between sequence semantics, multi-view graph structures, and adaptive expert selection strategies significantly enhances the model's ability to learn discriminative gene features for the prediction task.

3.5 Ablation Study

We conducted systematic ablation experiments to validate the contribution of three core components to the BioMOE-CDG framework: (1) DNAGPT-derived sequence embeddings, (2) the Mixture-of-Experts (MoE) architecture, and (3) the load-balancing loss. We compared the following four variants:

- **w/o DNAGPT**: Removes sequence embeddings, utilizing only gene expression and network features.
- **w/o Balance Loss**: Trains the MoE network without load-balancing constraints, relying solely on supervised loss.
- **w/o MoE**: Replaces the MoE architecture with a dual-view Chebyshev GCN encoder of equivalent hidden dimensions.
- **Full-Model**: An expanded framework with 6 experts (activating 3 per view) to test capacity limits.

Table 4 summarize the ablation study results in pan-cancer settings. Removing the DNAGPT embeddings (w/o DNAGPT) causes the most substantial performance degradation, with AUC dropping by 30.4% on STRING and AUPRC dropping by 11.2% on CPDB and 74.3% on STRING, demonstrating that sequence-level semantics provide critical biological insights complementary to conventional data. Removing the MoE module (w/o MoE) also leads to notable declines, with AUC decreasing by 5% on STRING and AUPRC decreasing by 5.38% on CPDB, confirming the importance of the Mixture-of-Experts architecture. The complete Full-Model achieves the best performance, with AUC of 0.943 (CPDB) and 0.930 (STRING), and AUPRC of 0.926 (CPDB) and 0.838 (STRING).

Table 2. Performance comparison of different methods across 15 cancer types (AUC)

Cancer	ChebNet	MTGCN	MNGCL	EMOGI	ECD-CDGI	DISHyper	DISFusion	DGCL_DWA	BioMOE-CDG
BLCA	0,946±0,000	0,950±0,001	0,948±0,000	0,906±0,002	0,935±0,001	0,898±0,002	0,937±0,002	0,950±0,000	0,947±0,004
BRCA	0,903±0,002	0,910±0,001	0,916±0,001	0,895±0,001	0,897±0,002	0,114±0,001	0,913±0,001	0,917±0,001	0,945±0,004
CESC	0,953±0,002	0,975±0,001	0,712±0,003	0,960±0,004	0,971±0,003	0,941±0,002	0,943±0,009	0,935±0,004	0,869±0,001
COAD	0,820±0,001	0,831±0,002	0,834±0,001	0,782±0,003	0,796±0,003	0,801±0,002	0,807±0,004	0,835±0,001	0, 900 ± 0, 013
ESCA	0,886±0,002	0,911±0,001	0,875±0,004	0,835±0,005	0,884±0,002	0,887±0,002	0,859±0,003	0,890±0,005	0, 947 ± 0, 004
HNSC	0,821±0,002	0,852±0,001	0,826±0,002	0,776±0,003	0,805±0,002	0,822±0,002	0,826±0,002	0,855±0,004	0, 923 ± 0, 004
KIRC	0,876±0,003	0,899±0,005	0,835±0,007	0,873±0,005	0,874±0,007	0,843±0,007	0,894±0,005	0,910±0,003	0, 925 ± 0, 019
KIRP	0,879±0,008	0, 963 ± 0, 004	0,875±0,018	0,885±0,012	0,937±0,002	0,870±0,006	0,918±0,005	0,962±0,010	0,913±0,009
LIHC	0,870±0,002	0,906±0,001	0,904±0,001	0,831±0,005	0,872±0,003	0,841±0,004	0,885±0,003	0,900±0,000	0, 948 ± 0, 005
LUAD	0,921±0,001	0,907±0,001	0,906±0,000	0,823±0,003	0,878±0,001	0,832±0,002	0,865±0,002	0,896±0,001	0, 952 ± 0, 006
LUSC	0,830±0,023	0,894±0,010	0,860±0,014	0,769±0,030	0,864±0,014	0,868±0,009	0, 924 ± 0, 002	0,914±0,007	0,885±0,043
PRAD	0,859±0,015	0,918±0,004	0,965±0,002	0,904±0,006	0,900±0,007	0,892±0,006	0,902±0,004	0,935±0,004	0,954±0,002
STAD	0,877±0,006	0,931±0,001	0,882±0,006	0,826±0,005	0,900±0,003	0,878±0,003	0,884±0,004	0,907±0,004	0, 948 ± 0, 009
THCA	0,761±0,004	0,827±0,004	0,844±0,003	0,745±0,007	0,804±0,004	0,852±0,003	0,822±0,004	0,844±0,002	0, 933 ± 0, 012
UCEC	0,845±0,003	0,902±0,003	0,903±0,002	0,855±0,004	0,883±0,003	0,849±0,003	0,881±0,002	0,902±0,001	0, 943 ± 0, 027

Table 3. Performance comparison of different methods across 15 cancer types (AUPRC)

Cancer	ChebNet	MTGCN	MNGCL	EMOGI	ECD-CDGI	DISHyper	DISFusion	DGCL_DWA	BioMOE-CDG
BLCA	0.648±0.010	0.661±0.007	0.613±0.011	0.528±0.026	0.569±0.026	0.429±0.012	0.586±0.018	0.680±0.006	0.790±0.062
BRCA	0.649±0.010	0.674±0.005	0.712±0.003	0.616±0.019	0.628±0.022	0.047±0.000	0.693±0.007	0.680±0.011	0.800±0.035
CESC	0.390±0.079	0.527±0.060	0.443±0.102	0.429±0.088	0.430±0.087	0.367±0.079	0.501±0.091	0.622±0.033	0.740±0.064
COAD	0.367±0.003	0.417±0.008	0.407±0.003	0.342±0.012	0.350±0.016	0.337±0.008	0.361±0.011	0.416±0.005	0.693±0.103
ESCA	0.436±0.006	0.503±0.013	0.372±0.022	0.360±0.023	0.426±0.026	0.365±0.016	0.404±0.023	0.510±0.016	0.747±0.060
HNSC	0.419±0.013	0.463±0.005	0.441±0.010	0.355±0.016	0.386±0.016	0.425±0.009	0.453±0.010	0.453±0.010	0.684±0.065
KIRC	0.307±0.018	0.382±0.023	0.307±0.034	0.288±0.026	0.311±0.028	0.283±0.029	0.313±0.022	0.351±0.012	0.730±0.096
KIRP	0.318±0.060	0.464±0.055	0.211±0.048	0.166±0.033	0.313±0.062	0.143±0.024	0.183±0.030	0.274±0.038	0.457±0.125
LIHC	0.401±0.010	0.495±0.013	0.473±0.011	0.356±0.023	0.435±0.023	0.350±0.017	0.481±0.016	0.491±0.008	0.751±0.055
LUAD	0.658±0.005	0.635±0.004	0.575±0.004	0.471±0.019	0.546±0.015	0.479±0.007	0.559±0.009	0.654±0.003	0.815±0.050
LUSC	0.301±0.048	0.312±0.034	0.215±0.049	0.176±0.035	0.240±0.049	0.183±0.043	0.292±0.046	0.347±0.046	0.589±0.122
PRAD	0.583±0.038	0.623±0.025	0.649±0.025	0.531±0.036	0.532±0.042	0.454±0.035	0.508±0.022	0.621±0.021	0.740±0.084
STAD	0.542±0.025	0.603±0.014	0.500±0.038	0.377±0.030	0.486±0.031	0.437±0.033	0.463±0.020	0.575±0.031	0.797±0.051
THCA	0.208±0.006	0.285±0.014	0.299±0.015	0.226±0.015	0.268±0.019	0.311±0.018	0.288±0.023	0.291±0.005	0.712±0.097
UCEC	0.382±0.008	0.480±0.019	0.415±0.006	0.345±0.026	0.393±0.029	0.300±0.020	0.409±0.021	0.517±0.035	0.740±0.124

Table 4. Ablation study results of Pan-Cancer Driver Gene Prediction

Configuration	CPDB		STRING	
	AUC	AUPRC	AUC	AUPRC
w/o DNAGPT	$0.8989_{\pm 0.0002}$	$0.8148_{\pm 0.0006}$	$0.6260_{\pm 0.0020}$	$0.0995_{\pm 0.0006}$
w/o Balance Loss	$0.9354_{\pm 0.0016}$	$0.8970_{\pm 0.0077}$	$0.9079_{\pm 0.0163}$	$0.7741_{\pm 0.1030}$
w/o MoE	$0.9360_{\pm 0.0015}$	$0.8722_{\pm 0.0089}$	$0.8798_{\pm 0.0158}$	$0.8001_{\pm 0.0858}$
Full-Model	$\mathbf{0.943}_{\pm \mathbf{0.0003}}$	$\mathbf{0.926}_{\pm \mathbf{0.0036}}$	$\mathbf{0.930}_{\pm \mathbf{0.0031}}$	$\mathbf{0.838}_{\pm \mathbf{0.0250}}$

4 Conclusion

In this study, we introduced BioMOE-CDG, a novel method for cancer driver gene prediction based on a sparse mixture-of-experts framework. By incorporating the pretrained biological sequence knowledge, we designed a gating network that dynamically adapts expert selection to diverse cancer characteristics. Experimental results demonstrate the effectiveness of our approach compared to baseline methods. This work provides a valuable framework for cancer driver gene identification and drug development. Future directions include integrating single-cell and clinical data to enable personalized treatment strategies.

Acknowledgments. This work is supported in part by the National Natural Science Foundation of China (No. 62472202, No. U25A20449, No. 62472108, No. U24A20256) and Nature Science Foundation of Yunnan Provice 202601AS070066.

References

1. Garraway, L.A., Lander, E.S.: Lessons from the cancer genome. Cell **153**(1), 17–37 (2013)
2. Lawrence, M.S., Stojanov, P., Mermel, C.H., et al.: Discovery and saturation analysis of cancer genes across 21 tumour types. Nature **505**(7484), 495–501 (2014)
3. Weinstein, J.N., Collisson, E.A., Mills, G.B., et al.: The cancer genome atlas pan-cancer analysis project. Nat. Genet. **45**(10), 1113–1120 (2013)
4. Zhang, J., Bajari, R., Andric, D., et al.: The international cancer genome consortium data portal. Nat. Biotechnol. **37**(4), 367–369 (2019)
5. Tate, J.G., Bamford, S., Jubb, H.C., et al.: COSMIC: the catalogue of somatic mutations in cancer. Nucleic Acids Res. **47**(D1), D941–D947 (2019)
6. Lawrence, M.S., Stojanov, P., Polak, P., et al.: Mutational heterogeneity in cancer and the search for new cancer-associated genes. Nature **499**(7457), 214–218 (2013)
7. Tamborero, D., Gonzalez-Perez, A., Lopez-Bigas, N.: OncodriveCLUST: exploiting the positional clustering of somatic mutations to identify cancer genes. Bioinformatics **29**(18), 2238–2244 (2013)
8. Adzhubei, I.A., Schmidt, S., Peshkin, L., et al.: A method and server for predicting damaging missense mutations. Nat. Methods **7**(4), 248–249 (2010)
9. Ng, P.C., Henikoff, S.: SIFT: predicting amino acid changes that affect protein function. Nucleic Acids Res. **31**(13), 3812–3814 (2003)

10. Yang, H., Wei, Q., Zhong, X., et al.: Cancer driver gene discovery through an integrative genomics approach in a non-parametric Bayesian framework. Bioinformatics **33**(4), 483–490 (2017)
11. Colaprico, A., Olsen, C., Bailey, M.H., et al.: Interpreting pathways to discover cancer driver genes with moonlight. Nat. Commun. **11**(1), 69 (2020)
12. Bashashati, A., Haffari, G., Ding, J., et al.: DriverNet: uncovering the impact of somatic driver mutations on transcriptional networks in cancer. Genome Biol. **13**(12), R124 (2012)
13. Cho, A., Shim, J.E., Kim, E., et al.: MUFFINN: cancer gene discovery via network analysis of somatic mutation data. Genome Biol. **17**(1), 129 (2016)
14. Leiserson, M.D.M., Vandin, F., Wu, H.T., et al.: Pan-cancer network analysis identifies combinations of rare somatic mutations across pathways and protein complexes. Nat. Genet. **47**(2), 106–114 (2015)
15. Wei, P.J., Zhang, D., Xia, J., et al.: LNDriver: identifying driver genes by integrating mutation and expression data based on gene-gene interaction network. BMC Bioinform. **17**(Suppl. 17), 467 (2016)
16. Song, J., Peng, W., Wang, F.: A random walk-based method to identify driver genes by integrating the subcellular localization and variation frequency into bipartite graph. BMC Bioinform. **20**(1), 238 (2019)
17. Song, J., Peng, W., Wang, F.: An entropy-based method for identifying mutual exclusive driver genes in cancer. IEEE/ACM Trans. Comput. Biol. Bioinf. **17**(3), 758–768 (2019)
18. Schulte-Sasse, R., Budach, S., Hnisz, D., et al.: Integration of multiomics data with graph convolutional networks to identify new cancer genes and their associated molecular mechanisms. Nat. Mach. Intell. **3**(6), 513–526 (2021)
19. Peng, W., Tang, Q., Dai, W., et al.: Improving cancer driver gene identification using multi-task learning on graph convolutional network. Briefings Bioinform. **23**(1), bbab432 (2022)
20. Wang, T., Zhuo, L., Chen, Y., et al.: ECD-CDGI: an efficient energy-constrained diffusion model for cancer driver gene identification. PLoS Comput. Biol. **20**(8), e1012400 (2024)
21. Peng, W., Xu, X.P., Dai, W., et al.: Predicting cancer driver genes via contrastive graph diffusion and dynamic weighting. J. Comput. Sci. Technol. **40**(6), 1650–1661 (2025)
22. Peng, W., Zhou, Z., Dai, W., et al.: Multi-network graph contrastive learning for cancer driver gene identification. IEEE Trans. Netw. Sci. Eng. **11**(4), 3430–3440 (2024)
23. Zhao, W., Gu, X., Chen, S., et al.: MODIG: integrating multi-omics and multi-dimensional gene network for cancer driver gene identification based on graph attention network model. Bioinformatics **38**(21), 4901–4907 (2022)
24. Zhang, D., Zhang, W., Zhao, Y., et al.: DNAGPT: a generalized pre-trained tool for versatile DNA sequence analysis tasks. arXiv preprint arXiv:2307.05628 (2023)
25. Kingma, D.P., Welling, M.: Auto-encoding variational bayes. arXiv preprint arXiv:1312.6114 (2013)
26. Shazeer, N., Mirhoseini, A., Maziarz, K., et al.: Outrageously large neural networks: the sparsely-gated mixture-of-experts layer. arXiv preprint arXiv:1701.06538 (2017)
27. Yates, A.D., Austine-Orimoloye, O., Azov, A.G., et al.: Ensembl 2026. Nucleic Acids Res. **54**(D1), D1053–D1060 (2026)

28. Wang, X., Yang, C.: MoE-health: a mixture of experts framework for robust multimodal healthcare prediction. In: Proceedings of the 16th ACM International Conference on Bioinformatics, Computational Biology, and Health Informatics, pp. 1–9 (2025)
29. Li, Y., Jiang, S., Hu, B., et al.: Uni-MoE: scaling unified multimodal LLMs with mixture of experts. IEEE Trans. Pattern Anal. Mach. Intell. (2025)
30. Du, Z., An, J., Tu, Y., et al.: Mixture-of-experts for open set domain adaptation: a dual-space detection approach. IEEE Trans. Artif. Intell. (2025)
31. Kamburov, A., Pentchev, K., Galicka, H., et al.: ConsensusPathDB: toward a more complete picture of cell biology. Nucleic Acids Res. **39**(Suppl_1), D712–D717 (2011)
32. Szklarczyk, D., Gable, A.L., Lyon, D., et al.: STRING v11: protein–protein association networks with increased coverage, supporting functional discovery in genome-wide experimental datasets. Nucleic Acids Res. **47**(D1), D607–D613 (2019)
33. Repana, D., Nulsen, J., Dressler, L., et al.: The Network of Cancer Genes (NCG): a comprehensive catalogue of known and candidate cancer genes from cancer sequencing screens. Genome Biol. **20**(1), 1 (2019)
34. Hamosh, A., Scott, A.F., Amberger, J.S., et al.: Online mendelian inheritance in man (OMIM), a knowledgebase of human genes and genetic disorders. Nucleic Acids Res. **33**(Suppl_1), D514–D517 (2005)
35. Kanehisa, M., Goto, S.: KEGG: kyoto encyclopedia of genes and genomes. Nucleic Acids Res. **28**(1), 27–30 (2000)
36. Deng, C., Li, H.D., Zhang, L.S., et al.: Identifying new cancer genes based on the integration of annotated gene sets via hypergraph neural networks. Bioinformatics **40**(Suppl._1), i511–i520 (2024)
37. Deng, C., Li, H., Wang, J.: Improving cancer gene prediction by enhancing common information between the PPI network and gene functional association. In: Proceedings of the AAAI Conference on Artificial Intelligence, vol. 39, pp. 137–145 (2025)

DIMIR: Deep Incomplete Multi-view Information Recovery for Breast Cancer Subtype Classification

Wei Lan[1], Yinghao Liu[1], Xuhua Yan[1(✉)], Cong Peng[1], Qingfeng Chen[1], Liangliang Liu[2], Min Li[3], and Yi Pan[4]

[1] School of Computer, Electronic and Information, Guangxi University, Guangxi 530004, China
{lanwei,qingfeng}@gxu.edu.cn, liuyinghao@st.gxu.edu.cn, 3200376951@qq.com

[2] College of Information and Management Science, Henan Agricultural University, Henan 450046, China
liangliu@henau.edu.cn

[3] School of Computer Science and Engineering, Central South University, Hunan 410083, China
limin@mail.csu.edu.cn

[4] Faculty of Computer Science and Control Engineering, Shenzhen University of Advanced Technology, Guangdong 518055, China
panyi@suat-sz.edu.cn

Abstract. Breast cancer is a major global health threat to women. Its molecular heterogeneity leads to distinct subtypes with different treatments. Traditional diagnostic methods using either single-omics data or whole-slide imaging (WSI) cannot fully capture tumor complexity. Although multimodal models have emerged, most rely on simple feature concatenation, ignoring differences between omics and imaging data. Moreover, missing values in omics data further limit clinical applicability. In this work, we introduce a Deep Incomplete Multi-view Information Recovery framework (DIMIR) for breast cancer subtype classification. DIMIR utilizes cross-attention and latent self-attention mechanisms to model relationships between multi-omics views and reconstruct missing omics views with a context-aware way. Then, it reconstructs missing omics views by learning high-level semantic representations across multiple views. Further, the reconstructed multi-omics views are used to train a subtype classification network that fully exploits multimodal discriminative information. Experiments on the Cancer Genome Atlas (TCGA) breast cancer demonstrate that DIMIR significantly outperforms state-of-the-art methods in cancer subtypes prediction and identifies biomarkers closely associated with cancer subtypes.

Keywords: Breast subtype classification · Multi-omics data · Whole-slide images · Multimodal fusion · Biomarker discovery

X. Cui et al. (Eds.): ISBRA 2026, LNBI 16690, pp. 125–136, 2027.
https://doi.org/10.1007/978-981-92-3716-6_10

1 Introduction

Breast cancer is one of the most prevalent malignant tumors among females globally, posing a significant threat to public health. Its molecular heterogeneity leads to substantial differences in biological characteristics, clinical manifestations, and treatment responses across various subtypes. Consequently, precise subtype classification is critical for personalized treatment strategies and prognostication.

Whole-slide images (WSIs) offer rich structural and morphological information for breast cancer subtype identification. Recent research has focused on developing computational models to exploit this information. Wang et al. [1] proposed a Connectivity-aware Graph Transformer (CGT) framework that constructs tissue graphs to represent intercellular topological connectivity and integrates local connectivity aggregation with spatial distance-aware self-attention. Liu et al. [2] developed a weakly supervised learning framework to predict molecular subtypes from H&E-stained WSIs by combining discriminative image block selection with multi-instance learning. In addition, Wang et al. [3] designed a two-stage hybrid networkâĂŞbased multi-classification model for breast cancer pathological images based on ResNet34 and transfer learning. Multi-omics data provide complementary molecular information and have shown strong potential for elucidating tumor mechanisms [4]. Therefore, a number of multi-omics integration methods have been developed. Lan et al. [5] proposed DeepKEGG, an interpretable multi-omics fusion model for cancer prediction and biomarker discovery. Huang et al. [6] developed the DSCCN model, which integrates multiple omics for breast cancer subtyping and employs sparse canonical correlation analysis to extract correlated features across different omics layers. Subsequently, Lan et al. [7] introduced MULGONET, an end-to-end deep learning framework that alleviates the problems of high dimensionality and limited interpretability commonly encountered in multi-omics analysis. scMoMtF [8] has been developed for single-cell multi-omics fusion. With advances in omics analysis technologies, growing attention has been directed toward integrating pathological images with multi-omics data to enhance both predictive performance and biological interpretability. In this context, Liu et al. [9] proposed a hybrid deep learning model that combines patients' genetic information with imaging features to predict breast cancer subtypes. Gao et al. [10] further developed the MRP system, which integrates pathological images and multi-omics data to simulate clinical assessment of responses to neoadjuvant therapy in breast cancer, incorporating cross-modal knowledge mining and temporal information embedding strategies. However, complete omics data is rarely available for every patient. This data incompleteness makes it difficult to train deep learning models effectively, hindering the learning of complex relationships and ultimately reducing model generalization and predictive accuracy. Data imputation combined with graph regularization has been successfully applied to single-cell RNA-seq data [11], providing a relevant basis for handling missing multi-omics views.

This work proposes a deep incomplete multi-omics view information recovery framework designed for breast cancer subtype classification. The overall architecture is illustrated in Fig. 1. Fusion of multi-views has been studied in clustering tasks [12], inspiring our cross-attention based fusion. It utilizes cross-attention and latent self-attention mechanisms to model complex inter-view relationships and reconstruct missing omics views with a context-aware way. By learning high-level semantic representations across multiple views, it reconstructs missing view features and leverages the inherent complementarity between diverse views. These reconstructed omics views are then integrated into a classification network to fully exploit multimodal discriminative information. Experimental results on the Cancer Genome Atlas (TCGA) breast cancer dataset demonstrate that DIMIR significantly outperforms state-of-the-art methods, achieving a classification accuracy of 96.0%. Furthermore, interpretability analysis indicates its effectiveness in identifying key biomarkers closely associated with cancer subtypes.

2 Materials and Methods

2.1 Multimodal Data Preprocessing

The input data is denoted as $X = \{X^{(1)}, X^{(2)}, \ldots, X^{(m)}\}$, where $X^{(v)}$ represents the v-th omics views and $X^{(1)}$ corresponds to the WSI-level features representation. To handle missing omics views, DIMIR constructs a mask matrix $M \in \{0,1\}^{n \times m}$ which indicates the absence of each data across all omics views.

2.2 Omics Reconstruction

Omics Embedding and Enhancement. The omics reconstruction stage aims to map heterogeneous omics data into a shared latent space and recover missing values. The DIMIR employs an omics embedding module to map each omics into a unified latent space. For the v-th omics view, the embedded representation $\hat{X}^{(v)}$ is defined as follows:

$$\hat{X}^{(v)} = M^{(v)} \odot E\left(X^{(v)}\right) + \left(1 - M^{(v)}\right) \odot t \tag{1}$$

where $E(\cdot)$ denotes a transformation consisting of a linear layer followed by layer normalization, ensuring each omics view can be mapped to a unified dimension D. $M^{(v)}$ denotes the v-th column of the mask matrix, $\odot$ represents the Hadamard product, and t is a learnable vector used to impute missing omics views. The resulting embeddings of all omics are stacked into a 3D tensor $X_s \in \mathbb{R}^{n \times m \times D}$.

During the encoding phase of DIMIR, a cross-view attention mechanism is introduced to enhance information flow across omics views. The specific implementation is as follows:

$$Attn\left(Q, K, V\right) = Concat\left(head_1, \ldots, head_h\right) W^O \tag{2}$$

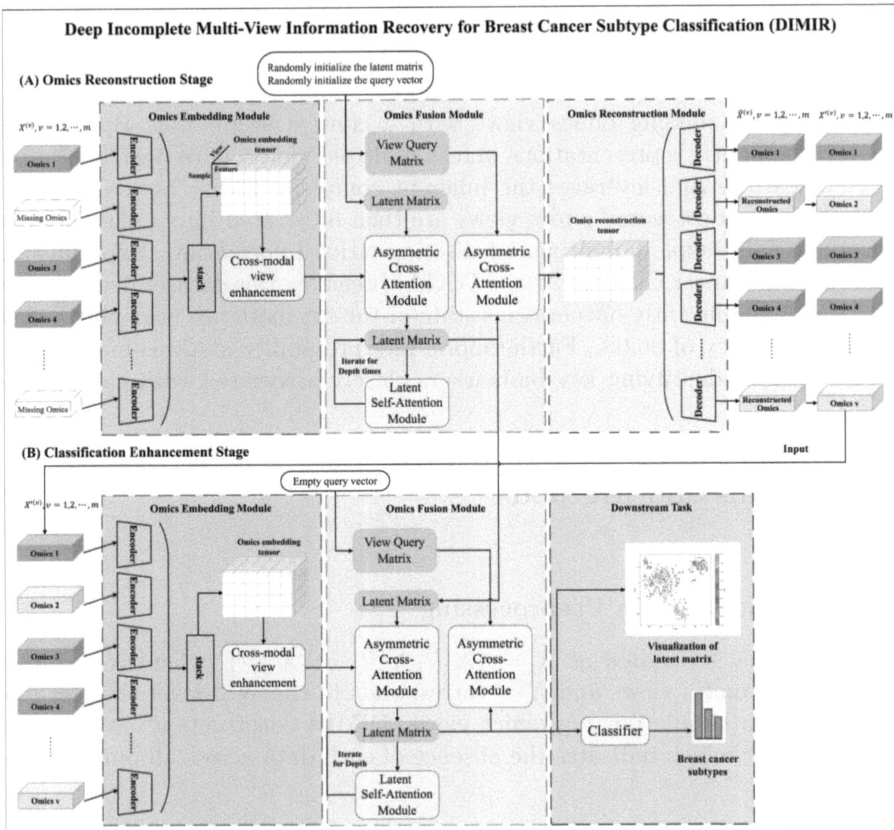

Fig. 1. The overall architecture of DIMIR. (A) Omics reconstruction stage: designed to restore missing omics views. (B) Classification enhancement stage: aimed at refining subtype prediction by leveraging the reconstructed omics views from the first stage.

$$head_i = Softmax\left(\frac{Q_i K_i^\top}{\sqrt{d_k}}\right) V_i \tag{3}$$

$$X_a = X_s + \alpha \cdot Attn\left(X_s, X_s, X_s\right) \tag{4}$$

where Q_i, K_i, V_i represent the query, key, and value matrices for the i-th attention head, which are obtained through learnable linear projections of the input X_s. $\sqrt{d_k}$ is the scaling factor used to maintain gradient stability, and W^O is the output projection matrix that integrates information from all h heads. α is used to balance the original omics views information and enhanced information.

Omics Fusion and Reconstruction. The omics fusion module compresses X_a into a low-dimensional latent space to capture complex intra-view relationships. It randomly initializes a latent matrix L_0 and compresses the augmented omics views into the latent space via an asymmetric cross-attention mechanism. Subsequently, it performs implicit modeling of the omics views through multiple latent self-attention layers to capture complex intra-view relationships:

$$L_{ca} = LayerNorm\left(L_0 + Attn\left(L_0, X_a, X_a\right)\right) \tag{5}$$

$$L_{la}^{(d)} = LayerNorm\left(L_{la}^{(d-1)} + Attn\left(L_{la}^{(d-1)}, L_{la}^{(d-1)}, L_{la}^{(d-1)}\right)\right) \tag{6}$$

where $L_{la}^{(0)} = L_{ca}$, $d = 1, \ldots, N$. N is the number of layers in the latent self-attention module. The final output $L_{la}^{(N)}$ represents the global multi-omics embedding used for disease subtype classification and omics reconstruction.

Then, it employs a learnable query mechanism to construct an omics-specific query vector library: $Q = \left\{q^{(1)}, q^{(2)}, \cdots, q^{(m)}\right\} \in \mathbb{R}^{m \times D}$. This library interacts with the latent space representations to reconstruct the omics embeddings. DIMIR builds a dynamic weight generation network for each omics type. The embedding of each omics is processed by its corresponding sub-network to obtain a scalar dynamic weight $\omega^{(v)}$, which is defined as follows:

$$\omega^{(v)} = Sigmoid\left(Linear\left(ReLU\left(Linear\left(\hat{X}^{(v)}\right)\right)\right)\right) \tag{7}$$

In addition, the dynamic weight $\omega^{(v)}$ is used to weight the query vector $q^{(v)}$, enabling it to account for the relative importance of each omics view. For each omics query vector $q^{(v)}$, the weighted query vector is defined as follows:

$$q\prime^{(v)} = \omega^{(v)} \times q^{(v)} \tag{8}$$

The omics query vector library is then updated as $Q' = \left\{q'^{(1)}, q'^{(2)}, \cdots, q'^{(m)}\right\}$.

DIMIR reconstructs the features for each omics view through interaction between the weighted query vectors and the latent space representation. The reconstructed omics is defined as follows:

$$\hat{X}_{rec} = Softmax\left(\frac{(Q'W_Q)(Q'W_K)^T}{\sqrt{D}}\right)\left(L_{la}^{(N)} W_V\right) \tag{9}$$

where W_Q, W_K and W_V are transformation matrices for the query, key, and value in cross-attention, and $\hat{X}_{rec}$ is the reconstructed 3D embedded tensor.

DIMIR employs an omics reconstruction module to process the reconstructed embeddings of each omics, which is defined as follows:

$$\bar{X}^{(v)} = Linear\left(GELU\left(Linear\left(\hat{X}_{rec}^{(v)}\right)\right)\right) \tag{10}$$

where $\hat{X}_{rec}^{(v)}$ denotes the reconstructed embedding of the v-th omics. The reconstructed omics view after embedding is defined as $\bar{X} = \left\{\bar{X}^{(1)}, \bar{X}^{(2)}, \cdots, \bar{X}^{(m)}\right\}$, where $\bar{X} \in \mathbb{R}^{n \times d_v}$, and $v = 1, 2, \ldots, m$.

2.3 Classification Enhancement

The classification enhancement stage integrates the original incomplete omics views with the reconstructed omics views to form the final input. The augmented input for each omics view is defined as follows:

$$X'^{(v)} = M^v \odot X^{(v)} + (1 - M^v) \odot \bar{X}^{(v)} \tag{11}$$

In the classification enhancement stage, each omics view is processed by its own embedding layer, which is consistent with the reconstruction stage. These representations are stacked into a 3D tensor and enhanced through the cross-view attention module to obtain X'_a. It is defined as follows:

$$\hat{X}'^{(v)} = E\left(X'^{(v)}\right) \tag{12}$$

$$X'_s = Stack\left(\hat{X}'^{(v)}\right) \in \mathbb{R}^{n \times m \times D} \tag{13}$$

$$X'_a = X'_s + \alpha \times Attn\left(X'_s, X'_s, X'_s\right) \tag{14}$$

Unlike the reconstruction stage, the fusion module in the classification stage no longer uses a randomly initialized latent matrix. Instead, it is initialized with $L_{la}^{(N)}$ obtained from the reconstruction phase. Then, it employs an asymmetric cross-attention mechanism to compress X'_a into the latent space, followed by a multi-layer latent self-attention module for implicit data modeling to obtain a high-quality latent matrix L'_{la}. It is defined as follows:

$$L'_{ca} = LayerNorm\left(L_{la}^{(N)} + Attn\left(L_{la}^{(N)}, X'_a, X'_a\right)\right) \tag{15}$$

$$L_{la}'^{(d)} = LayerNorm\left(L_{la}'^{(d-1)} + Attn\left(L_{la}'^{(d-1)}, L_{la}'^{(d-1)}, L_{la}'^{(d-1)}\right)\right) \tag{16}$$

where $L_{la}'^{(0)} = L'_{ca}$, $d = 1, \ldots, N$. N is the number of layers in the latent self-attention module.

Finally, L'_{la} is mapped to the classification space through a fully connected layer and transformed into a probability distribution $\hat{y}$ using the Softmax function. It is defined as follows:

$$\hat{y} = Softmax\left(Linear\left(L'_{la}\right)\right) \tag{17}$$

2.4 Loss Function

Reconstruction Loss. The reconstruction loss is used to calculate the discrepancy between the reconstructed omics views and the original omics views.

It is only used during the omics reconstruction phase and computed based on dynamic weights of each view.

$$\mathcal{L}_r = \frac{\sum_{v=1}^{m} \omega^{(v)} \sum_{b=1}^{B} \left(1 - M_b^{(v)}\right) \times \left(X_b^{(v)} - \bar{X}_b^{(v)}\right)^2}{\sum_{v=1}^{m} \sum_{b=1}^{B} \left(1 - M_b^{(v)}\right)} \tag{18}$$

where m denotes the number of views, $\omega^{(v)}$ represents the dynamic weight of the v-th view, $X_b^{(v)}$ is the v-th original omics view, $\bar{X}_b^{(v)}$ denotes the v-th reconstructed omics view, and M is the mask matrix.

View Consistency Loss. The view consistency loss is designed to enforce consistency among the latent representations of different omics views, by calculating the cosine similarity between each pair of views and comparing it to a target consistency value.

$$\mathcal{L}_{con} = \frac{1}{B} \sum_{b=1}^{B} \frac{1}{m(m-1)} \sum_{v_1 \neq v_2} BCE\left(\cos\left(\hat{X}^{(v_1)}, \hat{X}^{(v_2)}\right)\right) \tag{19}$$

where $\hat{X}^{(v_1)}$ and $\hat{X}^{(v_2)}$ represent the embedded representations of the v_1-th and v_2-th views, respectively, $\cos(\hat{X}^{(v_1)}, \hat{X}^{(v_2)})$ denotes the cosine similarity which is used to calculate the similarity between views. BCE represents the Binary Cross-Entropy loss, which calculates the difference between the similarity and the target consistency.

Graph Structure Regularization Loss. The graph structure regularization loss ensures the consistency of graph structure in the reconstructed omics and is used only during the omics reconstruction phase. It is defined as follows:

$$\mathcal{L}_g = \|\bar{A} - A\|_2^2 \tag{20}$$

where $\bar{A}$ represents the adjacency matrix of the reconstructed omics views constructed via K-nearest neighbors (KNN) to represent the local similarity between data points. Meanwhile, A represents the adjacency matrix of the original omics views constructed using the same KNN strategy. $\|\cdot\|_2^2$ is the squared Euclidean distance which is used to calculate the difference between the adjacency matrices of the reconstructed and original omics views.

Classification Loss. The classification loss is employed to train the model for classification tasks, enhancing accuracy by computing the classification error through the cross-entropy loss function. It is defined as follows:

$$\mathcal{L}_c = -\frac{1}{B} \sum_{b=1}^{B} \sum_{i=1}^{C} y_{b,i} \log\left(\hat{y}_{b,i}\right) \tag{21}$$

where B denotes the batch size and C denotes the number of classes. $y_{b,i}$ represents the true label of the b-th sample, and $\hat{y}_{b,i}$ denotes the predicted probability for class i.

Total Loss Function. The loss of the data reconstruction phase is defined as follows:

$$\mathcal{L}_{rec} = \mathcal{L}_r + \lambda_{con}\mathcal{L}_{con} + \lambda_g\mathcal{L}_g + \mathcal{L}_c \tag{22}$$

where λ_{con} and λ_g represent the weights for each loss term, controlling the contribution of each task to the total loss function.

The loss function for the classification training phase is defined as follows:

$$\mathcal{L}_{class} = \lambda_{con}\mathcal{L}_{con} + \mathcal{L}_c \tag{23}$$

3 Results

To validate the effectiveness of DIMIR, experiments are conducted on breast cancer dataset from The Cancer Genome Atlas (TCGA), including whole-slide images (WSI), copy number variation (CNV), DNA methylation, RNA-seq, and miRNA expression. We used complete-case patients with artificially created missingness and 5-fold cross-validation. In the experiment, the embedding dimension is set to 512, and the latent representation matrix is configured with a size of 256 × 512. The AdamW optimizer is used with an initial learning rate of 1e-4 and a weight decay coefficient of 1e-5. A dropout rate is set to 0.1. The batch size is set to 8. Furthermore, the α is set to 0.5.

3.1 Comparative Analysis

This work compares DIMIR with a variety of multi-omics integration and WSI analysis algorithms to evaluate its performance in breast cancer subtype classification. The methods are categorized as: Traditional Machine Learning (KNN, DTC), Multi-Omics Integration (VAE, MOGONET, MOGCN, DeepOmix, CustOmics), Multimodal Fusion (HGCN, MCFN), and Image-only (CLAM). As shown in Table 1, by integrating multi-omics and WSI data, DIMIR achieves a classification accuracy of 96.0% and improves performance by nearly 3% over the sub-optimal model MCFN. Compared to the imaging-only CLAM model, it achieves a performance gain of approximately 36%. It also outperforms traditional machine learning algorithms and other models based on multi-omics and whole-slide imaging data. These results strongly validate the effectiveness and robustness of DIMIR in breast cancer classification. By deeply integrating radiomics with multi-omics data, DIMIR comprehensively captures inter-modal correlations to enhance classification accuracy.

3.2 Ablation Analysis

To evaluate the contribution of each component in loss function, we conduct an ablation study by removing individual loss components from the complete loss function. As shown in Table 2, the complete loss function achieves the best performance across all metrics with an Accuracy of 0.960. In contrast, removing any loss components degraded model performance. Specifically, excluding the view

Table 1. Classification Results of Different Algorithms on the TCGA-BRCA Dataset.

Method	Accuracy	F1	Recall
KNN	0.776	0.671	0.632
DTC	0.881	0.855	0.838
VAE	0.751	0.576	0.667
MOGONET [13]	0.768	0.612	0.667
MOGCN [14]	0.641	0.261	0.334
DeepOmix [15]	0.633	0.258	0.334
GCN-LWF [16]	0.623	0.256	0.334
CustOmics [17]	0.878	0.851	0.838
HGCN [18]	0.916	0.895	0.912
MCFN [19]	0.928	0.851	0.905
CLAM [20]	0.701	0.707	0.668
DIMIR	**0.960**	**0.941**	**0.954**

consistency loss results in the most significant decrease in performance, reducing accuracy to 0.878. This emphasises the important role of this loss in aligning feature representations across different omics views. Furthermore, excluding graph structure regularization loss or reconstruction loss also leads to a noticeable decline in performance, confirming the necessity of each component for maintaining classification capability. These results demonstrate that the multi-component loss function improves feature representation from multiple angles. This enables DIMIR to effectively coordinate feature extraction, relationship modelling and cross-view representation, ultimately leading to significant improvements in the performance of breast cancer subtyping tasks.

Table 2. Classification results of different loss combinations on the TCGA-BRCA dataset.

Loss Type	Accuracy	F1	Recall
DIMIR(w/o Graph Structure Regularization)	0.940	0.928	0.938
DIMIR (w/o Reconstruction)	0.889	0.854	0.869
DIMIR (w/o View Consistency)	0.878	0.864	0.862
DIMIR	**0.960**	**0.941**	**0.954**

3.3 Biomarker Discovery

Based on the attention scores derived from multi-omics data, we select the top 10 high-attention features from each data type as potential biomarkers for cancer recurrence. A higher attention score indicates a greater contribution of the corresponding feature to breast cancer prognosis prediction. Table 3 lists the identified potential BRCA-related biomarkers determined by their attention scores. We validated these identified genes through a comprehensive literature review. ZHX3 [21], CISD3 [22], OPRM1 [23], SYNJ2 [24], SNX9 [25], PCGF2 [26] and HNRNPA0 [27] genes are well-documented in breast cancer or other malignancies, while others represent novel candidates requiring further investigation. The DIMIR not only demonstrates excellent performance in breast cancer subtyping tasks but also exhibits a strong ability to identify key features and screen potential biomarkers. This provides valuable support for precise diagnosis and treatment strategy development in breast cancer.

Table 3. The Top 10 Potential biomarkers identified.

Rank	ENSG Gene Symbol	Array Express	Evidence (DOI)
1	ENSG00000174306	ZHX3	10.2147/CMAR.S184340
2	ENSG00000277972	CISD3	10.21203/rs.3.rs-26134/v1
3	ENSG00000112038	OPRM1	10.1007/s13277-015-3113-z
4	ENSG00000078269	SYNJ2	10.1186/s12920-022-01266-0
5	ENSG00000124181	PLCG1	unknown
6	ENSG00000272047	GTF2H5	unknown
7	ENSG00000172209	GPR22	unknown
8	ENSG00000130340	SNX9	10.1242/jcs.188045
9	ENSG00000277258	PCGF2	10.1097/MD.0000000000030598
10	ENSG00000177733	HNRNPA0	10.18632/aging.202411

4 Conclusion

This work presents a deep incomplete multi-omics view information recovery framework designed for breast cancer subtype classification. The model integrates diverse omics views and recovers missing omics views through cross-attention and latent self-attention mechanisms. In the initial stage, DIMIR learns high-level semantic representations and reconstructs missing omics views features via latent self-attention. In the subsequent stage, the model is trained on the completed multi-omics data to optimize classification accuracy. This two-stage approach effectively leverages inter-view complementarity, mitigates the impact of data incompleteness, and enhances overall predictive performance. Comparing with state-of-the-art algorithms validates the effectiveness of DIMIR. In addition, literature validation is conducted on the breast cancer-related biomarkers identified by DIMIR, providing further biological understanding of the complex mechanisms underlying breast cancer.

Acknowledgments. This work is supported in part by the National Natural Science Foundation of China (U24A20256); the Natural Science Foundation of Guangxi (2024GXNSFFA010006); the Guangxi Bagui Young Elite Talent Development Program; the funding of Hunan Intelligent Rehabilitation Robot and Auxiliary Equipment Engineering Technology Research Center (2025AQ10); the project of Disease Prevention and Control of Guangxi (GXJKKJ2025YB019).

References

1. Wang, K., Zheng, F., et al.: Breast cancer classification from digital pathology images via connectivity-aware graph transformer. IEEE Trans. Med. Imaging **43**(8), 2854–2865 (2024)
2. Liu, H., Xu, W.D., et al.: Breast cancer molecular subtype prediction on pathological images with discriminative patch selection and multi-instance learning. Front. Oncol. **12**, 858453 (2022)
3. Wang, G., Jia, M., et al.: Multi-classification of breast cancer pathology images based on a two-stage hybrid network. J. Cancer Res. Clin. Oncol. **150**(12), 505 (2024)
4. Lan, W., Tang, Z., et al.: The large language models on biomedical data analysis: a survey. IEEE J. Biomed. Health Inform. **29**(6), 4486–4497 (2025)
5. Lan, W., Liao, H., et al.: Deepkegg: a multi-omics data integration framework with biological insights for cancer recurrence prediction and biomarker discovery. Briefings Bioinform. **25**(3), bbae185 (2024)
6. Huang, Y., Zeng, P., Zhong, C.: Classifying breast cancer subtypes on multi-omics data via sparse canonical correlation analysis and deep learning. BMC Bioinform. **25**(1), 132 (2024)
7. Lan, W., Tang, Z.: Mulgonet: an interpretable neural network framework to integrate multi-omics data for cancer recurrence prediction and biomarker discovery. Fundam. Res. (2025)
8. Lan, W., Ling, T., et al.: scmomtf: an interpretable multitask learning framework for single-cell multi-omics data analysis. PLoS Comput. Biol. **20**(12), e1012679 (2024)
9. Liu, T., Huang, J., et al.: A hybrid deep learning model for predicting molecular subtypes of human breast cancer using multimodal data. IRBM **43**(1), 62–74 (2022)
10. Gao, Y., Ventura-Diaz, S., et al.: An explainable longitudinal multi-modal fusion model for predicting neoadjuvant therapy response in women with breast cancer. Nat. Commun. **15**(1), 9613 (2024)
11. Lan, W., Chen, J.: Deep imputation bi-stochastic graph regularized matrix factorization for clustering single-cell RNA-sequencing data. IEEE Trans. Comput. Biol. Bioinform. (2024)
12. Lan, W., Guo, Y., et al.: Coordinator: semantic-coordinated dynamic fusion for multi-view clustering. Inf. Fusion 104239 (2026)
13. Wang, T., Shao, W., et al.: Mogonet integrates multi-omics data using graph convolutional networks allowing patient classification and biomarker identification. Nat. Commun. **12**(1), 3445 (2021)
14. Li, X., Ma, J., et al.: MoGCN: a multi-omics integration method based on graph convolutional network for cancer subtype analysis. Front. Genet. **13**, 806842 (2022)

15. Zhao, L., Dong, Q., et al.: Deepomix: a scalable and interpretable multi-omics deep learning framework and application in cancer survival analysis. Comput. Struct. Biotechnol. J. **19**, 2719–2725 (2021)
16. Luo, Y., Zhao, X., et al.: Low-rank tensor function representation for multi-dimensional data recovery. IEEE Trans. Pattern Anal. Mach. Intell. **46**(5), 3351–3369 (2023)
17. Benkirane, H., Pradat, Y., et al.: Customics: a versatile deep-learning based strategy for multi-omics integration. PLoS Comput. Biol. **19**(3), e1010921 (2023)
18. Hou, W., Lin, C., et al.: Hybrid graph convolutional network with online masked autoencoder for robust multimodal cancer survival prediction. IEEE Trans. Med. Imaging **42**(8), 2462–2473 (2023)
19. Ding, S., Li, J., et al.: Multimodal co-attention fusion network with online data augmentation for cancer subtype classification. IEEE Trans. Med. Imaging **43**(11), 3977–3989 (2024)
20. Lu, M.Y., Williamson, D.F., et al.: Data-efficient and weakly supervised computational pathology on whole-slide images. Nat. Biomed. Eng. **5**(6), 555–570 (2021)
21. You, Y., Ma, Y.: Attenuated ZHX3 expression serves as a potential biomarker that predicts poor clinical outcomes in breast cancer patients. Cancer Manag. Res. 1199–1210 (2019)
22. Li, X., Wang, Y., et al.: Identification of potential genes in her2+ breast cancer by co-expression network analysis. Res. Square (2020). https://doi.org/10.21203/rs.3.rs-26134/v1
23. Cieślińska, A., Sienkiewicz-Szłapka, E., et al.: μ-opioid receptor gene (oprm1) polymorphism in patients with breast cancer. Tumor Biol. **36**(6), 4655–4660 (2015)
24. Hou, W., Li, G.S., et al.: Synj2 is a novel and potential biomarker for the prediction and treatment of cancers: from lung squamous cell carcinoma to pan-cancer. BMC Med. Genomics **15**(1), 114 (2022)
25. Bendris, N., Stearns, C.J., et al.: Sorting nexin 9 negatively regulates invadopodia formation and function in cancer cells. J. Cell Sci. **129**(14), 2804–2816 (2016)
26. Zheng, Y., Lu, W., et al.: Identification of a novel ubiquitination related gene signature for patients with breast cancer. Medicine **101**(37), e30598 (2022)
27. Zhou, J., Guo, Y., et al.: Identification of therapeutic targets and prognostic biomarkers from the hnrnp family in invasive breast carcinoma. Aging **13**(3), 4503 (2021)

MPATDTI: A Meta-Path-Aware Transformer with Contrastive Learning for Drug-Target Interaction Prediction

Haoyuan Li[1], Haochen Zhao[2](✉), and Jianxin Wang[1]

[1] Hunan Provincial Key Lab on Bioinformatics, School of Computer Science and Engineering, Central South University, Changsha 410083, China
[2] Big Data Institute, Central South University, Changsha 410083, China
zhaohaochen@csu.edu.cn

Abstract. Drug–target interaction (DTI) prediction is fundamental to drug discovery and drug repositioning. Meta-path-based methods have shown strong performance by leveraging heterogeneous biomedical networks for DTI prediction. However, many existing approaches do not explicitly encode meta-path types during representation learning, and they often underutilize intermediate nodes along meta-path instances, making it difficult to distinguish different semantic roles of heterogeneous relations and to fully capture the informative context embedded in different paths. To address these issues, we propose MPATDTI, a Meta-Path-Aware Transformer framework for DTI prediction. MPATDTI encodes meta-path types and aggregates information from endpoints and intermediate nodes on meta-path instances to learn network-based representations for drugs and proteins. In addition, we use ChemBERTa and ESM-2 to extract intrinsic features from drug SMILES and protein sequences, respectively. We then use contrastive learning to align the network-based representations with the intrinsic features, and fuse them with a gating module. Finally, MPATDTI predicts DTIs based on the fused drug and protein representations. We evaluated MPATDTI on two benchmark datasets, and it consistently outperformed recent DTI prediction methods. In addition, we conducted ablation studies to evaluate the contribution of each module, and performed key hyper-parameter analysis to examine the sensitivity of the model. Overall, these results demonstrate that MPATDTI is effective and stable, and can serve as a practical tool for DTI prediction.

Keywords: metapath · DTIs prediction · transformer · contrastive learning

1 Introduction

Drug-target interaction prediction is a key task in drug discovery and drug repositioning. It aims to identify potential targets for a given compound and

X. Cui et al. (Eds.): ISBRA 2026, LNBI 16690, pp. 137–148, 2027.
https://doi.org/10.1007/978-981-92-3716-6_11

to support the study of drug mechanisms and side effects [1]. Despite recent progress, large-scale experimental validation of DTIs is still expensive and time-consuming. Moreover, the number of candidate drug–target pairs grow rapidly with the expanding chemical and biological space [2]. Therefore, computational models are widely used to prioritize promising interactions for further testing [3]. Among these, data-driven methods have become an important direction for improving the efficiency and scalability of DTI screening. In practice, an effective DTI model should achieve high accuracy under sparse observations and offer reasonable evidence for its predictions [4]. These requirements motivate continuous research on more reliable and more informative DTI prediction methods [5].

A variety of computational approaches have been developed for DTI prediction [6]. Early studies mainly relied on similarity measures and matrix factorization, which model DTIs as link prediction under predefined drug–drug and target–target similarities [7,8]. Later, machine learning and deep learning methods further improved performance by learning interaction patterns from known DTIs and auxiliary features, such as molecular descriptors and protein sequences [9]. More recently, graph-based models have received increasing attention, because they can naturally integrate diverse biomedical relations into a unified framework [10]. In particular, heterogeneous biomedical networks connect drugs, proteins, diseases, and other entities through multiple relation types, providing rich relational context for DTI prediction [11]. These advances make it promising to learn drug and protein representations by exploiting multi-relational network structure.

Meta-path-based learning is widely used to leverage heterogeneous biomedical networks for DTI prediction [12]. A meta-path describes a sequence of node and relation types, and it provides a clear way to capture multi-hop relations between drugs and proteins through other biomedical entities [13,14]. This design often improves performance and also offers a more interpretable view of how information is propagated in the network [15,16]. However, two challenges remain. First, many methods do not explicitly encode meta-path types during representation learning, which may blur the semantic differences among heterogeneous relation patterns and reduce the discriminability of learned representations [17]. Second, intermediate nodes within meta-path instances are often not fully utilized, making it difficult to fully model the important relational information carried by paths [18].

To address the above issues, we propose MPATDTI, a unified DTI prediction framework that combines meta-path-aware modeling with contrastive learning. Specifically, we build a heterogeneous biomedical network that connects drugs, proteins, diseases, and side effects through multiple relation types, and design a meta-path-aware Transformer to learn drug and protein representations by incorporating meta-path type signals and aggregating information along sampled meta-path instances. In addition, we use ChemBERTa to encode drug SMILES and ESM-2 to encode protein sequences, and fuse these semantic features with the network representations for prediction, enabling the framework to integrate heterogeneous biomedical network information with pretrained molecular and protein encoders. We further introduce contrastive learning to make representations more stable across different graph views and improve robustness and generalization in sparse DTI settings. Experimental results on benchmark datasets demonstrate that MPATDTI achieves strong predictive performance.

2 Materials and Methods

2.1 Benchmark Datasets

In this study, two public benchmark datasets were adopted to assess our method and to compare it with several representative DTI prediction approaches. The first benchmark, Hetero-A, was built based on DrugBank [19]. It contains 29,181 nodes and 663,893 edges. In this graph, nodes cover drugs, proteins, diseases, and drug side effects, and edges correspond to multiple biological or pharmacological relations among these entities. The second benchmark, Hetero-B, was collected from BioSnap together with additional disease-related resources [20]. Hetero-B includes 38,975 nodes and 364,713 edges, where the graph mainly involves drugs, proteins, and diseases. Similar to Hetero-A, its edges describe a set of key relationships used to support DTI modeling and evaluation.

2.2 Heterogeneous Graph and Meta-Path Definition

We represent the biomedical network as a heterogeneous graph $G = (\mathcal{V}, \mathcal{E})$, where $\mathcal{V}$ is the node set and $\mathcal{E}$ is the edge set. Each node $v \in \mathcal{V}$ has a semantic type, and each edge $e \in \mathcal{E}$ has a relation type. In our setting, the graph includes multiple biomedical entities such as drugs, proteins, diseases, and drug side effects, and the edges describe their known biological or pharmacological associations. Modeling the data as a heterogeneous graph lets us put different entity types and relations into one network. In this way, a drug and a protein may be related through either direct links or short paths that pass through other biomedical entities.

To characterize typical multi-hop semantics in G, we introduce meta-paths. A meta-path is a type-level schema that specifies an ordered sequence of node types connected by relation types, written as

$$\mathcal{P} : T_1 \xrightarrow{r_1} T_2 \xrightarrow{r_2} \cdots \xrightarrow{r_{L-1}} T_L, \tag{1}$$

where T_i denotes a node type, r_i denotes a relation type, and L is the length of the meta-path. Given a meta-path schema $\mathcal{P}$, a meta-path instance is a concrete path $(v_1, \ldots, v_L)$ in the graph whose node and relation types follow $\mathcal{P}$. Different meta-paths correspond to different connection patterns in the graph, and they can reveal useful clues for drug-target interaction prediction. We therefore use meta-paths to organize multi-hop information for representation learning.

2.3 Overall Framework

The overall framework of MPATDTI is shown in Fig. 1. We learn drug and protein representations from two complementary views, including the network view from a meta-path-aware transformer and the structure view from ChemBERTa and ESM-2. The two views are first aligned via contrastive learning and then fused to produce joint embeddings for interaction prediction.

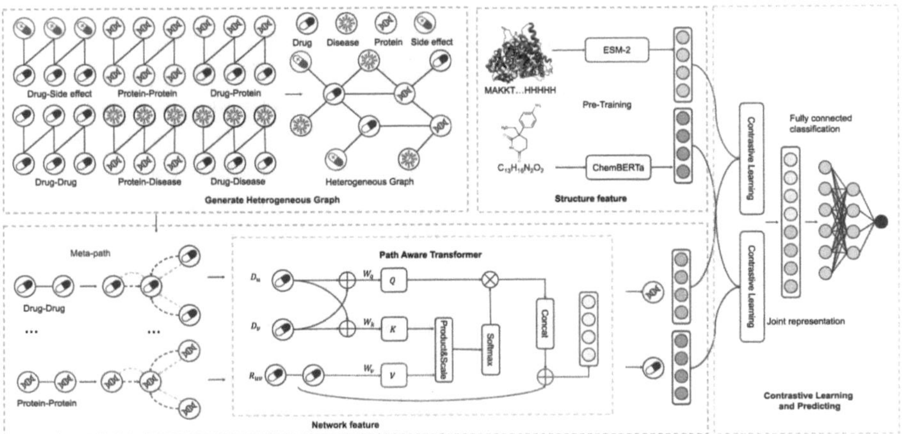

Fig. 1. A flow chart illustrating a method for predicting drug-target interaction.

2.4 Meta-Path-Aware Transformer for Network Representation

To learn structural representations of drugs and proteins from the heterogeneous graph, we design a meta-path-aware transformer module by integrating meta-path type information and intermediate-node semantics in a unified framework.

For a given center node u, we consider M predefined meta-path types, including drug-disease-drug, drug-drug, drug-side-effect-drug, protein-protein, protein-disease-protein. Under the type m, we sample up to P meta-path instances starting from u. The p-th instance connects u with an endpoint node $v_{m,p}$ through a sequence of intermediate nodes $\{x_{m,p,\ell}\}_{\ell=1}^{L}$, where L denotes the number of intermediate nodes in the sampled meta-path instance and ℓ is the index of the intermediate node. In the network channel, all node features are initialized as randomly initialized learnable embeddings.

We first aggregate intermediate-node features by mean pooling:

$$\bar{\mathbf{x}}_{m,p} = \frac{1}{L} \sum_{\ell=1}^{L} \mathbf{x}_{m,p,\ell}. \tag{2}$$

To explicitly encode meta-path type information, we introduce a learnable embedding $\mathbf{e}_m$ for each meta-path type. The path representation is then constructed as

$$\mathbf{r}_{m,p} = \mathbf{W}_r \left[\mathbf{e}_m \parallel \bar{\mathbf{x}}_{m,p}\right], \tag{3}$$

where $\mathbf{W}_r$ is a linear projection matrix.

Based on the path representation, we apply a path-aware attention mechanism. Let d_u and $d_{v_{m,p}}$ denote the features of the center node and the endpoint node, respectively. The query is generated from the path representation, while the key and value vectors are derived from the two endpoint nodes:

$$q_{m,p} = W_q r_{m,p}, \qquad k_u = W_k d_u, \qquad k_{v_{m,p}} = W_k d_{v_{m,p}}, \tag{4}$$

$$v_u = W_v d_u, \qquad v_{v_{m,p}} = W_v d_{v_{m,p}}. \tag{5}$$

The attention weights for the two endpoints are computed as

$$\alpha_{m,p,u} = \frac{\exp(q_{m,p}^\top k_u/\sqrt{d})}{\exp(q_{m,p}^\top k_u/\sqrt{d}) + \exp(q_{m,p}^\top k_{v_{m,p}}/\sqrt{d})}, \quad \alpha_{m,p,v_{m,p}} = 1 - \alpha_{m,p,u}, \tag{6}$$

where d is the hidden dimension. The instance representation is given by

$$h_{m,p} = W_o\left[\alpha_{m,p,u} v_u + \alpha_{m,p,v_{m,p}} v_{v_{m,p}} \parallel r_{m,p}\right]. \tag{7}$$

After encoding all instances, we aggregate them hierarchically. For each meta-path type,

$$\mathbf{h}_m = \sum_{p=1}^{P} \beta_{m,p} \mathbf{h}_{m,p}, \tag{8}$$

and across meta-path types,

$$\mathbf{z}_u^{\text{net}} = \sum_{m=1}^{M} \gamma_m \mathbf{h}_m, \tag{9}$$

where $\beta_{m,p}$ and γ_m are attention weights. The final representation $\mathbf{z}_u^{\text{net}}$ integrates meta-path semantics and structural information.

2.5 Structure Feature Extraction

Besides network topology, we further incorporate structure-related semantics from raw drug and protein inputs. For drugs, we extract molecular features from SMILES strings using a pretrained ChemBERTa encoder [21]. Given a SMILES sequence, it is first tokenized with a maximum length of 256 and then fed into the ChemBERTa model. The last-layer hidden representations are obtained and aggregated by mean pooling over the token dimension to produce the final drug structure representation.

For proteins, we use the pretrained ESM-2 model to encode amino-acid sequences [22]. Specifically, we adopt the variant `esm2_t33_650M_UR50D` and extract token representations from layer 33. Given a protein sequence, the model generates contextual embeddings for each residue. After removing the beginning and end special tokens, mean pooling is applied over the remaining tokens to obtain the protein structure representation.

In our experiments, ChemBERTa and ESM-2 are used as frozen encoders to extract structure embeddings in an offline manner. The obtained drug and protein structure representations provide complementary semantic information to the network view and will be used together with the network representations in the following modules.

2.6 Cross-View Alignment and Interaction Prediction

After obtaining the network representations and structure representations, we first align the two views via contrastive learning. For drugs (similarly for proteins), let $\mathbf{Z}^{net} \in \mathbb{R}^{N\times d}$ and $\mathbf{Z}^{str} \in \mathbb{R}^{N\times d}$ denote the normalized network and structure representations within a batch. We compute the cross-view similarity matrix as

$$\mathbf{S} = \frac{\mathbf{Z}^{net}(\mathbf{Z}^{str})^{\top}}{\tau}, \tag{10}$$

where τ is a temperature parameter.

We adopt a symmetric InfoNCE objective to align the two views:

$$\mathcal{L}_{cl} = \frac{1}{2}\left(-\frac{1}{N}\sum_{i=1}^{N}\log\frac{\exp(\mathbf{S}_{ii})}{\sum_{j=1}^{N}\exp(\mathbf{S}_{ij})} - \frac{1}{N}\sum_{i=1}^{N}\log\frac{\exp(\mathbf{S}_{ii})}{\sum_{j=1}^{N}\exp(\mathbf{S}_{ji})}\right). \tag{11}$$

After alignment, the joint representations are obtained by concatenation:

$$\mathbf{h}_d = [\mathbf{z}_d^{net} \,\|\, \mathbf{z}_d^{str}], \quad \mathbf{h}_p = [\mathbf{z}_p^{net} \,\|\, \mathbf{z}_p^{str}]. \tag{12}$$

For each drug–protein pair, we construct interaction features and apply a multilayer perceptron to predict the interaction probability $\hat{y}$.

The supervised objective is defined as the binary cross-entropy loss:

$$\mathcal{L}_{bce} = -\frac{1}{B}\sum_{i=1}^{B}\left(y_i \log \hat{y}_i + (1-y_i)\log(1-\hat{y}_i)\right). \tag{13}$$

The overall training objective is

$$\mathcal{L} = \mathcal{L}_{bce} + \lambda\mathcal{L}_{cl}, \tag{14}$$

where λ controls the weight of the contrastive term.

3 Results

3.1 Comparison with Related Methods

To evaluate the overall performance of the proposed MPATDTI framework, we conducted 10-fold cross-validation experiments on both Hetero-A and Hetero-B datasets. In each fold, nine subsets were used for training and the remaining subset was used for testing. MPATDTI was compared with several representative baseline methods, including metapath2vec [23], KGE_NFM [24], GIFDTI [25], DrugBAN [26], SGCL [27], GSL [28], SGMDTI [29] and BINDTI [30]. The corresponding results are illustrated in Fig. 2(a) and Fig. 2(b), where the performance on Hetero-A and Hetero-B is presented, respectively. As shown in the figure, MPATDTI achieves the best performance among all compared methods on both datasets. On the Hetero-A dataset, MPATDTI achieves an AUC of 0.9288 and an AUPR of 0.9208. On the Hetero-B dataset, it obtains an AUC of 0.9106 and an AUPR of 0.9158. Overall, MPATDTI achieves the best performance among all compared methods.

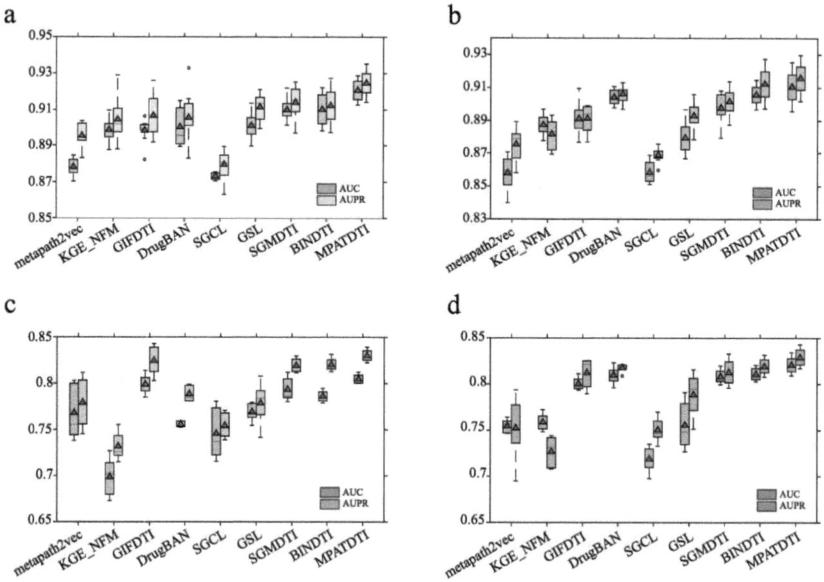

Fig. 2. Comparison of MPATDTI with baseline methods. (a) and (b) show the AUC and AUPR results under 10-fold cross-validation on the Hetero-A and Hetero-B datasets, respectively. (c) and (d) show the AUC and AUPR results under the drug cold-start and protein cold-start settings on the Hetero-A dataset, respectively.

3.2 Comparison of Cold-Start Performance

To further evaluate the generalization ability of MPATDTI in more challenging settings, we conducted cold-start experiments for both drugs and proteins on the Hetero-A dataset. In the drug cold-start setting, all drugs appearing in the test set were excluded from training, while in the protein cold-start setting, the proteins in the test set were not observed during training. The corresponding results are shown in Fig. 2(c) and Fig. 2(d). As can be seen, MPATDTI still achieves the best overall performance under both cold-start scenarios. In the drug cold-start setting, MPATDTI attains an average AUC of 0.8048 and an AUPR of 0.8298. In the protein cold-start setting, it obtains an average AUC of 0.8206 and an AUPR of 0.8287. These results show that MPATDTI achieves the best performance in both cold-start scenarios and maintains good robustness when predicting interactions for previously unseen drugs or proteins.

3.3 Ablation Study

To further evaluate the contribution of each component in MPATDTI, we conducted an ablation study on both Hetero-A and Hetero-B datasets. Specifically, we compared the full model with three degraded variants, including w/o pretrain, w/o path, and w/o CL. The results are listed in Table 1. As shown in the table, the complete MPATDTI model consistently achieves the best performance on both datasets, indicating that all modules contribute positively to the final prediction results. Among the three variants, removing the meta-path-aware module leads to the largest performance degradation. On Hetero-A, the AUC and AUPR decrease by approximately 3.80% and 3.49%, respectively. On Hetero-B, the corresponding decreases reach about 8.58% and 8.16%, further demonstrating the importance of meta-path-aware representation learning for capturing informative structural patterns in heterogeneous graphs. Removing the pretrained structure encoders also causes clear performance drops. Compared with the full model, the AUC and AUPR decrease by about 2.28% and 2.14% on Hetero-A, and by 5.42% and 4.63% on Hetero-B, suggesting that pretrained molecular and protein features provide useful complementary information for DTI prediction. In comparison, removing contrastive learning results in relatively smaller but still consistent declines, with AUC and AUPR decreasing by about 0.61% and 0.71% on Hetero-A, and 1.45% and 1.51% on Hetero-B. These results indicate that contrastive learning further improves the robustness and discriminability of the learned representations.

Table 1. Ablation study of MPATDTI on Hetero-A and Hetero-B.

Model	Hetero-A		Hetero-B	
	AUC	AUPR	AUC	AUPR
w/o pretrain	0.8998 (0.0113)	0.9049 (0.0141)	0.8612 (0.0173)	0.8734 (0.0185)
w/o path	0.8858 (0.0135)	0.8924 (0.0172)	0.8325 (0.0198)	0.8410 (0.0220)
w/o CL	0.9152 (0.0120)	0.9181 (0.0150)	0.8974 (0.0154)	0.9020 (0.0181)
MPATDTI	0.9208 (0.0053)	0.9247 (0.0068)	0.9106 (0.0096)	0.9158 (0.0091)

3.4 Case Study

To further evaluate the practical utility of MPATDTI in identifying potential DTIs, we conducted a case study on Acetylcholinesterase (AChE, UniProt ID: P22303), which is a well-known therapeutic target for Alzheimer's disease. Specifically, all candidate drugs were ranked according to their predicted interaction scores with AChE, and the top 15 predicted drugs are listed in Table 2. Among them, 13 out of the top 15 candidates were supported by previous studies, indicating that MPATDTI can effectively recover biologically meaningful drug-target associations. For the remaining two drugs without direct literature evidence, we further performed molecular docking to provide additional support. As shown in Fig. 3, the docking scores were -8.5 kcal/mol of DB09462 and -9.4 kcal/mol of DB00474, respectively, suggesting favorable binding affinities with AChE. These results further demonstrate the effectiveness of MPATDTI in discovering both known and potential novel DTIs.

Table 2. Top 15 predicted drugs associated with AChE (P22303).

Rank	Drug Name	DrugBank ID	PMID
1	Amantadine	DB00915	4674484
2	Memantine	DB01043	23657927
3	Choline	DB00122	16297435
4	Metamfetamine	DB01577	40444166
5	Mephentermine	DB01365	34391136
6	Tramadol	DB00193	28461881
7	Glycerin	DB09462	Unknown
8	Pargyline	DB01626	40620970
9	Amphetamine	DB00182	5037382
10	Progesterone	DB00396	6892055
11	Methohexital	DB00474	Unknown
12	Mecamylamine	DB00657	23603417
13	Cannabidiol	DB09061	35702400
14	Vildagliptin	DB04876	41619967
15	Diethylpropion	DB00937	19897080

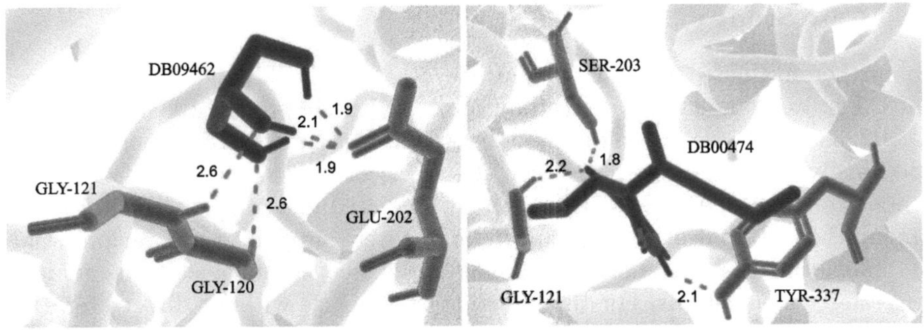

Fig. 3. Docking of DB09462 and DB00474 with acetylcholinesterase (AChE, P22303).

4 Conclusion

In this study, we proposed MPATDTI, a meta-path-aware framework with contrastive learning for drug–target interaction prediction. The model jointly exploits heterogeneous network information and structure-level semantics by combining a meta-path-aware Transformer with pretrained molecular and protein representations. In addition, cross-view contrastive learning helps improve the consistency and robustness of the learned representations. Experimental results on two benchmark datasets demonstrate that MPATDTI achieves strong predictive performance and maintains good generalization ability under cold-start settings. The case study further shows that the proposed method can identify both known and potential novel drug–target interactions. Overall, MPATDTI provides an effective framework for DTI prediction and offer useful support for drug discovery and drug repositioning. Nevertheless, two limitations remain. First, the performance of the model depends on the completeness of the heterogeneous biomedical network and the quality of pretrained representations. Second, the biological interpretability of the prediction results is still limited and requires further investigation.

Funding. This work was supported in part by the National Natural Science Foundation of China (Grant Nos. 62572488 and 62502541). This work was also carried out in part using computing resources at the High Performance Computing Center of Central South University.

References

1. Luo, Y., Xiaotong Zhao, M., Zhou, Y.F., Yong Li, X., Peng, Z.Y., He, X., Deng, H.: A network integration approach for drug-target interaction prediction and computational drug repositioning from heterogeneous information. Nat. Commun. **8**, 1–13 (2017)
2. Brian Walsh, Sameh K Mohamed, and Vít Nováček. Biokg: A knowledge graph for relational learning on biological data. In *Proceedings of the 29th ACM International Conference on Information & Knowledge Management*, pages 3173–3180, 2020

3. Peng, L., Liu, X., Chen, M., Liao, W., Mao, J., Zhou, L.: Mgndti: A drug-target interaction prediction framework based on multimodal representation learning and the gating mechanism. J. Chem. Inf. Model. **64**(16), 6684–6698 (2024)
4. Kun Huang, Cao Xiao, Lucas M Glass, and Jimeng Sun. Moltrans: molecular interaction transformer for drug–target interaction prediction. *Bioinformatics*, 37(6):830–836, 2021
5. Bredel, M., Jacoby, E.: Chemogenomics: an emerging strategy for rapid target and drug discovery. Nat. Rev. Genet. **5**, 262–275 (2004)
6. Xie, C.-L., Zhao, H.-C., Wang, J.-X.: Mvcasyn: Predicting synergistic drug combinations based on multi-view learning and cross-attention mechanism. J. Comput. Sci. Technol. **40**(6), 1626–1638 (2025)
7. Ran Zhang, Zhanjie Wang, Xuezhi Wang, Zhen Meng, and Wenjuan Cui. Mhtan-dti: Metapath-based hierarchical transformer and attention network for drug–target interaction prediction. *Briefings in Bioinformatics*, 24(2):bbad079, 2023
8. Zhao, H., Ni, P., Zhao, Q., Liang, X., Ai, D., Erhardt, S., Wang, J., Li, Y., Wang, J.: Identifying the serious clinical outcomes of adverse reactions to drugs by a multi-task deep learning framework. Communications Biology **6**(1), 870 (2023)
9. Zhou, D., Zenghui, X., Li, W., Xie, X., Peng, S.: Multidti: drug-target interaction prediction based on multi-modal representation learning to bridge the gap between new chemical entities and known heterogeneous network. Bioinformatics **37**(23), 4485–4492 (2021)
10. Hakime Öztürk, Elif O. Olmez, and Arzucan Özgür. Deepdta: deep drug-target binding affinity prediction. *Bioinformatics*, 34(issue supplement 13):i821–i829, 2018
11. Tsubaki, M., Tomii, K., Sese, J.: Compound-protein interaction prediction with end-to-end learning of neural networks for graphs and sequences. Bioinformatics **35**(2), 309–318 (2019)
12. Lim, S., et al.: A review on compound-protein interaction prediction methods: data, format, representation and model. Comput. Struct. Biotechnol. J. **19**, 1541–1556 (2021)
13. Fei Guo, Renchu Guan, Yaohang Li, Qi Liu, Xiaowo Wang, Can Yang, and Jianxin Wang. Foundation models in bioinformatics. *National science review*, 12(4):nwaf028, 2025
14. Zhao, H., Zhong, J., Liang, X., Xie, C., Wang, S.: Application of machine learning in drug side effect prediction: databases, methods, and challenges. Front. Comp. Sci. **19**(5), 195902 (2025)
15. Kai-Yue Gao et al. Interpretable drug target prediction using deep neural representation. In *Proceedings of the International Joint Conference on Artificial Intelligence (IJCAI)*, pages 3371–3377, 2018
16. Zhao, H., Li, B., Xie, C., Duan, G.: A multi-modal feature fusion method enhanced by dynamic sample graphs for predicting drug responses. Big Data Mining and Analytics **9**(2), 580–595 (2026)
17. Hongzhun Wang, Feng Huang, Zhankun Xiong, and Wen Zhang. A heterogeneous network-based method with attentive meta-path extraction for predicting drug–target interactions. *Briefings in Bioinformatics*, 23(4):bbac184, 2022
18. Yanyi Chu, Aman Chandra Kaushik, Xiangeng Wang, Wei Wang, Yufang Zhang, Xiaoqi Shan, Dennis Russell Salahub, Yi Xiong, and Dong-Qing Wei. Dti-cdf: a cascade deep forest model towards the prediction of drug-target interactions based on hybrid features. *Briefings in Bioinformatics*, 22(1):451–462, 2021

19. David S Wishart, Craig Knox, An Chi Guo, Dean Cheng, Savita Shrivastava, Dan Tzur, Bijaya Gautam, and Murtaza Hassanali. Drugbank: a knowledgebase for drugs, drug actions and drug targets. *Nucleic acids research*, 36(suppl_1):D901–D906, 2008
20. Sukannya Purkayastha, Ishani Mondal, Sudeshna Sarkar, Pawan Goyal, and Jitesh K Pillai. Drug-drug interactions prediction based on drug embedding and graph auto-encoder. In *2019 IEEE 19th International Conference on Bioinformatics and Bioengineering (BIBE)*, pages 547–552. IEEE, 2019
21. Chithrananda, S., Grand, G.: and Bharath Ramsundar. Large-scale self-supervised pretraining for molecular property prediction, Chemberta (2020)
22. Sapir Israeli and Yoram Louzoun. Single-residue linear and conformational b cell epitopes prediction using random and esm-2 based projections. *Briefings in Bioinformatics*, 25(2):bbae084, 03 2024
23. Yuxiao Dong, Nitesh V Chawla, and Ananthram Swami. metapath2vec: Scalable representation learning for heterogeneous networks. In *Proceedings of the 23rd ACM SIGKDD international conference on knowledge discovery and data mining*, pages 135–144, 2017
24. Ye, Q., et al.: A unified drug-target interaction prediction framework based on knowledge graph and recommendation system. Sci. Rep. **12**(1), 6775 (2021)
25. Qian Zhao et al. Gifdti: Prediction of drug-target interactions based on global molecular and intermolecular interaction representation learning. *bioRxiv*, 2022
26. Bai, P., Miljković, F., John, B., Haifeng, L.: Interpretable bilinear attention network with domain adaptation improves drug-target prediction. Nature Machine Intelligence **5**(2), 126–136 (2023)
27. Li, Y., Qiao, G., Gao, X., Wang, G.: Supervised graph co-contrastive learning for drug-target interaction prediction. Bioinformatics **38**(10), 2847–2854 (2022)
28. Zixuan, E.: Guojun Qiao, Guangyu Wang, and Yilong Li. Graph structure learning network for drug-target interaction prediction. bioRxiv, Gsl-dti (2024)
29. Li, H., et al.: Sgmdti: A unified framework for drug-target interaction prediction by semantic-guided meta-path method. In Jing Tang, Xin Lai, Zhipeng Cai, Wei Peng, and Yanjie Wei, editors, *Bioinformatics Research and Applications*, pages 314–324, Singapore, 2026. Springer Nature Singapore
30. Peng, L., et al.: BINDTI: a bi-directional intention network for drug-target interaction identification based on attention mechanisms. IEEE J. Biomed. Health Inform. **29**(3), 1602–1612 (2025)

Drug-Target-Disease Association Prediction Based on Multi-Modal Feature Fusion Transformer

Wenjun Li[1], Han Xiao[1], Wanjun Ma[2], Yiting Zhou[1], Ju Xiang[1], Cuicui Liu[3], Xiwei Tang[2], and Weijun Liang[4](✉)

[1] Hunan Provincial Key Laboratory of Intelligent Processing of Big Data on Transportation, Changsha University of Science and Technology, Changsha 410076, Hunan, China

[2] School of Computer, Hunan First Normal University, Changsha 410205, Hunan, China

[3] School of Information Engineering, Changsha Medical University, Changsha 410219, Hunan, China

[4] Department of Respiratory Medicine, Changsha Central Hospital, Changsha 410000, Hunan, China

lwj9601221@outlook.com

Abstract. Drug repositioning is an effective strategy for identifying new therapeutic uses for existing drugs, thereby reducing research and development costs and shortening clinical validation timelines. Despite advancements in deep learning-based drug-target interaction prediction methods, most models are limited to simple binary relationship modeling and fail to capture the complex tripartite associations among drugs, targets, and diseases. Furthermore, current methods struggle with heterogeneous data integration and feature representation, leading to restricted generalization capabilities for novel entities. To address these challenges, this study introduces TripleMTrans, a novel multimodal Transformer model that incorporates drug character embeddings (Word2Vec), rule-based target features, and disease-therapeutic relationship matrices to create a unified multidimensional feature space. The model employs multi-head self-attention mechanisms to dynamically capture complex correlations across heterogeneous features, enabling end-to-end prediction of potential therapeutic relationships. Experimental results demonstrate that TripleMTrans achieves exceptional performance on the Stanford BioSNAP dataset (AUC = 0.9992, Recall = 0.9990, AUPR = 0.9985), significantly outperforming existing mainstream methods. This model not only enhances prediction accuracy but also offers a new technical approach and theoretical foundation for mechanism-based drug discovery.

Keywords: Drug-Target-Disease Association · Word2Vec · Transformer · Multimodal

X. Cui et al. (Eds.): ISBRA 2026, LNBI 16690, pp. 149–161, 2027.
https://doi.org/10.1007/978-981-92-3716-6_12

1 Introduction

Traditional de novo drug discovery increasingly faces clinical setbacks and mechanistic uncertainties, while drug repositioning—identifying new therapeutic uses for existing drugs—has emerged as a complementary strategy to expand treatment indications [1–3]. These contrasting trends highlight a shift in biomedicine: as traditional discovery struggles, drug repositioning redefines therapy through "new uses for old drugs." The "double-ten dilemma"—a decade-long development cycle coupled with billion-dollar investments—has long been recognized and has intensified in recent years [4,5]. Deloitte's 2024 report shows top-20 pharma R&D returns plummeting to 1.2%, a nearly 70% decline since 2010 [6]. This trend underscores that, despite advances in disease understanding, tumor heterogeneity and complex neurodegenerative networks still cause even precision therapies to often fail [7–9]. The traditional hypothesis-driven paradigm reveals its inefficiency against such biological complexity [10].

The value of drug repositioning lies in its innovative transformation of existing knowledge systems. Unlike de novo drug discovery, repositioning leverages the safety data of marketed drugs or clinical-stage compounds, providing an inherent "risk buffer" advantage [11]. Moreover, real-world evidence from long-term clinical use serves as a unique "biological probe" for exploring new indications. Recent technological innovations have introduced unparalleled tools for "signal mining": single-cell sequencing, AI-driven molecular docking, and knowledge graphs that amalgamate multi-dimensional data [12,13]. By integrating diverse data sources, computational methods can effectively predict new applications for existing drugs. The current predominant computational strategies primarily utilize three core technologies: matrix decomposition, network analysis, and multimodal feature fusion, collectively forming a comprehensive framework for drug repositioning [14,15]. Despite these advances, current methods still face challenges that hinder clinical translation. The cold start problem is prevalent, as models struggle to incorporate newly added drugs or targets [16]. The scarcity of high-quality labeled data and reliance on unverified negative samples introduce noise bias [17]. Furthermore, insufficient model generalization means many models excel on randomly partitioned test sets but decline markedly when confronted with new drugs or target proteins [18].

To address these issues, this paper proposes a multimodal Transformer-based drug repositioning method called TripleMTrans (Triple Multimodal Transformer), which generates drug name embeddings using character-level Word2Vec, extracts rule-based target features from protein names, and constructs disease-drug relationship matrices. These low-dimensional vectors serve as initial node features and are input into a multimodal Transformer-based triplet classification model to predict drug-gene-disease associations. Experimental results demonstrate that our method surpasses existing mainstream techniques across various evaluation metrics, achieving exceptional performance (AUC = 0.9992, Recall = 0.9990) with greater predictive accuracy and robustness. By integrating features of drug molecular structures, gene target embeddings, and disease phenotypes, the model develops a cross-modal biomedical entity representation system, overcoming the limitations of traditional single-dimensional feature modeling methods and significantly enhancing prediction performance.

2 Methods

This study aims to develop a multimodal Transformer-based method for drug repositioning, focusing on predicting potential associations among drugs, targets, and diseases. The overall framework is illustrated in Fig. 1.

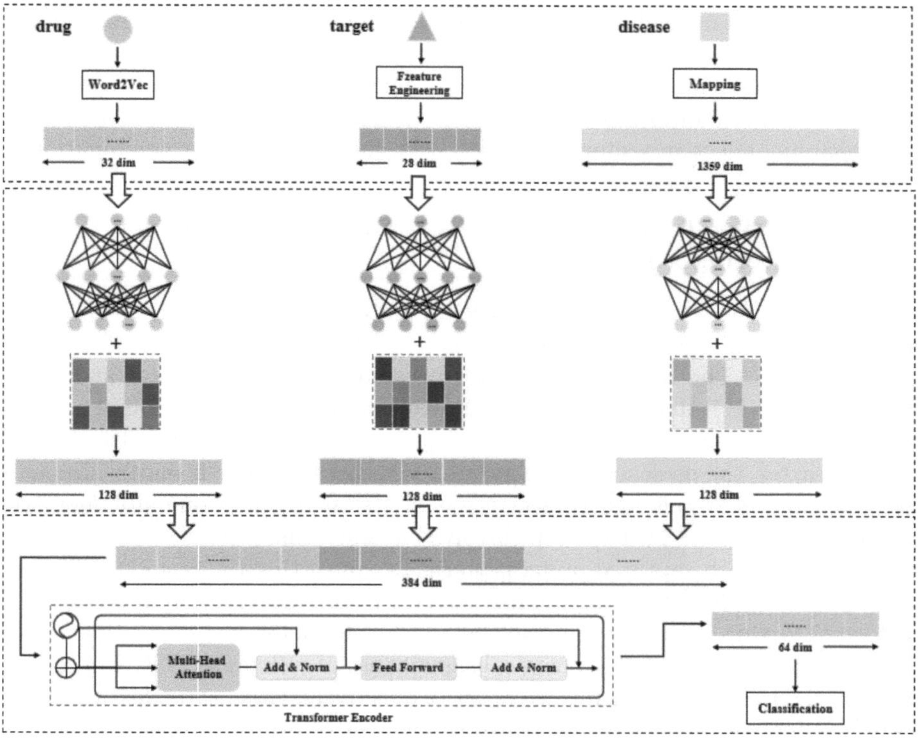

Fig. 1. TripleMTrans Framework Diagram.

2.1 Drug Feature Extraction Using Word2Vec

The first column containing drug names was analyzed: missing values were removed, entries converted to strings, and duplicate names eliminated to ensure unique identifiers. Each unique drug name was then tokenized into a list of lowercase characters. We employed the Skip-gram model within Word2Vec, which employs a self-supervised mechanism where the center character predicts its context characters, demonstrating enhanced ability to capture semantic relationships of local character combinations within limited contexts. The model maximizes the conditional probability $P(c|v)$ of context characters c given a center character v. Its three-layer architecture consists of an input layer (one-hot vector o_v), a hidden layer producing a low-dimensional vector $h = W^T o_v$, and an output layer computing context scores via $u_c = W'^T h$ followed by Softmax:

$$P(c \mid v; \theta) = \frac{\exp(\mathbf{u}_c \cdot \mathbf{v}_v)}{\sum_{n \in V} \exp(\mathbf{u}_n \cdot \mathbf{v}_v)}.$$

To generate drug name vectors, we employed a character vector averaging strategy: each drug name is decomposed into character sequences, the corresponding character vectors are retrieved from the vocabulary and averaged to form the final embedding; if all characters are out-of-vocabulary, a zero vector is used. This approach balances local character-level semantics with overall name representation, enabling effective vector generation even for rare character combinations.

2.2 Extracting Target Features Using a Rule-Based Manual Feature Engineering Method

In this study, we created a 28-dimensional feature vector by extracting fundamental statistical features, character type statistics, and ASCII encoding from protein names. The first feature type consisted of basic statistical attributes (dimensions 0-11) that describe the global characteristics of protein names, including name length, the presence of digits and uppercase letters, the type of final character, the presence of underscores, whether the name is purely alphanumeric, counts of vowels and consonants, and statistics on unique alphanumeric characters. The second feature type involved forward character encoding (dimensions 12-19), which captured prefix patterns by converting the first eight characters to their ASCII codes, with names shorter than eight characters being zero-padded. The third feature type involved reverse character encoding (dimensions 20-27), which focused on the biological significance of suffixes by ASCII-encoding the last eight characters in reverse order. Collectively, these three feature types facilitate lightweight and efficient pattern analysis of protein names.

2.3 Creating Disease-Drug Mappings

In biomedical relationship modeling, the disease-drug association matrix serves as a co-occurrence-based feature representation method. This method constructs a binary adjacency matrix that explicitly represents therapeutic relationships between diseases and drugs. The row vectors correspond to specific diseases, with each dimension mapped to a drug entity. If a known therapeutic relationship exists between disease d_i and drug t_j, the value at dimension j is set to 1; otherwise, it is 0.

This representation offers interpretability and relationship preservation, as each dimension retains the semantic information of original associations. Unlike learned embeddings, this explicit representation requires no training and is directly usable for similarity calculations, offering advantages in cold-start scenarios. This method establishes a structured representation of therapeutic knowledge, converting discrete disease-drug relationships into a numerical feature space suitable for machine learning algorithms.

2.4 Transformer-Based Drug-Target-Disease Association Prediction Model

We propose a Transformer model for predicting drug-target-disease associations.

Feature Processing. Input comprises drug, gene, and disease indices with feature vectors. Three linear layers map them to 128-dim for alignment. Learnable embeddings are fused, concatenated into a 384-dim vector, and a sequence dimension is added for Transformer input.

Multi-Head Self-Attention (MHSA). The multi-head self-attention mechanism captures interaction patterns by computing attention in parallel across multiple subspaces. Given an input matrix $X \in \mathbb{R}^{n \times d_{\text{model}}}$ with $d_{\text{model}} = 384$, we split it into $h = 2$ heads, each operating on a 192-dimensional subspace. For the i-th head, learned weight matrices $W_i^Q, W_i^K \in \mathbb{R}^{d_{\text{model}} \times d_k}$ and $W_i^V \in \mathbb{R}^{d_{\text{model}} \times d_v}$ project X into queries, keys, and values, where $d_k = d_v = d_{\text{model}}/h = 192$. The attention output is then computed via scaled dot-product and Softmax:

$$\text{head}_i = \text{softmax}\left(\frac{(XW_i^Q)(XW_i^K)^\top}{\sqrt{d_k}}\right)(XW_i^V). \tag{1}$$

Outputs from all heads are concatenated and linearly projected to produce the final multi-head representation. This architecture enables the model to focus on diverse feature interaction patterns across distinct subspaces.

Feed Forward Network(FFN). The Feed Forward Network (FFN) serves as a post-processing module for the attention mechanism, performing non-linear transformations and dimensional mapping to enhance expressive capacity. Its mathematical formulation is:

$$FFN(x) = \max(0, xW_1 + b_1)W_2 + b_2 \tag{2}$$

where W_1, W_2, b_1, b_2 are shared across all positions. This structure projects input features into a higher-dimensional space, introduces non-linearity via ReLU, and then projects back to the target dimension, capturing global feature patterns efficiently.

Residual Connections and Layer Normalization. To mitigate gradient vanishing and stabilize training, each sublayer employs residual connections and layer normalization. Layer normalization is applied before the sublayer operation, followed by residual addition: Output = Sublayer(LayerNorm(Input)) + Input. This design ensures stable feature distributions while preserving original semantic information, enhancing both training efficiency and representational capacity.

2.5 Feature Compression and Classification

The high-dimensional features from the Transformer encoder are compressed to 64 dimensions via a linear layer with ReLU activation and Dropout for regularization. These refined features are then mapped to a one-dimensional space through another linear layer and passed through a Sigmoid function to produce a probability score, indicating the confidence of an association within the drug-gene-disease triad. This compression reduces redundancy while preserving discriminative information, enhancing generalization and classification performance. The final association probability is computed as $\hat{y} = \sigma\big(W_2\,\mathrm{ReLU}(W_1 z + b_1) + b_2\big)$, where z denotes the compressed representation from the Transformer encoder, W_1, W_2, b_1, b_2 are learnable parameters, and σ is the Sigmoid function. The model is trained by minimizing the binary cross-entropy loss $\mathcal{L} = -\big[\,y \log \hat{y} + (1 - y) \log(1 - \hat{y})\,\big]$, where $y \in \{0, 1\}$ is the ground-truth label indicating whether the triplet represents a genuine association.

3 Experiment and Result

3.1 Dataset Introduction

The core data for this study was obtained from the Stanford BioSNAP dataset, a reputable public resource for biomedical network analysis [19]. We focused on two major subnetworks: the drug-target interaction (DTI) network, containing experimentally validated interactions between drugs and human target proteins, and the target-disease association (TDA) network, linking targets to diseases with biological context. The dataset comprises 1359 drug nodes, 514 target nodes, 5497 disease nodes, 15140 drug-target edges, and 426138 target-disease edges. This heterogeneous network, constructed through hierarchical associations, enables multi-hop inference pathways. All edges are biologically annotated and have undergone multi-level verification, ensuring data quality and network consistency, thus providing essential support for drug repositioning research.

3.2 Experimental Configuration

A drug–target–disease triplet is considered positive if a known drug–target interaction and a known target–disease association jointly connect the three entities in BioSNAP. Negative triplets are formed by independently sampling one drug, one target, and one disease uniformly from their respective pools; any triplet matching a known association is discarded. Training is conducted with a 1:1 positive-to-negative ratio to avoid class imbalance. To ensure full reproducibility, we set a uniform random seed of 42 across Python, NumPy, and PyTorch. Device detection automatically prioritizes GPU acceleration, falling back to CPU when necessary. We used a learning rate of 0.0001 to balance convergence speed and stability, which helps mitigate gradient oscillations in the Transformer architecture. Binary cross-entropy was employed as the loss function, and the Adam optimizer was utilized for parameter updates owing to its adaptive learning rate and stable convergence properties. On an experimental platform equipped with an NVIDIA RTX 3060 GPU, TripleMTrans completes full training in approximately two hours; its lightweight design offers potential high-throughput capability for large-scale virtual screening.

3.3 Evaluation Metrics

To thoroughly assess the performance of our proposed model in predicting drug-target-disease associations, we employed several widely recognized classification and ranking evaluation metrics. These metrics evaluate the model's predictive capability from various perspectives, as outlined below:

Accuracy(ACC). Accuracy measures the proportion of correctly classified samples among all samples, providing an intuitive overview of overall model performance:

$$ACC = \frac{TP + TN}{TP + FP + FN + TN} \tag{3}$$

where TP, TN, FP, and FN denote true positives, true negatives, false positives, and false negatives, respectively.

Precision. Precision quantifies the reliability of positive predictions by measuring the proportion of actual positive samples among all samples predicted as positive:

$$Precision = \frac{TP}{TP + FP} \tag{4}$$

Recall. Recall, also known as sensitivity or true positive rate, measures the proportion of actual positive samples that are correctly identified by the model:

$$Recall = \frac{TP}{TP + FN} \tag{5}$$

F1-Score(F1). The F1-score is the harmonic mean of precision and recall, providing a balanced assessment when both metrics are critical:

$$F1 = 2.\frac{Precision.Recall}{Precision + Recall} \tag{6}$$

Area Under the ROC Curve (AUC). AUC measures the area under the ROC curve (TPR vs. FPR), assessing overall discriminative ability. It is robust to class imbalance by focusing on ranking rather than absolute classification.

Area Under the Precision-Recall Curve (AUPR). AUPR measures the area under the Precision-Recall curve, capturing the precision–recall trade-off. It is especially informative for imbalanced datasets: higher values indicate better precision retention at high recall.

3.4 Experimental Results

Our multimodal Transformer-based model demonstrated exceptional performance on the standard test set for drug-target-disease interaction prediction, achieving the following metrics: AUC = 0.9992, Accuracy (ACC) = 0.9966, F1-Score (F1) = 0.9966, Precision = 0.9942, and Recall = 0.9990. All experiments utilized a consistent data splitting strategy, dividing the original dataset into an 80% training set, a 10% validation set, and a 10% test set. During training, mini-batches of 32 samples were employed, with data order randomized within each epoch. The model was trained on the training set and evaluated on the validation set after each epoch, with the best-performing model selected for final evaluation on the test set. All evaluation metrics were computed using standard formulas, without any manual weight adjustments or post-processing methods.

Comparative Experiments. To validate the effectiveness of our method, we compared it with several state-of-the-art deep learning models: DeepDTA (CNN-based for drug-target affinity) [20], GraphDTA (GCN for molecular graphs combined with protein sequence CNN) [21], DeepPurpose (modular framework with pretrained drug/target encoders)DeepPurpose [22], DRKG (knowledge graph embedding with RotatE) [23], and Decagon (relation-specific GCN for multi-relational networks) [24]. All models were trained and tested on identical data splits to ensure fairness.

As shown in Table 1, our TripleMTrans significantly outperforms all baselines across all metrics, achieving ACC = 0.9966, Precision = 0.9942, Recall = 0.9990, F1 = 0.9966, AUC = 0.9992, and AUPR = 0.9985. The near-perfect recall and AUC demonstrate its exceptional ability to capture true associations while maintaining high precision, effectively addressing class imbalance. The balanced performance stems from multimodal feature fusion (Word2Vec, rule-based features, disease-drug matrix) and Transformer's cross-modal attention, which together enable robust discriminative representation for drug-target-disease triplets.

Figure 2 visualizes the ROC and Precision-Recall curves. TripleMTrans maintains strong performance across most thresholds, and its PR curve remains above 0.99 even at high recall levels, which compares favorably with the baselines. These curves generally align with the numerical results in Table 1 and further illustrate the stability of our model under different threshold settings.

Table 1. Comparative Experiments Result

Model	ACC	Precision	Recall	F1	AUC	AUPR
DeepDTA	0.8632	0.8415	0.9102	0.8743	0.9215	0.8904
GraphDTA	0.8917	0.8673	0.9348	0.9001	0.9436	0.9127
DeepPurpose	0.9024	0.8891	0.9237	0.9059	0.9482	0.9215
DRKG	0.9268	0.9012	0.9614	0.9303	0.9675	0.9489
Decagon	0.9415	0.9236	0.9687	0.9455	0.9763	0.9621
TripleMTrans	**0.9966**	**0.9942**	**0.9990**	**0.9966**	**0.9992**	**0.9985**

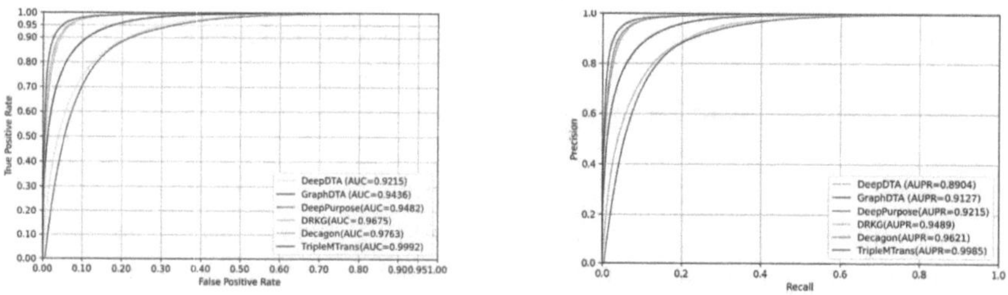

(a) ROC curves (b) PR curves

Fig. 2. ROC and PR curves of different models on the test set.

Ablation Experiment. To assess the influence of each module on the final performance of the proposed method, we conducted a systematic ablation study. This involved sequentially removing key components from the model and evaluating their effects on predictive performance. The detailed experimental design is presented in Table 2:

Table 3 illustrates the performance comparison of various model configurations on the test set.

The results show that the inclusion of each module has significantly enhanced the model's overall performance. Notably, the introduction of disease feature mapping has yielded the most substantial improvement, underscoring the importance of precise disease representation in predicting drug-target-disease associations. Additionally, protein feature extraction and drug feature extraction provide essential structural information about targets and chemical information about drugs, respectively, ensuring the comprehensiveness of multimodal features. Furthermore, the Transformer feature alignment module significantly improves the semantic consistency of cross-modal interactions by projecting heterogeneous features into a unified semantic space, thereby enhancing the model's generalization ability.

Table 2. Ablation Experiment Design

Experimental Group	Model Configuration Description
- Word2Vec	Replace Word2Vec with randomly initialized node vectors
- Feature Engineering	Replace manual protein feature engineering with randomly initialized node vectors
- Feature Mapping	Replace disease feature mapping with randomly initialized node vectors
- Transformer Linear	Remove linear layers from Transformer; use raw inputs directly
Full Model	Complete model with all components

Table 3. Ablation Experiment Result

Model	ACC	Precision	Recall	F1	AUC	AUPR
-Word2Vec	0.8921	0.8455	0.9512	0.8943	0.9612	0.9527
-Feature Engineering	0.9380	0.9217	0.9583	0.9397	0.9588	0.9491
-Feature Mapping	0.8723	0.8261	0.9325	0.8762	0.9476	0.9338
-TransformerLinear	0.9547	0.9482	0.9619	0.9550	0.9763	0.9684
Full Model	**0.9966**	**0.9942**	**0.9990**	**0.9966**	**0.9992**	**0.9985**

4 Discussion

4.1 Comparative Experimental Analysis

To assess performance, we compared TripleMTrans against five established models (DeepDTA, GraphDTA, DeepPurpose, DRKG, and Decagon) using identical data splits and positive/negative samples. Since these baselines were designed for different tasks, we adapted them for triplet classification.

DeepDTA and GraphDTA, originally regression models for binding affinity, were modified by concatenating the drug–target logit with a disease one-hot vector and adding a binary classification head. For DeepPurpose, its built-in drug and target encoders were used, while disease features were processed through an encoder of the same architecture; the three embeddings were fused via fully connected layers with default hyperparameters, and the classification head was fine-tuned. DRKG's RotatE triplet scoring (negative distance) was adopted, with the decision threshold optimized on the training set. Decagon's multi-relational GCN was extended to DTI and TDA relations, and node embeddings were fed into a dot-product decoder to produce triplet scores.

TripleMTrans significantly outperformed all baselines. It achieved an accuracy of 0.9966 (a 5.51% improvement over Decagon's 0.9415), precision of 0.9942 (vs. DeepPurpose 0.8891 and GraphDTA 0.8673), recall of 0.9990, and an F1 score of 0.9966, surpassing DRKG (0.9303) and Decagon (0.9455). AUC reached

0.9992 and AUPR 0.9985, confirming robust discriminative capability and class-imbalance adaptability. We attribute this to (1) multimodal features capturing complementary drug–target–disease information, and (2) the Transformer's cross-attention effectively modeling non-linear triplet interactions. We acknowledge that a single random split may introduce optimistic bias and that temporal or entity hold-out evaluation was not performed. However, the character-level embeddings combined with rule-based features inherently support generalization to novel entities, and the ablation study validates each component's contribution, keeping the results convincing.

4.2 Ablation Experiment Analysis

We conducted systematic ablation studies to quantify the contribution of each model component. Removing drug feature extraction (Word2Vec) reduced accuracy to 0.8435, underscoring its role in capturing molecular structure semantics. Eliminating protein feature extraction decreased recall to 0.9583, highlighting the importance of target structural features. Most notably, removing disease feature mapping caused substantial performance degradation (F1 dropping to 0.8762, AUPR to 0.9338), indicating its critical role in modeling pathological mechanisms. Even with all multimodal features retained, omitting the feature alignment mechanism limited performance (AUC decreased to 0.9763, F1 loss increased to 4.16%), demonstrating the necessity of a unified semantic space for cross-modal integration. The complete model achieved optimal performance (ACC = 0.9966, AUPR = 0.9985, Recall = 0.9990, AUC = 0.9992), confirming that the synergistic interaction of all modules—disease mapping for pathological modeling, drug/protein features for structural representation, and feature alignment for semantic consistency—collectively enables robust and accurate drug-target-disease association prediction.

5 Conclusion

In this study, we propose TripleMTrans, a multimodal Transformer-based drug repositioning framework that integrates drug, target, and disease features to achieve accurate prediction of drug-gene-disease associations. By combining character-level Word2Vec embeddings, rule-based protein features, and disease-drug association matrices within a Transformer architecture, the model effectively captures complex cross-modal relationships among biomedical entities. Experimental results demonstrate that TripleMTrans significantly outperforms existing methods across multiple evaluation metrics, achieving superior predictive accuracy and robustness. The model effectively addresses key challenges in current approaches, including the integration of heterogeneous data sources, cold-start problems with novel entities, and insufficient generalization performance. Ablation studies further validate the contribution of each multimodal component to overall prediction capability.

Despite the excellent performance achieved by TripleMTrans under the current triplet-level random split, several limitations should be acknowledged. First, the model has not been evaluated under entity-level splits (i.e., holding out entire drugs, targets, or diseases), and therefore its cold-start generalization capability remains unverified. Second, no case-level biomedical validation based on attention weights or feature importance has been provided. Third, both drug and target features rely on name strings, which makes the model potentially sensitive to non-standardized naming or missing entity information. These issues constitute the core directions for future work, including constructing entity-level evaluation benchmarks and retraining all models accordingly, identifying key modality contributions through attention visualization, and integrating structural information from molecular graphs and sequences to enhance feature robustness.

Acknowledgements. This work was supported in part by the National Key Research and Development Program of China (Grant No. 2024YFB2605500), the National Natural Science Foundation of China (Grant Nos. 62372066 and 62272309), and the Practical Innovation and Entrepreneurship Capacity Enhancement Program for Postgraduate Students of Changsha University of Science and Technology (Grant No. CLSJCX25066).

References

1. Van Dyck, C.H., et al.: LECANEMAB in early Alzheimer's disease. N. Engl. J. Med. **388**(1), 9–21 (2023)
2. Solomon, S.D., et al.: Dapagliflozin in heart failure with mildly reduced or preserved ejection fraction. N. Engl. J. Med. **387**(12), 1089–1098 (2022)
3. Verma, S.: Potential mechanisms of sodium-glucose co-transporter 2 inhibitor-related cardiovascular benefits. Am. J. Med. **132**(10), S39–S48 (2019)
4. Pushpakom, S., et al.: Drug repurposing: progress, challenges and recommendations. Nat. Rev. Drug Discov. **18**(1), 41–58 (2019)
5. Schlander, M., Hernandez-Villafuerte, K., Cheng, C.Y., Mestre-Ferrandiz, J., Baumann, M.: How much does it cost to research and develop a new drug? A systematic review and assessment. Pharmacoeconomics **39**(11), 1243–1269 (2021). https://doi.org/10.1007/s40273-021-01065-y
6. Fernald, K.D., Förster, P.C., Claassen, E., van de Burgwal, L.H.: The pharmaceutical productivity gap-incremental decline in R&D efficiency despite transient improvements. Drug Discov. Today **29**(11), 104160 (2024)
7. Ramón y Cajal, S., et al.: Clinical implications of intratumor heterogeneity: challenges and opportunities. J. Mol.r Med. **98**(2), 161–177 (2020)
8. Thakur, S., Dhapola, R., Sarma, P., Medhi, B., Reddy, D.H.: Neuroinflammation in Alzheimer's disease: current progress in molecular signaling and therapeutics. Inflammation **46**(1), 1–17 (2023)
9. Pich, O., Bailey, C., Watkins, T.B., Zaccaria, S., Jamal-Hanjani, M., Swanton, C.: The translational challenges of precision oncology. Cancer Cell **40**(5), 458–478 (2022)
10. Sadri, A.: Is target-based drug discovery efficient? discovery and "off-target" mechanisms of all drugs. J. Med. Chem. **66**(18), 12651–12677 (2023). https://doi.org/10.1021/acs.jmedchem.2c01737

11. Nossier, E.S., Anwar, M.M., El-Zahabi, M.A.: Recent advances in drug repositioning and rediscovery for different therapeutic activities utilizing updated technological approaches. Mol. Diversity, 1–28 (2025)
12. Jagadeesh, K.A., et al.: Identifying disease-critical cell types and cellular processes by integrating single-cell RNA-sequencing and human genetics. Nat. Genet. **54**(10), 1479–1492 (2022)
13. Zhao, H., et al.: Benchmarking ai-powered docking methods from the perspective of virtual screening. Nat. Mach. Intell. **7**(3), 509–520 (2025)
14. Yang, X., Yang, G., Chu, J.: The computational drug repositioning without negative sampling. IEEE/ACM Trans. Comput. Biol. Bioinf. **20**(2), 1506–1517 (2022)
15. Korotcov, A., Tkachenko, V., Russo, D.P., Ekins, S.: Comparison of deep learning with multiple machine learning methods and metrics using diverse drug discovery data sets. Mol. Pharm. **14**(12), 4462–4475 (2017)
16. Liu, Y., Wu, M., Miao, C., Zhao, P., Li, X.L.: Neighborhood regularized logistic matrix factorization for drug-target interaction prediction. PLoS Comput. Biol. **12**(2), e1004760 (2016)
17. Yang, Z., et al.: Does negative sampling matter? A review with insights into its theory and applications. IEEE Trans. Pattern Anal. Mach. Intell. (2024)
18. Wang, X., Zhu, M., Bo, D., Cui, P., Shi, C., Pei, J.: AM-GCN: adaptive multichannel graph convolutional networks. In: Proceedings of the 26th ACM SIGKDD International Conference on Knowledge Discovery & Data Mining, pp. 1243–1253 (2020)
19. Song, T., Zhang, X., Ding, M., Rodriguez-Paton, A., Wang, S., Wang, G.: Deep-Fusion: a deep learning based multi-scale feature fusion method for predicting drug-target interactions. Methods **204**, 269–277 (2022)
20. Öztürk, H., Özgür, A., Ozkirimli, E.: DeepDTA: deep drug-target binding affinity prediction. Bioinformatics **34**(17), i821–i829 (2018)
21. Nguyen, T., Le, H., Quinn, T.P., Nguyen, T., Le, T.D., Venkatesh, S.: Graphdta: predicting drug-target binding affinity with graph neural networks. Bioinformatics **37**(8), 1140–1147 (2021)
22. Huang, K., Fu, T., Glass, L.M., Zitnik, M., Xiao, C., Sun, J.: DeepPurpose: a deep learning library for drug-target interaction prediction. Bioinformatics **36**(22–23), 5545–5547 (2020)
23. Ioannidis, V.N., et al.: DRKG-drug repurposing knowledge graph for covid-19. arXiv preprint arXiv:2010.09600 (2020)
24. Zitnik, M., Agrawal, M., Leskovec, J.: Modeling polypharmacy side effects with graph convolutional networks. Bioinformatics **34**(13), i457–i466 (2018)

MORM: Multi-omics-Guided Region Mining and Cross-Modal Interaction for Multimodal Survival Prediction

Yan Li[1], Xin Xu[2], Jiadi Luo[3], Qingchun Liang[3(✉)], and Shaoliang Peng[1(✉)]

[1] College of Computer Science and Electronic Engineering, Hunan University, Changsha 410082, Hunan, China
slpeng@hnu.edu.cn

[2] College of Intelligence Science and Technology, National University of Defense Technology, Changsha 410073, China

[3] Department of Pathology, The Second Xiangya Hospital, Central South University, Changsha 410011, Hunan, China
503079@csu.edu.cn

Abstract. Accurate survival prediction is essential for precision oncology, yet most existing multimodal methods encode pathology and omics data independently and fuse them only at a late stage, preventing molecular information from explicitly guiding region-level pathology modeling. This limitation makes it difficult to identify pathological regions that are truly relevant to prognosis under patient-specific molecular heterogeneity. To address this issue, we propose MORM, a Multi-Omics-guided Region Mining framework with cross-modal interaction for multimodal survival prediction. MORM first learns omics representations from mRNA expression and DNA methylation data, and uses the fused omics context to score and select prognosis-relevant WSI regions. The retained regions are then summarized into a compact set of visual prototypes through prototype aggregation, followed by prototype-omics cross-attention to capture structured cross-modal associations for survival risk estimation. Experiments on TCGA-BRCA, TCGA-GBMLGG, and TCGA-LUAD achieve C-index scores of 0.740 ± 0.033, 0.858 ± 0.020, and 0.678 ± 0.031, respectively, consistently outperforming representative baseline methods. These results demonstrate that introducing molecular guidance before pathology abstraction provides a more effective paradigm than conventional late-fusion multimodal survival frameworks.

Keywords: Multimodal survival prediction · Multi-omics-guided region mining · Computational pathology

1 Introduction

Accurate survival prediction is important for precision oncology, as it supports patient risk stratification and individualized treatment planning [10]. With the

X. Cui et al. (Eds.): ISBRA 2026, LNBI 16690, pp. 162–173, 2027.
https://doi.org/10.1007/978-981-92-3716-6_13

rapid development of digital pathology and high-throughput sequencing technologies, multimodal survival modeling based on whole slide images (WSIs) and molecular data has attracted increasing attention [13]. More recent studies have further explored stronger multimodal integration strategies for cancer survival prediction [11].Recent studies have shown that combining histopathology with omics information can improve prognostic modeling compared with single-modality approaches, including representative methods such as MCAT [1], PORPOISE [2], SurvPath [6], and HEALNet [4].

Despite these advances, most existing multimodal survival methods still follow a paradigm of independent modality encoding followed by fusion at a later stage [1,2,4,6]. Under this design, pathology and omics representations interact only after pathology regions have already been selected, summarized, or abstracted. As a result, molecular information cannot explicitly guide region-level pathology modeling. This limitation is nontrivial for survival prediction, because visually salient regions are not always the most prognostically informative, especially under substantial inter-patient molecular heterogeneity [15]. Therefore, the key challenge is not only how to fuse pathology and omics representations, but also how to allow molecular information to guide which pathology regions should be retained for downstream survival modeling [9].

To address this issue, we propose MORM, a Multi-Omics-guided Region Mining framework with cross-modal interaction for multimodal survival prediction. MORM moves molecular guidance ahead of pathology abstraction. Specifically, it first encodes mRNA expression and DNA methylation into modality-specific representations and fuses them into a unified omics context. This omics representation is then used to score WSI patches and select prognosis-relevant pathology regions through hard region mining. The retained regions are further summarized into a compact set of visual prototypes, followed by prototype-omics interaction for survival risk estimation.

We evaluate MORM on three TCGA cohorts, including BRCA, GBMLGG, and LUAD [14]. Experimental results show that MORM achieves C-index scores of 0.740 ± 0.033, 0.858 ± 0.020, and 0.678 ± 0.031, respectively, outperforming representative baselines such as DeepSurv [8], MCAT [1], SurvPath [6], Porpoise [2], and HealNet [4]. Ablation studies further verify the contribution of omics-guided scoring, hard region mining, prototype aggregation, and cross-modal interaction. These results suggest that introducing molecular guidance before pathology abstraction provides a more effective paradigm for multimodal survival prediction.

The main contributions of this work are summarized as follows:

1. We propose MORM, a multimodal survival prediction framework that introduces molecular guidance before pathology abstraction, enabling patient-specific omics information to explicitly guide pathology region selection.
2. We develop a unified modeling pipeline that integrates omics-guided region scoring, hard region mining, prototype aggregation, and prototype-omics cross-modal interaction for multimodal survival modeling.

3. Extensive experiments on three TCGA cohorts demonstrate that MORM consistently outperforms representative baselines, while ablation studies verify the effectiveness of each proposed component.

2 Related Work

WSI-Based and Omics-Based Survival Modeling. WSI-based survival prediction is commonly formulated under the multiple instance learning (MIL) framework, where a slide is represented as a bag of patches and aggregated into a slide-level representation [12,18]. In parallel, omics-based survival models such as DeepSurv estimate patient risk from molecular features alone [8]. Although these approaches are effective within their respective modalities, they cannot jointly model the complementary pathological and molecular information required for more comprehensive survival prediction.

Multimodal Survival Prediction. To integrate pathology and molecular data, recent studies have proposed multimodal survival frameworks. MCAT introduces co-attention between WSI and genomic features [1], PORPOISE performs pan-cancer histology-genomic integration via multimodal learning [2], SurvPath models dense interactions between biological pathways and histology [6], and HEALNet explores multimodal fusion for heterogeneous biomedical data [4]. Despite their effectiveness, many existing multimodal survival methods still follow a paradigm of modality-specific encoding followed by cross-modal fusion at a later stage [17]. Under this design, molecular information is introduced only after pathology regions have already been selected or abstracted, which limits its ability to guide region-level pathology modeling. Different from these approaches, MORM introduces molecular guidance before pathology abstraction by using fused omics representations to guide pathology region scoring and selection, followed by prototype-based abstraction and prototype-omics interaction for survival prediction.

3 Method

Given a patient, MORM takes as input a set of WSI patch features $H = \{h_1, h_2, \ldots, h_n\}$, an mRNA expression profile x^{rna}, and a DNA methylation profile x^{meth}, and outputs a survival risk score optimized by the Cox partial likelihood. Unlike conventional multimodal survival frameworks that introduce omics information only after pathology features have been aggregated, MORM moves molecular guidance ahead of pathology abstraction, enabling patient-specific omics context to directly influence pathology region modeling.

Specifically, MORM first encodes mRNA and DNA methylation data into modality-specific embeddings and fuses them into a unified omics representation. This fused omics context is then used to score WSI patch features and select prognosis-relevant pathology regions through hard region mining. The retained regions are further summarized into a compact set of visual prototypes, which interact with omics tokens via cross-attention to model structured cross-modal associations. Finally, the resulting slide-level representation is concatenated with the fused omics representation for survival risk prediction (Fig. 1).

3.1 Multimodal Feature Extraction

MORM begins by encoding multimodal inputs, including mRNA expression, DNA methylation, and WSI patch features, into their corresponding latent representations.

Omics Encoding. Given an mRNA expression profile $x^{rna} \in R^{d_r}$ and a DNA methylation profile $x^{meth} \in R^{d_m}$, we employ two modality-specific encoders to obtain their latent embeddings:

$$z_{rna} = E_{rna}(x^{rna}), \qquad z_{meth} = E_{meth}(x^{meth}), \tag{1}$$

where $E_{rna}(\cdot)$ and $E_{meth}(\cdot)$ denote learnable encoders, and $z_{rna}, z_{meth} \in R^d$.

To capture complementary molecular information across modalities, we further fuse the two embeddings into a unified omics representation:

$$z_{omics} = F_{omics}(z_{rna}, z_{meth}), \tag{2}$$

where $F_{omics}(\cdot)$ is implemented as an MLP-based fusion module. The resulting z_{omics} serves as a patient-specific molecular context for subsequent region selection and cross-modal interaction.

Pathology Encoding. A whole slide image is represented as a bag of patch-level features:

$$H = \{h_1, h_2, \ldots, h_n\}, \qquad h_i \in R^d, \tag{3}$$

where each patch feature h_i is extracted by a patch encoder from the corresponding WSI region.

These multimodal representations, including z_{rna}, z_{meth}, z_{omics}, and H, provide the foundation for the subsequent omics-guided region selection and cross-modal modeling.

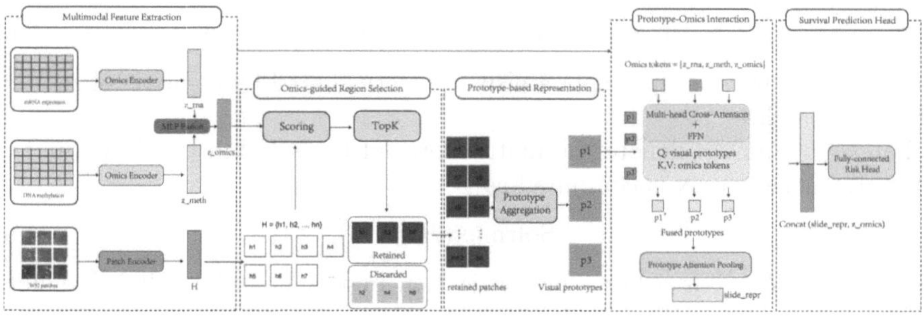

Fig. 1. Overall framework of MORM. The model first encodes mRNA expression, DNA methylation, and WSI patch features, then performs omics-guided region selection, prototype-based representation learning, prototype-omics interaction, and final survival risk prediction.

3.2 Omics-Guided Region Selection

Conventional WSI-based survival models usually rank pathology patches using visual information alone, which may be insufficient for identifying prognosis-relevant regions under patient-specific molecular heterogeneity. To overcome this limitation, MORM performs pathology region selection under explicit molecular guidance.

Given the patch feature set $H = \{h_1, h_2, \ldots, h_n\}$ and the fused omics representation z_{omics}, we compute an omics-conditioned score for each patch:

$$s_i = S(h_i, z_{omics}), \tag{4}$$

where $S(\cdot)$ is a learnable scoring function implemented on the concatenated feature $[h_i; z_{omics}]$. The score quantifies how well each pathology region matches the patient-specific molecular context.

We then retain only the top-K scored patches:

$$H^{sel} = \text{TopK}(H, \{s_i\}_{i=1}^{n}), \tag{5}$$

where $H^{sel} = \{h_{i_1}, h_{i_2}, \ldots, h_{i_K}\}$ and $K \ll n$. By filtering pathology regions before prototype abstraction and cross-modal interaction, this design not only suppresses redundant or noisy WSI patches, but also allows downstream pathology modeling to focus on regions that are more likely to be prognostically informative in the given molecular context.

3.3 Prototype-Based Representation

Although omics-guided region selection removes many irrelevant patches, the retained set H^{sel} may still contain redundancy, since multiple patches often correspond to similar local tissue patterns. MORM therefore further abstracts the selected patches into a small set of visual prototypes.

Given the selected patch set

$$H^{sel} = \{h_{i_1}, h_{i_2}, \ldots, h_{i_K}\}, \tag{6}$$

we construct a prototype set

$$P = \{p_1, p_2, \ldots, p_M\}, \qquad p_j \in R^d, \quad M \ll K, \tag{7}$$

where each prototype represents a visual pattern shared by a subset of retained pathology patches.

Let $H^{sel} \in R^{K \times d}$ denote the matrix form of the selected patch features. A soft assignment matrix is computed as

$$A = \text{Softmax}(H^{sel} W_p), \tag{8}$$

where $W_p \in R^{d \times M}$ is a learnable projection matrix and $A \in R^{K \times M}$ denotes the patch-to-prototype assignment weights. Each prototype is then obtained as a weighted combination of the selected patches:

$$p_j = \sum_{k=1}^{K} A_{k,j}\, h_{i_k}, \qquad j = 1, \ldots, M. \tag{9}$$

3.4 Prototype-Omics Interaction and Survival Prediction

Based on the prototype set $P = \{p_1, p_2, \ldots, p_M\}$, MORM models the associations between representative pathology patterns and molecular states through cross-modal interaction. Instead of directly interacting with all retained patches, this interaction is performed at the prototype level.

Specifically, we construct an omics token set by combining the modality-specific and fused omics embeddings:

$$T^{omics} = [z_{rna}, z_{meth}, z_{omics}], \tag{10}$$

where z_{rna} and z_{meth} preserve modality-specific molecular characteristics, while z_{omics} provides a unified omics context. We then use the visual prototypes as queries and the omics tokens as keys and values in a multi-head cross-attention module:

$$P' = \text{MHCA}(Q = P,\ K = T^{omics},\ V = T^{omics}) + P, \tag{11}$$

followed by a feed-forward network for feature refinement.

The refined prototypes are aggregated into a slide-level pathology representation through attention pooling:

$$z_{slide} = \text{Pool}(P'). \tag{12}$$

We then concatenate the slide-level pathology representation with the fused omics representation:

$$z = [z_{slide}; z_{omics}], \tag{13}$$

and feed it into a fully connected prediction head to estimate the patient-specific survival risk:

$$\hat{r} = f_{risk}(z). \tag{14}$$

The model is optimized using the Cox partial likelihood loss for right-censored survival data [3].

4 Experiments

4.1 Datasets

We evaluated the proposed method on three TCGA cohorts, including BRCA, GBMLGG, and LUAD. For each cohort, multimodal data were collected from The Cancer Genome Atlas (TCGA), including mRNA expression, DNA methylation, whole slide images (WSIs), and corresponding survival annotations.

For multimodal survival modeling, the mRNA and DNA methylation modalities were constructed from the corresponding TCGA molecular profiles, while the pathology modality was represented by patch-level features extracted from preprocessed WSIs. To ensure cross-modal consistency, only patients with all three modalities and valid survival information were retained. The final cohort statistics are summarized in Table 1.

Table 1. Statistics of the three TCGA cohorts used in this study.

Statistic	BRCA	GBMLGG	LUAD
Number of patients	403	332	371
WSI feature dimension	384	384	384
Number of DNA methylation features	20,977	20,977	20,977
Number of mRNA features	19,908	19,908	19,908
Censored/uncensored	339/64	205/127	234/137
Median follow-up time (months)	37.40	31.92	31.28

Table 1 summarizes the statistics of the three cohorts. The final BRCA, GBMLGG, and LUAD cohorts contain 403, 332, and 371 patients, respectively. The mRNA and DNA methylation feature dimensions are 19,908 and 20,977 for all three cohorts, while the extracted WSI feature dimensionality is 384 for BRCA, GBMLGG and LUAD. We also report the numbers of censored and uncensored patients, together with the median follow-up time, to characterize the survival distributions of the three cohorts.

4.2 Experimental Setup

All experiments were conducted under a unified five-fold cross-validation protocol on each cohort. MORM jointly modeled mRNA expression, DNA methylation, and WSI data, and performance was evaluated by the concordance index (C-index), reported as mean$\pm$standard deviation over the five folds.

The model was trained with AdamW for at most 60 epochs, with early stopping (patience = 10) based on the validation Cox partial likelihood loss. Hyperparameters were tuned independently for each cohort, where the learning rate was selected from {0.0001, 0.0003, 0.0005}, the weight decay from $\{0, 10^{-5}, 10^{-4}, 5 \times 10^{-4}\}$, and the dropout ratios for the WSI, omics, and fusion modules from {0.1, 0.25, 0.4}. Other structural parameters were fixed during training.

4.3 Baselines

We compared MORM with representative omics-only, WSI-only, and multimodal survival prediction methods. DeepSurv [8] was used as the omics-only baseline. The WSI-only baselines included ILRA [16], ABMIL [5], and TransMIL [12]. The multimodal baselines included MCAT [1], SurvPath [6], Porpoise [2], and HealNet [4]. All methods were evaluated under the same five-fold cross-validation protocol for fair comparison.

As shown in Table 2, MORM achieves the highest C-index across all three TCGA cohorts, consistently outperforming both single-modal and multimodal baselines. On the BRCA dataset, it reaches 0.740 ± 0.033, outperforming the strongest multimodal baseline HealNet by 0.005 and the best WSI-only method

Table 2. C-index comparison of omics-only, WSI-only, and multimodal methods on the three TCGA cohorts. The best result in each column is highlighted in bold.

Category	Method	BRCA	GBMLGG	LUAD
Omics-only	DeepSurv	0.638 ± 0.092	0.833 ± 0.031	0.625 ± 0.017
WSI-only	ILRA	0.629 ± 0.021	0.839 ± 0.028	0.627 ± 0.054
	ABMIL	0.622 ± 0.041	0.837 ± 0.023	0.623 ± 0.063
	TransMIL	0.636 ± 0.050	0.840 ± 0.035	0.628 ± 0.029
Multimodal	MCAT	0.728 ± 0.061	0.846 ± 0.027	0.645 ± 0.031
	SurvPath	0.715 ± 0.074	0.833 ± 0.033	0.630 ± 0.046
	Porpoise	0.729 ± 0.023	0.844 ± 0.020	0.652 ± 0.046
	HealNet	0.735 ± 0.062	0.843 ± 0.031	0.657 ± 0.040
	MORM (Ours)	**0.740±0.033**	**0.858±0.020**	**0.678±0.031**

TransMIL by 0.104, which highlights the effectiveness of multi-omics guidance in selecting prognostically relevant pathological regions. On GBMLGG, MORM scores 0.858 ± 0.020, surpassing the leading omics-only model DeepSurv by 0.025 and the top multimodal baseline MCAT by 0.012. This improvement can be attributed to the prototype-omics cross-attention mechanism, which captures structured cross-modal associations for accurate risk estimation. Even on the more challenging LUAD dataset, MORM still leads with 0.678 ± 0.031, outperforming HealNet by 0.021, demonstrating its robustness across different cancer types.

Multimodal methods generally outperform both omics-only and WSI-only approaches across all datasets, confirming the complementary nature of molecular and pathological information in survival prediction. MORM also consistently outperforms late-fusion multimodal baselines such as SurvPath and Porpoise, supporting our core hypothesis that introducing molecular guidance before pathology abstraction yields better results than conventional late-stage fusion. The consistent performance gains on three distinct cancer cohorts further validate that our multi-omics-guided region mining framework effectively alleviates patient-specific molecular heterogeneity, enabling more accurate and generalizable survival prediction.

4.4 Ablation Study

Fusion and Modality Combination Ablation. To investigate the effect of different fusion strategies and modality combinations, we compared the proposed full model (*current_wsi_rna_meth*) with conventional early fusion and late fusion under the same three-modality setting, as well as three dual-modality variants, including WSI+mRNA, WSI+DNA methylation, and mRNA+DNA methylation.

As shown in Table 3, the proposed full model achieves the best performance on all three cohorts, reaching 0.740 ± 0.033, 0.858 ± 0.020, and 0.678 ± 0.031 on

Table 3. Ablation results of different fusion strategies and modality combinations. W, R, and M denote WSI, mRNA, and DNA methylation, respectively. The best result in each column is highlighted in bold.

Setting	BRCA	GBMLGG	LUAD
Fusion strategy			
Current (W+R+M)	**0.740±0.033**	**0.858±0.020**	**0.678±0.031**
Late fusion (W+R+M)	0.665 ± 0.086	0.839 ± 0.028	0.654 ± 0.040
Early fusion (W+R+M)	0.670 ± 0.061	0.837 ± 0.028	0.633 ± 0.044
Modality combination			
Late fusion (W+M)	0.691 ± 0.030	0.838 ± 0.032	0.645 ± 0.053
Late fusion (W+R)	0.701 ± 0.062	0.824 ± 0.028	0.654 ± 0.039
Late fusion (R+M)	0.681 ± 0.012	0.837 ± 0.029	0.640 ± 0.036

BRCA, GBMLGG, and LUAD, respectively. Both conventional early fusion and late fusion yield consistently inferior results, indicating that the proposed multimodal modeling strategy is more effective than directly combining modalities at an early or late stage.

All dual-modality variants also perform worse than the full three-modality model, suggesting that WSI, mRNA, and DNA methylation provide complementary information for survival prediction. We also observe that the relative effectiveness of dual-modality combinations varies across cancer types: WSI+mRNA performs better on BRCA and LUAD, whereas WSI+DNA methylation is slightly more competitive on GBMLGG. Nevertheless, the full three-modality model remains the best-performing configuration overall.

Component Ablation. We further performed component ablation to evaluate the contribution of each module in MORM. In each ablation setting, one component was removed from the full model while keeping the remaining pipeline unchanged. Specifically, *w/o co-attention* removes the prototype-omics cross-modal interaction module and directly uses the pathology representation for downstream prediction. *w/o prototype aggregation* bypasses the prototype abstraction step and directly uses the retained pathology patches for subsequent modeling. *w/o hard mining* removes the TopK-based hard patch selection step in the region selection module. *w/o omics-guided scoring* removes the omics-conditioned scoring function and replaces it with pathology-only scoring for region selection.

As shown in Table 4, the full MORM model achieves the best performance on all three cohorts, with the highest average C-index of 0.759. Removing any component leads to a clear performance drop, confirming that each module contributes to the overall effectiveness of the framework.

Notably, removing omics-guided scoring causes the largest degradation, reducing the average C-index to 0.704. This highlights the importance of early molecular guidance in selecting prognosis-relevant pathological regions, as the performance drop is especially pronounced on BRCA (from 0.740 to 0.633).

Table 4. Component ablation results of MORM on the BRCA, GBMLGG, and LUAD cohorts. Avg denotes the average C-index across the three cohorts. The best result in each column is highlighted in bold.

Setting	BRCA	GBMLGG	LUAD	Avg
Full model	**0.740±0.033**	**0.858±0.020**	**0.678±0.031**	**0.759**
w/o co-attention	0.670 ± 0.081	0.842 ± 0.026	0.642 ± 0.056	0.718
w/o prototype aggregation	0.652 ± 0.045	0.842 ± 0.020	0.646 ± 0.070	0.713
w/o hard mining	0.670 ± 0.096	0.837 ± 0.026	0.633 ± 0.067	0.713
w/o omics-guided scoring	0.633 ± 0.084	0.839 ± 0.027	0.641 ± 0.060	0.704

Removing prototype aggregation or hard mining also reduces the average C-index to 0.713, showing that both compact visual abstraction and focused learning on informative patches are critical for robust prediction. Meanwhile, removing co-attention lowers the average C-index to 0.718, indicating that explicit prototype-omics interaction helps refine multimodal alignment and improve predictive power.

These results collectively demonstrate that the performance gain of MORM arises from the joint contribution of all four components, validating the rationality and necessity of our integrated design.

4.5 Kaplan–Meier Analysis

To further evaluate the clinical stratification ability of MORM, we divided patients into high-risk and low-risk groups according to the median predicted risk score and plotted Kaplan–Meier survival curves for the three TCGA cohorts [7]. As shown in Fig. 2, the two risk groups are clearly separated on BRCA,

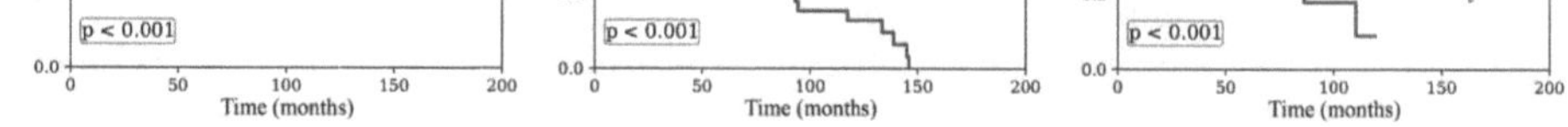

Fig. 2. Kaplan–Meier survival curves of the high-risk and low-risk groups stratified by the predicted risk scores of MORM on the BRCA, GBMLGG, and LUAD cohorts. Patients were divided into two groups according to the median predicted risk score. The separation between the two groups is statistically significant on all three cohorts based on the log-rank test.

GBMLGG, and LUAD, indicating that the risk scores produced by MORM can effectively stratify patients with distinct survival outcomes.

In particular, the high-risk group consistently exhibits worse survival probability than the low-risk group across all three cohorts. The log-rank test shows statistically significant differences between the two groups, with $p < 0.001$ on BRCA, GBMLGG, and LUAD. These results indicate that MORM not only improves C-index performance, but also provides meaningful survival stratification ability.

5 Conclusion

In this work, we proposed MORM, a multimodal survival prediction framework that introduces molecular guidance before pathology abstraction to address the limitations of conventional late-fusion methods. By using fused omics representations to guide both pathology region selection and cross-modal modeling, MORM learns more prognostically relevant multimodal representations. Experiments on three TCGA cohorts show that MORM consistently outperforms representative baselines. Ablation studies and Kaplan-Meier analysis further validate the effectiveness of each key component and the clinical utility of the proposed framework. Overall, our results demonstrate that integrating molecular guidance into region-level pathology modeling offers a promising direction for multimodal survival prediction in precision oncology.

Acknowledgements. This work was supported by National Key R&D Program of China 2022YFC3400400, 2023YFC3503400; NSFC-FDCT Grants 62361166662; The Innovative Research Group Project of Hunan Province 2024JJ1002; Key R&D Program of Hunan Province 2023GK2004, 2023SK2059, 2023SK2060; Top 10 Technical Key Project in Hunan Province 2023GK1010; Key Technologies R&D Program of Guangdong Province (2023B1111030004 to FFH). The Funds of State Key Laboratory of Chemo and Biosensing, the National Supercomputing Center in Changsha http://nscc.hnu.edu.cn/, and Peng Cheng Lab.

References

1. Chen, R.J., et al.: Multimodal co-attention transformer for survival prediction in gigapixel whole slide images. In: Proceedings of the IEEE/CVF International Conference on Computer Vision, pp. 4015–4025 (2021)
2. Chen, R.J., et al.: Pan-cancer integrative histology-genomic analysis via multimodal deep learning. Cancer Cell **40**(8), 865–878 (2022)
3. Cox, D.R.: Regression models and life-tables. J. Roy. Stat. Soc.: Ser. B (Methodol.) **34**(2), 187–202 (1972)
4. Hemker, K., Simidjievski, N., Jamnik, M.: HEALNET: multimodal fusion for heterogeneous biomedical data. Adv. Neural. Inf. Process. Syst. **37**, 64479–64498 (2024)
5. Ilse, M., Tomczak, J., Welling, M.: Attention-based deep multiple instance learning. In: International Conference on Machine Learning, pp. 2127–2136. PMLR (2018)

6. Jaume, G., Vaidya, A., Chen, R.J., Williamson, D.F., Liang, P.P., Mahmood, F.: Modeling dense multimodal interactions between biological pathways and histology for survival prediction. In: Proceedings of the IEEE/CVF Conference on Computer Vision and Pattern Recognition, pp. 11579–11590 (2024)
7. Kaplan, E.L., Meier, P.: Nonparametric estimation from incomplete observations. J. Am. Stat. Assoc. **53**(282), 457–481 (1958)
8. Katzman, J.L., Shaham, U., Cloninger, A., Bates, J., Jiang, T., Kluger, Y.: DeepSURV: personalized treatment recommender system using a cox proportional hazards deep neural network. BMC Med. Res. Methodol. **18**(1), 24 (2018)
9. Marouf, A.A., Rokne, J.G., Alhajj, R.: Integrating multi-omics and medical imaging in artificial intelligence-based cancer research: an umbrella review of fusion strategies and applications. Cancers **17**(22), 3638 (2025)
10. Parvaiz, A., Nasir, E.S., Fraz, M.M.: From pixels to prognosis: a survey on AI-driven cancer patient survival prediction using digital histology images. J. Imaging Inf. Med. **37**(4), 1728–1751 (2024)
11. Raza, M., Azam, A., Qaiser, T., Rajpoot, N.: PS3: a multimodal transformer integrating pathology reports with histology images and biological pathways for cancer survival prediction. In: Proceedings of the IEEE/CVF International Conference on Computer Vision, pp. 22175–22186 (2025)
12. Shao, Z., Bian, H., Chen, Y., Wang, Y., Zhang, J., Ji, X., et al.: TRANSMIL: transformer based correlated multiple instance learning for whole slide image classification. Adv. Neural. Inf. Process. Syst. **34**, 2136–2147 (2021)
13. Wang, S., Zhang, S., Lai, H., Huo, W., Zhang, Q.: Pomp: pathology-omics multimodal pre-training framework for cancer survival prediction. In: Proceedings of the Thirty-Fourth International Joint Conference on Artificial Intelligence, pp. 7813–7821 (2025)
14. Weinstein, J.N., et al.: The cancer genome atlas pan-cancer analysis project. Nat. Genet. **45**(10), 1113–1120 (2013)
15. Wekesa, J.S., Kimwele, M.: A review of multi-omics data integration through deep learning approaches for disease diagnosis, prognosis, and treatment. Front. Genet. **14**, 1199087 (2023)
16. Xiang, J., Zhang, J.: Exploring low-rank property in multiple instance learning for whole slide image classification. In: The Eleventh International Conference on Learning Representations (2023)
17. Xu, Y., Zhou, F., Zhao, C., Wang, Y., Yang, C., Chen, H.: Distilled prompt learning for incomplete multimodal survival prediction. In: Proceedings of the Computer Vision and Pattern Recognition Conference, pp. 5102–5111 (2025)
18. Zhang, H., et al.: DTFD-MIL: double-tier feature distillation multiple instance learning for histopathology whole slide image classification. In: Proceedings of the IEEE/CVF Conference on Computer Vision and Pattern Recognition, pp. 18802–18812 (2022)

GENE-M1: Cross-Species Genomic Discovery Enhanced by a Taxon-Specific Mixture-of-Experts Model

Yuhang Li[1], Jiaqi Tang[1,2], Jianmin Chen[1], Yourui Han[1], Xueque Shang[1], and Bolin Chen[1(✉)]

[1] School of Computer Science, Northwestern Polytechnical University, Xi'an 710072, Shaanxi, China
blchen@nwpu.edu.cn
[2] The Hong Kong University of Science and Technology, Hong Kong SAR, China

Abstract. Existing genomic foundation models have advanced cross-species sequence modeling, but they largely process all genomes through a uniform architecture. Such one-size-fits-all designs overlook the hierarchical organization of biological taxonomy, making taxon-specific features harder to separate and weakening both fine-grained classification and out-of-distribution generalization to unseen species. To address this, **GENE-M1** is introduced as a novel Mixture-of-Experts (MoE) framework whose architecture is strictly governed by biological taxonomy. The framework is built on three core components: (1) a hierarchical expert architecture that instantiates specialized modules for taxonomic ranks (Domain, Kingdom, Phylum, Class) to enable taxon-specific processing; (2) a dynamic router that activates taxonomy-aligned expert branches for each sequence, enabling hierarchical feature extraction; and (3) a progressive training strategy that transfers knowledge from higher to lower taxonomic ranks for stable optimization. **GM-DATA** is also constructed as a large-scale, taxonomically aligned benchmark comprising 294 species across 5 kingdoms, 18 phyla, and 62 classes, providing broad and balanced coverage of major clades. In addition, a held-out evaluation set, **GM-DATA**(eval), containing 15 unseen species, is included for rigorous cross-species evaluation. Extensive experiments on this benchmark show that **GENE-M1** significantly outperforms state-of-the-art baselines in few-shot classification and unsupervised clustering, demonstrating that explicit taxonomic alignment is key to robust and interpretable genomic representation learning.

Keywords: Cross-species genomics · Mixture-of-Experts (MoE) · Taxon-specific modeling · Genomic Discovery

1 Introduction

With the rapid development of high-throughput sequencing technologies, genomic data are being generated at unprecedented scale across diverse species,

X. Cui et al. (Eds.): ISBRA 2026, LNBI 16690, pp. 174–185, 2027.
https://doi.org/10.1007/978-981-92-3716-6_14

creating new opportunities for large-scale genomic discovery [1–4]. Meanwhile, genomic foundation models [5–10] have substantially advanced genomic representation learning and enabled a wide range of downstream applications, including promoter and enhancer prediction, transcription-factor binding analysis, and variant-effect prioritization.

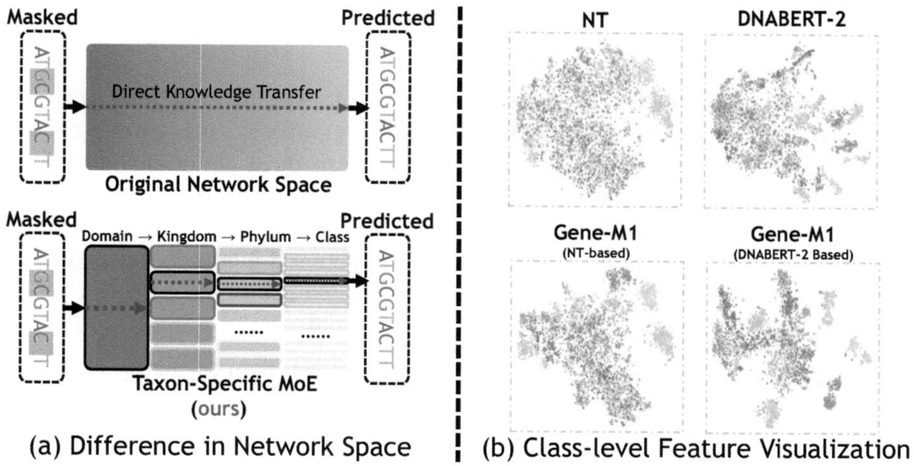

Fig. 1. Motivation. (a) Baseline models process genomic data with a single shared network, lacking expert specialization and suffering from feature interference across taxa. In contrast, **Gene-M1** introduces taxon-specific experts aligned with biological hierarchy, enabling disentangled and specialized representations. (b) At the Class level, feature visualizations show that baseline models collapse diverse taxa into overlapping clusters, while **Gene-M1** produces well-separated, biologically meaningful clusters, demonstrating stronger taxon-specific customization and alignment with taxonomy.

However, existing models, such as DNABERT [5], DNABERT-2 [6], Nucleotide Transformer (NT) [7], HyenaDNA [8], and DNABERT-S [9], typically use a single shared architecture for genomic sequences from all species. This **one-size-fits-all** design overlooks the substantial evolutionary divergence and taxon-specific characteristics of genomic data (Fig. 1(a)), often leading to **feature interference** across taxa, weak cross-species generalization, and representations that are poorly aligned with biological taxonomy (Fig. 1(b)).

To address these limitations, **Gene-M1** is proposed as a novel Mixture-of-Experts (MoE [11]) framework explicitly aligned with the biological taxonomic hierarchy (Domain → Kingdom → Phylum → Class) [12,13], as illustrated in Fig. 1(a). Specifically, **Gene-M1** incorporates hierarchical experts specialized for different taxonomic levels, a router that dynamically activates taxonomically consistent expert routes, and a progressive training strategy that transfers coarse-grained knowledge to finer-grained levels (Secs. 2.1–2.3). This design enables the model to better capture taxon-specific genomic patterns while preserving biologically meaningful hierarchical structure.

To support this study, a new large-scale genomic dataset is constructed from NCBI [14], comprising 294 representative species organized into 5 Kingdoms, 18 Phyla, and 62 Classes. Compared with prior resources that are often dominated by bacteria and limited to a few coarse categories, **GM-Data** provides broader and more balanced taxonomic coverage, including underrepresented groups such as Archaea and Plants. For rigorous evaluation of cross-species generalization, **GM-Data**(eval) is further constructed, containing 15 entirely unseen species spanning 4 Kingdoms, 10 Phyla, and 15 Classes. The remaining 279 species constitute the training set, **GM-Data**(train).

Extensive experiments on supervised few-shot classification and unsupervised clustering show that **Gene-M1** consistently outperforms state-of-the-art genomic foundation models. Notably, the gains are most pronounced at finer taxonomic levels, where cross-species discrimination is particularly challenging. Further analysis shows that different taxonomic levels provide complementary signals for representation learning, and that the proposed hierarchy-aware design yields more biologically interpretable taxonomic separation.

In summary, the main contributions are threefold:

- **Gene-M1** is proposed as the first genomics MoE framework explicitly aligned with biological taxonomy, integrating hierarchical experts, dynamic routing, and progressive training to improve generalization and interpretability.
- Extensive experiments demonstrate that **Gene-M1** improves generalization to unseen species in cross-species gene classification and yields more discriminative, taxonomy-aligned embeddings in clustering analysis.
- **GM-Data** is curated and released as a large-scale, taxonomically structured genomic dataset for the development and evaluation of taxon-aware foundation models.

2 Methodology

In this section, **Gene-M1** is presented as a taxonomy-aligned Mixture-of-Experts framework that systematically addresses cross-species genomic modeling through three interconnected components: (1) a hierarchical expert architecture (Sect. 2.1) that processes sequences along biological taxonomy from Domain to Class levels, (2) a weighted routing mechanism (Sect. 2.2) that dynamically combines class-specific features through supervised learning [15], and (3) a coarse-to-fine training strategy (Sect. 2.3) that progressively transfers knowledge while preventing feature interference. The overview of the structure is shown in Fig. 2. In practice, **Gene-M1** is instantiated on top of two representative genomic foundation models, NT [7] and DNABERT-2 [6]. This integrated approach enables **Gene-M1** to capture both universal genomic patterns and taxon-specific characteristics while maintaining parameter efficiency and biological interpretability.

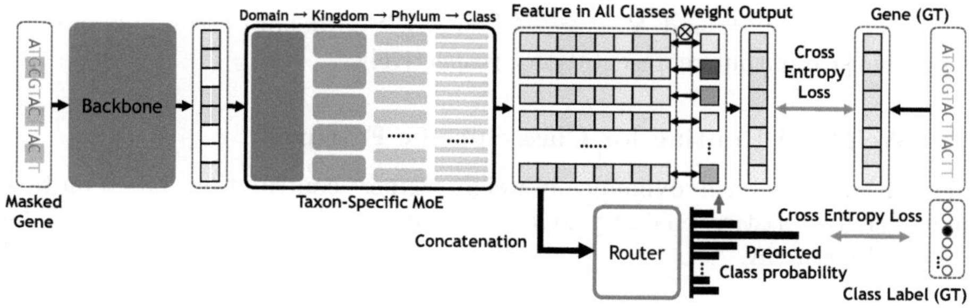

Fig. 2. Overview of the training process of **GENE-M1**. The model is trained on **GM-DATA**(train), a hierarchical dataset derived from cross-species reference genomes, using a progressive freeze–unfreeze paradigm that refines knowledge from Domain → Kingdom → Phylum → Class. The objective combines masked language modeling (MLM) with router supervision to ensure taxonomy-aligned expert selection and robust cross-species generalization.

2.1 Taxon-Specific Mixture-of-Experts

To address the limitations of one-size-fits-all genomic foundation models, a hierarchical Mixture-of-Experts (MoE) [16] architecture is introduced to explicitly mirror biological taxonomic organization. The framework decomposes the representation learning process along the natural hierarchy of life—Domain → Kingdom → Phylum → Class—thereby enabling specialized processing at each taxonomic level.

Hierarchical Expert Architecture. Given hidden representations $\mathcal{H} \in \mathbb{R}^{B\times L\times D}$ from the backbone (batch size B, sequence length L, hidden dimension D), we instantiate a set of expert networks $\{E_\ell^{(i)}\}_{i=1}^{N_\ell}$ for each taxonomic level $\ell \in \{\text{Domain}, \text{Kingdom}, \text{Phylum}, \text{Class}\}$, where N_ℓ is the number of taxa at level ℓ.

Each expert module applies normalization, a residual connection, and a dimension-reducing projection (ratio $r = N_\ell$):

$$\begin{aligned} E_\ell^{(i)}(\mathbf{h}) &= f_{\text{proj}}^{(\ell,i)}\big(\mathbf{h} + \text{Dropout}(\text{LayerNorm}(\mathbf{h}))\big), \\ f_{\text{proj}}^{(\ell,i)}(\mathbf{x}) &= \text{GELU}\left(\mathbf{W}^{(\ell,i)}\mathbf{x}\right), \quad \mathbf{W}^{(\ell,i)} \in \mathbb{R}^{D\times D/r}. \end{aligned} \tag{1}$$

This design ensures parameter efficiency while preserving cross-species representational capacity.

Taxonomy-Aligned Composition. To progressively integrate taxonomic signals, sequences traverse the hierarchical experts via function composition ($\circ$) and feature-wise concatenation ($\bigoplus$):

$$\mathbf{Y} = E_{\text{Class}}^{(k)} \circ \bigoplus_{j=1}^{N_{\text{Phylum}}} E_{\text{Phylum}}^{(j)} \circ \bigoplus_{i=1}^{N_{\text{Kingdom}}} E_{\text{Kingdom}}^{(i)} \circ E_{\text{Domain}}(\mathbf{X}), \tag{2}$$

where $\mathbf{X} \in \mathbb{R}^{B \times L \times D}$ and $\mathbf{Y} \in \mathbb{R}^{B \times L \times \frac{D}{N_{\text{Class}}} \times N_{\text{Class}}}$ denote the input and the comprehensive output representations, respectively.

2.2 Weighted Routing for Class-Specific Features

The routing mechanism dynamically weights expert contributions based on taxonomic characteristics, enabling adaptive feature combinations aligned with the biological hierarchy.

Context-Aware Routing. Given concatenated representations $\mathbf{Y}$ from class experts, routing weights $\mathbf{s}$ are computed via a linear classifier: $\mathbf{s} = \mathbf{W}_{\text{router}} \cdot \text{Flatten}(\mathbf{Y})$, where $\mathbf{W}_{\text{router}} \in \mathbb{R}^{N_{\text{Class}} \times (B \cdot L \cdot D)}$ denotes learnable parameters. These weights are normalized via softmax with temperature scaling $\tau > 0$ to produce a distribution α over experts:

$$\alpha_i = \frac{\exp(s_i/\tau)}{\sum_{j=1}^{N_{\text{Class}}} \exp(s_j/\tau)}. \tag{3}$$

Lower τ values promote peaked distributions for specialization, while higher values encourage uniform utilization. To ensure taxonomic consistency, the router is supervised during training using a cross-entropy loss:

$$\mathcal{L}_{\text{router}} = -\frac{1}{B} \sum_{b=1}^{B} \sum_{i=1}^{N_{\text{Class}}} y_{b,i} \log \left(\frac{\exp(s_{b,i})}{\sum_{j=1}^{N_{\text{Class}}} \exp(s_{b,j})} \right), \tag{4}$$

where $y_{b,i}$ is the one-hot taxonomic label for sequence b at the class level. This supervision encourages the router to prioritize experts corresponding to the ground-truth taxonomic classification.

Weighted Feature Concatenation. The final representation is obtained by weighting and concatenating class-specific features according to the learned routing weights:

$$\mathbf{Z} = \bigoplus_{i=1}^{N_{\text{Class}}} \alpha_i \cdot \mathbf{Y}^{(i)}, \tag{5}$$

where $\mathbf{Y}^{(i)}$ denotes the portion of $\mathbf{Y}$ corresponding to class expert i (with dimensionality D/N_{Class}), and $\mathbf{Z} \in \mathbb{R}^{B \times L \times D}$ is the final routed representation. This weighted concatenation ensures that the model can adaptively combine taxonomic features based on the input sequence, with experts receiving higher weights for sequences that match their taxonomic specialization. The resulting representation $\mathbf{Z}$ captures both universal genomic patterns and taxon-specific characteristics, providing a rich feature set for downstream tasks.

2.3 Taxon Coarse-to-Fine Learning

A progressive training strategy is adopted to mimic evolutionary specialization, transferring knowledge from coarse to fine taxonomic levels [17].

Sequential Training with Layer Freezing. Training proceeds sequentially through four phases. At each phase t, the parameters θ_t are optimized while all previously trained parameters $\theta_{<t}$ remain frozen:

$$\theta_l^* = \arg\min_{\theta_t} \mathcal{L}(\theta_t|\theta_{<t} \text{ frozen}), \quad t = 1, \ldots, 4 \tag{6}$$

The sequence follows the taxonomic hierarchy: ($t = 1$) Domain → ($t = 2$) Kingdom → ($t = 3$) Phylum → ($t = 4$) Class, with each level initialized from its parent and trained on increasingly specialized data subsets. This sequential freezing strategy ensures stable optimization by preventing feature interference between taxonomic levels, as each level specializes based on fixed representations from coarser levels.

Multi-objective Optimization. The training objective combines masked language modeling with router supervision:

$$\mathcal{L}_{\text{total}} = \lambda_{\text{mlm}}\mathcal{L}_{\text{mlm}} + \lambda_{\text{router}}\mathcal{L}_{\text{router}}, \tag{7}$$

where $\mathcal{L}_{\text{mlm}}$ is the standard masked language modeling loss and $\mathcal{L}_{\text{router}}$ is the routing supervision loss defined in Sect. 2.2. The hyperparameters λ_{mlm} and λ_{router} balance the two objectives.

This coarse-to-fine learning approach ensures that the model progressively incorporates taxonomic specialization while maintaining the stability of previously learned representations, effectively addressing feature interference and enabling robust cross-species generalization.

3 Experiments and Results

This section presents a comprehensive experimental evaluation of **Gene-M1**. A large-scale, taxonomically structured dataset (**GM-Data**) is first constructed, and principled training and test partitions are established to ensure strict cross-species evaluation. Training configurations and experimental settings are then described, including backbone models and task definitions. Finally, the framework is assessed from three complementary perspectives—cross-species gene classification, cross-species gene clustering, and experimental analysis—providing a systematic evaluation of predictive accuracy, representation quality, and the role of hierarchical modeling.

3.1 Data Construction

Data Collection and Composition. **GM-Data** is constructed from the NCBI RefSeq database [14], comprising 294 representative species spanning 5 kingdoms, 18 phyla, and 62 classes. All genomes are processed using a standardized pipeline: after filtering, non-ATCG characters are replaced with N, and sequences are segmented into 6,000 bp fragments with 100 bp overlaps. The resulting fragments are then merged and converted into a HuggingFace dataset, yielding a high-quality resource for model training and evaluation.

Training and Test Partitioning. The dataset is partitioned into 279 training species and 15 held-out species for evaluation. The test species are phylogenetically diverse and remain entirely unseen during training, ensuring strict cross-species evaluation. The full taxonomic hierarchy from Domain to Class is preserved in both splits, enabling systematic assessment at multiple taxonomic levels.

Taxonomic Coverage Comparison. As shown in Table 1, **GM-DATA** exhibits substantially better taxonomic balance than existing benchmarks. Unlike prior datasets that are strongly dominated by bacteria (74–78%), **GM-DATA** maintains a more even distribution across kingdoms (Fungi: 13%, Animalia: 22%, Plantae: 16%, Bacteria: 34%, Archaea: 15%). It also preserves the full biological hierarchy (Domain → Kingdom → Phylum → Class), enabling multi-granularity learning and enhancing biological interpretability.

Table 1. Comparison of genomic datasets.

Dataset	Total Species	Training/Test Split	Taxonomic Levels
DNABERT-2	135	135/0	7 coarse groups
NT	850	850/0	6 coarse groups
Ours	294	279/15	5 Kingdoms, 18 Phyla, 62 Classes

3.2 Settings

Training Configuration. For optimization, AdamW [18] is used with an initial learning rate of 1×10^{-3}, together with a cosine learning rate scheduler and a 10% warm-up phase. The effective batch size is set to 64 through gradient accumulation. Gradient clipping (maximum norm = 1.0) and mixed-precision training are applied to improve stability and efficiency. The overall training objective is empirically designed to jointly optimize the masked language modeling (MLM) loss and the router supervision loss, with weights $\lambda_{\text{mlm}} = 1.0$ and $\lambda_{\text{router}} = 0.2$, respectively.

3.3 Tasks

The proposed framework is evaluated under two complementary protocols: cross-species gene classification on unseen species and cross-species gene clustering to assess the taxonomy alignment of the learned embeddings. For clearer comparison, the evaluated models are organized into three groups: **Group 1** includes the backbone models, **Group 2** consists of other representative DNA foundation models, and **Group 3** contains the **GENE-M1**-enhanced variants built upon the backbone models.

Table 2. Model performance (macro-F1, ↑) at different taxonomic levels and shot numbers. The best results are highlighted in bold, and the second best are underlined. ↑ indicates that higher F1 scores are better.

Level	Shots	Group 1		Group 2		Group 3	
		NT	DNABERT-2	DNABERT-S	HyenaDNA	GENE-M1(NT Based)	GENE-M1(DNABERT-2Based)
Kingdom	1-shot	47.67%	46.08%	<u>51.16%</u>	19.25%	39.79%	**77.42%**
	2-shot	44.59%	<u>54.22%</u>	52.70%	24.37%	43.12%	**75.14%**
	5-shot	39.86%	68.06%	<u>74.04%</u>	24.72%	51.05%	**85.36%**
	10-shot	57.55%	72.82%	<u>79.49%</u>	32.83%	61.34%	**87.52%**
	20-shot	66.75%	79.30%	<u>83.06%</u>	36.53%	78.15%	**91.20%**
Phylum	1-shot	24.79%	22.09%	33.70%	8.44%	**60.04%**	<u>58.20%</u>
	2-shot	23.59%	35.60%	45.69%	11.15%	<u>51.91%</u>	**62.40%**
	5-shot	30.80%	42.79%	51.05%	13.79%	<u>53.76%</u>	**74.33%**
	10-shot	36.88%	45.28%	<u>60.54%</u>	17.76%	56.93%	**75.41%**
	20-shot	50.96%	53.19%	63.60%	21.90%	<u>79.75%</u>	**80.34%**
Class	1-shot	14.48%	15.82%	<u>26.45%</u>	4.12%	23.21%	**47.45%**
	2-shot	10.91%	29.29%	<u>37.04%</u>	5.89%	31.90%	**60.56%**
	5-shot	18.46%	34.34%	48.05%	9.21%	<u>48.28%</u>	**71.73%**
	10-shot	26.22%	41.27%	50.62%	13.01%	<u>54.87%</u>	**73.26%**
	20-shot	36.34%	44.58%	55.91%	14.69%	<u>65.47%</u>	**78.84%**

Evaluation on Cross-Species Gene Classification. Downstream performance on **GM-DATA**(eval) is evaluated through three hierarchical classification tasks at the kingdom, phylum, and class levels, enabling a systematic assessment of cross-species classification capability across different taxonomic granularities. Performance is measured using the macro-averaged F1 score, which balances precision and recall across classes and is particularly suitable for imbalanced taxonomic distributions [19]. In addition, few-shot training regimes (1-shot, 2-shot, 5-shot, 10-shot, and 20-shot) are adopted, in which models are trained with only a small number of labeled samples before evaluation. Such few-shot settings provide a rigorous test of the base model's adaptability and robustness in cross-species scenarios [20].

As shown in Table 2, **GENE-M1** achieves state-of-the-art (SOTA) performance across all few-shot training settings on the hierarchical classification tasks. Notably, at the class level, the macro-averaged F1 score exceeds that of DNABERT-2 [6] by more than 25% under every few-shot condition, highlighting the advantage of taxonomy-aligned modeling for fine-grained cross-species classification. The most pronounced and consistent improvements are observed at the class level, where fine-grained discrimination is inherently more challenging. In comparison with coarser taxonomic ranks, **GENE-M1** delivers larger and more consistent gains at this level, highlighting its advantage in modeling subtle taxon-specific variations. Since the evaluation is performed on **GM-DATA**(eval), which contains only previously unseen species, these improvements provide direct evidence of the enhanced cross-species generalization capability of **GENE-M1**.

Evaluation on Cross-Species Gene Clustering. Unsupervised cross-species clustering is performed on **GM-DATA**(eval) to evaluate whether taxonomic structure can be recovered from embedding similarity alone. DNA embeddings produced by baseline models and **Gene-M1** are projected into a shared latent space, followed by k-means [21], to assess whether unseen species form compact intra-taxon clusters with clear inter-taxon boundaries.

Table 3. Model performance across taxonomic levels with clustering evaluation metrics (↑ indicates higher is better). Best results are highlighted in bold, and second best are underlined.

Level	Metric↑	Group 1		Group 2		Group 3	
		NT	DNABERT-2	DNABERT-S	HyenaDNA	**Gene-M1**(NT Based)	**Gene-M1**(DNABERT-2Based)
Kingdom	ACC	44.63%	40.38%	<u>54.38%</u>	41.63%	44.38%	**60.25%**
	NMI	15.05%	9.19%	<u>26.27%</u>	14.83%	18.41%	**45.48%**
	ARI	12.63%	7.44%	<u>18.48%</u>	11.29%	13.39%	**31.41%**
Phylum	ACC	42.85%	30.50%	38.30%	26.60%	<u>47.80%</u>	**56.55%**
	NMI	37.38%	21.47%	31.24%	23.65%	<u>43.72%</u>	**57.98%**
	ARI	24.10%	11.56%	18.22%	11.46%	<u>28.22%</u>	**40.54%**
Class	ACC	34.20%	23.53%	29.87%	19.83%	<u>37.03%</u>	**44.83%**
	NMI	33.09%	23.64%	27.52%	17.96%	<u>39.84%</u>	**56.20%**
	ARI	17.48%	10.02%	13.37%	7.16%	<u>22.09%</u>	**32.66%**

As shown in Table 3, performance is evaluated using three standard clustering metrics: Clustering Accuracy (ACC), Normalized Mutual Information (NMI), and Adjusted Rand Index (ARI). **Gene-M1** achieves state-of-the-art results across all metrics and taxonomic levels, with the most substantial gains observed at the class level. This suggests that existing models tend to produce overlapping clusters with less distinct boundaries at fine-grained levels, whereas **Gene-M1** effectively mitigates feature interference, resulting in more compact intra-class distributions and clearer inter-class separation. This observation is further supported by the visualizations in Fig. 3.

These findings provide strong evidence that **Gene-M1** enhances cross-species generalization by disentangling lineage-specific signals within a unified hierarchical framework. By progressively refining representations from coarse (kingdom) to fine-grained (class) levels, the model not only reduces ambiguity in distinguishing closely related taxa but also yields embeddings that remain biologically meaningful for unseen species.

3.4 Ablation Study and Analysis

An ablation analysis is conducted to assess how hierarchical depth influences representation quality. As shown in Fig. 4, the embeddings evolve progressively from coarse to fine: representations at the Domain level remain entangled, whereas the Kingdom and Phylum layers exhibit clearer boundaries, and the Class layer achieves the most distinct separation.

Quantitative clustering results in Table 4 further confirm this trend, with ACC, NMI, and ARI consistently improving as the hierarchy deepens. These results suggest that deeper hierarchical expert modeling progressively refines

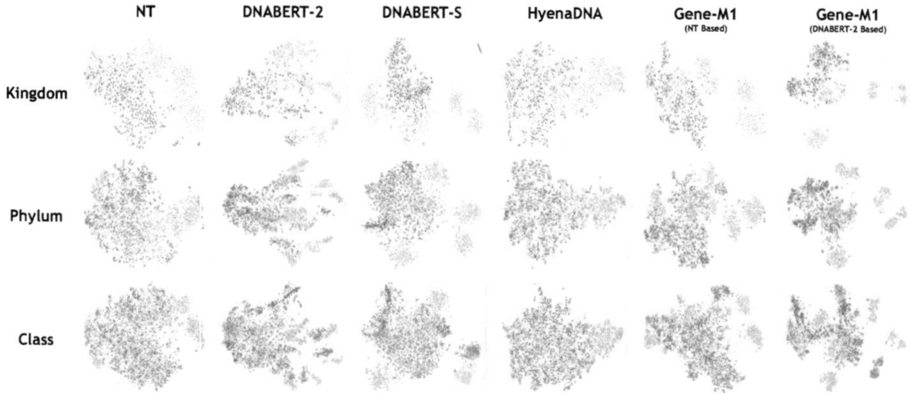

Fig. 3. T-SNE visualizations of sequence embeddings across Kingdom, Phylum, and Class. Compared with baselines, **GENE-M1** produces clearer, more separable clusters aligned with taxonomy.

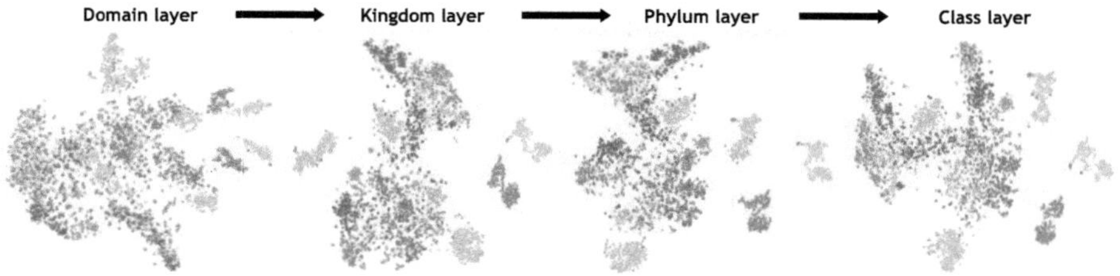

Fig. 4. T-SNE visualizations of embeddings from different hierarchical levels (Domain, Kingdom, Phylum, Class) in **GENE-M1 (DNABERT-2 Based)**, showing progressive refinement from coarse to fine-grained taxonomy.

genomic representations and improves fine-grained discrimination across taxa. This progressive disentanglement of taxonomic structure indicates stronger taxonomy-aware representation learning.

To probe expert allocation, the routing weight heatmap (Fig. 5) reveals sparse, distinct activation pathways across species. Crucially, the absence of solid vertical bands confirms the model successfully avoids expert collapse, adaptively allocating taxon-specific channels rather than uniform weights. By isolating specialized biological signals, this weighted routing fosters stable specialization, minimizes cross-expert interference, and substantially boosts fine-grained classification accuracy.

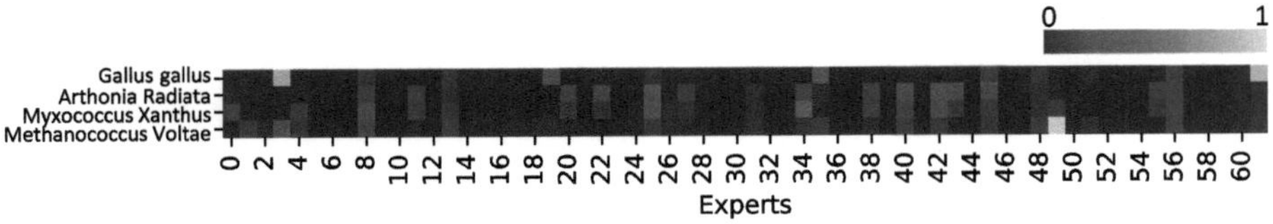

Fig. 5. Router weights heatmap.

Table 4. Performance across taxonomic levels with clustering evaluation metrics. The best results are highlighted in bold, and the second best are underlined.

Level	Metric↑	Layers			
		Domain	Kingdom	Phylum	Class
Kingdom	ACC	58.13%	<u>60.00%</u>	59.50%	**60.25%**
	NMI	26.87%	36.62%	<u>41.58%</u>	**45.48%**
	ARI	19.69%	**31.98%**	30.16%	<u>31.34%</u>
Phylum	ACC	36.35%	41.15%	<u>46.85%</u>	**56.55%**
	NMI	30.17%	44.32%	<u>50.16%</u>	**57.98%**
	ARI	16.37%	26.21%	<u>31.55%</u>	**40.54%**
Class	ACC	28.07%	35.80%	<u>44.03%</u>	**44.83%**
	NMI	25.90%	43.38%	<u>50.84%</u>	**56.20%**
	ARI	11.84%	21.75%	<u>30.36%</u>	**32.66%**

4 Conclusion

In summary, **Gene-M1** is presented as a taxon-specific Mixture-of-Experts framework for genomics. By structurally mirroring biological hierarchy, the model disentangles taxon-specific features and achieves superior cross-species generalization. Extensive experiments show that **Gene-M1** not only outperforms state-of-the-art baselines but also yields biologically meaningful and interpretable representations, thereby enabling more effective analysis of cross-species genomic data.

Acknowledgements. This work was supported by the National Natural Science Foundation of China under Grant Nos. 62433016, 61972320, the National Key R&D Program of China under Grant No. 2021YFA1000402, and the Fundamental Research Funds for the Central Universities under Grant Nos. D5000250279, G25KY0612610.

References

1. Reuter, J.A., Spacek, D.V., Snyder, M.P.: High-throughput sequencing technologies. Mol. Cell **58**(4), 586–597 (2015)
2. Lee, J.Y.: The principles and applications of high-throughput sequencing technologies. Dev. Reprod. **27**(1), 9 (2023)

3. Ambardar, S., Gupta, R., Trakroo, D., Lal, R., Vakhlu, J.: High throughput sequencing: an overview of sequencing chemistry. Indian J. Microbiol. **56**(4), 394–404 (2016)
4. Hu, T., Chitnis, N., Monos, D., Dinh, A.: Next-generation sequencing technologies: an overview. Hum. Immunol. **82**(11), 801–811 (2021)
5. Ji, Y., Zhou, Z., Liu, H., Davuluri, R.V.: DNABERT: pre-trained bidirectional encoder representations from transformers model for DNA-language in genome. Bioinformatics **37**(15), 2112–2120 (2021)
6. Zhou, Z., Ji, Y., Li, W., Dutta, P., Davuluri, R.V., Liu, H.: DNABERT-2: efficient foundation model and benchmark for multi-species genomes. In: The Twelfth International Conference on Learning Representations (2024). https://openreview.net/forum?id=oMLQB4EZE1
7. Dalla-Torre, H., et al.: Nucleotide transformer: building and evaluating robust foundation models for human genomics. Nat. Methods **22**(2), 287–297 (2025)
8. Nguyen, E., et al.: Hyenadna: long-range genomic sequence modeling at single nucleotide resolution. Adv. Neural. Inf. Process. Syst. **36**, 43177–43201 (2023)
9. Zhou, Z., et al.: DNABERT-S: learning species-aware DNA embedding with genome foundation models. arXiv preprint arXiv:2402.08777 (2024)
10. Shao, B., Yan, J.: A long-context language model for deciphering and generating bacteriophage genomes. Nat. Commun. **15**(1), 9392 (2024)
11. Cai, W., Jiang, J., Wang, F., Tang, J., Kim, S., Huang, J.: A survey on mixture of experts in large language models. IEEE Trans. Knowl. Data Eng. (2025)
12. Shazeer, N., et al.: Outrageously large neural networks: the sparsely-gated mixture-of-experts layer. arXiv preprint arXiv:1701.06538 (2017)
13. Ruggiero, M.A., et al.: A higher level classification of all living organisms. PLoS ONE **10**(4), e0119248 (2015)
14. Geer, L.Y., et al.: The NCBI biosystems database. Nucleic Acids Res. **38**(suppl_1), D492–D496 (2010)
15. Yang, B., Guo, C., Ma, Yu., Jensen, C.S.: Toward personalized, context-aware routing. VLDB J. **24**(2), 297–318 (2015). https://doi.org/10.1007/s00778-015-0378-1
16. Ng, J.W., Deisenroth, M.P.: Hierarchical mixture-of-experts model for large-scale gaussian process regression. arXiv preprint arXiv:1412.3078 (2014)
17. Fidler, S., Boben, M., Leonardis, A.: A coarse-to-fine taxonomy of constellations for fast multi-class object detection. In: Daniilidis, K., Maragos, P., Paragios, N. (eds.) European Conference on Computer Vision, pp. 687–700. Springer (2010). https://doi.org/10.1007/978-3-642-15555-0_50
18. Loshchilov, I., Hutter, F.: Decoupled weight decay regularization. arXiv preprint arXiv:1711.05101 (2017)
19. Goutte, C., Gaussier, E.: A probabilistic interpretation of precision, recall and f-score, with implication for evaluation. In: Losada, D.E., Fernández-Luna, J.M. (eds.) European conference on information retrieval, pp. 345–359. Springer (2005). https://doi.org/10.1007/978-3-540-31865-1_25
20. Wang, Y., Yao, Q., Kwok, J.T., Ni, L.M.: Generalizing from a few examples: a survey on few-shot learning. ACM Comput. Surv. (CSUR) **53**(3), 1–34 (2020)
21. He, L., Li, K.: Mitigating hallucinations in LLM using k-means clustering of synonym semantic relevance. Authorea Preprints (2024)

scCT: Mapping Single-Cell Data to Human Reference Atlases to Identify Deviated Cell States

Yuman Li, Zikang Yin, Yanhong Wu(✉), and Jin Gu(✉)

Department of Automation, MOE Key Lab of Bioinformatics, BNRIST Bioinformatics Division, Tsinghua University, Beijing 100084, China
wuyh20@tsinghua.org.cn, jgu@tsinghua.edu.cn

Abstract. With the rapid development of large-scale single-cell atlases, accurate reference mapping has become essential for deciphering cellular heterogeneity and identifying disease-specific states. However, current methods frequently struggle to balance batch effect correction with the preservation of true biological variation, particularly in highly heterogeneous datasets. To address this, we introduce scCT, a novel single-cell **C**ell **T**ype mapping method that leverages an encoder–decoder architecture and cyclic adversarial training to explicitly decouple technical noise from biological signals. By capturing the underlying distribution of normal data to construct an integrated reference atlas, scCT facilitates the one-step, fine-tuning-free projection of query datasets into a shared latent space. Within this space, scCT detects unmatched disease populations as deviated states.

Comprehensive evaluations across public breast, pancreas, and peripheral blood mononuclear cell (PBMC) datasets demonstrate that scCT outperforms state-of-the-art methods. Furthermore, applying scCT to map hepatocellular carcinoma (HCC) cells onto a healthy liver reference successfully identified cell state deviations within the tumor microenvironment. Similarly, mapping systemic lupus erythematosus (SLE) data onto a normal PBMC reference revealed a distinct classical monocyte subpopulation driven by the upregulation of interferon-associated genes. Together, these results demonstrate that scCT enables robust mapping and sensitive detection of disease-associated cell state alterations, offering broad utility for both basic and translational single-cell research. Code and Supplementary data are available at http://lifeome.net/software/scCT.

Keywords: single-cell atlas · reference mapping · adversarial networks · batch effect correction · deviated-state identification

1 Introduction

With advancements in sequencing technologies, it has become possible to resolve human heterogeneity at the single-cell level. As sequencing data continues to

X. Cui et al. (Eds.): ISBRA 2026, LNBI 16690, pp. 186–198, 2027.
https://doi.org/10.1007/978-981-92-3716-6_15

accumulate, efforts have been made to construct reference datasets [1–3]. A critical challenge is how to map newly generated data onto these reference atlases. Unlike integration methods that aim to merge new data with reference datasets [4,5], reference mapping approaches leverage models to capture the distribution of the original reference data [6]. These methods embed new datasets into the reference space without modifying the reference itself, enabling consistent annotation of incoming datasets using publicly available data.

Drawing inspiration from the human genome reference, a human single-cell reference atlas should not only annotate cell types but also detect abnormal states in disease and identify differences between disease and healthy states. To achieve this, it is essential to accurately represent new datasets. Existing reference mapping approaches include cVAE-based methods, such as scArches [7] and scPoli [8], which use conditional variational autoencoders (cVAEs) to learn the distribution of reference data. These methods embed new data into the reference space by fine-tuning newly added network nodes. Another category involves VAE-based methods, such as scAtlasVAE [9], which learn a batch-invariant encoder and decoder to embed new data into the reference space. Additionally, anchor-based methods like Seurat_RPCA [10] align datasets by identifying shared anchors. Statistical approaches, such as Symphony [11], model data using Gaussian distributions and align new datasets to the closest Gaussian center before embedding them into the reference space. Recent large-scale models, such as scGPT [12], also utilize this principle by learning the distribution of the data. VAE-based methods rely on large datasets to shape a probability distribution, a mechanism that inherently struggles to perfectly disentangle biological signals from batch noise. A poorly estimated distribution leaves batch effects entangled, resulting in under-correction and falsely labeling normal data as diseased. In contrast, distribution-alignment methods often over-correct, mixing disease and normal data.

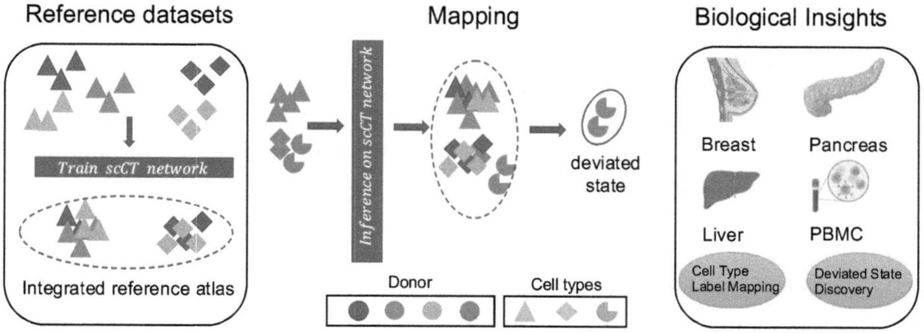

Fig. 1. Overflow and downstream applications of the scCT framework.

In this study, we propose a novel reference-based single-cell **C**ell **T**ype mapping method (sc**CT**), built upon an encoder-decoder framework with cyclic adversarial training. Unlike conventional methods, scCT explicitly models the joint distribution of the gene expression data and its latent representation and decouples technical noise from biological signals by optimizing a minimax objective: maximizing batch confusion via gradient reversal while minimizing cell-type classification error. Through this process, a robust, integrated reference atlas is constructed. For new query data, scCT performs direct mapping via a single inference step without requiring fine-tuning. In the resulting latent space, disease data that lacks a corresponding match in normal data is well-represented as isolated clusters. By acting as a diagnostic "CT scan" at the cellular level, this approach ensures accurate cell-type annotation and highlights deviated cell states, revealing alterations in diseased cells (see Fig. 1). Evaluations on public Breast, Pancreas and PBMC datasets demonstrate scCT's superiority over state-of-the-art methods. Furthermore, we apply scCT to align tumor-derived liver cells with normal liver reference, successfully identifying Hallmarks pathway-supported cell state deviations. Finally, mapping systemic lupus erythematosus (SLE) data onto a normal PBMC reference uncovered a distinct classical monocyte subpopulation with upregulated interferon-associated genes.

2 Method

2.1 Architecture of the ScCT Framework

scCT is fundamentally based on an encoder-decoder architecture trained via adversarial networks (see Fig. 2). The input to scCT consists of single-cell gene expression matrices from multiple batches ($X_{batch\ n}$). An encoder (E) is utilized to map them into a shared latent embedding space, producing latent representations ($Z_{gen\ n}$). Subsequently, a generator (G) reconstructs the gene expression ($\hat{X}_{batch\ n}$) from these latent embeddings. Moreover, we adopt a cyclic adversarial training framework inspired by CycleGAN [13]. This framework employs three distinct discriminators (D_{xx}, D_{zz}, and D_{xz}): D_{xx} and D_{zz} enforce cycle consistency in the data space and latent space, respectively, by distinguishing real samples from their cyclic reconstructions (e.g., comparing real data X with its reconstruction $G(E(X))$). Meanwhile, D_{xz} aligns the joint distribution of the input and its latent representation by distinguishing between encoded data pairs and generated latent pairs. By cycling the data through these mappings, the model preserves the essential biological features of the original data.

To effectively remove technical batch effects while preserving biological signals, two classifiers are applied to the latent embeddings. The *BatchClassifier* is connected to the latent space via a gradient reversal layer (GRL) [14]. During backpropagation, the GRL reverses the gradients, making the embeddings ($Z_{gen\ n}$) indistinguishable across different batches. Concurrently, the *CellTypeClassifier* is connected via a gradient forward layer, which standardly minimizes the cell type classification error. This dual-classifier strategy ensures a delicate balance: the adversarial training with the *BatchClassifier* successfully removes batch-specific biases, while the *CellTypeClassifier* guarantees that the resulting batch-corrected latent space strictly retains essential cell type identities.

For highly efficient new data mapping, new single-cell data is directly projected into the shared latent space via inference through the pre-trained Encoder (E), without requiring any fine-tuning. In this space, query cells with corresponding reference types integrate seamlessly into the reference atlas. Conversely, novel or disease-specific cells lacking reference matches form isolated, query-specific clusters.

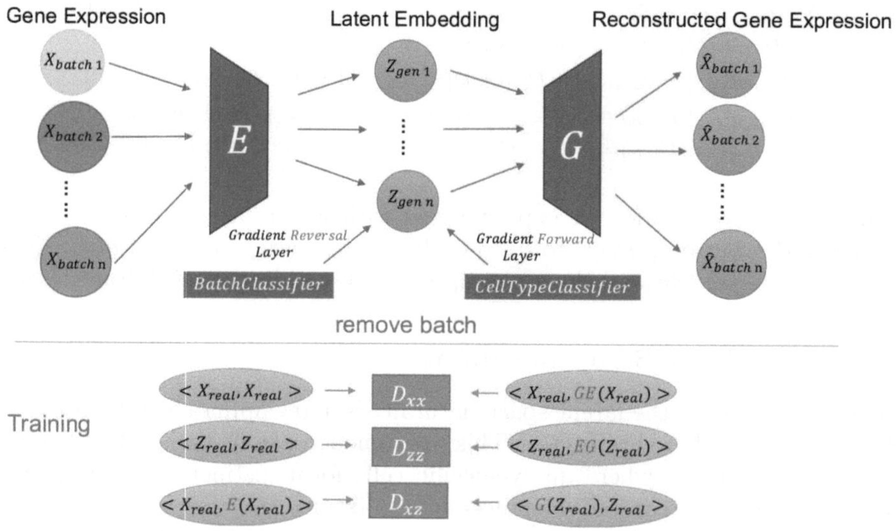

Fig. 2. Architecture of the scCT framework and adversarial training strategy.

2.2 Adversarial Training Strategy

The training strategy of scCT is formulated as a minimax optimization problem to achieve an equilibrium among all components. Optimized concurrently within the same objective level, D_{xz} (λ_{adv}) drives E and G to explicitly model the joint distribution of x and z, while D_{xx} and D_{zz} (λ_{cycle}) enforce cycle consistency to guarantee robust bidirectional mappings. Crucially, while both auxiliary classifiers (C_{batch} and C_{cell}) are optimized to achieve maximum accuracy in their prediction tasks, they impose opposing constraints on the encoder E: it must simultaneously maximize the batch classification error ($-\lambda_{batch}$) to remove technical noise and minimize the cell-type classification error ($+\lambda_{cell}$) to retain intrinsic biological signals, ensuring the latent embedding Z achieves an optimal state: decoupled from batch effects while preserving biological heterogeneity.

To stabilize the early stages of this complex adversarial training, we employ a dynamic weight scheduling strategy. During an initial warm-up phase, λ_{batch} and λ_{cell} are set to zero, allowing E and G to prioritize feature extraction and cycle consistency. Subsequently, these weights are linearly increased to their base values. By jointly optimizing these objectives with the dynamic schedule, scCT effectively integrates multi-batch datasets, ensuring that the learned latent representations are robust, unbiased, and consistent across all batches.

$$\begin{aligned}\min_{G,E,C_{cell}} \max_{D_{xz},D_{zz},D_{xx},C_{batch}} & \{\lambda_{adv} V(D_{xz},E,G) + \lambda_{cycle}\left[V(D_{zz},E,G) + V(D_{xx},E,G)\right] \\ & -\lambda_{batch}\mathcal{L}_{batch}(E,C_{batch}) + \lambda_{cell}\mathcal{L}_{cell}(E,C_{cell})\} \\ V(D_{xz},E,G) &= \mathbb{E}_{x\sim p_x}\left[\log D_{xz}(x,E(x))\right] + \mathbb{E}_{z\sim p_z}\left[\log\left(1 - D_{xz}(G(z),z)\right)\right] \\ V(D_{zz},E,G) &= \mathbb{E}_{z\sim p_z}\left[\log D_{zz}(z,z)\right] + \mathbb{E}_{z\sim p_z}\left[\log\left(1 - D_{zz}(z,E(G(z)))\right)\right] \\ V(D_{xx},E,G) &= \mathbb{E}_{x\sim p_x}\left[\log D_{xx}(x,x)\right] + \mathbb{E}_{x\sim p_x}\left[\log\left(1 - D_{xx}(x,G(E(x)))\right)\right] \\ \mathcal{L}_{batch}(E,C_{batch}) &= \mathbb{E}_{x\sim p_x}\left[\text{CrossEntropyLoss}\left(C_{batch}(E(x)), y_{batch}\right)\right] \\ \mathcal{L}_{cell}(E,C_{cell}) &= \mathbb{E}_{x\sim p_x}\left[\text{CrossEntropyLoss}\left(C_{cell}(E(x)), y_{cell}\right)\right]\end{aligned}$$

In the ablation studies, we experimented with setting λ_{batch} or λ_{cell} to zero, or setting the warm-up steps to 0, to evaluate the roles of the *BatchClassifier*, the *CellTypeClassifier*, and the warm-up strategy within the scCT framework.

2.3 Deviated Cell States Identification

For new query data, the latent space naturally isolates unmatched disease data while integrating shared cell types. This phenomenon can be easily identified via UMAP visualization, where query-specific cells form distinct, isolated groups separate from the integrated reference-query mixtures.

To quantitatively evaluate deviated cell states, we employ the Milo framework [15] to model cell counts within overlapping K-Nearest Neighbors (KNN) neighborhoods using a Negative Binomial (NB) generalized linear model. For a given neighborhood i, the Differential Abundance (DA) log fold change is derived from the condition-specific expected cell counts μ:

$$\text{DAlogFC}_i = \log_2\left(\frac{\text{Ratio}_{query}}{\text{Ratio}_{ref}}\right) = \log_2\left(\frac{\mu_{i,query}/N_{query}}{\mu_{i,ref}/N_{ref}}\right)$$

where N represents the total cell count serving as an offset for each condition. A larger positive DAlogFC score indicates a higher degree of abnormality, revealing neighborhoods significantly dominated by query cells that represent disease-associated or novel cellular subpopulations.

3 Result

3.1 scCT Accurately Detects Deviated States Across Complex Batches

We conducted simulation experiments on the Breast [16], Pancreas [17–21] and PBMC [22] datasets, to evaluate the ability to detect out-of-reference cell states. We selected a specific batch as the query data (the "UC Irvine cohort" for Breast,

"CEL-Seq2" for Pancreas and "ye-lupus-normal" for PBMC) and removed a designated cell type from the remaining reference. We then mapped the query data onto the reference to assess whether the "missing" cell type in the query could be successfully identified as deviated states using the DAlogFC metric. We tested this across the top 15 most abundant cell types. Compared to existing methods, scCT demonstrated the best identification performance, particularly excelling in detecting the top 3 most abundant cell types (see Fig. 3).

To visually demonstrate this, we examined basal cells, the most abundant cell type in the Breast dataset. Specifically, we removed basal cells from the reference and then mapped the query cells into the scCT latent embedding, enabling us to assess how different methods handle this out-of-reference scenario. We visualized the mapping results of basal cells to compare representative methods (see Fig. 4). scAtlasVAE [9] exhibited inadequate batch correction, whereas Symphony [11] suffered from severe over-correction, leading to the confounding of distinct cell types. While scArches_scPoli [8] achieved reasonable performance, scCT demonstrated the optimal performance by effectively removing batch effects while preserving biological variance and cell type identities.

3.2 Ablation Studies

To best validate our model, we evaluated the top 3 cell types in two datasets. We conducted ablation studies by removing the *BatchClassifier*, the *CellTypeClassifier*, and the dynamic warm-up strategy (see Fig. 5). Removing the *BatchClassifier* caused the most significant performance drop by failing to resolve technical noise across batches, while removing the *CellTypeClassifier* concurrently led to lost some biological signals. Furthermore, training the model without the dynamic warm-up strategy caused severe instability and poor convergence during the early adversarial phases, as the encoder was prematurely penalized before learning meaningful feature representations. Together, these results demonstrate that both the dual-classifier architecture and the dynamic scheduling are crucial for achieving optimal batch correction while preserving biological heterogeneity.

3.3 scCT Identifies Cell State Alterations in Hepatocellular Carcinoma

To evaluate scCT's performance on real-world data and demonstrate its clinical relevance, we apply it to hepatocellular carcinoma (HCC). Given HCC's pronounced heterogeneity and clinical urgency, we aim to precisely identify its deviated cell states at single-cell resolution.

We constructed a normal liver reference using the Guilliams2022 dataset [23], which provides unified, high-resolution cell-type labels. We then mapped a HCC dataset (Lu2022 [24]) onto this healthy reference. By acting as a diagnostic "CT scan" at the cellular level, scCT not only ensures accurate cell-type annotation but also highlights deviated cell states.

Specifically, the joint latent embedding colored by sample source (see Fig. 6A) reveals that cells from the Lu2022 dataset exhibit significant state deviations,

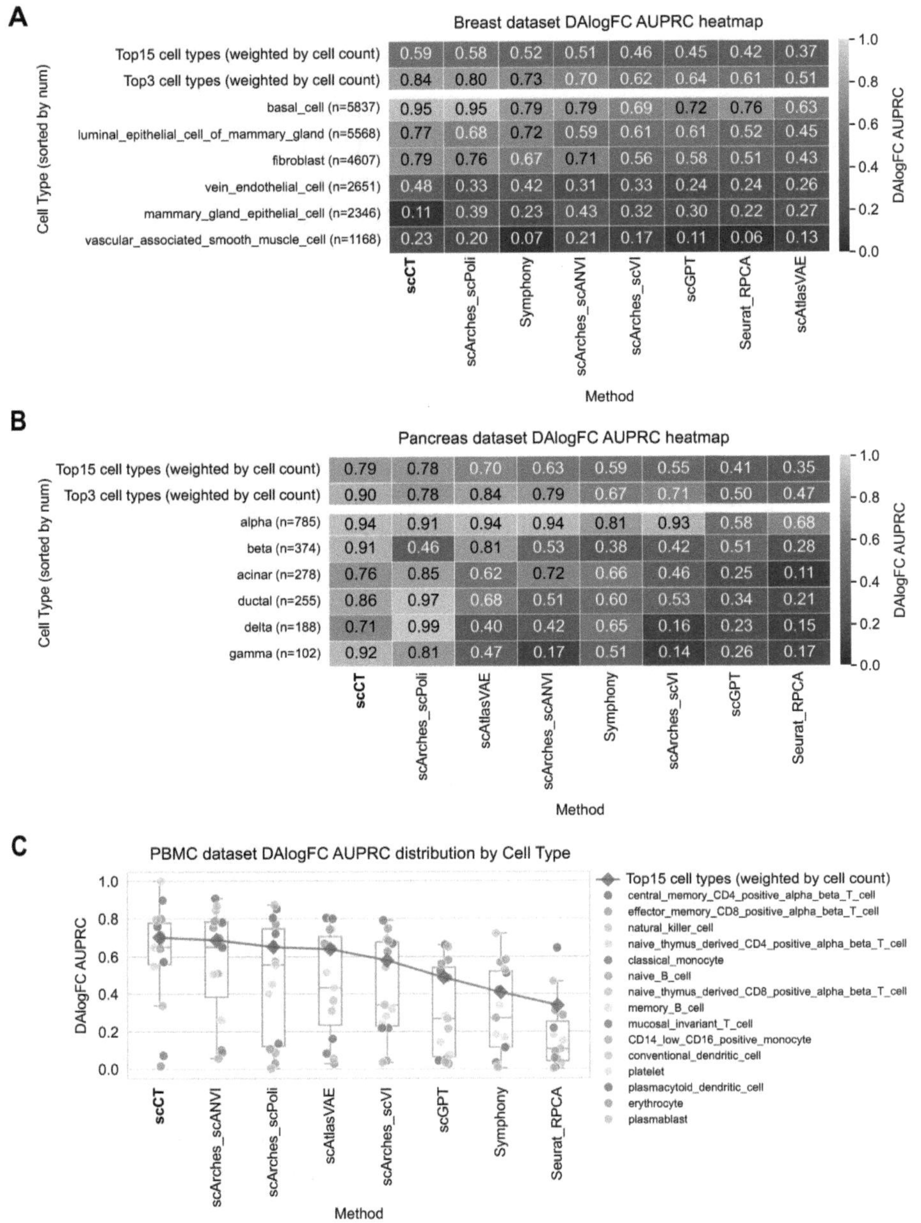

Breast	scCT	scArches_scPoli	Symphony	scArches_scANVI	scArches_scVI	scGPT	Seurat_RPCA	scAtlasVAE
Top15 cell types (weighted by cell count)	0.59	0.58	0.52	0.51	0.46	0.45	0.42	0.37
Top3 cell types (weighted by cell count)	0.84	0.80	0.73	0.70	0.62	0.64	0.61	0.51
basal_cell (n=5837)	0.95	0.95	0.79	0.79	0.69	0.72	0.76	0.63
luminal_epithelial_cell_of_mammary_gland (n=5568)	0.77	0.68	0.72	0.59	0.61	0.61	0.52	0.45
fibroblast (n=4607)	0.79	0.76	0.67	0.71	0.56	0.58	0.51	0.43
vein_endothelial_cell (n=2651)	0.48	0.33	0.42	0.31	0.33	0.24	0.24	0.26
mammary_gland_epithelial_cell (n=2346)	0.11	0.39	0.23	0.43	0.32	0.30	0.22	0.27
vascular_associated_smooth_muscle_cell (n=1168)	0.23	0.20	0.07	0.21	0.17	0.11	0.06	0.13

Pancreas	scCT	scArches_scPoli	scAtlasVAE	scArches_scANVI	Symphony	scArches_scVI	scGPT	Seurat_RPCA
Top15 cell types (weighted by cell count)	0.79	0.78	0.70	0.63	0.59	0.55	0.41	0.35
Top3 cell types (weighted by cell count)	0.90	0.78	0.84	0.79	0.67	0.71	0.50	0.47
alpha (n=785)	0.94	0.91	0.94	0.94	0.81	0.93	0.58	0.68
beta (n=374)	0.91	0.46	0.81	0.53	0.38	0.42	0.51	0.28
acinar (n=278)	0.76	0.85	0.62	0.72	0.66	0.46	0.25	0.11
ductal (n=255)	0.86	0.97	0.68	0.51	0.60	0.53	0.34	0.21
delta (n=188)	0.71	0.99	0.40	0.42	0.65	0.16	0.23	0.15
gamma (n=102)	0.92	0.81	0.47	0.17	0.51	0.14	0.26	0.17

Fig. 3. Performance comparison of out-of-reference detection across mapping methods. (A) Breast dataset: DAlogFC AUPRC heatmap for the top 15 and top3 most abundant cell types (weighted by cell count); per-cell-type results are additionally shown for cell types with more than 1,000 cells. (B) Pancreas dataset: DAlogFC AUPRC heatmap with the same evaluation protocol; per-cell-type results are additionally shown for cell types with more than 100 cells. (C) PBMC dataset: distribution of DAlogFC AUPRC across cell types for each method; the red curve indicates the weighted average over the top 15 most abundant cell types.

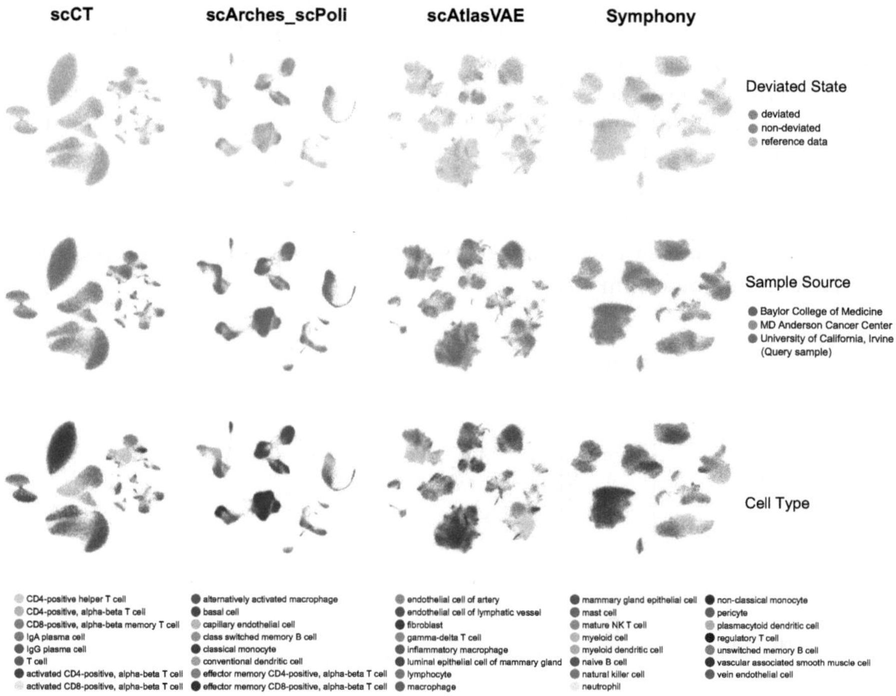

Fig. 4. UMAP visualizations of out-of-reference basal-cell mapping across methods.

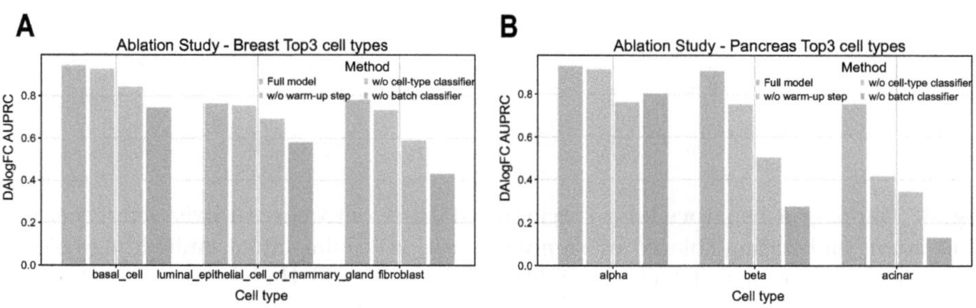

Fig. 5. Ablation study of scCT components for out-of-reference detection performance on the top 3 most abundant cell types. (A) Results on Breast. (B) Results on Pancreas.

primarily within Hepatocytes, Cholangiocytes, Endothelial cells, and a subset of Myeloid cells (see Fig. 6B), which also quantitatively confirmed by the Differential Abundance (DA) log-Fold Change metric (see Fig. 6C).

Finally, to biologically validate these state deviations, we evaluated Hallmarks gene set scores across the Lu2022 cell types (see Fig. 6D). Pathway analysis reveals distinct functional compartmentalization within the HCC microenvironment: Hepatocytes and Cholangiocytes are driven by cellular stress and

DNA repair mechanisms; Myeloid lineagesare dominated by IL6/JAK/STAT3-mediated inflammatory responses; and Endothelial cells selectively upregulate TGF-β signaling, consistent with a microenvironment-driven vascular remodeling/activation state. Taking together, these pathway patterns support that the deviated cells detected by scCT correspond to genuine biological adaptations in the hepatocellular carcinoma microenvironment.

Overall, scCT maps HCC cells onto a healthy liver reference and reveals biologically coherent, pathway-supported state deviations across key compartments of the HCC microenvironment.

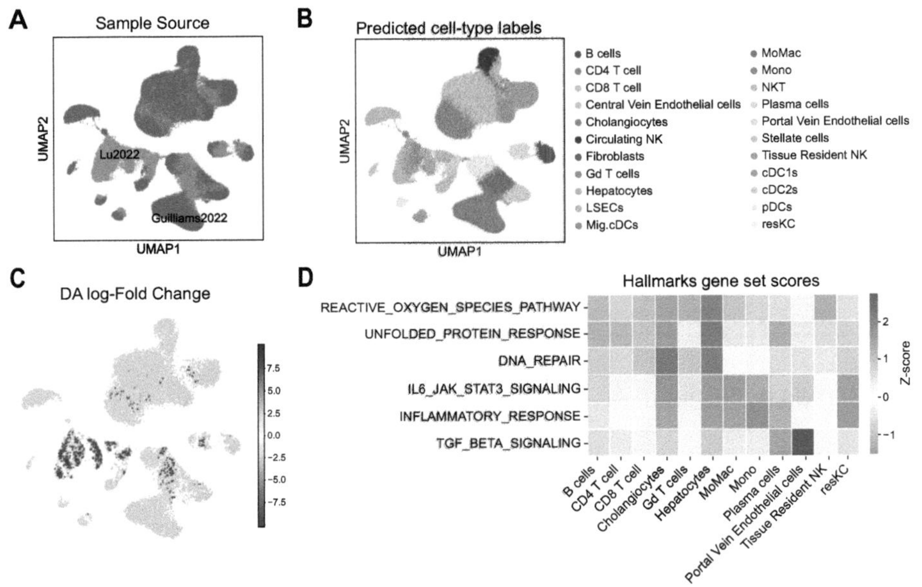

Fig. 6. Mapping a hepatocellular carcinoma dataset onto normal liver reference. (A) Joint latent embedding colored by sample source. (B) Joint latent embedding colored by predicted cell types. (C) DA log-fold change score. (D) Hallmarks gene set scores across Lu2022 cell types, shown for cell types with more than 1,000 cells.

3.4 scCT Mapping Uncovers a Distinct Interferon-Activated Classical Monocyte Subpopulation in SLE

A comprehensive and reliable blood reference is of great importance for immunological and clinical research. Large-scale peripheral blood mononuclear cell (PBMC) datasets aggregate numerous samples, providing a stable foundation characterized by relatively small batch effects, in contrast to the Breast and Pancreas datasets evaluated earlier.

We constructed a robust PBMC reference to facilitate the analysis of complex clinical query data. Then, we applied scCT to map a Systemic Lupus Erythematosus (SLE) [25] dataset onto PBMC reference. SLE is a blood-related autoimmune disease with diverse etiologies and high heterogeneity, making clinical diagnosis often challenging. Through scCT mapping, we successfully transferred high-resolution labels from the reference, upgrading the annotations to a much finer granularity (see Fig. 7A,B).

Moreover, the DAlogFC score revealed a distinct subpopulation of classical monocytes (see Fig. 7C). To biologically validate this specific subpopulation, we performed differential gene expression analysis and identified canonical interferon-associated genes, including *IFI44L*, *ISG15*, and *IFI6*. Consistent with the landmark findings in recent large-scale SLE single-cell studies, which highlighted a strong, cell type-specific Type I interferon signature [25]. As shown in Fig. 7E, *IFI44L*, *ISG15*, and *IFI6* were significantly upregulated in the SLE dataset. Crucially, while a baseline elevation of ISGs was observed globally across all cell types (Fig. 7D, bottom), the most dramatic and specific upregulation was pinpointed exactly within the classical monocyte subpopulation identified by our DA analysis (Fig. 7D, top). This demonstrates that scCT accurately resolves disease-specific, hyper-responsive pathogenic cell states.

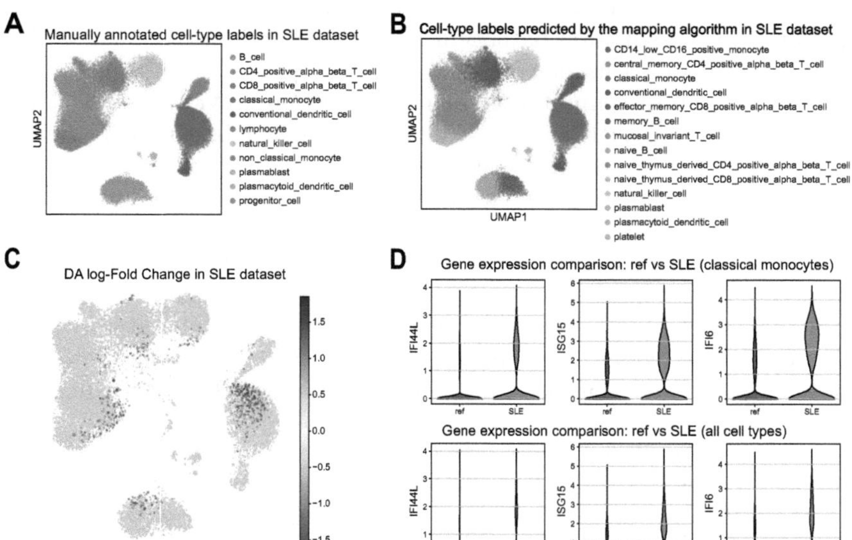

Fig. 7. Mapping an SLE dataset onto a normal PBMC reference. (A) Original cell-type annotations in the SLE dataset. (B) Cell-type labels transferred by scCT from the PBMC reference. (C) DA log-fold change scores highlighting a deviated classical monocyte subpopulation. (D) Expression of representative interferon-stimulated genes.

Overall, scCT mapping transfers finer-grained cell-type labels from the PBMC reference and pinpoints an interferon-activated classical monocyte subpopulation in SLE, linking this deviated state to Type I interferon signature.

4 Discussion

In this study, we developed scCT, an encoder–decoder reference-mapping method with cyclic adversarial training that separates technical batch effects from biological signals, enabling one-step mapping of query data onto a reference without fine-tuning. In the learned latent space, scCT supports accurate label transfer and highlights deviated, disease-specific cell states—like a "cellular CT scan".

Evaluations across both simulated and real-world scenarios underscore the robustness and versatility of our approach. In simulation experiments, scCT consistently outperformed state-of-the-art methods, achieving an optimal balance between batch effect removal and the conservation of true biological variation.

Building upon this strong foundational performance, we demonstrated the clinical utility of scCT by constructing comprehensive healthy reference atlases for human liver and peripheral blood mononuclear cells (PBMCs). By projecting complex clinical disease datasets onto these healthy reference, scCT accurately identified critical deviated cellular states. These real-world applications validate the power of scCT to discover pathogenic cell subsets and provide high-resolution insights into disease pathogenesis.

Despite the robust computational batch correction provided by scCT, inherent batch effects across current public datasets remain substantial. To construct optimal and highly reliable reference atlases moving forward, we emphasize the importance of experimental standardization at the data source to minimize technical variations, as exemplified by high-quality PBMC datasets. Furthermore, as single-cell technologies rapidly evolve, extending the scCT framework to integrate multi-omic modalities, such as spatial transcriptomics [26], will be a crucial next step for capturing a more comprehensive view of cellular states. Looking ahead, we plan to expand our current liver and PBMC references into a comprehensive "pan-tissue" database, ultimately advancing precision medicine [27].

Acknowledgments. This study was funded by the National Natural Science Foundation of China (NSFC) (Nos. 62133006, 92568303), Xinjiang Uygur Autonomous Region Key R & D Program (No. 2024B03039), the Beijing Natural Science Foundation (No. Z230015) and the Tsinghua University Research Program of Precision Medicine.

Disclosure of Interests. The authors have no competing interests to declare that are relevant to the content of this article.

A Appendix

Implementation and Efficiency. scCT was evaluated on an NVIDIA RTX 3090 GPU. We conducted simulation experiments on the Breast [16], Pancreas

[17–21] and PBMC [22] datasets, to evaluate the ability to detect out-of-reference cell states. We selected a specific batch as the query data (the "UC Irvine cohort" for Breast, "CEL-Seq2" for Pancreas and "ye-lupus-normal" for PBMC) and removed a designated cell type from the remaining reference. All models were trained on a unified set of selected highly variable genes. Benchmark methods were implemented using their default parameter settings, and performance was evaluated on 50-dimensional embeddings for all methods.

For the Breast dataset(the training dataset contains on average $\sim 1.25 \times 10^5$ cells, while the query dataset contains $\sim 2.8 \times 10^4$ cells.), the average total training time is approximately 26 min, with a mean epoch time of about 5 s over the default 300 epochs. The average peak GPU memory usage during training is approximately 1.8 GB. Inference is substantially more efficient than training. On average, inference on the training dataset requires about 3 s, while inference on the query dataset requires about 0.7 s. The average peak GPU memory usage during inference is only about 0.36 GB. These results indicate that the main computational cost of scCT lies in model training rather than inference; once training is completed, cell mapping can be performed very quickly.

Hyperparameters are adjusted according to the degree of batch-effect heterogeneity in the dataset: for high-quality PBMC datasets with weaker batch effects, we set $\{\lambda_{adv}, \lambda_{cycle}, \lambda_{batch}, \lambda_{cell}\}$ to $\{1.0, 0.5, 0.25, 0.25\}$ with no warm-up. For datasets with stronger batch effects and greater heterogeneity (e.g., Breast and Pancreas), we increase λ_{batch} and λ_{cell} to 0.4 and introduce a 10-epoch warm-up phase to stabilize adversarial training. A 10-epoch ramp-up period is applied in all configurations. Code and Supplementary data are available at http://lifeome.net/software/scCT.

References

1. Snyder, M.P., Lin, S., Posgai, A., et al.: The human body at cellular resolution: the NIH human biomolecular atlas program. Nature **574**(7777), 187–192 (2019)
2. Rozenblatt-Rosen, O., Shin, J.W., Rood, J.E., et al.: Building a high-quality human cell atlas. Nat. Biotechnol. **39**(2), 149–153 (2021)
3. Regev, A., Teichmann, S.A., Lander, E.S., et al.: Science forum: the human cell atlas. eLife **6**, e27041 (2017). https://doi.org/10.7554/eLife.27041
4. Luecken, M.D., Büttner, M., Chaichoompu, K., et al.: Benchmarking atlas-level data integration in single-cell genomics. Nat. Methods **19**(1), 41–50 (2022)
5. Polański, K., Young, M.D., Miao, Z., et al.: BBKNN: fast batch alignment of single cell transcriptomes. Bioinformatics **36**(3), 964–965 (2019)
6. Lotfollahi, M., Hao, Y., Theis, F.J., Satija, R.: The future of rapid and automated single-cell data analysis using reference mapping. Cell **187**(10), 2343–2358 (2024)
7. Lotfollahi, M., Naghipourfar, M., Luecken, M.D., et al.: Mapping single-cell data to reference atlases by transfer learning. Nat. Biotechnol. **40**(1), 121–130 (2022)
8. De Donno, C., Hediyeh-Zadeh, S., Moinfar, A.A., et al.: Population-level integration of single-cell datasets enables multi-scale analysis across samples. Nat. Methods **20**(11), 1683–1692 (2023)
9. Xue, Z., Wu, L., Tian, R., et al.: Integrative mapping of human CD8+ T cells in inflammation and cancer. Nat. Methods **22**(2), 435–445 (2025)

10. Stuart, T., Butler, A., Hoffman, P., et al.: Comprehensive integration of single-cell data. Cell **177**(7), 1888-1902.e21 (2019)
11. Kang, J.B., Nathan, A., Weinand, K., et al.: Efficient and precise single-cell reference atlas mapping with Symphony. Nat. Commun. **12**(1), 5890 (2021)
12. Cui, H., Wang, C., Maan, H., et al.: scGPT: toward building a foundation model for single-cell multi-omics using generative AI. Nat. Methods **21**(8), 1470–1480 (2024). https://doi.org/10.1038/s41592-024-02201-0
13. Zhu, J.Y., Park, T., Isola, P.: Unpaired image-to-image translation using cycle-consistent adversarial networks. In: 2017 IEEE International Conference on Computer Vision (ICCV), pp. 2242–2251 (2017)
14. Ganin, Y., Lempitsky, V.: Unsupervised Domain Adaptation by Backpropagation. In: Proceedings of the 32nd International Conference on Machine Learning, vol. 37, pp. 1180–1189. PMLR, Lille, France (2015)
15. Dann, E., Henderson, N.C., Teichmann, S.A., et al.: Differential abundance testing on single-cell data using k-nearest neighbor graphs. Nature Biotechnol. **40**(2), 245–253 (2022). https://doi.org/10.1038/s41587-021-01033-z
16. Kumar, T., Nee, K., Wei, R., et al.: A spatially resolved single-cell genomic atlas of the adult human breast. Nature **620**(7972), 181–191 (2023)
17. Segerstolpe, Å., Palasantza, A., Eliasson, P., et al.: Single-cell transcriptome profiling of human pancreatic islets in health and type 2 diabetes. Cell Metab. **24**(4), 593–607 (2016). https://doi.org/10.1016/j.cmet.2016.08.020
18. Grün, D., Muraro, M.J., Boisset, J.C., et al.: De novo prediction of stem cell identity using single-cell transcriptome data. Cell Stem Cell **19**(2), 266–277 (2016)
19. Muraro, M.J., Dharmadhikari, G., Grün, D., et al.: A single-cell transcriptome atlas of the human pancreas. Cell Syst. **3**(4), 385-394.e3 (2016)
20. Baron, M., Veres, A., Wolock, S.L., et al.: A single-cell transcriptomic map of the human and mouse pancreas reveals inter- and intra-cell population structure and others. Cell Syst. **3**(4), 346-360.e4 (2016)
21. Lawlor, N., George, J., Bolisetty, M., et al.: Single-cell transcriptomes identify human islet cell signatures and reveal cell-type-specific expression changes in type 2 diabetes. Genome Res. **27**(2), 208–222 (2017)
22. Dann, E., Cujba, A.M., Oliver, A.J., et al.: Precise identification of cell states altered in disease using healthy single-cell references. Nat. Genet. **55**(11), 1998–2008 (2023). https://doi.org/10.1038/s41588-023-01523-7
23. Guilliams, M., Bonnardel, J., Haest, B., et al.: Spatial proteogenomics reveals distinct and evolutionarily conserved hepatic macrophage niches. Cell **185**(2), 379–396.e38 (2022). https://doi.org/10.1016/j.cell.2021.12.018
24. Lu, Y., Yang, A., Quan, C., et al.: A single-cell atlas of the multicellular ecosystem of primary and metastatic hepatocellular carcinoma. Nat. Commun. **13**(1), 4594 (2022). https://doi.org/10.1038/s41467-022-32283-3
25. Perez, R.K., Gordon, M.G., Subramaniam, M., et al.: Single-cell RNA-seq reveals cell type–specific molecular and genetic associations to lupus. Science **376**(6589), eabf1970 (2022). https://doi.org/10.1126/science.abf1970
26. Börner, K., Blood, P.D., Silverstein, J.C., et al.: Human BioMolecular atlas program (HuBMAP): 3D human reference atlas construction and usage. Nat. Methods **22**(4), 845–860 (2025). https://doi.org/10.1038/s41592-024-02563-5
27. Rood, J.E., Maartens, A., Hupalowska, A., et al.: Impact of the human cell atlas on medicine. Nat. Med. **28**(12), 2486–2496 (2022)

Predicting Drug Synergy via Cross-modal Contrastive Learning and Masked Multi-omics Hypergraphs

Zhiyong Li, Xinqiang Wen, Chengqian Lu, Xixi Yang, Xuan Lin, and Xiangmao Meng(✉)

School of Computer Science, Xiangtan University, Xiangtan 411105, China
mxmanhui@xtu.edu.cn

Abstract. Drug combinations are essential in precision oncology to overcome monotherapy resistance, reduce toxicity, and enhance therapeutic efficacy. However, identifying highly synergistic pairs is hindered by the combinatorial explosion problem, making traditional experimental screening extremely expensive. Furthermore, existing computational models often fail to simultaneously and effectively integrate multi-modal drug data and multi-omics cell line profiles. To overcome these limitations, we propose CMMOSyn, a novel framework for predicting drug synergy via cross-modal contrastive learning and masked multi-omics hypergraphs. Specifically, CMMOSyn leverages cross-modal contrastive pre-training on large-scale databases to generate generalizable drug representations, effectively addressing the limited drug scale in combinatorial datasets. Concurrently, a Transformer-based masking mechanism is applied for multi-omics cell line feature fusion. These integrated representations are used to construct a drug-cell line hypergraph, which employs a subgraph sampling strategy to capture the high-order neighborhood topology of densely connected drugs and refine node features. Ultimately, CMMOSyn predicts synergy scores based on these refined representations. Extensive experiments demonstrate that CMMOSyn outperforms state-of-the-art baseline models across three benchmark datasets. Additionally, case studies on three cell lines highlight its practical utility in discovering unknown combinations.

Keywords: Drug Synergy Prediction · Hypergraph Neural Networks · Contrastive Learning · Multi-omics Fusion

1 Introduction

Drug combination therapy is a clinical strategy using two or more drugs simultaneously to maximize therapeutic efficacy [1]. Synergistic combination therapy enhances efficacy and mitigates adverse reactions, while its multi-target action delays or prevents drug resistance and improves long-term patient outcomes [2]. Combination therapy outperforms monotherapy for complex diseases, but experimentally identifying synergistic pairs is impractical due to the vast combinatorial space, highlighting the need for accurate computational models [3, 4].

X. Cui et al. (Eds.): ISBRA 2026, LNBI 16690, pp. 199–210, 2027.
https://doi.org/10.1007/978-981-92-3716-6_16

Machine learning methods, including support vector machines (SVM) and random forests (RF), are widely applied to predict drug combinations using chemical and biological features. For example, ComboFM [5] formulates drug, dose, and cell line data as a fifth-order tensor to capture multi-way interactions and reconstruct dose-response matrices. To address data imbalance and high dimensionality, ForSyn [6] utilizes a multi-layer cascade architecture integrating class balancing and dimensionality reduction modules. Although foundational, these conventional methods are generally limited by their inability to automatically capture highly complex non-linear relationships.

Advancements in deep learning have established a new paradigm for drug combination prediction [7], enabling end-to-end feature extraction from high-dimensional data to model complex relationships. DeepSynergy [8], an early deep learning model, utilized a feedforward neural network (FNN) to predict synergy scores by concatenating chemical descriptors of drug pairs with cell line gene expression profiles. Subsequent models adopted more advanced architectures. TranSynergy [9] applied a self-attention Transformer to model gene interactions using network-propagated drug targets and cell-line gene dependencies. MARSY [10] introduced a multi-task dual-encoder framework to simultaneously predict combination scores and single-drug responses, utilizing distinct encoders to extract drug pair features and capture drug-cell line synergies.

Graph Neural Networks (GNNs) are increasingly utilized in biomedical research to model complex biological interactions. For instance, DeepDDS [11] employs Graph Convolutional Networks (GCNs) to extract molecular embeddings for synergy prediction. To capture broader topological contexts, NEWMIN [12] utilizes biased random walks and Word2vec on heterogeneous networks to learn topology-aware drug representations. Similarly, Muthene [13] models complex heterogeneous interactions by processing pre-defined meta-paths via a heterogeneous GCN with BiGRU aggregators and graph attention networks (GAT), further enhancing predictions through a multi-task auxiliary objective. Moving beyond pairwise connections, HypergraphSynergy [14] employs a hypergraph neural network (HGNN) [15] to explicitly capture high-order relationships within drug-drug-cell line triplets. Extending this paradigm, HypertranSynergy [16] integrates coarse-grained features extracted by an HGNN with fine-grained distant dependencies captured by a Transformer. However, while these advanced graph and hypergraph architectures excel at capturing topological relationships, their predictive power is heavily bottlenecked by the limited comprehensiveness of single-modality initial node features.

To address the inherent dimensional and coverage limitations of single-modality data, integrating multimodal data is essential for comprehensively modeling complex interaction mechanisms. For example, AuDNNsynergy [17] employs pre-trained autoencoders to extract cell-line gene expression, genetic mutation, and copy number variation (CNV) features, combining them with physicochemical drug properties. Similarly, MMCL-CDR [18] aligns multi-omics and morphology features via contrastive learning, concatenating them with GCN-extracted drug representations. However, such multimodal methods typically rely on simple concatenation or shallow fusion, failing to capture the complex, high-order topological interactions among distinct biological entities.

We propose CMMOSyn, a hypergraph neural network integrating cross-modal contrastive learning and masked multi-omics fusion for drug synergy prediction. Specifically, to establish highly expressive node initializations, CMMOSyn extracts robust drug representations through a cross-modal contrastive encoder with gated fusion and unifies multi-omics cell line profiles via a Transformer-based masked autoencoder. These calibrated embeddings are then used to initialize a synergy hypergraph. Within this framework, an active-node-centric subgraph sampling strategy is designed to explicitly model localized high-order topological dependencies, progressively refining node representations for highly accurate synergy prediction.

2 Materials

We evaluated our model on three benchmark datasets: O'Neil [19] (23,062 samples, 38 drugs, 39 cell lines), NCI-ALMANAC [20] (304,549 samples, 104 drugs, 60 cell lines), and DrugComb [21] (739,964 samples, 8,397 drugs, 2,320 cell lines). Following MARSY, we resolved replicate inconsistencies in DrugComb by retaining samples with $\geq 60\%$ score agreement and a standard deviation ≤ 0.1, adopting the median as the consensus synergy score. We adopt Smean as the primary metric to evaluate drug combinations within the DrugComb dataset. By incorporating monotherapy baseline sensitivities (mean AUC) into the Combination Sensitivity Score (CSS), Smean effectively balances synergistic interaction with biological efficacy. This choice ensures the model prioritizes combinations demonstrating a genuine therapeutic surplus relative to their single-drug backgrounds. Finally, to guarantee permutation invariance without data leakage, all training samples were augmented by swapping drug orders strictly after the train-test split. SMILES strings retrieved from PubChem [22] were processed via RDKit into 2D molecular graphs and Morgan fingerprints. For the graph modality, we constructed feature matrices using one-hot encoded physicochemical properties for nodes, such as atomic number and hybridization, and for edges, including bond type and conjugation. For the fingerprint modality, we generated 2048-dimensional binary Morgan fingerprints with a radius of 2 to capture local topological substructures.

In this study, the multi-omics profiles of cancer cell lines, including gene expression, gene mutation, and CNV, were obtained from the Cancer Cell Line Encyclopedia (CCLE) [23] via the Broad Institute DepMap portal. Specifically, gene expression profiles were represented by log2-transformed transcripts per million (TPM) values derived from RNA-seq data. Gene mutation data were processed into a binary feature matrix, where 1 indicates a deleterious or hotspot mutation in a specific gene, and 0 otherwise. Additionally, gene-level relative copy number values were extracted to construct the CNV profiles. Finally, the continuous omics features (gene expression and CNV) were standardized using z-score normalization.

3 Methods

CMMOSyn is a hypergraph neural network featuring subgraph sampling that integrates a multi-omics cell line encoder and a pre-trained multimodal drug encoder. The overall architecture of CMMOSyn, illustrated in Fig. 1, comprises four primary modules:

(1) dual-branch encoder pre-training for multimodal drugs and multi-omics cell lines; (2) synergy hypergraph construction initialized by the pre-trained representations; (3) hypergraph representation learning refined by an active-node-centric subgraph sampling strategy; and (4) final drug combination synergy prediction.

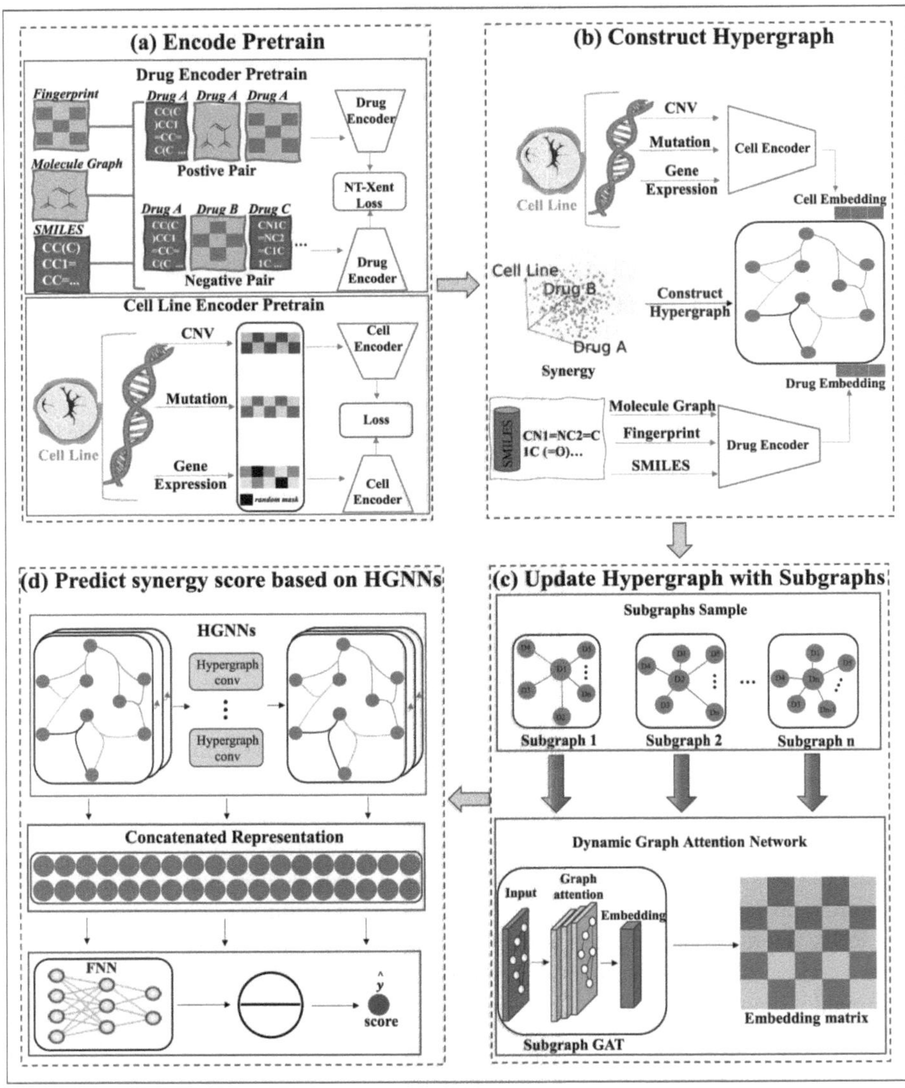

Fig. 1. The overall architecture of CMMOSyn.

3.1 Cross-modal Drug and Multi-omics Cell Line Encoder Pre-training

To integrate the multi-omics profiles of cancer cell lines, we developed the Tri-Omics Multiway Masked Transformer (Tri-OMT) encoder. The model employs a gene-centric tokenization strategy to align the multimodal inputs into a unified 512-dimensional latent space. The standardized continuous features, including gene expression and CNV, are projected into 512-dimensional continuous vectors via two independent linear projection layers. The binarized somatic mutation matrix is mapped using a learnable discrete state embedding dictionary with a size of two by 512. For each gene, the three modality-specific embeddings are summed element-wise with a trainable global gene identity embedding to construct a fused token. A trainable cell token is prepended to the input sequence to aggregate the global cell-line representation.

$$T_i = E_{id}(i) + \left(W_{exp}g_i + b_{exp}\right) + (W_{env}c_i + b_{env}) + E_{mut}(m_i) \tag{1}$$

where T_i represents the final fused multi-omics token representation for the i-th gene. $E_{id}(i)$ represents the global gene identity embedding, which is used to anchor the specific biological entity in the sequence. g_i and c_i denote the standardized continuous values for gene expression and CNV, respectively. W_{exp}, b_{exp} and W_{env}, b_{env} are the weight matrices and bias terms of the independent linear projection layers, which are used to map the scalar values into high-dimensional vectors. $\mathrm{m_i}$ is the binary somatic mutation status, and $E_{mut}(m_i)$ denotes the discrete state embedding extracted from the learnable dictionary based on the mutation status.

During the self-supervised pre-training, we employ an asymmetric random masking strategy. We randomly mask 15% of the gene expression tokens while maintaining the upstream genomic variants, including mutations and CNVs, completely visible. The sequence is then processed by a 6-layer Multiway Transformer backbone with 8 attention heads. To address the distinct statistical distributions of the continuous expression or CNV data and the discrete mutation inputs, each layer shares a global multi-head self-attention module but routes the outputs to modality-specific feed-forward network experts. The model is optimized by minimizing the mean squared error between the reconstructed and original expression values at the masked positions. Following pre-training, the 512-dimensional vector corresponding to the cell token is extracted as the final joint multi-omics representation.

We construct a multimodal drug encoder via cross-modal contrastive pre-training and a gated fusion mechanism. For each drug, SMILES strings are processed using RDKit to generate 2D molecular graphs and Morgan fingerprints. To extract modality-specific representations, we employ three distinct neural architectures: (1) a 4-layer Transformer encoder with 8 attention heads and a 512-dimensional hidden state processes the tokenized SMILES strings to capture sequence-level semantic dependencies; (2) a 3-layer GCN equipped with ReLU activations and batch normalization encodes the molecular graphs by propagating atom and bond features; and (3) a 2-layer MLP projects the high-dimensional sparse Morgan fingerprints into 512-dimensional dense continuous vectors.

During the self-supervised pre-training phase, representations of the same drug from any two distinct modalities form a positive pair, while those from different drugs in the same mini-batch serve as negative pairs. We optimize the encoders using the Normalized Temperature-scaled Cross-Entropy (NT-Xent) loss to enforce‘ semantic alignment across the sequence, graph, and fingerprint modalities within a shared latent space:

$$\mathcal{L}_{NT-Xent} = -log\frac{exp\left(sim\left(x_{di}, x_{di}^{+}\right)/\tau\right)}{\sum_{j=1}^{N} exp\left(sim\left(x_{di}, x_{dj}\right)/\tau\right)} \tag{2}$$

where x_{di} and x_{di}^{+} represent the feature representations extracted from the same drug in different modalities, and they constitute a positive sample pair. x_{dj} Represents the characterization of another drug in the same training batch as negative samples. Sim(,) denotes Cosine Similarity, which is used to compute the angle between two high-dimensional vectors in the latent space. τ is the temperature coefficient, which is used to adjust the penalty strength of the model on difficult negative samples. Following pre-training and alignment, the ultimate drug representations are dynamically aggregated via a gated fusion module.

3.2 Construct Hypergraph

Once the independent pre-training phases for both the cell line and drug encoders are complete, the resulting embeddings are utilized to initialize the node attributes for the downstream hypergraph architecture. Specifically, the cell token embedding derived from the Tri-OMT encoder serves as the initial feature vector for each cell line node, while the aggregated output from the gated fusion module acts as the initial feature vector for each drug node. By mapping the multi-omics profiles and multimodal drug features into a unified latent space, these extracted representations provide the foundational node features required to model the high-order synergistic interactions in the subsequent drug-drug-cell line hypergraph.

To model the high-order interactions among drugs and cell lines, we construct a synergistic hypergraph based on the previous node features. Specifically, a hyperedge is instantiated for each sample exhibiting a synergy score above a predefined threshold, concurrently connecting the respective triplet of entities (Drug A, Drug B, and Cell Line). This hypergraph topology explicitly captures the complex, non-pairwise dependencies inherent in drug combinations, facilitating effective message passing across heterogeneous nodes and yielding more discriminative feature representations.

When each drug combination sample is represented by a hyperedge, the entire drug combination dataset can be represented as a hypergraph $G = (V, E, Z)$. Where, $V = v_d \cup v_c$ represents the set of nodes, where v_d and v_c denote the sets of drug entities and cell line entities, respectively. $E \subseteq v_d \times v_d \times v_c$ is defined as the set of hyperedges, with each hyperedge representing the synergistic relationship among a drug-drug-cell line triplet. $Z \in R^{|E| \times |E|}$ is a diagonal matrix containing the weights corresponding to each hyperedge. Thus, the feature matrix for the hypergraph nodes is represented as: $X = \begin{bmatrix} X_D \\ X_C \end{bmatrix} \in R^{|V| \times n}$, where n is dimensionality of the features.

3.3 Subgraph Sampling

To capture localized topological dependencies and refine drug representations, we introduce an active-node-centric subgraph sampling mechanism. Specifically, high-degree drug nodes within the hypergraph are first identified as active nodes. For each active node, we extract its 1-hop ego-network to isolate its immediate structural context. A multi-head GAT is then deployed to dynamically update the embeddings of these active nodes. By computing attention weights across distinct representation subspaces, the GAT adaptively aggregates neighborhood features and fuses them with the central node's intrinsic embedding, ultimately yielding a highly contextualized representation.

3.4 Hypergraph Neural Networks and Prediction

HGNNs generalize the message-passing paradigm of traditional GNNs from pairwise links to higher-order relationships. Specifically, the hypergraph convolutional layer updates a given node's representation by aggregating information from all other nodes incident to the same hyperedge. Stacking multiple such layers enables the final node embeddings to explicitly capture the complex multi-way interactions inherent in the hypergraph topology.

In the $l-th$ layer of HGNNs, the embedding representations of all drug and cell line nodes, denoted as $H^{(l)}$, are calculated according to the following iterative propagation rule:

$$H^{(l)} = \sigma\left(O^{-1}YZB^{-1}Y^{T}H^{(l-1)}\Theta^{(l-1)}\right) \tag{3}$$

where $Y \in \mathbb{R}^{|V|\times|E|}$ is the incidence matrix of the hypergraph, and Z is the diagonal hyperedge weight matrix defined. $O \in R^{|V|\times|V|}$ and $B \in \mathrm{R}^{|E|\times|E|}$ are the degree matrices for nodes and hyperedges, respectively. Θ^{l-1} represents the learnable weight matrix for the current layer. σ denotes the ReLU activation function. The initial embedding H^{0} is initialized using the feature matrix X from the hypergraph.

Through L iterations of message passing, the HGNN effectively updates the node embeddings by aggregating representations from k-hop neighbors, fully leveraging the complex triplet relationships between drugs and cell lines. To predict the synergy score for a specific combination triplet (Drug A, Drug B, and Cell Line), the corresponding refined node embeddings h_{d_A}, h_{d_B}, and h_c are extracted from the final HGNN outputs, concatenated, and then fed into a three-layer FNN.

$$\hat{y}_{ddc} = \mathrm{FNN}\left(h_{d_A}\|h_{d_B}\|h_c\right) \tag{4}$$

where $\hat{y}_{ddc}$ represents the predicted synergy score for the given combination.

4 Results

4.1 Comparison Experiments

To rigorously evaluate CMMOSyn, we conducted experiments on three benchmark datasets: DrugComb, O'Neil, and NCI-ALMANAC, comparing its performance against seven established baselines. Traditional machine learning methods (SVM and RF) were evaluated under identical experimental protocols, while deep learning baselines (DeepSynergy [8], HypergraphSynergy [14], HypertranSynergy [16], MARSY [10], and TAG-C [24]) were implemented using the optimal hyperparameters specified in their original literature. All models were assessed via 5-fold cross-validation repeated five times, with standard deviations reported to ensure statistical stability. Predictive accuracy and correlation were quantified using Pearson Correlation Coefficient (PCC), Spearman Correlation Coefficient (SCC), Root Mean Square Error (RMSE), and the Coefficient of Determination (R^2) [25]. Empirical results show that CMMOSyn consistently outperforms all baselines across the three benchmark datasets and four evaluation metrics.

As detailed in Table 1, CMMOSyn outperforms the leading baseline, TAG-C, on the DrugComb dataset, achieving a 5.22% absolute increase in SCC and an 8.59% improvement in R^2. Furthermore, CMMOSyn maintains superior predictive accuracy across two additional benchmark datasets (Table 2 and Table 3). These empirical results validate the model's robustness and highlight its practical utility for prioritizing synergistic drug combinations in precision oncology.

Table 1. Results of 5-fold cross-validation repeated five times on the DrugComb dataset.

Models	RMSE↓	PCC↑	SCC↑	R2↑
RF	12.987 ± 1.723	0.646 ± 0.021	0.599 ± 0.029	0.486 ± 0.032
SVM	10.671 ± 1.373	0.779 ± 0.022	0.766 ± 0.026	0.554 ± 0.020
DeepSynergy	9.143 ± 0.882	0.843 ± 0.017	0.803 ± 0.015	0.576 ± 0.022
HypergraphSynergy	8.957 ± 0.971	0.858 ± 0.024	0.809 ± 0.028	0.594 ± 0.026
HypertranSynergy	8.421 ± 0.713	0.866 ± 0.014	0.822 ± 0.019	0.637 ± 0.024
MARSY	8.424 ± 0.851	0.864 ± 0.023	0.836 ± 0.018	0.622 ± 0.024
TAG-C	8.396 ± 0.741	0.869 ± 0.018	0.843 ± 0.024	0.710 ± 0.017
CMMOSyn	**8.022 ± 0.462**	**0.885 ± 0.045**	**0.887 ± 0.070**	**0.771 ± 0.014**

Table 2. Results of 5-fold cross-validation repeated five times on the O'Neil dataset.

Models	RMSE↓	PCC↑	SCC↑	R^2↑
RF	17.490 ± 0.693	0.652 ± 0.067	0.581 ± 0.071	0.455 ± 0.063
SVM	19.922 ± 0.751	0.503 ± 0.098	0.480 ± 0.058	0.311 ± 0.069
DeepSynergy	15.912 ± 1.531	0.733 ± 0.116	0.642 ± 0.102	0.592 ± 0.085
HypergraphSynergy	14.372 ± 0.085	0.784 ± 0.017	0.723 ± 0.022	0.612 ± 0.019
HypertranSynergy	13.771 ± 0.068	0.812 ± 0.021	0.773 ± 0.016	0.642 ± 0.014
MARSY	15.522 ± 0.093	0.761 ± 0.030	0.632 ± 0.024	0.624 ± 0.028
TAG-C	13.071 ± 0.127	0.839 ± 0.046	0.852 ± 0.037	0.711 ± 0.035
CMMOSyn	**8.592 ± 0.067**	**0.879 ± 0.127**	**0.877 ± 0.054**	**0.853 ± 0.023**

Table 3. Results of 5-fold cross-validation repeated five times on the NCI-ALMANAC dataset.

Models	RMSE↓	PCC↑	SCC↑	R^2↑
RF	57.390 ± 2.551	0.442 ± 0.055	0.371 ± 0.067	0.295 ± 0.051
SVM	59.713 ± 1.282	0.414 ± 0.042	0.366 ± 0.051	0.254 ± 0.049
DeepSynergy	44.912 ± 5.810	0.661 ± 0.075	0.581 ± 0.068	0.472 ± 0.072
HypergraphSynergy	43.653 ± 3.261	0.701 ± 0.062	0.622 ± 0.069	0.513 ± 0.058
HypertranSynergy	46.721 ± 1.659	0.647 ± 0.046	0.595 ± 0.039	0.469 ± 0.051
MARSY	44.137 ± 2.136	0.675 ± 0.041	0.613 ± 0.039	0.503 ± 0.028
TAG-C	42.033 ± 1.192	0.712 ± 0.022	0.630 ± 0.034	0.535 ± 0.033
CMMOSyn	**38.572 ± 5.011**	**0.768 ± 0.135**	**0.686 ± 0.032**	**0.601 ± 0.121**

4.2 Ablation Study

To assess the contributions of CMMOSyn's key components, we conducted an ablation study by comparing the full model with several structurally simplified variants. Specifically, we constructed three ablation settings, namely CMMOSyn-DM, CMMOSyn-CM, and CMMOSyn-DM-CM, in which the pre-trained multimodal drug encoder, the multi-omics cell line encoder, or both were replaced with lightweight alternatives, namely a basic GCN for drug representation learning and a two-layer MLP for cell line feature encoding. As shown in Table 4, replacing both encoders results in the most substantial performance drop, underscoring the importance of integrating multimodal drug information with multi-omics cellular representations. Moreover, the single-module ablation results indicate that the two encoders make complementary contributions to predictive performance, jointly strengthening the model's accuracy and representation quality (Fig. 2).

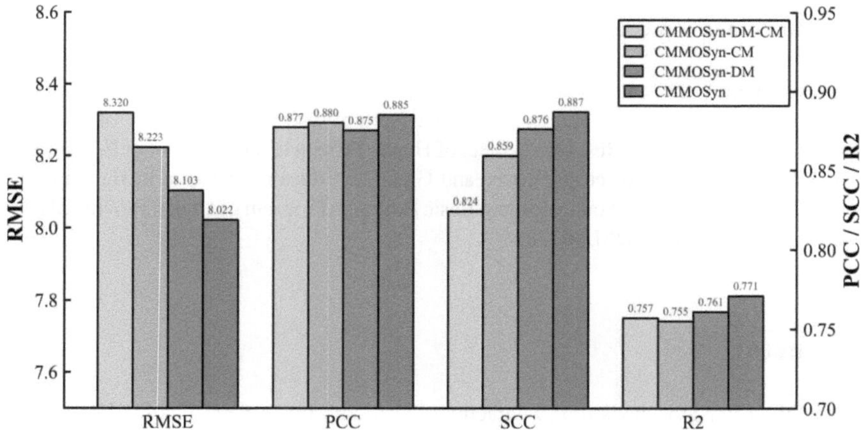

Fig. 2. Ablation Study of CMMOSyn Components on the DrugComb Dataset.

4.3 Case Study

To further assess the practical utility of CMMOSyn in prioritizing previously unobserved synergistic drug combinations, we applied the fully trained model to predict drug-pair–cell-line triplets not included in the training set. Using three selected cell lines, namely CRL-1740, SNB-75, and A375, as case studies, we identified several high-confidence candidate drug pairs and further examined their biological plausibility based on evidence from previous studies.

For example, Dactolisib, a dual PI3K/mTOR inhibitor, is a plausible synergistic partner of Topotecan in CRL-1740 cells. Mechanistically, Dactolisib suppresses the PI3K/AKT/mTOR signaling axis and may also interfere with DNA damage response pathways, thereby potentially enhancing the cytotoxic effect of Topotecan. This combination may be particularly relevant in CRL-1740 cells, where PTEN deletion is associated with constitutive activation of the PI3K/AKT/mTOR pathway [26, 27]. In A375 cells, the combination of Sorafenib and Vemurafenib has been reported to enhance melanoma cell sensitivity by promoting ferroptosis-mediated accumulation of reactive oxygen species [28]. In addition, Ruxolitinib, a BBB-penetrant JAK1/2 inhibitor, may act synergistically with Temozolomide in glioblastoma multiforme by suppressing IFN-driven JAK/STAT signaling, thereby reducing glioma invasion and potentially sensitizing tumor cells to Temozolomide [29]. Since EGFR is frequently over activated in GBM and contributes to tumor cell proliferation and survival, this prediction is also biologically reasonable.

5 Conclusions

In this study, we propose CMMOSyn, a hypergraph framework for drug synergy prediction. To mitigate data sparsity, CMMOSyn employs dual-branch self-supervised pre-training for node initialization. For drugs, a cross-modal contrastive encoder with gated fusion aligns SMILES, molecular graphs, and fingerprints. For cell lines, a Tri-Omics Multiway Masked Transformer (Tri-OMT) integrates multi-omics profiles via asymmetric masking. Finally, these robust embeddings initialize the hypergraph, where active-node-centric subgraph sampling captures high-order topological dependencies for accurate synergy prediction.

Acknowledgments. This work was supported by the National Natural Science Foundation of China (No.62202502), the Hunan Provincial Natural Science Foundation of China (No. 2025JJ60422), the Scientific Research Project of Hunan Provincial Department of Education (No. 24B0151), the Research Project on Degree and Graduate Education Reform in Hunan Province (No. 2025JGYB189) and the Young Student Basic Research Program of Hunan Provincial Natural Science Foundation (No. 2026JJ90278).

References

1. Van Mil, J.W.: Stockley's drug interactions, 11th edn. Int. J. Clin. Pharm. **38**, 1003–1004 (2016)

2. Jia, J., Zhu, F., Ma, X., Cao, Z.W., Li, Y.X., Chen, Y.Z.: Mechanisms of drug combinations: interaction and network perspectives. Nat. Rev. Drug Discovery **8**, 111–128 (2009)
3. Wu, L., et al.: Machine learning methods, databases and tools for drug combination prediction. Brief Bioinform. **23** (2022)
4. Pourmousa, M., et al.: AI-driven discovery of synergistic drug combinations against pancreatic cancer. Nat. Commun. **16**, 4020 (2025)
5. Julkunen, H., et al.: Leveraging multi-way interactions for systematic prediction of pre-clinical drug combination effects. Nat. Commun. **11**, 6136 (2020)
6. Wu, L., et al.: A hybrid deep forest-based method for predicting synergistic drug combinations. Cell Reports Methods 3 (2023)
7. Baptista, D., Ferreira, P.G., Rocha, M.: A systematic evaluation of deep learning methods for the prediction of drug synergy in cancer. PLoS Comput. Biol. **19**, e1010200 (2023)
8. Preuer, K., Lewis, R.P.I., Hochreiter, S., Bender, A., Bulusu, K.C., Klambauer, G.: DeepSynergy: predicting anti-cancer drug synergy with Deep Learning. Bioinformatics **34**, 1538–1546 (2018)
9. Liu, Q., Xie, L.: TranSynergy: Mechanism-driven interpretable deep neural network for the synergistic prediction and pathway deconvolution of drug combinations. PLoS Comput. Biol. **17**, e1008653 (2021)
10. El Khili, M.R., Memon, S.A., Emad, A.: MARSY: a multitask deep-learning framework for prediction of drug combination synergy scores. Bioinformatics **39** (2023)
11. Wang, J., Liu, X., Shen, S., Deng, L., Liu, H.: DeepDDS: deep graph neural network with attention mechanism to predict synergistic drug combinations. Briefings Bioinform. **23**, bbab390 (2022)
12. Yu, L., Xia, M., An, Q.: A network embedding framework based on integrating multiplex network for drug combination prediction. Briefings Bioinform. **23**, bbab364 (2022)
13. Yue, Y., Liu, Y., Hao, L., Lei, H., He, S.: Improving therapeutic synergy score predictions with adverse effects using multi-task heterogeneous network learning. Briefings Bioinform. **24**, bbac564 (2023)
14. Liu, X., Song, C., Liu, S., Li, M., Zhou, X., Zhang, W.: Multi-way relation-enhanced hypergraph representation learning for anti-cancer drug synergy prediction. Bioinformatics **38**, 4782–4789 (2022)
15. Feng, Y., You, H., Zhang, Z., Ji, R., Gao, Y.: Hypergraph neural networks. Proceedings of the AAAI Conference on Artificial Intelligence **33**, 3558–3565 (2019)
16. Wang, W., et al.: A granularity-level information fusion strategy on hypergraph transformer for predicting synergistic effects of anticancer drugs. Briefings in Bioinformatics 25 (2024)
17. Zhang, T., Zhang, L., Payne, P.R.O., Li, F.: Synergistic Drug Combination Prediction by Integrating Multiomics Data in Deep Learning Models. In: Markowitz, J. (ed.) Translational Bioinformatics for Therapeutic Development, pp. 223–238. Springer, US, New York, NY (2021)
18. Li, Y., Guo, Z., Gao, X., Wang, G.: MMCL-CDR: enhancing cancer drug response prediction with multi-omics and morphology images contrastive representation learning. Bioinformatics 39 (2023)
19. O'Neil, J., et al.: An unbiased oncology compound screen to identify novel combination strategies. Mol. Cancer Ther. **15**, 1155–1162 (2016)
20. Holbeck, S.L., et al.: The national cancer institute ALMANAC: a comprehensive screening resource for the detection of anticancer drug pairs with enhanced therapeutic activity. Cancer Res. **77**, 3564–3576 (2017)
21. Zagidullin, B., et al.: DrugComb: an integrative cancer drug combination data portal. Nucleic Acids Res. **47**, W43–W51 (2019)
22. Kim, S., et al.: PubChem 2019 update: improved access to chemical data. Nucleic Acids Res. **47**, D1102–D1109 (2019)

23. Ghandi, M., et al.: Next-generation characterization of the cancer cell line encyclopedia. Nature **569**, 503–508 (2019)
24. Zhang, J., Chen, S.-L., Wang, Y.-C.: Systematic prediction of synergistic drug combinations through network-based deep learning framework. Expert Syst. Appl. **270**, 126566 (2025)
25. Zeng, X., Zhong, K.-Y., Jiang, B., Li, Y.: Fusing sequence and structural knowledge by heterogeneous models to accurately and interpretively predict drug–target affinity. Molecules **28**, 8005 (2023)
26. Demel, H.-R., et al.: Effects of topoisomerase inhibitors that induce DNA damage response on glucose metabolism and PI3K/Akt/mTOR signaling in multiple myeloma cells. Am. J. Cancer Res. **5**, 1649 (2015)
27. Maira, S.-M., et al.: Identification and characterization of NVP-BEZ235, a new orally available dual phosphatidylinositol 3-kinase/mammalian target of rapamycin inhibitor with potent in vivo antitumor activity. Mol. Cancer Ther. **7**, 1851–1863 (2008)
28. Tang, F., Li, S., Liu, D., Chen, J., Han, C.: Sorafenib sensitizes melanoma cells to vemurafenib through ferroptosis. Transl Cancer Res **9**(3), 1584–1593 (2020)
29. Goker Bagca, B., Ozates, N.P., Biray Avci, C.: Ruxolitinib enhances cytotoxic and apoptotic effects of temozolomide on glioblastoma cells by regulating WNT signaling pathway-related genes. Med. Oncol. **40**, 37 (2022)

A Unified Benchmark and Conditional Sequence Modeling Framework for Future Influenza Evolution Prediction

Zhuolun Li[1], Xulinyi Huang[1], Jiayu Yang[1], Qianyao Lin[1], Xiaohua Wan[2], Yuxiao Cui[3], Shabir Madhi[4], Fa Zhang[2](✉), and Dongxu Zhang[1](✉)

[1] Xiamen University, Xiamen 361102, Fujian, China
zhangdongxu@xmu.edu.cn
[2] Beijing Institute of Technology, Beijing 100081, China
zhangfa@bit.edu.cn
[3] Changchun University of Science and Technology, Changchun, China
[4] University of the Witwatersrand, Johannesburg, South Africa

Abstract. Vaccination remains the most effective strategy for seasonal influenza prevention, but vaccine strain selection depends on anticipating future circulating variants before they are fully observed. This is challenging because influenza viruses evolve rapidly and existing studies often use heterogeneous datasets, targets, and evaluation settings.

We formulate future influenza evolution prediction as a conditional sequence modeling problem and present a unified benchmark, with an initial release on influenza A/H1N1 hemagglutinin (HA). The benchmark distinguishes raw and aligned sequence layers, separates hard and soft target definitions, and adopts leakage-safe rolling evaluation.

We instantiate the benchmark with a representative conditional seq2seq framework that combines pretrained protein representations, prevalence signals, and a compact multi-objective training objective. The resulting study provides a reproducible basis for systematic comparison in future influenza forecasting research.

Keywords: Influenza forecasting · Vaccine strain selection · Protein language models · Time extrapolation · Benchmark · Multi-objective learning

1 Introduction

Seasonal influenza remains a major global health burden, with modeling studies estimating hundreds of thousands of influenza-associated respiratory deaths each year worldwide [5]. Vaccination is the most important population-level intervention for controlling seasonal influenza, and vaccine strain selection is therefore not only a virological problem, but also a matter of direct public-health importance.

However, influenza control faces a fundamental challenge: vaccination is the best preventive strategy, yet influenza viruses evolve rapidly and their future

X. Cui et al. (Eds.): ISBRA 2026, LNBI 16690, pp. 211–221, 2027.
https://doi.org/10.1007/978-981-92-3716-6_17

direction is difficult to predict. Antigenic drift in key surface proteins such as hemagglutinin (HA) can progressively erode immunity against previously circulating strains [8,15]. Because vaccine composition must be determined months before the epidemic season, viral populations may continue to evolve during the lead time, increasing the risk of mismatch and limited future coverage [1,16]. Recent studies further show that later or more timely vaccine-strain selection can improve the match between selected vaccine viruses and subsequently circulating seasonal strains, and can improve evolutionary forecast accuracy in A/H3N2 settings [4,11].

Traditional influenza prediction and vaccine-strain selection rely on surveillance, phylogenetic analysis, serological assays, antigenic cartography, and expert judgment. These approaches remain indispensable, but they are not naturally optimized for large-scale future-distribution prediction from sequence data alone. Meanwhile, recent learning-based studies have started to model antigenic change, dominance, and candidate vaccine strain ranking, and protein foundation models provide reusable large-scale sequence representations [3,7,9,10,12,13]. However, these studies often use different datasets, targets, time splits, and metrics, making fair comparison difficult.

Motivated by this gap, we organize future influenza evolution prediction as a benchmark problem and instantiate it with a representative conditional sequence modeling framework. Our initial study focuses on H1N1-HA, distinguishes raw and aligned sequence layers, adopts strict rolling evaluation, and supports common comparison of model representations, forecasting backbones, and training objectives. The experiments reported in this manuscript focus on the current one-step H1N1-HA release, while the benchmark design leaves room for broader multi-horizon extensions.

The main contributions are summarized as follows.

- We cast influenza evolution forecasting as a strict time-extrapolation task and construct a unified H1N1-HA benchmark. The benchmark supports rolling splits, multi-horizon prediction, hard/soft supervision, and evaluation on both full-sequence and high-variability subset spaces.
- We introduce a conditional sequence modeling framework that combines protein foundation model representations with historical prevalence signals for future position-level prediction.
- We formalize a multi-objective learning strategy that jointly considers distribution fitting, conservative substitution preference, evolutionary plausibility, and temporal consistency.
- We provide an initial benchmark-based evaluation framework for systematic comparison of forecasting methods and future AI-assisted influenza sequence-forecasting studies.

2 Problem Formulation

We define future influenza evolution prediction as a conditional sequence modeling problem. Let x_t denote a current influenza sequence observed at time t, and let $p_{t-w+1:t}$ denote a historical prevalence window composed of the prevalence vectors from the previous w time bins. The predictive goal is to model the future sequence or position-level distribution at a horizon K:

$$p(x_{t+K} \mid x_t, p_{t-w+1:t}).$$

This formulation emphasizes two principles. First, prediction must be strictly prospective: only information available up to time t may be used during training, model selection, and evaluation setup. Second, the target should not be understood only as reconstruction of a single future sample, but more generally as prediction of the future population distribution over residues or sequences.

We use four paired definitions throughout the benchmark. The raw sequence layer keeps the original records after subtype and protein filtering. The aligned sequence layer maps records to a stable residue coordinate system for position-level prediction. A hard target treats one future representative sequence as the direct token-level label. A soft target aggregates future samples within a target window into empirical residue distributions. Unless otherwise noted, position-level tasks and subset metrics are reported in the aligned coordinate system.

These definitions separate the primary predictive task from downstream views. The main output is the aligned position-level future distribution. Candidate scores and budget-matched future coverage then assess whether these forecasts can support sequence-level ranking.

3 Benchmark and Task Design

The benchmark combines two complementary data roles. Sequence repositories provide residue-level influenza records with subtype labels, collection dates, and sequence identifiers; in this study these records are gathered from GISAID and NCBI GenBank [2,14]. Surveillance summaries provide temporal prevalence context rather than additional sequence labels. We use CDC-linked summaries from systems such as FluView and NREVSS, within the broader US influenza virologic surveillance landscape described in [6]. This separation makes clear which data source defines residues and which one defines the prevalence condition.

The present release focuses on influenza A/H1N1 HA. This choice gives a well-sampled HA forecasting task with public surveillance context and a clear need for aligned residue coordinates. It is also a conservative first case: A/H3N2 has stronger antigenic complexity and remains an important extension, but using H1N1-HA first allows the benchmark protocol, leakage controls, and model comparison machinery to be validated before broader subtype expansion (Fig. 1).

We first filter the raw collection by subtype and then split records by protein, retaining HA as the main branch. Temporal metadata are normalized into a consistent week/year representation. Invalid records include entries without usable subtype, protein, sequence, or collection-date metadata; duplicate records with conflicting metadata; sequences with non-amino-acid ambiguity that cannot be represented by the benchmark vocabulary; and sequences that are too short to map reliably. In the aligned release, sequences shorter than 0.8 times the selected

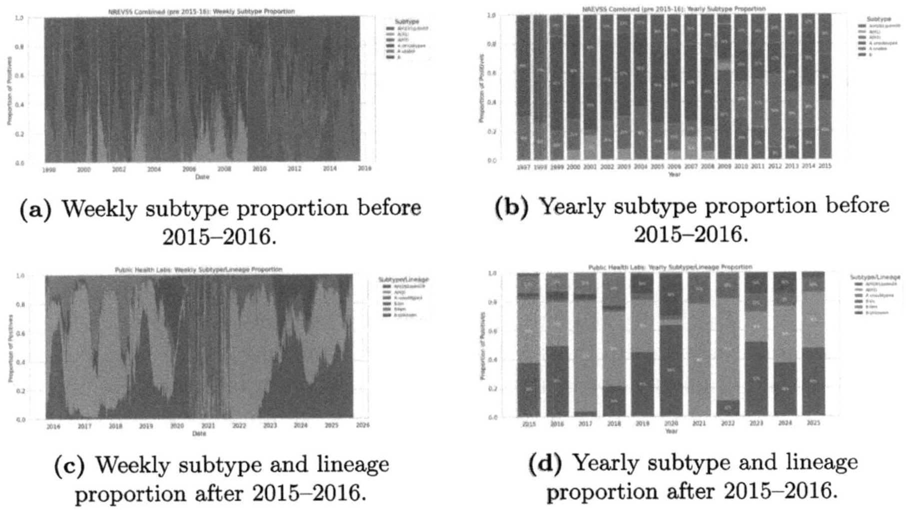

(a) Weekly subtype proportion before 2015–2016.

(b) Yearly subtype proportion before 2015–2016.

(c) Weekly subtype and lineage proportion after 2015–2016.

(d) Yearly subtype and lineage proportion after 2015–2016.

Fig. 1. Subtype composition patterns observed in surveillance summaries across different time scales. Panels (a) and (b) show weekly and yearly subtype proportions in the pre-2015–2016 period, while panels (c) and (d) summarize public-health laboratory reports in the later period. Together, these views illustrate strong temporal variation in dominant influenza subtypes and lineages, motivating a benchmark that emphasizes time-aware forecasting rather than static train-test evaluation.

group reference length are excluded before reference mapping. Traceable identifiers are retained so that processed records remain linked to their original sources.

Because raw HA sequences are not strictly length-consistent, raw token indices cannot safely serve as residue definitions. We retain the raw layer for provenance and inspection, and construct an aligned layer for modeling and evaluation. The aligned layer uses reference mapping within subtype groups and marks deletions or unmapped residues with a missing character. This avoids confounding a tokenizer position with a biological residue coordinate.

The benchmark adopts a strict rolling-window protocol. For each decision time t, the training set uses only observations available before t, validation is selected from a temporally later but still historical interval, and testing is carried out on a future target window. No information from the future window is allowed to influence training, hyperparameter selection, or score calibration. This design is intended to measure genuine time extrapolation rather than interpolation over randomly mixed samples. Figure 2 illustrates the benchmark protocol together with the representative rolling-window training and forecasting workflow used in this study.

Each run produces standardized outputs at three levels: aligned position-level predictive distributions, sequence-level candidate scores and rankings, and season-level coverage summaries under fixed candidate budgets. In addition, structured run summaries are retained to support cross-model comparison under

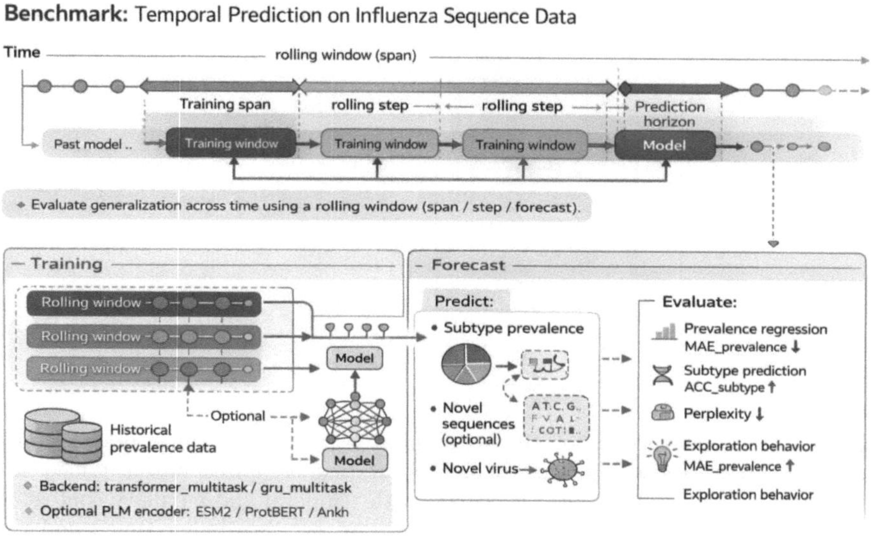

Fig. 2. Overview of the benchmark protocol and rolling-window forecasting framework. The upper panel shows the time-aware evaluation setting, where the training span advances with a fixed rolling step and predictions are assessed on a future horizon. The lower panel summarizes the representative training and forecasting workflow: historical sequence and prevalence information are used to train a model within each rolling window, and the resulting model is evaluated on future prediction windows under unified benchmark metrics.

identical split definitions. The submitted benchmark package records the split definitions, preprocessing filters, selected high-variability positions, run configurations, and metric tables so that later comparisons can reuse the same protocol.

4 Representative Modeling Framework

The proposed framework takes as input the current sequence together with a historical prevalence window describing recent population dynamics. The sequence is represented at the token level, while the prevalence history is encoded as a time-indexed condition signal. In this way, the model predicts not an unconditional future sequence distribution, but a future distribution conditioned on both sequence context and recent epidemiological composition.

At the representation level, we use protein foundation models as a shared sequence encoding basis. Their role is not merely to increase parameter count, but to import contextual substitution regularities and broader sequence priors learned from large-scale protein corpora. On top of these encoders, the default forecasting backbone in the current benchmark is a conditional seq2seq model. After preprocessing and alignment, HA sequences are tokenized and passed to a pretrained protein encoder, which is then fine-tuned jointly with the forecasting backbone under the benchmark training protocol. The backbone receives

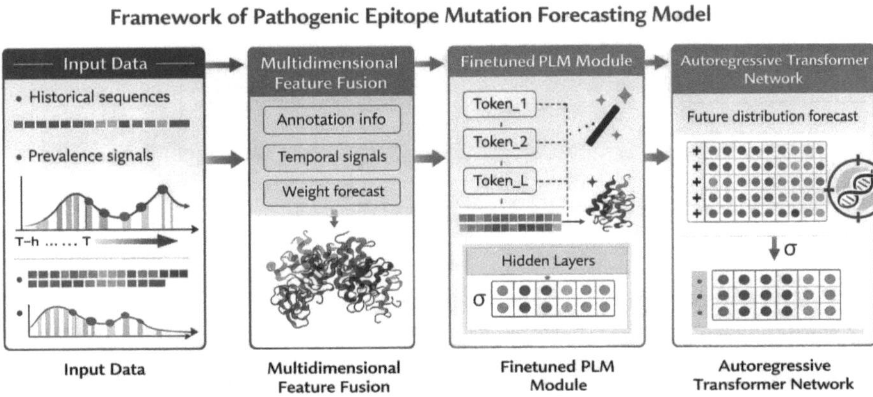

Fig. 3. Schematic overview of the representative modeling framework. Historical sequence observations and prevalence signals are first organized into a unified input representation. These inputs are then fused with temporal and auxiliary context features, encoded by a pretrained protein language model that is fine-tuned under the benchmark protocol, and passed to a downstream sequence forecasting backbone to produce future mutation or residue-distribution predictions. The figure is intended as a high-level architectural overview rather than a one-to-one specification of every compared backbone.

both sequence-derived features and prevalence-conditioned context, and produces future residue distributions on aligned positions. We do not regard this architecture as the only admissible design; rather, it serves as a representative and stable default model class for benchmarked comparison. In this manuscript, we refer to this default configuration as the conditional seq2seq forecasting framework. Figure 3 gives a schematic view of the representative modeling pipeline, including sequence and prevalence inputs, multidimensional feature fusion, pretrained protein encoding with fine-tuning, and the downstream sequence forecasting backbone.

Although the supervised target is evaluated position by position, the model is not a purely independent site model. Each position-level logit is produced from the encoded full HA sequence and the prevalence condition, so distant residues can influence the prediction through the pretrained representation and the seq2seq backbone. We therefore treat epistatic effects as context captured by the sequence encoder, while explicit higher-order epistasis tests are left for future benchmark extensions.

The framework supports hard-target and soft-target supervision under single- and multi-horizon settings. Let $\mathbf{z}_{i,l} \in \mathbb{R}^{|V|}$ be the logits for sample i and aligned position l, and let $p_{i,l} = \text{softmax}(\mathbf{z}_{i,l})$. We use $y_{i,l}$ for a hard future residue, $q_{i,l}$ for a soft empirical future distribution, and $m_{i,l}$ for the mask over valid aligned positions.

The training objective is

$$\mathcal{L} = \lambda_{\text{dist}}\mathcal{L}_{\text{dist}} + \lambda_{\text{blosum}}\mathcal{L}_{\text{blosum}} + \lambda_{\text{eve}}\mathcal{L}_{\text{eve}} + \lambda_{\text{temp}}\mathcal{L}_{\text{temp}}. \tag{1}$$

The distribution term is masked negative log-likelihood for hard targets and masked KL divergence for soft targets:

$$\mathcal{L}_{\text{dist}} = \begin{cases} -\frac{1}{M}\sum_{i,l} m_{i,l} \log p_{i,l}(y_{i,l}), & \text{hard}, \\ \frac{1}{M}\sum_{i,l} m_{i,l} D_{\text{KL}}(q_{i,l} \| p_{i,l}), & \text{soft}, \end{cases} \tag{2}$$

where $M = \sum_{i,l} m_{i,l}$. The remaining terms add lightweight biological and temporal regularization:

$$\begin{aligned} \mathcal{L}_{\text{blosum}} &= -\frac{1}{M}\sum_{i,l} m_{i,l} \sum_{a \in V} p_{i,l}(a) S(a, y_{i,l}), \\ \mathcal{L}_{\text{eve}} &= \frac{1}{M}\sum_{i,l} m_{i,l} D_{\text{KL}}(p_{i,l} \| \pi_{i,l}), \\ \mathcal{L}_{\text{temp}} &= \frac{1}{M}\sum_{i,l} m_{i,l} D_{\text{KL}}(p_{i,l}^{(t+1|t)} \| p_{i,l}^{(t|t-1)}). \end{aligned} \tag{3}$$

Here S is a BLOSUM similarity score. The prior $\pi_{i,l}$ is estimated from historical data or an auxiliary evolution-aware model. The first regularizer rewards conservative near-miss substitutions, the second discourages implausible residue distributions, and the third discourages abrupt distributional jumps. In the current release, this loss setting is fixed across the main valid runs; the empirical comparison below is therefore a backbone and representation comparison rather than a loss-component ablation.

To connect position-level forecasting with downstream evaluation, we map position-level predictions to sequence-level candidate scores. Candidates are then ranked by predicted future relevance and compared under fixed Top-K budgets, linking residue forecasting with future coverage analysis in one protocol.

5 Evaluation Protocol

Evaluation compares learned models against simple but informative baselines, including persistence forecasts, dominant-sequence history rules, frequency-driven selection, and budget-matched random baselines. When available, seasonal recommendation references are also included as external comparators.

Metrics are grouped into three families. Position-level distribution quality is measured by Top-k accuracy, NLL, Brier score, and ECE. Sequence-level ranking, when evaluated explicitly, is measured by MRR, NDCG, and Coverage@K. Season-level summaries report budget-matched future coverage under fixed candidate budgets. Model selection uses only historical validation windows, and final performance is aggregated across rolling windows rather than inferred from a single split.

All position metrics are reported on the full aligned sequence and on a high-variability subset. The subset is selected only from the training split by normalized residue entropy in aligned coordinates; the main reported runs use the top

50 sites with minimum coverage 200. This subset is a mutation-enriched stress test, not a claim that all selected sites are known antigenic sites. Overlap with curated HA epitope or structural annotations is an important future extension for connecting the benchmark more directly to antigenic and functional plausibility.

6 Experiments and Analysis

The current paper package is organized around the first H1N1-HA benchmark release and is intended to support benchmark validation, backbone comparison, and representative-model selection. In total, 54 runs were collected under a shared loss setting and reduced train/validation limits. Among them, 36 runs have valid non-zero subset metrics and are used in the main comparisons. A valid run is one for which the aligned high-variability mask is non-empty and the subset metrics are actually evaluated. The remaining 18 zero-subset runs are excluded because their subset fields do not correspond to a valid evaluated residue subset. Because the available result package reports $K = 1$ metrics, the following analysis should be viewed as an initial benchmark release rather than a complete multi-horizon study.

We first evaluate whether future influenza evolution is statistically learnable under strict rolling evaluation. Table 1 summarizes backbone-level performance using only valid runs. The results are highly non-uniform. The conditional seq2seq backbone is clearly superior to all other tested architectures, achieving the best mean validation NLL (0.187), mean subset NLL (0.267), mean subset Top-1 accuracy (0.945), and competitive calibration. By contrast, the next strongest backbone, autoregressive transformer, remains far behind, with a mean subset NLL of 2.175 and subset Top-1 of 0.521. The remaining backbones cluster near chance-level Top-1 performance in both the full and subset spaces. These results indicate that under the current benchmark protocol, future position-distribution prediction is learnable, but strong performance depends substantially on the choice of forecasting backbone.

Table 1. Backbone comparison for $K = 1$ prediction. Values are means over valid runs with non-zero subset metrics; lower NLL/ECE and higher Top-1 are better.

Backbone	n	Val NLL	Subset NLL	Subset Top-1	Val ECE
Cond. Seq2Seq	6	0.187	0.267	0.945	0.101
AR Transformer	6	1.658	2.175	0.521	0.178
SeqVAE	6	2.935	2.892	0.103	0.012
Temp. Transformer	6	2.937	2.894	0.103	0.015
Graph Attention	6	2.937	2.893	0.103	0.014
Temp. GRU	6	2.938	2.895	0.103	0.015

We next examine protein foundation model choice under the conditional seq2seq backbone. Table 2 shows that the ESM2 family consistently outperforms the tested Ankh models. The current best valid run is obtained by ESM2-35M, which achieves a validation NLL of 0.110, subset NLL of 0.153, subset Top-1 of 0.988, and validation ECE of 0.090. Although ESM2-150M is marginally better in subset NLL (0.152 vs. 0.153), ESM2-35M remains more attractive as the main-paper model because it is the best valid run overall and provides the most balanced combination of likelihood, accuracy, and calibration among the valid seq2seq candidates. We do not interpret this as evidence that smaller protein models are generally superior. The pattern may reflect the limited training budget, fine-tuning stability, dataset size, and the position-level forecasting objective used in this release.

Table 2. PFM comparison under the conditional seq2seq backbone for $K = 1$ prediction. Each row reports the best valid run for that PFM under the shared training setting.

PFM	Val NLL	Subset NLL	Subset Top-1	Val ECE
ESM2-35M	**0.110**	0.153	**0.988**	**0.090**
ESM2-150M	0.126	**0.152**	0.982	0.100
ESM2-8M	0.135	0.159	0.981	0.107
Ankh-Base	0.196	0.301	0.941	0.113
ESM2-650M	0.209	0.246	0.983	0.149
Ankh-Large	0.345	0.591	0.793	0.045

The current recommended main model is therefore the ESM2-35M plus conditional seq2seq configuration. These results should be interpreted in a benchmark-first setting. The main value of the current study is not to claim a final best model or a complete loss ablation, but to show that the benchmark can distinguish architectures and support stable representative-model selection.

7 Conclusion

This paper presents a unified benchmark and conditional sequence modeling framework for future influenza evolution prediction. Rather than treating the problem as a static sequence task or reporting isolated model performance on a single split, we organize it as a prevalence-conditioned time-extrapolation problem with rolling evaluation, multi-horizon settings, hard and soft target definitions, and high-variability subset analysis.

The main conclusions are not limited to the score of one model under one configuration. More fundamentally, our study supports three claims: future influenza position-distribution prediction is a meaningful and learnable task; benchmark standardization is necessary for credible comparison in this area; and pretrained protein representations together with conditional sequence modeling are promising ingredients for improving future evolution prediction. At the same time, the current release is limited to H1N1-HA, available $K = 1$ runs, and a shared multi-objective loss setting; broader subtype coverage, multi-horizon evaluation, loss-component ablation, and structural or functional plausibility metrics remain important future extensions. We hope that this work provides a reproducible starting point for larger-scale model comparison and future AI-assisted influenza forecasting research.

Acknowledgements. This work was supported by the National Natural Science Foundation of China General Program under Grant No. 62472365 and the Xiamen Municipal Natural Science Foundation General Program under Grant No. 3502Z202473003.

References

1. Agor, J.K., Özaltın, O.Y.: Models for predicting the evolution of influenza to inform vaccine strain selection. Human Vaccines Immunotherapeutics **14**(3), 678–683 (2018). https://doi.org/10.1080/21645515.2017.1423152
2. Clark, K., Karsch-Mizrachi, I., Lipman, D.J., Ostell, J., Sayers, E.W.: GenBank. Nucleic Acids Res. **44**(D1), D67–D72 (2016). https://doi.org/10.1093/nar/gkv1276
3. Gao, C., Wen, F., Guan, M., Hatuwal, B., Li, L., Praena, B., Tang, C.Y., Zhang, J., Luo, F., Xie, H., Webby, R., Tao, Y.J., Wan, X.F.: MAIVeSS: streamlined selection of antigenically matched, high-yield viruses for seasonal influenza vaccine production. Nat. Commun. **15**, 1128 (2024). https://doi.org/10.1038/s41467-024-45145-x
4. Huddleston, J., Bedford, T.: Timely vaccine strain selection and genomic surveillance improve evolutionary forecast accuracy of seasonal influenza A/H3N2. eLife **14**, RP104282 (2025). https://doi.org/10.7554/eLife.104282
5. Iuliano, A.D., et al.: Estimates of global seasonal influenza-associated respiratory mortality: a modelling study. Lancet **391**(10127), 1285–1300 (2018). https://doi.org/10.1016/S0140-6736(17)33293-2
6. Jester, B., Schwerzmann, J., Mustaquim, D., Aden, T., Brammer, L., Humes, R., Shult, P., Shahangian, S., Gubareva, L., Xu, X., Miller, J., Jernigan, D.: Mapping of the US domestic influenza virologic surveillance landscape. Emerg. Infect. Dis. **24**(7), 1300–1306 (2018). https://doi.org/10.3201/eid2407.180028
7. Lin, Z., Akin, H., Rao, R., Hie, B., Zhu, Z., Lu, W., Santos Costa, A., Fazel-Zarandi, M., Sercu, T., Candido, S., et al.: Evolutionary-scale prediction of atomic-level protein structure with a language model. Science **379**(6637), 1123–1130 (2023). https://doi.org/10.1126/science.ade2574
8. Łuksza, M., Lässig, M.: A predictive fitness model for influenza. Nature **507**, 57–61 (2014). https://doi.org/10.1038/nature13087
9. Perofsky, A.C., Nelson, M.I.: The challenges of vaccine strain selection. eLife **9**, e62955 (2020). https://doi.org/10.7554/eLife.62955
10. Rives, A., Meier, J., Sercu, T., Goyal, S., Lin, Z., Liu, J., Guo, D., Ott, M., Zitnick, C.L., Ma, J., Fergus, R.: Biological structure and function emerge from scaling unsupervised learning to 250 million protein sequences. Proc. Natl. Acad. Sci. U.S.A. **118**(15), e2016239118 (2021). https://doi.org/10.1073/pnas.2016239118

11. de Rooij, A.J.H., Lempers, V.J.C., Park, Y., Vicic, N., Han, A.X., Russell, C.A., Rudin, D.: Reproducible and later vaccine strain selection can improve vaccine match to A/H3N2 seasonal influenza viruses. npj Vaccines **10**, 243 (2025). https://doi.org/10.1038/s41541-025-01292-w
12. Shah, S.A.W., Palomar, D.P., Barr, I., Poon, L.L.M., Quadeer, A.A., McKay, M.R.: Seasonal antigenic prediction of influenza A H3N2 using machine learning. Nat. Commun. **15**, 3833 (2024). https://doi.org/10.1038/s41467-024-47862-9
13. Shi, W., Wohlwend, J., Wu, M., et al.: Influenza vaccine strain selection with an AI-based evolutionary and antigenicity model. Nat. Med. **31**, 3862–3870 (2025). https://doi.org/10.1038/s41591-025-03917-y
14. Shu, Y., McCauley, J.: GISAID: Global initiative on sharing all influenza data–from vision to reality. Eurosurveillance **22**(13), 30494 (2017). https://doi.org/10.2807/1560-7917.ES.2017.22.13.30494
15. Smith, D.J., Lapedes, A.S., de Jong, J.C., Bestebroer, T.M., Rimmelzwaan, G.F., Osterhaus, A.D.M.E., Fouchier, R.A.M.: Mapping the antigenic and genetic evolution of influenza virus. Science **305**(5682), 371–376 (2004). https://doi.org/10.1126/science.1097211
16. Tricco, A.C., et al.: Comparing influenza vaccine efficacy against mismatched and matched strains: a systematic review and meta-analysis. BMC Med. **11**, 153 (2013). https://doi.org/10.1186/1741-7015-11-153

SecPredNet: Joint Modeling of PLM Embeddings and Physicochemical Features for Signal Peptide Secretion Efficiency Prediction

Xiao Liang[1], Haochen Zhao[2], Chengchao Shen[1(✉)], and Jianxin Wang[1]

[1] Hunan Provincial Key Lab on Bioinformatics, School of Computer Science and Engineering, Central South University, Changsha 410083, China
scc.cs@csu.edu.cn
[2] Big Data Institute, Central South University, Changsha 410083, China

Abstract. Signal peptides (SPs) are short N-terminal sequences that direct proteins to the secretory pathway and strongly influence secretion efficiency. In recombinant protein production, selecting an appropriate SP is critical for improving yield and reducing cost. However, current screening of high-efficiency signal peptides still relies heavily on labor-intensive trial-and-error experiments, creating a strong need for accurate computational prediction methods. However, the existing traditional machine learning methods rely on handcrafted physicochemical descriptors and often fail to capture complex sequence patterns, whereas current deep learning approaches still do not fully exploit the structural priors and evolutionary knowledge embedded in large-scale pretrained protein language models (PLMs). To bridge this gap, we propose SecPredNet, a hybrid framework for signal peptide secretion efficiency prediction. SecPredNet integrates structure-aware sequence representations extracted by the PLM with residue-level physicochemical features derived from AAindex, and employs a gating module to adaptively fuse the two modalities. Experimental results on three secretion datasets show that the proposed model consistently outperforms traditional physicochemical methods and single-modal deep learning baselines. These results demonstrate the value of jointly modeling protein language representations and physicochemical features for secretion efficiency prediction. The codes of SecPredNet are available at https://github.com/liangxiaodata/SecPredNet.

Keywords: Signal peptide · Secretion efficiency prediction · Protein language model · Physicochemical features · Feature fusion

1 Introduction

Signal peptides (SPs) are short N-terminal sequences that guide proteins to cellular secretion pathways and play a central role in protein translocation across

X. Cui et al. (Eds.): ISBRA 2026, LNBI 16690, pp. 222–233, 2027.
https://doi.org/10.1007/978-981-92-3716-6_18

membranes [1,2]. In recombinant protein production, the choice of signal peptide can substantially influence secretion efficiency, thereby affecting production yield and cost [3]. As a result, the identification and design of high-efficiency SPs have become important for optimizing industrial protein expression. However, current screening strategies still rely heavily on experimental trial-and-error, which is time-consuming, labor-intensive, and expensive.

Recently, machine learning, deep learning, and foundation models have been increasingly applied to bioinformatics and biomedical prediction tasks [4–7]. In the field of signal peptides, machine learning and deep learning approaches have also been widely used in a variety of signal peptide-related tasks. Representative models such as SignalP 5.0 [8] and Deepsig [9], based on recurrent neural networks(RNN) [10] and convolutional neural networks(CNN) [11], respectively, were developed for signal peptide category prediction from sequence information. More recently, PLM-based methods such as SignalP 6.0 [12] and USPNet [13] have further improved prediction performance. In addition, Wu et al. [14] developed an attention-based Transformer model trained on Swiss-Prot [15] data to generate novel signal peptides, and SecretoGen [16] further demonstrated that generative transformers trained on large-scale natural signal peptide sequences can assist in selecting efficient signal peptide candidates. In contrast, studies on signal peptide secretion efficiency prediction remain limited. Existing efforts mainly fall into two categories: traditional machine learning methods based on handcrafted physicochemical features, and deep learning approaches based on sequence data. For example, Grasso et al. [17] showed that residue composition and physicochemical descriptors provide useful information for this task, and that combining these features with a Random Forest model [18] can achieve promising performance. However, such methods rely heavily on manual feature engineering and have limited ability to model complex nonlinear sequence patterns. More recently, Li et al. [19] explored several deep learning architectures, including CNN [11], LSTM [20], Transformer [21], and GRU [22], and found that transfer learning based on CNN achieved the best performance for signal peptide secretion efficiency prediction. Their results suggest that transfer learning can help alleviate the data scarcity problem by leveraging knowledge from source-domain data. However, this strategy still depends strongly on the choice of source-domain data, and its generalizability across different target domains remains to be further validated.

To address these limitations, we propose SecPredNet, a hybrid deep learning framework for signal peptide secretion efficiency prediction. Inspired by [23], SecPredNet integrates two complementary modalities: structure-aware sequence representations derived from the Implicit Structure Model (ISM) [24], a PLM that captures latent structural topologies from sequences; and residue-level physicochemical descriptors obtained from AAindex [25], a comprehensive database of amino acid indices that encodes diverse physicochemical properties of amino acids. To effectively combine these heterogeneous features, we further introduce a gating mechanism that adaptively balances the contributions of the two branches. In this way, the model can jointly leverage global contextual semantics from pre-trained sequence representations and local biophysical priors from physicochemical descriptors. Experimental results on three benchmark datasets demonstrate that SecPredNet achieves competitive and robust performance. Further analyses demonstrate that the model achieves superior performance in practical screening tasks, including effective candidate prioritization and robust false positive reduction. These results suggest that SecPredNet is an effective computational tool for signal peptide performance prediction and the rational design of high-efficiency signal peptides.

2 Materials and Methods

2.1 Dataset and Task Definition

In this study, signal peptide secretion efficiency prediction is formulated as a supervised regression task under a given host–protein setting. Given a signal peptide sequence, the model aims to predict its secretion efficiency score for the target protein in the corresponding host system. In essence, the task is to learn the quantitative relationship between signal peptide characteristics and secretion efficiency. It should be noted that the definition of the secretion efficiency score may vary across different datasets.

To comprehensively evaluate SecPredNet, we employed three datasets collected under different host–protein settings.

- **BS-AmyQ dataset.** This dataset contains experimental secretion data for multiple signal peptides in the α-amylase (AmyQ) expression system of *Bacillus subtilis.* It was introduced by Grasso et al. [17] and contains 4,421 signal peptides, with 3,095 samples for training and 1,326 samples for testing. The secretion efficiency score is defined as a weighted average (WA) score derived from bin-based ranking in high-throughput screening, where a lower WA value indicates higher secretion efficiency.
- **BS-Cut dataset.** This dataset contains experimental secretion data for multiple signal peptides in the Cutinase expression system of *Bacillus subtilis.* The raw data were obtained from SPSED [26], which summarizes the screening results reported by Brockmeier et al. [27]. After data cleaning, 168 distinct signal peptides were retained. The secretion efficiency score is defined based on the experimentally measured secretion level of Cutinase and was further standardized using Z-score normalization before model training.
- **BA-PG dataset.** This dataset contains experimental secretion data for multiple signal peptides in the protein-glutaminase (PG) expression system of *Bacillus amyloliquefaciens.* It was collected from Li et al. [19] and contains 151 distinct signal peptides. The secretion efficiency score is defined based on the experimentally measured secretion level of PG and was further standardized using Z-score normalization before model training.

2.2 Model Overview

The overall architecture of SecPredNet is illustrated in Fig. 1. The model consists of four modules: sequence encoding, physicochemical encoding, feature fusion, and prediction. Given an input signal peptide sequence, the sequence branch uses ISM to extract contextual embeddings, while the physicochemical branch represents each residue using AAIndex descriptors and encodes residue-level physicochemical patterns. The two feature streams are then integrated by a learnable gating mechanism, and the fused representation is fed into a multilayer perceptron (MLP) regressor to produce the final secretion score.

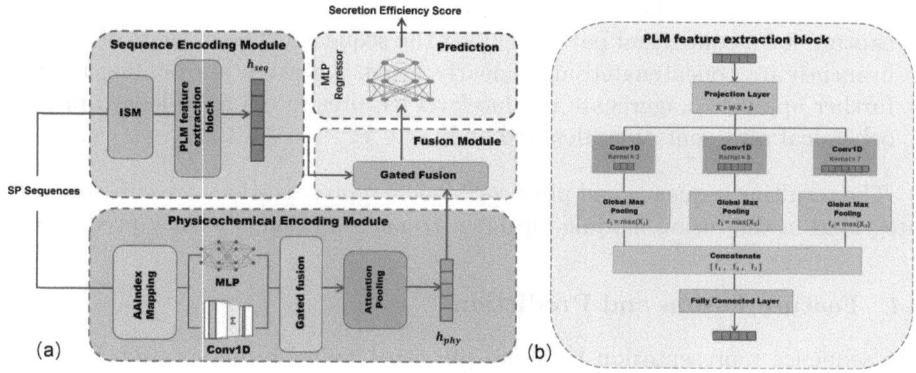

Fig. 1. Overview of the proposed SecPredNet framework. (a) The overall framework of SecPredNet. (b) Detailed architecture of the PLM feature extraction block used in the sequence encoding module.

2.3 Feature Encoding

To capture complementary information from both sequence semantics and explicit physicochemical properties, we design a dual-branch feature encoding strategy in SecPredNet. Specifically, the model extracts sequence-level representations from a pre-trained protein language model and physicochemical representations from residue-level AAIndex descriptors.

- **Sequence Encoding Module.** Before encoding, each input sequence is truncated or padded to a fixed length of 50 residues. The input signal peptide sequence is then fed into ISM to obtain contextualized residue-level embeddings. In the Sequence Encoding Module, these embeddings are further processed by a PLM feature extraction block. Specifically, the high-dimensional residue embeddings are first passed through a projection layer to obtain a compact latent representation. The projected features are then delivered to three parallel one-dimensional convolutional [28] branches with kernel sizes

of 3, 5, and 7, respectively, to capture local sequence patterns at different receptive-field scales. The output of each branch is summarized by global max pooling to retain the most informative responses. Finally, the pooled features are concatenated and passed through a fully connected layer, yielding the final sequence representation, denoted as $\mathbf{h}_{seq} \in \mathbb{R}^d$, where d denotes the dimensionality of the learned feature representation.
- **Physicochemical Encoding Module.** To explicitly characterize residue-level physicochemical properties, each amino acid is mapped to a 566-dimensional AAindex descriptor vector, yielding an AAindex feature matrix for the signal peptide. A dual-branch encoder is then adopted. One branch uses an MLP to learn nonlinear transformations of residue-wise physicochemical features, while the other uses a one-dimensional convolutional network to capture local contextual patterns along the sequence. The outputs of the two branches are concatenated and linearly fused. An attention pooling layer is further applied to aggregate residue-level features into a fixed-length physicochemical representation, denoted as $\mathbf{h}_{phy} \in \mathbb{R}^d$.

The resulting sequence and physicochemical representations are subsequently integrated in the fusion module for downstream secretion efficiency prediction.

2.4 Feature Fusion and Prediction

The sequence representation $\mathbf{h}_{seq}$ and physicochemical representation $\mathbf{h}_{phy}$ are integrated using a learnable gating mechanism. Specifically, a scalar gate is generated from the concatenation of the two representations and used to adaptively balance their contributions:

$$\mathbf{h}_{fuse} = \text{LayerNorm}\left(g\mathbf{h}_{seq} + (1-g)\mathbf{h}_{phy}\right), \tag{1}$$

where $g = \sigma(\mathbf{W}_g[\mathbf{h}_{seq}; \mathbf{h}_{phy}] + b_g)$ is a learnable gate, $\sigma(\cdot)$ denotes the sigmoid function, and LayerNorm$(\cdot)$ denotes layer normalization. The fused representation is then fed into an MLP regressor to predict the secretion efficiency score.

For model optimization, different objectives were used according to dataset size. For the BS-AmyQ dataset, which contains relatively more samples, the model was trained using the mean squared error (MSE) loss. For the smaller BS-Cut and BA-PG datasets, we further introduced a margin ranking loss to improve the consistency of relative secretion-efficiency ordering between samples. The final training objective is:

$$\mathcal{L} = \mathcal{L}_{\text{MSE}} + \lambda\mathcal{L}_{\text{rank}}, \tag{2}$$

where λ was set to 1 in our experiments. For the margin ranking loss, the margin hyperparameter m was set to 0.1. The ranking loss penalizes incorrectly ordered sample pairs within a mini-batch and encourages the model to assign higher predicted scores to samples with higher experimentally measured secretion efficiency.

3 Experiments and Results

3.1 Performance Evaluation

To evaluate the effectiveness of SecPredNet for signal peptide secretion efficiency prediction, we compared it with two representative baselines from previous studies, namely the handcrafted feature-based random forest model proposed by Grasso et al. [17] and the deep learning model reported by Li et al. [19] Since the BS-AmyQ dataset already provides an official train–test split, all methods were evaluated under this predefined split. In contrast, the BS-Cut and BA-PG datasets are much smaller in scale. To obtain a more reliable and robust evaluation, we adopted 5-fold cross-validation on these two datasets and report the average results across the five folds.

Table 1. Performance comparison of different methods on three signal peptide secretion efficiency prediction datasets.

Datasets	Models	MSE ↓	RMSE ↓	Pearson ↑	Spearman ↑
BS-AmyQ	SecPredNet	**0.854**	**0.924**	**0.906**	**0.885**
	Grasso et al. [17]	1.238	1.113	0.862	0.853
	Li et al. [19]	2.209	1.486	0.195	0.198
BS-Cut	SecPredNet	**0.886±0.414**	**0.909±0.245**	**0.487±0.217**	**0.513±0.196**
	Grasso et al. [17]	1.057±0.549	1.002±0.243	0.259±0.191	0.380±0.138
	Li et al. [19]	1.116±0.456	1.034±0.239	0.110±0.320	0.176±0.297
BA-PG	SecPredNet	**0.968±0.264**	**0.975±0.135**	**0.409±0.117**	**0.423±0.186**
	Grasso et al. [17]	1.048±0.277	1.015±0.139	0.157±0.307	0.190±0.299
	Li et al. [19]	0.975±0.203	0.985±0.105	0.181±0.276	0.114±0.195

Note: BS-AmyQ was evaluated using the official train–test split, while BS-Cut and BA-PG were evaluated by 5-fold cross-validation. The results of Grasso et al. and Li et al. were reproduced using their released code under the same evaluation settings.

As shown in Table 1, SecPredNet consistently achieved the best performance across all three datasets on all four evaluation metrics, demonstrating its effectiveness in simultaneously improving regression accuracy and ranking consistency under different host–protein settings. Compared with the second-best model, SecPredNet achieved clear improvements in both prediction error and correlation metrics, including a 31.0% reduction in MSE on BS-AmyQ, a 16.2% reduction on BS-Cut, and the largest gains in ranking performance on BA-PG, where Spearman correlation improved by 122.6%. Notably, SecPredNet also remained superior on the two smaller datasets, BS-Cut and BA-PG, indicating that the structural and evolutionary prior knowledge encoded in the pre-trained protein language model helps maintain robust performance when labeled data are limited. Overall, these results highlight the advantage of jointly modeling pre-trained sequence representations and physicochemical features for practical signal peptide screening, where both accurate efficiency estimation and reliable candidate ranking are essential.

3.2 Feature Representation Visualization

To visually assess the quality of the learned feature representations, we employ t-distributed Stochastic Neighbor Embedding (t-SNE) [29] to project the high-dimensional fused representations obtained after the fusion module and before the regression head for the BS-AmyQ test set into a two-dimensional space, as shown in Fig. 2. Each point represents one signal peptide sample, and the color of each point corresponds to its true secretion efficiency score WA.

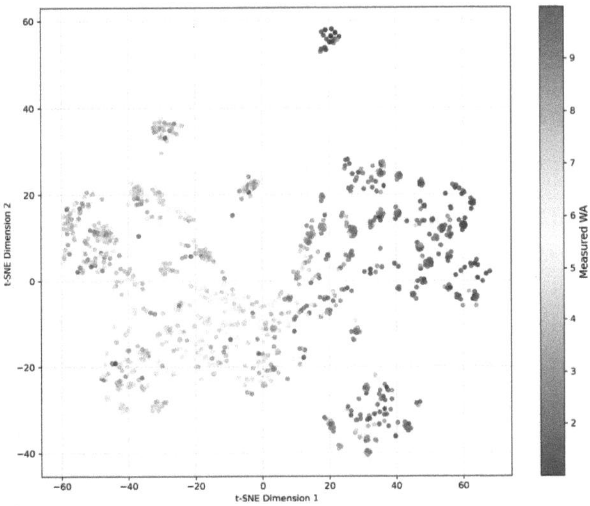

Fig. 2. t-SNE visualization of signal peptide representations learned by SecPredNet.

As illustrated in Fig. 2, the learned representations exhibit an evident structured distribution in the embedded space. Signal peptides with similar secretion efficiency values tend to be located closer to each other, while those with substantially different WA values are more likely to occupy distant regions. In particular, samples with relatively high WA values are mainly distributed in the left part of the plot, whereas samples with low WA values are more frequently observed in the right part, revealing a noticeable gradient-like transition of secretion efficiency across the representation space. This suggests that the proposed model SecPredNet is capable of capturing informative features associated with secretion performance and organizing signal peptide samples according to their functional similarity.

Overall, the t-SNE visualization on the BS-AmyQ test set provides intuitive evidence that the learned feature space preserves meaningful relationships among signal peptides and supports the effectiveness of the proposed model in representing secretion efficiency-related patterns.

3.3 Ablation Study

To investigate the contribution of different components in SecPredNet, we conducted an ablation study on the BS-AmyQ benchmark dataset by examining the performance of different model variants.

Table 2. Ablation results of different model variants on the BS-AmyQ benchmark dataset.

Models	MSE ↓	RMSE ↓	Pearson ↑	Spearman ↑
AAIndex only	1.1756	1.0842	0.8687	0.8483
Sequence only	0.8800	0.9381	0.9029	0.8796
Sequence + AAIndex (Concat)	0.8672	0.9312	0.9048	0.8834
SecPredNet(ESM2)	0.8936	0.9453	0.9018	0.8790
SecPredNet	**0.8542**	**0.9242**	**0.9064**	**0.8849**

The evaluated variants are defined as follows: **AAIndex only** denotes the model that uses only the physicochemical encoding module to extract AAIndex-derived physicochemical features for prediction; **Sequence only** denotes the model that uses only the sequence encoding module to extract sequence features for prediction; **Sequence + AAIndex (Concat)** denotes the model that uses both sequence features and physicochemical features and fuses them by direct concatenation; **SecPredNet(ESM2)** denotes the complete SecPredNet model in which ISM is replaced by ESM2-650M [30] as the pre-trained sequence encoder; and **SecPredNet** denotes the full proposed model, which combines ISM-derived sequence representations with AAIndex-based physicochemical features and adaptively integrates the two feature types through the gated fusion module.

As shown in Table 2, **Sequence only** substantially outperformed **AAIndex only** across all evaluation metrics, indicating that pre-trained sequence representations provide stronger predictive power than physicochemical descriptors alone. Meanwhile, **Sequence + AAIndex (Concat)** further improved over **Sequence only**, suggesting that AAIndex features provide complementary information to sequence-derived representations. Compared with direct concatenation, **SecPredNet** achieved the best performance on all four metrics, demonstrating the advantage of the proposed gated fusion strategy for integrating heterogeneous features. In addition, **SecPredNet** consistently outperformed **SecPredNet(ESM2)**, indicating that the structure-enhanced PLM produces more informative representations than a purely sequence-based pre-trained PLM.

Overall, the ablation results confirm that both multi-source feature modeling and gated fusion contribute positively to the final performance of SecPredNet, while the ISM-based sequence encoder further enhances the quality of the learned sequence representations.

4 High-Efficacy Screening and False Positive Control

Beyond overall regression accuracy, practical signal peptide screening requires a model to perform well in two key scenarios: identifying highly efficient candidates and avoiding false positive selection among low-efficiency samples. To evaluate SecPredNet from this perspective, we further analyzed its behavior on two subsets of the test set of the BS-AmyQ dataset.

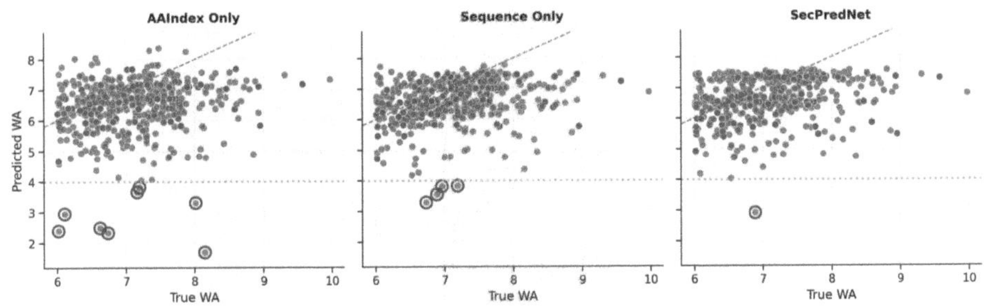

Fig. 3. Performance comparison of different models on low-secreting signal peptides in the test set of the BS-AmyQ dataset (True WA > 6). Samples predicted below the threshold (WA = 4) are regarded as false positives.

First, we evaluate model performance on the subset of low-secreting signal peptides with true WA values greater than 6. In this setting, samples predicted below the screening threshold (WA = 4) can be regarded as false positives, because they may be mistakenly selected as promising candidates. As shown in Fig. 3, the AAIndex only and Sequence only models both produced multiple false positive predictions, whereas SecPredNet yielded only one such case. This result indicates that SecPredNet is more effective at suppressing overly optimistic predictions for poor secretors, which is important for reducing unnecessary experimental validation. This advantage is attributable to the joint modeling strategy in SecPredNet, where pre-trained sequence representations capture overall secretion-related patterns and physicochemical descriptors provide explicit biophysical constraints, together helping the model avoid assigning unrealistically favorable scores to low-efficiency samples.

Second, we analyzed high-secreting signal peptides with true WA values lower than 2, which represent the most desirable candidates in secretion optimization. As shown in Fig. 4, SecPredNet achieved the lowest MSE and the highest Spearman correlation among the compared models in this subset. In addition, its prediction distribution is more concentrated around the ideal trend, suggesting better ranking consistency for top-performing signal peptides. This property is particularly valuable in practical applications, where reliable prioritization of the best candidates is often more important than exact score fitting alone. This advantage is attributable to the complementary design of SecPredNet, where

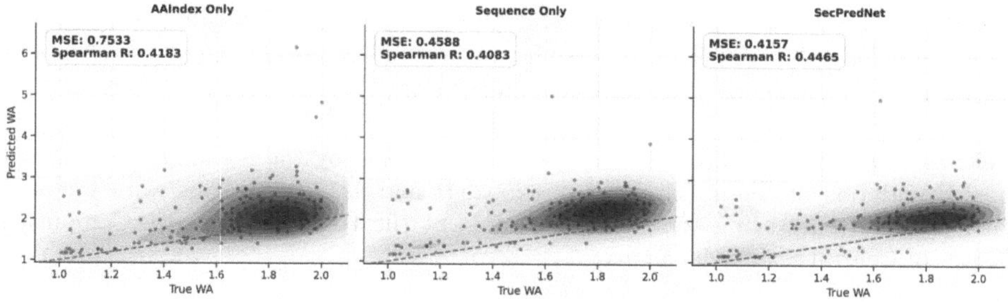

Fig. 4. Performance comparison of different models on high-secreting signal peptides in the test set of the BS-AmyQ dataset (True WA < 2).

sequence embeddings capture high-efficiency sequence patterns and physicochemical features further refine the prediction through residue-level biophysical cues.

Overall, these results show that SecPredNet provides favorable practical performance on both high-efficacy screening and false positive control. It not only improves the identification of highly efficient signal peptides, but also reduces the risk of selecting poor secretors as false positives, thereby making it more useful for realistic screening and optimization workflows.

5 Discussion and Conclusion

In this work, we propose SecPredNet, a novel framework for signal peptide secretion efficiency prediction, which effectively integrates pre-trained PLM features and physicochemical features. A major strength of SecPredNet is introducing pre-trained PLM representations into this task, which enables the model to capture structural and evolutionary priors beyond conventional handcrafted descriptors. Furthermore, by jointly modeling PLM-based sequence representations and AAIndex-based physicochemical features, SecPredNet provides a more comprehensive representation of signal peptides from both sequence-structure and physicochemical perspectives, thus enhancing prediction accuracy and ranking reliability. The experimental results on three datasets further confirm the effectiveness of this framework. SecPredNet consistently achieves superior performance across different host–protein settings, including the two smaller datasets, demonstrating its robustness under limited-data conditions. These findings underscore the practical value of combining protein pre-trained knowledge with explicit physicochemical descriptors for screening high-efficiency signal peptides.

Nevertheless, our current study does not fully exploit cross-host and cross-protein data for model training and adaptation. As a result, the transferability of SecPredNet across different secretion systems remains underexplored, which may limit its generalization ability in very low-data resource settings. In future work, we plan to combine transfer learning and few-shot learning to enable more effective cross-domain pretraining and target-domain fine-tuning. This would allow knowledge learned from diverse host–protein secretion systems to be better transferred to scenarios with limited labeled data.

Acknowledgement. This work was supported in part by the National Natural Science Foundation of China (Grant Nos. 62502541 and 62572488). This work was also carried out in part using computing resources at the High Performance Computing Center of Central South University.

References

1. Rapoport, T.A.: Protein translocation across the eukaryotic endoplasmic reticulum and bacterial plasma membranes. Nature **450**(7170), 663–669 (2007)
2. Blobel, G., Dobberstein, B.: Transfer of proteins across membranes. i. presence of proteolytically processed and unprocessed nascent immunoglobulin light chains on membrane-bound ribosomes of murine myeloma. J. Cell Biol. **67**(3), 835–851 (1975)
3. Chen, X., Fu, W., Luo, Y., Cui, C., Suppavorasatit, I., Liang, L.: Protein deamidation to produce processable ingredients and engineered colloids for emerging food applications. Comprehensive Rev. Food Sci. Food Saf. **20**(4), 3788–3817 (2021)
4. Guo, F., Guan, R., Li, Y., Liu, Q., Wang, X., Yang, C., Wang, J.: Foundation models in bioinformatics. National Sci. Rev. **12**(4), nwaf028 (2025)
5. Zhao, H., Zhong, J., Liang, X., Xie, C., Wang, S.: Application of machine learning in drug side effect prediction: databases, methods, and challenges. Front. Comp. Sci. **19**(5), 195902 (2025)
6. Xie, C.L., Zhao, H.C., Wang, J.X.: Mvcasyn: predicting synergistic drug combinations based on multi-view learning and cross-attention mechanism. J. Comput. Sci. Technol. **40**(6), 1626–1638 (2025)
7. Zhao, H., Ni, P., Zhao, Q., Liang, X., Ai, D., Erhardt, S., Wang, J., Li, Y., Wang, J.: Identifying the serious clinical outcomes of adverse reactions to drugs by a multi-task deep learning framework. Commun. Biol. **6**(1), 870 (2023)
8. Almagro Armenteros, J.J., et al.: Signalp 5.0 improves signal peptide predictions using deep neural networks. Nature Biotechnol. **37**(4), 420–423 (2019)
9. Savojardo, C., Martelli, P.L., Fariselli, P., Casadio, R.: Deepsig: deep learning improves signal peptide detection in proteins. Bioinformatics **34**(10), 1690–1696 (2018)
10. Rumelhart, D.E., Hinton, G.E., Williams, R.J.: Learning internal representations by error propagation. In: Parallel Distributed Processing: Explorations in the Microstructure of Cognition, vol. 1, pp. 318–362 (1986)
11. LeCun, Y., Bottou, L., Bengio, Y., Haffner, P.: Gradient-based learning applied to document recognition. Proc. IEEE **86**(11), 2278–2324 (1998)
12. Teufel, F., et al.: Signalp 6.0 predicts all five types of signal peptides using protein language models. Nature Biotechnol. **40**(7), 1023–1025 (2022)
13. Shen, J., Yu, Q., Chen, S., Tan, Q., Li, J., Li, Y.: Unbiased organism-agnostic and highly sensitive signal peptide predictor with deep protein language model. Nature Comput. Sci. **4**(1), 29–42 (2024)
14. Wu, Z., Yang, K.K., Liszka, M.J., Lee, A., Batzilla, A., Wernick, D., Weiner, D.P., Arnold, F.H.: Signal peptides generated by attention-based neural networks. ACS Synth. Biol. **9**(8), 2154–2161 (2020)

15. Boeckmann, B., Bairoch, A., Apweiler, R., Blatter, M.C., Estreicher, A., Gasteiger, E., Martin, M.J., Michoud, K., O'Donovan, C., Phan, I., et al.: The swiss-prot protein knowledgebase and its supplement trembl in 2003. Nucleic Acids Res. **31**(1), 365–370 (2003)
16. Teufel, F., Stahlhut, C., Refsgaard, J., Nielsen, H., Winther, O., Madsen, D.: Secretogen: towards prediction of signal peptides for efficient protein secretion. In: NeurIPS 2023 Generative AI and Biology, GenBio) Workshop (2023)
17. Grasso, S., Dabene, V., Hendriks, M.M., Zwartjens, P., Pellaux, R., Held, M., Panke, S., Van Dijl, J.M., Meyer, A., van Rij, T.: Signal peptide efficiency: from high-throughput data to prediction and explanation. ACS Synth. Biol. **12**(2), 390–404 (2023)
18. Breiman, L.: Random forests. Mach. Learn. **45**(1), 5–32 (2001)
19. Li, Z., Wang, M., Li, J., Ding, Y., Wang, L., Peng, C., Li, Y., Lu, F., Liu, Y.: Transfer learning for designing efficient signal peptides to improve the secretion level of recombinant protein in bacillus amyloliquefaciens. J. Agric. Food Chem. **73**(27), 17080–17092 (2025)
20. Hochreiter, S., Schmidhuber, J.: Long short-term memory. Neural Comput. **9**(8), 1735–1780 (1997)
21. Vaswani, A., et al.: Attention is all you need. Advances in neural information processing systems **30** (2017)
22. Cho, K., et al.: Learning phrase representations using rnn encoder–decoder for statistical machine translation. In: Proceedings of the 2014 Conference on Empirical Methods in Natural Language Processing (EMNLP), pp. 1724–1734 (2014)
23. Zhao, H., Li, B., Xie, C., Duan, G.: A multi-modal feature fusion method enhanced by dynamic sample graphs for predicting drug responses. Big Data Mining Anal. **9**(2), 580–595 (2026)
24. Ouyang-Zhang, J., Gong, C., Zhao, Y., Krähenbühl, P., Klivans, A.R., Diaz, D.J.: Distilling structural representations into protein sequence models. bioRxiv, pp. 2024–11 (2024)
25. Kawashima, S., Kanehisa, M.: Aaindex: amino acid index database. Nucleic Acids Res. **28**(1), 374–374 (2000)
26. Peng, C., Guo, Y., Ren, S., Li, C., Liu, F., Lu, F.: Spsed: a signal peptide secretion efficiency database. Front. Bioeng. Biotechnol. **9**, 819789 (2022)
27. Brockmeier, U., Caspers, M., Freudl, R., Jockwer, A., Noll, T., Eggert, T.: Systematic screening of all signal peptides from bacillus subtilis: a powerful strategy in optimizing heterologous protein secretion in gram-positive bacteria. J. Mol. Biol. **362**(3), 393–402 (2006)
28. Kim, Y.: Convolutional neural networks for sentence classification. In: Proceedings of the 2014 Conference on Empirical Methods in Natural Language Processing (EMNLP), pp. 1746–1751 (2014)
29. Van der Maaten, L., Hinton, G.: Visualizing data using t-sne. J. Mach. Learn. Res. **9**(11) (2008)
30. Lin, Z., Akin, H., Rao, R., Hie, B., Zhu, Z., Lu, W., Smetanin, N., Verkuil, R., Kabeli, O., Shmueli, Y., et al.: Evolutionary-scale prediction of atomic-level protein structure with a language model. Science **379**(6637), 1123–1130 (2023)

AFLink Enables Multiview Analysis of Atrial Fibrillation Genes Through Integrating Heterogeneous Functional Genomic Data

Cuixiang Lin(✉), Menglong Wang, Yating Tang, and Ruiqi He

School of Mathematics and Computational Science, National Center for Applied Mathematics in Hunan, Xiangtan University, Xiangtan, Hunan 411105, People's Republic of China
lincx@xtu.edu.cn

Abstract. Atrial fibrillation (AF) is a complex heart disease with its genetic etiology remaining unclear. Integrating heterogeneous functional genomic data holds promise for the identification of AF risk genes. Here, we present AFLink, a web server that deploys a rich collection of genomic data along with statistical/computational approaches for interrogating candidate AF genes. AFLink integrates a variety of multi-omics data along with AF-specific functional gene networks constructed in this work. First, we curated a set of AF genes and AF-related tissue-specific genomic data, including atrial appendage-specific regulatory networks, heart-specific gene-enhancer interactions, expression Quantitative Trait Loci (eQTL), gene expression data from AF and control samples, AF-associated miRNAs, and other omics data including protein-protein interaction, Gene Ontology, human phenotype ontology and gene-drug interactions. Second, we constructed an AF-specific functional gene network. To construct this network, we integrated AF-associated RNA-seq datasets and genomic interaction data, computed pairwise features, curated gene pair labels, and trained an XGBoost model to predict AF-specific functional associations. Finally, we implemented methods to evaluate the relevance of given genes to AF from network and molecular landscape analysis. With this web server, users can input their genes of interest and explore how the genes are related to AF based on functional data at different molecular levels. AFLink is freely available at: https://diseaselinks.com/AFLink/.

Keywords: atrial fibrillation · heterogeneous functional genomics · web server · biological networks · network analysis · molecular landscape

1 Introduction

Atrial fibrillation (AF) is a complex and polygenic heart disease characterized by irregular and often rapid heart rhythms, which can lead to serious complications such as stroke, heart failure, and other cardiovascular disorders [1,2].

X. Cui et al. (Eds.): ISBRA 2026, LNBI 16690, pp. 234–246, 2027.
https://doi.org/10.1007/978-981-92-3716-6_19

Despite extensive research, the precise genetic etiology of AF remains incompletely understood, with many risk-associated loci not yet functionally validated [3,4]. Although genome-wide association studies (GWAS) have identified numerous susceptibility loci, the causal genes and their underlying molecular mechanisms remain largely elusive [5]. Novel genes contributing to the pathogenesis of AF continue to be discovered, suggesting that the genetic architecture of AF is much more intricate than previously anticipated [6]. Furthermore, risk genes may exert their effects at different molecular levels, including transcriptional regulation, protein-protein interactions, post-transcriptional modifications, and epigenetic alterations [7]. Therefore, integrating heterogeneous functional genomic data, such as gene expression profiles, protein interaction networks, regulatory elements, and non-coding RNA interactions is a promising and systematic approach to pinpointing risk genes of diseases [8].

Existing studies aimed at identifying AF risk genes often rely on a single type of genomic or genetic data, such as GWAS summary statistics or differential expression, which may overlook critical interactions and regulatory mechanisms [9,10]. For instance, while GWAS can highlight genomic loci associated with AF, they do not directly implicate specific genes or pathways. Similarly, transcriptomic studies may reveal differentially expressed genes in AF patients but fail to distinguish between causal drivers and secondary effects of the disease. Moreover, efforts to integrate different types of functional genomic data, such as combining protein-protein interaction networks with regulatory genomics remains limited, leaving a significant gap in comprehensively understanding AF pathogenesis [11]. The multi-omics approach that systematically integrates diverse biological layers is therefore essential to uncover the full spectrum of genetic contributors to AF [12].

To address these challenges, we developed AFLink based on curated multi-omics data and an AF-specific functional gene network constructed in this work. AFlink is a comprehensive and user-friendly web server designed to evaluate the association of a queried gene with AF from comprehensive network and molecular landscape analysis.

First, AFLink investigates the gene's connectivity with curated AF risk genes through multiple biological networks, including: 1)AF-specific functional gene networks, which capture disease-relevant interactions; 2)Protein-protein interaction (PPI) networks, highlighting potential physical and functional partnerships with known AF-associated proteins; 3)Regulatory networks of the atrial appendage, providing insights into tissue-specific transcriptional regulation; 4)Interactions with AF-associated microRNAs (miRNAs), revealing post-transcriptional regulatory mechanisms that may influence AF susceptibility.

Second, AFLink performs a comprehensive molecular landscape analysis to assess gene-AF associations from multiple dimensions. It integrates differential expression analysis across independent datasets to ensure robustness against batch effects and cohort-specific biases [13]. To provide a holistic view, the platform integrates six complementary perspectives: (i) functional annotations detailing the gene's mechanistic role in AF; (ii) GWAS associations to identify

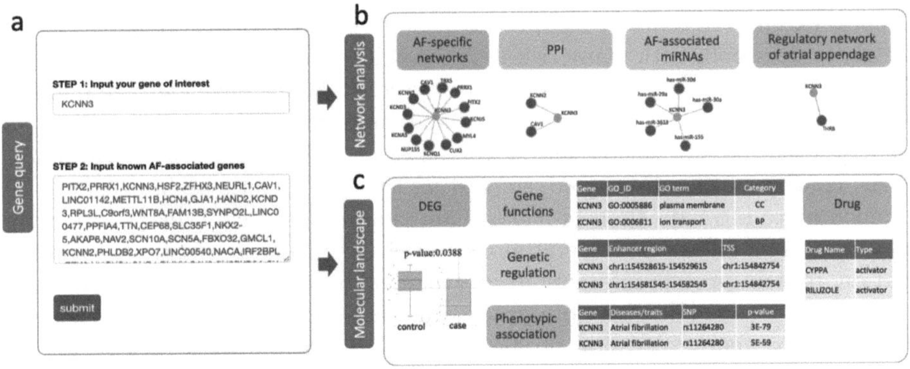

Fig. 1. Overview of integrative analysis by AFLink. (**A**) Gene query of AFLink. (**B**) Network visualization of interactions with known AF-associated genes or miRNAs in multiple biological networks. (**C**) Molecular landscape analysis from differential expression, gene function, gene regulation, phenotypic association, and drug-target interaction.

proximity to AF-linked genomic loci; (iii) Heart-specific eQTLs from GTEx to uncover regulatory variants in cardiac tissues; (iv) Enhancer-gene interactions to highlight distal modulation of AF risk; (v) Human phenotype annotations to link genes with clinical manifestations; and (vi) Drug-gene interactions from DGIdb [14] to explore therapeutic or repurposing potential.

By consolidating diverse genomic and functional data into a unified platform, AFLink empowers researchers to efficiently prioritize candidate genes, generate mechanistic hypotheses, and accelerate the discovery of novel therapeutic targets for AF. This integrative approach represents a significant advancement over conventional single-data-type analyses, providing a more holistic understanding of AF genetics.

2 Construction of AFLink

AFLink is a comprehensive computational platform designed to systematically investigate the association between candidate genes and atrial fibrillation (AF) by integrating known AF risk genes, heterogeneous genomic data, and AF-specific biological networks.

AFLink integrates (I) a variety of omics data, including AF risk genes, AF gene expression datasets, protein-protein interactions, AF-associated miRNAs, regulatory network of atrial appendage collected from public domains, and (II) AF-specific functional gene networks (AF-FGNs) constructed in this work. The details of these data are described below.

2.1 Collection of Multi-omics Data

Curated AF Risk Genes. The identification and characterization of AF risk genes play a pivotal role in understanding the genetic basis of atrial fibrillation (AF) and its underlying molecular mechanisms. These genes are crucial for studying the association between genetic variants and AF susceptibility, providing valuable insights for both research and clinical applications. To ensure a comprehensive and reliable collection of AF-related genes, we systematically curated AF risk genes from multiple authoritative sources, including OMIM (Online Mendelian Inheritance in Man), large-scale genome-wide association studies (GWAS), and peer-reviewed published literature.

To maintain high confidence in our gene selection, we applied stringent criteria, requiring that each gene be supported by at least two independent published studies to minimize false positives and enhance reproducibility. The supporting references for each gene were meticulously compiled and are provided in Resource option of AFLink for further validation and transparency. Through this rigorous approach, we successfully identified and consolidated a total of 124 AF risk genes, forming a robust dataset for subsequent analyses.

AF-Associated Gene Expression. To systematically investigate the molecular underpinnings of atrial fibrillation (AF), we have curated ten gene expression datasets from public repositories (GEO accession ids: GSE128188, GSE79768, GSE41177, GSE115574, GSE2240, and GSE143924). The primary purpose of integrating these datasets is twofold. First, we will perform a comprehensive meta-analysis to identify robust and consistent differentially expressed genes (DEGs) between AF and control patients across diverse cohorts. Second, leveraging these DEGs, we will construct a sophisticated AF-specific gene functional network. This will be achieved by calculating pairwise genomic features, such as Pearson correlation coefficients of expression patterns, to infer functional relationships and co-regulation. This integrated approach aims to uncover central hubs and key functional modules driving AF pathogenesis, ultimately revealing potential diagnostic biomarkers and therapeutic targets (Table 1).

Table 1. Datasets of AF patients' gene expression used in construction of AF-FGNs.

Dataset	#genes	#samples	Tissue
GSE128188	13144	10	atrial appendage
GSE79768	21755	14	atrium
GSE41177	21755	32	left atrium
GSE115574	21755	28	atrium
GSE2240	13101	21	right atrium
GSE143924	7298	15	epicardial adipose tissue

Biological Networks. The visualization of the association of the queried gene with AF-biomarkers in different types of biological networks would help reveal its role in the association with AF. The biological networks include protein-protein interactions, gene-miRNAs interactions, regulatory network of atrial appendage. The analysis includes network visualization of queried genes with AF associated genes in biological networks which are detailed below.

protein-Protein Interactions. Protein-protein interactions are utilized to analyze the association of the queried gene with AF risk genes. PPI are obtained from the STRING database, which provides high quality proteinâĂŞprotein associations [15].

AF-Associated miRNAs. To analyze the association with AF-associated miRNAs, we collected AF-associated miRNAs from HMDD database [16] and miRNA-target interaction networks from miRTarBase [17].

Regulatory Network of Atrial Appendage. The regulatory network of atrial appendage is also considered in AFLink analysis. The network contains 1,888,413 pairs of regulatory relationship. We obtained the network from the GRAND database [18].

2.2 AF-Specific Functional Gene Networks (AF-FGNs)

Unlike conventional gene prioritization tools, AFLink not only aggregates existing genetic evidence but also constructs disease-specific interaction networks to uncover novel mechanistic insights into AF pathogenesis. We constructed AF-FGNs by integrating RNA-seq gene expression data from atrial fibrillation studies along with multiple genomic interaction datasets collected above using the advanced XGBoost algorithm [19]. The methodology is summarized as follows.

First, to represent functional relationships between genes in a pairwise manner, Pearson correlation coefficients (PCC) were computed for all gene pairs across each expression dataset. It is worth noting that lowly expressed genes were filtered out from each dataset, resulting in a qualified expression matrix. Additionally, six pairwise genomic features were incorporated from the GIANT platform [8], covering: protein-protein interactions (from MINT [20], IntAct [21], and BioGRID [22]), chemical and genetic perturbation data, shared $3'$ UTR miRNA binding motifs (MSigDB [23]), and co-occurrence of transcription factor binding sites (Jaspar [24]).

Next, functionally related (positive) and unrelated (negative) gene pairs were curated using established methods [8,25]. Positives were defined as gene pairs co-annotated within the same Gene Ontology biological process (limited to experimental evidence codes: EXP, IDA, IPI, IMP, IGI, IEP) or KEGG pathway. Redundant pairs were removed. Negatives were selected following the same benchmark procedure as in the previous studies [26,27].

Finally, the XGBoost algorithm was implemented to model and predict AF-FGNs. Selected for its suitability for non-linear modelling, scalability, and robust performance documented in the literature [26,28], an XGBoost model was trained on our dataset of features and labeled gene pairs. This trained model was then employed to compute co-function probability scores for all gene pairs to construct the AF-FGNs.

2.3 Multi-view Analysis of AFLink

AFLink further incorporates multi-omics validation and interactive visualization to enhance the interpretability and reliability of its findings based on curated multi-omics data and AF-FGNs. In the search page of AFLink, users can input their genes of interest (Fig. 1a). The returned results of AFLink include visualization interactions with AF risk genes in multiple biological networks, and a comprehensive molecular landscape, including differential expression analysis, gene function, gene regulation, phenotypic association, and associated drugs of queried genes. The multi-view analysis is detailed below.

(I) **Network analysis.**

AFLink enables visualization of interactions with biomarkers of AF in multiple biological networks. The networks include protein interactions, functional gene interactions of AF-FGNs, interactions between AF-associated miRNAs and genes, and regulatory interactions of the atrial appendage (Fig. 1b). In the figure, the green node denotes the gene of interest, and the dark gray nodes denote AF-related genes or miRNAs.

(II) **Molecular landscape analysis.**

Differential gene expression analysis. AFLink provides visualization of differential gene expression analysis of queried genes. Visualization of association with AF from multiple gene expression datasets utilizing t-test. Differential gene expression between AF and control samples is statistically tested. A p-value of less than 0.05 is considered statistically significant. Four expression datasets, i.e. GSE115574, GSE2240, GSE143924 and GSE79768, are used in the analysis (Fig. 1c);

Gene Function. AFLink also offers the gene function of queried genes (Fig. 1c). The information, which includes gene function or biological processes, locations in the cell they carry out, is obtained from Gene Ontology (GO) [29].

Gene Regulation. For queried genes, AFLink provides regulatory elements information derived from AF-associated tissues. The genetic regulatory elements include eQTLs and heart-specific enhancers. eQTL information about the left ventricle and atrial appendage is from Genotype-Tissue Expression (GTEx) [30]. And the heart-specific gene-enhancer interactions were predicted by FENRIR framework [25] (Fig. 1c).

Phenotypic Association. AFLinks provides phenotypic association from GWAS and HPO. Phenotypic association includes GWAS, which describes SNP-trait associations, and Human Phenotype Ontology (HPO) [31] provides phenotypic abnormalities of human diseases. These two resources can assist researchers studying the evidence of the queried genes associated with AF (Fig. 1c).

Drug-Target Interaction. AFLink provides relevant drug targets for further studies. It retrieves and displays information on potential drug targets for the given gene by querying the Drug Gene Interaction Database (DGIdb) [14]. For each interaction, it provides supporting data like the source database and the interaction type, such as activator, blocker, modulator and inhibitor (Fig. 1c).

2.4 Implementation of AFLink

AFLink is built on the Apache HTTP server (v2.4.41), the front-end development is based on HTML5, and the back-end implementation uses both PHP (v.7.4.3) and Python 3.6. Network visualization is implemented using d3 JavaScript script. The network analysis results are intuitively visualized and can be downloaded as text files. To assist researchers to be familiar with the website, we also provide the help documents on the website. In addition, AFLink also provides substantial resources, including evidence and visualization for collected AF-associated genes and miRNAs, gene expression data of AF, PPI, construction process of AF-specific networks, and regulatory networks of atrial appendage.

3 Results

3.1 The Performance of AF-FGNs

We subsequently evaluated the predictive capability of AF-FGNs for atrial fibrillation (AF)-associated genes based on ridge regression. As illustrated in Fig. 2, AF-FGNs achieved strong classification performance. In ROC analysis (Fig. 2A), the AUROC reached 0.9397, which is substantially higher than the random baseline (AUC=0.5), indicating that AF-FGNs can effectively discriminate AF-associated from non-associated gene pairs [19,32]. In PR analysis (Fig. 2B), the AUPRC was 0.6061, indicating that the model maintained a balanced trade-off between precision and recall under imbalanced data settings, consistent with

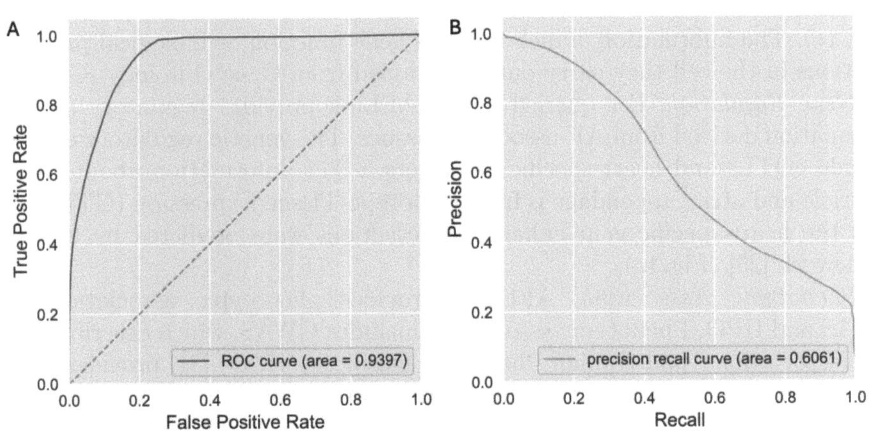

Fig. 2. The network performance of modeling AF-FGNs based on XGBoost. (**A**) ROC curve of the model. (**B**) Precision recall curve of the model (The ratio of positive and negative samples is 1:20).

prior observations in disease gene prediction tasks [33]. Together, these results highlight the robustness of AF-FGNs in distinguishing positive from negative gene pairs.

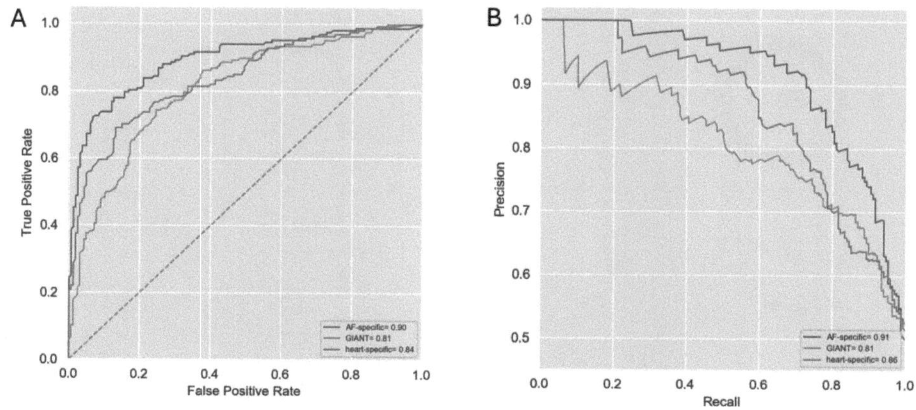

Fig. 3. Comparison of different FGNs' performance in predicting AF-associated genes based on ridge regression. (**A**) AUROCs of using three networks to predict AF-associated genes. (**B**) AUPRCs of using three networks to predict AF-associated genes.

We further compared AF-FGNs against other functional gene networks, including the global GIANT network and the heart-specific TissueNexus network, using ridge regression for AF gene prioritization. As shown in Fig. 3, AF-FGNs achieved the highest AUROC (0.90) compared to GIANT (0.81) and TissueNexus (0.84) (Fig. 3A). This indicates superior discriminatory power in identifying AF-associated genes. For AUPRC (Fig. 3B), the heart-specific TissueNexus network obtained the highest value (0.85), slightly surpassing AF-FGNs (0.81) and GIANT (0.81), which aligns with the notion that tissue-specific contexts can enhance predictive precision [34]. Statistical assessment with 10-fold cross-validation and DeLong tests confirmed that AUROC improvements of AF-FGNs over GIANT and TissueNexus were significant ($p < 0.01$ and $p < 0.05$, respectively) [35].

Beyond quantitative performance, AF-FGNs showed strong biological validity. The top-ranked candidates included PITX2, KCNN3, TTN, and SCN5A, which are well-established AF susceptibility genes supported by GWAS and functional studies [36]. Notably, PITX2 at chromosome 4q25 has been repeatedly confirmed as the most significant locus for AF [37], and ion channel genes such as KCNN3 and SCN5A have been implicated in arrhythmia pathogenesis [38]. These results illustrate that AF-FGNs not only achieves strong computational metrics but also captures key molecular players in AF pathophysiology.

AF-FGNs also prioritized several novel candidates lacking previous AF annotations. Network-based disease gene discovery strategies are widely applied to uncover such genes [39,40]. Integrating multi-omics information has further

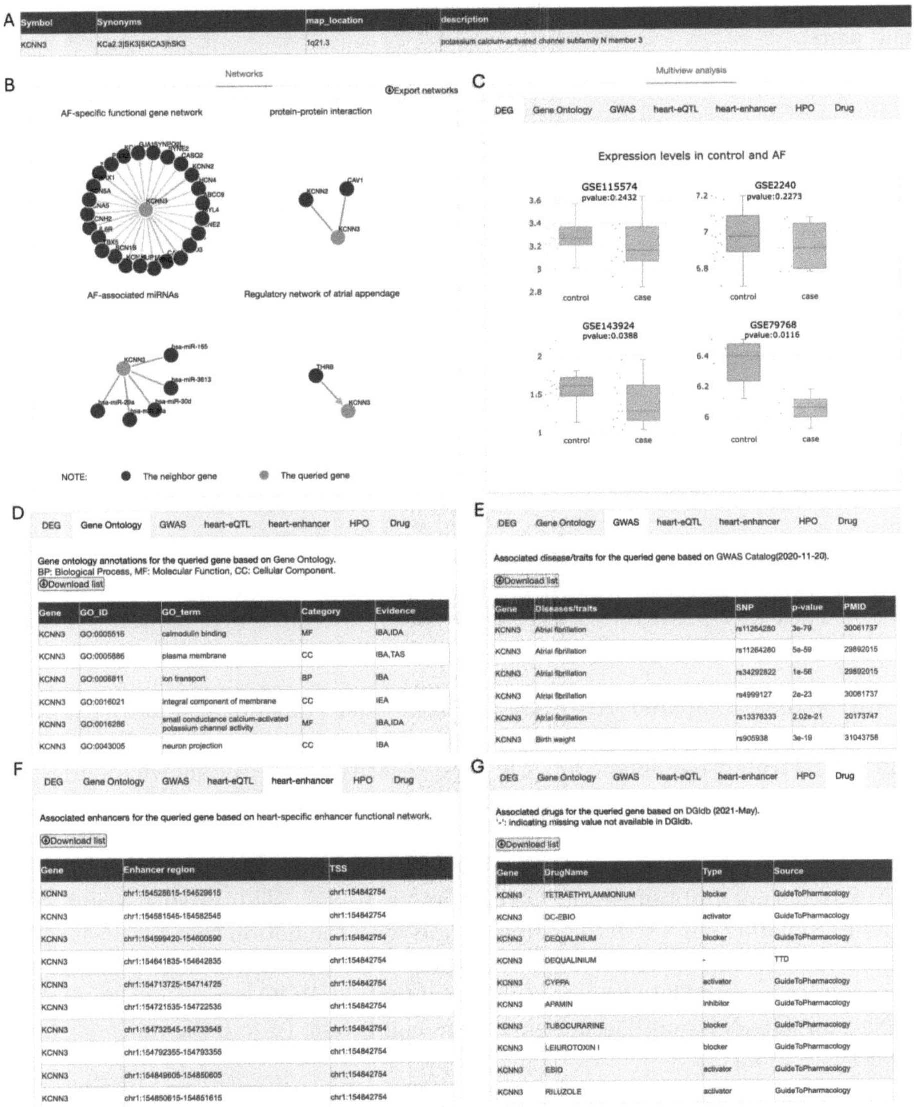

Fig. 4. Results of integrative analysis by AFLink. (**A**) The basic information of queried gene. (**B**) Interaction with known AF-associated genes in multiple biological networks. (**C**) Differential expression analysis including datasets of GSE115574, GSE2240, GSE143924 and GSE79768. (**D**) Gene ontology annotations for the queried gene. (**E**) Associated disease/traits for the queried gene based on GWAS Catalog. (**F**) Associated enhancers for the queried gene based on heart-specific enhancer functional network. (**G**) Associated drugs for the queried gene based on DGIdb. phenotypic association, and drug-target interaction.

proven effective in enhancing prediction of AF risk loci and uncovering causal mechanisms [4]. Importantly, cross-population studies show that AF risk loci are largely polygenic and benefit from integrative modeling approaches [41]. These findings support the potential of AF-FGNs in revealing novel biology that complements traditional GWAS signals.

From a translational perspective, integration with curated resources such as STRING and BioGRID supports that disease- or tissue-specific networks provide a more biologically relevant context than global networks [42]. The development of AF-related bioinformatics platforms indicates that functional network-based resources can be effectively translated into user-friendly websites for disease research and clinical application [43,44]. Similar to successful platforms in other cardiovascular and neurological diseases, AF-FGNs could serve as the foundation for an AF-focused online knowledgebase, improving accessibility of genetic and molecular insights for the wider research community [45–47].

AF-FGNs shows both superior performance and predictive validity. These findings underscore the utility of disease-specific functional gene networks in AF gene discovery and highlight the feasibility of extending such networks into online resources to support the AF research community.

3.2 A Case Study to Analyze the Association of Genes with AF

To illustrate the usage of AFLink, we take *KCNN3* as an example to analyze its association with AF [27]. The query first returns the description of KCNN3 (Fig. 4A). The other analysis results obtained by AFLink show that it functionally interacts with AF genes like *PITX2, etc.* (Fig. 4B) [37]; its encoded protein interacts with known AF genes *KCNN2* and *CAV1* (Fig. 4B) [22]; it shows significantly lower expression in AF patients compared with control samples in the datasets GSE79768 and GSE143924 (Fig. 4C); it participates in potassium ion transmembrane transport and functions at plasma membrane, neuron projection, and ion transport (Fig. 4D); it has multiple SNPs associated with AF (Fig. 4E); it interacts with 10 enhancer regions from heart-specific enhancer functional networks (Fig. 4F). These evidences suggest that *KCNN3* could be a promising candidate gene for AF. Based on drug-target interaction, researchers can narrow down its list of target drugs (Fig. 4G). As an activator of KCNN3, riluzole can significantly lower incidence of new-onset AF [48].

4 Conclusions

AFLink is a free platform to comprehensively analyze whether a gene of interest is functionally associated with AF. It allows researchers to obtain new insights by analyzing the gene of interest based on AF-specific functional interactions, AF-associated proteins, miRNAs, and gene regulation, differential gene expression, gene function, phenotypic association, and drug-target interaction. It is expected that AFLink would facilitate researchers in the identification of candidate genes and therapeutic targets for AF. In the future, we will keep on integrating AF-associated data to keep AFLink up to date.

Acknowledgment. This work was supported in part by the National Natural Science Foundation of China [No. 62302426].

References

1. Andersen, J.H., Andreasen, L., Olesen, M.S.: Atrial fibrillation-a complex polygenetic disease. Eur. J. Hum. Genet. **29**(7), 1051–1060 (2021)
2. Kirchhof, P., Benussi, S., Kotecha, D., Ahlsson, A., et al.: 2016 esc guidelines for the management of atrial fibrillation developed in collaboration with eacts. Eur. Heart J. **37**(38), 2893–2962 (2016)
3. Nielsen, J.B., Thorolfsdottir, R.B., Fritsche, L.G., Zhou, W., et al.: Biobank-driven genomic discovery yields new insight into atrial fibrillation biology. Nat. Genet. **50**(9), 1234–1239 (2018)
4. Owais, A., Barney, M., Ly, O.T., Brown, G.: Genetics and pharmacogenetics of atrial fibrillation: a mechanistic perspective. JACC: Basic Transl. Sci **9**(7), 918–934 (2024)
5. Roberts, J.D., Gollob, M.H.: A contemporary review on the genetic basis of atrial fibrillation. Methodist Debakey Cardiovasc. J. **10**(1), 18–24 (2014)
6. Lubitz, S.A., Lunetta, K.L., Lin, H., Arking, D.E., et al.: Novel genetic markers associate with atrial fibrillation risk in europeans and japanese. J. Am. Coll. Cardiol. **63**(12), 1200–1210 (2014)
7. Zhou, D., Yang, K., Hu, J., Shi, J.: Noncoding rnas in atrial fibrillation: current status and prospect. J. Cardiovasc. Pharmacol. **75**(1), 10–17 (2020)
8. Greene, C.S., Krishnan, A., Wong, A.K., Ricciotti, E., et al.: Understanding multicellular function and disease with human tissue-specific networks. Nat. Genet. **47**(6), 569–576 (2015)
9. Nakano, Y.: Genome and atrial fibrillation. J. Arrhythmia **39**(3), 303–309 (2023)
10. van Ouwerkerk, A.F., Bosada, F.M., van Duijvenboden, K., Hill, M.C., et al.: Identification of atrial fibrillation associated genes and functional non-coding variants. Nat. Commun. **10**(1), 4755 (2019)
11. Zhu, C., Preissl, S., Ren, B.: Single-cell multimodal omics: the power of many. Nat. Methods **17**, 11–14 (2020)
12. Karczewski, K.J., Snyder, M.P.: Integrative omics for health and disease. Nat. Rev. Genet. **19**(5), 299–310 (2018)
13. Leek, J.T., Scharpf, R.B., Bravo, H.C., Simcha, D., et al.: Tackling the widespread and critical impact of batch effects in high-throughput data. Nat. Rev. Genet. **11**(10), 733–739 (2010)
14. Freshour, S.L., Kiwala, S., Cotto, K.C., Coffman, A.C., et al.: Integration of the drug–gene interaction database (dgidb 4.0) with open crowdsource efforts. Nucleic Acids Res. **49**(D1), D1144–D1151 (2021)
15. Szklarczyk, D., Kirsch, R., Koutrouli, M., Nastou, K., et al.: The string database in 2023: protein-protein association networks and functional enrichment analyses for any sequenced genome of interest. Nucleic Acids Res. **51**(D1), D638–D646 (2023)
16. Huang, Z., Shi, J., Gao, Y., Cui, C., et al.: Hmdd v3.0: a database for experimentally supported human microrna-disease associations. Nucleic Acids Res. **47**(D1), D1013–D1017 (2019)
17. Huang, H.Y., Lin, Y.C., Li, J., Huang, K.Y., et al.: mirtarbase 2020: updates to the experimentally validated microrna-target interaction database. Nucleic Acids Res. **48**(D1), D148–D154 (2020)

18. Ben Guebila, M., Lopes-Ramos, C.M., Weighill, D., Sonawane, A.R., et al.: Grand: a database of gene regulatory network models across human conditions. Nucleic Acids Res. **50**(D1), D610–D621 (2022)
19. Chen, T., Guestrin, C.: Xgboost: a scalable tree boosting system. ACM (2016)
20. Licata, L., Briganti, L., Peluso, D., Perfetto, L., et al.: Mint, the molecular interaction database: 2012 update. Nucleic Acids Res. **40**(Database issue), D857–D861 (2012)
21. Orchard, S., Ammari, M., Aranda, B., Breuza, L., et al.: The mintact project–intact as a common curation platform for 11 molecular interaction databases. Nucleic Acids Res. **42**(Database issue), D358–D363 (2014)
22. Oughtred, R., Rust, J., Chang, C., Breitkreutz, B.J., et al.: The biogrid database: a comprehensive biomedical resource of curated protein, genetic, and chemical interactions. Protein Sci. **30**(1), 187–200 (2021)
23. Subramanian, A., Tamayo, P., Mootha, V.K., Mukherjee, S., et al.: Gene set enrichment analysis: a knowledge-based approach for interpreting genome-wide expression profiles. Proc. Natl. Acad. Sci. U. S. A. **102**(43), 15545–15550 (2005)
24. Castro-Mondragon, J.A., Riudavets-Puig, R., Rauluseviciute, I., Lemma, R.B., et al.: Jaspar 2022: the 9th release of the open-access database of transcription factor binding profiles. Nucleic Acids Res. **50**(D1), D165–D173 (2022)
25. Chen, X., Zhou, J., Zhang, R., Wong, A.K., et al.: Tissue-specific enhancer functional networks for associating distal regulatory regions to disease. Cell Syst. **12**(4), 353-362.e6 (2021)
26. Lin, C.X., Li, H.D., Deng, C., Liu, W., et al.: An integrated brain-specific network identifies genes associated with neuropathologic and clinical traits of alzheimer's disease. Brief Bioinform. **23**(1), bbab522 (2022)
27. Ellinor, P.T., Lunetta, K.L., Glazer, N.L., Pfeufer, A., et al.: Common variants in kcnn3 are associated with lone atrial fibrillation. Nat. Genet. **42**(3), 240–244 (2010)
28. Li, H.D., Bai, T., Sandford, E., Burmeister, M., et al.: Baihui: cross-species brain-specific network built with hundreds of hand-curated datasets. Bioinformatics **35**(14), 2486–2488 (2019)
29. Ashburner, M., Ball, C.A., Blake, J.A., Botstein, D., et al.: Gene ontology: tool for the unification of biology. the gene ontology consortium. Nat. Genet. **25**(1), 25–29 (2000)
30. Lonsdale, J., Thomas, J., Salvatore, M., Phillips, R., et al.: The genotype-tissue expression (gtex) project. Nat. Genet. **45**, 580–585 (2013)
31. Köhler, S., Gargano, M., Matentzoglu, N., Carmody, L.C., et al.: The human phenotype ontology in 2021. Nucleic Acids Res. **49**(D1), D1207–D1217 (2021)
32. Pey, J., Planes, F.J.: Direct calculation of elementary flux modes satisfying several biological constraints in genome-scale metabolic networks. Bioinformatics **30**(15), 2197–2203 (2014)
33. Lotfollahi, M., Susmelj, A.K., De Donno, C., Hetzel, L., et al.: Predicting cellular responses to complex perturbations in high-throughput screens. Mol. Syst. Biol. **19**(6), e11517 (2023)
34. Assum, I., Krause, J., Scheinhardt, M.O., Müller, C., et al.: Tissue-specific multiomics analysis of atrial fibrillation. Nat. Commun. **13**(1), 441 (2022)
35. DeLong, E.R., DeLong, D.M., Clarke-Pearson, D.L.: Comparing the areas under two or more correlated receiver operating characteristic curves: a nonparametric approach. Biometrics **44**(3), 837–845 (1988)

36. Yuan, S., Chen, J., Ruan, X., Li, Y., et al.: Cross-population gwas and proteomics improve risk prediction and reveal mechanisms in atrial fibrillation. Nat. Commun. **16**, 6426 (2025)
37. Gudbjartsson, D., Arnar, D., Helgadottir, A., Gretarsdottir, S., et al.: Variants conferring risk of atrial fibrillation on chromosome 4q25. Nature **448**, 353–357 (2007)
38. Zito, E., Bianchini, L., Sommariva, E., Costa, M., et al.: The genetic mechanisms and pathology of atrial fibrillation: A narrative review. Biomedicines **13**(3), 654 (2025)
39. Fu, S., Feng, Z., Li, A., Ma, Z., et al.: Using integrative bioinformatics approaches and machine-learning strategies to identify potential signatures for atrial fibrillation. Int. J. Cardiol. Heart Vasc. **56**, 101592 (2025)
40. Lyu, Z., Yang, J., Xu, Z., Wang, W.: Predicting the risk of ischemic stroke in patients with atrial fibrillation using heterogeneous drug-protein-disease network-based deep learning (2024)
41. Vad, O.B., Monfort, L.M., Paludan-Müller, C., Kahnert, K., et al.: Rare and common genetic variation underlying atrial fibrillation risk. JAMA Cardiol. **9**(8), 732–740 (2024)
42. Ganegoda, G., Wang, J., Wu, F.X., Li, M.: Prediction of disease genes using tissue-specified gene-gene network. BMC Syst. Biol. **8**(Suppl 3), S3 (2014)
43. Kern, F., Fehlmann, T., Keller, A.: On the lifetime of bioinformatics web services. Nucleic Acids Res. **48**(22), 12523–12533 (2020)
44. Habineza, T., Ribeiro, A.H., Gedon, D., Behar, J.A., et al.: End-to-end risk prediction of atrial fibrillation from the 12-lead ecg by deep neural networks. J. Electrocardiol. **81**, 193–200 (2023)
45. Zou, R., Zhang, D., Lv, L., Shi, W., et al.: Bioinformatic gene analysis for potential biomarkers and therapeutic targets of atrial fibrillation-related stroke. J. Transl. Med. **17**(1), 45 (2019)
46. Yang, G., Zhuang, X., Khan, H., Haldar, S., et al.: Fully automatic segmentation and objective assessment of atrial scars for long-standing persistent atrial fibrillation patients using late gadolinium-enhanced mri. Med. Phys. **45**(4), 1562–1576 (2018)
47. Scarsoglio, S., Saglietto, A., Gaita, F., Ridolfi, L.: Computational fluid dynamics modelling of left valvular heart diseases during atrial fibrillation. PeerJ 4 (2016)
48. Lal, J.C., Mao, C., Zhou, Y., Gore-Panter, S.R., et al.: Transcriptomics-based network medicine approach identifies metformin as a repurposable drug for atrial fibrillation. Cell Rep. Med. **3**(10), 100749 (2022)

Reconstructing Qwen3 into Qwen3-Protein: A Versatile Biophysics-Grounded Protein Language Foundation Model for PTMs and Downstream Tasks

Yiyu Lin[1], Sen Yang[1], Jiahui Wu[1], Huaiyang Sun[1], Hao Wu[1], Lun Zhu[1(✉)], and Yan Wang[2(✉)]

[1] School of Computer Science and Artificial Intelligence Aliyun School of Big Data School of Software, Changzhou University, Changzhou 213164, China
zl@cczu.edu.cn

[2] Key Laboratory of Symbol Computation and Knowledge Engineering of Ministry of Education, College of Computer Science and Technology, Jilin University, Changchun 130012, China
wy6868@jlu.edu.cn

Abstract. Post-translational modifications (PTMs) and their intricate crosstalk networks are essential for driving complex cellular functions, yet their experimental validation remains highly resource-intensive. Current computational frameworks face fundamental biophysical limitations, particularly unidirectional constraints and a representational gap between one-dimensional sequence semantics and three-dimensional folding physics. To overcome these bottlenecks, we introduce Qwen3-Protein, a biophysics-grounded foundation model systematically reconstructed and rigorously retrained on a million-scale dataset specifically for PTM prediction. Our architecture features four fundamental innovations. First, it fuses ESM-C and SaProt embeddings to create robust multimodal protein representations. Second, a novel Bidirectional GatedDeltaNet establishes a global, non-causal structural receptive field with O(N) linear complexity, breaking traditional unidirectional sequence modeling constraints. Third, the Fast Linear Algebra Scalable Hybrid Conformal Geometric Algebra (Flash-CGA) network natively maps Euclidean coordinates into a 5D conformal manifold, guaranteeing strict translational and rotational invariance while utilizing geometric invariants to physically gate biochemical semantic streams. Finally, a Crosstalk-Aware Asymmetric Uncertainty Loss (CAAULoss) mitigates extreme statistical class imbalance and mathematically simulates the complex synergistic and antagonistic logic inherent in biological networks. Empirically, Qwen3-Protein establishes new state-of-the-art performance, achieving an average 7.7% improvement in the Matthews correlation coefficient (MCC) across 16 distinct PTM categories. The framework also allows seamless adaptation to downstream tasks through targeted model tuning, driving substantial MCC enhancements of 5.8% in PTM crosstalk prediction and 4.8% in identifying kinase-specific modifications. Crucially, in silico perturbations validate the model's intrinsic capacity to autonomously uncover dynamic

Y. Lin, S. Yang, J. Wu—These authors contributed equally to this work.

X. Cui et al. (Eds.): ISBRA 2026, LNBI 16690, pp. 247–260, 2027.
https://doi.org/10.1007/978-981-92-3716-6_20

network associations, shifting the paradigm from isolated site identification to a holistic, system-level interpretation.

Keyword: Post-translational modification · Protein language model · GNN

1 Introduction

Posttranslational modifications (PTMs) play a pivotal role in expanding proteomic diversity and regulating complex cellular processes [1]. Beyond acting as isolated molecular switches, these modifications frequently operate within intricate networks known as PTM crosstalk, where the modification status of one residue directly influences adjacent or spatially distant sites [2]. This synergistic regulation generates a sophisticated modification code that drives critical physiological functions. Because experimental validation of these dynamic networks demands tremendous resources and time, developing robust computational frameworks is highly essential [3]. Despite the accumulation of vast proteomic data, accurately predicting both individual modification sites and their interconnected crosstalk events remains a formidable challenge. Overcoming this limitation requires innovative computational architectures capable of integrating complex structural geometries and rich semantic sequence representations to fully decipher the regulatory grammar of proteins [4].

While recent protein language models have advanced post-translational modification (PTM) prediction, existing frameworks exhibit fundamental biophysical limitations. For instance, PTMGPT2 employs a decoder-only, autoregressive GPT-2 architecture for prompt-based label generation [5]; however, its unidirectional masked self-attention inherently precludes modeling the global, non-causal spatial dependencies of folded polypeptides. To incorporate structural context, MTPrompt-PTM utilizes a multi-task framework built upon a structure-aware protein language model [6]. Current models rely on 1D convolutions, which fail to capture 3D protein folding features. Furthermore, they cannot accurately simulate the complex cooperative and competitive interactions in biological signaling networks. Therefore, there is an urgent need for a new foundation model that breaks the 1D sequence limitations, bridges the 1D-3D gap, and incorporates biophysical logic to fully decode multi-site PTM networks [7].

To transcend the physical and biological limitations inherent in causal natural language models when modeling complex biomolecular topologies, we introduce Qwen3-Protein, a pioneering foundation model that systematically reconstructs the highly sparse, 80-billion-parameter Qwen3-Next framework into a biophysics-grounded paradigm tailored specifically for post-translational modification (PTM) prediction, having been rigorously retrained on a million-scale protein sequence dataset. By strictly aligning computational topology with structural biology, Qwen3-Protein introduces four fundamental architectural innovations. First, we fuse ESM-C sequence embeddings with Saprot structural embeddings to construct multi-modal protein representations. Second, breaking the unidirectional constraints of traditional sequence modeling, we propose the Bidirectional GatedDeltaNet (Bi-GatedDeltaNet); this mechanism symmetrically concatenates forward and backward hidden states to establish a global, non-causal structural receptive field, enabling the capture of full-length, long-range spatial dependencies across the polypeptide chain while maintaining strict O(N) linear complexity. Third, to bridge the representational chasm between one-dimensional sequences and three-dimensional folding physics, we replace the conventional semantic attention mechanism with a Fast Linear Algebra Scalable Hybrid Conformal Geometric Algebra (Flash-CGA) network. This dual-stream $O(N \cdot K)$ interaction module natively maps Euclidean coordinates into the five-dimensional conformal manifold G(4,1) via factorized tensor product approximations, thereby guaranteeing strict translational and rotational invariance; crucially, it extracts geometric invariants to physically gate the higher-order biochemical semantic stream, ensuring that spatial interactions are governed by genuine physical proximity rather than mere semantic similarity. Finally, to address the extreme statistical class imbalance of PTM sites and mathematically simulate the complex synergistic and antagonistic logic gates inherent in biological signaling networks, we design the Crosstalk-Aware Asymmetric Uncertainty Loss (CAAULoss). This multi-task optimization objective synergizes an asymmetric probabilistic hard-margin shift to eliminate the gradient dominance caused by ubiquitous negative samples, dynamic heteroscedastic uncertainty weighting for task balancing, and a Frobenius norm penalty that explicitly enforces empirically validated PTM crosstalk priors during gradient descent. Taken together, these innovations transform Qwen3-Protein from a general-purpose sequence processor into a physics- and biology-constrained foundation model, establishing a highly scalable computational paradigm for decoding multi-site biochemical modification networks. The architectural diagram of the Qwen3-protein model is shown in Fig. 1.

Engineered as a universal PTM foundation model, Qwen3-Protein demonstrates exceptional capabilities and consistently outperforms current leading models across diverse predictive benchmarks. Most notably, the architecture achieves an average improvement of 7.7% in the Matthews correlation coefficient (MCC) for site prediction across 16 distinct PTM categories. Furthermore, the framework allows seamless adaptation to downstream tasks through targeted model tuning, which drives substantial MCC enhancements of 5.8% in PTM crosstalk prediction and 4.8% in the identification of modifications specific to kinases. Collectively, these empirical gains strongly substantiate the overall efficacy and broad utility of the model. Crucially, Qwen3-Protein exhibits remarkable robustness by sustaining high accuracy on intrinsically challenging targets, including proteins with low pLDDT structural confidence scores or profound evolutionary conservation. Beyond isolated site prediction, the model demonstrates a systemic comprehension of complex PTM networks. It autonomously uncovers dynamic biological associations, such as competitive or synergistic coordination between distinct modifications, a capability rigorously validated via comprehensive in silico knockout simulations.

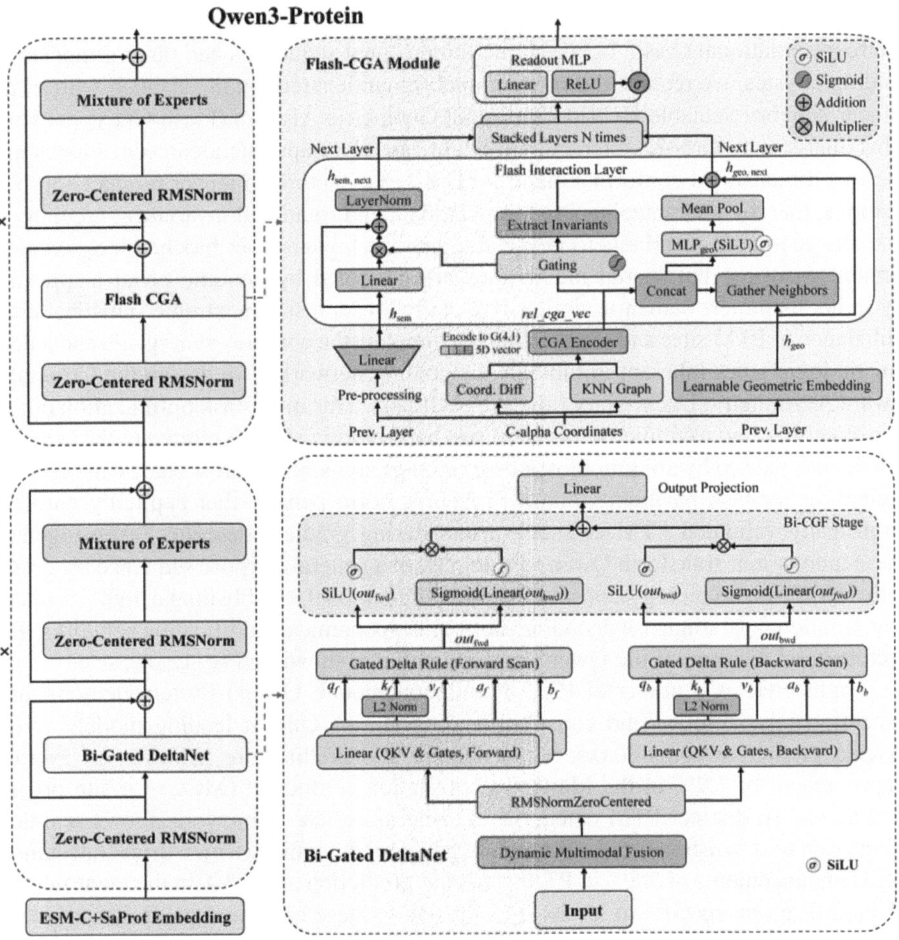

Fig. 1. The architecture of the Qwen3-Protein model

2 Methods

2.1 Dataset Construction

To construct the Qwen3-protein dataset, we curated experimentally validated sequences from the UniProt and UniRef databases alongside previously published datasets [8]. Following rigorous homology reduction, the finalized dataset encompasses 16 prevalent types of post-translational modifications (PTMs). In total, the dataset comprises 6,268,442 protein sequences, yielding 2,507,376 positive and 3,761,066 negative samples. These sequences were subsequently partitioned into training and independent test sets at a ratio of 10:1. Furthermore, for downstream fine-tuning tasks, we adopted the dataset published in DeepPCT [9] for PTM crosstalk prediction, and the established DCPPS dataset [10] for kinase-specific PTM prediction.

2.2 Multimodal Embedding

To robustly capture the complex determinants of post-translational modifications (PTMs), this study extracts dual-modality protein representations by fusing sequence-based embeddings from ESM-C [11] with structure-aware embeddings from Saprot [12]. While ESM-C leverages masked language modeling to efficiently encode deep evolutionary information and long-range dependencies directly from raw sequences—bypassing the need for time-consuming multiple sequence alignments—Saprot introduces a "structure-aware vocabulary" that integrates Foldseek-derived tokens to explicitly capture the local 3D geometric environment of each residue. Synergizing ESM-C's evolutionary propensity with Saprot's structural feasibility yields a highly complementary, multi-modal representation. This fusion effectively maps both the local sequence motifs and 3D conformational constraints driving PTMs, thereby mitigating single-modality ambiguity and significantly improving the accuracy and robustness of PTM site prediction.

2.3 Model Architecture

We introduce Qwen3-Protein, a highly specialized framework for multi-task post-translational modification (PTM) site prediction that extends the Qwen3-Next [13] architecture to model protein sequences as a complex biochemical language. To explicitly capture both localized sequence motifs and intricate long-range functional dependencies, we overhaul the baseline to natively process multimodal inputs comprising ESM-C evolutionary sequences and SaProt structural embeddings. At the architectural core, we replace the standard Gated DeltaNet with a Bidirectional Gated DeltaNet (Bi-Gated DeltaNet), which employs a dual-stream recursive state scanning mechanism (causal and anti-causal) coupled with a Bidirectional Cross-Gating Fusion (Bi-CGF) layer for robust global context extraction. Furthermore, to overcome the spatial limitations of conventional attention, we propose a Fast Linear Algebra Scalable Hybrid Conformal Geometric Algebra (Flash-CGA) network. Operating within a G(4,1) conformal metric space, Flash-CGA explicitly decouples feature interactions into a low-rank geometric flow based on relative C_α coordinates and a high-rank semantic flow, ensuring rigorous, translation-invariant spatial awareness with linear computational scalability. Finally, to mitigate extreme class imbalance and strictly enforce the biological theory of PTM crosstalk, we optimize the network using a novel Crosstalk-Aware Asymmetric Uncertainty Loss (CAAULoss). This objective elegantly unifies asymmetric hard thresholding, task-specific heteroscedastic uncertainty weighting, and empirical penalties regularized by biological priors, ensuring our simultaneous predictions remain statistically robust and biologically plausible.

Bidirectional GatedDeltaNet. To overcome the spatial constraints of unidirectional causal attention in traditional large language models while sustaining paramount computational efficiency in multi-task prediction of protein post-translational modifications (PTMs), we innovatively introduce the Bidirectional Gated DeltaNet (Bi-Gated

DeltaNet) as our core modeling engine. To comprehensively capture both local biochemical microenvironments and long-range amino acid contexts, this flagship multimodal architecture pioneeringly embeds an O(N) linear-complexity recurrent engine—the Gated Delta Rule—within a dual-stream bidirectional framework [14]. This breakthrough effectively dismantles the quadratic computational bottleneck inherent to traditional self-attention mechanisms. Furthermore, it dynamically aligns evolutionarily conserved ESM-C features with 3D geometrically aware SaProt features under a constant memory overhead. The data flow seamlessly advances through three distinct stages: multimodal fusion, bidirectional recurrent scanning, and cross-gated feature modulation, thereby accurately mapping the intricate spatial folding interaction networks between the protein's N- and C-termini. By leveraging this mechanism, Bi-Gated DeltaNet yields highly contextualized, 3D-aware, high-fidelity joint representations with a global receptive field. This enables the model to pinpoint and selectively amplify the subtle motif variations and spatial dependencies governing multi-task PTM propensities, ultimately delivering state-of-the-art feature representations for downstream classification tasks and substantially elevating biological predictive accuracy.

Initially, to circumvent the attenuation of high-frequency signals often caused by conventional late-fusion concatenation, the module takes the ESM-C derived sequence features E_{esm} and the SaProt derived structural features E_{saprot} as inputs. We introduce a Sigmoid-based, modality-specific information gain gate to regulate this process. For the t-th residue, the dynamically fused representation X_t is obtained through the Hadamard product of the gating weights and the original features. This representation is then projected into a unified dimensional space d_{model} via a linear transformation paired with a SiLU activation function. The process is defined as follows:

$$X_t = SiLU(W_{esm}(E_{esm}^t \odot \sigma(W_{ge}E_{esm}^t)) + W_{esm}\left(E_{saprot}^t \odot \sigma\left(W_{gs}E_{saprot}^t\right)\right) \quad (1)$$

The fused features are ultimately aligned via a zero-mean RMSNorm layer to ensure numerical stability for bidirectional propagation in subsequent deep layers. Subsequently, the fused representation X enters a dual-stream gated Delta recurrent scanning phase, where it is projected into two independent recurrent inference systems: a forward stream (N-terminus to C-terminus) and a backward stream (C-terminus to N-terminus). Taking the forward information flow as an instance, the input sequence is linearly mapped into the query vector $\overrightarrow{Q_t}$, key vector $\overrightarrow{K_t}$, and value vector $\overrightarrow{V_t}$. Simultaneously, the network dynamically generates a forget gate $\overrightarrow{\alpha_t}$ to rapidly erase redundant or stale memories, alongside an update gate $\overrightarrow{\beta_t}$ for precise feature writing. To prevent numerical explosion caused by matrix outer products, L2 norm normalization is strictly enforced on the key vectors. The update of the forward recurrent memory state matrix $\overrightarrow{S_t}$ strictly follows the gated Delta rule:

$$\overrightarrow{S_t} = \overrightarrow{\alpha_t} \odot \overrightarrow{S_{t-1}} + \overrightarrow{\beta_t} \odot \left(\overrightarrow{K_t} \otimes \left(\overrightarrow{V_t} - \overrightarrow{K_t}^T \overrightarrow{S_{t-1}}\right)\right) \quad (2)$$

The forward scanning output is then generated as follows:

$$\overrightarrow{O_t} = \overrightarrow{Q_t}\,\overrightarrow{S_t}\# \quad (3)$$

Conversely, the backward stream executes a perfectly symmetrical reverse scan to yield the backward representation $\overleftarrow{O_t}$.. This mechanism enables the model to adaptively manage memory while directionally injecting critical structural mutation information. Finally, to overcome the semantic fragmentation typically caused by the naive concatenation of hidden states in conventional bidirectional large models, we introduce a Bidirectional Cross-Gated Fusion (Bi-CGF) mechanism in the deeper layers of the network. This mechanism utilizes the global context of one direction as a modulator to dynamically filter the feature output of the opposite direction, thereby simulating complex protein spatial crosstalk effects. Specifically, the forward output is modulated by a gate derived from the backward features, and the backward output is similarly modulated by the forward features. The summation of these two modulated representations is then projected through a linear layer to produce the final output O_t^{final}, mathematically formulated as:

$$O_t^{fwd\_mod} = SiLU\left(\overrightarrow{O_t}\right) \odot \sigma\left(W_{cross}^{b}\overleftarrow{O_t}\right) \quad (4)$$

$$O_t^{bwd\_mod} = SiLU\left(\overleftarrow{O_t}\right) \odot \sigma\left(W_{cross}^{f}\overrightarrow{O_t}\right) \quad (5)$$

$$O_t^{final} = W_{out}\left(O_t^{fwd_{mod}} + O_t^{bwd_{mod}}\right)\# \quad (6)$$

This final representation seamlessly unifies the global physicochemical properties of amino acids, evolutionary conservation, and 3D spatial topological folding principles.

Fast Linear Algebra Scalable Hybrid Conformal Geometric Algebra Network. The Fast Linear Algebra Scalable Hybrid Conformal Geometric Algebra Network (Flash-CGA) module is designed to efficiently decipher the complex spatial topology and biochemical semantic interactions within protein structures. The core innovation of this module lies in its ability to overcome the prohibitive computational barriers associated with multivector geometric products in traditional Geometric Algebra (GA) networks [15]. By replacing the computationally expensive full geometric product with a lightweight factorized tensor product approximation, Flash-CGA achieves “flash"-level computational scalability suitable for million-scale molecular datasets. Furthermore, this architecture innovatively constructs a synergistic dual-stream mechanism. It not only inherently guarantees the strict translation invariance essential for 3D molecular modeling by embedding relative spatial coordinates into the 5D conformal geometric algebra (CGA) space G(4,1), but also dynamically gates the high-dimensional semantic feature flow using the extracted physical invariant geometric features. This design elegantly bridges the gap between spatial topology and biochemical semantics, ensuring that biochemical semantic expressions are consistently constrained and guided by rigorous local physical geometric structures.

To realize this process, the model first receives the 3D C-alpha coordinates of the protein, X, alongside pre-trained semantic feature embeddings, $H_{sem}^{(0)}$ After constructing a K-nearest neighbor (KNN) graph to capture local topological structures, the module computes the relative translation vector $\Delta x_{ij} = x_j - x_i$ between a target node i and its neighbor j. To encode both direction and distance within a unified mathematical framework, this relative coordinate is mapped into the conformal space G(4,1) with the metric signature (+, +, +, +, -). Specifically, through a specialized up-projection, the relative vector is encoded into a 5D conformal vector V_{ij}, , where the first three dimensions correspond to the Euclidean spatial components, and the latter two dimensions correspond to the combinations of origin and infinity basis vectors (e_0, e_∞) representing the homogeneous coordinate and the squared distance:

$$V_{ij} = \left[\Delta x_{ij}^{(1)}, \Delta x_{ij}^{(2)}, \Delta x_{ij}^{(3)}, 1, 0.5\|\Delta x_{ij}\|^2\right]\# \quad (7)$$

This CGA vector serves as an immutable, purely geometric input driving the subsequent feature propagation within the Flash Interaction Layers. For the feature update at layer l, to circumvent the $O_{(d_{geo}^2)}$ time complexity of the standard geometric product, the geometric stream employs an efficient alternative: it concatenates the neighboring geometric hidden state $H_{geo,j}^{(l)}$ with the relative CGA vector V_{ij}, processes this through a Multi-Layer Perceptron (MLP_{geo}) to learn transformation rules, and subsequently aggregates these to obtain the geometric update increment for the target node:

$$\Delta H_{\text{geo},i}^{(l)} = \frac{1}{K}\sum_{j\in\mathcal{N}(i)} \text{MLP}_{\text{geo}}\left(\left[H_{\text{geo},j}^{(l)} \| V_{ij}\right]\right)\# \quad (8)$$

The geometric state is then updated via a residual connection as $H_{geo}^{(l+1)} = H_{geo}^{(l)} + \Delta H_{geo,i}^{(l)}$. Upon acquiring the updated geometric topological information, the model modulates the semantic stream via a Geometric Gating mechanism. To ensure the rotation invariance of the features, the module applies an absolute value operation to the geometric hidden state to extract a scalar invariant, $I_{geo}^{(l+1)} = \left|H_{geo}^{(l)}\right|$. This invariant is fed into a bottleneck network equipped with a Sigmoid activation to generate a gating matrix G^l with values bounded in (0,1). Finally, the semantic features $H_{sem}^{(l)}$ undergo a linear transformation, are element-wise modulated by this geometric gating matrix, and complete the high-rank semantic stream update through Layer Normalization (LayerNorm) and a residual connection:

$$H_{\text{sem}}^{(l+1)} = LayerNorm\left(H_{\text{sem}}^{(l)} + G^{(l)} \odot \text{Linear}\left(H_{\text{sem}}^{(l)}\right)\right)\# \quad (9)$$

Through this iterative, layer-by-layer cross-stream interaction, Flash-CGA produces representations that deeply fuse 3D spatial structures with high-dimensional biochemical knowledge while maintaining exceptional computational efficiency and strict translation invariance. This significantly enhances the accuracy and robustness of downstream protein property predictions, such as Post-Translational Modification (PTM) probability forecasting.

Crosstalk-Aware Asymmetric Uncertainty Loss. To accurately predict protein post-translational modification (PTM) sites, we formulate a novel global optimization objective tailored for the Qwen3-Protein-based multi-task classifier, termed Crosstalk-Aware Asymmetric Uncertainty Loss (CAAULoss). This loss function is specifically designed to address three primary challenges inherent in multi-PTM prediction. First, it incorporates an asymmetric probability truncation mechanism to mitigate extreme positive-negative sample imbalances. Second, it employs adaptive task-weighting based on heteroscedastic uncertainty to balance the varying convergence rates and learning difficulties across different modification types. Finally, as a core innovation, CAAULoss translates known biological PTM crosstalk priors into a differentiable regularization penalty, thereby explicitly guiding the model to capture authentic synergistic or mutually exclusive relationships among multiple modifications [16].

Formally, the computational workflow of CAAULoss begins with calculating the Asymmetric Loss (ASL) for each independent PTM prediction task. Let $y^{(k)}$ denote the ground-truth label for the k-th task, and $p^{(k)}$ represent the predicted probability of the positive class. To filter out redundant gradients generated by an overwhelming number of easily distinguishable negative samples, we introduce a hard thresholding margin, m, applied to the negative sample probability $1 - p^{(k)}$. The shifted negative probability is defined as $\tilde{p}_{-}^{(k)} = \max(1-p^{(k)} - m, 0)$. By decoupling the positive and negative focusing parameters, γ_{+} and γ_{-}, the base loss for a single task is formulated as:

$$L_{\text{ASL}}^{(k)} = -y^{(k)}(1 - p^{(k)})^{\gamma_{+}} log(p^{(k)}) - (1 - y^{(k)})(1 - \tilde{p}_{-}^{(k)})^{\gamma_{-}} \log\left(\tilde{p}_{-}^{(k)}\right)\# \tag{10}$$

Subsequently, to balance the gradient contributions across the K classification heads during multi-task learning, we integrate a dynamic weighting mechanism driven by heteroscedastic uncertainty. The model maintains a learnable log-variance parameter, $\log(\sigma_k^2)$, for each task k. By utilizing the precision (the inverse of the variance) as a dynamic weight, the model adaptively down-weights tasks with high inherent noise, thereby optimizing the joint training trajectory. The uncertainty-weighted multi-task base loss is expressed as:

$$L_{\text{task}} = \sum_{k=1}^{K}\left(\frac{1}{2\sigma_k^2} L_{\text{ASL}}^{(k)} + \frac{1}{2}\log\left(\sigma_k^2\right)\right)\# \tag{11}$$

Finally, to inject domain-specific biological priors into the learning process, we compute the empirical correlation matrix, C_{emp}, of the predicted probabilities across all tasks within the current batch. Given a $K \times K$ biological prior correlation matrix, C_{prior} and a binary mask matrix, M, indicating high-confidence crosstalk relationships, we construct a crosstalk penalty term by measuring the discrepancy between the empirical predictions and the biological priors. This penalty is quantified using the squared Frobenius norm, modulated by a regularization hyperparameter λ_{cross}. The final global objective function, CAAULoss, optimized during backpropagation is defined as:

$$L_{\text{total}} = L_{\text{task}} + \lambda_{\text{cross}} \| M \odot \left(C_{\text{emp}} - C_{\text{prior}}\right) \|_F^2\# \tag{12}$$

2.4 Hyperparameter Configuration

For the training of Qwen3-Protein, we employed the AdamW optimizer with a peak learning rate of 0.0004. We utilized a learning rate scheduling strategy that combines linear warmup with cosine annealing decay. Specifically, the model was trained for a maximum of 100,000 steps, which included 5,000 warmup steps, using a global batch size of 1,024. For model fine-tuning, we primarily utilize the Low-Rank Adaptation (LoRA) method. To ensure reproducibility, the comprehensive hyperparameter configurations, along with the source code and model weights, will be made publicly accessible via GitHub and Hugging Face. Furthermore, all training and fine-tuning procedures were executed on a hardware cluster comprising 16 NVIDIA H100 GPUs. In terms of task evaluation metric selection, we adopted several of the most commonly employed metrics in the field of bioinformatics.

3 Results

3.1 Ablation Experiment

In this study, we utilized protein representations derived from ESM-C and SaProt as our multimodal embeddings. An ablation study evaluating state-of-the-art protein language models (PLMs) on the O-glycosylation dataset (Fig. 2A) demonstrates that this specific combination yields the optimal performance, outperforming the second-best configuration by 2.5% in terms of the MCC. Furthermore, these results validate the superiority of multimodal embeddings over unimodal counterparts that rely exclusively on sequence information, underscoring the complementary benefits of integrating sequential and structural features.

Additionally, we introduced three novel modules to our architecture and quantified their respective contributions to the overall performance enhancement (Fig. 2B). Evaluated by the MCC metric, the Bidirectional GatedDeltaNet outperforms the standard GatedDeltaNet by 3.7%. Similarly, Flash-CGA surpasses the baseline channel attention mechanism by 3.4%, and the proposed CAAULoss achieves a 2.6% improvement over the standard causal cross-entropy loss.

3.2 Model Comparison and Paradigm Validation

For our comparative analysis, we selected two recently introduced general-purpose models—PTMGPT2 and MTPrompt-PTM—as baselines to evaluate Qwen3-Protein. Qwen3-Protein achieved state-of-the-art (SOTA) performance across 16 standard PTM site prediction tasks, significantly outperforming the second-best models by average margins of 7.7%, 6.6%, and 6.6% in MCC, AUC, and AP, respectively. Furthermore, when fine-tuned for the downstream task of PTM crosstalk prediction, Qwen3-Protein surpassed the strongest baseline, DeepPCT, yielding a 5.8% improvement in MCC. Finally, upon adaptation to kinase-specific PTM site prediction tasks, Qwen3-Protein exceeded the second-best baseline DCPPS by 4.8% in MCC. Collectively, these empirical results compellingly validate the paradigm shift represented by Qwen3-Protein: transitioning from a specialized PTM site predictor to a versatile foundation model. This demonstrates that the model intrinsically captures the interdependencies among modifications rather than treating them as isolated events. To further elucidate the underlying mechanisms, we generated attention score maps of PTM crosstalk sequences for Qwen3-Protein (Fig. 2C). The analysis revealed that while predicting a specific PTM site, the model concurrently allocates significant attention weights to associated crosstalk sites. This provides computational evidence of the model's systemic understanding of PTM networks. The comprehensive experimental results are summarized in Table 1; notably, due to strict space constraints, all comparative data have been consolidated into a single table.

Table 1. Performance comparison of Qwen3-Protein across various tasks. Here, ↑MCC indicates the margin of improvement achieved by Qwen3-Protein over the second-best model.

Task	Name	MCC	AUC	AP	↑MCC	↑AUC	↑AP
PTMs	O-Glycosylation	0.837	0.960	0.922	**8.3%**	**6.2%**	**6.5%**
	N-Phosphorylation	0.745	0.938	0.909	**5.9%**	**7.0%**	**6.2%**
	Succinylation	0.560	0.861	0.658	**7.9%**	**6.7%**	**5.8%**
	S-Carboxyethylation	0.622	0.874	0.883	**6.2%**	**4.8%**	**5.0%**
	S-Sulfhydration	0.580	0.879	0.851	**7.1%**	**8.0%**	**8.4%**
	S-Nitrosylation	0.602	0.891	0.815	**8.6%**	**6.4%**	**7.5%**
	O-Phosphorylation	0.711	0.970	0.802	**10.0%**	**8.6%**	**8.2%**
	Hydroxylation	0.878	0.944	0.926	**13.0%**	**7.7%**	**8.1%**
	SUMOylation	0.903	0.949	0.960	**6.9%**	**4.4%**	**5.3%**
	Methylation	0.908	0.942	0.968	**8.1%**	**6.4%**	**5.9%**
	Malonylation	0.766	0.885	0.874	**5.8%**	**5.0%**	**6.2%**
	Ubiquitination	0.405	0.705	0.814	**4.5%**	**6.2%**	**4.9%**
	Glutarylation	0.811	0.937	0.926	**9.2%**	**9.5%**	**8.5%**
	Amidation	0.834	0.848	0.766	**8.0%**	**7.9%**	**7.2%**
	S-Palmitoylation	0.454	0.486	0.490	**6.5%**	**5.3%**	**6.0%**
	Formylation	0.519	0.410	0.333	**7.6%**	**5.8%**	**6.2%**
PCT	PTM1 to PTM2	0.320	0.828	0.346	**5.8%**	**4.6%**	**5.6%**
Kinase-Specific	Phosphorylation	0.612	0.929	0.558	**4.8%**	**3.9%**	**4.0%**

To mitigate the noise introduced by low-confidence protein structures, SaProt employs a structure-aware masking strategy. Specifically, 3Di tokens in regions with pLDDT scores below 70 are replaced by a mask token ("#"), effectively reducing these uncertain regions to a purely sequence-based representation. To evaluate the impact of structural quality, we stratified the dataset into three cohorts based on pLDDT scores (Fig. 2D). Qwen3-Protein consistently outperforms the baseline model, PTMGPT2, across all categories. Notably, Qwen3-Protein sustains its performance advantage even within the pLDDT < 70 cohort, demonstrating its distinct superiority in predicting PTM sites for low-confidence protein structures.

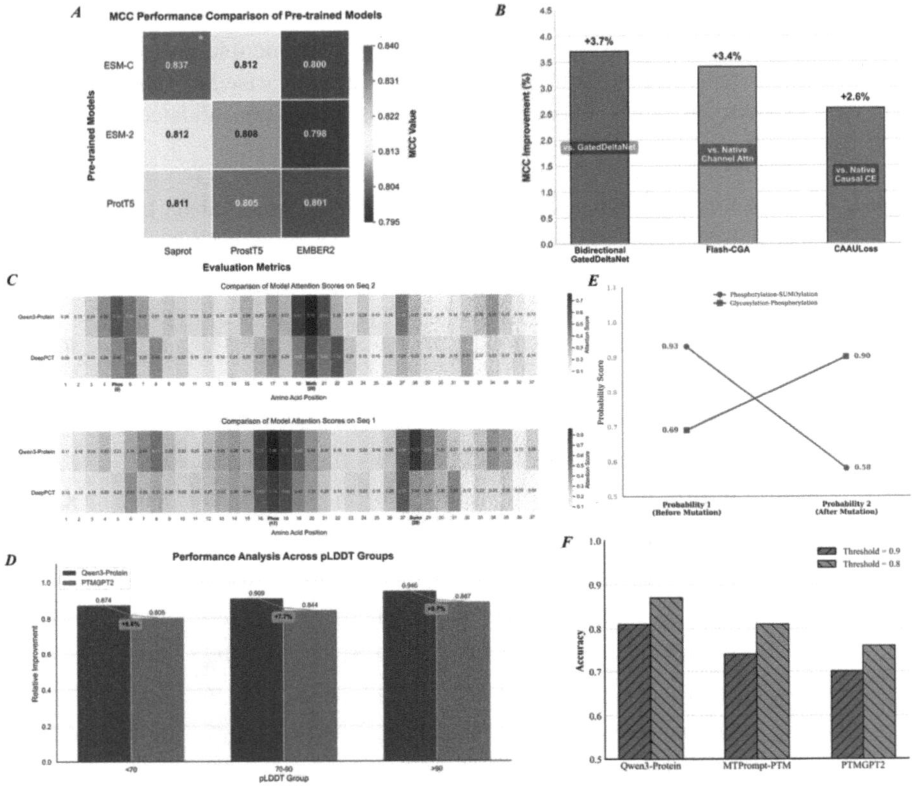

Fig. 2. Performance comparison across models and validation of the proposed paradigm.

Deciphering context-dependent correlations in post-translational modifications (PTMs) is essential for advancing from isolated site prediction to a holistic system-level understanding [17]. Rather than relying on post hoc statistical correlations of static predictions, Qwen3-Protein inherently captures network dynamics during inference through its attention mechanism and shared latent space. To verify this, we used in silico perturbations to probe the conditional probabilities learned by the model. We designed knockout experiments on unseen sequences to assess dynamic associations, from synergistic to competitive regulation. By mutating specific modification sites to alanine, we observed the subsequent probability changes in related PTMs (Fig. 2E). In the first sequence featuring phosphorylation and SUMOylation, "knocking out" the phosphorylation site substantially reduced the predicted SUMOylation probability, reflecting a synergistic (positive) correlation captured by the model. Conversely, in the second sequence involving glycosylation and phosphorylation, mutating the glycosylation site significantly increased the phosphorylation probability, pointing to a competitive (negative) mechanism. These results confirm that this "network" is not an external graph mapped out after the fact, but an intrinsic logic embedded in the model's weights, allowing it to simulate the causal impact of modifying a single node (site) on the overall system. Ultimately, Qwen3-Protein proves highly effective at inferring functional PTM crosstalk, demonstrating its potential for full-scale network-level interpretation.

Evolutionary conservation within protein sequences serves as a robust indicator of functional significance [18]. Post-translational modifications (PTMs) occurring at highly conserved residues typically represent evolutionarily ancient and vital regulatory mechanisms, indispensable for core signal transduction and cellular homeostasis. Conversely, PTMs situated in rapidly evolving regions may reflect species-specific adaptations or stochastic noise. Given that prioritizing conserved sites is critical for identifying high-confidence regulatory switches, we stratified the phosphorylation dataset based on conservation scores utilizing the well-established ConSurf tool (at thresholds of >0.8 and >0.9, respectively) to conduct a comparative analysis [19]. As illustrated in Fig. 2F, benchmarking results demonstrate that Qwen3-Protein achieves the highest accuracy across both conservation thresholds. This exceptional performance not only underscores the model's proficiency in identifying critical conserved PTM sites but also validates its capacity to transcend localized site prediction, advancing toward a system-level understanding of regulatory networks [20].

4 Conclusion

In summary, we introduce Qwen3-Protein, a biophysics-grounded foundation model that shifts PTM prediction from isolated site identification to holistic, network-level interpretation. By integrating multimodal embeddings with our novel Bi-GatedDeltaNet and Flash-CGA architectures, the model achieves linear-complexity, translation-invariant sequence modeling that explicitly bridges 1D semantics with 3D folding physics. Furthermore, the proposed CAAULoss successfully mitigates extreme class imbalances while mathematically enforcing empirical crosstalk priors. Empirically, Qwen3-Protein establishes new state-of-the-art performance across 16 PTM categories, demonstrating exceptional robustness on low-confidence structures and highly conserved functional regions. Most notably, in silico perturbations validate its intrinsic capacity to decipher complex synergistic and competitive modification dynamics. This scalable paradigm significantly advances the computational decoding of multi-site biochemical networks, providing a robust framework for future biomolecular engineering.

Acknowledgements. This research was funded by Natural Science Foundation of Jiangsu Province of China (Grant No. BK20230626), the National Natural Science Foundation of China (Grant No. 62502053), supported by National Students' platform for innovation and entrepreneurship training program (Grant No. 202510292035).

References

1. Walsh, C.T., Garneau-Tsodikova, S., Gatto, G.J., Jr.: Protein posttranslational modifications: the chemistry of proteome diversifications. Angew. Chem. Int. Ed. **44**, 7342–7372 (2005)
2. Deribe, Y.L., Pawson, T., Dikic, I.: Post-translational modifications in signal integration. Nat. Struct. Mol. Biol. **17**, 666–672 (2010)

3. Venne, A.S., Kollipara, L., Zahedi, R.P.: The next level of complexity: Crosstalk of posttranslational modifications. Proteomics **14**, 513–524 (2014)
4. Deep Learning in Proteomics - Wen - 2020 - PROTEOMICS - Wiley Online Library,
5. Shrestha, P., Kandel, J., Tayara, H., Chong, K.T.: Post-translational modification prediction via prompt-based fine-tuning of a GPT-2 model. Nat. Commun. **15**, 6699 (2024)
6. Han, Y., He, F., Shao, Q., Wang, D., Xu, D.: MTPrompt-PTM: a multi-task method for post-translational modification prediction using prompt tuning on a structure-aware protein language model. Biomolecules **15**, 843 (2025)
7. Heritz, J.A., et al.: Integrating deep learning for post-translational modifications crosstalk on Hsp90 and drug binding. J. Biol. Chem. **301** (2025)
8. Ahmad, S., et al.: The UniProt Consortium: The UniProt website API: facilitating programmatic access to protein knowledge. Nucleic Acids Res. **53**, W547–W553 (2025)
9. Huang, Y.-X., Liu, R.: Improved prediction of post-translational modification crosstalk within proteins using DeepPCT. Bioinformatics. **40**, btae675 (2024)
10. Liu, M., Wang, X., Sun, Z.-L., Yang, X., Chen, X.: DCPPS: prediction of kinase-specific phosphorylation sites using dynamic embedding and cross-representation interaction. Interdiscip. Sci. Comput. Life Sci. **17**, 1056–1073 (2025)
11. Hayes, T., et al.: Simulating 500 million years of evolution with a language model. Science **387**, 850–858 (2025)
12. Su, J., Han, C., Zhou, Y., Shan, J., Zhou, X., Yuan, F.: SaProt: Protein Language Modeling with Structure-aware Vocabulary, https://www.biorxiv.org/content/https://doi.org/10.1101/2023.10.01.560349v5 (2024)
13. Yang, A., et al.: Qwen3 Technical Report, http://arxiv.org/abs/2505.09388 (2025)
14. Yang, S., Kautz, J., Hatamizadeh, A.: Gated Delta Networks: Improving Mamba2 with Delta Rule, http://arxiv.org/abs/2412.06464 (2025)
15. UniProNet: A Universal PTM Site Prediction Model with an Equivariant Graph Neural Network and Multimodal Fusion. https://ieeexplore.ieee.org/abstract/document/11356504
16. Joshi, S.: A Comprehensive Review of Qwen and DeepSeek LLMs: Architecture, Performance and Applications. https://papers.ssrn.com/abstract=5267655 (2025)
17. Leutert, M., Entwisle, S.W., Villén, J.: Decoding post-translational modification crosstalk with proteomics. Mol. Cell. Proteomics **20**, 100129 (2021)
18. Philippe, H., Lopez, P.: On the conservation of protein sequences in evolution. Trends Biochem. Sci. **26**, 414–416 (2001)
19. Armon, A., Graur, D., Ben-Tal, N.: ConSurf: an algorithmic tool for the identification of functional regions in proteins by surface mapping of phylogenetic information1. J. Mol. Biol. **307**, 447–463 (2001)
20. Chung, C.-R., et al.: DbPTM 2025 update: comprehensive integration of PTMs and proteomic data for advanced insights into cancer research. Nucleic Acids Res. **53**, D377–D386 (2025)

Dynamic Spatiotemporal Graph Learning of EEG for Multi-type Epileptiform Event Detection

Sheng Liu[1,2,3], Mingyu Wang[4], Yanjie Wei[3], Linxia Xiao[3(✉)], and Shizhong Lian[4(✉)]

[1] Southern University of Science and Technology, Shenzhen, China
[2] Faculty of Computer Science and Artificial Intelligence, Shenzhen University of Advanced Technology, Shenzhen, China
[3] Center for High Performance Computing, Shenzhen Institutes of Advanced Technology, Chinese Academy of Sciences, Shenzhen, China
lx.xiao@siat.ac.cn
[4] Department of Neurosurgery, The First Hospital of Shanxi Medical University, Taiyuan, China
13934236496@163.com

Abstract. Multi-type epileptiform events, including spike and ripple activities in electroencephalogram (EEG), are important biomarkers for seizure detection; however, their accurate detection is challenging due to complex spatio-temporal dynamics and multi-scale oscillatory patterns. To address these challenges, we propose a unified framework that integrates clinically motivated multi-band decomposition with dynamic spatio-temporal representation learning for accurate classification of EEG signals. Specifically, EEG signals are first decomposed into multiple frequency branches, followed by a branch-aware wavelet enhancement module to emphasize transient oscillatory patterns. A multi-scale temporal convolution module is then employed to capture diverse temporal dynamics across different time scales. Finally, a dynamic spatio-temporal graph reasoning module constructs sample-adaptive spatial and temporal graphs and performs joint propagation to model inter-channel interactions and temporal dependencies. Extensive experiments conducted on both a private clinical dataset and the public TUEV dataset demonstrate that the proposed method consistently outperforms existing state-of-the-art approaches in epileptic event detection. These results highlight its effectiveness in capturing clinically relevant EEG patterns and its potential for assisting automated epilepsy diagnosis.

Keywords: Spatiotemporal Graph Learning · Epileptiform Event Detection · Multi-Scale Temporal Modeling · Multi-Band EEG Decomposition

X. Cui et al. (Eds.): ISBRA 2026, LNBI 16690, pp. 261–272, 2027.
https://doi.org/10.1007/978-981-92-3716-6_21

1 Introduction

Electroencephalography (EEG) is a non-invasive technique for recording neural activity, widely used in epilepsy detection, neuroscience research, and cognitive assessment [4]. In clinical practice, seizure detection largely relies on identifying interictal epileptiform discharges (IEDs), particularly spikes and sharp waves, which are established biomarkers of epileptogenic activity. As illustrated in Fig. 1, spikes are brief transients lasting approximately 20–70 ms, while ripples typically span 70–200 ms. Their frequency, spatial distribution, and morphology are closely associated with epileptic events, making accurate detection crucial for reliable diagnosis and long-term monitoring [11,12]. Moreover, emerging evidence indicates that high-frequency oscillations [19], such as ripples, together with spikes, provide complementary and more specific insights into epileptogenic processes, further enhancing seizure characterization and localization.

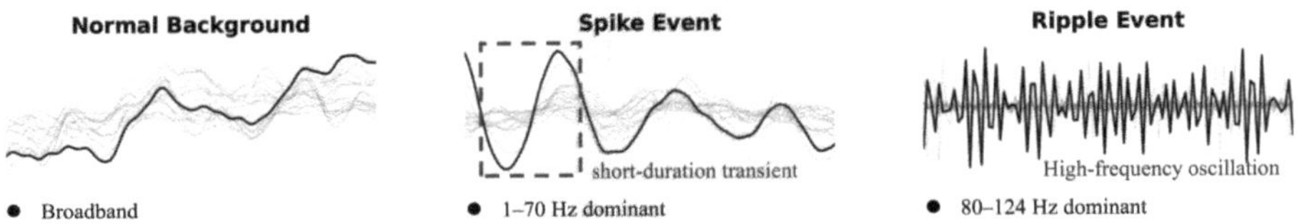

Fig. 1. Representative EEG patterns of normal background, spike, and ripple events. Spike events exhibit short-duration transient discharges, while ripple events are characterized by high-frequency oscillations.

Reliable detection of epileptiform events in clinical practice remains highly challenging [2,6]. These events are typically characterized by low amplitude, short duration, and substantial inter-patient variability, while EEG recordings are often contaminated by artifacts such as muscle activity and environmental noise and complex background rhythms, further obscuring pathological patterns. Traditional approaches, including band-pass filtering and multi-band spectral analysis, attempt to enhance discriminative features using frequency-specific information [9,22]. However, clinically relevant biomarkers such as spikes and ripples are defined not only by frequency components but also by their spatio-temporal context across channels, which is difficult for these methods to capture. Consequently, the sensitivity and generalization of these methods are extremely dependent on predefined frequency bands or handcrafted representation.

In recent years, with the rapid development of deep learning and signal processing techniques, significant progress has been made in automated EEG analysis [13,14]. Representative models, including Convolutional Neural Networks (CNN) [1], Long Short-Term Memory (LSTM) [7], Gated Recurrent Units (GRU) [17], Graph Neural Networks (GNNs) [3], and Transformer-based methods [23], have been widely used to extract spatiotemporal features for brain activity classification [8,18]. In addition, functional connectivity analysis [20] and graph-based approaches [8,21] have further improved modeling of inter-channel relationships.

Despite these advances, existing methods still struggle to capture the highly dynamic and transient nature of epileptic spikes and ripple activities, largely due to their reliance on fixed frequency representations or static connectivity patterns. Moreover, temporal models often have limited capacity in modeling long-range dependencies under noisy clinical conditions, while most graph-based approaches fail to account for time-varying inter-channel interactions. These limitations highlight the need for dynamic spatio-temporal graph modeling for accurate EEG-based spike and ripple detection.

To address these challenges, we propose a unified framework for epileptiform event detection from EEG signals, termed Dynamic Spatiotemporal Graph Learning Network (DSTGNet). The proposed method integrates clinically motivated multi-band decomposition, waveform enhancement, multi-scale temporal modeling, and dynamic spatio-temporal graph reasoning in a unified architecture. By constructing sample-adaptive spatial and temporal graphs, the model effectively captures the evolving inter-channel interactions and transient propagation patterns of epileptic spikes and ripples, leading to more discriminative representations for accurate event detection.

The main contributions of this work are summarized as follows:

- We introduce a clinically inspired multi-band EEG representation with branch-aware waveform enhancement, enabling adaptive refinement of transient oscillatory activities such as spikes and ripple discharges while preserving fine-grained signal characteristics;
- We design a multi-scale temporal encoding module to effectively model heterogeneous temporal patterns of epileptic events, ranging from sharp spikes to high-frequency ripple activities;
- We propose a dynamic spatio-temporal graph learning module that constructs sample-adaptive spatial and temporal graphs and performs joint message propagation, effectively modeling time-varying inter-channel dependencies and seizure-related propagation dynamics.

2 Methodology

2.1 Overview

To enable more accurate detection of epileptiform events in complex EEG signals, we propose a epileptiform event detection framework from EEG signals, which integrates clinically motivated multi-band decomposition with dynamic spatio-temporal representation learning. As illustrated in Fig. 2, the proposed framework consists of four sequential stages. Given an input EEG segment, multi-band decomposition is first performed to separate frequency-specific components, which are further refined by a branch-aware wavelet enhancement module to emphasize transient oscillatory activities, such as spikes and high-frequency ripple patterns. The enhanced representations are then processed by a multi-scale temporal convolution module to capture heterogeneous temporal dynamics across different time scales. Subsequently, a dynamic spatio-temporal graph reasoning module is constructed to model sample-adaptive inter-channel interactions together with temporal dependencies in a unified manner. Finally, the learned representation is fed into a classification head to generate the detection result.

2.2 Data Preprocessing

To better capture frequency-specific patterns and enhance the representation of epileptiform activities, we adopt a multi-band preprocessing strategy. Each EEG recording is segmented into fixed-length windows and decomposed into three frequency branches via band-pass filtering. The low-frequency branch (1–70 Hz) preserves spike-related activity, the ripple-related branch (80–124 Hz) captures fast oscillatory patterns, and the full-band branch (1–124 Hz) retains the overall waveform morphology.

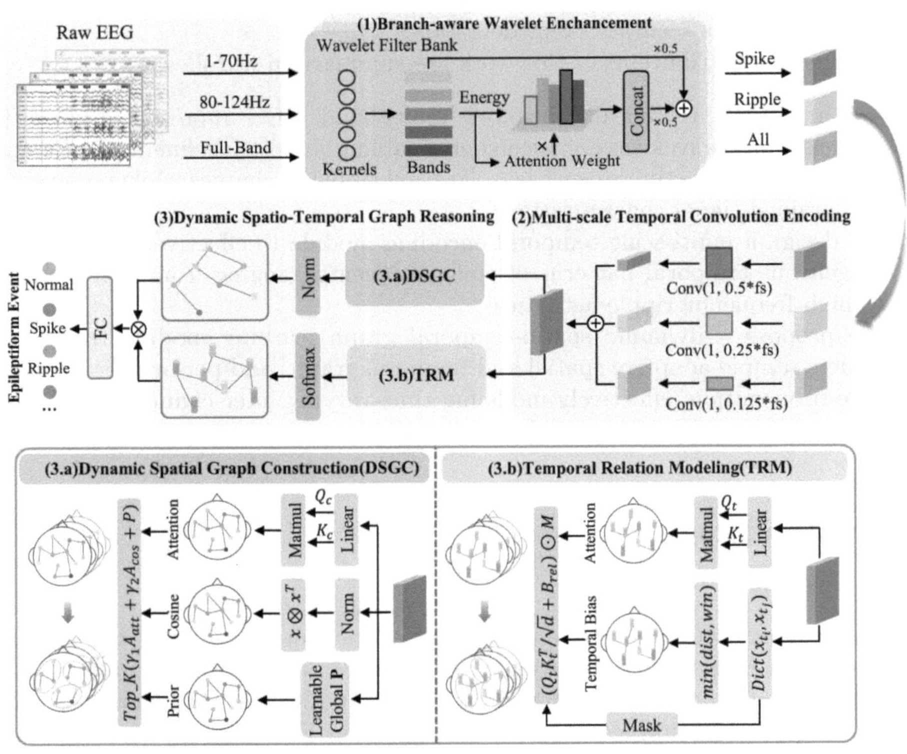

Fig. 2. Overall architecture of the proposed DSTGNet. The framework consists of (1) branch-aware wavelet enhancement for multi-band feature extraction, (2) multi-scale temporal convolution encoding for hierarchical temporal modeling, and (3) dynamic spatio-temporal graph reasoning, including (3.a) dynamic spatial graph construction (DSGC) and (3.b) temporal relation modeling (TRM), to capture adaptive spatial and temporal dependencies.

Formally, given an EEG segment $\mathbf{S} \in \mathbb{R}^{C \times T}$, where C and T denote the number of channels and temporal samples, the three branches are defined as

$$\mathbf{X}^{(1)} = \mathcal{B}_{1\sim70}(\mathbf{S}), \quad \mathbf{X}^{(2)} = \mathcal{B}_{80\sim124}(\mathbf{S}), \quad \mathbf{X}^{(3)} = \mathcal{B}_{1\sim124}(\mathbf{S}), \tag{1}$$

where $\mathcal{B}_{a\sim b}(\cdot)$ denotes band-pass filtering within $[a, b]$ Hz. The final input is constructed as

$$\mathbf{X} = \text{Stack}\big(\mathbf{X}^{(1)}, \mathbf{X}^{(2)}, \mathbf{X}^{(3)}\big) \in \mathbb{R}^{3 \times C \times T}. \tag{2}$$

Channel-wise standardization is applied independently to each branch. This design provides a physiologically meaningful multi-view representation for subsequent modeling.

2.3 Branch-Aware Wavelet Enhancement

Although multi-band decomposition provides coarse spectral separation, epileptic EEG patterns remain highly transient and non-stationary within each branch. In particular, spikes correspond to short-duration sharp transients, while fast ripple activities are localized in high-frequency bands. Fixed band-pass filtering alone is therefore insufficient to capture fine-grained time-frequency variations.

To address this, we introduce a branch-aware wavelet enhancement module with branch-specific kernels. Each branch is enhanced according to its physiological characteristics: the low-frequency branch emphasizes spike morphology, the high-frequency branch focuses on ripple oscillations, and the full-band branch preserves global waveform structure. For each branch $\mathbf{X}^{(m)}$, the enhanced representation is

$$\tilde{\mathbf{X}}^{(m)} = f_{\text{wave}}^{(m)}(\mathbf{X}^{(m)}). \tag{3}$$

To stabilize the transformation and preserve original signal characteristics, a residual fusion mechanism is applied. This design enables adaptive enhancement of transient patterns while maintaining waveform fidelity.

2.4 Multi-scale Temporal Convolution Encoding

After branch-wise enhancement, the signals are fed into a multi-scale temporal convolution module. Epileptiform events exhibit diverse temporal characteristics, ranging from short spikes to longer rhythmic discharges, making a single receptive field insufficient.

To capture this variability, we employ multiple temporal convolution branches with different kernel sizes. Given sampling rate f_s, the kernel sizes are defined as $k_i = \lfloor \alpha_i f_s \rfloor$, where $\alpha_i \in \{0.5, 0.25, 0.125\}$. For $f_s = 250$ Hz, this corresponds to $k_i \in \{125, 62, 31\}$.

Each branch applies a convolution with kernel size $(1 \times k_i)$, extracting features along the temporal dimension while preserving channel-wise independence. Larger kernels model long-range dependencies, whereas smaller kernels capture transient events.

The outputs of all branches are concatenated along the temporal dimension and compressed using power-based pooling:

$$\mathbf{Z} = f_{\text{temp}}(\tilde{\mathbf{X}}), \quad \mathbf{Z} \in \mathbb{R}^{C \times T'}. \tag{4}$$

The pooling operation computes logarithmic signal energy, providing a more robust representation for EEG analysis.

2.5 Dynamic Spatio-Temporal Graph Reasoning

To capture dependencies beyond local temporal patterns, we model EEG signals using a dynamic spatio-temporal graph, where spatial and temporal relationships are adaptively inferred from input features, enabling sample-specific modeling of inter-channel interactions and temporal evolution.

Dynamic Spatial Graph Construction. Instead of using predefined adjacency matrices, we construct a sample-adaptive spatial graph from the encoded representation $\mathbf{Z} \in \mathbb{R}^{C \times T'}$, where each channel is treated as a node. Pairwise affinities are computed using attention and similarity measures, together with a learnable global prior

$$\mathbf{L}_s = \gamma_1 \mathbf{A}_{att} + \gamma_2 \mathbf{A}_{cos} + \mathbf{P}. \tag{5}$$

The resulting graph is sparsified and normalized to suppress noisy connections, yielding $\tilde{\mathbf{A}}_s$. This formulation allows the model to capture dynamic inter-channel synchronization patterns associated with epileptiform activity.

Temporal Relation Modeling. Temporal dependencies are modeled by treating each time step as a node. A lightweight attention mechanism with relative positional bias is used to capture temporal relations:

$$\mathbf{L}_t = \frac{\mathbf{Q}_t \mathbf{K}_t^\top}{\sqrt{d}} + \mathbf{B}_{rel}. \tag{6}$$

A locality constraint is further imposed to emphasize short-range continuity, yielding the normalized temporal adjacency $\tilde{\mathbf{A}}_t$. This reflects the fact that epileptiform events typically exhibit short-duration and locally continuous temporal patterns.

Joint Spatio-Temporal Propagation. Given the spatial and temporal graphs, feature propagation is performed as:

$$\mathbf{Z}_{st} = \tilde{\mathbf{A}}_s \mathbf{Z} \tilde{\mathbf{A}}_t + \mathbf{Z}. \tag{7}$$

This operation aggregates information across correlated channels and temporally related steps. A residual connection is introduced to preserve local features and stabilize training. The output is then projected as:

$$\mathbf{H} = \text{GELU}(\mathbf{Z}_{st} \mathbf{W}_o). \tag{8}$$

Epileptic seizures are characterized by abnormal synchronization and propagation of neural activity across brain regions. The proposed dynamic graph formulation allows the model to adaptively capture such evolving inter-channel dependencies and temporal progression, rather than relying on fixed connectivity patterns.

2.6 Epileptiform Event Classification

The graph-refined representation $\mathbf{H}$ is flattened and fed into a linear classifier to obtain the final prediction: $\hat{\mathbf{y}} = f_{\text{cls}}(\mathbf{H})$. The model is trained end-to-end using the cross-entropy loss:

$$\mathcal{L}_{cls} = -\sum_{k=1}^{K} y_k \log \hat{y}_k. \tag{9}$$

3 Experiments and Results

3.1 Dataset

All experiments are implemented in PyTorch with Python 3.10 and conducted on an NVIDIA A6000 GPU. The learning rate and batch size are set to 3×10^{-4} and 32, respectively, and the model is trained for 100 epochs. To evaluate both accuracy and generalization capability, we conduct experiments on a private clinical dataset and the publicly available TUEV dataset [10].

Private Dataset. This dataset contains EEG recordings from 18 patients with a total duration of approximately 2.78 h. The signals are acquired using 19 channels at a sampling rate of 250 Hz, with annotations for two types of epileptiform events: spike and ripple.

TUEV Dataset. The TUEV dataset is a subset of the TUH EEG (TUEG) corpus, containing annotated EEG segments categorized into six classes: (1) spike and sharp wave (SPSW), (2) generalized periodic epileptiform discharges (GPED), (3) periodic lateralized epileptiform discharges (PLED), (4) eye movement (EYEM), (5) artifact (ARTF), and (6) background (BCKG). The recordings use 23 channels with a sampling rate of 256 Hz.

3.2 Performance Evaluation

To quantitatively evaluate model performance, we employ Precision, Recall, and F1-score, which respectively measure detection accuracy, sensitivity, and their harmonic balance. All reported results are averaged over five independent runs to ensure robustness and stability. We compare DSTGNet with several representative baseline models, including the graph-based ATDGNN [16], the CNN-based Inception [5], and the conventional CBraMod [15]. These baselines are selected to cover different mainstream methodological paradigms for EEG analysis, including graph-based modeling of inter-channel dependencies, convolutional architectures for temporal feature extraction, and traditional signal processing-based approaches. Such a diverse set of baselines enables a comprehensive evaluation of the proposed method across different modeling perspectives. All models are implemented and evaluated under consistent experimental settings for fair comparison.

Table 1. Performance comparison across private and TUEV datasets.

Model	Private Dataset			TUEV Dataset		
	Precision	Recall	F1-score	Precision	Recall	F1-score
DSTGNet(Ours)	**0.9845**	**0.9882**	**0.9863**	**0.9522**	**0.9399**	**0.9458**
ATDGNN [16]	0.9605	0.9646	0.9626	0.9455	0.9369	0.9412
Inception [5]	0.9765	0.9546	0.9654	0.8472	0.8177	0.8322
CBraMod [15]	0.9368	0.9343	0.9356	0.7294	0.6920	0.7103

As shown in Table 1, the experimental results demonstrate that the proposed DSTGNet consistently achieves superior performance across both datasets. On the private dataset, DSTGNet attains the best results in all evaluation metrics, with a Precision of 0.9845, Recall of 0.9882, and F1-score of 0.9863, significantly outperforming competing methods such as ATDGNN, Inception, and CBraMod. Notably, the high Recall indicates its strong capability in capturing epileptiform events, while the balanced F1-score reflects robust overall performance.

On the TUEV dataset, DSTGNet also delivers the highest performance, achieving a Precision of 0.9522, Recall of 0.9399, and F1-score of 0.9458. Compared with other baselines, it maintains a clear advantage, demonstrating better generalization ability across different datasets and more complex multi-class scenarios. Overall, these results validate the effectiveness of DSTGNet in modeling the spatiotemporal dynamics of EEG signals and accurately detecting epileptiform events.

To evaluate the model's interpretability, we compare background activity with epileptic events, using spike events as representative pathological discharges. Figure 3 visualizes the spatiotemporal connectivity evolution of a 1-second EEG segment across five 0.2 s windows. Under an absolute thresholding strategy, the Normal background (Fig. 3a) exhibits a sparse, weak, and randomly distributed topology, accurately reflecting a healthy desynchronized baseline. Conversely, the Spike event (Fig. 3b) demonstrates a distinct, highly localized dynamic process. Following a relatively quiet pre-onset phase (Frame 1), a sudden hypersynchronous burst erupts in Frames 2 and 3, characterized by dense functional coupling predominantly at the right hemisphere (e.g. F4, FP2) and midline (e.g., Cz) channels. This pathological network subsequently dissipates in Frames 4 and 5. These results confirm that our model successfully captures the microscopic spatial propagation and focal onset of epileptic discharges.

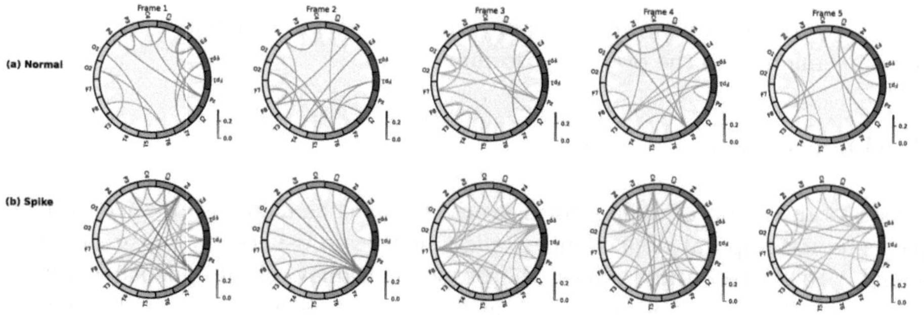

Fig. 3. Dynamic spatial connectivity evolution for (a) Normal background and (b) Spike event. The 1-second EEG segment is divided into five consecutive 0.2 s windows. Edge colors represent the different channels, with darker red line indicating stronger functional coupling.

3.3 Ablation Study

We conduct an ablation study on the TUEV dataset, with results averaged over five runs. As shown in Fig. 4(a), the full DSTGNet consistently achieves the best performance across all evaluation metrics, demonstrating the effectiveness of integrating wavelet decomposition, temporal modeling, and spatial graph learning. Removing any component leads to noticeable performance degradation, verifying that each module contributes to the overall model capability. Figure 4(b) further provides a fine-grained analysis of the contribution of each component across different metrics. Notably, removing the temporal relation graph results in the most significant drop in Recall and F1-score, highlighting its critical role in capturing dynamic temporal dependencies in EEG signals. In contrast, the removal of the dynamic spatial graph mainly affects Precision, indicating its effectiveness in suppressing spatial noise and reducing false positives.

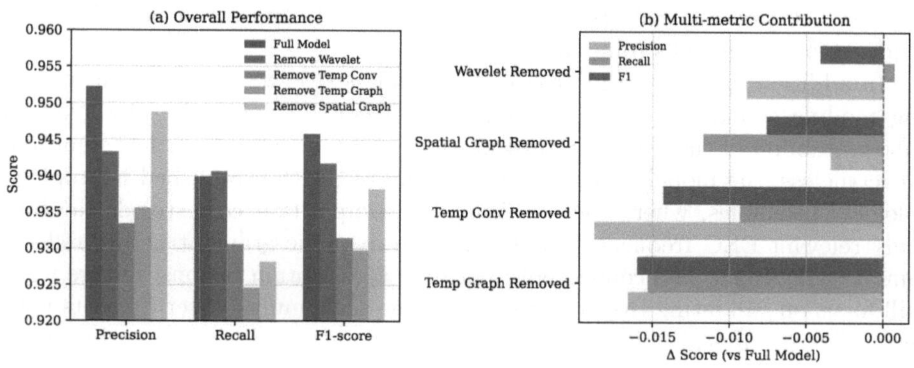

Fig. 4. Ablation study on the TUEV dataset. (a) Overall performance comparison of different model variants. (b) Multi-metric performance degradation (ΔPrecision, ΔRecall, and ΔF1) after removing each component.

These observations confirm that different components contribute in a complementary manner to the overall performance.

4 Discussion

Accurate detection of epileptiform events remains challenging due to the complex spatio-temporal dependencies and multi-scale oscillatory nature of EEG signals. To address these issues, the proposed framework of epileptiform event detection effectively addresses several key challenges in epileptic EEG modeling by jointly integrating frequency-aware decomposition, temporal dynamics modeling, and dynamic spatio-temporal graph reasoning within a unified architecture. Specifically, the multi-band decomposition combined with branch-aware wavelet enhancement improves the representation of transient and low-amplitude oscillatory activities, such as epileptic spikes and ripple events, which are often difficult to identify in raw EEG signals. Meanwhile, the multi-scale temporal convolution module enables the capture of heterogeneous temporal patterns ranging from short-duration spike discharges to longer ripple activities, thereby enhancing temporal sensitivity across multiple time scales. More importantly, the dynamic spatio-temporal graph reasoning module provides sample-adaptive modeling of inter-channel dependencies and propagation patterns, allowing the model to move beyond static connectivity assumptions and better reflect the evolving nature of epileptic brain activity. As a result, the proposed method achieves more discriminative and clinically meaningful representations, leading to consistent improvements over existing approaches.

Despite the promising performance of the proposed method, several limitations remain. The model is evaluated on a limited number of datasets, including a single-center private dataset and one public benchmark dataset, which may not fully capture the diversity of EEG recordings across different clinical settings, patient populations, and acquisition conditions. Nevertheless, it is worth noting that the two adopted datasets differ in recording environments and data distributions, which partially reflects cross-domain variability and provides preliminary evidence of the model's robustness.

In addition, although the proposed dynamic spatio-temporal graph reasoning module can model evolving inter-channel dependencies, the physiological interpretability of the learned representations still requires further investigation. Nevertheless, the model design is partially aligned with established neurophysiological principles, where the multi-band decomposition corresponds to clinically relevant EEG frequency bands, and the dynamic graph structure reflects time-varying functional connectivity patterns across brain regions. Future work will focus on validating the framework on large-scale multi-center datasets with more diverse clinical conditions, as well as enhancing clinical interpretability by explicitly linking the learned dynamic graph patterns to neurophysiological mechanisms underlying epileptic spike and ripple generation.

5 Conclusion

In this work, we proposed a multi-type epileptiform event detection framework based on dynamic spatio-temporal graph learning. The DSTGNet integrates clinically motivated multi-band decomposition, branch-aware waveform enhancement, multi-scale temporal convolution encoding, and dynamic spatio-temporal graph reasoning into a single architecture, enabling comprehensive characterization of spectral information, temporal dynamics, and inter-channel dependencies. By constructing sample-adaptive spatio-temporal graphs, the model effectively captures the evolving propagation patterns of epileptic discharges, particularly transient spike and ripple activities that are difficult to detect using conventional approaches. Comprehensive evaluations on both a private clinical dataset and the public TUEV benchmark demonstrate that the proposed approach consistently outperforms state-of-the-art methods, indicating strong robustness and generalization across different recording conditions and event distributions. These findings suggest that dynamic graph-based modeling provides an effective and scalable solution for capturing clinically relevant EEG dynamics.

Acknowledgements. This work was partly supported by the National Natural Science Foundation of China (62303442), Guangdong Basic, Applied Basic Research Foundation (2025A1515010423, 2024A1515140078) and National Key Clinical Discipline Construction Project,[2023]26-1, and the Shenzhen Basic Research Fund (KQTD2020 0820113106007, ZDSYS20220422103800001). We would also like to thank the funding support by the Key Laboratory of Quantitative Synthetic Biology, Chinese Academy of Sciences under grant no. CKL075.

Disclosure of Interests. The authors declare that they have no competing interests.

References

1. Assali, I., Blaiech, A.G., Abdallah, A.B., Khalifa, K.B., Carrere, M., Bedoui, M.H.: CNN-based classification of epileptic states for seizure prediction using combined temporal and spectral features. Biomed. Signal Process. Control **82**, 104519 (2023)
2. Fabbri, L., et al.: Spikes on ripples are better interictal biomarkers of epilepsy than spikes or ripples. Brain commun. **7**(1), fcaf056 (2025)
3. Fan, X., et al.: EEG-based seizure detection and type classification with structured state space modeling and graph neural networks. In: 2025 IEEE International Conference on Bioinformatics and Biomedicine (BIBM), pp. 4613–4619. IEEE
4. He, C., Yu, X., Zhang, Y., Li, Y., Jiang, N.: Wearable EEG devices in the detection of mild cognitive impairment: a systematic review. NPJ Digital Med. (2026)
5. Ismail Fawaz, H., et al.: InceptionTime: finding alexnet for time series classification. Data Min. Knowl. Disc. **34**(6), 1936–1962 (2020)
6. Li, Z., Wan, Y., Xu, L., Su, W., Wang, P., Zhou, X.: A diffusion model and few-shot learning framework for EEG abnormality classification and cerebral infarction assessment. IEEE Trans. Comput. Social Syst. (2026)
7. Lu, X., Wen, A., Sun, L., Wang, H., Guo, Y., Ren, Y.: An epileptic seizure prediction method based on CBAM-3D CNN-LSTM model. IEEE J. Trans. Eng. Health Med. **11**, 417–423 (2023)

8. Mohammed, A.H., Cabrerizo, M., Pinzon, A., Yaylali, I., Jayakar, P., Adjouadi, M.: Graph neural networks in EEG spike detection. Artif. Intell. Med. **145**, 102663 (2023)
9. Mu, J., et al.: Automatic detection for epileptic seizure using graph-regularized nonnegative matrix factorization and Bayesian linear discriminate analysis. Biocybernetics Biomed. Eng. **41**(4), 1258–1271 (2021)
10. Obeid, I., Picone, J.: The temple university hospital EEG data corpus. Front. Neurosci. **10**, 196 (2016)
11. Remakanthakurup Sindhu, K., Staba, R., Lopour, B.A.: Trends in the use of automated algorithms for the detection of high-frequency oscillations associated with human epilepsy. Epilepsia **61**(8), 1553–1569 (2020)
12. Shi, W., et al.: Spike ripples localize the epileptogenic zone best: an international intracranial study. Brain **147**(7), 2496–2506 (2024)
13. Tautan, A.M., Andrei, A.G., Smeralda, C.L., Vatti, G., Rossi, S., Ionescu, B.: Unsupervised learning from EEG data for epilepsy: a systematic literature review. Artif. Intell. Med. **162**, 103095 (2025)
14. Uyanik, H., Sengur, A., Salvi, M., Tan, R., Tan, J.H., Acharya, U.R.: Automated detection of neurological and mental health disorders using EEG signals and artificial intelligence: a systematic review. Wiley Interdisciplinary Rev.: Data Min. Knowl. Discovery **15**(1), e70002 (2025)
15. Wang, J., et al.: CBRamod: a criss-cross brain foundation model for EEG decoding. arXiv preprint arXiv:2412.07236 (2024)
16. Xiao, M., Zhu, Z., Xie, K., Jiang, B.: MEEG and at-DGNN: improving EEG emotion recognition with music introducing and graph-based learning. In: 2024 IEEE International Conference on Bioinformatics and Biomedicine (BIBM), pp. 4201–4208. IEEE
17. Xu, G., Guo, W., Wang, Y.: Subject-independent EEG emotion recognition with hybrid spatio-temporal GRU-conv architecture. Med. Biolog. Eng. Comput. **61**(1), 61–73 (2023)
18. Xu, Z., Wang, T., Cao, J., Bao, Z., Jiang, T., Gao, F.: BECT spike detection based on novel EEG sequence features and LSTM algorithms. IEEE Trans. Neural Syst. Rehabil. Eng. **29**, 1734–1743 (2021)
19. Ye, H., Chen, C., Weiss, S.A., Wang, S.: Pathological and physiological high-frequency oscillations on electroencephalography in patients with epilepsy. Neurosci. Bull. **40**(5), 609–620 (2024)
20. Zhang, Y., Liu, X., Tang, P., Zhang, Z.: SGMDD: subgraph neural network-based model for analyzing. In: Bioinformatics Research and Applications: 19th International Symposium, ISBRA 2023, Wrocław, Poland, October 9–12, 2023, Proceedings, vol. 14248, p. 364. Springer Nature (2023)
21. Zhao, H., et al.: St-DecNet: a spatio-temporal graph learning framework for epileptic seizure prediction via dynamic effective connectivity in EEGs. IEEE Trans. Instrum. Measur. (2025)
22. Zhou, S., Hu, D., Gao, F., Jiang, T., Cao, J.: Automatic EEG-based spike ripples detection with multi-band frequency analysis. In: 2024 IEEE International Symposium on Circuits and Systems (ISCAS), pp. 1–5. IEEE
23. Zhu, R., Pan, W.X., Liu, J.X., Shang, J.L.: Epileptic seizure prediction via multidimensional transformer and recurrent neural network fusion. J. Trans. Med. **22**(1), 895 (2024)

HCPDA: Identification of PiRNA-Disease Association Based on Heterogeneous Graph Attention and Contrastive Learning

Yajun Liu[1](✉), Yongliang Wang[1], Fan Zhang[1], Yulian Ding[2], and Xuefeng Cui[3]

[1] Shaanxi Key Laboratory for Network Computing and Security Technology, School of Computer Science and Engineering, Xi'an University of Technology, Xi'an, China
liuyajun@xaut.edu.cn

[2] Center for High Performance Computing, Shenzhen Institutes of Advanced Technology, Chinese Academy of Sciences, Shenzhen, China

[3] School of Computer Science and Technology, Shandong University, Qingdao, China

Abstract. Identifying potential piRNA-disease associations (PDAs) is instrumental in advancing our understanding of pathogenesis and catalyzing the development of precision medicine. However, highly sparse PDA data with experimentally validated remains a hurdle for computational models, and intricate dependencies are not fully captured yet by existing PDA methods. In this study, we propose a novel method based on heterogeneous graph attention and contrastive learning for predicting potential PDAs. First, a heterogeneous information network is constructed by integrating the known PDA network, piRNA sequence similarity, and disease semantic similarity. Based on this network, a fusion design of hierarchical attention mechanism and transformer encoder was proposed. In addition, a dual-view contrastive learning strategy is applied at the piRNA-disease pair level. Experiments on benchmark datasets demonstrate that the proposed method significantly outperforms state-of-the-art approaches in PDA prediction. Further case studies confirm its effectiveness in identifying biologically meaningful associations.

Keywords: piRNA · disease · association identification · heterogeneous graph · contrastive learning

1 Overview

Piwi-interacting RNAs (piRNAs) are a subclass of small non-coding RNAs that bind to PIWI proteins. They are closely involved in the onset and progression of various diseases and show great potential as diagnostic biomarkers and therapeutic targets. Existing studies have demonstrated that piRNAs regulate tumor immune evasion [1], pyroptosis [2], and cancer signaling pathways [3], and thus play valuable roles in tumor molecular subtyping and prognostic evaluation. Since biological experiments are costly and time-consuming, it is urgent to develop efficient computational models for systematic prediction of piRNA-disease associations (PDAs).

X. Cui et al. (Eds.): ISBRA 2026, LNBI 16690, pp. 273–286, 2027.
https://doi.org/10.1007/978-981-92-3716-6_22

Although biological experimental data have accumulated rapidly in recent years, currently available PDA data remain very limited. Wei et al. [4] constructed the first PDA benchmark dataset based on the piRDisease [5] database, in which known PDAs account for only 5.48% of all potential association pairs. Another dataset from MNDR v3.0 [6] shows a similar sparsity of merely 5.26%. Such severe data sparsity highlights the importance of exploiting computational methods to mine novel PDAs.

Existing PDA prediction methods can be divided into three categories: traditional machine learning, deep learning, and graph neural networks. Early traditional machine learning methods such as iPiDi-PUL [4] can only achieve preliminary prediction performance, failing to capture complex nonlinear relationships and relying heavily on abundant labeled samples. Subsequently, deep learning methods including piRDA [7], MSRDA [8], and MRDPDA [9] have been proposed, which automatically learn feature representations from multi-source data based on convolutional neural networks, stacked autoencoders, and DeepFM.

In recent years, researchers have modeled biological systems as heterogeneous networks and formulated PDA prediction as a heterogeneous graph link prediction task, making graph neural networks (GNNs) the mainstream research paradigm. GNN-based methods such as iPiDA-GCN [10], iPiDA-SWGCN [11], and PUTransGCN [12] can effectively capture topological characteristics and adopt positive-unlabeled learning to alleviate the shortage of negative samples. Nevertheless, these methods still have room for improvement in cross-dataset generalization ability.

In the past five years, contrastive learning has exhibited outstanding performance in label-sparse scenarios by virtue of its self-supervised representation learning advantages, and has been widely applied to various bioinformatics tasks, such as histological image reconstruction [13] and multi-omics data fusion [14]. In the field of PDA prediction, methods including CLPiDA [15] and iPiDA_CL [16] have initially introduced contrastive learning and validated its effectiveness. However, existing approaches still struggle to adapt to sparse heterogeneous networks and cannot sufficiently model the representations of PDAs.

Building on the above research, this paper proposes a novel PDA prediction method that integrates heterogeneous graph representation learning and contrastive learning. Firstly, a heterogeneous information network is constructed by integrating known PDA associations, piRNA sequence similarity, and disease semantic similarity. Secondly, the heterogeneous graph attention mechanism is adopted to mine structural correlations, and a Transformer-based semantic fusion module is employed to model complex dependencies among meta-paths. Finally, a dual-view contrastive learning strategy is introduced to mitigate the adverse effects of data sparsity, enabling full exploration of heterogeneous biological information to identify potential PDAs.

The main contributions can be summarized in three points:

(1) A fusion architecture of hierarchical attention and Transformer encoder is constructed to realize multi-level modeling of complex heterogeneous graph structures.
(2) A joint optimization strategy combining class balance loss, contrastive loss and regularization is designed, which improves the model's ability to identify minority samples and enhances its robustness on imbalanced datasets.

(3) An end-to-end dual-view contrastive learning model was applied to PDA problem, and generalization ability of methods was verified on three datasets.

2 Materials and Methods

As shown in Fig. 1, the framework of HCPDA consists of 3 main parts. They are construction of heterogeneous graph, heterogeneous graph attention network and contrastive learning module.

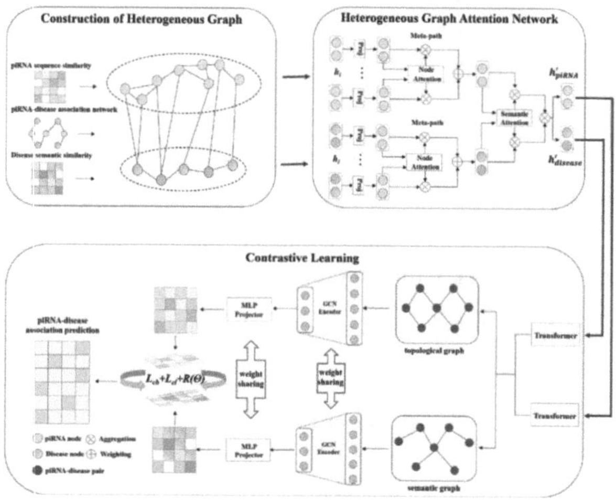

Fig. 1. Framework of HCPDA.

2.1 Benchmark Datasets

To construct reliable benchmark datasets for PDA prediction, we manual review piRNA disease association data from three databases, piRDisease, MNDR v3.0 and RNADisease v4.0 [17].

The first PDA benchmark data is downloaded by Wei et al., which is derived from piRDisease. It has 5,002 experimentally validated PDAs involving 4,350 piRNAs and 21 diseases. Moreover, refer to Hou et al., 11,981 PDAs with experimental validation from MNDR v3.0 were considered. These associations involve 10,149 distinct piRNAs and 19 disease types.

RNADisease v4.0 is a repository for RNA-disease association. Compared with earlier versions, RNADisease v4.0 significantly expands the scale of collected data and currently covers 18 RNA types, 117 species and 4,090 diseases. After removing duplicated records and inconsistent annotations, 9,502 high-confidence PDAs are retained from this database, which involve 8,205 piRNAs and 15 diseases. The confirmed associations constitute only 7.72% of all theoretically possible pairs.

To further support sequence-based similarity analysis, the corresponding piRNA sequences were retrieved from piRBase v3.0 [18] by aligning piRNA identifiers across databases. Two standardized datasets are used for subsequent heterogeneous network construction. The statistical distribution of samples across different disease categories is shown in Fig. 2. A portion of the associations is unique to specific database.

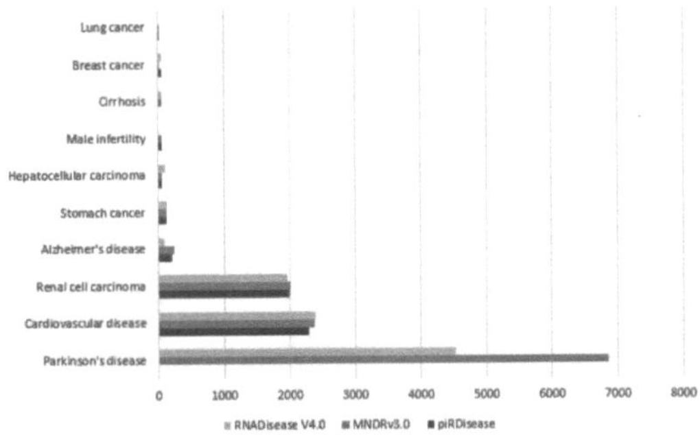

Fig. 2. Statistical distribution of samples across different disease categories.

2.2 Heterogeneous Network Construction

Based on a standardized PDA dataset, we construct a heterogeneous information network, and it is formally defined as:

$$G = (V, E) \tag{1}$$

$$V = V_p \bigcup V_d \tag{2}$$

$$E = E_{pd} \bigcup E_{pp} \bigcup E_{dd} \tag{3}$$

where V denotes the set of nodes representing piRNA node V_p and disease node V_d. E represents the set of edges describing three association types. They are PDA edges E_{pd}, piRNA similarity edges E_{pp} and Disease semantic similarity edges E_{dd}.

Each piRNA node V_p corresponds to a unique piRNA sequence obtained from the curated dataset. Disease nodes V_d represent distinct MeSH disease entities. PDA edges E_{pd} represent PDAs from the dataset.

piRNA similarity edges E_{pp} is constructed by similarity calculation by Smith-Waterman algorithm, which is widely used for local sequence comparison. piRNA similarity $W_{ps}(p_i, p_j)$ between the i-th piRNA node and j-th piRNA node is computed as:

$$W_{ps}(p_i, p_j) = \frac{SW(p_i, p_j)}{\sqrt{SW(p_i, p_i) \times SW(p_j, p_j)}} \tag{4}$$

where the $SW(p_i, p_j)$ is the sequence alignment value between the i-th piRNA and j-th piRNA.

Disease similarity edges E_{dd} is created by disease semantic similarity W_{ds}. Using MeSH information, a directed acyclic graph (DAG) is constructed based on hierarchical descriptors, in which nodes represent disease terms and the edges represent the relationship between the current node and its ancestors. $DAG_{d_i} = \left(d, T_{d_i}, E_{d_i}\right)$ describes the structure of the i-th disease d_i, where T_{d_i} indicates the set of nodes including all ancestors of d_i as well as itself, and E_{d_i} stands for the corresponding direct edges. $D_{d_i}(t)$ denotes the semantic contribution of disease term t ∈ $\mathrm{T_{d_i}}$ related to the i-th disease and can be written as follows:

$$D_{d_i}(t) = \begin{cases} 1 & if\ t = ith\ disease \\ max\left\{\Delta \times D_{d_i}\left(t^{'}\right)\middle|t^{'} \in children\ of\ t\right\} & otherwise \end{cases} \tag{5}$$

where Δ is the semantic contribution factor ($\Delta = 0.5$).

Disease similarity $\mathrm{W}_{ds}\left(d_i, d_j\right)$ between the i-th disease node and j-th disease node can be defined as follows:

$$\mathrm{W}_{ds}\left(d_i, d_j\right) = \frac{\sum_{t \in T_{d_i} \cap T_{d_j}} \left(D_{d_i}(t) + D_{d_j}(t)\right)}{\sum_{t \in T_{d_i}} D_{d_i}(t) + \sum_{t \in T_{d_j}} D_{d_j}(t)} \tag{6}$$

2.3 Hierarchical Attention Representation Learning

Due to the heterogeneous structure and multi-relation characteristics of the piRNA-disease network, simple aggregation strategies may fail to capture the complex semantic relationships. To address this issue, we design a hierarchical attention representation learning framework. It integrates node-level attention and semantic-level attention to get node representation by dynamically aggregating from heterogeneous neighbors.

Meta-Path Construction. Meta-paths are widely used to describe high-order semantic relationships in heterogeneous networks. In our study, meta-paths are defined as an alternating sequence of node types and relation types:

$$P = N_1, R_1, N_2, R_2, \ldots, N_L \tag{7}$$

where N_i represents the node type and R_i represents the relation type connecting two adjacent nodes. L denotes the length of the meta-path. To balance semantic interpretability and computational efficiency, only three-hop neighbors are considered here.

Node-Level Attention. For each meta-path, dynamic meta-path instances were generated based on node feature similarity. The similarity between two nodes was calculated using cosine similarity.

Starting from a target node, its neighbors were traversed according to the meta-path definition. At each step, the top 3 neighbors with the highest similarity scores were selected as candidate nodes for the next hop. If fewer than three neighbors existed, all valid neighbors were retained. By iteratively applying this strategy along the meta-path, a set of dynamic meta-path instances was generated. Within each meta-path instance, a node-level attention mechanism was applied to measure the importance of neighboring nodes. Specifically, the attention coefficient between the target node i and its neighbor j under meta-path P is computed as:

$$e_{ij}^P = LeakyReLU\left(a_P^T\left[W_P h_i || W_P h_j\right]\right) \tag{8}$$

where W_P and a_P are learnable attention parameters associated with meta-path P. The negative slope of LeakyReLU is fixed to 0.01 throughout the experiments. The normalized attention weight is obtained through the Softmax function:

$$a_{ij}^{P} = \frac{exp\left(e_{ij}^{p}\right)}{\sum_{j' \in N_i^P} exp\left(e_{ij'}^{p}\right)} \tag{9}$$

Finally, the node representation h_i^P under meta-path P is computed as:

$$h_i^P = \sum\nolimits_{j \in N_i^P} a_{ij}^P h_j \tag{10}$$

Semantic-Level Attention. Different meta-paths capture distinct semantic contexts, and contribute unequally to the final node representation. Therefore, a semantic-level attention mechanism was employed to learn the relative importance of each meta-path.

The node representations generated under different meta-paths is first projected into a shared semantic space by MLP and is computed as:

$$z_i^P = ReLU\left(Wh_i^P + b\right) \tag{11}$$

where W and b are learnable attention parameters of MLP.

The importance score of each meta-path was then calculated, and normalization using the Softmax function. The node representation $h_{i'}$ of node i is obtained as:

$$h_{i'} = \sum_{P} \beta_P z_i^P \tag{12}$$

where β_P represents the normalized attention weight of meta-path P.

Meta-Path-Aware Transformer Encoder. Although hierarchical attention captures local semantic information, it may still be insufficient to model long-range dependencies and complex cross-path interactions in heterogeneous networks. To further capture complex dependencies between piRNA and disease nodes and compensate for the lack of structural information, we employ a transformer-based encoder based on meta-path. Taking the piRNA representation $h_{p'}$ and disease representation $h_{d'}$ as inputs, this module incorporates Laplacian positional embedding (PE) of meta-path-based subgraphs to output node embeddings with strong discriminative capability and structural relevance.

Inspired by Zhang et.al.[19] and Dwivedi et al.[20], we use a transformer encode combines multi-head self-attention and Laplacian PE to encode nodes. First, homogeneous subgraphs are constructed for each meta-path in the heterogeneous graph, and global structural coordinates are assigned to each node via Laplacian eigen decomposition. Subsequently, node semantic representations are fused with Laplacian PE from multiple meta-paths, and then fed into the multi-head self-attention mechanism. This enables the model to capture complex interactive relationships across diverse meta-paths. The final node embeddings h_i^* of node i contains both local semantic information and global structural context, providing a powerful representation for PDA prediction.

2.4 Dual-View Contrastive Learning

To further enhance the robustness of pair representations and alleviate the sparsity of known PDAs, we introduce a dual-view contrastive learning strategy operating on piRNA-disease pairs. Inspired by Li et.al.[21], the proposed model constructs two complementary views of the pairwise network and jointly optimizes their representations through supervised contrastive objectives.

piRNA-Disease Pair Representation. Given a piRNA node p and a disease node d, we construct a piRNA-disease pair node (PDP) by concatenating their learned embeddings:

$$h_i^{pdp} = [h_p^* || h_d^*] \tag{13}$$

where h_p and h_d denote the final embeddings of piRNA and disease respectively. The PDP representation h_i^{pdp} captures both molecular and disease-level characteristics and serves as the fundamental unit for association prediction.

Construction of Dual-View Pair Graphs. To capture complementary topology and semantic relationships among piRNA-disease pairs, two graphs are constructed.

The topology graph is constructed on the structural connectivity. Two PDP nodes are connected if they share a common biological component, which is the same piRNA or same disease. The topology graph is defined as:

$$G^t = (A^t, X^{pdp}) \tag{14}$$

where A^t denotes the adjacency matrix, X^{pdp} is the PDP representation matrix.

The semantic graph reflects similarity relationships between PDP nodes. We compute the cosine similarity between PDP representations and connect the two most similar nodes in the embedding space. These connections are encoded into a predicted association matrix A^s, which is calculated as following:

$$A_{ij}^s = \begin{cases} 1 if\, pdp_j \in top2(pdp_i) \\ 0 otherwise \end{cases} \tag{15}$$

The semantic graph is defined as:

$$G^s = (A^s, X^{pdp}) \tag{16}$$

This semantic view captures potential associations inferred from feature similarity, thereby complementing the structural information encoded in the topological graph.

Dual-View Contrastive Learning. Two independent graph encoders are employed to learn representations from the topology and semantic graphs. Topology-view representation z_i^t and semantic-view representation z_i^s are computed as follows:

$$z_i^t = GCN_t(G^t) \tag{17}$$

$$z_i^s = GCN_s(G^s) \tag{18}$$

To encourage consistency between the two views, we adopt a supervised cross-view contrastive objective. For a PDP node i, its positive sample set P_i includes the corresponding node in the other view and neighboring nodes that share the same class label. The supervised contrastive loss for the topology view is defined as:

$$L_{cl}^{t} = -\sum_{i=1}^{N_{pdp}} \log \frac{\sum_{j \in P_i} \exp(\mathrm{sim}(z_t^i, z_s^j)/\tau)}{\sum_{k \in \{P_i \cup N_i\}} \exp(\mathrm{sim}(z_t^i, z_s^k)/\tau)} \tag{19}$$

where N_i is the negative sample set, τ is the temperature parameter. Similarly, the semantic-view contrastive loss can be defined as L_{cl}^{s}. It symmetrically contrasts semantic-view embeddings against topology-view embeddings.

The final training objective combines classification loss, dual-view contrastive losses, and regularization. The overall optimization objective is calculated as:

$$L = L_{ce} + \lambda L_{cl}^{t} + (1 - \lambda) L_{cl}^{s} + \gamma R(\Theta) \tag{20}$$

where L_{ce} is the binary cross-entropy loss for PDA prediction, λ balances the two contrastive objectives and γ controls the regularization term.

Through this dual-view contrastive learning mechanism, the model encourages consistent representations across complementary views. This design effectively improves the discriminative ability of piRNA-disease pair representations and alleviates the impact of sparse association data.

3 Results and Discussion

3.1 Experiment and Hyper-Parameters Selection

To verify the performance and generalization ability of model, five-fold cross-validation on three datasets is used. All experiments were conducted on a workstation equipped with an NVIDIA GeForce RTX 4070 GPU, an i7-10700KF CPU, 32GB RAM, and 4.5TB of storage. To evaluate the model, we employed the area under the receiver operating characteristic curve (AUC) and under the precision-recall curve (AUPR) as key metrics. The model achieved larger areas under both curves, indicating optimal predictive performance.

The predictive accuracy is influenced by multiple hyperparameters. They were determined empirically or optimized through performance evaluations in this study. Take embedding dimension for example, we sequentially evaluated embedding dimensions from 64 to 1024 by fixed all other parameters. As shown in Fig. 3, performance consistently increases and peaks at a dimension of 256.

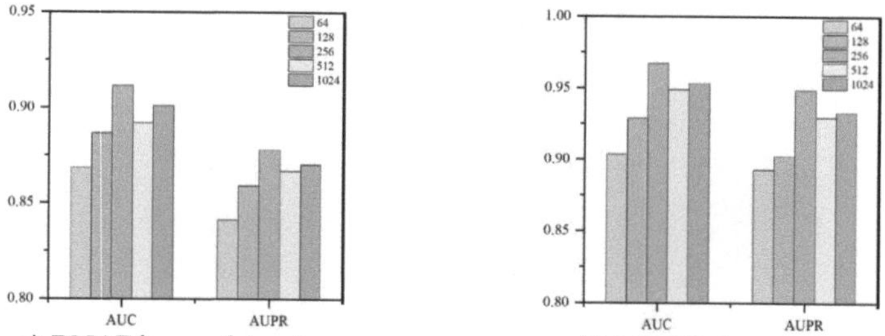

a) RNADisease dataset b) MNDR dataset

Fig. 3. Impact of feature dimension on performance.

Take contrastive objective weight λ for another example, we evaluated a candidate set ranging from 0 to 1 with an increment of 0.2. Figure 4 depicts the resulting performance fluctuations in terms of AUC and AUPR across the RNADisease v4.0 and MNDR v3.0 datasets. It suggests that the model predictive capacity steadily enhances with increasing λ. The model attained its best perform when λ reached 0.8.

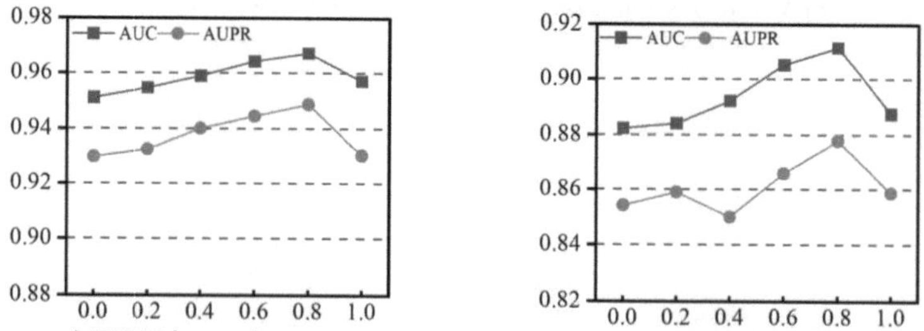

a) RNADisease dataset b) MNDR dataset

Fig. 4. Impact of hyperparameter λ on performance.

3.2 Performance Evaluation

To comprehensively evaluate the model performance, we performed five-fold cross-validation on all benchmark datasets described in Sect. 2.1, with results illustrated in Fig. 5. HCPDA achieves average AUC of 0.9963 and AUPR of 0.9961 on piRDisease, 0.9123 AUC and 0.8607 AUPR on RNADisease, and 0.9746 AUC and 0.9611 AUPR on MNDR.

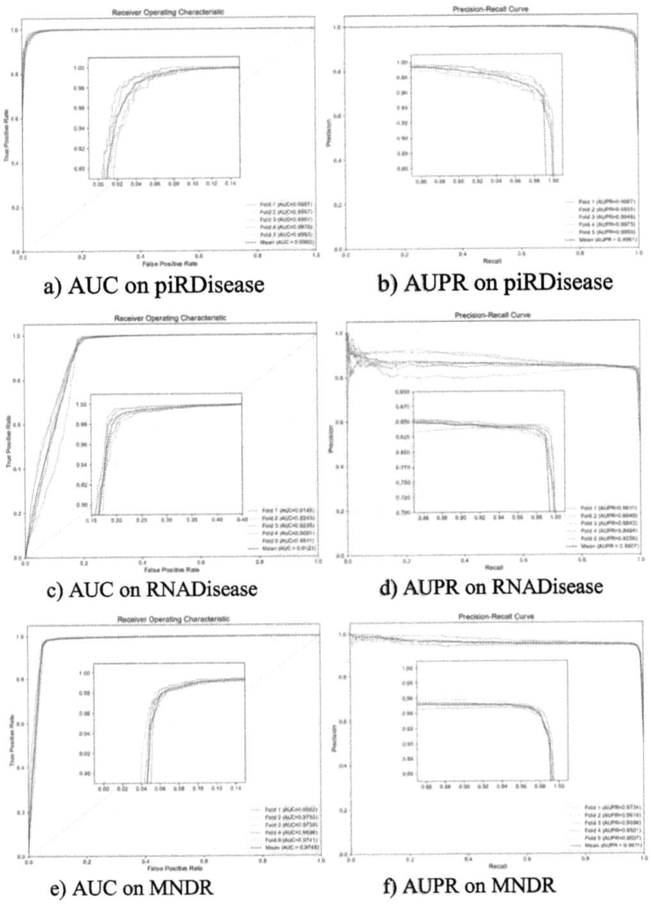

Fig. 5. AUC and AUPR Curves of HCPDA in three datasets.

The results show that HCPDA maintains stable and high prediction performance across all datasets with small variance in both AUC and AUPR, verifying its robustness under diverse data scenarios. Notably, HCPDA achieves balanced AUC and AUPR even under severe association sparsity.

3.3 Comparison with Other Methods

To further evaluate the effectiveness of HCPDA, a comparative experiment against five representative methods across two benchmark datasets was done. The representative methods were categorized into three groups. iPiDi-PUL is a traditional machine learning method, and piRDA is a PDA tool based on non-graph structured deep learning. iPiDA-GCN, iPiDA-SWGCN and PUTransGCN are all GNN-based approaches.

On both RNADisease and MNDR datasets, GNN-based methods outperformed traditional and non-graph deep learning approaches, demonstrating GNN's advantage in modeling heterogeneous graph interactions. However, their limited AUPR on RNADisease indicates room for improved generalization. All methods showed high AUC but relatively low AUPR, reflecting challenges from severe class imbalance in PDA prediction.

On RNADisease, HCPDA achieved an AUPR of 0.8607, a 26.25% improvement over the second-best PUTransGCN. While its AUC was slightly lower than PUTransGCN and iPiDA-SWGCN, it remained high, showing balanced performance. On MNDR, HCPDA achieved the best AUC and AUPR among all methods.

3.4 Ablation Experiment

To investigate the contribution of individual components in the HCPDA, a ablation study on two datasets. The complete model is denoted as HCPDA, and four variants were evaluated to verify the effectiveness of each key module:

- HCPDA w/o contrastive learning (CL): the model retains the hierarchical attention and graph convolution structure but removes the contrastive learning module.
- HCPDA w/o semantic view: only the topology-based graph is used with intra-view contrastive learning.
- HCPDA w/o topological view: only the semantic graph is used with intra-view contrastive learning.
- HCPDA w/o Transformer: the model retains contrastive learning but removes the meta-path-aware transformer encoder module.

As shown in Table 2, models using only one view perform significantly worse than the full HCPDA, indicating complementary topological adjacency information and semantic attribute features—multi-view fusion enables multi-dimensional PDA capture. Additionally, the contrastive learning module consistently improves performance on both datasets: by pulling same-class first-order neighbors closer and pushing different-class features apart in the embedding space, it enhances discriminative capability and alleviates PDA data sparsity. Finally, the meta-path-aware transformer is critical for capturing long-range dependencies and global context. Overall, ablation results show that all modules work together to ensure robust and accurate PDA prediction.

Table 1. The performance comparison among six methods.

Method	RNADisease		MNDR	
	AUC	AUPR	AUC	AUPR
iPiDi-PUL	0.7842	0.1652	0.6653	0.6550
piRDA	0.9122	0.3385	0.4939	0.5116
iPiDA-GCN	0.8852	0.4275	0.7149	0.7036
iPiDA-SWGCN	0.9203	0.4615	0.8178	0.8151
PUTransGCN	**0.9301**	0.5982	0.8532	0.6436
HCPDA	0.9123	**0.8607**	**0.9746**	**0.9611**

Table 2. The performance comparison in ablation experiment.

Method	RNADisease		MNDR		
	AUC	AUPR		AUC	AUPR
HCPDA w/o CL	0.8923	0.8541		0.9358	0.9094
HCPDA w/o semantic view	0.8690	0.8231		0.9045	0.8823
HCPDA w/o topological view	0.8755	0.8384		0.8916	0.8736
HCPDA w/o transformer	0.8903	0.8415		0.9248	0.9054
HCPDA	**0.9123**	**0.8607**		**0.9746**	**0.9611**

3.5 Case Study

To assess the generalization of our model, we conducted case study on two representative diseases and followed the steps in iPiDA-sHN [22]. These diseases are Alzheimer's disease (AD) and Renal Cell Carcinoma (RCC). The top five piRNA associated with these two diseases are listed in Table 3 Eight identified piRNAs associated with two diseases have been validated by literature mining. These prediction results demonstrate the effectiveness of the proposed method. The unverified piRNA-disease relationships can be considered as candidates and investigated in the further research.

Table 3. The top 5 predicted piRNAs for AD and RCC.

piRNA	AD	Evidence	piRNA	RCC	Evidence
piR-hsa-1207	Yes	PMID:28127595	piR-hsa-30978	Yes	PMID:26071182
piR-hsa-2106	No		piR-hsa-10732	Yes	PMID:26071182
piR-hsa-28131	Yes	PMID:28127595	piR-hsa-5773	Yes	PMID:25998508
piR-hsa-2107	Yes	PMID:28127595	piR-hsa-3161	Yes	PMID:26071182
piR-hsa-10009	No		piR-hsa-9186	Yes	PMID:26071182

4 Conclusion

In this study, we proposed a novel PDA prediction model based on hierarchical attention representation learning and contrastive learning. Comprehensive experimental results on three benchmark datasets demonstrate that HCPDA achieves high predictive accuracy and robustness. We believe that it will facility functional exploration of piRNAs in disease diagnosis and therapeutic development.

We will further enhance the model performance and applicability in the future. For instance, the new development of graph contrastive learning algorithms can be exploited to construct multi-modal frameworks. It will incorporate diverse sources of biological information such as piRNA expression profiles, target gene interactions.

Code availability: https://github.com/Liangzaiz/HCPDA.

5 Funding Acknowledgments.

This work was supported by the National Key R&D Program of China (Grant No. 2025YFA0923200), the National Natural Science Foundation of China (Grant Nos. 62533015, 62072283 and 62402489) and the Guangdong Basic and Applied Basic Research Foundations (Grant No. 2023A1515110570).

Disclosure of Interests. The authors have no competing interests to declare that are relevant to the content of this article.

References

1. Zhong, Y., et al.: "Small extracellular vesicle piR-hsa-30937 derived from pancreatic neuroendocrine neoplasms upregulates CD276 in macrophages to promote immune evasion **12**(7), 840–853 (2024)
2. Liao, Z., et al.: pir-HSA-216911 inhibit pyroptosis in hepatocellular carcinoma by suppressing TLR4 initiated GSDMD activation. **11**(1), 11 (2025)
3. Shaker, F.H., Sanad, E.F., Elghazaly, H., Hsia, S.M., Hamdy, N.M.: piR-823 tale as emerging cancer-hallmark molecular marker in different cancer types: a step-toward ncRNA-precision **398**(1), 47–68 (2025)
4. Wei, H., Xu, Y., Liu, B.: iPiDi-PUL: identifying Piwi-interacting RNA-disease associations based on positive unlabeled learning. (in English). Brief. Bioinf. **22**(3), 10 (2021). Art. no. bbaa058
5. Muhammad, A., Waheed, R., Khan, N. A., Jiang, H., D, X. J.: Song, "piRDisease v1. 0: a manually curated database for piRNA associated diseases **2019**, baz052 (2019)
6. Ning, L., et al.: MNDR v3. 0: mammal ncRNA–disease repository with increased coverage and annotation, **49**(D1), D160-D164 (2021)
7. Ali, S. D., Tayara, H., Chong, K. T. J. C., Journal, S. B.: Identification of piRNA disease associations using deep learning, **20**, 1208–1217 (2022)
8. Zheng, K., Liang, Y., Liu, Y.-Y., Yasir, M., Wang, P.: A decision support system based on multi-sources information to predict piRNA-disease associations using stacked autoencoder. Soft Comput. **26**(20), 11007–11016 (2022). 10 Jan 2022
9. Liu, Y., et al.:"MRDPDA: a multi-Laplacian regularized deepFM model for predicting piRNA-disease associations, **28**(17), e70046 (2024)
10. Hou, J., Wei, H., Liu, B. J. P. C. B.: iPiDA-GCN: identification of piRNA-disease associations based on graph convolutional network **18**(10), e1010671 (2022)
11. Hou, J., Wei, H., Liu, B. J. P. C. B.: iPiDA-SWGCN: identification of piRNA-disease associations based on supplementarily weighted graph convolutional network **19**(6), e1011242 (2023)
12. Chen, Q., Zhang, L., Liu, Y., Qin, Z., Zhao, T. J. B. i. B. : PUTransGCN: identification of piRNA-disease associations based on attention encoding graph convolutional network and positive unlabelled learning **25**(3), bbae144 (2024)
13. Li, L., et al.: FineST: contrastive learning integrates histology and spatial transcriptomics for nuclei-resolved ligand-receptor analysis (2026)
14. Guo, Y., Mallona, I., Robinson, M. D., Li, L. J. P. C. B.: BiCLUM: bilateral contrastive learning for unpaired single-cell multi-omics integration **22**(2), e1013932 (2026)

15. Hu, X., Zhang, Y., Zhang, J., Deng, L.: CLPiDA: a contrastive learning approach for predicting potential PiRNA-disease associations. In: 2023 IEEE International Conference on Bioinformatics and Biomedicine (BIBM), Istanbul, Turkiye, pp. 159–164 (2023)
16. Hu, X., et al.: Unraveling disease-associated PIWI-interacting RNAs with a contrastive learning methods. J. Chem. Inf. Model. **65**(9), 4687–4697 (2025)
17. Chen, J., et al.: RNADisease v4. 0: an updated resource of RNA-associated diseases, providing RNA-disease analysis, enrichment and prediction **51**(D1), D1397-D1404 (2023)
18. Wang, J., et al.: piRBase: integrating piRNA annotation in all aspects **50**(D1), D265-D272 (2022)
19. Zhang, R., Wang, Z., Wang, X., Meng, Z., Cui, W. J. B. I. B : MHTAN-DTI: metapath-based hierarchical transformer and attention network for drug–target interaction prediction **24**(2), bbad079 (2023)
20. Dwivedi, V. P., Bresson, X.: A generalization of transformer networks to graphs. arXiv preprint arXiv:2012.09699, 2020
21. Li, Y., Qiao, G., Gao, X., Wang, G. J. B.:"Supervised graph co-contrastive learning for drug–target interaction prediction. **38**(10), 2847–2854 (2022)
22. Wei, H., Ding, Y. X., Liu, B.: iPiDA-sHN: identification of Piwi-interacting RNA-disease associations by selecting high quality negative samples. (in English). Comput. Biol. Chem. Article **88**(107361), 7 (2020)

Predicting CRISPR-Cas13d On-Target Efficacy via Deep Learning

Zhendong Liu[1](✉), Jiamin Jiang[1], Hao Zhang[2], Rui Jiang[3], Jingran Niu[1], Xiao Liu[1], Tengbo Zhao[1], and Hebing Chen[4]

[1] Shanghai Polytechnic University, Shanghai, China
zdliu@sspu.edu.cn
[2] Jilin University, Changchun, China
[3] Tsinghua University, Beijing, China
[4] Academy of Military Medical Science, Beijing, China

Abstract. The CRISPR-Cas13d system holds immense potential for RNA-targeted therapy. However, accurate prediction of on-target efficacy remains a bottleneck due to the complex interplay between sequence composition and dynamic RNA structures. Here, we introduce LJDeep, a novel deep learning framework that integrates a pre-trained RNA foundation model with a Dual-Stream Transformer architecture. Unlike traditional methods, LJDeep explicitly models the biological interaction between guide and target RNAs through a learnable physics-aware embedding and a Bidirectional Cross Attention module. This architecture effectively captures both local thermodynamic constraints and long-range structural contexts, extending beyond simple sequence matching to explicitly model the global spatial dependencies of RNA interactions. Benchmarking on a systematic dataset demonstrates that LJDeep achieves state-of-the-art performance with an AUROC of 0.91 and a PCC of 0.79. LJDeep exhibits superior generalization across Perfect Match and mismatch scenarios, providing a robust computational engine for high-precision RNA editing.

Keywords: CRISPR-Cas13d · deep learning · on-target effects · feature fusion · large language models

1 Introduction

The characterization of CRISPR-Cas systems has fundamentally transformed biomedical and biotechnological fields [1]. Originally discovered in microbial immune systems, these systems have been ingeniously applied to precise genome editing [2–4]. Following the transcription and processing of pre-crRNA into mature guide RNAs (gRNAs) [5,6], Cas enzymes are directed to cleave homologous genomic regions. While Type II CRISPR-Cas9 utilizes a dual-RNA complex for DNA targeting [7–10], and Type V Cas12 expands utility via a single crRNA [11,12], Cas13 represents a breakthrough expansion by specifically cleaving RNA. This enables reversible transcriptomic interference without altering

X. Cui et al. (Eds.): ISBRA 2026, LNBI 16690, pp. 287–299, 2027.
https://doi.org/10.1007/978-981-92-3716-6_23

DNA and introduces novel diagnostic applications due to its collateral cutting activity [13].

Optimizing gRNA design is critical to maximize on-target efficacy and minimize unintended impacts. However, unlike DNA-targeting tools, Cas13 gRNA design must account for the complex and variable structural features of RNA [14]. Early Cas13 research heavily relied on large-scale screening and empirical rules [14,15], often hindered by an incomplete understanding of key design parameters [13,16,17]. To address these limitations, computational models leveraging genomic sequence characteristics have successfully enhanced Cas9 platforms [18–20]. Yet, the unique RNA-targeting properties of Cas13d present distinct challenges that these initial models cannot address [21].

Initial machine learning approaches for Cas13d, such as CASowary, incorporated manually engineered features like k-mer frequency and target complementarity [22]. Concurrently, Wessels et al. conducted massive parallel screens, identifying positions 15–21 as a critical seed region [14]. This led to the creation of the first empirical scoring models, providing a foundation for subsequent deep learning developments [23]. However, these models struggle to automatically capture complex sequence-structure hierarchical relationships. Breakthroughs emerged with DeepCas13, which integrated hybridization free energy and secondary structure using a CNN-RNN framework [24]. Building on this, the TIGER model utilized CNNs to effectively capture mismatch position dependence and dosage control [25].

Despite these advancements, current technologies overlook crucial structural contexts. The design efficiency of gRNA is highly dependent on local target RNA structures; for instance, stem-loop structures at the target's 5′ proximal flanking sequence (PFS) can reduce Cas13d binding affinity by over 50%, while the exact spatial positioning of mismatches dictates distinct mechanisms of inhibition [26]. These intricate structure-function relationships make it exceptionally challenging to accurately predict editing efficacy, highlighting three major bottlenecks: data scarcity, insufficient quantification of RNA structures, and the inadequate integration of multi-source sequence-structure information [27].

To address these limitations, we developed LJDeep, a dual-stream Transformer model featuring learnable physics-aware embeddings to capture spatial constraints and non-linear mismatch tolerances in Cas13d binding. LJDeep utilizes a bidirectional cross-attention layer with segment position bias to quantify spatial gradients in target interactions, while leveraging RNA foundation models to bypass manual feature engineering. Validated on 118,267 gRNAs, LJDeep significantly outperforms traditional and state-of-the-art computational tools by effectively integrating structural insights.

2 Results

As illustrated in Fig. 1, the workflow for LJDeep integrates RNA-FM semantic features and physics-aware sequence representations to predict targeting efficacy. We evaluated LJDeep against traditional machine learning and recent deep learning models using a systematic dataset of 118,267 CRISPR-Cas13d pairs [25]. All metrics were computed via 16-fold cross-validation with gene-level isolation to ensure robustness. Section 2.1 details these baseline comparisons, while Sect. 2.2 assesses our specific architectural innovations.

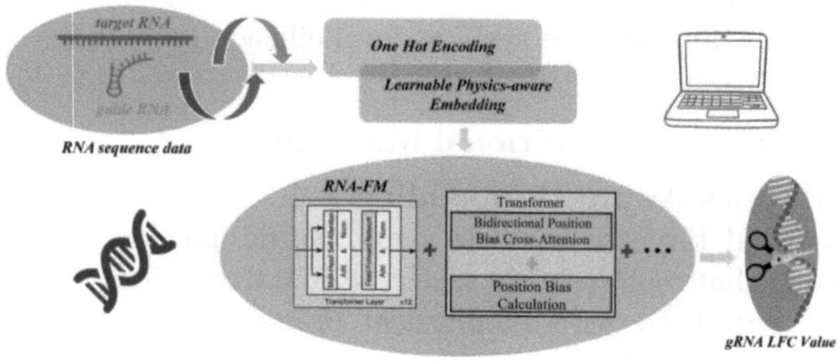

Fig. 1. Overview of the workflow for LJDeep.

2.1 Comparison with Other Models

To comprehensively assess LJDeep's predictive capabilities, we compared it against traditional machine learning methods and recent deep learning models. For this baseline performance comparison, we focused specifically on Perfect Match (PM) guide RNAs. This ensures a standardized evaluation of on-target efficacy, isolating the predictions from the confounding effects of mismatch tolerance which are analyzed separately. To ensure absolute fairness, all baseline deep learning models were retrained from scratch using identical 16-fold cross-validation splits.

LJDeep outperforms all baselines in classification in Table 1. While traditional methods fail to capture hierarchical relationships and recent models like DeepCas13 or TIGER neglect systematic mismatches or global structural contexts, LJDeep effectively simulates dynamic RNA interactions via bidirectional cross-attention and base-pairing encoding. Its superior robustness under class imbalance further underscores the necessity of automated sequence-structure feature learning over heuristic or local-only approaches.

Table 1. Performance comparison of LJDeep with other models.

Metric	LJDeep	TIGER	DeepCas13	Adaboost	Random Forest	XGBoost
AUROC (Mean ± SD)	0.91 ± 0.01	0.89 ± 0.01	0.84 ± 0.03	0.78 ± 0.03	0.82 ± 0.03	0.83 ± 0.03
AUPRC (Mean ± SD)	0.84 ± 0.02	0.82 ± 0.03	0.78 ± 0.04	0.72 ± 0.03	0.76 ± 0.02	0.77 ± 0.03
PCC (Mean ± SD)	0.79 ± 0.01	0.77 ± 0.02	0.62 ± 0.05	0.54 ± 0.04	0.58 ± 0.03	0.53 ± 0.04
SCC (Mean ± SD)	0.65 ± 0.01	0.65 ± 0.02	0.60 ± 0.02	0.48 ± 0.05	0.56 ± 0.04	0.52 ± 0.04

The most groundbreaking aspect, however, is observed in the regression task. While traditional methods fail to capture non-linear variations in binding energy and TIGER lacks global structural integration, LJDeep leverages its dual-stream Transformer and RNA-FM fusion to model complex biophysical dynamics. This approach enables LJDeep to transcend the shallow sequence-activity associations of baseline methods and provide systems-level efficacy predictions.

2.2 Comparison with Traditional Methods

Learnable Physics-Aware Embedding. To capture interactive effects between gRNA and target RNA base pairs, we designed a learnable physics-aware embedding that replaces rigid scalars with a dynamically fine-tuned interaction matrix. Initialized with biophysical priors, this matrix automatically learns non-linear mismatch penalties and context-dependent thermodynamics during training. Table 2 shows that this biophysical-aware approach outperforms traditional one-hot encoding, confirming that the base-pairing encoder effectively captures deep interaction features between gRNA and target RNA sequences.

Table 2. Comparison of learnable physics-aware embedding and traditional encoding.

Encoding Method	AUROC	AUPRC	PCC	SCC
Traditional Encoding	0.81 ± 0.03	0.78 ± 0.04	0.62 ± 0.05	0.60 ± 0.04
Learnable Physics-aware Embedding	0.91 ± 0.01	0.84 ± 0.02	0.79 ± 0.01	0.65 ± 0.01

RNA Large Language Model. RNA-FM, a 12-layer bidirectional Transformer, extracts functional signatures by aggregating contextual dependencies and pairwise interactions [29]. LJDeep integrates these high-dimensional embeddings via linear projection and cross-attention to capture implicit RNA secondary structures. Table 3 reveals a consistent performance decline across all metrics when RNA-FM features are removed in our ablation study. This confirms that RNA-FM effectively enhances the model's comprehension of complex structure-function relationships, providing more accurate predictions than traditional manual feature engineering.

Table 3. Comparison of RNA-FM feature integration and non-integration.

Integration Strategy	AUROC	AUPRC	PCC	SCC
Not integrated with RNA-FM	0.85 ± 0.03	0.80 ± 0.04	0.64 ± 0.03	0.71 ± 0.04
Integrated with RNA-FM	0.91 ± 0.01	0.84 ± 0.02	0.79 ± 0.01	0.65 ± 0.01

Dual-Stream Transformer Architecture. We propose a dual-stream Transformer to independently encode gRNA and target RNA sequences, integrating an RNA-FM cross-attention layer to extract structural contexts. A subsequent bidirectional cross-attention mechanism, utilizing segment and multi-dimensional position biases, models global sequence interactions. Table 4 demonstrates that this bidirectional architecture significantly outperforms unidirectional and standard multi-head self-attention, confirming its critical role in enhancing predictive accuracy and biological interpretability.

Table 4. Comparison of Attention Mechanisms.

Attention Mechanism	AUROC	AUPRC	PCC	SCC
Multi-Head Self-Attention	0.85 ± 0.04	0.79 ± 0.05	0.55 ± 0.06	0.58 ± 0.05
Cross Attention	0.85 ± 0.03	0.80 ± 0.04	0.61 ± 0.05	0.62 ± 0.04
Bidirectional Cross Attention	0.91 ± 0.01	0.84 ± 0.02	0.79 ± 0.01	0.65 ± 0.01

3 Discussion

Our results suggest that traditional sequence-based models overlook targeting efficiency as a complex emergent property of dynamic gRNA-target interactions. By moving beyond simple complementarity matching, our base pairing weight matrix reveals that mismatches and matches at specific positions contribute nonlinearly to binding energy [32]. Contextual embeddings from RNA-FM further demonstrate that remote interactions and structural folding (e.g., pseudoknots) significantly influence target accessibility. This validates our dual-stream Transformer architecture, which simulates cooperative conformational adjustments and reveals that target RNA actively regulates binding site formation via structural feedback [33]. For practical gRNA design, we recommend aggressively filtering out highly fragmented mismatch patterns (RDM/RTM) and prioritizing stable localized duplexes (PM or SM) to mitigate prediction risks.

However, limitations remain. Current technology excludes RNA-protein interaction effects, such as HEPN domain binding of Cas13d, which can alter target folding energy by up to -5 kcal/mol [33,34]. Future iterations could integrate 3D Graph Neural Networks or protein structural embeddings to explicitly quantify these Cas13d-induced microenvironments. Additionally, reliance on static sequence data may cause specificity loss for low-frequency mutations. Future iterations will integrate these biophysical insights and extend model inputs beyond the 23-nt protospacer to refine predictions in PFS-sensitive flanking contexts.

4 Materials and Methods

4.1 Data Preparation

To ensure a robust foundation, this study utilizes the systematic CRISPR-Cas13d dataset published by Wessels et al. in Nature Biotechnology [25]. This benchmark includes 118,267 gRNAs (10,000 perfectly matched and 108,600 engineered variants) covering 16 essential human genes. Raw data were obtained from NCBI GEO (accession GSE232228). Following the original literature, we employed median ratio normalization and the ComBat algorithm for activity correction and batch effect handling. All sequences were uniformly converted to 23-nt RNA sequences, with insufficient positions padded with 'N'. To decouple targeting efficacy from biological gene essentiality, we performed gene-wise Z-score normalization on the LFC values as shown in Eq. (1).

$$y'_{i,g} = \frac{y_{i,g} - \mu_g}{\sigma_g} \tag{1}$$

where μ_g and σ_g denote the mean and standard deviation of LFCs for gene g. This step ensures the model captures intrinsic targeting efficacy rather than gene-specific survival effects. However, this gene-wise normalization cannot entirely eliminate confounding micro-effects from dynamic intracellular RNA expression abundance or transient structural accessibility.

In addition to standard one-hot encoding, we preprocessed sequences using an innovative learnable physics-aware embedding scheme. This involves a dynamic 4×4 learnable interaction matrix, W_{pair}, which maps base combinations between gRNA and target RNA to capture biological interaction characteristics. To accelerate convergence, W_{pair} is initialized with biophysical priors reflecting the fundamental thermodynamic stability and hydrogen bond availability of RNA structural interactions [35]. Specifically, baseline weights are assigned hierarchically: C-G pairs (three hydrogen bonds, highest stability) at 3.0, A-U pairs (two hydrogen bonds) at 2.0, G-U wobble pairs (thermodynamically weaker than Watson-Crick pairs) at 1.0, and unmapped mismatches at 1.0. During training, gradient descent fine-tunes these weights as a learnable parameter tensor, enabling the network to discover context-specific spatial and thermodynamic variations that static assignments cannot encapsulate (Figs. 2 and 3).

4.2 Description of the Model

Traditional serial architectures often struggle with insufficient feature representation and inadequate positional modeling when handling high-dimensional sequence data. To address these limitations, we propose LJDeep, which balances local details with global dependencies through two core modules: dual-path feature extraction and fusion, and bidirectional position bias cross-attention. The overall processing flow of the model is illustrated in Fig. 4.

In the dual-path feature extraction module, a symmetric Transformer encoder independently processes each sequence. A learnable linear transformation first maps the 4D base encoding to dense vectors. To incorporate spatial context, we apply standard sine-cosine positional encoding, where *pos* denotes the sequence index, i the dimension index, and d the model dimension. Finally, a four-layer multi-head self-attention mechanism and feedforward network compute internal dependencies to generate position-aware representations.

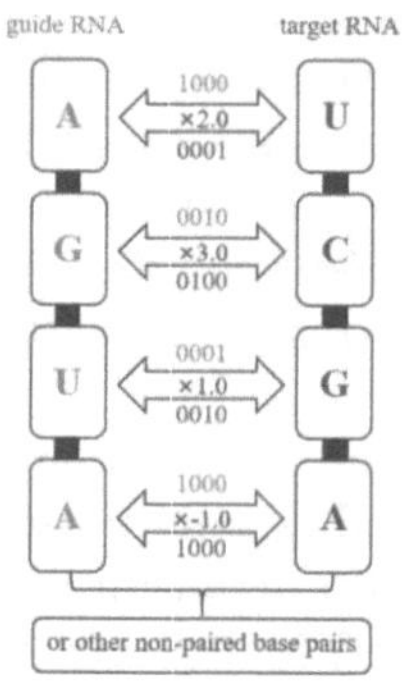

Fig. 2. Base Pairing encoding rules, illustrating initialized biophysical priors that differentiate Watson-Crick matches, wobble pairs, and mismatches.

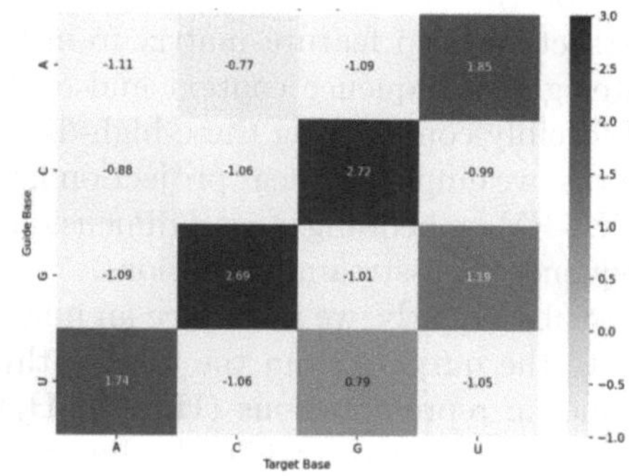

Fig. 3. Heatmap of interaction matrix weights. Darker shades (red) indicate higher penalty weights, while lighter shades (yellow) represent lower weights. (Color figure online)

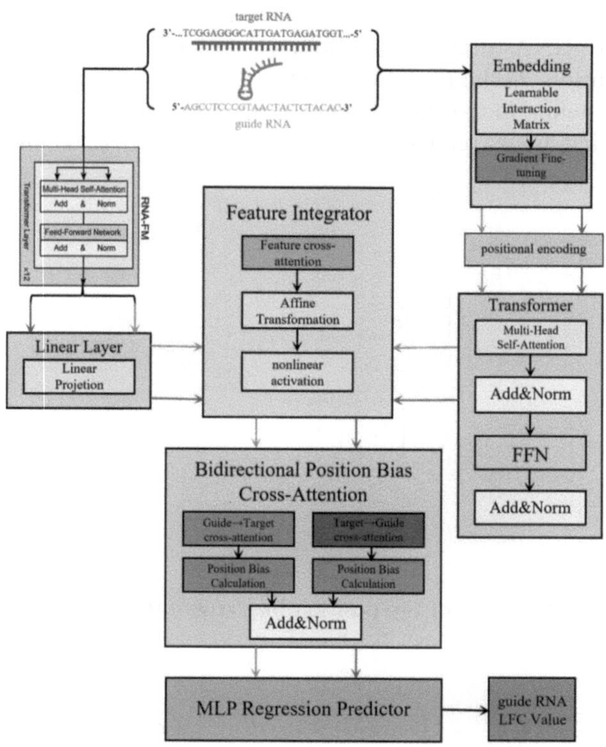

Fig. 4. Overall architectural model of the LJDeep structure. Abbreviations: FFN, Feed-Forward Network; LFC, Log2 Fold Change; RNA-FM, RNA Foundation Model.

For the RNA-FM feature pathway, the pre-trained RNA-FM model first extracts a deep feature matrix from the input RNA sequence, which encapsulates global sequence context and evolutionary constraint information. Instead of forcibly compressing these high-dimensional features using convolutional networks, we employ a linear projection layer to smoothly map the 1200-dimensional RNA-FM embeddings to a d-dimensional space ($d = 128$), aligning with the main sequence dual-stream dimensions.

Subsequently, we introduce an innovative cross-modal attention layer to integrate the outputs from the dual pathways. In this module, the position-aware sequence representations ($\mathbf{H}_g$ and $\mathbf{H}_t$) generated by the Transformer encoder serve as the Query, while the linearly projected RNA-FM features ($\mathbf{P}_g^{fm}$ and $\mathbf{P}_t^{fm}$) serve as the Key and Value. The mathematical operation is defined in Eq. (2).

$$\mathbf{F}_i = \text{LayerNorm}\left(\mathbf{H}_i + \text{softmax}\left(\frac{(\mathbf{H}_i\mathbf{W}_Q)(\mathbf{P}_i^{fm}\mathbf{W}_K)^T}{\sqrt{d_k}}\right)\mathbf{P}_i^{fm}\mathbf{W}_V\right) \tag{2}$$

where $i \in \{g, t\}$ and $\mathbf{W}_{Q,K,V}$ are learnable weights. The resulting $\mathbf{F}_i$ unifies global semantics with local structural constraints into a high-dimensional vector. To simulate gRNA-target recognition, we implement a bidirectional position-bias cross-attention mechanism. Addressing the limits of traditional positional encoding in modeling long-range dependencies, we utilize a piecewise bias function in Fig. 5 that maps relative distance d to a specific bias value, as defined in Eq. (3).

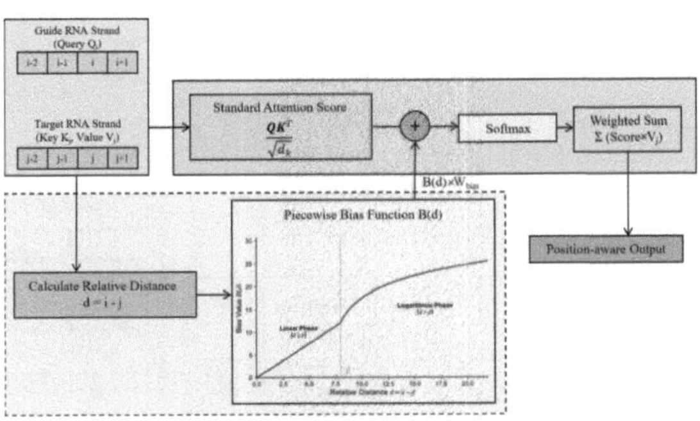

Fig. 5. Architecture of the position-bias cross-attention mechanism.

$$B(d) = \begin{cases} \text{sign}(d) \times \alpha \cdot d & \text{if } d \leq \beta \\ \gamma \cdot \log(1 + d - \beta) & \text{if } d > \beta \end{cases} \tag{3}$$

where α, β and γ are learnable parameters that control the linear slope, piecewise boundaries, and logarithmic curvature, respectively. Furthermore, we use the target encoding as the query and the gRNA encoding as the key-value to update the target representation. This design is mathematically implemented as shown in Eq. (4).

$$\mathbf{CrossAttn}_{g\to t} = \text{softmax}\left(\frac{\mathbf{Q}_g\mathbf{K}_t^T}{\sqrt{d_k}}\right)\mathbf{V}_t \tag{4}$$

Finally, the bidirectional cross-attention results are residual connected with the original input and then processed through LayerNorm. The proposed fusion computation is shown in Eq. (5).

$$\mathbf{Score} = \frac{\mathbf{QK}^T}{\sqrt{d_k}} + \mathbf{W}_{bias} \times B(\Delta pos) \tag{5}$$

where $\mathbf{W}_{bias}$ is the learnable bias weight matrix, and $B(\Delta pos)$ represents the relative positional bias output from the aforementioned piecewise function. The pseudo-code of LJDeep is shown in Algorithm 1.

Algorithm 1. LJDeep Workflow

Input: Guide RNA sequence S_g, Target RNA sequence S_t, Pre-trained RNA-FM, dimension d.
Output: Predicted on-target efficiency score Y_{pred}.

Initialize feature matrices $\mathbf{E}_g^{seq}, \mathbf{E}_t^{seq} \leftarrow \emptyset$
for $i \leftarrow 1$ to 23 **do**
    $\mathbf{E}_g^{seq}[i] \leftarrow \text{LearnablePhysicsEmbedding}(s_{gi}, s_{ti}, \mathbf{W}_{pair})$
    $\mathbf{E}_t^{seq}[i] \leftarrow \text{LearnablePhysicsEmbedding}(s_{ti}, s_{gi}, \mathbf{W}_{pair})$
end for
$\mathbf{E}_g^{fm}, \mathbf{E}_t^{fm} \leftarrow \text{RNA\_FM}(S_g, S_t)$
$\mathbf{P}_g^{fm}, \mathbf{P}_t^{fm} \leftarrow \text{LinearProjection}(\mathbf{E}_g^{fm}, \mathbf{E}_t^{fm})$
Calculate positional encoding **PE** for all positions
$\mathbf{H}_g \leftarrow \text{TransformerEncoder}(\mathbf{E}_g^{seq} + \mathbf{PE})$
$\mathbf{H}_t \leftarrow \text{TransformerEncoder}(\mathbf{E}_t^{seq} + \mathbf{PE})$
$\mathbf{F}_g \leftarrow \text{LayerNorm}(\mathbf{H}_g + \text{CrossAttention}(\mathbf{Q} = \mathbf{H}_g, \mathbf{K} = \mathbf{P}_g^{fm}, \mathbf{V} = \mathbf{P}_g^{fm}))$
$\mathbf{F}_t \leftarrow \text{LayerNorm}(\mathbf{H}_t + \text{CrossAttention}(\mathbf{Q} = \mathbf{H}_t, \mathbf{K} = \mathbf{P}_t^{fm}, \mathbf{V} = \mathbf{P}_t^{fm}))$
for $i, j \leftarrow 1$ to 23 **do**
    Calculate piecewise bias $B(|i-j|)$ based on α, β, γ
    $\mathbf{A}_{g\to t}[i][j] \leftarrow \text{Softmax}\left(\frac{\mathbf{Q}_g[i]\mathbf{K}_t[j]^T}{\sqrt{d_k}} + \mathbf{W}_{bias} \cdot B\right)$
    $\mathbf{A}_{t\to g}[j][i] \leftarrow \text{Softmax}\left(\frac{\mathbf{Q}_t[i]\mathbf{K}_g[j]^T}{\sqrt{d_k}} + \mathbf{W}_{bias} \cdot B\right)$
end for
$\mathbf{O}_{g\to t} \leftarrow \text{LayerNorm}(\mathbf{A}_{g\to t} \cdot \mathbf{V}_t + \mathbf{F}_g)$
$\mathbf{O}_{t\to g} \leftarrow \text{LayerNorm}(\mathbf{A}_{t\to g} \cdot \mathbf{V}_g + \mathbf{F}_t)$
$\mathbf{O} \leftarrow \text{Concatenate}(\mathbf{O}_{g\to t}, \mathbf{O}_{t\to g})$
$Y_{pred} \leftarrow \text{RegressionOutputLayer}(\mathbf{O})$
return Y_{pred}

4.3 Training of the Model

All models were trained and executed on the Windows platforms, employing Scikit-learn resources under Python version 3.10.18. We utilized a batch size of 256 gRNAs during model training. The training process utilized an initial learning rate of 1e-4, which was reduced by 20% every five epochs. For the RNA-FM large language model, we extracted the hidden states from the penultimate layer (the 11th layer) as the feature representation. This layer was chosen because it retains rich semantic information while avoiding potential bias towards specific pre-training tasks. Consequently, each nucleotide position is transformed into a 1,200-dimensional feature vector.

The loss function was defined as a combination of the mean squared error (MSE) for regression tasks and a symmetry constraint loss term to enforce consistency between the bidirectional attention matrices. Specifically, let $\mathbf{A}_{g\to t}$ and $\mathbf{A}_{t\to g}$ denote the attention matrices from the Guide → Target and Target → Guide flows, respectively. The symmetry constraint loss is computed as the Frobenius norm of their difference, which is shown in Eq. (6). The total loss is shown in Eq. (7).

$$\mathcal{L}_{sym} = ||\mathbf{A}_{g\to t} - \mathbf{A}_{t\to g}||_F^2 \tag{6}$$

$$\mathcal{L}_{total} = \mathcal{L}_{mse} + \lambda\mathcal{L}_{sym} \tag{7}$$

where λ is a hyperparameter set to 0.1 based on a grid search ($\lambda \in \{0.01, 0.05, 0.1, 0.5, 1.0\}$). We acknowledge that in vivo structural interactions are inherently asymmetric due to the steric constraints imposed by the Cas13d HEPN domain and independent target mRNA folding. Therefore, $\mathcal{L}_{sym}$ is not intended to mirror this biological reality, but rather serves as a crucial mathematical regularization. Without this soft constraint, bidirectional attention optimization is highly susceptible to directional mode collapse, where the network overfits to a single attention flow. Thus, $\mathcal{L}_{sym}$ acts purely as a computational stabilizer to ensure balanced feature representations. To suppress overfitting, L2 regularization and dropout (rate 0.3) were applied, with parameters determined strictly within the training folds via grid search to prevent data leakage.

4.4 Performance Evaluation

We evaluate classification performance using AUROC and AUPRC, derived from the True Positive Rate ($TPR = TP/(TP + FN)$), False Positive Rate ($FPR = FP/(FP + TN)$), and Precision ($TP/(TP + FP)$). For the regression task, we utilize the Pearson Correlation Coefficient (PCC) and Spearman Correlation Coefficient (SCC) to assess the linear and monotonic relationships between predicted scores (y') and experimental LFC values (y), as defined in Eq. (8):

$$PCC = \frac{\sum_{i=1}^{n}(y_i - \bar{y})(y'_i - \bar{y}')}{\sqrt{\sum_{i=1}^{n}(y_i - \bar{y})^2 \sum_{i=1}^{n}(y'_i - \bar{y}')^2}}, \quad SCC = 1 - \frac{6\sum_{i=1}^{n} d_i^2}{n(n^2 - 1)} \tag{8}$$

where d_i represents the difference between the ranks of paired observations and n is the sample size. These metrics provide a comprehensive framework for validating LJDeep's predictive accuracy across both discrete efficacy categories and continuous activity gradients.

5 Conclusions

LJDeep demonstrates high versatility and robustness, with experimental results validating the necessity and effectiveness of its architectural innovations in the Cas13d system. By combining a base-pair specificity weight matrix with advanced attention mechanisms, the model adeptly captures complex sequence nuances and interactive dependencies essential for precise genome editing. LJDeep's integration of deep learning with large-scale genomic data allows it to surpass traditional models in accuracy and efficiency, providing a scalable analytical framework for optimizing RNA-targeted therapeutics. Future research will focus on refining the LJDeep architecture and extending this methodology to other CRISPR systems, such as Cas9 and Cas12, to broaden its impact across diverse clinical and basic research applications. Adapting to DNA-targeting Cas9 and Cas12 will inherently require substituting the current RNA-FM with a pre-trained DNA foundation model.

References

1. Barber, H.M., Pater, A.A., Gagnon, K.T., Damha, M.J., O'Reilly, D.: Chemical engineering of CRISPR–Cas systems for therapeutic application. Nat. Rev. Drug Discovery **24**(3), 209–230 (2025)
2. Horvath, P., Barrangou, R.: CRISPR/Cas, the immune system of bacteria and archaea. Science **327**(5962), 167–170 (2010)
3. Rodriguez-Carrascal, D.: CRISPR-Cas Systems: origins and their impact on functional genomic. Science **8**, 100069 (2025)
4. Li, Y., et al.: Comparison of CRISPR/Cas and Argonaute for nucleic acid tests. Trends Biotechnol. **41**(5), 595–599 (2023)
5. Jinek, M., Chylinski, K., Fonfara, I., Hauer, M., Doudna, J.A., Charpentier, E.: A programmable dual-RNA–guided DNA endonuclease in adaptive bacterial immunity. Science **337**(6096), 816–821 (2012)
6. Deltcheva, E., et al.: CRISPR RNA maturation by trans-encoded small RNA and host factor RNase III. Nature **471**(7340), 602–607 (2011)
7. Li, T., et al.: CRISPR/Cas9 therapeutics: progress and prospects. Signal Transduct. Target. Ther. **8**(1), 36 (2023)
8. Zhuo, C., et al.: Spatiotemporal control of CRISPR/Cas9 gene editing. Signal Transduct. Target. Ther. **6**(1), 238 (2021)
9. Doudna, J.A., Charpentier, E.: The new frontier of genome engineering with CRISPR-Cas9. Science **346**(6213), 1258096 (2014)
10. Chen, J.: Trans-nuclease activity of Cas9 activated by DNA or RNA target binding. Nat. Biotechnol. , 1–11 (2024)
11. Jedrzejczyk, D.J., et al.: CRISPR-Cas12a nucleases function with structurally engineered crRNAs: SynThetic trAcrRNA. Sci. Rep. **12**(1), 12193 (2022)

12. Chen, J., et al.: DNA target binding-induced pre-crRNA processing in type II and V CRISPR-Cas systems. Nucleic Acids Res. **53**(3), gkae1241 (2025)
13. Abudayyeh, O.O., et al.: RNA targeting with CRISPR–Cas13. Nature **550**(7675), 280–284 (2017)
14. Wessels, H.H., et al.: Massively parallel Cas13 screens reveal principles for guide RNA design. Nat. Biotechnol. **38**(6), 722–727 (2020)
15. Zhang, F.: Development of CRISPR-Cas systems for genome editing and beyond. Q. Rev. Biophys. **52**, e6 (2019)
16. Molina Vargas, A.M., et al.: New design strategies for ultra-specific CRISPR-Cas13a-based RNA detection with single-nucleotide mismatch sensitivity. Nucleic Acids Res. **52**(2), 921–939 (2024)
17. Yang, H., Patel, D.J.: Structures, mechanisms and applications of RNA-centric CRISPR–Cas13. Nat. Chem. Biol. **20**(6), 673–688 (2024)
18. Stemmer, M., et al.: CCTop: an intuitive, flexible and reliable CRISPR/Cas9 target prediction tool. PLoS ONE **10**(4), e0124633 (2015)
19. Hsu, P.D., et al.: DNA targeting specificity of RNA-guided Cas9 nucleases. Nat. Biotechnol. **31**(9), 827–832 (2013)
20. Muhammad Rafid, A.H., et al.: CRISPRpred (SEQ): a sequence-based method for sgRNA on target activity prediction using traditional machine learning. BMC Bioinformatics **21**(1), 223 (2020)
21. Gupta, R., et al.: Cas13d: a new molecular scissor for transcriptome engineering. Front. Cell Develop. Biol. **10**, 866800 (2022)
22. Krohannon, A., et al.: CASowary: CRISPR-Cas13 guide RNA predictor for transcript depletion. BMC Genomics **23**(1), 172 (2022)
23. Stirn, A.A.: Representation Learning for CRISPR-Cas13d Efficacy and Single-Cell RNA Sequencing Data, Columbia University (2025)
24. Cheng, X., et al.: Modeling CRISPR-Cas13d on-target and off-target effects using machine learning approaches. Nat. Commun. **14**(1), 752 (2023)
25. Wessels, H.H., et al.: Prediction of on-target and off-target activity of CRISPR–Cas13d guide RNAs using deep learning. Nat. Biotechnol. **42**(4), 628–637 (2024)
26. Kuo, H.C., et al.: Massively parallel profiling of RNA-targeting CRISPR-Cas13d. Nat. Commun. **15**(1), 498 (2024)
27. Wu, K.E., Zou, J.Y., Chang, H.: Machine learning modeling of RNA structures: methods, challenges and future perspectives. Briefings Bioinfo. **24**(4), bbad210 (2023)
28. Zhang, J., Lang, M., Zhou, Y., Zhang, Y.: Predicting RNA structures and functions by artificial intelligence. Trends Genet. **40**(1), 94–107 (2024)
29. Chen, J.: Interpretable RNA foundation model from unannotated data for highly accurate RNA structure and function predictions (2022). arXiv:2204.00300 arXiv preprint
30. Bouchal, T., et al.: Importance of base-pair opening for mismatch recognition. Nucleic Acids Res. **48**(20), 11322–11334 (2020)
31. Ferrer, J., Dimitrova, N.: Transcription regulation by long non-coding RNAs: mechanisms and disease relevance. Nat. Rev. Mol. Cell Biol. **25**(5), 396–415 (2024)
32. Marklund, E., Ke, Y., Greenleaf, W.J.: High-throughput biochemistry in RNA sequence space: predicting structure and function. Nat. Rev. Genet. **24**(6), 401–414 (2023)
33. Ishikawa, J., et al.: Structural insights into RNA-guided RNA editing by the Cas13b–ADAR2 complex. Nature Struct. Molecul. Biol., 1–12 (2025)

34. Boorla, V.S., Maranas, C.D.: CatPred: a comprehensive framework for deep learning in vitro enzyme kinetic parameters. Nat. Commun. **16**(1), 2072 (2025)
35. Riley, A.T., et al.: Generative and predictive neural networks for the design of functional RNA molecules. Nat. Commun. **16**(1), 4155 (2025)

GradGE: Gradient-Augmented Genetic Evolution for Prediction of SARS-CoV-2 Variants with Enhanced Immune Escape Potentials

Ziming Liu, Jialu Zuo, Yikai Li, and Jian Zu(✉)

School of Mathematics and Statistics, Xi'an Jiaotong University, Xi'an 710049, Shaanxi, China
{lzmlzm,zjljy,liyikai}@stu.xjtu.edu.cn, jianzu@xjtu.edu.cn

Abstract. Predicting the evolutionary trends of SARS-CoV-2 antigens is of significant importance for pandemic prevention and vaccine design, with the receptor-binding domain (RBD) of the spike protein serving as a critical antigenic site. Due to the high complexity of mutation patterns within RBD sequences, quantifying the functional changes induced by potential mutations and predicting future high-risk variant sequences are critical but challenging. To address this, we propose **GradGE** (**Grad**ient-Augmented **G**enetic **E**volution), a genetic algorithm designed to predict future unseen high-risk variants with enhanced immune escape potentials. GradGE employs an ESM-2-based deep neural network as the oracle model to quantify immune escape score. It then integrates multiple biological priors into a standard genetic algorithm to simulate the sequence evolutionary process, generating novel RBD sequences with superior immune escape scores. Besides, we design a novel metric **MRP** (**M**utation **R**ecall and **P**recision), in order to select similar sequences with real high-risk ones automatically. Through internal validation in feature space and retrospective simulations, we characterized the distribution of generated unseen sequences and identified both real-world and potential future critical mutation sites. The consistency across multiple experimental results demonstrates that GradGE effectively improves the prediction performance for variants with strong immune escape potential, providing vital technical support for future variant forecasting. Our code and dataset are available at https://github.com/MaxLiu245/GradGE.

Keywords: GradGE · Genetic Algorithm · Biological Priors · Receptor Binding Domains · Sequence Prediction · Immune Escape Potential

1 Introduction

Although the global threat of COVID-19 has significantly diminished through worldwide efforts, organizations such as the World Health Organization (WHO)

X. Cui et al. (Eds.): ISBRA 2026, LNBI 16690, pp. 300–317, 2027.
https://doi.org/10.1007/978-981-92-3716-6_24

and the European Centre for Disease Prevention and Control (ECDC) continue to monitor its prevalence to provide guidance for pandemic early warning and the prediction of future high-risk variants. With the development of sequencing and deep mutational scanning (DMS) technologies, researchers have accumulated critical viral antigenic DMS data, consisting of antigen sequences and their associated laboratory-measured functional scores. These datasets capture the evolutionary trends of SARS-CoV-2 antigens and are important for forecasting evolutionary trajectories, predicting potential outbreaks, and optimizing vaccine design. However, given the rapid mutation rate and diversity of viral antigen sequences, accurately simulating evolutionary paths and predicting potential emerging variants within a large sequence space remains a formidable challenge in bioinformatics.

Currently, various tools for the evolution and generation of viral sequences have been proposed. Early methods primarily relied on random mutation simulations or Markov Chain models. In recent years, deep learning based evolutionary strategies have become mainstream. One prominent category involves model-based optimization (MBO), such as AdaLead [21] and PEX [18], which balance exploration and exploitation utilizing a surrogate model within a local fitness landscape. Other strategies incorporate reinforcement learning [1,15,20,27], or high-throughput screening with genetic algorithms (GA) [4,10].

In contrast to these discrete search-based evolutionary methods, another significant approach involves using gradient ascent [8] to obtain sequences with higher functional scores. However, existing gradient-based methods, such as ReLSO [2] and LatentDE [24], require additional model training to reconstruct biological sequences from hidden latent variables. The corresponding reconstruction models, such as VAE [6,13,23], VED [15], and even large-capacity transformers [25], significantly increase computational costs. Furthermore, deriving gradients for discrete one-hot encoding poses serious recovery and convergence issues. While techniques like Gumbel-Softmax reparameterization [11,14] enable gradient computation for continuous encoding, they remain incompatible with most mainstream pretrained models, requiring specialized architectures to update these continuous representations.

In this study, we propose **GradGE** (**Grad**ient-Augmented **G**enetic **E**volution), an algorithm designed to overcome the limitations of traditional evolutionary methods, such as limited exploration in gradient-based search and high computational cost. By integrating biological priors with an ESM-2-based [19] oracle model, GradGE simulates nature-inspired evolutionary trajectories under selective pressure. Through gradient ascent via soft tokens, our algorithm enables directed mutations toward optimal regions of the fitness landscape, facilitating the precise prediction of future high-risk variants with enhanced immune escape potential. The main contributions of this work include:

1. We developed GradGE, a novel evolutionary algorithm that combines genetic algorithms with biological priors and gradient-guided directed mutations to effectively explore potential future high-risk sequences.

2. We introduced a soft token-based gradient ascent strategy, enabling the optimization of discrete biological sequences without the need for complex reconstruction models.
3. We designed the **MRP** (Mutation Recall and Precision) metric, a novel automated criterion that accelerates the identification of potential emerging high-risk sequences from the vast candidate pool.

2 Materials and Methods

2.1 Dataset

This study utilizes two datasets: (1) the SARS-CoV-2 RBD DMS dataset [9,10,22], and (2) the HR-CoV meta dataset of 41 known high-risk SARS-CoV-2 lineages. The former is a publicly available DMS dataset [10] with RBD amino acid sequences and their corresponding binding scores, while the latter is a dataset with high-risk lineage metadata collected and cleaned in this work by integrating various public databases.

SARS-CoV-2 RBD DMS Dataset. The primary dataset for oracle model training and feature space visualization is the SARS-CoV-2 RBD DMS dataset [9,10,22], containing 19,132 unique RBD sequences of length 201, covering positions from 331 to 531 on the spike protein. Each sequence includes 1 to 8 substitution mutations and is associated with nine binary binding labels $V \in \{0,1\}^9$. The labels are derived via Gaussian mixture models [10], evaluating the binding or escape capacity against the human ACE2 receptor and eight monoclonal antibodies. A label of 1 indicates high immune escape potential, providing a comprehensive functional profile for fitness evaluation.

HR-CoV: High-Risk Variant Meta-dataset. In this study, we automatically built HR-CoV, a meta-dataset of high-risk SARS-CoV-2 lineages and their key mutation sites from public databases, serving as high-risk benchmarks for comparison and visualization. Standard high-risk lineage information was collected from ECDC. Using the CoV-Spectrum [3] API, we retrieved RBD substitution mutations and consensus sequences for 41 high-risk lineages, primarily including Omicron subvariants, early variants of concern (VOCs) and variants of interest (VOIs). Notably, according to current WHO rules, these lineages are now categorized as de-escalated variants (DEVs), while variants under monitoring (VUMs) focus on emerging lineages such as NB.1.8.1, XFG and BA.3.2 (as of February 2026). For the complete HR-CoV dataset, please refer to our code repository.

2.2 Fitness Prediction Oracle

We adopt the fitness definition to measure the immune escape score of RBD sequences and the classification model f from previous work [10,19]. The checkpoint and evaluation results are provided in [10]. The fitness of a RBD sequence S

is defined as a comprehensive metric of its binding affinity to the ACE2 receptor and eight antibodies. Specifically, it is defined as the mean of the classification probabilities provided by f: p_1 to bind ACE2, and $p_j (j = 2, \cdots, 9)$ to escape eight antibodies, as provided by the classification model:

$$\text{fitness}(S) \stackrel{def}{=} \frac{1}{9}\sum_{i=1}^{9} p_i, \quad \text{where } [p_1, \ldots, p_9] = \text{softmax}(f(S)). \tag{1}$$

By integrating nine scores related to immune escape, the fitness prediction model f quantifies the strength of an RBD sequence's immune escape potential. This model is utilized in our proposed algorithm to simulate the pressure of natural selection. The prediction results of the fitness model for early VOCs and Omicron subvariants is consistent with the evolution trajectory of SARS-CoV-2, confirming the steady increase in the immune escape potential among variants.

Note that although this fitness definition is inherently static, our framework is designed to be agnostic to a fixed oracle. As will be detailed in the next section, any differentiable network can substitute the current model to capture evolving immune responses in practical applications.

2.3 Overview of GradGE: Framework and Algorithm

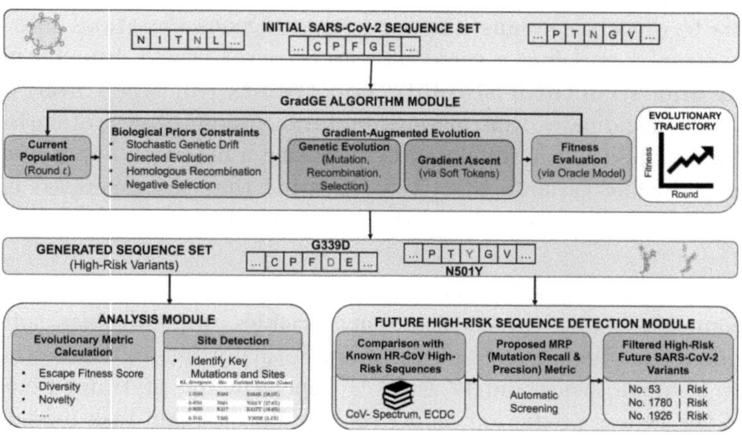

Fig. 1. The framework of GradGE. The whole framework consists of five main components. (1) Building initial SARS-CoV-2 sequence set. (2) GradGE algorithm module. (3) Generated sequence set, i.e., high-risk variants. (4) Analysis module. (5) Future high-risk sequence detection module with HR-CoV and MRP metric.

We propose GradGE (Gradient-Augmented Genetic Evolution), a genetic algorithm to predict high-risk SARS-CoV-2 variants with enhanced immune escape potential. As illustrated in Fig. 1, GradGE significantly extends the vanilla genetic algorithm by introducing two critical enhancements: (1) the integration of four core biological priors to rationally constrain the search space, and (2) the application of directed gradient ascent via soft tokens. The algorithm simulates nature-inspired evolutionary trajectories, where biological sequences are iteratively refined toward higher fitness regions of the mutational landscape, while maintaining biophysical stability constraints. In the following sections, we provide a detailed explanation of the two main modules of the framework, and the implementation of the algorithm.

Biological Prior Constraints. To simulate the complex evolution of SARS-CoV-2 sequences, GradGE extends the vanilla genetic algorithm by incorporating four core biological priors [10,15,24,26]. The ablation studies to claim their individual contributions are provided in Appendix A. First, **stochastic genetic drift** introduces random point mutations naturally occurring during viral replication and transmission, providing genetic diversity in different stages to explore potential candidates within the sequence space. Second, **directed evolution and immune escape** driven by immune selection pressure [24] assume that sequences mutate directionally towards a higher fitness score defined in Eq. 1. Our algorithm utilizes gradient information $\nabla\mathcal{J}$, where $\mathcal{J} = |f(S) - T|$, to force biological sequences to directionally mutate at key sites (e.g., RBD high-risk sites), thereby rapidly simulating the process of achieving immune escape score T. Third, **homologous recombination** [10] usually occurs when different variants co-infect a host or exist in the same environment, simulated via crossover operations to quickly combine dispersed advantageous mutations into a single offspring, thereby enabling a rapid increase in viral fitness. Finally, **negative selection and structural stability constraints** [15] origin from purifying selection, which indicates that massive mutations might lose protein folding or ACE2 binding ability. It is simulated by imposing a mutation upper bound L to filter out unfeasible variants effectively, ensuring that the generated biological sequences maintain biophysical and structural stability.

Gradient Ascent via Soft Tokens. Unlike non-differentiable one-hot encoding or computationally expensive latent variables, we introduce soft tokens enabling direct gradient-based optimization. Formally, let $|\mathcal{V}|$ denote the vocabulary size of amino acids and $W \in \mathbb{R}^{V \times d}$ represent the pretrained embedding matrix of the fitness prediction model (or any downstream task model), where d is the embedding dimension. A discrete sequence S of length 201 can be represented as a sequence of one-hot vectors $X \in \{0,1\}^{201 \times |\mathcal{V}|}$. The continuous soft token representation $E \in \mathbb{R}^{201 \times d}$ is obtained via a linear projection:

$$E = XW. \tag{2}$$

During the directed evolution phase, we perform gradient ascent directly in this continuous embedding space to optimize the objective $\mathcal{J} = |f(S) - T|$. The perturbed soft token embedding E' is updated as:

$$E' = E - \eta * \text{sign}(\nabla_E \mathcal{J}(E)), \tag{3}$$

where η is the step size. Since E' is a continuous matrix that no longer strictly corresponds to discrete one-hot vectors, we can recover the sequence S' by projecting each perturbed token vector back to the discrete vocabulary space. For the i-th position in the sequence, the recovered discrete token index $\hat{x}_i$ is determined by finding the nearest neighbor in the embedding matrix W using cosine similarity:

$$\hat{x}_i = \arg \max_{v \in \{1,\dots,\mathcal{V}\}} \left(e_{adv}^{(i)} \cdot w_v \right), \tag{4}$$

where $e_{adv}^{(i)} \in \mathbb{R}^d$ is the i-th row vector of E_{adv}, and $w_v \in \mathbb{R}^d$ is the embedding vector for the v-th token in the vocabulary. This operation allows us to map the gradient-optimized soft tokens back to valid biological sequences S' without requiring an auxiliary decoder.

This strategy can recover sequences without additional computational cost and act as a plug-and-play module, requiring only a standard embedding layer present in most of the mainstream protein language models [5,6,19].

Algorithm 1: GradGE: Gradient-Augmented Genetic Evolution

Input : Wild type sequence S_{wt}, target fitness score T, population size N, maximum generations G, and mutation upper bound L

Output: Optimized pool of high-risk protein sequences P_{risk}

$P \leftarrow \{\text{Mutate}(S_{wt})\}$ **for** $g = 1$ **to** G **do**

  $V_{adv} \leftarrow \emptyset$;

  for *each* $S_i \in P$ **do** $V_{adv} \leftarrow V_{adv} \cup \{\text{Reconstruct}(E_{S_i} - \eta \cdot \text{sign}(\nabla_E |f(S_i) - T|))\}$

  $V_{ga} \leftarrow \emptyset$;

  for $(S_a, S_b) \in$ *Shuffle*$(P \cup V_{adv})$ **do**

    $V_{ga} \leftarrow V_{ga} \cup \{\text{Mutate}(\text{Crossover}(S_a, S_b))\}$

  end

  $P_{valid} \leftarrow \{S \in (P \cup V_{adv} \cup V_{ga}) \mid \text{Dist}(S, S_{wt}) \leq L\}$;

  for *each* $S_j \in P_{valid}$ **do** $\text{score}_j \leftarrow f(S_j)$ $P \leftarrow \text{SelectTop}(P_{valid}, \text{score}, N)$

end

return P;

GradGE Algorithm. By integrating the core biological priors and gradient ascent via soft tokens, GradGE achieves directed evolution toward high-risk immune escape regions while maintaining biological evolution trajectories. The detailed algorithm is shown in Fig. 1 and Algorithm 1. Theoretically, an upper bound on the step size η ensures that soft tokens do not recover unstable amino acids. See Appendix B for details.

2.4 Evaluation Metrics

Sequence Optimization Metrics. Assume that the initial sequence set is $\mathbf{S}_0$, and generated sequence set at each round is $\mathbf{S} = \{S_1, \cdots, S_K\}$. To monitor the evolution of generated sequences across multiple evolution rounds, we employ mainly six metrics: (1) average fitness score: $\frac{1}{K}\sum_{i=1}^{K}\text{fitness}(S_i)$, (2) diversity: $\text{med}(\{d(S_i, S_j) \mid i < j\})$, (3) novelty: $\text{med}_{s \in \mathbf{S}}(\{\min_{s' \in \mathbf{S}_0} d(s, s')\})$, (4) perplexity (PPL), (5) number of identified high-risk mutations (IM), and (6) number of identified high-risk sites (IS). d denotes Hamming distance and med denotes the median. More details of the first four metrics can refer to [15] and Sect. 3.3. The last two metrics IM and IS are designed only for detecting future high-risk variants.

Sequence Similarity Metric: MRP. Current methods for identifying high-risk variants often rely soley on subjective criteria or simple mutation counts. We then propose **MRP** (Mutation Recall and Precision), a quantitative metric that evaluates the similarity between a predicted sequence and a known high-risk one, using the alignment between predicted (S_{pred}) and known (S_{known}) high-risk mutation sets. Besides, this metric incorporates two weighting schemes to balance task difficulty related to the length of S_{known}. When $|S_{known}|$ is small, the weight punishes noisy (non high-risk) mutations for precision; when $|S_{known}|$ is large, it shifts to encourage signal recovery. The weighting schemes ensures evaluation fairness by normalizing task difficulty across varying mutation scales.

MRP is defined as:

$$\text{MRP}(\alpha) \overset{\text{def}}{=} \alpha\text{MR} + (1 - \alpha)\text{MP} * p, \tag{5}$$

where mutation recall $\text{MR} = \frac{|S_{pred} \cap S_{known}|}{|S_{known}|}$ is the rate of high-risk mutations recovered by the generated sequence, representing the algorithm's capability to reproduce known threats. Mutation precision $\text{MP} = \frac{|S_{pred} \cap S_{known}|}{|S_{pred}|}$ is the proportion of high-risk mutations in the generated sequence that are previously known, representing the precision in distinguishing true high-risk mutations from background genetic noise.

1. **MP Balanced Weighting**: To balance MR and MP, $\alpha \overset{\text{def}}{=} \frac{1}{1+e^{-0.5(|S_{known}|-10)}}$ is designed to adaptively adjust based on the size of the known high-risk mutation set, i.e., $|S_{known}|$. For simpler tasks ($|S_{known}| < 10$), α decreases to prioritize MP, preventing the inflation of recall through excessive off-target mutations. For more complex tasks ($|S_{known}| > 10$), α increases to encourage recovery of critical mutations.
2. **MP Decay Weighting**: Simultaneously, an exponential penalty term $p \overset{\text{def}}{=} e^{-\lambda \Delta S}$ is introduced into MP to suppress redundant mutations, where $\Delta S \overset{\text{def}}{=} \max(0, |S_{pred}| - |S_{pred} \cap S_{known}|)$ represents the count of non high-risk mutations. The penalty coefficient $\lambda = \frac{1}{|S_{known}|+1}$ scales inversely with task scale: smaller $|S_{known}|$ values trigger a more sensitive penalty to discourage noise, while larger sets allow for more flexibility.

Furthermore, the MRP metric avoids penalizing necessary epistatic pairs because it directly measures similarity against actual high-risk variants, which inherently encompass these compensatory mutations as valid targets.

3 Results

3.1 Overall Performance

Table 1. Benchmarking GradGE against evolutionary optimization baselines on the future variant prediction task. Bold values indicate the optimal, and underline values indicate the suboptimal. Other metrics don't have the optimal.

Method	Future Variants Prediction Task					
	Fitness (Avg) ↑	Diversity	Novelty	PPL	IM	IS
PEX [18]	0.7948	8.0	7.0	1.62	1	42
AdaLead [21]	0.8652	15.0	7.0	1.63	**12**	31
GA [10]	0.8289	35.0	8.0	1.64	2	41
GradGE	<u>0.9074</u>	24.0	8.0	1.63	**12**	21
– Max Muations=15	**0.9263**	19.0	8.0	1.62	<u>8</u>	15

We show the generation results of three baseline algorithms and GradGE to generated future high risk variants from 15 initial sequences. The compared algorithms are traditional genetic algorithm (GA) [10] and traditional evolutionary sequence optimization methods PEX [18] and AdaLead [21]. We claim that our baselines are model-based optimization (MBO) algorithms to ensure a fair evaluation with a single oracle, as recent deep generative models or large-scale protein design models employ fundamentally different generation paradigms, and newer MBO approaches often introduce additional modules such as auxiliary decoders [15] or multi-oracle ensembles [26]. We evaluate all algorithms under same conditions with the same initial sequence set, a fixed random seed of 42, and an evolutionary process spanning 20 rounds with maximum mutation count of 30, and maximum 2,048 sequences per round. The initial set contains 15 sequences, which are available in this repository. Although evaluated retrospectively, this setup effectively simulates prospective prediction by iteratively optimizing simple initial sequences without any prior knowledge of unseen high-risk mutations, successfully identifying future emerged lineages that were completely absent from the initial dataset. We report the results of the last round in table 1.

Table 1 shows that GradGE outperforms baseline methods in most key metrics. Specifically, GradGE achieves the highest average fitness (0.9074) and IM (12), indicating its superior ability to generate high-risk variants with enhanced immune escape potential. Notably, when setting max mutation count from 30 to 15, the fitness further improves to 0.9263, while maintaining a competitive balance between PPL and IS, i.e., biological plausibility and search efficiency, proving the algorithm's effectiveness in directed sequence optimization. For other metrics like diversity and novelty, they are not deterministic indicators of quality. Instead, they capture the structural heterogeneity of the generated population, offering higher-level insights into the diverse high-risk population the algorithm identifies beyond the fitness peaks.

Furthermore, to systematically quantify the contributions of the four biological priors integrated into GradGE, we conducted a comprehensive ablation study (detailed quantitative metrics and KL divergence distributions are provided in Appendix A, Table 3 and Fig. 6). The analysis reveals that removing stochastic genetic drift causes the model to overfit to historically advantageous mutations, significantly losing exploration capability. Without gradient-guided directed evolution, the framework reduces to a blind random search, causing the average fitness to drop to 0.7947. Omitting homologous recombination traps lineages in local optima, while removing negative selection constraints allows for biophysically distorted evolutionary paths. This confirms that all four priors are essential for simulating realistic viral evolution effectively.

3.2 Experimental Setting for GradGE

To demonstrate the capability of the proposed algorithm in generating high-risk sequences, GradGE follows the experimental setup of GA [10]. Starting from an initial sequence set as described in Sect. 3.1, the algorithm generates new sequences through multiple iterative rounds. The initial set includes 15 known high-risk sequences, thus incorporating significant prior information regarding critical high-risk mutations. The primary experimental parameters are set as follows: a random seed of 42, an initial population of 15 sequences that expand to 1,484 after perturbation, and 20 rounds of parallel evolution. In addition, a maximum of 2,048 new sequences are saved per round. The target fitness score is set to a maximum value of 1.0, with a saving threshold for sequence fitness in the range of $[0.7, 1.0]$ and a mutation count limit of $L = 30$. Finally, GradGE yields 13,730 high-risk sequences within the $[0.7, 1.0]$ fitness range. Compared to the wild type sequence of RBD, these sequences exhibit an average mutation count of 12.33, ranging from 1 to 30.

3.3 Population Metrics and Evolutionary Trajectory

Figure 2 compares GradGE population metrics with baseline methods over 20 evolutionary rounds. As shown in Fig. 2a, GradGE exhibits superior convergence and optimization efficiency, with its average fitness better than all baselines and converging near 0.9 after the 15th round. While sequence perplexity shown in Fig. 2b) reflects a slight upward trend across all methods, GradGE maintains a lower PPL than the GA baseline, indicating better adherence to the biological distributions defined by the protein language model. Furthermore, GradGE demonstrates a robust balance between exploration and stability. Unlike PEX and AdaLead, which show stagnating or fluctuating diversity, GradGE achieves a consistent increase in population diversity (Fig. 2c) and maintains a stable and high level of novelty (Fig. 2d). These results confirm GradGE's capability to effectively navigate the fitness landscape, guiding the population toward high-risk, diverse, and biologically plausible sequence regions.

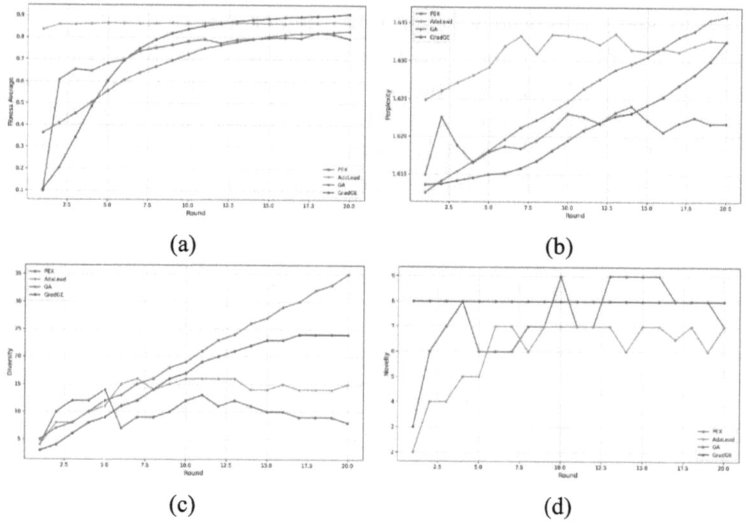

Fig. 2. Population metrics per round. (a) Average fitness score. (b) Perplexity. (c) Diversity. (d) Novelty.

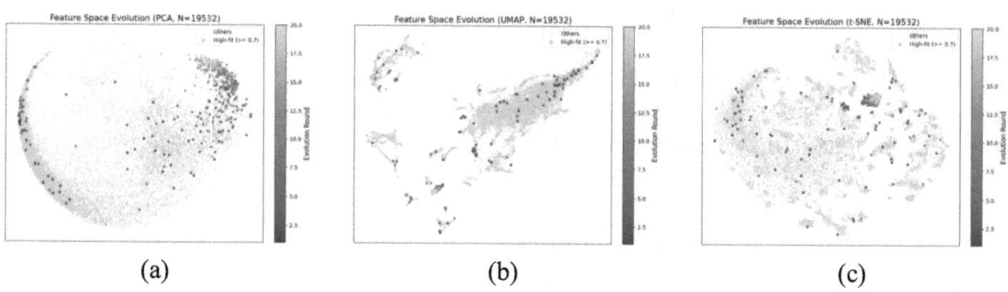

Fig. 3. Evolutionary trajectories in feature space. Grey and orange dots represent original DMS samples with fitness scores below and above 0.7. The color trend from purple to yellow denotes the evolutionary trajectory, with final yellow samples highly overlapping with high-fitness orange regions: (a) PCA [7] (Color figure online), (b) UMAP [17], (c) t-SNE [16].

Figure 3 visualizes the evolution of generated sequences in the feature space across 20 rounds. Using the original DMS dataset as the gray background, the plot illustrates the algorithm's trajectory from stochastic exploration to directed optimization. The color gradient shifting from purple to yellow represents the effective evolutionary trajectory towards high-fitness region.

3.4 Identification of High-Risk Mutations and Sites

We calculated the KL divergence between the amino acid distributions of the 13,730 generated sequences and the initial 1,484 sequences at each site

($N = 201$), as shown in Fig. 4. Therefore, higher KL divergence values indicate greater mutational richness and uncertainty at a given position. The sites highlighted in red denote 12 positions where GradGE successfully identifies real world high-risk mutations. Ranked by KL divergence, these high-risk mutations are E484K, N501Y, K417T, Y505H, G446S, S373P, T478K, G339D, Q498R, N440K, S477N, and Q414K, which existed widely in previous high-risk RBD sequences.

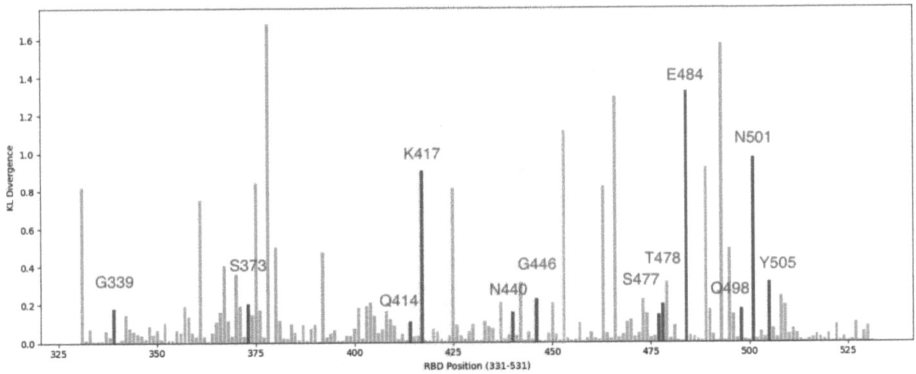

Fig. 4. KL divergence distribution across RBD sequence sites. Higher values indicate greater mutational richness, with red bars marking confirmed high-risk mutations captured by the algorithm. (Color figure online)

Table 2 details the identified high-risk mutations. Other mutations noted as Log-odds > 0 indicate amino acids whose occurrence frequencies increase significantly in the generated population, reflecting their enrichment under selective pressure. Beyond confirmed substitutions, GradGE identified 21 critical sites (e.g. Q493, S375, K444) that find novel enriched mutations distinct from known variants. These findings highlight the algorithm's capacity to predict potential immune-escape enhancers that deserve continuous monitoring.

3.5 Selection of Similar Novel Sequences with MRP

Furthermore, GradGE aims to detect unseen sequences similar to real high-risk ones. We then calculated the MRP metric between the optimized candidates and 41 known high-risk lineages (see Sects. 2.1 and 2.4). We set the MRP threshold as 0.6, where scores above this level indicate significant mutational similarity to real high-risk variants. Under this criterion, 1,297 generated sequences are identified as highly similar to known lineages. Notably, sequence No. 1780 exhibits exceptional alignment, achieving MRP > 0.6 across five dominant Omicron lineages (BA.4, BA.5, BF.7, BQ.1, and XAY). It shared 11 to 12 critical mutations with each, including a core set of ten fully consistent substitutions such as E484A, N501Y, and Y505H.

Table 2. Top ranked confirmed high-risk mutations captured by GradGE: KL divergence and mutational enrichment at corresponding SARS-CoV-2 antigenic sites.

KL Rank	KL divergence	Site	Enriched Mutation (Gains)	Log-odds > 0	Log-odds < 0
3	1.3194	E484	E484K (28.0%)	A(5.7%), C(1.3%), G(0.1%), I(0.5%), K(28.4%), R(0.6%), S(2.1%), T(0.4%), Y(2.8%)	/
6	0.9701	N501	N501Y (27.6%)	E(0.1%), H(0.6%), S(0.2%), Y(28.0%)	/
8	0.9035	K417	K417T (18.6%)	A(0.3%), I(0.1%), N(5.9%), S(0.2%), T(18.7%)	/
19	0.3141	Y505	Y505H (5.4%)	A(1.2%), D(0.4%), F(0.2%), G(0.2%), H(5.5%), I(2.1%), L(1.1%), M(0.7%), N(1.0%), P(0.7%), S(0.3%), V(1.5%)	K(0.1%), T(0.1%)
23	0.2271	G446	G446S (5.9%)	A(0.3%), D(0.5%), H(1.6%), K(0.3%), P(0.3%), R(0.2%), S(6.1%)	/
28	0.2001	S373	S373P (5.3%)	A(0.5%), D(0.3%), E(1.4%), G(0.3%), L(1.3%), P(5.5%), Y(0.3%)	R(0.1%)
29	0.1980	T478	T478K (5.5%)	A(1.6%), E(0.4%), K(5.7%), R(1.1%), S(1.2%)	/
35	0.1788	G339	G339D (5.6%)	A(0.4%), D(5.7%), F(0.1%), L(0.1%), N(0.1%), Q(0.6%), S(0.2%)	/
36	0.1751	Q498	Q498R (3.7%)	D(0.3%), H(0.2%), K(0.1%), N(1.9%), P(1.7%), R(3.9%)	/
41	0.1575	N440	N440K (5.5%)	D(0.2%), G(0.9%), K(5.7%)	/
46	0.1412	S477	S477N (2.8%)	D(2.8%), E(0.2%), H(0.2%), M(0.2%), N(3.0%), R(0.9%)	/
55	0.1073	Q414	Q414K (3.1%)	A(0.1%), E(0.3%), G(0.2%), H(0.2%), I(0.1%), K(3.2%), L(0.5%), R(0.1%), S(0.2%)	N(0.1%)

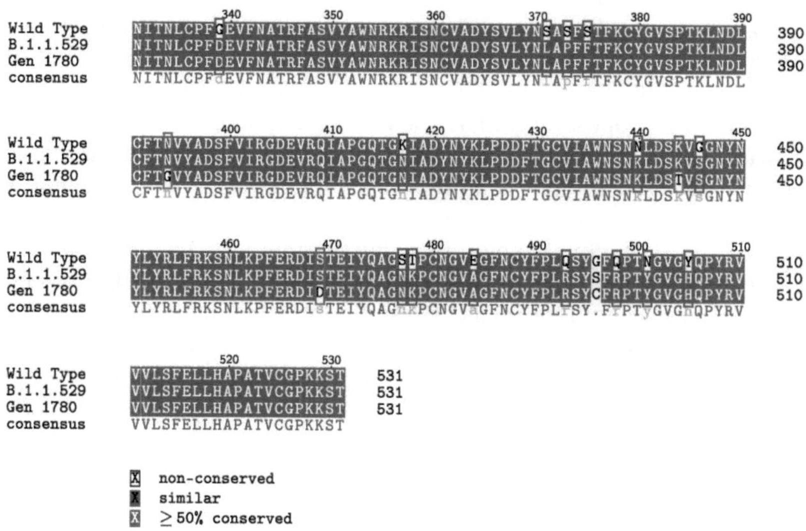

Fig. 5. Comparison of mutation sites among the RBD wild type sequence (top), standard Omicron B.1.1.529 with 15 mutations (middle), and selected generated sequence No. 1780 (bottom).

The comparative analysis in Fig. 5 further illustrates the algorithm's predictive precision. Sequence No. 1780 captured exactly 14 mutations present in the standard Omicron B.1.1.529 (red boxes), with G496S being the only omission (white background). Crucially, GradGE also identified three novel mutations (green boxes): N394G, K444T, and S469D. While K444T is a recognized high-risk mutation in lineages like BQ.1 and CH.1.1, S469D represents a novel, unrecorded substitution. Additionally, we verifies the 3D structure of this sequence using AlphaFold2 [12], which exhibits a strong overall pLDDT score, where details are provided in Appendix C. These results demonstrate that GradGE not only accurately detects high-risk sequences but also has the prospective capability to identify emerging mutational sites that deserve future monitoring.

To evaluate the biological validity of these identified sequences, we predicted the 3D structures of selected high-risk variants using AlphaFold2 [12]. As visualized in Appendix C (Fig. 7), sequence No. 1780 exhibits a tightly correlated predicted alignment error (PAE) matrix and achieves an overall pLDDT score of 85.9, with its core architecture exceeding 90. This structural-level validation confirms that GradGE generates variants that are not only mathematically optimal for immune escape but also preserve a natural, biophysically stable 3D fold.

4 Conclusion

Sequence optimization methods and gradient ascent have provided novel insights for viral antigenic evolution and future variant prediction. However, existing methods often only consider increasing the fitness scores with directed optimization, making it difficult to simulate nature-inspired evolutionary trajectories. In this study, we proposed GradGE, a genetic algorithm that integrates biological priors with gradient ascent via soft tokens, in order to predict future high-risk sequences. Through comprehensive comparisons with baseline methods, we demonstrate that our approach exhibits superior performance in fitness convergence and mutational exploration. Furthermore, by introducing the MRP metric, we provide an adaptive automated criterion for identifying emerging variants from vast candidate pools. These findings highlight the importance of incorporating gradient-augmented evolution into future high-risk sequence detection, offering critical insights for public health and supporting the development of pandemic early-warning strategies.

A Ablation Study on Biological Priors

To systematically quantify the specific contributions of the four biological priors in the GradGE algorithm, we conduct an ablation study under the same conditions mentioned in Sect. 3.1. We independently remove each of the four priors to evaluate their individual impacts on the evolutionary process. The performance of the full GradGE (baseline) compared with the four ablation strategies is presented in Table 3.

Table 3. Ablation study of the four biological priors in GradGE, evaluated at last round. Bold values indicate the optimal, and underline values indicate the suboptimal.

Ablation Strategy	Runtime (s)	Fitness (Avg)	High-Risk Pool Size	Avg Mutations	MRP Matches
Baseline (Full GradGE)	6497.03	<u>0.9281</u>	25,443	10.05	247
w/o Stochastic Genetic Drift	2920.43	**0.9294**	22,695	11.79	3,344
w/o Directed Evolution	424.18	0.7947	3,877	6.14	97
w/o Homologous Recombination	3472.01	0.8762	10,574	11.18	349
w/o Negative Selection	3609.57	0.9203	25,509	10.20	264

B Theoretical Proof of the Stability Bounds of Soft Token Recovery via Semantic Manifolds

To address potential concerns regarding the vulnerability of latent space projection to bad amino acids (e.g., mapping to unstable mutations when the step size η is large), we provide a formal mathematical proof. This proof demonstrates that our soft token recovery mechanism, operating within the pre-trained ESM-2 embedding manifold, is intrinsically robust against arbitrary hard truncation.

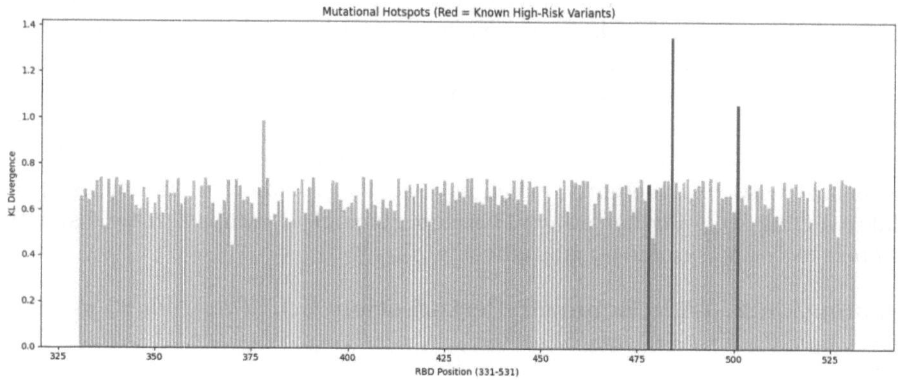

Fig. 6. KL divergence across RBD sequence sites without the drift prior. It demonstrates extreme concentration on a few historical sites, losing exploration capability.

B.1 Definitions

Definition 1. (Vocabulary Space). *Let $\mathcal{V}$ be the vocabulary of amino acids, and $V = |\mathcal{V}| = 20$ be the size of the vocabulary.*

Definition 2. (Latent Space Representation). *Let $W \in \mathbb{R}^{V \times d}$ denote the pre-trained embedding matrix of the ESM-2 model. For any amino acid $v \in \mathcal{V}$, its corresponding embedding vector is $w_v \in \mathbb{R}^d$.*

Definition 3. (Variables).

- *$x \in \mathcal{V}$: The original amino acid at the current sequence position.*
- *$v_{safe} \in \mathcal{V}$: A valid, homologous mutation that is physicochemically compatible with x and maintains protein structural stability (e.g., Leucine to Isoleucine).*
- *$v_{bad} \in \mathcal{V}$: A destructive, arbitrary mutation that severely conflicts with the physicochemical properties of x, potentially leading to protein unfolding or loss of function.*

Definition 4. (Perturbation Representation). *The continuous vector after gradient ascent is defined as $e_{adv} = w_x + \eta\Delta$, where $\eta > 0$ is the step size and $\Delta = -sign(\nabla_E \mathcal{J})$ is the gradient-guided perturbation direction.*

B.2 Assumptions and Justifications

Assumption 1. (A1: Semantic Manifold of ESM-2 (Core Assumption).). *In the pre-trained ESM-2 space, the dot product of amino acids with similar physicochemical and evolutionary properties is significantly larger than that of conflicting amino acids. So there exists a strictly positive Semantic Gap (S_{gap}):*

$$S_{gap} \triangleq (w_x \cdot w_{safe}) - (w_x \cdot w_{bad}) \gg 0 \tag{6}$$

This property is not a mathematical coincidence but a geometric inevitability dictated by the masked language modeling (MLM) objective over 250 million protein sequences. Replacing a hydrophobic residue (x) with another hydrophobic residue (v_{safe}) generally preserves the structural syntax, yielding a low loss. Conversely, replacing it with a highly charged residue (v_{bad}) in a hydrophobic core generates severe conflict and high loss. To minimize the global MLM loss, the neural network inherently forces w_x and w_{safe} closer in the latent space while pushing w_{bad} further away. Therefore, biological compatibility is strictly mapped to cosine similarity, guaranteeing $S_{gap} \gg 0$.

Assumption 2. (A2: Bounded Perturbation Δ.). *The gradient direction $\Delta = -sign(\nabla_E \mathcal{J})$ is a bounded vector.*

In Eq. (3), we extract the gradient direction using the sign$(\cdot)$ function. Therefore, $\Delta \in \{-1, 1\}^d$, making its L2 norm strictly bounded to $\sqrt{d}$.

Assumption 3. (A3: Boundedness of $(w_{bad} - w_{safe})$.). *The embedding matrix of ESM-2, $W \in \mathbb{R}^{V \times d}$, is a converged and fixed parameter matrix consisting of finite real numbers. Furthermore, the vocabulary $\mathcal{V}$ is a rigidly finite set ($V \approx 20$). By the mathematical properties of finite sets, the maximum pairwise distance between any two elements in $\{w_v \mid v \in \mathcal{V}\}$ is strictly finite. Therefore, the difference vector $(w_{bad} - w_{safe})$ is rigorously bounded.*

B.3 Theorem Derivation

Theorem 1. (The Safe Bound for Anti-Arbitrary Truncation.). *For the soft token recovery mechanism to produce a destructive, arbitrary mutation (v_{bad}), the gradient step size η must exceed a strict theoretical upper bound defined by the ESM-2 semantic manifold.*

Proof. According to the cosine nearest-neighbor recovery mechanism (Eq. 4), a destructive truncation occurs if and only if the perturbed vector e_{adv} is closer to w_{bad} than to w_{safe} in the latent space. Mathematically, this requires

$$e_{adv} \cdot w_{bad} > e_{adv} \cdot w_{safe}. \tag{7}$$

Using $e_{adv} = w_x + \eta\Delta$ gets $(w_x + \eta\Delta) \cdot w_{bad} > (w_x + \eta\Delta) \cdot w_{safe}$.

Expanding the dot products as

$$w_x \cdot w_{bad} + \eta(\Delta \cdot w_{bad}) > w_x \cdot w_{safe} + \eta(\Delta \cdot w_{safe}). \tag{8}$$

Rearranging the terms to isolate the perturbation components parameterized by η on the left side, and the pre-trained semantic components on the right side:

$$\eta(\Delta \cdot w_{bad} - \Delta \cdot w_{safe}) > w_x \cdot w_{safe} - w_x \cdot w_{bad}. \tag{9}$$

By definition (A1), the right side of the inequality is exactly the Semantic Gap, S_{gap}. Factoring the left side yields $\eta[\Delta \cdot (w_{bad} - w_{safe})] > S_{gap}$.

Since Δ, $w_{bad} - w_{safe}$ are bounded vectors by definition (A1, A2, A3), the difference in their dot products has a theoretical maximum. Let $C = \max_{v_{bad}, v_{safe}} [\Delta \cdot (w_{bad} - w_{safe})] < \infty$ represent the maximum possible projection gain along the gradient direction, and C is a constant relevant to ESM-2.

Therefore, the necessary condition for a destructive mapping to occur is

$$\eta > \frac{S_{gap}}{C} \tag{10}$$

■

C Structural Validation of High-Risk Variant No. 1780

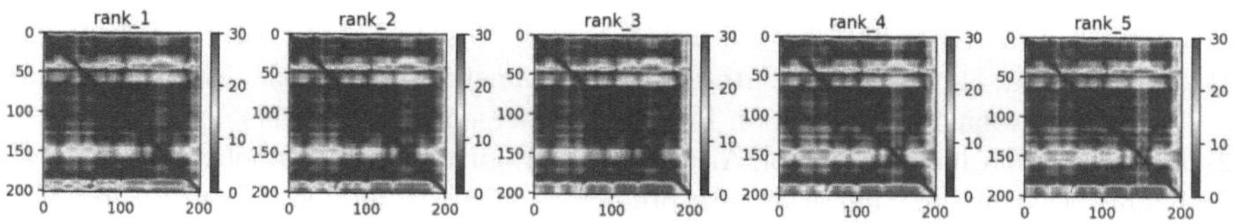

(a) PAE matrix of 5 runs by AlphaFold2.

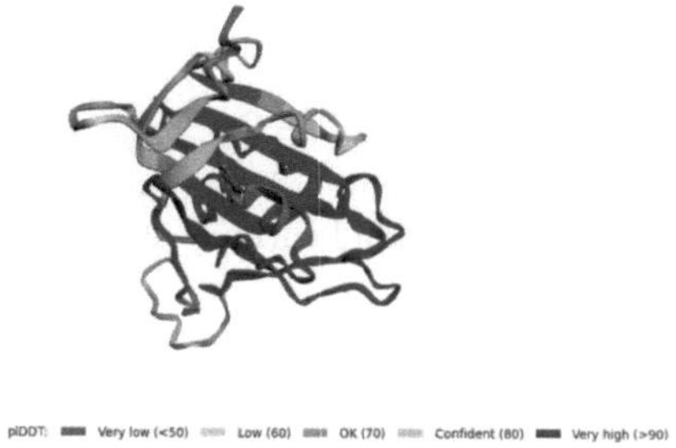

(b) Predicted 3D structure.

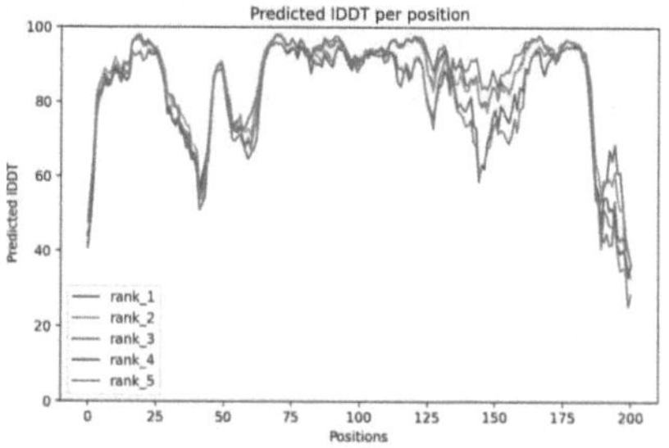

(c) pLDDT scores of 5 runs.

Fig. 7. Structural-level validation of the variant No. 1780. The PAE matrix (a) confirms a stable global topology. The 3D structure (b) shows a natural fold with high confidence scores in blue. The core architecture exhibits pLDDT > 90, (c) The slight decrease at the two ends of the sequence is due to the natural flexibility of unanchored ends. (Color figure online)

References

1. Angermueller, C., Dohan, D., Belanger, D., Deshpande, R., Murphy, K., Colwell, L.: Model-based reinforcement learning for biological sequence design. In: International Conference on Learning Representations (2020)
2. Castro, E., Godavarthi, A., Rubinfien, J., Givechian, K., Bhaskar, D., Krishnaswamy, S.: Transformer-based protein generation with regularized latent space optimization. Nature Mach. Intell. **4**(10), 840–851 (2022)
3. Chen, C., et al.: CoV-Spectrum: analysis of globally shared SARS-CoV-2 data to identify and characterize new variants. Bioinformatics **38**(6), 1735–1737 (2021)
4. Chen, J., Nie, Z., Wang, Y., Wang, K., Xu, F., Hu, Z., et al.: Running ahead of evolution-AI-based simulation for predicting future high-risk SARS-CoV-2 variants. Int. J. High Perf. Comput. Appl. **37**(6), 650–665 (2023)
5. Elnaggar, A., Heinzinger, M., Dallago, C., Rehawi, G., Wang, Y., Jones, L., et al.: ProtTrans: toward understanding the language of life through self-supervised learning. IEEE Trans. Pattern Anal. Mach. Intell. **44**(10), 7112–7127 (2022)
6. Frazer, J., Notin, P., Dias, M., Gomez, A., Min, J.K., Brock, K., et al.: Disease variant prediction with deep generative models of evolutionary data. Nature **599**(7883), 91–95 (2021)
7. Gewers, F.L., Ferreira, G.R., Arruda, H.F.D., Silva, F.N., Comin, C.H., Amancio, D.R.: Principal component analysis: a natural approach to data exploration. ACM Comput. Surv. **54**(4) (2021)
8. Goodfellow, I.J., Shlens, J., Szegedy, C.: Explaining and Harnessing Adversarial Examples (2015)
9. Greaney, A.J., Starr, T.N., Barnes, C.O., Weisblum, Y., Schmidt, F., Caskey, M., et al.: Mapping mutations to the SARS-CoV-2 RBD that escape binding by different classes of antibodies. Nat. Commun. **12**(1), 4196 (2021)
10. Han, W., Chen, N., Xu, X., Sahil, A., Zhou, J., Li, Z., et al.: Predicting the antigenic evolution of SARS-COV-2 with deep learning. Nat. Commun. **14**(1), 3478 (2023)
11. Jang, E., Gu, S., Poole, B.: Categorical reparameterization with Gumbel-Softmax. In: International Conference on Learning Representations (2017)
12. Jumper, J., Evans, R., Pritzel, A., Green, T., Figurnov, M., Ronneberger, O., et al.: Highly accurate protein structure prediction with AlphaFold. Nature **596**(7873), 583–589 (2021)
13. Kingma, D.P., Welling, M.: Auto-Encoding Variational Bayes (2022)
14. Kusner, M.J., Hernández-Lobato, J.M.: GANS for sequences of discrete elements with the Gumbel-softmax distribution (2016). https://arxiv.org/abs/1611.04051
15. Lee, M., Vecchietti, L.F., Jung, H., Ro, H., Cha, M., Kim, H.M.: Robust optimization in protein fitness landscapes using reinforcement learning in latent space. In: Proceedings of the 41st International Conference on Machine Learning. ICML'24, JMLR.org (2024)
16. van der Maaten, L., Hinton, G.: Visualizing data using t-SNE. J. Mach. Learn. Res. **9**(86), 2579–2605 (2008)
17. McInnes, L., Healy, J., Saul, N., Grossberger, L.: UMAP: uniform manifold approximation and projection. J. Open Source Softw. **3**(29), 861 (2018)
18. Ren, Z., Li, J., Ding, F., Zhou, Y., Ma, J., Peng, J.: Proximal exploration for model-guided protein sequence design. In: Chaudhuri, K., Jegelka, S., Song, L., Szepesvari, C., Niu, G., Sabato, S. (eds.) Proceedings of the 39th International Conference on Machine Learning. Proceedings of Machine Learning Research, vol. 162, pp. 18520–18536. PMLR (2022)

19. Rives, A., Meier, J., Sercu, T., Goyal, S., Lin, Z., Liu, J., et al.: Biological structure and function emerge from scaling unsupervised learning to 250 million protein sequences. Proc. Natl. Acad. Sci. **118**(15), e2016239118 (2021)
20. Schulman, J., Wolski, F., Dhariwal, P., Radford, A., Klimov, O.: Proximal policy optimization algorithms (2017). https://arxiv.org/abs/1707.06347
21. Sinai, S., Wang, R., Whatley, A., Slocum, S., Locane, E., Kelsic, E.D.: AdaLead: a simple and robust adaptive greedy search algorithm for sequence design (2020). https://arxiv.org/abs/2010.02141
22. Starr, T.N., Greaney, A.J., Hilton, S.K., Ellis, D., Crawford, K.H.D., Dingens, A.S., et al.: Deep mutational scanning of SARS-CoV-2 receptor binding domain reveals constraints on folding and ACE2 binding. Cell **182**(5), 1295-1310.e20 (2020)
23. Thadani, N.N., Gurev, S., Notin, P., Youssef, N., Rollins, N.J., Ritter, D., et al.: Learning from prepandemic data to forecast viral escape. Nature **622**(7984), 818–825 (2023)
24. Tran, T.V.T., Khang Ngo, N., Thanh Duy Nguyen, V., Hy, T.S.: LatentDE: latent-based directed evolution for protein sequence design. Mach. Learn.: Sci. Techn. **6**(1), 015070 (2025)
25. Vaswani, A., Shazeer, N., Parmar, N., Uszkoreit, J., Jones, L., Gomez, A.N.: Attention is all you need. In: Advances in Neural Information Processing Systems, vol. 30, Curran Associates, Inc (2017)
26. Wang, L., Wang, Y., Qiu, C., Xiao, L., Liu, X., Chen, J.: Heuristic multi-site optimization for protein sequence design using masked protein language models. bioRxiv (2025)
27. Wang, Y., Tang, H., Huang, L., Pan, L., Yang, L., Yang, H., et al.: Self-play reinforcement learning guides protein engineering. Nature Mach. Intell. **5**(8), 845–860 (2023)

Memory-Aware and Coarse-to-Fine Representation Learning for Medication Recommendation

Ziwei Ma, Xianghan Wang, Jingzhong Ning, and Yijia Zhang(✉)

Information Science and Technology College, Dalian Maritime University, Dalian 116026, Liaoning, China
zhangyijia@dlmu.edu.cn

Abstract. Medication recommendation plays a vital role in healthcare, aiming to provide appropriate medication plan for patients based on their medical records. However, existing methods often ignore patients' historical prescription information when modeling patient representations. At the same time, when modeling drug knowledge, they mainly focus on relationships between drugs while overlooking molecular information. These limitations lead to suboptimal recommendation performance. In this work, we propose **M**emory-aware and **C**oarse-to-fine Representation Learning for **M**edication **R**ecommendation (MCMR). Specifically, we design a memory-aware patient representation module that learns patient representations by integrating historical prescription and current clinical information. Furthermore, we design a coarse-to-fine drug representation module that captures comprehensive drug knowledge by jointly modeling entity-level drug relationships and molecular-level drug characteristics. Extensive experiments on the public MIMIC-III and MIMIC-IV datasets show that MCMR achieves superior performance. Our code is available at: https://github.com/WinniaMA/MCMR.

Keywords: Medication Recommendation · Graph Neural Network · Electronic Health Record

1 Introduction

Medication recommendation is a challenging task in intelligent healthcare, providing effective support for clinical medication decision-making. The task aims to recommend appropriate medication combinations for patients based on their electronic health records (EHRs) [3,16].

Existing methods for medication recommendation are generally divided into two categories: (1) Instance-based models [5,19], which recommend medication plans based on a patient's current health condition. However, these methods usually ignore historical clinical records, leading to incomplete patient representations and thus suboptimal medication recommendations. (2) Longitudinal

X. Cui et al. (Eds.): ISBRA 2026, LNBI 16690, pp. 318–330, 2027.
https://doi.org/10.1007/978-981-92-3716-6_25

methods [7,11,17,20], which utilize longitudinal diagnosis and procedure information from both historical and current visits for medication recommendation. However, despite the substantial progress achieved by existing methods, they still suffer from the following limitations:

Issue 1: Ignoring the Patient's Previous Prescription Information. Previous prescription information reflects the patient's health condition after medication and provides important clues for future treatment. Ignoring such historical prescriptions may lead to an incomplete understanding of the patient's health state, thereby resulting in biased medication recommendations.

Issue 2: Limited Integration of Molecular-Level Information with Relational Drug Knowledge. Existing methods mainly model drug knowledge based on coarse-grained relationships between drug entities, such as co-occurrence and drug-drug interaction (DDI) relationships, while failing to effectively incorporate fine-grained molecular properties into relational drug knowledge modeling, thereby limiting the ability to capture comprehensive medication characteristics and resulting in suboptimal medication recommendation performance.

To address these issues, we propose Memory-aware and Coarse-to-fine Representation Learning for Medication Recommendation. Specifically, we model the patient's current diagnosis and procedure information, while leveraging historical diagnoses, procedures, and prescriptions to construct a dynamic memory bank for memory-aware patient representation learning. Furthermore, by integrating inter-drug relational information and molecular-level drug characteristics, we learn more comprehensive drug representations for medication recommendation. In summary, our contributions can be summarized in three aspects:

- We propose a memory-aware patient representation learning module that utilizes current medical information and previous prescriptions, with a dynamic memory bank designed to capture key historical information for accurate patient representation.
- We design a coarse-to-fine drug representation learning module that integrates entity-level drug relationships and molecular-level information to learn more comprehensive drug representations.
- Extensive experiments on the public datasets MIMIC-III and MIMIC-IV demonstrate that MCMR consistently outperforms state-of-the-art methods and achieves superior performance in medication recommendation.

2 Related Works

2.1 Drug Recommendation

Existing studies on medication recommendation can be divided into two categories: instance-based methods and longitudinal methods. Instance-based methods recommend drugs based only on the patient's current diagnoses and procedures. LEAP [19] first encode the patient's current diagnoses and then use a recurrent decoder to generate candidate drugs. However, instance-based methods do not consider historical medical records, they have limited ability to capture the patient's longitudinal health condition. To address this problem, longitudinal methods further leverage historical medical records for medication recommendation. DMNC [7] uses LSTMs and memory units to encode medical sequences for medication prediction. GameNet [11] and DAINet [20] leverage dual-RNNs to learn patient representations based on all historical diagnoses and procedures. Overall, despite the progress made by these methods, they still overlook historical prescription information, which limits accurate patient representation learning.

2.2 Molecule Representation Learning

Molecular representation learning aims to learn meaningful representations of drug molecules that can capture their pharmacological properties [14,15]. Traditional methods represent drug molecules using handcrafted molecular descriptors [8] or molecular fingerprints [4,10]. These representations summarize molecular structures into fixed feature vectors and are widely used in drug discovery and bioinformatics.

These advances have also been introduced into medication recommendation. Some studies incorporate molecular information to enhance drug representation learning. SafeDrug [17] utilizes molecular graphs to improve safety-aware medication recommendation, while MoleRec [18] further explores molecular structure information for drug representation learning. However, these methods still have limited ability to integrate relational drug knowledge with molecular information. In our work, we fuse drug entity-level relations and molecular-level characteristics to construct more complete drug knowledge for comprehensive drug representations.

3 Problem Formulation

3.1 Electronic Health Record (EHR)

Electronic health records (EHRs) contain longitudinal medical information of patients. For each patient, the EHR is represented as a visit sequence $\mathcal{V} = [\mathrm{V}^{(1)}, \mathrm{V}^{(2)}, \ldots, \mathrm{V}^{(T)}]$, where $\mathrm{V}^{(t)} = \{\mathbf{d}^{(t)}, \mathbf{p}^{(t)}, \mathbf{m}^{(t)}\}$ denotes the t-th visit consisting of diagnosis, procedure, and medication codes. Specifically, $\mathbf{d}^{(t)} \in \{0,1\}^{|\mathcal{D}|}$, $\mathbf{p}^{(t)} \in \{0,1\}^{|\mathcal{P}|}$, and $\mathbf{m}^{(t)} \in \{0,1\}^{|\mathcal{M}|}$ are multi-hot vectors representing diagnoses, procedures, and medications, respectively, where $|\mathcal{D}|$, $|\mathcal{P}|$, and $|\mathcal{M}|$ denote the cardinalities of the corresponding code sets, and T is the total number of visits.

3.2 EHR Graph and DDI Graph

To model drug knowledge, we construct an EHR graph and a DDI graph. The EHR graph is derived from real-world medication records and reflects drug co-prescription relationships. The DDI graph is built from known drug-drug interaction knowledge and reflects known interaction relationships between drugs. We use $\mathbf{A}_{\mathrm{e}} \in \mathbb{R}^{|\mathcal{M}| \times |\mathcal{M}|}$ and $\mathbf{A}_{\mathrm{d}} \in \mathbb{R}^{|\mathcal{M}| \times |\mathcal{M}|}$ to denote the adjacency matrices of the EHR graph and the DDI graph, respectively (Fig. 1).

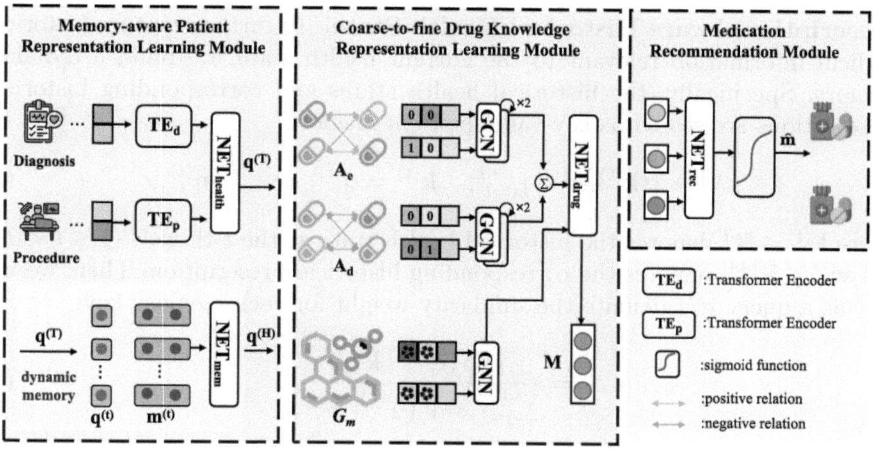

Fig. 1. The overall architecture of MCMR.

4 Method

4.1 Memory-Aware Patient Representation Learning Module

The goal of this module is to model both the patient's current health state and the prescription-aware historical health state. To achieve this, we model patient information from two aspects: current visit encoding and dynamic memory of historical medical information.

Current Health State. For the current visit, we use the diagnosis and procedure information to capture the patient's current health state. Specifically, the diagnosis codes $\mathbf{d}^{(T)} \in \mathbb{R}^{|\mathcal{D}|}$ and procedure codes $\mathbf{p}^{(T)} \in \mathbb{R}^{|\mathcal{P}|}$ are embedded using two independent embedding matrices $\mathbf{W}_{\mathrm{d}} \in \mathbb{R}^{|\mathcal{D}|\times d}$ and $\mathbf{W}_{\mathrm{p}} \in \mathbb{R}^{|\mathcal{P}|\times d}$, yielding $\mathbf{e}_{\mathrm{d}}^{(T)}$ and $\mathbf{e}_{\mathrm{p}}^{(T)}$, respectively. After that, two independent Transformer-based [13] encoders are employed to separately capture their semantic features and dependencies:

$$\hat{\mathbf{e}}_{\mathrm{d}}^{(\mathrm{T})} = \mathrm{Transformer}_{\mathrm{d}}(\mathbf{e}_{\mathrm{d}}^{(\mathrm{T})}), \quad \hat{\mathbf{e}}_{\mathrm{p}}^{(\mathrm{T})} = \mathrm{Transformer}_{\mathrm{p}}(\mathbf{e}_{\mathrm{p}}^{(\mathrm{T})}), \tag{1}$$

where $\hat{\mathbf{e}}_{\mathrm{d}}^{(\mathrm{T})} \in \mathbb{R}^{\mathrm{d}}$ and $\hat{\mathbf{e}}_{\mathrm{p}}^{(\mathrm{T})} \in \mathbb{R}^{\mathrm{d}}$ are the encoded diagnosis and procedure features, respectively. Finally, we concatenate $\hat{\mathbf{e}}_{\mathrm{d}}^{(\mathrm{T})}$ and $\hat{\mathbf{e}}_{\mathrm{p}}^{(\mathrm{T})}$ and obtain the current patient health state representation through health state network $\mathrm{Net}_{\mathrm{health}}$.

$$\mathbf{q}^{(\mathrm{T})} = \mathrm{Net}_{\mathrm{health}}[\hat{\mathbf{e}}_{\mathrm{d}}^{(\mathrm{T})}; \hat{\mathbf{e}}_{\mathrm{p}}^{(\mathrm{T})}], \tag{2}$$

where $\mathbf{q}^{(\mathrm{T})} \in \mathbb{R}^{\mathrm{d}}$, and $\mathrm{Net}_{\mathrm{health}} : \mathbb{R}^{2\mathrm{d}} \rightarrow \mathbb{R}^{\mathrm{d}}$ is a feed-forward neural network.

Prescription-Aware Historical Health State. To further capture historical medical information relevant to the current health state, we build a dynamic memory. Specifically, the historical health states and corresponding historical prescriptions are stored as key-value pairs in memory:

$$\mathcal{M} = \{(\mathbf{k}^{(t)}, \mathbf{v}^{(t)})\}_{t=1}^{T-1}, \quad \mathbf{k}^{(t)} = \mathbf{q}^{(t)}, \ \mathbf{v}^{(t)} = \mathbf{m}^{(t)}, \tag{3}$$

where $\mathbf{k}^{(t)} \in \mathbb{R}^d$ denotes the historical health state at the t-th visit $(1 \leq t < T)$, and $\mathbf{v}^{(t)} \in \mathbb{R}^{|\mathcal{M}|}$ denotes the corresponding historical prescription. Then, we use $\mathbf{q}^{(T)}$ as a query to calculate the similarity weight for each memory key:

$$\alpha_t = \frac{\exp\left(\mathbf{q}^{(T)\top}\mathbf{k}^{(t)}\right)}{\sum_{j=1}^{T-1}\exp\left(\mathbf{q}^{(T)\top}\mathbf{k}^{(j)}\right)}. \tag{4}$$

Based on this, the historical health state and historical prescription are retrieved by weighted aggregation:

$$\tilde{\mathbf{q}}^{(h)} = \sum_{t=1}^{T-1}\alpha_t\mathbf{k}^{(t)}, \quad \tilde{\mathbf{m}}^{(h)} = \sum_{t=1}^{T-1}\alpha_t\mathbf{m}^{(t)}, \tag{5}$$

where $\tilde{\mathbf{q}}^{(h)} \in \mathbb{R}^d$ and $\tilde{\mathbf{m}}^{(h)} \in \mathbb{R}^{|\mathcal{M}|}$ denote the retrieved historical health state and historical prescription, respectively.

Finally, we fuse the retrieved historical health state and prescription information to obtain the prescription-aware historical health state:

$$\mathbf{q}^{(H)} = \mathrm{Net}_{\mathrm{mem}}\left([\tilde{\mathbf{q}}^{(h)}; \tilde{\mathbf{m}}^{(h)}]\right), \tag{6}$$

where $\mathbf{q}^{(H)} \in \mathbb{R}^d$, and $\mathrm{Net}_{\mathrm{mem}} : \mathbb{R}^{d+|\mathcal{M}|} \to \mathbb{R}^d$ is a feed-forward neural network.

Overall, the patient representation module outputs the current health state representation $\mathbf{q}^{(T)}$ and the prescription-aware historical health state representation $\mathbf{q}^{(H)}$ for the subsequent drug recommendation module.

4.2 Coarse-to-Fine Drug Knowledge Representation Learning Module

In medication recommendation, accurately and comprehensively modeling drug knowledge is essential for learning informative drug representations. Existing methods usually focus on relational knowledge between drug entities, which leads to incomplete drug representations. To address this limitation, we propose a coarse-to-fine drug knowledge representation learning module that integrates drug knowledge from entity-level drug relations and molecular-level characteristics.

Entity-Level Drug Knowledge Modeling. Drug relations support the identification of effective drug combinations while helping avoid potentially harmful ones. To model these relationships, we construct two graphs: the EHR graph and the DDI graph. Based on the adjacency matrices of the EHR graph and the DDI graph, we initialize the drug embedding matrix as $\mathbf{E}_{\mathrm{m}} \in \mathbb{R}^{|\mathcal{M}| \times \mathrm{d}}$ and employ graph convolutional networks (GCNs) [6] to capture relational information from the two graphs:

$$\mathbf{H}_{\mathrm{e}} = \mathrm{GCN}_{\mathrm{e}}(\mathbf{A}_{\mathrm{e}}, \mathbf{E}_{\mathrm{m}}), \quad \mathbf{H}_{\mathrm{d}} = \mathrm{GCN}_{\mathrm{d}}(\mathbf{A}_{\mathrm{d}}, \mathbf{E}_{\mathrm{m}}), \tag{7}$$

where $\mathbf{H}_{\mathrm{e}} \in \mathbb{R}^{|\mathcal{M}| \times \mathrm{d}}$ and $\mathbf{H}_{\mathrm{d}} \in \mathbb{R}^{|\mathcal{M}| \times \mathrm{d}}$ represent the drug embeddings learned from co-prescription patterns and DDI knowledge [1], respectively. To balance them, we integrate $\mathbf{H}_{\mathrm{e}}$ and $\mathbf{H}_{\mathrm{d}}$ as:

$$\mathbf{H}_{\mathrm{r}} = \mathbf{H}_{\mathrm{e}} - \lambda \mathbf{H}_{\mathrm{d}}, \tag{8}$$

where $\mathbf{H}_{\mathrm{r}} \in \mathbb{R}^{|\mathcal{M}| \times \mathrm{d}}$ denotes the relational drug representation, and λ is a learning hyperparameter.

Molecular-Level Drug Representation Learning. To incorporate intrinsic chemical characteristics, we further model drug molecules using molecular graphs. Specifically, let $\mathcal{G}_m = \{\mathcal{G}_i\}_{i=1}^{|\mathcal{M}|}$ denote the set of molecular graphs for all drugs, where each molecular graph $\mathcal{G}_i = (\mathcal{V}_i, \mathcal{E}_i)$ consists of atoms as nodes and chemical bonds as edges. We employ a graph neural network to encode these molecular graphs and obtain molecular-level drug representations:

$$\mathbf{H}_{\mathrm{m}} = \mathrm{GNN}_{\mathrm{mol}}(\mathcal{G}_m), \tag{9}$$

where $\mathbf{H}_{\mathrm{m}} \in \mathbb{R}^{|\mathcal{M}| \times \mathrm{d}}$ denotes the molecular-level representation of all drugs.

Coarse-To-Fine Drug Representation Fusion. Finally, we integrate drug knowledge from entity-level and molecular-level to obtain comprehensive drug representations:

$$\mathbf{M} = \mathrm{Net}_{\mathrm{drug}}([\mathbf{H}_{\mathrm{m}}; \mathbf{H}_{\mathrm{r}}]), \tag{10}$$

where $\mathbf{M} \in \mathbb{R}^{|\mathcal{M}| \times \mathrm{d}}$ denotes the final drug representation matrix and $\mathrm{Net}_{\mathrm{drug}} : \mathbb{R}^{2\mathrm{d}} \rightarrow \mathbb{R}^{\mathrm{d}}$ is a feed-forward neural network. Through this coarse-to-fine modeling strategy, we provide more comprehensive drug knowledge for medication recommendation.

4.3 Medication Recommendation Module

Based on the patient representation and drug knowledge representation, we perform medication recommendation for the current visit. Specifically, the current health state representation $\mathbf{q}^{(\mathrm{T})}$ is used to retrieve relevant drug knowledge from the drug representation matrix $\mathbf{M}$:

$$\mathbf{o} = \mathrm{softmax}(\mathbf{M}\mathbf{q}^{(\mathrm{T})})^{\top}\mathbf{M}, \tag{11}$$

where $\mathbf{o} \in \mathbb{R}^{\mathrm{d}}$ is the retrieved drug knowledge relevant to the current health state. After that, we concatenate $\mathbf{q}^{(\mathrm{T})}$, $\mathbf{q}^{(\mathrm{H})}$, $\mathbf{o}$. The predicted medication combination is obtained through a recommendation network:

$$\hat{\mathbf{m}} = \sigma\left(\mathrm{Net}_{\mathrm{rec}}([\mathbf{q}^{(\mathrm{T})}; \mathbf{q}^{(\mathrm{H})}; \mathbf{o}])\right), \tag{12}$$

where $\hat{\mathbf{m}} \in [0,1]^{|\mathcal{M}|}$ denotes the predicted probability of medication recommendation, $\mathrm{Net}_{\mathrm{rec}} : \mathbb{R}^{3\mathrm{d}} \rightarrow \mathbb{R}^{|\mathcal{M}|}$ is a feed-forward neural network, and $\sigma(\cdot)$ denotes the sigmoid function.

4.4 Training

We train the model with the binary cross-entropy loss $\mathcal{L}_{bce}$, the multi-label margin loss $\mathcal{L}_{multi}$, and the DDI loss $\mathcal{L}_{ddi}$. The first two losses improve prediction accuracy, while the DDI loss reduces unsafe drug combinations based on the DDI adjacency matrix $\mathbf{A}_{\mathrm{d}}$.

$$\mathcal{L}_{bce} = -\sum_{i=1}^{|\mathcal{M}|} \mathbf{y}_i \log(\mathbf{m}_i) + (1 - \mathbf{y}_i)\log(1 - \mathbf{m}_i), \tag{13}$$

$$\mathcal{L}_{multi} = \sum_{\substack{i,j: \\ \mathbf{m}_i=1, \mathbf{m}_j=0}} \frac{\max\left(0, 1 - (\mathbf{m}_i - \mathbf{m}_j)\right)}{|\mathcal{M}|}, \tag{14}$$

where $\mathbf{m}_i$ and $\mathbf{y}_i$ are the i-th entries.

$$\mathcal{L}_{ddi} = \sum_{i=1}^{|\mathcal{M}|}\sum_{j=1}^{|\mathcal{M}|} \mathbf{A}_{\mathrm{d}}[i,j] \cdot \mathbf{m}_i \cdot \mathbf{m}_j. \tag{15}$$

We combine the three losses to train the model:

$$\mathcal{L} = \beta \cdot \left(\alpha\mathcal{L}_{bce} + (1-\alpha)\mathcal{L}_{multi}\right) + (1-\beta) \cdot \mathcal{L}_{ddi}, \tag{16}$$

where α and β are hyperparameters that balance the contributions of different loss terms, and are set to 0.8 and 0.9, respectively.

5 Experiments

5.1 Comparison with Other Methods

The following baselines are used for comparison with our method: Logistic regression (LR), Ensemble Classifier Chain (ECC) [9], RETAIN [2], LEAP [19], DMNC [7], GameNet [11], SafeDrug [17], 4SDrug [12], MoleRec [18], DAI-Net [20]. To validate the overall performance of MCMR, we compared it with several strong baselines. Table 1 shows that MCMR consistently achieves superior performance.

Table 1. Performance Comparison on MIMIC-III (top) and MIMIC-IV (bottom). The best and second best score results are **highlighted in bold** and underlined respectively, under t-tests, at the level of 95% confidence level.

Method	DDI↓	Jaccard↑	F1↑	PRAUC↑
LR	0.0816 ± 0.0007	0.4924 ± 0.0030	0.6509 ± 0.0027	0.7589 ± 0.0026
ECC [9]	0.0817 ± 0.0007	0.4856 ± 0.0031	0.6438 ± 0.0028	0.7590 ± 0.0026
RETAIN [2]	0.0871 ± 0.0013	0.4866 ± 0.0034	0.6471 ± 0.0032	0.7593 ± 0.0035
LEAP [19]	$\underline{0.0760 \pm 0.0008}$	0.4540 ± 0.0027	0.6158 ± 0.0025	0.6598 ± 0.0026
DMNC [7]	0.0801 ± 0.0011	0.4550 ± 0.0031	0.6160 ± 0.0031	0.6757 ± 0.0029
GameNet [11]	0.0859 ± 0.0005	0.5037 ± 0.0015	0.6601 ± 0.0014	0.7673 ± 0.0024
SafeDrug [17]	0.0773 ± 0.0006	0.5126 ± 0.0028	0.6691 ± 0.0023	0.7655 ± 0.0022
4SDrug [12]	0.0868 ± 0.0011	0.5132 ± 0.0027	0.6695 ± 0.0024	0.7678 ± 0.0026
MoleRec [18]	0.0817 ± 0.0008	0.5218 ± 0.0033	0.6767 ± 0.0029	0.7725 ± 0.0027
DAINet [20]	0.0843 ± 0.0007	$\underline{0.5361 \pm 0.0017}$	$\underline{0.6893 \pm 0.0023}$	$\underline{0.7835 \pm 0.0021}$
MCMR	$\mathbf{0.0733 \pm 0.0006}$	$\mathbf{0.5402 \pm 0.0018}$	$\mathbf{0.6929 \pm 0.0024}$	$\mathbf{0.7980 \pm 0.0020}$

Method	DDI↓	Jaccard↑	F1↑	PRAUC↑
LR	0.0775 ± 0.0009	0.4527 ± 0.0031	0.6012 ± 0.0025	$\underline{0.7286 \pm 0.0023}$
ECC [9]	0.0689 ± 0.0004	0.4378 ± 0.0018	0.5835 ± 0.0021	0.7219 ± 0.0020
RETAIN [2]	0.0842 ± 0.0005	0.4207 ± 0.0021	0.5753 ± 0.0017	0.6798 ± 0.0013
LEAP [19]	$\underline{0.0674 \pm 0.0006}$	0.4152 ± 0.0023	0.5689 ± 0.0020	0.6053 ± 0.0026
DMNC [7]	0.0823 ± 0.0012	0.4021 ± 0.0021	0.5512 ± 0.0023	0.3956 ± 0.0021
GameNet [11]	0.0810 ± 0.0007	0.4621 ± 0.0016	0.6153 ± 0.0012	0.7256 ± 0.0021
SafeDrug [17]	0.0679 ± 0.0005	0.4670 ± 0.0036	0.6192 ± 0.0021	0.7078 ± 0.0012
4SDrug [12]	0.0832 ± 0.0003	0.4813 ± 0.0011	0.6291 ± 0.0012	0.6989 ± 0.0019
MoleRec [18]	0.0731 ± 0.0008	0.4748 ± 0.0022	0.6269 ± 0.0018	0.7172 ± 0.0016
DAINet [20]	0.0763 ± 0.0008	$\underline{0.4857 \pm 0.0030}$	$\underline{0.6363 \pm 0.0017}$	$\underline{0.7301 \pm 0.0015}$
MCMR	$\mathbf{0.0644 \pm 0.0004}$	$\mathbf{0.4888 \pm 0.0019}$	$\mathbf{0.6448 \pm 0.0029}$	$\mathbf{0.7445 \pm 0.0027}$

Specifically, LR is a traditional machine learning method, so it has limited ability to capture complex dependencies. LEAP only uses the current diagnoses, so it cannot learn a comprehensive patient representation from longitudinal clinical records. ECC, RETAIN, DMNC, 4SDrug, these methods use historical clinical records, but they do not perceive historical prescription information, so their patient representations are still incomplete. In contrast, MCMR explicitly introduces previous prescriptions into the dynamic memory, which helps the model better capture the patient's long-term treatment pattern. On the drug side, GameNet only uses drug relation information, while SafeDrug MoleRec and DAINet use molecular information but do not model drug relations sufficiently. Therefore, these methods learn incomplete drug knowledge. MCMR jointly models drug relations and molecular information, so it learns more complete drug representations from coarse to fine. Overall, because MCMR has both prescription-aware patient modeling and more comprehensive drug knowledge modeling, it shows better overall recommendation ability.

5.2 Ablation Study

Table 2. Ablation study results on MIMIC-III and MIMIC-IV.

Method	MIMIC-III			MIMIC-IV		
	Jaccard	F1	PRAUC	Jaccard	F1	PRAUC
MCMR	**0.5402**	**0.6929**	**0.7980**	**0.4888**	**0.6448**	**0.7425**
w/o PA	0.5254	0.6809	0.7730	0.4693	0.6256	0.7275
w/o EL	0.5322	0.6863	0.7828	0.4746	0.6346	0.7358
w/o ML	0.5264	0.6817	0.7740	0.4649	0.6863	0.7231

As shown in Table 2, the ablation results indicate that each component improves the performance of MCMR. When the prescription-aware component (PA) is removed, the performance drops on both MIMIC-III and MIMIC-IV, which indicates that incorporating historical prescription information helps the model better capture patients' medication patterns. Removing the entity-level drug knowledge (EL) or molecular-level drug knowledge (ML) also leads to lower results, indicating that both relational and molecular drug information provide useful complementary knowledge for drug representation learning. Overall, the full model achieves the best performance on the two datasets.

5.3 Parameter Sensitivity Analysis

As shown in Table 3, we further analyze the sensitivity of the hyperparameters α and β on MIMIC-III and MIMIC-IV. Overall, MCMR achieves the best performance when $\beta = 0.8$ and $\alpha = 0.9$. Specifically, decreasing β improves the overall recommendation performance, indicating that excessively emphasizing the DDI

Table 3. Parameter sensitivity analysis of α and β on MIMIC-III and MIMIC-IV.

Parameters	MIMIC-III			MIMIC-IV		
	Jaccard	F1	PRAUC	Jaccard	F1	PRAUC
$\beta = 0.8,\ \alpha = 0.9$	**0.5402**	**0.6929**	**0.7908**	**0.4888**	**0.6448**	**0.7425**
$\beta = 0.85,\ \alpha = 0.9$	0.5314	0.6858	0.7841	0.4693	0.6298	0.7318
$\beta = 0.9,\ \alpha = 0.8$	0.5297	0.6842	0.7826	0.4631	0.6240	0.7252
$\beta = 0.9,\ \alpha = 0.85$	0.5363	0.6900	0.7880	0.4743	0.6345	0.7341

loss may negatively affect recommendation accuracy. In addition, larger α values generally lead to better results, suggesting that the binary cross-entropy loss contributes more effectively to medication prediction than the multi-label margin loss in our framework. These results demonstrate that properly balancing prediction accuracy and DDI regularization is important for achieving optimal medication recommendation performance.

Table 4. Case study of medication recommendation results for a representative patient with two visits. For each visit, we report the true prescription and the predicted drug set from different models. We also report C/U/M counts (Correct/Unseen/Missed) for each model.

Visit	Ground Truth and Total	MCMR and C/U/M	MoleRec and C/U/M	SafeDrug and C/U/M
1	A12C, N01A, C07A, N02B, A06A, N02A, A02B, B01A, C10A, N05B, C03C, M01A, J01C, D06A and 14	N01A, C07A, N02B, A06A, N02A, A02B, B01A, C10A, J01C and 9/2/3	A12C, N01A, C07A, N02B, A06A, N02A, A02B, B01A, C10A and 9/3/2	A06A, N02A, C07A, B01A, N05B, A02B, C10A, M01A and 8/0/5
2	N02B, A06A, B05C, A12C, C07A, C03C, A12B, N07A, A12A, C02D, A01A, C10A, N05C, B01A, C01E, N05B, N02A, A02B, M01A, N01A and 20	A12C, C07A, B05C, N02B, A12B, N05C, C02D, N07A, A02B, A06A, C01E, C10A, N05B, C03C, A01A, N01A and 16/2/2	N02B, C02D, A12A, C07A, A06A, N05B, A01A, B05C, N07A, A12C, N05C, C10A, A12B, C03C and 14/3/3	N02B, A06A, B05C, A12C, C07A, C03C, A12B, N07A, A12A, C02D and 10/6/4

5.4 Case Study

To further show the practical effectiveness of our model, we conduct a case study on a representative patient from the MIMIC-III test set. As shown in Table 4, the patient has two visits, and we compare our method with SafeDrug and MoleRec. During the first visit, the patient is diagnosed with renal malignant neoplasm, dilated cardiomyopathy, congestive heart failure, and other chronic diseases. During the second visit, the patient is further diagnosed with cardiac diseases and chronic pulmonary problems. Overall, MCMR achieves the best results on both visits, with 9 correct predictions in the first visit and 16 correct predictions in the second visit. In the second visit, MCMR misses only 2 drugs and predicts 2 unseen drugs. Most methods correctly recommend several common drugs, such as N02B, A06A, B05C, and A12C. However, our method still shows better overall performance. This is mainly because MCMR can better capture the patient's prescription history and make better use of comprehensive drug knowledge.

5.5 Analysis of Visit Length

We further analyze model performance under different numbers of patient visits. The results are shown in Fig. 2. Since most patients in the MIMIC-III dataset have fewer than five visits, we evaluate the models on the first five visits. For comparison, we include two baseline methods, SafeDrug and MoleRec. Figure 2 shows that MCMR achieves the best performance across all visit settings. The main reason is that MCMR explicitly models historical prescription information when learning patient representations. This helps the model better capture the patient's treatment pattern and medication dependency across visits. In contrast, SafeDrug and MoleRec do not consider historical prescriptions when modeling the patient state. As a result, their patient representations are less complete, which limits recommendation performance.

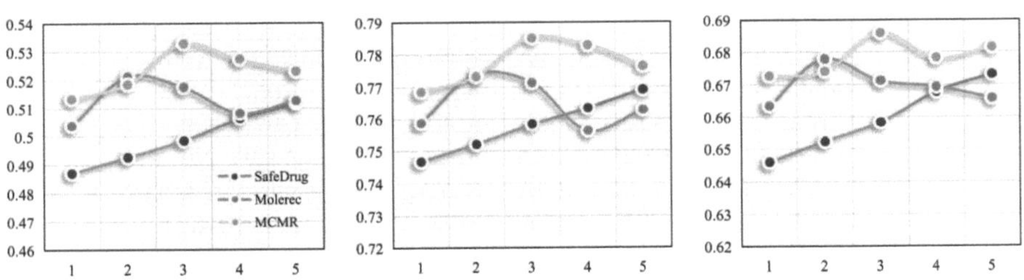

(a) Jaccard (b) PRAUC (c) F1

Fig. 2. The impact of historical visit counts on various models is illustrated using MIMIC-III dataset.

6 Conclusion

In this work, we propose MCMR for medication recommendation. MCMR addresses two important limitations in existing methods. On the patient side, it introduces historical prescription information through a dynamic memory to learn prescription-aware patient representations. On the drug side, it integrates entity-level drug relations and molecular-level drug knowledge to learn more complete drug representations.

Experimental results on MIMIC-III and MIMIC-IV show that MCMR achieves better performance than strong baseline methods. The ablation study further shows that each component contributes to the final performance. The case study and visit-length analysis also demonstrate that MCMR can better capture patient treatment patterns and provide more accurate medication recommendations. Overall, MCMR provides an effective way to jointly model patient history and multi-level drug knowledge for medication recommendation.

Acknowledgements. This work is supported by grant from the Natural Science Foundation of China (No. 62572089).

Disclosure of Interests. The authors have no competing interests to declare that are relevant to the content of this article.

References

1. Chen, J., Zhang, L., Cheng, K., Jin, B., Lu, X., Che, C.: Predicting drug-target interaction via self-supervised learning. IEEE/ACM Trans. Comput. Biol. Bioinf. **20**(5), 2781–2789 (2022)
2. Choi, E., Bahadori, M.T., Sun, J., Kulas, J., Schuetz, A., Stewart, W.: Retain: an interpretable predictive model for healthcare using reverse time attention mechanism. Adv. Neural. Inf. Process. Syst. **29** (2016)
3. Cowie, M.R., et al.: Electronic health records to facilitate clinical research. Clin. Res. Cardiol. **106**(1), 1–9 (2017)
4. Duvenaud, D.K., Maclaurin, D., Iparraguirre, J., Bombarell, R., Hirzel, T., Aspuru-Guzik, A., Adams, R.P.: Convolutional networks on graphs for learning molecular fingerprints. Adv. Neural. Inf. Process. Syst. **28** (2015)
5. Gong, F., Wang, M., Wang, H., Wang, S., Liu, M.: Smr: medical knowledge graph embedding for safe medicine recommendation. Big Data Research **23**, 100174 (2021)
6. Kipf, T.N., Welling, M.: Semi-supervised classification with graph convolutional networks (2016). arXiv:1609.02907 arXiv preprint
7. Le, H., Tran, T., Venkatesh, S.: Dual memory neural computer for asynchronous two-view sequential learning. In: Proceedings of the 24th ACM SIGKDD International Conference on Knowledge Discovery & Data Mining, pp. 1637–1645 (2018)
8. Mauri, A., Consonni, V., Pavan, M., Todeschini, R., et al.: Dragon software: an easy approach to molecular descriptor calculations. Match **56**(2), 237–248 (2006)
9. Read, J., Pfahringer, B., Holmes, G., Frank, E.: Classifier chains for multi-label classification. Mach. Learn. **85**(3), 333–359 (2011)
10. Rogers, D., Hahn, M.: Extended-connectivity fingerprints. J. Chem. Inf. Model. **50**(5), 742–754 (2010)
11. Shang, J., Xiao, C., Ma, T., Li, H., Sun, J.: GameNet: graph augmented memory networks for recommending medication combination. In: The Thirty-Third AAAI Conference on Artificial Intelligence, AAAI 2019, pp. 1126–1133. AAAI Press (2019)
12. Tan, Y., Kong, C., Yu, L., Li, P., Chen, C., Zheng, X., Hertzberg, V.S., Yang, C.: 4SDrug: symptom-based set-to-set small and safe drug recommendation. In: Proceedings of the 28th ACM SIGKDD Conference on Knowledge Discovery and Data Mining, pp. 3970–3980 (2022)
13. Vaswani, A., et al.: Attention is all you need. In: Advances in Neural Information Processing Systems, vol. 30 (2017)

14. Wang, P., Fu, Y., Zhou, Y., Liu, K., Li, X., Hua, K.A.: Exploiting mutual information for substructure-aware graph representation learning. In: IJCAI. pp. 3415–3421 (2020)
15. Wang, S., Li, Z., Zhang, S., Jiang, M., Wang, X., Wei, Z.: Molecular property prediction based on a multichannel substructure graph. IEEE Access **8**, 18601–18614 (2020)
16. Wang, Y., et al.: Soft prompt transfer for zero-shot and few-shot learning in EHR understanding. In: Advanced Data Mining and Applications - 19th International Conference, ADMA 2023, Shenyang, China, August 21-23, 2023, Proceedings, Part III, pp. 18–32. Springer (2023)
17. Yang, C., Xiao, C., Ma, F., Glass, L., Sun, J.: SafeDrug: dual molecular graph encoders for recommending effective and safe drug combinations. In: Proceedings of the Thirtieth International Joint Conference on Artificial Intelligence, pp. 3735–3741. ijcai.org (2021)
18. Yang, N., et al.: MoleRec: combinatorial drug recommendation with substructure-aware molecular representation learning. In: Houben, G. (ed.) Proceedings of the ACM Web Conference 2023, pp. 4075–4085. ACM (2023)
19. Zhang, Y., Chen, R., Tang, J., Stewart, W.F., Sun, J.: LEAP: learning to prescribe effective and safe treatment combinations for multimorbidity. In: Proceedings of the 23rd ACM SIGKDD International Conference on Knowledge Discovery and Data Mining, pp. 1315–1324 (2017)
20. Zou, X., He, X., Zheng, X., Zhang, W., Chen, J., Tang, C.: Dai-net: Dual adaptive interaction network for coordinated medication recommendation. IEEE J. Biomed. Health Info. **28**(10), 6201–6211 (2024)

SpaAGMF: Adaptive Gated Multi-scale Fusion of Histology and Spatial Transcriptomics for Cancer Region Classification

Yunfeng Mao and Wenwen Min(✉)

School of Information Science and Engineering, Yunnan University, Kunming, China
minwenwen@ynu.edu.cn

Abstract. Accurate classification of cancer tissue regions (CTR) in spatial transcriptomics is critical for understanding tumor heterogeneity and informing clinical treatment decisions. However, current computational methods struggle to bridge the semantic gap between high-dimensional transcriptomic profiles and complex histological images, while also being hindered by inherent noise and significant batch effects across clinical samples and sequencing platforms, thereby limiting their generalizability. To address these challenges, we propose SpaAGMF, a novel adaptive gated multi-scale fusion framework. SpaAGMF integrates a pre-trained pathology foundation model to extract semantic histological features and employs a bidirectional contrastive learning strategy to align these visual patterns with transcriptomic profiles in a shared latent space. A core component of SpaAGMF is the Multi-Scale Gated Representation Extractor (MS-GRE), which uses a gated multi-head attention mechanism to adaptively fuse micro-scale details with macro-scale neighborhood contexts. We evaluated SpaAGMF on five spatial transcriptomics datasets encompassing various cancer types and sequencing platforms. Extensive experiments demonstrate that SpaAGMF consistently outperforms state-of-the-art methods in cross-sample, cross-platform and cross-batch classification tasks. Our source code is available at https://github.com/wenwenmin/SpaAGMF.

Keywords: Spatial Transcriptomics · Cancer Tissue Regions · Contrastive Learning · Multi-Scale Representation · Multimodal Fusion

1 Introduction

Accurate classification of cancer tissue regions (CTR) is critical for formulating effective treatment strategies [6]. Specifically, it not only improves the long-term survival rate of patients and reduces treatment-related side effects, but also provides essential support for oncology research, including the analysis of tumor microenvironment and the deciphering of tumor heterogeneity [5]. Traditionally, CTR classification relies on pathologists to manually annotate histological images, which may result in misjudgment due to visual similarities

X. Cui et al. (Eds.): ISBRA 2026, LNBI 16690, pp. 331–343, 2027.
https://doi.org/10.1007/978-981-92-3716-6_26

between tumor and healthy tissues. With the advancement of deep learning, several studies have employed computer vision models to automatically identify CTR [3]. However, relying solely on image information makes it difficult to overcome classification biases caused by morphological similarities and staining variations across different platforms and batches [17].

The advent of Spatial Transcriptomics (ST) introduces a new perspective on this challenging task. By delivering high-throughput gene expression profiles alongside spatial coordinates, ST data can be integrated with histological images to comprehensively characterize tissue regions in terms of both molecular signatures and histomorphological context [16,19]. However, effectively integrating ST data with histological images remains challenging for three main reasons: (i) Cross-modal semantic gap: semantic and statistical differences between histological images and gene expression profiles make simple fusion strategies insufficient to capture intrinsic associations between morphology and biological function. (ii) Inherent noise: ST data inherently contain noise, including technical errors from spatial localization and random variations across sequencing platforms and batches [21]. (iii) Domain shift and generalization constraints: batch effects arising from different patients, sequencing platforms and batches often hinder model generalization to unseen samples, cross-platform and cross-batch settings [11]. Existing methods such as SpaCRD [24], SpaCell-Plus [18], iStar [27] and GCN-based spatial resolution inference [25] incorporate histological images and ST data but rely on relatively simple or shallow integration strategies that are generally inadequate to address the aforementioned challenges.

In this paper, we propose SpaAGMF, a multimodal framework that integrates histological morphology and gene expression via contrastive alignment and adaptive gated multi-scale fusion (Fig. 1). Specifically, SpaAGMF adopts the UNI2 pathology foundation model [2] to extract high-level histological features and employs contrastive learning [13] to project both modalities into a shared latent space for cross-modal alignment and batch effect mitigation. Furthermore, we propose a Multi-Scale Gated Representation Extractor (MS-GRE) that uses gated multi-head attention on the aligned embeddings to capture micro- and macro-scale spatial contexts, selectively emphasizing task-relevant interactions while suppressing noise. The main contributions of this study are summarized as follows:

- We introduce SpaAGMF, a unified multimodal framework that employs adaptive gated fusion to integrate histology and ST data for precise CTR classification.
- We leverage UNI2, a pathology foundation model pre-trained on large-scale histology images, along with contrastive learning, to align modalities in a shared space and mitigate batch effects.
- We design the MS-GRE that adaptively combines micro-scale patterns and macro-scale spatial context, enhancing generalization and robustness.
- Extensive experiments on five spatial transcriptomics datasets demonstrate that SpaAGMF outperforms state-of-the-art baselines in cross-sample, cross-platform, and cross-batch CTR classification tasks.

2 Method

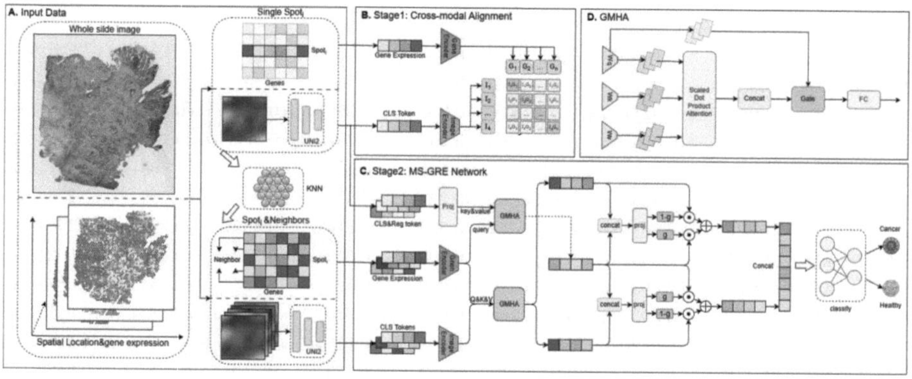

Fig. 1. Schematic of the proposed framework with a two-stage training strategy. (A) Multimodal input processing from whole slide images and spatial transcriptomics. (B) Stage 1: Cross-modal alignment using bidirectional InfoNCE loss. (C) Stage 2: The MS-GRE network, featuring gene-guided gated cross-attention for micro-scale features and neighborhood-aware gated self-attention for macro-scale context. (D) Detailed architecture of the GMHA module.

2.1 Cross-Modal Alignment

Feature Extraction and Preprocessing. For each spatial spot, we crop a histology image patch centered at its spatial coordinate from the corresponding whole-slide image. The patch diameter is defined as $D = \frac{d_{\text{phys}}}{r} \times s$, where d_{phys} denotes the physical diameter of the spot, r denotes the pixel resolution of the full-resolution histological image, and s denotes the image scaling factor.

Let $\mathcal{I} = \{I_i \in \mathbb{R}^{D \times D \times 3}\}_{i=1}^{n}$ denote the set of cropped histology image patches for all n spots. To reduce computational overhead, we employ UNI2 as a frozen feature extractor to obtain high-level histological representations:

$$\mathbf{T}_i = f_{\text{UNI2}}(I_i) = \{\mathbf{t}_{i,cls}, \mathbf{t}_{i,reg_1}, \ldots, \mathbf{t}_{i,reg_m}\}, \quad i = 1, \ldots, n, \tag{1}$$

where $\mathbf{t}_{i,cls}$ represents the CLS token capturing global patch-level semantics, and $\mathbf{t}_{i,reg_1}, \ldots, \mathbf{t}_{i,reg_m}$ denote the register tokens ($m = 8$), which preserve fine-grained spatial information and will be utilized in subsequent micro-scale attention to capture detailed histological patterns [4]. The patch-level representation is defined as $\mathbf{x}_i^{\text{img}} = \mathbf{t}_{i,cls}$.

In parallel, for the raw gene expression data, we first perform normalization and select the common genes across the dataset, followed by the selection of highly variable genes (HVGs). The normalization and HVG selection

Table 1. Quantitative performance of cross-sample CTR classification on the CRC cohort. Best and second-best results are **bolded** and underlined, respectively. Results are reported as mean ± standard deviation across five random seeds.

Slice	Metric	Methods							
		Ours	SpaCRD	SpaCell-Plus	MEATRD	STANDS	iStar	STAGE	TESLA
CRC_A1	AUC	**0.985**±0.000	0.967±0.003	0.952±0.006	0.503±0.005	0.486±0.018	0.461±0.016	0.374±0.091	0.341±0.000
	AP	**0.958**±0.001	0.921±0.013	0.866±0.020	0.270±0.003	0.269±0.014	0.258±0.004	0.212±0.035	0.230±0.000
	F1	**0.888**±0.003	0.886±0.005	0.632±0.053	0.266±0.013	0.267±0.027	0.262±0.042	0.135±0.073	0.246±0.000
CRC_A2	AUC	**0.970**±0.002	0.944±0.009	0.945±0.003	0.515±0.005	0.502±0.010	0.525±0.045	0.469±0.135	0.341±0.000
	AP	**0.935**±0.003	0.889±0.022	0.891±0.009	0.329±0.006	0.325±0.020	0.329±0.031	0.299±0.063	0.276±0.000
	F1	**0.863**±0.003	0.861±0.005	0.731±0.009	0.323±0.005	0.315±0.028	0.362±0.038	0.279±0.101	0.198±0.001
CRC_B1	AUC	**0.945**±0.001	0.836±0.030	0.861±0.003	0.506±0.004	0.502±0.009	0.512±0.002	0.474±0.039	0.502±0.000
	AP	**0.974**±0.001	0.853±0.037	0.937±0.001	0.686±0.003	0.688±0.008	0.693±0.002	0.654±0.023	0.687±0.000
	F1	**0.912**±0.003	0.893±0.004	0.841±0.010	0.691±0.002	0.686±0.005	0.049±0.011	0.683±0.015	0.641±0.000
CRC_B2	AUC	**0.963**±0.000	0.922±0.009	0.891±0.010	0.549±0.004	0.516±0.019	0.501±0.001	0.518±0.089	0.429±0.000
	AP	**0.978**±0.001	0.955±0.011	0.948±0.003	0.743±0.004	0.719±0.014	0.710±0.001	0.717±0.059	0.682±0.000
	F1	**0.939**±0.003	0.906±0.009	0.520±0.052	0.723±0.003	0.715±0.008	0.007±0.003	0.721±0.036	0.559±0.000
CRC_C1	AUC	**0.936**±0.002	0.894±0.013	0.867±0.004	0.747±0.016	0.514±0.016	0.731±0.003	0.553±0.095	0.490±0.000
	AP	**0.778**±0.011	0.683±0.022	0.730±0.012	0.511±0.021	0.268±0.018	0.446±0.002	0.284±0.046	0.252±0.000
	F1	**0.791**±0.014	0.726±0.016	0.635±0.021	0.476±0.008	0.271±0.035	0.593±0.003	0.283±0.070	0.384±0.000
CRC_C2	AUC	**0.922**±0.003	0.895±0.015	0.873±0.022	0.543±0.007	0.487±0.016	0.656±0.008	0.483±0.082	0.415±0.002
	AP	0.825±0.021	**0.847**±0.027	0.812±0.057	0.441±0.006	0.415±0.012	0.517±0.006	0.415±0.052	0.391±0.003
	F1	**0.867**±0.002	0.820±0.021	0.766±0.028	0.456±0.010	0.413±0.019	0.674±0.006	0.402±0.069	0.365±0.000
CRC_D1	AUC	**0.852**±0.008	0.787±0.011	0.824±0.008	0.503±0.008	0.492±0.022	0.708±0.018	0.535±0.067	0.495±0.000
	AP	**0.967**±0.003	0.935±0.005	0.958±0.003	0.865±0.008	0.858±0.007	0.917±0.005	0.872±0.021	0.860±0.000
	F1	**0.939**±0.002	0.904±0.014	0.580±0.053	0.869±0.002	0.857±0.004	0.691±0.038	0.871±0.008	0.770±0.000
CRC_D2	AUC	**0.784**±0.006	0.633±0.017	0.698±0.039	0.469±0.018	0.505±0.028	0.622±0.019	0.494±0.017	0.489±0.000
	AP	**0.967**±0.002	0.937±0.009	0.954±0.008	0.901±0.007	0.914±0.008	0.933±0.003	0.908±0.006	0.911±0.000
	F1	**0.945**±0.004	0.363±0.073	0.638±0.191	0.912±0.001	0.913±0.001	0.548±0.071	0.912±0.002	0.212±0.000
CRC_E1	AUC	**0.984**±0.001	0.957±0.007	0.969±0.003	0.544±0.004	0.526±0.027	0.472±0.032	0.500±0.126	0.743±0.000
	AP	**0.959**±0.002	0.937±0.001	0.938±0.006	0.403±0.007	0.389±0.024	0.360±0.013	0.374±0.106	0.538±0.000
	F1	**0.936**±0.005	0.893±0.011	0.842±0.048	0.410±0.010	0.384±0.040	0.294±0.032	0.356±0.121	0.692±0.000
CRC_E2	AUC	**0.988**±0.001	0.961±0.017	0.984±0.004	0.890±0.011	0.502±0.023	0.462±0.027	0.464±0.044	0.410±0.000
	AP	**0.989**±0.001	0.939±0.038	0.986±0.004	0.867±0.021	0.550±0.030	0.530±0.007	0.514±0.019	0.500±0.000
	F1	**0.956**±0.002	0.935±0.012	0.896±0.021	0.833±0.011	0.538±0.019	0.174±0.094	0.506±0.023	0.569±0.000
CRC_G1	AUC	**0.904**±0.002	0.862±0.022	0.850±0.014	0.511±0.006	0.495±0.009	0.739±0.005	0.509±0.097	0.437±0.000
	AP	**0.751**±0.010	0.653±0.032	0.679±0.027	0.168±0.005	0.159±0.004	0.397±0.001	0.163±0.031	0.146±0.000
	F1	**0.716**±0.011	0.635±0.027	0.398±0.101	0.173±0.016	0.153±0.006	0.570±0.003	0.146±0.045	0.183±0.000
CRC_G2	AUC	**0.919**±0.004	0.891±0.014	0.905±0.013	0.554±0.014	0.506±0.008	0.723±0.014	0.518±0.162	0.455±0.000
	AP	**0.814**±0.006	0.708±0.047	0.778±0.012	0.240±0.012	0.212±0.011	0.410±0.014	0.260±0.150	0.192±0.000
	F1	**0.748**±0.007	0.715±0.016	0.440±0.071	0.256±0.017	0.206±0.014	0.563±0.019	0.232±0.179	0.261±0.000

steps are implemented using standard Scanpy preprocessing functions, including `sc.pp.normalize_total`, `sc.pp.log1p`, and `sc.pp.highly_variable_genes`. Unless otherwise specified, we set $G = 3000$ HVGs in all experiments, whereas for the Xenium dataset, we retain all identified HVGs. Accordingly, we denote the processed gene expression profile of the i-th spot as $\mathbf{x}_i^{\text{gene}} \in \mathbb{R}^G$.

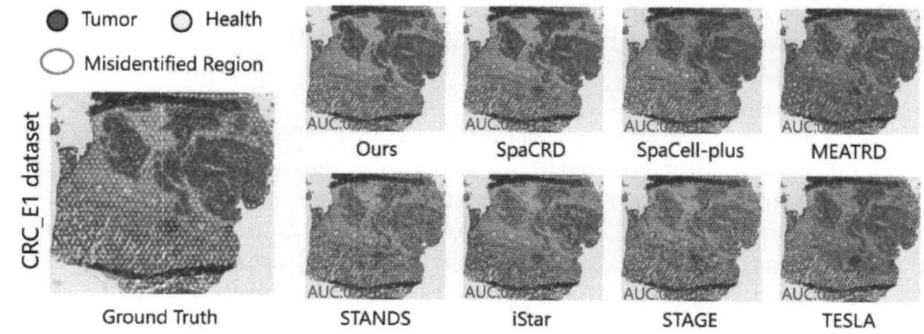

Fig. 2. Cross-sample CTR classification on CRC_E1 dataset. Ground truth (left) and predictions from eight methods with AUC scores. Red/white dots: tumor/healthy regions. Blue contours: misidentified areas. Green contours: annotated cancer regions. (Color figure online)

Dual-Encoder Projection and Contrastive Alignment. To project histological and transcriptomic features into a common embedding space, we utilize a dual-encoder architecture comprising lightweight multi-layer perceptrons (MLPs), $f_{\text{img}}(\cdot)$ and $f_{\text{gene}}(\cdot)$, to map $\mathbf{x}_i^{\text{img}}$ and $\mathbf{x}_i^{\text{gene}}$ into embeddings $\mathbf{z}_i^{\text{img}}, \mathbf{z}_i^{\text{gene}} \in \mathbb{R}^{128}$. The projected embeddings are ℓ_2-normalized prior to similarity computation. Following the CLIP paradigm [15], we define the cross-modal similarity between the i-th gene embedding and the j-th image embedding using a scaled dot-product:

$$S_{ij} = \frac{1}{\tau} \frac{\mathbf{z}_i^{\text{gene}} \cdot \mathbf{z}_j^{\text{img}}}{\|\mathbf{z}_i^{\text{gene}}\|_2 \, \|\mathbf{z}_j^{\text{img}}\|_2}, \tag{2}$$

where $\tau = 0.07$ is a temperature parameter controlling the sharpness of the distribution. To align these modalities, we apply a bidirectional InfoNCE loss that optimizes the similarity of matched image-gene pairs (S_{ii}) originating from the same spatial spot against mismatched pairs (S_{ij} for $i \neq j$):

$$\mathcal{L}_{\text{g2i}} = -\frac{1}{n}\sum_{i=1}^{n} \log \frac{\exp(S_{ii})}{\sum_{j=1}^{n}\exp(S_{ij})}, \quad \mathcal{L}_{\text{i2g}} = -\frac{1}{n}\sum_{i=1}^{n} \log \frac{\exp(S_{ii})}{\sum_{j=1}^{n}\exp(S_{ji})}. \tag{3}$$

The final contrastive objective is defined as the weighted sum $\mathcal{L}_{\text{contrast}} = \lambda_{\text{g2i}}\mathcal{L}_{\text{g2i}} + \lambda_{\text{i2g}}\mathcal{L}_{\text{i2g}}$, with both weights λ_{g2i} and λ_{i2g} set to 0.5 in all experiments.

2.2 Multi-scale Gated Representation Extractor

Following cross-modal alignment, our proposed MS-GRE leverages gated mechanisms to jointly extract and fuse micro-scale and macro-scale representations in a single end-to-end framework.

Table 2. Performance comparison on breast cancer datasets under cross-sample (STHBC) and cross-platform&batch (IDC, ViHBC, XeHBC) settings.

Slice	Metric	Methods							
		Ours	SpaCRD	SpaCell-Plus	MEATRD	STANDS	iStar	STAGE	TESLA
STHBC_A	AUC	**0.981**±0.004	0.972±0.008	0.869±0.031	0.773±0.003	0.539±0.058	0.592±0.008	0.550±0.051	0.767±0.001
	AP	**0.997**±0.001	0.996±0.002	0.978±0.006	0.954±0.001	0.890±0.021	0.917±0.002	0.901±0.013	0.952±0.000
	F1	0.934±0.000	**0.962**±0.005	0.939±0.008	0.921±0.001	0.883±0.006	0.318±0.029	0.910±0.010	0.768±0.001
STHBC_B	AUC	**0.995**±0.001	0.988±0.002	0.963±0.018	0.877±0.016	0.547±0.082	0.656±0.007	0.615±0.074	0.435±0.001
	AP	**0.977**±0.003	0.968±0.004	0.881±0.075	0.728±0.018	0.247±0.042	0.408±0.011	0.293±0.059	0.220±0.000
	F1	**0.922**±0.005	0.922±0.025	0.631±0.068	0.730±0.017	0.238±0.050	0.473±0.016	0.286±0.065	0.000±0.000
STHBC_C	AUC	**0.873**±0.020	0.809±0.021	0.777±0.032	0.770±0.005	0.508±0.038	0.535±0.007	0.455±0.066	0.602±0.004
	AP	**0.935**±0.010	0.922±0.008	0.898±0.017	0.877±0.004	0.729±0.011	0.757±0.004	0.709±0.038	0.783±0.007
	F1	0.803±0.043	0.826±0.018	0.642±0.131	**0.835**±0.000	0.731±0.023	0.132±0.026	0.738±0.028	0.568±0.150
STHBC_D	AUC	**0.969**±0.003	0.964±0.004	0.866±0.012	0.806±0.004	0.522±0.049	0.542±0.004	0.563±0.109	0.387±0.005
	AP	**0.967**±0.003	0.967±0.004	0.856±0.011	0.727±0.004	0.480±0.052	0.523±0.005	0.526±0.093	0.443±0.001
	F1	0.633±0.006	**0.903**±0.004	0.731±0.041	0.708±0.004	0.462±0.053	0.157±0.012	0.540±0.094	0.351±0.000
STHBC_E	AUC	**0.955**±0.005	0.928±0.005	0.836±0.022	0.472±0.001	0.500±0.018	0.598±0.008	0.514±0.042	0.574±0.001
	AP	**0.962**±0.007	0.924±0.009	0.869±0.021	0.543±0.001	0.597±0.008	0.659±0.008	0.604±0.042	0.622±0.001
	F1	**0.791**±0.013	0.685±0.131	0.784±0.027	0.572±0.005	0.578±0.012	0.341±0.020	0.579±0.026	0.462±0.001
STHBC_F	AUC	**0.926**±0.004	0.914±0.006	0.820±0.025	0.524±0.004	0.520±0.024	0.603±0.022	0.510±0.051	0.462±0.001
	AP	**0.981**±0.001	0.978±0.002	0.950±0.008	0.849±0.002	0.845±0.012	0.885±0.006	0.871±0.019	0.848±0.001
	F1	0.914±0.004	**0.933**±0.004	0.922±0.006	0.835±0.001	0.841±0.009	0.380±0.054	0.851±0.008	0.662±0.002
STHBC_G	AUC	0.919±0.002	**0.929**±0.002	0.856±0.010	0.780±0.011	0.517±0.033	0.611±0.009	0.489±0.036	0.613±0.000
	AP	0.879±0.004	**0.889**±0.002	0.792±0.017	0.674±0.012	0.365±0.027	0.468±0.011	0.346±0.018	0.418±0.000
	F1	**0.783**±0.014	0.778±0.010	0.625±0.007	0.608±0.011	0.357±0.030	0.378±0.024	0.355±0.033	0.494±0.003
STHBC_H	AUC	**0.987**±0.002	0.974±0.004	0.912±0.011	0.558±0.003	0.555±0.057	0.660±0.008	0.489±0.040	0.613±0.000
	AP	**0.967**±0.004	0.951±0.006	0.852±0.016	0.345±0.003	0.349±0.048	0.459±0.014	0.338±0.031	0.418±0.000
	F1	0.693±0.038	**0.783**±0.028	0.726±0.024	0.390±0.010	0.341±0.053	0.534±0.007	0.321±0.036	0.474±0.000
IDC	AUC	**0.882**±0.016	0.756±0.024	0.854±0.022	0.509±0.000	0.466±0.024	0.513±0.003	0.564±0.059	0.506±0.069
	AP	**0.892**±0.014	0.763±0.018	0.874±0.019	0.562±0.000	0.514±0.013	0.562±0.003	0.593±0.047	0.517±0.051
	F1	**0.785**±0.032	0.750±0.007	0.767±0.033	0.553±0.001	0.538±0.021	0.059±0.012	0.595±0.040	0.322±0.027
ViHBC	AUC	**0.909**±0.014	0.867±0.019	0.875±0.017	0.521±0.000	0.583±0.049	0.602±0.014	0.439±0.024	0.685±0.004
	AP	**0.938**±0.012	0.909±0.014	0.933±0.013	0.661±0.000	0.702±0.039	0.721±0.010	0.581±0.012	0.764±0.004
	F1	**0.883**±0.010	0.858±0.011	0.814±0.054	0.661±0.000	0.683±0.023	0.340±0.039	0.638±0.014	0.673±0.009
XeHBC	AUC	**0.928**±0.006	0.855±0.022	0.679±0.257	0.511±0.001	0.500±0.020	0.587±0.003	0.517±0.021	0.337±0.004
	AP	**0.857**±0.014	0.723±0.045	0.544±0.025	0.369±0.002	0.374±0.126	0.449±0.003	0.379±0.018	0.327±0.001
	F1	**0.760**±0.025	0.704±0.021	0.547±0.003	0.381±0.002	0.361±0.022	0.337±0.009	0.385±0.022	0.207±0.001

Gated Multi-head Attention. MS-GRE utilizes GMHA [14] for adaptive information aggregation. The projected query is partitioned into $\tilde{\mathbf{Q}} = [\mathbf{Q}_a, \mathbf{Q}_g]$, where $\mathbf{Q}_a$ computes the standard attention output $\mathbf{O}$, and $\mathbf{Q}_g$ generates a gating signal. The intermediate output is then element-wise modulated via $\mathbf{O}_{\text{gated}} = \mathbf{O} \odot \sigma(\mathbf{Q}_g)$, with σ representing the sigmoid function. The final multi-head representation is computed as:

$$\text{GMHA}(\mathbf{Q}, \mathbf{K}, \mathbf{V}) = \mathbf{W}_o \,\text{Concat}(\mathbf{O}_{\text{gated}}), \tag{4}$$

where $\mathbf{W}_o$ is the learnable weight matrix for the final linear projection.

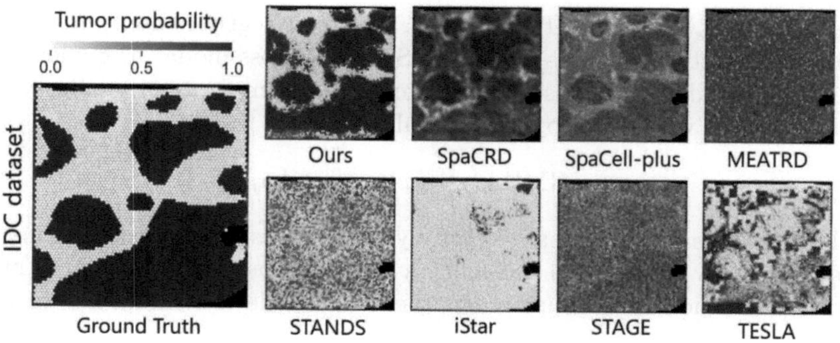

Fig. 3. Cross-platform&batch tumor probability prediction on IDC dataset. Ground truth (left) and predicted tumor probability maps from eight methods. Color intensity: 0 (health) to 1 (tumor). SpaAGMF produces sharper tumor boundaries compared with baseline methods.

Macro-scale Contextual Representation Modeling. Since pathological phenotypes highly depend on spatial interactions among neighboring spots, MS-GRE first performs macro-scale representation learning to capture this tissue-level context, a concept also explored in recent graph-based ST models [12].

For each central spot, we consider a neighborhood consisting of k spatially adjacent spots identified via k-nearest neighbors (KNN) based on spatial coordinates. From the alignment stage, we collect the aligned gene embeddings and CLS-level histology embeddings:

$$\mathbf{G} = \{\mathbf{z}_0^{\text{gene}}, \dots, \mathbf{z}_k^{\text{gene}}\}, \quad \mathbf{H} = \{\mathbf{z}_0^{\text{cls}}, \dots, \mathbf{z}_k^{\text{cls}}\}, \tag{5}$$

where $\mathbf{z}_0^{\text{gene}}$ and $\mathbf{z}_0^{\text{cls}}$ denote the embeddings of the central spot. We then concatenate them into a unified sequence $\mathbf{X} = [\mathbf{G}, \mathbf{H}]$ and feed it into GMHA:

$$[\mathbf{G}', \mathbf{H}'] = \text{GMHA}(\mathbf{X}, \mathbf{X}, \mathbf{X}). \tag{6}$$

The element-wise gating dynamically regulates contextual contributions, enabling robust aggregation while suppressing noisy neighborhood signals. The macro-scale representations for the central spot are then extracted as $\mathbf{r}_{\text{macro}}^{\text{gene}} = \mathbf{G}'_0, \mathbf{r}_{\text{macro}}^{\text{cls}} = \mathbf{H}'_0$.

Micro-scale Gene-Guided Representation Modeling. Building upon the macro-scale contextual embeddings, MS-GRE refines spot-level features via gene-guided micro-scale modeling. At this scale, token-level visual embeddings ($\mathbf{T}_i$) extracted from the pre-trained vision foundation model UNI2 are used to capture fine-grained histological patterns.

All tokens are projected into the shared contrastive embedding space:

$$\mathbf{p}_j = f_{\text{proj}}(\mathbf{t}_{i,j}), \quad j = 0, 1, \dots, m, \tag{7}$$

where $\mathbf{t}_{i,0} = \mathbf{t}_{i,cls}$ is the CLS token, $\mathbf{t}_{i,1}, \ldots, \mathbf{t}_{i,m}$ are register tokens, and $f_{\text{proj}}(\cdot)$ is a linear projection layer, as defined in Sect. 2.1 Cross-modal Alignment.

A gene-guided gated cross-attention mechanism integrates the aligned gene embedding $\mathbf{z}_i^{\text{gene}}$ with the projected visual tokens:

$$\mathbf{r}_{\text{micro}} = \text{GMHA}\big(\mathbf{z}_i^{\text{gene}}, \{\mathbf{p}_j\}_{j=0}^{m}, \{\mathbf{p}_j\}_{j=0}^{m}\big). \tag{8}$$

The learnable gating signal selectively emphasizes histological regions that are both visually salient and molecularly relevant, producing a refined micro-scale representation that complements the macro-scale contextual features.

Gated Multi-Scale Integration and Classification. To effectively combine micro-scale and macro-scale representations, MS-GRE introduces a *gated multi-scale integration* mechanism that adaptively balances fine-grained features and neighborhood-level contextual information.

Specifically, two gating networks are employed to modulate the contributions of micro-scale and macro-scale features:

$$\mathbf{g}_1 = \sigma\big(f_1([\mathbf{r}_{\text{micro}}, \mathbf{r}_{\text{macro}}^{\text{gene}}])\big), \quad \mathbf{g}_2 = \sigma\big(f_2([\mathbf{r}_{\text{micro}}, \mathbf{r}_{\text{macro}}^{\text{cls}}])\big), \tag{9}$$

where $f_1(\cdot)$ and $f_2(\cdot)$ are lightweight perceptrons and σ denotes the sigmoid activation.

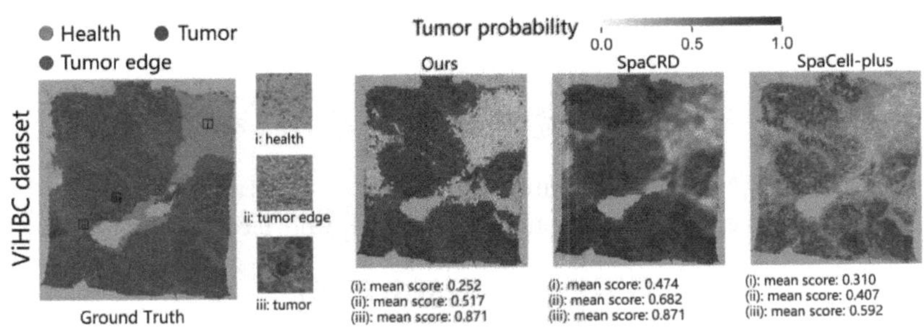

Fig. 4. Predicted cancer probability distributions across three tissue microenvironments in the ViHBC dataset. (Left) Ground truth annotations with magnified insets for (i) health, (ii) tumor-edge, and (iii) tumor tissues. (Right) Predicted probability heatmaps and corresponding mean scores for our method, SpaCRD, and SpaCell-Plus.

The unified multi-scale representation is defined as

$$\mathbf{h}_1 = \mathbf{g}_1 \odot \mathbf{r}_{\text{micro}} + (1 - \mathbf{g}_1) \odot \mathbf{r}_{\text{macro}}^{\text{gene}}, \tag{10}$$

$$\mathbf{h}_2 = \mathbf{g}_2 \odot \mathbf{r}_{\text{micro}} + (1 - \mathbf{g}_2) \odot \mathbf{r}_{\text{macro}}^{\text{cls}}. \tag{11}$$

Finally, $\mathbf{h}_{\text{unified}} = [\mathbf{h}_1, \mathbf{h}_2]$ is fed into an MLP-based classification head to predict the cancer probability $\hat{y}_i$ for each spot. The entire framework is optimized end-to-end using a Binary Cross-Entropy (BCE) loss supervised by the ground-truth annotation y_i:

$$\mathcal{L}_{\text{cls}} = -\frac{1}{n}\sum_{i=1}^{n}\big(y_i \log(\hat{y}_i) + (1-y_i)\log(1-\hat{y}_i)\big). \tag{12}$$

3 Experiment

3.1 Experiment Setup

Datasets and Evaluation. We evaluated SpaAGMF on five diverse spatial transcriptomics datasets encompassing distinct cancer types and sequencing platforms. To assess cross-sample generalization, we utilized two multi-slice datasets: the CRC datasets (Colorectal Cancer, 12 Visium slices) [20] and the STHBC datasets (Breast Cancer, 8 ST slices) [1]. To further evaluate cross-platform robustness against domain shifts, we employed three single-slice breast cancer datasets: XeHBC (Xenium) [9], ViHBC (Visium) [26], and IDC (Visium) [28].Classification performance was measured using the Area Under the ROC Curve (AUC), Average Precision (AP), and F1-score. For all baselines and our method, the F1-score was computed using a fixed decision threshold of 0.5.

Baselines. We benchmarked SpaAGMF against seven representative methods: six multimodal approaches (SpaCRD, SpaCell-Plus, iStar, MEATRD [23], STANDS [22], TESLA [8]) that integrate histological images with ST data, and one ST-only baseline (STAGE [10]).

3.2 Cross-Sample Cancer Region Classification

We evaluated SpaAGMF on the multi-slice CRC and STHBC datasets via leave-one-out cross-sample validation. As detailed in Tables 1 and 2, and visualized in Fig. 2, SpaAGMF outperforms other baseline methods in terms of overall performance. This demonstrates its robust generalization in reliably identifying cancer regions across unseen tissue samples.

3.3 Cross-Platform and Cross-Batch Cancer Region Classification

To assess cross-platform and cross-batch robustness, SpaAGMF was first trained on the STHBC datasets and then evaluated on three datasets: IDC, ViHBC, and XeHBC. As shown in Table 2 and Fig. 3, SpaAGMF achieves leading AUC, AP, and F1-scores compared to all baselines, confirming its generalization and reliability across diverse experimental platforms and heterogeneous datasets.

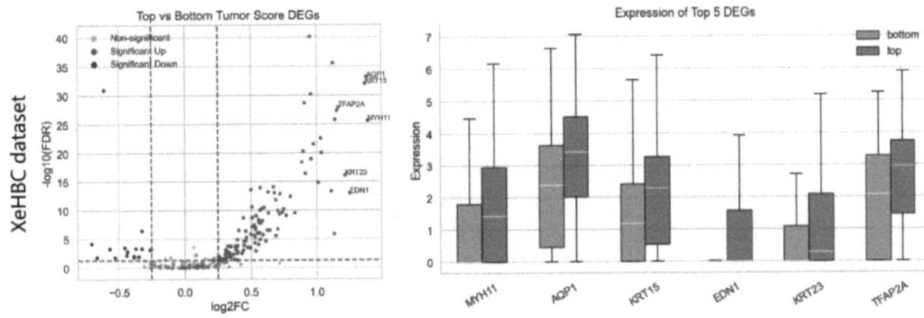

Fig. 5. Biomarker identification on XeHBC dataset. Differential gene expression: volcano plot (left) and box plots of top 6 DEGs (right) between spots in the top and bottom 20% of the predicted tumor scores.

3.4 Downstream Analysis

Profiling Spatial Heterogeneity and Microenvironmental Transitions. To explore the biological relevance of the prediction scores, we analyzed their spatial distribution across the tumor microenvironment in the ViHBC dataset. As shown in Fig. 4, our model exhibits a clearer spatial gradient compared with SpaCRD and SpaCell-Plus. The prediction scores are highest in the tumor regions, intermediate at the tumor boundary, and lowest in the healthy regions. This pattern suggests that the model captures the gradual transition from normal to malignant tissue, reflecting the spatial heterogeneity of the tumor microenvironment.

Table 3. Ablation study evaluating the contribution of individual SpaAGMF components across multiple test datasets.

Group	Dataset	Metric	Ours	w/o Gene	w/o Image	w/o CMA	w/o MS-GRE	w/o GMHA
Cross-sample	CRC	AUC	**0.928**	0.816	0.892	0.922	0.925	**0.928**
		AP	**0.908**	0.723	0.881	0.896	0.903	0.904
		F1	**0.877**	0.664	0.819	0.867	0.872	0.872
	STHBC	AUC	**0.950**	0.921	0.863	0.942	0.922	**0.950**
		AP	**0.958**	0.920	0.880	0.951	0.924	0.955
		F1	**0.813**	0.807	0.733	0.809	0.808	0.798
Cross-platform &batch	IDC	AUC	**0.917**	0.709	0.849	0.701	0.787	0.907
		AP	**0.926**	0.736	0.848	0.696	0.778	0.919
		F1	**0.854**	0.704	0.762	0.711	0.746	0.837
	ViHBC	AUC	**0.932**	0.580	0.750	0.779	0.870	0.914
		AP	**0.956**	0.717	0.775	0.851	0.910	0.946
		F1	**0.901**	0.731	0.817	0.798	0.870	0.879
	XeHBC	AUC	**0.935**	0.886	0.530	0.891	0.893	0.928
		AP	**0.871**	0.782	0.398	0.816	0.809	0.854
		F1	**0.798**	0.758	0.539	0.678	0.747	0.755

Biomarker Discovery. In addition, we evaluated the potential of SpaAGMF for biomarker discovery. As shown in Fig. 5, the spots in the XeHBC dataset were stratified into high-score (top 20%) and low-score (bottom 20%) groups based on the predicted tumor scores. Differential gene expression (DEG) analysis was then performed between these two groups using the Wilcoxon rank-sum test. Genes were ranked according to their $\log_2$(fold change) values, and the top six genes—*MYH11*, *AQP1*, *KRT15*, *TFAP2A*, *KRT23*, and *EDN1*—were selected for visualization using box plots. Notably, these genes have previously been reported to be associated with tumor progression, suggesting that SpaAGMF goes beyond mere classification to capture biological representations [7,29].

3.5 Ablation Studies

As detailed in Table 3, removing any core component of SpaAGMF degrades overall performance. In particular, relying solely on a single modality causes severe performance degradation, highlighting the necessity of multimodal fusion. Furthermore, removing the cross-modal alignment (CMA) or MS-GRE yields substantial declines in cross-platform and cross-batch evaluations, underscoring their crucial roles in domain generalization. Finally, the GMHA module stabilizes multimodal fusion, particularly under cross-platform settings. Overall, these results demonstrate that our adaptive gated multi-scale fusion approach is important for robust CTR classification.

4 Conclusions

We introduced SpaAGMF, an adaptive multi-scale fusion framework designed for accurate CTR classification. By coupling contrastive cross-modal alignment with the MS-GRE module, SpaAGMF effectively integrates transcriptomic and histological features. Extensive evaluations reveal its improved generalization and robustness across multi-slice and cross-platform settings compared to existing baselines, although its F1-score leaves room for further threshold optimization. Furthermore, its predicted scores reveal spatial gradients across tissue regions, reflecting tumor heterogeneity and microenvironmental transitions, while facilitating biologically meaningful biomarker discovery.

Acknowledgements. The work was supported in part by the National Natural Science Foundation of China (62262069).

References

1. Andersson, A., et al.: Spatial deconvolution of her2-positive breast tumors reveals novel intercellular relationships. bioRxiv, pp. 2020–07 (2020)
2. Chen, R.J., et al.: Towards a general-purpose foundation model for computational pathology. Nat. Med. **30**(3), 850–862 (2024)

3. Coudray, N., et al.: Classification and mutation prediction from non-small cell lung cancer histopathology images using deep learning. Nat. Med. **24**(10), 1559–1567 (2018)
4. Darcet, T., Oquab, M., Mairal, J., Bojanowski, P.: Vision transformers need registers (2024). https://arxiv.org/abs/2309.16588
5. De Visser, K.E., Joyce, J.A.: The evolving tumor microenvironment: from cancer initiation to metastatic outgrowth. Cancer Cell **41**(3), 374–403 (2023)
6. Fitzgerald, R.C., Antoniou, A.C., Fruk, L., Rosenfeld, N.: The future of early cancer detection. Nat. Med. **28**(4), 666–677 (2022)
7. Guo, Z., et al.: Water channel protein AQP1 in cytoplasm is a critical factor in breast cancer local invasion. J. Exp. Clin. Cancer Res. **42**(1), 49 (2023)
8. Hu, J., et al.: Deciphering tumor ecosystems at super resolution from spatial transcriptomics with tesla. Cell Syst. **14**(5), 404–417 (2023)
9. Janesick, A., et al.: High resolution mapping of the tumor microenvironment using integrated single-cell, spatial and in situ analysis. Nat. Commun. **14**(1), 8353 (2023)
10. Li, S., Gai, K., Dong, K., Zhang, Y., Zhang, S.: High-density generation of spatial transcriptomics with stage. Nucleic Acids Res. **52**(9), 4843–4856 (2024)
11. Millard, N., et al.: Batch correcting single-cell spatial transcriptomics count data with crescendo improves visualization and detection of spatial gene patterns. Genome Biol. **26**(1), 36 (2025)
12. Min, W., Fang, D., Chen, J., Zhang, S.: SpaMask: dual masking graph autoencoder with contrastive learning for spatial transcriptomics. PLoS Comput. Biol. **21**(4), e1012881 (2025)
13. Min, W., Shi, Z., Zhang, J., Wan, J., Wang, C.: Multimodal contrastive learning for spatial gene expression prediction using histology images. Brief. Bioinform. **25**(6), bbae551 (2024)
14. Qiu, Z., et al.: Gated attention for large language models: Non-linearity, sparsity, and attention-sink-free (2025)
15. Radford, A., et al.: Learning transferable visual models from natural language supervision. In: International Conference on Machine Learning, pp. 8748–8763. PMLR (2021)
16. Shi, Z., Xue, S., Min, W.: Geometry-informed multimodal fusion network for enhancing high-density spatial transcriptomics from histology images. Eng. Appl. Artif. Intell. **162**, 112647 (2025)
17. Stacke, K., Eilertsen, G., Unger, J., Lundström, C.: Measuring domain shift for deep learning in histopathology. IEEE J. Biomed. Health Inform. **25**(2), 325–336 (2020)
18. Tan, X., Su, A., Tran, M., Nguyen, Q.: SpaCell: integrating tissue morphology and spatial gene expression to predict disease cells. Bioinformatics **36**(7), 2293–2294 (2020)
19. Tian, L., Chen, F., Macosko, E.Z.: The expanding vistas of spatial transcriptomics. Nat. Biotechnol. **41**(6), 773–782 (2023)
20. Valdeolivas, A., et al.: Profiling the heterogeneity of colorectal cancer consensus molecular subtypes using spatial transcriptomics. NPJ Precis. Oncol. **8**(1), 10 (2024)
21. Wang, Y., et al.: Sprod for de-noising spatially resolved transcriptomics data based on position and image information. Nat. Methods **19**(8), 950–958 (2022)
22. Xu, K., et al.: Detecting anomalous anatomic regions in spatial transcriptomics with stands. Nat. Commun. **15**(1), 8223 (2024)
23. Xu, K., et al.: MEATRD: multimodal anomalous tissue region detection enhanced with spatial transcriptomics (2025)

24. Xue, S., Wan, J., Zhang, L., Min, W.: SpaCRD: multimodal deep fusion of histology and spatial transcriptomics for cancer region detection. In: Proceedings of the AAAI Conference on Artificial Intelligence, vol. 40, pp. 11523–11531 (2026)
25. Xue, S., Zhu, F., Chen, J., Min, W.: Inferring single-cell resolution spatial gene expression via fusing spot-based spatial transcriptomics, location, and histology using GCN. Brief. Bioinform. **26**(1), bbae630 (2025)
26. Yang, Y., et al.: STAIG: spatial transcriptomics analysis via image-aided graph contrastive learning for domain exploration and alignment-free integration. Nat. Commun. **16**(1), 1067 (2025)
27. Zhang, D., et al.: Inferring super-resolution tissue architecture by integrating spatial transcriptomics with histology. Nat. Biotechnol. **42**(9), 1372–1377 (2024)
28. Zhao, E., et al.: Spatial transcriptomics at subspot resolution with bayesspace. Nat. Biotechnol. **39**(11), 1375–1384 (2021)
29. Zhu, Y., et al.: ARHGEF2/EDN1 pathway participates in er stress-related drug resistance of hepatocellular carcinoma by promoting angiogenesis and malignant proliferation. Cell Death Dis. **13**(7), 652 (2022)

Motif-Aware Graph Attention Networks for Hemolytic Peptide Prediction

Qiaozhen Meng[1(✉)], Bangguo Tan[1], Yuchen Ma[1], and Fei Guo[2(✉)]

[1] School of Computer Science, Xiangtan University, Xiangtan, China
qiaozhenm@xtu.edu.cn

[2] School of Computer Science, Central South University, Changsha, China
guofei@csu.edu.cn

Abstract. Accurate early assessment of hemolytic risk is critical for the development of therapeutic peptides, a promising class of drug candidates. Current in vitro hemolysis assays yield reliable results but are labor intensive and costly, limiting their application in large scale screening. Computational methods offer an efficient alternative, but existing approaches typically rely on global sequence or structural features, overlooking the local motif patterns that capture functional patterns. Here, we propose Motif-Hemol, a novel framework that integrates Motif priors with structural and sequential representations for hemolytic peptide prediction. Specifically, we employ a graph attention network (GAT) to model structural information, where residues are represented as nodes and multiple complementary edge types are constructed to capture diverse spatial relationships. To effectively incorporate motif information, we introduce a motif-aware attention bias that enhances interactions among residues within the same motif, enabling the model to capture functionally relevant local substructures. In addition, a bidirectional gated recurrent unit (BiGRU) is utilized to model long-range sequence dependencies, providing global contextual information complementary to structural features. Extensive experiments demonstrate that Motif-Hemol achieves state-of-the-art performance, with a Matthews correlation coefficient (MCC) of 0.65. Ablation studies demonstrate the effectiveness of each component. Further analyses on node representations, edge construction strategies and peptide lengths provide deeper insights into the factors influencing model performance. Motif-Hemol provides an effective tool for hemolytic peptide prediction and shows potential for large-scale virtual screening in early-stage therapeutic peptide discovery.

Keywords: Peptide · Hemolytic Prediction · Multi-modal · Motif · Deep learning

1 Introduction

Peptides are bioactive molecules with molecular weights between small-molecule drugs and protein therapeutics [1]. They offer advantages such as high selectivity, low immunogenicity and good biocompatibility [2]. Since the introduction of

X. Cui et al. (Eds.): ISBRA 2026, LNBI 16690, pp. 344–355, 2027.
https://doi.org/10.1007/978-981-92-3716-6_27

insulin in 1922 [3], over 80 peptide drugs have been approved by the FDA for treating diseases ranging from metabolic disorders to cancer [4]. Despite these successes, clinical translation of peptide drugs remains challenging. In particular, hemolytic activity is a major safety concern for intravenously administered peptides. These peptides may disrupt red blood cell membranes, leading to hemoglobin leakage and hemolysis [5]. Severe hemolysis can result in anemia, kidney injury, or even death. Therefore, accurate early prediction of hemolytic risk is essential.

The hemolytic activity of peptides is governed by multiple structural factors, including amino acid sequence composition, net charge, hydrophobicity distribution, secondary structure propensity, and self assembly capacity [6]. Hemolytic activity varies significantly across different peptides. Current in vitro hemolysis assays are reliable but labor intensive and costly, limiting their use for large scale screening. Deep learning has shown great success in protein function prediction [7], suggesting that computational approaches can offer an efficient solution for hemolytic activity assessment.

Existing computational methods for hemolytic peptide prediction can be broadly categorized into sequence-based, pre-trained language model (PLM)-based, and structure-based approaches. Sequence-based methods rely on amino acid sequences and employ representations such as one-hot encoding, position-specific scoring matrices (PSSMs), and handcrafted physicochemical descriptors [8–10]. Although these features are interpretable and computationally efficient, they are limited in capturing long-range dependencies and higher-order sequence patterns. Recent advances in PLMs, such as ProtBERT [11] and ESM series [12,13], have enabled the learning of deep contextual representations from large-scale protein corpora, effectively modeling complex residue dependencies. AMPDeep utilizes ProtBERT embeddings to improve prediction performance [14]. Similarly, PeptideBERT employs transformer-based architectures to learn informative peptide representations for downstream prediction tasks [15]. Structure-based methods incorporate spatial and physicochemical information, including secondary structure and solvent accessibility, to capture conformational characteristics [16]. With the advent of accurate protein structure prediction tools such as AlphaFold2 [13] and RoseTTAFold [17], 3D structural information has become increasingly accessible, enabling the modeling of spatial relationships among residues. To further improve predictive performance, recent studies have explored multi-modal approaches that integrate sequence-based, structural-based and PLM-based representations to leverage their complementary information [18,19]. However, these approaches still lack explicit modeling of biologically meaningful sequence priors.

Specific short peptide fragments, typically 3–10 amino acids in length, are known to play critical roles in membrane disruption and hemolytic activity [20]. Existing methods that incorporate motif information typically rely on constructing handcrafted sequence features based on motif occurrence [21] or applying post-hoc adjustments. HemoPI2 integrates motifs by adding one to the predicted probability when a known motif is present [22]. However, simple additive adjustment fails to capture synergistic interactions among motif residues and their surrounding environment.

Motivated by these considerations, we propose Motif-Hemol, a framework that integrates motif priors and long-range sequence dependencies for hemolytic peptide prediction. Specifically, we employ a graph attention network (GAT) to model structural information, where residues serve as nodes and multiple edge types are used to capture complementary spatial relationships. To incorporate motif priors, we introduce a motif-aware attention mechanism that enhances interactions among residues within the same motif. In addition, a bidirectional gated recurrent unit (BiGRU) is adopted to capture global sequence context, complementing the structural representation. Extensive experiments demonstrate that our method achieves state-of-the-art performance, with an MCC of 0.65, and that each component contributes to the overall performance.

2 Materials and Methods

2.1 Dataset

We utilize the HemoPI2 benchmark dataset [22], which represents the most comprehensive collection of experimentally validated hemolytic peptides to date. The dataset comprises 1,926 unique peptide sequences with measured hemolytic concentrations (HC_{50} values), sourced from DBAASP v3 [23] and Hemolytik [24] databases. The dataset excludes peptides containing non-natural amino acids or those with fewer than six residues. The peptides with $HC_{50} \leq 100$ μM were labeled as hemolytic (positive class, $n = 891$), while those with $HC_{50} > 100$ μM were classified as non-hemolytic (negative class, $n = 1,035$).

2.2 Model Overview

In our study, we propose Motif-Hemol, a multi-modal framework that enhances peptide representation by integrating sequence and structural information under the guidance of motif priors. As illustrated in Fig. 1, the model comprises three main components:

(i) **Structural Graph Construction** represents peptides as residue-level graphs with complementary spatial edges, capturing multiple types of spatial relationships among residues;
(ii) **Motif-guided Functional Enhancement** incorporates motif priors into the graph attention network to enhance interactions among residues within functionally relevant fragments, guiding the model to focus on biologically meaningful local substructures.
(iii) **Global Sequence Context Encoding** captures long-range dependencies along the peptide sequence using a bidirectional GRU (BiGRU), allowing each residue representation to incorporate global contextual information.

2.3 Structural Graph Construction

The structural graph is constructed with residues as nodes and edges defined based on different residue-wise relationships. To capture complementary spatial relationships, we adopt three edge construction strategies following GearNet [25]:

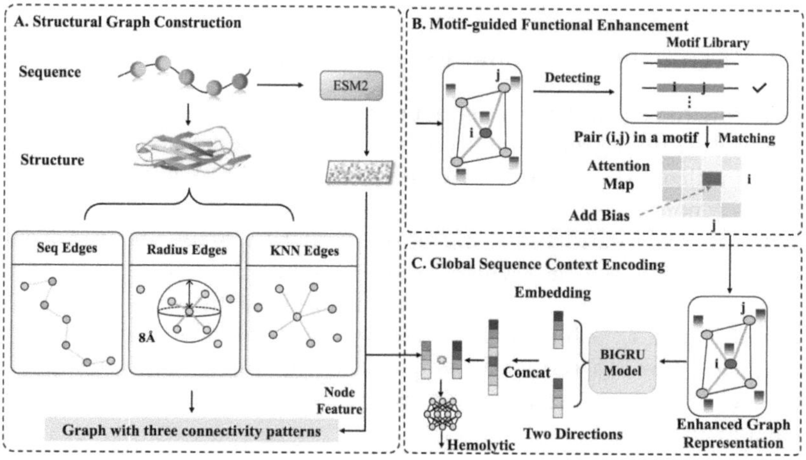

Fig. 1. Overview of the proposed Motif-Hemol framework. The framework integrates structural information and sequential context through a graph-based representation learning approach. A. Structural graph construction. Starting from a peptide sequence, residue-level embeddings are generated using ESM2. A multi-relational graph is then constructed based on structural information, incorporating three types of edges: sequential edges, radius edges and KNN edges. B. Motif-guided functional enhancement module. A motif library is precomputed from known hemolytic and non-hemolytic peptides. For each residue pair (i, j), a bias term is introduced into the attention mechanism of the GAT if they falls within the same motif fragment. C. Global sequence context encoding. After the graph module, the representations are passed to a bidirectional GRU to capture long-range sequence dependencies. The forward and backward hidden states are concatenated to produce context-aware representations, which complement the local structural features learned from the graph. The fused representations are then used for hemolytic activity prediction.

(i) Sequential Edges: Adjacent residues are connected to preserve backbone topology and sequential neighborhood information. For any $1 \le i < L$, a sequential edge is added if the residues are within a predefined sequential distance threshold d_{seq}. We set $d_{seq} = 2$, limiting sequential edges to immediately adjacent residues along the backbone. (ii) Radius Edges: Residues are connected if their 3D Euclidean distance falls within a threshold d_{str}, reflecting spatial proximity and potential physical interactions within the peptide conformation. For any residues i and j, a radius edge is added if the distance between their Cα atoms is within d_{str}. We set $d_{str} = 8$ Å to capture spatially proximal interactions. (iii) K-Nearest Neighbor (KNN) Edges: Each residue is connected to its K=5 nearest neighbors in 3D space, ensuring graph connectivity while incorporating a broader local structural context.

For each residue, node features are extracted using ESM-2 [12]. The corresponding 3D structures are predicted by ESMFold [12]. The structural graph is encoded by a graph attention network (GAT), which learns adaptive attention weights to aggregate information from neighboring residues.

2.4 Motif-Guided Functional Enhancement

To incorporate biologically meaningful prior knowledge, we explicitly model functional motifs to guide representation learning. We construct a curated motif library, We utilized the MERCI tool to mine motifs that highly correlated with hemolytic or non-hemolytic activity across the dataset. To enrich this prior library, motifs were extracted using both standard scheme and the Koolman-Röhm classification scheme, which groups residues by their physicochemical properties, and reduce redundancy by retaining representative motifs. For a given sequence of length L, a binary mask vector is generated by scanning for exact motif matches: the i-th residue is assigned 1 if it falls within a matched motif interval, and 0 otherwise. This motif-aware representation is then integrated into the model as prior guidance.

The second step, also the most critical one, is to incorporate the extracted motif priors into the graph attention network. To this end, we introduce a motif-aware attention bias within the GAT architecture to explicitly enhance interactions among residues within the same motif fragment, thereby capturing functionally relevant local substructures. Specifically, when the binary mask vector values for residues i and j are both 1, and these residues further belong to the same motif region, an additional bias term b_{ij}^{motif} is added to the attention score calculation. Here, a motif region is defined as a contiguous fragment corresponding to one of the extracted motif patterns extracted from the first step. This bias increases the likelihood of information flow between biologically relevant residues. Formally, the attention coefficient α_{ij} is computed as:

$$\alpha_{ij} = \frac{\exp\left(\text{LeakyReLU}\left(\mathbf{a}^{\top}[\mathbf{W}\mathbf{h}_i \parallel \mathbf{W}\mathbf{h}_j]\right) + b_{ij}^{\text{motif}}\right)}{\sum_{k \in \mathcal{N}_i} \exp\left(\text{LeakyReLU}\left(\mathbf{a}^{\top}[\mathbf{W}\mathbf{h}_i \parallel \mathbf{W}\mathbf{h}_k]\right) + b_{ik}^{\text{motif}}\right)} \tag{1}$$

where $\mathbf{h}_i$ denotes the feature representation of residue i, $\mathbf{W}$ is a learnable weight matrix for linear feature transformation, $\boldsymbol{a}$ is the attention weight vector, $||$ denotes concatenation, and $\mathcal{N}_i$ is the set of neighbors of node i. The bias term b_{ij}^{motif} is set to two if residues i and j belong to the same motif, and zero otherwise.

2.5 Global Sequence Context Encoding

Although graph attention effectively captures local residue interactions, peptide functionality often depends on relationships between distant residues along the sequence. To complement the local structural modeling capability of the graph module, we introduce a global context aggregation model to capture long-range dependencies across the peptide sequence.

The model is implemented with a BiGRU network. Given a peptide of length L with residue embeddings $\mathbf{e}_1, \mathbf{e}_2, \ldots, \mathbf{e}_L$, the forward GRU processes the sequence from 1 to L, producing hidden states $\overrightarrow{\mathbf{h}}_i$, while the backward GRU processes from L to 1, producing $\overleftarrow{\mathbf{h}}_i$. The final hidden state for residue i is obtained by concatenating the two directional outputs: $\mathbf{h}_i = [\overrightarrow{\mathbf{h}}_i | \overleftarrow{\mathbf{h}}_i]$, thereby capturing both preceding and following contextual information. The resulting hidden states $\mathbf{h}_1, \ldots, \mathbf{h}_L$ are then passed through a projection layer to produce a compact sequence-level embedding for subsequent fusion.

To preserve original sequence-level information, we introduce a residual connection that complements the global contextual embedding. The fused representation is subsequently fed into a MLP classifier to predict whether the peptide is hemolytic or non-hemolytic.

2.6 Evaluation Metrics

We evaluate model performance using sensitivity (Sn), specificity (Sp), accuracy (Acc), Matthews correlation coefficient (MCC), and area under the ROC curve (AUC). Sn and Sp measure the ability to correctly identify hemolytic and non-hemolytic peptides, respectively. Accuracy reflects overall correctness, MCC provides a balanced measure for imbalanced data, and AUC evaluates discriminative ability across thresholds.

3 Results

In this section, we evaluate the proposed model for hemolytic peptide prediction. We first compare its performance with state-of-the-art methods on benchmark datasets, followed by analyses of different node representations and graph construction strategies. We further conduct ablation studies to assess the contribution of each component and analyze performance across varying lengths.

3.1 Comparison with Existing Methods

We evaluate the proposed method against state-of-the-art baselines on the independent test dataset. As shown in Table 1, our method achieves 82.5% accuracy and an MCC of 0.650, along with an AUC of 0.882. Compared to the strongest baseline, HEMOPI2 with random forest, Motif-Hemol consistently improves performance, particularly in MCC, a key metric for imbalanced classification. Notably, our method achieves a well-balanced trade-off between sensitivity and specificity, with a difference of only 4.1%.

When grouped by representation type, multi-modal methods consistently outperform single-modal approaches. Sequence-based methods, such as HEMOPI2 with random forest, perform best among their category, while structure-only methods lag behind. PLM-based methods achieve competitive

Table 1. Performance comparison of Motif-Hemol with state-of-the-art methods on the independent test dataset.

Peptide representation	Method	Configuration	Sp(%)	Sn(%)	Acc(%)	MCC	AUC
Sequence-based	HEMOPI [8]	D1	16.7	**90.8**	58.4	0.099	0.538
		D2	59.9	60.8	60.3	0.207	0.662
		ModelAll	49.2	69.8	58.8	0.194	0.669
	HemoPred [9]	Default	31.5	<u>87.0</u>	57.2	0.221	-
	Plisson et al. [26]	XGBC	69.0	61.4	70.0	0.470	0.740
	Ansari et al. [27]	Embedding + Bi-LSTM	73.3	32.3	54.5	0.07	0.512
	QSVM [28]	HemoPI-1	**92.7**	13.0	50.0	0.095	0.642
		HemoPI-2	73.2	49.8	60.6	0.234	0.701
		HemoPI-3	81.0	41.5	59.8	0.243	0.705
	HEMOPI2 (Without MERCI)	RF	76.5	86.9	<u>82.1</u>	<u>0.640</u>	**0.888**
	HEPAD [21]	Hmp2-RBF SVM	60.1	66.0	62.5	0.257	0.683
Structure-based	HAPPENN [16]	Main-dataset	53.7	84.9	68.1	0.402	0.736
PLM-based	AMPDeep	Prot-BERT- BFD	67.0	53.0	59.0	0.413	0.602
	HEMOPI2 (Without MERCI)	ESM2-t6	76.1	84.0	79.5	0.591	0.870
Multi-modal	ConsAMP- Hemo [18]	S1	46.9	59.2	52.6	0.611	0.518
		S2	56.0	60.9	58.3	0.169	0.620
	Motif-Hemol	ESM2-t33	<u>84.4</u>	80.3	**82.5**	**0.650**	<u>0.882</u>

Note: Bold values indicate the best performance, and underlined values indicate the second-best performance.

results but remain inferior to multi-modal models. These results highlight the complementary nature of different representations, which our method effectively integrates through motif-guided attention and global sequence modeling.

3.2 Effects of Representations and Graph Edges

To gain insight into the effectiveness of our model, we analyze the contribution of two key factors: node representations and graph edge construction strategies. The former examines the effect of different protein language models as residue-level node features, while the latter evaluates the necessity of each spatial edge type.

Node Feature Representations. Recent advances in protein language models (PLMs) have introduced a variety of architectures, pretraining strategies, and training corpora, each offering distinct advantages in capturing sequence-level features. To assess how different PLMs influence hemolytic peptide prediction within our graph-based framework, we compare four representative models: ESM2-t33, ProtT5, Ankh-Large, and ESMC-600M [11,29]. Each PLM is used to generate residue-level embeddings that serve as initial node features in the structural graph. As shown in Fig. 2, the comparison reveals that ESM2-t33 consistently outperforms the other PLMs, achieving the highest AUC and MCC. This suggests that ESM2-t33 produces more discriminative residue-level representations, which are critical for the subsequent graph attention mechanism to capture functionally relevant interactions.

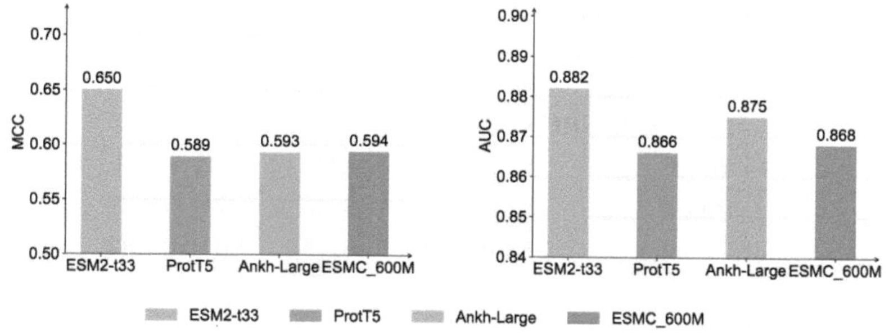

Fig. 2. Comparison of different protein language models for node feature representations in terms of MCC (left) and AUC (right).

Graph Edge Construction. While node features provide initial residue representations, graph edges determine how spatial and chemical information propagates across the peptide structure. Using ESM2-t33 as the backbone, we evaluate seven edge combinations to identify the most effective connectivity for hemolysis prediction. As shown in Fig. 3, the combination of sequential, radius, and KNN edges achieves the best performance.

The results reveal that incorporating spatial edges consistently improves performance over the Seq-only configuration, highlighting the importance of three-dimensional structural information in hemolytic activity prediction. This observation aligns with the biophysical understanding that hemolytic peptides exert their function through structural conformations rather than sequence alone [6].

Moreover, the three edge types provide complementary connectivity: sequential edges preserve backbone continuity, radius edges capture local spatial proximity, and KNN edges ensure balanced neighborhood construction across residues. The superior performance of the combined setting indicates that model-

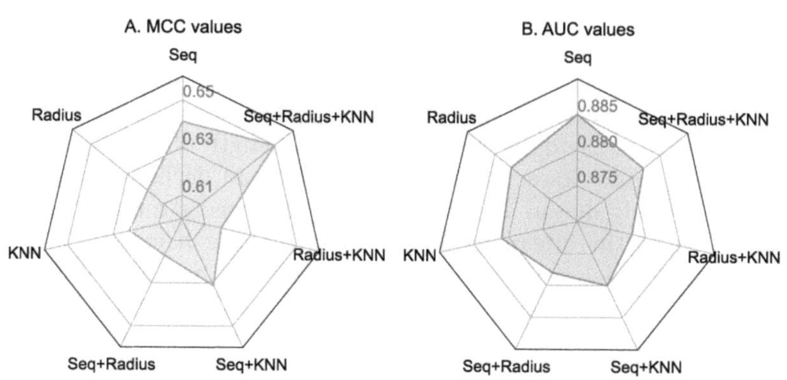

Fig. 3. Comparison of different graph edge construction strategies in terms of MCC (left) and AUC (right).

Table 2. Ablation study of the Motif-Hemol architecture

Configuration	Sp (%)	Sn (%)	Acc (%)	MCC	AUC
w/o Motif & BiGRU	82.5	78.1	80.5	0.607	0.860
w/o Motif	82.1	78.8	80.6	0.611	0.864
w/o BiGRU	82.5	77.7	80.3	0.604	0.877
Motif-Hemol	**84.4**	**80.3**	**82.5**	**0.650**	**0.882**

ing hemolytic activity benefits from integrating these complementary structural relationships.

3.3 Ablation Study of Model Components

We conducted ablation experiments to assess the contribution of the two core components in Motif-Hemol: the motif-guided functional enhancement module and the global sequence context encoding module. Starting from the full model (Motif-Hemol), we created three variants: (i) removing both modules (w/o Motif & BiGRU), (ii) removing only the motif-guided module (w/o Motif), and (iii) removing only the BiGRU module (w/o BiGRU).

As shown in Table 2, removing both modules leads to a substantial performance drop, with AUC decreasing from 0.882 to 0.860 and MCC from 0.650 to 0.607. Removing either component individually also results in clear degradation. Notably, the model without the motif-guided module achieves an AUC of 0.864 and MCC of 0.611, while the model without the BiGRU module achieves 0.877 and 0.604, respectively. These results indicate that both modules contribute to the overall performance.

3.4 Performance on Peptides of Varying Lengths

We further evaluated model performance across peptides of varying sequence lengths. As shown in Fig. 4, the model achieves the best performance on peptides with 10–20 residues, with an MCC of 0.72 and an AUC of 0.91, which aligns with both the majority of the dataset and the typical length of hemolytic peptides. Performance is slightly lower for shorter peptides and declines for longer ones (>30 residues), likely due to data scarcity and increased structural complexity. This trend reflects the inherent difficulty of predicting hemolytic activity for underrepresented and complex peptide classes rather than a limitation of the model itself.

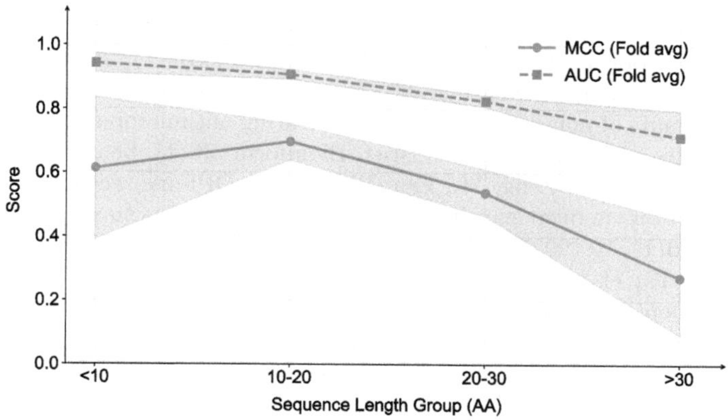

Fig. 4. Impact of sequence length on model predictive performance.

4 Conclusion

In this study, we proposed Motif-Hemol, a multi-modal framework for hemolytic peptide prediction that integrates sequence and structural information. The model consists of a motif-guided module that enhances interactions among functionally relevant residues and a bidirectional GRU that captures global sequence context and long-range dependencies. Ablation studies confirm the contribution of both components. Further analyses demonstrate the complementary role of different edge types and show that the model performs best on peptides of moderate length, consistent with the typical length distribution of hemolytic peptides. While the current motif integration strategy achieves performance gains, more effective approaches remain an important direction for future work.

Acknowledgments. This work was supported by the Hunan Provincial Natural Science Foundation of China (2025JJ60387). This study was also supported in part by the High-Performance Computing Center of Central South University.

Disclosure of Interests. The authors declare no conflict of interest.

References

1. Xiao, W., et al.: Advance in peptide-based drug development: delivery platforms, therapeutics and vaccines. Signal Transduct. Target. Ther. **10**(1), 74 (2025)
2. Lau, J.L., Dunn, M.K.: Therapeutic peptides: historical perspectives, current development trends, and future directions. Bioorganic Med. Chem. **26**(10), 2700–2707 (2018)
3. Vecchio, I., Tornali, C., Bragazzi, N.L., Martini, M.: The discovery of insulin: an important milestone in the history of medicine. Front. Endocrinol. **9**, 613 (2018)
4. Zheng, B., Wang, X., Guo, M., Tzeng, C.-M.: Therapeutic peptides: recent advances in discovery, synthesis, and clinical translation. Int. J. Mol. Sci. **26**(11), 5131 (2025)

5. Ma, X., et al.: A review of antimicrobial peptides: structure, mechanism of action, and molecular optimization strategies. Fermentation **10**(11), 540 (2024)
6. Kumar, A., Chadha, S., Sharma, M., Kumar, M.: Deciphering optimal molecular determinants of non-hemolytic, cell-penetrating antimicrobial peptides through bioinformatics and random forest. Brief. Bioinform. **26**(1), bbaf049 (2025)
7. Wang, W., Shuai, Y., Zeng, M., Fan, W., Li, M.: DPFunc: accurately predicting protein function via deep learning with domain-guided structure information. Nat. Commun. **16**(1), 70 (2025)
8. Chaudhary, K., et al.: A web server and mobile app for computing hemolytic potency of peptides. Sci. Rep. **6**(1), 22843 (2016)
9. Win, T.S., Malik, A.A., Prachayasittikul, V., Wikberg, J.E.S., Nantasenamat, H., Shoombuatong, W.: Hemopred: a web server for predicting the hemolytic activity of peptides. Future Med. Chem. **9**(3), 275–291 (2017)
10. Perveen, G., Alturise, F., Alkhalifah, T., Khan, Y.D.: Hemolytic-pred: a machine learning-based predictor for hemolytic proteins using position and composition-based features. Digital Health **9**, 20552076231180740 (2023)
11. Elnaggar, A., et al.: ProtTrans: toward understanding the language of life through self-supervised learning. IEEE Trans. Pattern Anal. Mach. Intell. **44**(10), 7112–7127 (2021)
12. Lin, Z., et al.: Evolutionary-scale prediction of atomic-level protein structure with a language model. Science **379**(6637), 1123–1130 (2023)
13. Hayes, T., et al.: Simulating 500 million years of evolution with a language model. Science **387**(6736), 850–858 (2025)
14. Salem, M., Arshadi, A.K., Yuan, J.S.: AMPDeep: hemolytic activity prediction of antimicrobial peptides using transfer learning. BMC Bioinform. **23**(1), 389 (2022)
15. Guntuboina, C., Das, A., Mollaei, P., Kim, S., Farimani, A.B.: PeptideBERT: a language model based on transformers for peptide property prediction. The Journal of Physical Chemistry Letters **14**(46), 10427–10434 (2023)
16. Timmons, P.B., Hewage, C.M.: Happenn is a novel tool for hemolytic activity prediction for therapeutic peptides which employs neural networks. Sci. Rep. **10**(1), 10869 (2020)
17. Baek, M., et al.: Accurate prediction of protein structures and interactions using a three-track neural network. Science **373**(6557), 871–876 (2021)
18. Xie, P., et al.: ConsAMPHemo: a computational framework for predicting hemolysis of antimicrobial peptides based on machine learning approaches. Protein Sci. **34**(7), e70087 (2025)
19. Yang, S., Piao, X.: HemoDL: hemolytic peptides prediction by double ensemble engines from rich sequence-derived and transformer-enhanced information. Anal. Biochem. **690**, 115523 (2024)
20. Vens, C., Rosso, M.-N., Danchin, E.G.J.: Identifying discriminative classification-based motifs in biological sequences. Bioinformatics **27**(9), 1231–1238 (2011)
21. Chen, S.-H., Jen-Chieh, Yu., Lin, Y.-H., Kuo, S.-C., Ni, K., Chen, C.-T.: HEPAD: enhancing hemolytic peptide prediction with adaptive feature engineering and diverse sequence descriptors. BMC Bioinform. **26**(1), 234 (2025)
22. Rathore, A.S., Kumar, N., Choudhury, S., Mehta, N.K., Raghava, G.P.S.: Prediction of hemolytic peptides and their hemolytic concentration. Commun. Biol. **8**(1), 176 (2025)
23. Pirtskhalava, M., et al.: DBAASP v3: database of antimicrobial/cytotoxic activity and structure of peptides as a resource for development of new therapeutics. Nucleic Acids Res. **49**(D1), D288–D297 (2021)

24. Gautam, A., et al.: Hemolytik: a database of experimentally determined hemolytic and non-hemolytic peptides. Nucleic Acids Res. **42**(D1), D444–D449 (2014)
25. Zhang, Z., et al.: Protein representation learning by geometric structure pretraining. arXiv preprint arXiv:2203.06125 (2022)
26. Plisson, F., Ramírez-Sánchez, O., Martínez-Hernández, C.: Machine learning-guided discovery and design of non-hemolytic peptides. Sci. Rep. **10**(1), 16581 (2020)
27. Ansari, M., White, A.D.: Serverless prediction of peptide properties with recurrent neural networks. J. Chem. Inf. Model. **63**(8), 2546–2553 (2023)
28. Kavitha, S.S., Kaulgud, N.: Quantum machine learning for support vector machine classification. Evol. Intell. **17**(2), 819–828 (2024)
29. Elnaggar, A., et al.: Ankh: optimized protein language model unlocks general-purpose modelling. arXiv preprint arXiv:2301.06568 (2023)

Identifying Nuclear Export Signals from Large-Scale Candidate Pools with a Deep Reranking Method

Zhixuan Piao, Xiaoyong Pan, and Hong-Bin Shen(✉)

Shanghai Jiao Tong University, Shanghai 200240, China
{piaozx2001,2008xypan,hbshen}@sjtu.edu.cn

Abstract. Nuclear export signals (NESs) are short peptide motifs that mediate CRM1/exportin-1-dependent nuclear export, but their computational prediction remains difficult because validated NESs are limited, diverse, and often hard to distinguish from NES-like hydrophobic segments. We formulate NES identification as a candidate retrieval and recommendation problem and propose a two-stage framework in which candidates are first generated by consensus-based matching and then re-ranked by a deep model. For second-stage training, we combine a biologically motivated hard label with an IoU-based soft label, enabling the model to learn both binary discrimination and spatial agreement with annotated NES regions. The reranking model integrates pretrained protein language model representations with local and global sequence-context modeling, and is optimized for top-ranked candidate prioritization under severe class imbalance. On the DUB dataset benchmark, our method achieved motif-level area under the receiver operating characteristic curve (AUROC) and average precision (AP) of 0.719 and 0.654, respectively, and outperformed reproduced baselines under a unified evaluation protocol at the candidate, protein, and motif levels. These results indicate that overlap-aware deep reranking provides an effective strategy for practical NES recommendation.

Keywords: Nuclear export signal · consensus matching · candidate reranking · protein language model

1 Introduction

Nuclear export signals (NESs) are short peptide motifs that mediate CRM1/exportin-1-dependent transport from the nucleus to the cytoplasm [8,14]. Because NES-dependent trafficking is involved in diverse processes such as transcriptional regulation, cell-cycle control, antiviral response, and tumor-related signaling [17], accurate NES identification is important for understanding protein localization and for guiding downstream functional studies.

Despite their biological importance, computational prediction of NESs remains difficult. Classical CRM1-dependent NESs are short hydrophobic motifs

X. Cui et al. (Eds.): ISBRA 2026, LNBI 16690, pp. 356–368, 2027.
https://doi.org/10.1007/978-981-92-3716-6_28

with variable spacers, whereas experimentally validated NESs are limited and highly diverse. Although several NES-related databases have collected experimentally supported CRM1 cargo proteins, the number of proteins with sufficiently precise and reliable NES annotations for model development remains limited [1,4,6,10,18]. Most existing predictors follow a two-step strategy: candidate retrieval by consensus templates or regular expressions, followed by statistical or machine-learning classification. Representative methods such as NetNES [2], NESsential [5], Wregex [15,16], NESmapper [9], and LocNES [19] have advanced the field, while NoLogo [12] further highlighted the diversity of NES patterns. Nevertheless, current methods still suffer from high false-positive rates and limited robustness across datasets.

In this work, we formulate NES identification as a candidate retrieval and recommendation problem and focus on a two-stage framework in which candidate NES segments are first generated by consensus-based matching and then reranked by a deep model. For second-stage training, we introduce both hard and soft supervision: the hard label is defined by the overlap between the biologically critical $\Phi 2$–$\Phi 4$ region and an annotated NES, whereas the soft label is defined by the intersection-over-union (IoU) between the full candidate segment and the annotated NES region. Based on these labels, we train a deep reranking model that combines pretrained protein language model ESM2 [13] representations with local and global sequence-context modeling, with particular emphasis on the quality of top-ranked recommendations rather than pure global ranking.

We evaluate our method on the benchmark set and compare it with representative previous predictors. Beyond motif-level benchmark performance, we also assess candidate-level discrimination and protein-level retrieval behavior, which are more directly relevant to practical NES recommendation. The results show that our method achieves competitive motif-level performance while strongly enriching true positives near the top of the ranked list. We further show, in a later Results and Discussion section, that some NES-containing proteins cannot be recovered by consensus matching, and we use an adapted A2KA module from NLSExplorer to explore whether attention-based proposal signals may help highlight non-canonical NES candidates missed by template-based retrieval [11]. This exploratory analysis is included only to illustrate the limitations of consensus-based recall and a possible direction for future improvement.

2 Methods

2.1 Datasets

Training Set. The training set was constructed following the LocNES data organization strategy, based on experimentally curated CRM1-cargo proteins collected from NESdb [18] and ValidNESs [4]. We used the accession list reported in the LocNES study as the primary starting point and further collected newer NESdb entries not covered by the original resource. To obtain a high-confidence set for second-stage training, we performed homology reduction with CD-HIT [3] at an 80% sequence identity threshold and excluded proteins with unreliable

NES annotations, including entries labeled as in doubt in NESdb or lacking explicit functional export signal annotation. The final training set contained 209 proteins with 255 annotated NES segments.

Benchmark Set. The DUB dataset [7] was used as the independent benchmark set. It contains 110 experimentally tested NES-related peptide segments from 56 deubiquitinases (DUBs), including 32 functional NES motifs and 78 non-functional motifs according to nuclear export assay annotations. Each tested peptide is 19–22 amino acids long, and the labels are defined at the motif/segment level. In our evaluation, the 32 functional motifs were treated as benchmark positives, whereas the 78 non-functional motifs were used as experimentally supported negatives. To avoid information leakage, the full-length benchmark sequences were collected and used to perform homology reduction on the training set. Homologous training proteins overlapping with the benchmark sequences were removed before model training. The DUB dataset was used only for independent testing and homology filtering, and was not involved in model training or hyperparameter selection.

2.2 Candidate Retrieval

We first retrieved NES candidate segments by regular-expression matching based on the modified Kosugi consensus patterns. Specifically, the following three consensus patterns were used: $\Phi1$-$X_{1,2,3}$-$\Phi2$-$[\hat{}W]_2$-$\Phi3$-$[\hat{}W]$-$\Phi4$; $\Phi1$-$X_{2,3}$-$\Phi2$-$[\hat{}W]_3$-$\Phi3$-$[\hat{}W]$-$\Phi4$; and $\Phi1$-X_2-$\Phi2$-X-$[\hat{}W]_2$-$\Phi3$-$[\hat{}W]_2$-$\Phi4$, where X denotes any amino acid, [^W] denotes any amino acid except Trp, and Ala or Thr is allowed once at either $\Phi1$ or $\Phi2$.

For each matched consensus pattern, a 15-aa candidate segment was constructed by aligning its C-terminus to the $\Phi4$ position. If fewer than 15 residues were available on the N-terminal side, the candidate segment was started from the first residue of the protein sequence. A candidate was regarded as positive if its $\Phi2$–$\Phi4$ interval overlapped an annotated NES region; otherwise, it was regarded as negative. This pipeline extracted 3,893 candidates (1,025 positives and 2,868 negatives) from 209 training proteins and 1,367 candidates (150 positives and 1,217 negatives) from the benchmark set.

2.3 Candidate Label Assignment

For second-stage training, we first assigned a hard binary label to each candidate segment following the definition used in LocNES. Specifically, a candidate was treated as positive if its $\Phi2 - \Phi4$ region overlapped an annotated NES region; otherwise, it was treated as negative. This hard label provides a biologically motivated binary supervision signal for candidate classification. In addition, we assigned each candidate an IoU-based soft label, defined as the maximum intersection-over-union (IoU) between the candidate segment and any annotated

NES region. This soft label was introduced to further reflect the degree of spatial agreement between a candidate and the ground-truth NES. Accordingly, the candidate set was supervised by both hard binary labels and IoU-based soft labels.

2.4 Deep Candidate Reranking Model

Model Architecture. The second-stage model was designed to score and rerank each candidate segment by integrating task-specific sequence features with pretrained protein language model representations. The overall architecture of the second-stage reranking model is illustrated in Fig. 1.

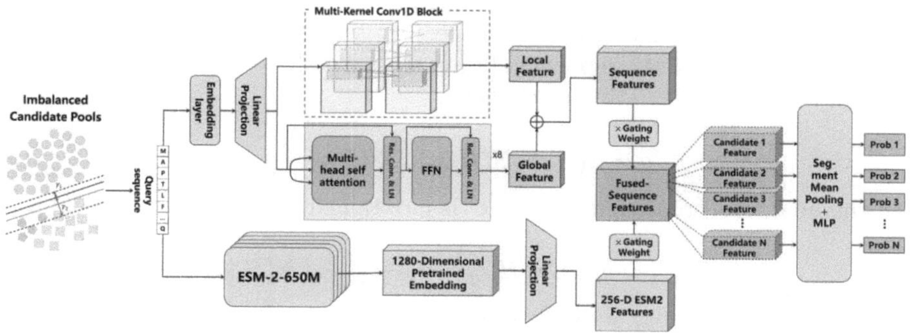

Fig. 1. Architecture of the second-stage candidate reranking model. The model combines local and global sequence-context features with projected ESM2 representations through competitive gated fusion, and then scores candidate NES segments by segment mean pooling followed by an MLP.

Given a protein sequence of length L, each residue was first tokenized and mapped through an embedding layer and a linear projection, yielding a residue-level sequence representation. Positional encoding was then added to preserve order information. Let x denote the input amino-acid token sequence, and let $X^{(0)} \in \mathbb{R}^{L\times d}$ denote the initial sequence representation.

$$X^{(0)} = \mathrm{PE}\big(W_{seq}(\mathrm{Emb}(x))\big) \quad (1)$$

where $\mathrm{Emb}(\cdot)$ denotes the amino-acid embedding layer, W_{seq} is a linear projection matrix, and $\mathrm{PE}(\cdot)$ denotes positional encoding.

To capture complementary contextual information, the sequence branch consisted of two parallel feature extraction modules. The local module comprised three parallel two-layer 1D convolutional branches with kernel sizes 3, 5, and 7, respectively, enabling the model to capture short-range residue patterns at different receptive fields. In parallel, the global module was implemented as an 8-layer multi-head Transformer encoder, which was used to model long-range dependencies across the full sequence. The outputs of the local and global modules, $H_{local} \in \mathbb{R}^{L\times d}$ and $H_{global} \in \mathbb{R}^{L\times d}$, were then summed element-wise to form the enhanced sequence representation $H_{seq} \in \mathbb{R}^{L\times d}$.

$$H_{local} = \mathrm{CNN}^3(X^{(0)}) + \mathrm{CNN}^5(X^{(0)}) + \mathrm{CNN}^7(X^{(0)}) \tag{2}$$

$$H_{seq} = H_{local} + \mathrm{Transformer}(X^{(0)}) \tag{3}$$

Instead of directly concatenating the high-dimensional ESM2 residue embeddings with the sequence-branch features, we first projected the pretrained language-model representations into the same hidden space as the sequence representation. Specifically, let $E_{esm} \in \mathbb{R}^{L\times d_{esm}}$ denote the precomputed residue-level ESM2 embedding and let $H_{esm} = W_{esm}(E_{esm}) \in \mathbb{R}^{L\times d}$ denote its projected representation in the shared hidden space. The sequence-derived representation and the projected ESM2 representation were normalized separately and fused through a competitive gating mechanism:

$$g = \sigma\big(W_g\big[\mathrm{LN}(H_{seq}); \mathrm{LN}(H_{esm})\big]\big) \tag{4}$$

and the final fused representation was then obtained by

$$H_{joint} = g \odot \mathrm{LN}(H_{seq}) + (1-g) \odot \mathrm{LN}(H_{esm}) \tag{5}$$

where $\sigma(\cdot)$ is the sigmoid activation function, $\mathrm{LN}(\cdot)$ denotes layer normalization, $[;]$ denotes channel-wise concatenation, and $\odot$ denotes element-wise multiplication. The gate $g \in \mathbb{R}^{L\times d}$ adaptively balances the contributions of the sequence and ESM2 feature streams.

This competitive fusion mechanism allows the model to determine, at each residue position and feature channel, whether the downstream decision should rely more heavily on task-specific sequence features or pretrained language-model representations. A post-fusion normalization layer was further applied to stabilize the fused features.

For each candidate segment $c = [s, e]$, the fused residue features within the segment boundaries were mean-pooled to obtain a fixed-length segment representation $Z_c \in \mathbb{R}^d$. The resulting segment-level representation was then fed into a multilayer perceptron to produce the final candidate score $\hat{p}_c$. Candidate segments from the same protein were ranked according to $\hat{p}_c$.

$$Z_c = \left(\frac{1}{e-s+1}\right)\sum_{i=s}^{e} H_{joint,i} \tag{6}$$

$$\hat{p}_c = \sigma\big(\mathrm{MLP}(Z_c)\big) \tag{7}$$

Training Objective and Optimization Strategy. The second-stage model was optimized using five-fold cross-validation with identical random initialization across folds. To make training difficulty comparable, we attempted to maintain a similar positive-to-negative candidate ratio across folds. Because the candidate pool still contained many irrelevant or weakly overlapping segments, training remained highly imbalanced and was dominated by easy negatives. To address this issue, we incorporated focal loss and dynamic positive re-weighting into the optimization design.

Let z_{pc} denote the logit of candidate c from protein p, and let $\hat{p}_{pc} = \sigma(z_{pc})$ denote the corresponding predicted score. To prevent proteins with many candidate segments from dominating optimization, losses were first averaged over candidates within each protein and then averaged across proteins in the mini-batch. For a mini-batch $\mathcal{B}$, the protein-balanced loss $\mathcal{L}$ was defined as

$$\mathcal{L} = \frac{1}{|\mathcal{B}|} \sum_{p \in \mathcal{B}} \frac{1}{|C_p|} \sum_{c \in C_p} w_{pc}\, \ell(z_{pc}, y_{pc}) \tag{8}$$

where C_p denotes the candidate set of protein p, y_{pc} the training target, w_{pc} the sample weight, and $\ell(\cdot)$ the focal loss with logits.

Instead of standard binary cross-entropy, we adopted a focal-style loss

$$\begin{aligned} \ell_{\mathrm{BCE}}(z, y) &= -y \log \sigma(z) - (1 - y) \log \big(1 - \sigma(z)\big) \\ \ell(z, y) &= \ell_{\mathrm{BCE}}(z, y) \cdot \big|y - \sigma(z)\big|^{\gamma} \end{aligned} \tag{9}$$

which is compatible with both binary hard labels and continuous IoU-based soft labels. Training was therefore performed jointly with the hard label $y^h_{pc} \in \{0, 1\}$ and the soft IoU label y^s_{pc}:

$$\mathcal{L}_{hard} = \frac{1}{|\mathcal{B}|} \sum_{p \in \mathcal{B}} \frac{1}{|C_p|} \sum_{c \in C_p} w^h_{pc}\, \ell(z_{pc}, y^h_{pc}) \tag{10}$$

$$\mathcal{L}_{soft} = \frac{1}{|\mathcal{B}|} \sum_{p \in \mathcal{B}} \frac{1}{|C_p|} \sum_{c \in C_p} w^s_{pc}\, \ell(z_{pc}, y^s_{pc}) \tag{11}$$

$$\mathcal{L}_{scan} = \mathcal{L}_{hard} + \lambda_{soft} \mathcal{L}_{soft} \tag{12}$$

To further emphasize informative candidates, we applied a positive-oriented reweighting strategy in which candidates whose soft labels exceeded a predefined IoU threshold were assigned larger weights, while the others retained unit weight. In this formulation, γ controls the suppression of easy examples in focal loss, λ_{soft} controls the contribution of the soft-supervision branch, and the positive weight is set in a fold-specific manner according to the positive-to-negative candidate ratio. The loss-related hyperparameters, including γ and λ_{soft}, were selected by Optuna-based hyperparameter search according to validation AP. The individual effects of focal loss and dynamic reweighting are analyzed in the ablation study.

The model was optimized using Adam. The initial learning rate, batch size, maximum epoch number, dropout rate, and early-stopping patience were treated as tunable hyperparameters and selected according to validation AP. During training, a ReduceLROnPlateau scheduler monitored validation AP and reduced the learning rate by a tunable factor when performance plateaued, with a lower bound of 10^{-6}. Early stopping was also based on validation AP, and the checkpoint with the best validation AP was used for final evaluation. Unless otherwise specified, the same hyperparameter selection strategy and training procedure were used for all ablation variants to ensure fair comparison. All experiments were implemented in PyTorch 2.0.0 and conducted on an NVIDIA RTX 3090 GPU.

2.5 Evaluation Metrics

Benchmark performance was evaluated at three complementary levels: candidate, protein, and motif.

Candidate-Level Metrics. At the candidate level, binary reference labels were assigned according to Sect. 2.2. Based on the candidate scores produced by the second-stage reranking model, we reported Average Precision (AP) and Area Under the Receiver Operating Characteristic Curve (AUROC). AP is particularly informative under severe class imbalance, whereas AUROC measures overall ranking performance across all thresholds.

Protein-Level Metrics. At the protein level, candidate segments for each protein were ranked by predicted score. Evaluation was restricted to proteins containing at least one annotated NES. For a given k, the top-k candidates of each protein were selected, and we reported *Hit@k* and *Recall@k* with $k \in \{1, 3, 5\}$. In the current implementation, a predicted candidate was regarded as covering an annotated NES only when its $\Phi2 - \Phi4$ region overlapped the annotated NES region.

Let P denote the set of proteins containing at least one annotated NES, let G_p denote the set of annotated NESs for protein p, and let $\mathrm{Top}_k(p)$ denote the top-k predicted candidate segments for protein p. Under the above overlap criterion, protein-level *Hit@k* and *Recall@k* were defined as

$$\mathrm{ov}(c, g) = \mathbf{1}\big(|c \cap g| > 0\big) \tag{13}$$

$$\mathrm{Hit@}k = \frac{1}{|P|} \sum_{p \in P} \mathbf{1}\left(\sum_{g \in G_p} \mathbf{1}\Big(\max_{c \in \mathrm{Top}_k(p)} \mathrm{ov}(c, g) = 1 \Big) > 0 \right) \tag{14}$$

$$\mathrm{Recall@}k = \frac{\sum_{p \in P} \sum_{g \in G_p} \mathbf{1}\big(\max_{c \in \mathrm{Top}_k(p)} \mathrm{ov}(c, g) = 1 \big)}{\sum_{p \in P} |G_p|} \tag{15}$$

Motif-Level Metrics. At the motif level, each predicted candidate was assigned, when possible, to the single annotated motif with which it achieved the largest IoU, provided that this maximum IoU was greater than zero. The score of each motif was defined as the highest predicted score among its assigned candidates; motifs without any assigned candidate were given a score of zero. AUROC and AP were then computed from the resulting motif-level scores and labels to assess whether functional motifs could be ranked ahead of negative or decoy motifs.

3 Results and Discussion

3.1 Overall Performance on the DUB Dataset Benchmark

The DUB dataset is the independent benchmark originally used in the LocNES study and therefore provides the most direct reference for evaluating our method against previous NES predictors. However, published results on this dataset were mainly reported at the motif level for LocNES, NESsential, and Wregex. Therefore, direct comparison with previously reported benchmark results was restricted to the motif level, whereas a reproduced multi-level comparison was additionally performed for methods that could be reevaluated under our unified setting.

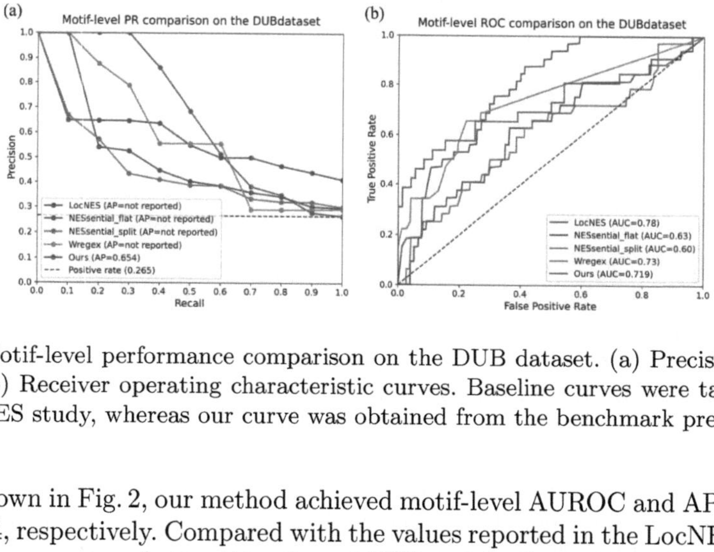

Fig. 2. Motif-level performance comparison on the DUB dataset. (a) Precision–recall curves. (b) Receiver operating characteristic curves. Baseline curves were taken from the LocNES study, whereas our curve was obtained from the benchmark predictions.

As shown in Fig. 2, our method achieved motif-level AUROC and AP of 0.719 and 0.654, respectively. Compared with the values reported in the LocNES study, this performance was better than that of NESsential_flat and NESsential_split, but remained below the reported LocNES and Wregex results. Thus, in terms of overall motif-level ranking, our model remained slightly inferior to the strongest published baselines.

However, practical NES prediction is not determined solely by global ranking quality. With a positive rate of 0.265, the motif-level AP of 0.654 corresponds to an approximately 2.47-fold improvement over the random baseline, indicating substantial enrichment of functional motifs near the top of the ranked list. This observation is consistent with the low-recall region of the PR curve and the low-FPR region of the ROC curve, suggesting favorable head-ranking behavior for recommendation-oriented use.

Table 1. Reproduced multi-level comparison under our unified evaluation protocol on the DUB dataset

Method	Candidate		Hit			Recall			Motif	
	AUROC	AP	@1	@3	@5	@1	@3	@5	AUROC	AP
NESmapper	0.634	0.108	0.350	0.500	0.600	0.269	**0.462**	0.538	0.655	0.418
NoLogo	0.567	0.047	0.250	0.300	0.350	0.192	0.269	0.308	0.514	0.330
Wregex3.0	0.587	0.296	0.350	0.550	0.600	0.269	0.500	0.538	0.605	0.404
Ours	**0.789**	**0.332**	**0.450**	**0.600**	**0.750**	**0.346**	**0.462**	**0.654**	**0.719**	**0.654**

To complement the published motif-level comparison, Table 1 summarizes a reproduced comparison under our unified evaluation setting. Under this setting, our method achieved the best candidate-level AUROC and AP, the best protein-level $Hit@1, 3, 5$, and the best motif-level AUROC and AP among the reproduced baselines, while matching the best reproduced *Recall*@3. These results indicate that our method provides stronger candidate discrimination, better top-ranked protein retrieval, and better motif-level prioritization than the reproduced alternatives.

Overall, the DUB dataset benchmark suggests that our method remains competitive at the published motif level and, more importantly, is well suited to practical NES recommendation.

3.2 Ablation Study

To investigate the contribution of different components in the second-stage reranking model, we conducted an ablation study in which the first-stage candidates were fixed to those generated by consensus matching and only the second-stage training strategy was varied. Specifically, we compared five variants: A1 with hard labels only, A2 with hard and soft supervision, A3 with focal loss added to A2, A4 with both focal loss and dynamic weighting, and A5 with dynamic weighting only.

The ablation results provide quantitative evidence for the contribution of each training component. Compared with hard-label supervision alone (A1), introducing IoU-based soft supervision (A2) improved candidate-level AUROC by 0.010, Hit@1 by 0.060, Recall@1 by 0.046, and motif-level AP by 0.010. These results indicate that overlap-aware soft labels provide useful ranking information beyond binary discrimination.

On top of A2, adding focal loss (A3) further improved the quality of top-ranked recommendations, increasing Hit@1 by 0.040, Recall@1 by 0.031, and candidate-level AP by 0.019. In contrast, dynamic weighting alone (A5) achieved better global ranking metrics at the candidate and motif levels, but did not outperform A3 on top-k recommendation metrics. Combining focal loss and dynamic weighting (A4) did not bring additional gains, suggesting that these two imbalance-oriented strategies are not simply additive (Table 2).

Table 2. Ablation study of the second-stage reranking model. The first-stage consensus-matching candidates were fixed across all variants, and only the supervision and imbalance-aware training strategies were varied.

Variant	Candidate		Hit			Recall			Motif	
	AUROC	AP	@1	@3	@5	@1	@3	@5	AUROC	AP
A1	0.822 ±0.030	0.265 ±0.069	0.360 ±0.107	0.670 ±0.051	0.730 ±0.040	0.277 ±0.082	0.546 ±0.038	0.631 ±0.031	0.699 ±0.024	0.518 ±0.066
A2	0.832 ±0.011	0.269 ±0.041	0.420 ±0.075	**0.690** ±0.049	0.780 ±0.040	0.323 ±0.058	**0.577** ±0.042	**0.685** ±0.045	0.709 ±0.010	0.528 ±0.060
A3	0.823 ±0.016	0.288 ±0.054	**0.460** ±0.058	**0.690** ±0.074	**0.790** ±0.020	**0.354** ±0.045	0.562 ±0.058	**0.685** ±0.015	0.707 ±0.008	0.553 ±0.049
A4	0.822 ±0.039	0.266 ±0.027	0.380 ±0.068	0.670 ±0.060	0.750 ±0.045	0.292 ±0.052	0.546 ±0.038	0.654 ±0.034	0.713 ±0.034	0.527 ±0.023
A5	**0.845** ±0.026	**0.294** ±0.050	0.420 ±0.068	0.650 ±0.071	0.720 ±0.040	0.323 ±0.052	0.554 ±0.067	0.639 ±0.039	**0.718** ±0.023	**0.570** ±0.066

Overall, these results suggest that the main improvements in the second-stage reranking model come from overlap-aware soft supervision and imbalance-aware optimization. Since practical NES recommendation emphasizes the accuracy of top-ranked candidates, we selected A3 as the final configuration because it achieved the best top-ranked recommendation performance while maintaining competitive AP and AUROC.

3.3 A Supplementary Exploration of Attention-Based Candidate Discovery

Although our method showed competitive reranking performance, we observed that some NES-containing proteins could not be recalled by consensus matching under any reasonable parameter setting. In such cases, second-stage reranking becomes ineffective because no biologically relevant candidate is provided to the scorer. This limitation may reflect a broader discovery bias in NES research: existing consensus rules are derived from previously annotated NESs and therefore tend to favor signals resembling already known patterns. As a result, non-canonical NESs may be systematically under-recalled (Table 3).

Motivated by this observation, we performed a supplementary exploration using the A2KA module originally introduced in NLSExplorer [11]. After adapting it to the NES task, we pretrained A2KA in a weakly supervised manner

Table 3. Failure cases of consensus matching under top-$k = 999$.

Protein	Consensus candidates	Annotated NES	Recovered
A0A1W5HKL7	$(43, 57), (92, 106), (103, 117), \ldots$	$(77, 91)$	No
A0A1W5HLB9	$(1, 12), (11, 25), (42, 56), (157, 171), \ldots$	$(76, 90)$	No
P56693	$(78, 92), (99, 113), (148, 162), \ldots$	$(134, 145)$	No

on Swiss-Prot proteins, where proteins annotated with both nuclear and cytoplasmic localization were treated as positives and the remaining proteins as negatives. The resulting checkpoint was then applied to full-length proteins to generate residue-level attention response vectors. We found that these attention scores could in some cases highlight annotated NES regions even when consensus matching failed to recover meaningful candidates. Representative examples are shown in Fig. 3. In particular, for the three proteins shown in Fig. 3(d)–(f), consensus matching generated candidate segments, but none overlapped the annotated NES region even under a highly permissive setting (top-k = 999).

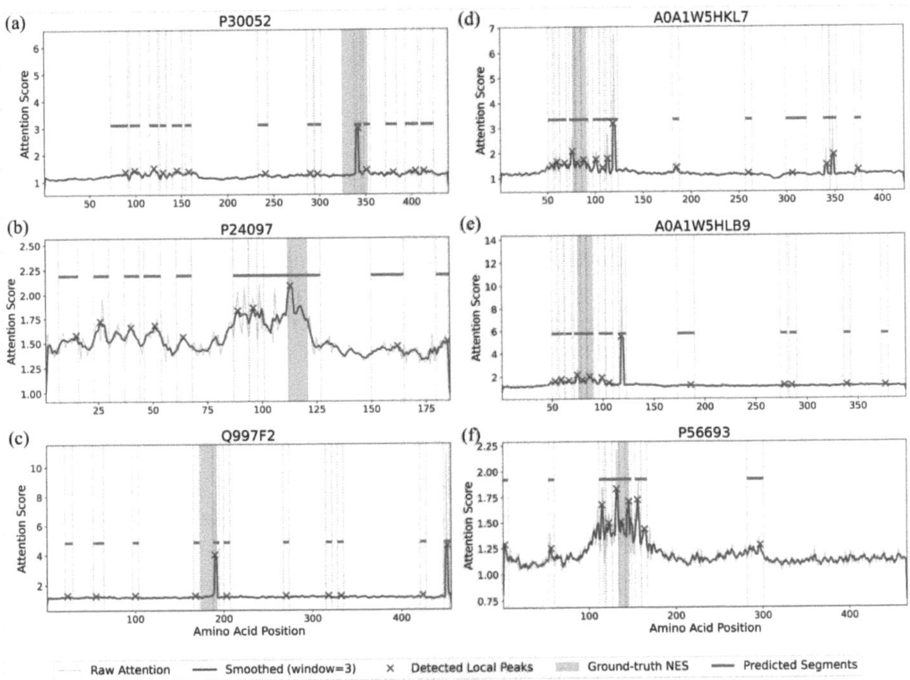

Fig. 3. Representative local attention peak profiles of the adapted A2KA model on NES-containing proteins. Panels (a)–(c) show cases in which local attention peaks align with annotated NES regions, whereas panels (d)–(f) show proteins whose annotated NESs were not recovered by consensus matching but were still highlighted by A2KA-derived local peaks.

Although this analysis does not yet provide a validated replacement for consensus-based candidate retrieval, it suggests that attention-based proposal signals may offer a complementary route for identifying non-canonical NES candidates. This exploratory result points to a promising future direction: using learning-based proposal models to complement consensus matching when template-based recall is intrinsically limited.

4 Conclusion

In this work, we presented a recommendation-oriented framework for NES identification that combines consensus-based candidate retrieval with deep reranking. By introducing overlap-aware dual supervision, the model can better prioritize biologically relevant candidates in a highly imbalanced search space. Experimental results on the DUB dataset showed that our method remained competitive at the published motif level and achieved strong candidate-level and protein-level retrieval performance. Our ablation study further showed that IoU-based soft supervision consistently improved performance, while focal loss was particularly helpful for enhancing top-ranked recommendations. These findings support deep reranking with biologically grounded supervision as an effective strategy for practical NES prediction.

We also found that some annotated NESs may remain unrecovered by consensus matching even when downstream reranking is effective. Exploratory analysis with an adapted A2KA module suggested that learning-based proposal signals may help identify candidate regions missed by template-based retrieval, especially for potentially non-canonical NESs. This points to a promising direction for future work.

References

1. la Cour, T., Gupta, R., Rapacki, K., Skriver, K., Poulsen, F.M., Brunak, S.: NESbase version 1.0: a database of nuclear export signals. Nucleic Acids Res. **31**(1), 393–396 (2003)
2. la Cour, T., Kiemer, L., Mølgaard, A., Gupta, R., Skriver, K., Brunak, S.: NetNES: analysis and prediction of leucine-rich nuclear export signals. Protein Eng. Des. Sel. **17**(6), 527–536 (2004)
3. Fu, L., Niu, B., Zhu, Z., Wu, S., Li, W.: CD-HIT: accelerated for clustering the next-generation sequencing data. Bioinformatics **28**(23), 3150–3152 (2012)
4. Fu, S.C., Huang, H.C., Horton, P., Juan, H.F.: ValidNESs: a database of validated leucine-rich nuclear export signals. Nucleic Acids Res. **41**(D1), D338–D343 (2013)
5. Fu, S.C., Imai, K., Horton, P.: Prediction of leucine-rich nuclear export signal containing proteins with NESsential. Nucleic Acids Res. **39**(16), e111 (2011)
6. Fung, H.Y.J., Niesman, A., Chook, Y.M.: An update to the CRM1 cargo/NES database NESdb. Mol. Biol. Cell **32**(6), 467–469 (2021)
7. García-Santisteban, I., Bañuelos, S., Rodríguez, J.A.: A global survey of CRM1-dependent nuclear export sequences in the human deubiquitinase family. Biochem. J. **441**(1), 209–217 (2012)
8. Görlich, D., Kutay, U.: Transport between the cell nucleus and the cytoplasm. Annu. Rev. Cell Dev. Biol. **15**, 607–660 (1999)
9. Kosugi, S., Yanagawa, H., Terauchi, R., Tabata, S.: NESmapper: accurate prediction of leucine-rich nuclear export signals using activity-based profiles. PLoS Comput. Biol. **10**(9), e1003841 (2014)
10. Lee, Y., Baumhardt, J.M., Pei, J., Chook, Y.M., Grishin, N.V.: pCRM1exportome: database of predicted CRM1-dependent nuclear export signal (NES) motifs in cancer-related genes. Bioinformatics **36**(3), 961–963 (2019)

11. Li, Y.F., Pan, X., Shen, H.B.: Discovering the nuclear localization signal universe through a deep learning model with interpretable attention units. Patterns **6**(6), 101262 (2025)
12. Liku, M.E., Legere, E.A., Moses, A.M.: NoLogo: a new statistical model highlights the diversity and suggests new classes of CRM1-dependent nuclear export signals. BMC Bioinform. **19**(1), 65 (2018)
13. Lin, Z., Akin, H., Rao, R., et al.: Evolutionary-scale prediction of atomic-level protein structure with a language model. Science **379**(6637), 1123–1130 (2023). https://doi.org/10.1126/science.ade2574
14. Pemberton, L.F., Paschal, B.M.: Mechanisms of receptor-mediated nuclear import and nuclear export. Traffic **6**(3), 187–198 (2005)
15. Prieto, G., Fullaondo, A., Rodriguez, J.A.: Prediction of nuclear export signals using weighted regular expressions (Wregex). Bioinformatics **30**(9), 1220–1227 (2014)
16. Prieto, G., Rodríguez, J.A., Fullaondo, A.: Enhancing prediction of short linear protein motifs with Wregex 3.0. Comput. Struct. Biotechnol. J. **23**, 2978–2984 (2024)
17. Turner, J.G., Dawson, J., Sullivan, D.M.: Nuclear export of proteins and drug resistance in cancer. Biochem. Pharmacol. **83**(8), 1021–1032 (2012)
18. Xu, D., Grishin, N.V., Chook, Y.M.: NESdb: a database of NES-containing CRM1 cargoes. Mol. Biol. Cell **23**(18), 3673–3676 (2012)
19. Xu, D., et al.: LocNES: a computational tool for locating classical NESs in CRM1 cargo proteins. Bioinformatics **31**(9), 1357–1365 (2015)

Identifying Spatial Domains via Hierarchical Fusion of Multi-scale Biological Priors

Zhihao Ping[1], Wei Peng[1(✉)], Wei Dai[1], Xingyu Zhou[1], Xiaodong Fu[1], Wei Lan[2], Li Liu[1], and Lijun Liu[1]

[1] Faculty of Information Engineering and Automation, Kunming University of Science and Technology, Kunming 650050, China
weipeng@kust.edu.cn

[2] Guangxi Key Laboratory of Multimedia Communications and Network Technology, Guangxi University, Nanning 530004, China

Abstract. Spatial domain identification in spatial transcriptomics using deep learning models has great potential for revealing the spatial distribution of cells and gene expression patterns within tissues, thereby facilitating the understanding of complex biological processes and disease mechanisms. However, cell populations with similar functions in tissues often form stable spatial structures through complex molecular regulation and intercellular interactions. Therefore, spatial domain identification requires the integration of multi-scale information, including gene expression regulation, cell–cell interactions, and tissue structural organization. To address this challenge, we propose SpaMBP, a multi-view contrastive learning framework with hierarchical node representation learning that integrates multi-scale biological information. SpaMBP systematically models spatial transcriptomics data from three complementary levels: gene scale, microscopic scale, and macroscopic scale. We evaluate SpaMBP on several spatial transcriptomics datasets, including the human dorsolateral prefrontal cortex and human breast cancer datasets. Experimental results demonstrate that, in most cases, SpaMBP out-performs other state-of-the-art methods. The code and data are available at: https://github.com/weiba/SpaMBP.

Keywords: Spatial Transcriptomics · Spatial Domain Identification · Multi-scale Biological Prior Modeling · Hierarchical Representation Learning

1 Introduction

Spatial transcriptomics (ST) has emerged as a transformative frontier in biomedical research, transcending the limitations of traditional transcriptomics by shifting the focus from "what genes are expressed" to "where they are expressed" within the native tissue architecture. By mapping molecular profiles to precise anatomical coordinates, ST facilitates the construction of spatially resolved maps that delineate cell types and their distinct molecular characteristics. This spatial context is vital for deciphering the functional organization of biological systems, such as the mapping of complex neural circuits

X. Cui et al. (Eds.): ISBRA 2026, LNBI 16690, pp. 369–380, 2027.
https://doi.org/10.1007/978-981-92-3716-6_29

in neuroscience or the elucidation of spatiotemporal dynamics in developmental biology [1]. Furthermore, characterizing spatial tissue organization is essential for understanding disease pathology, including tumor heterogeneity and the intricate interactions within the immune microenvironment, thereby laying the foundation for novel clinical diagnostics and therapeutic strategies [2].

The rapid evolution of high-resolution platforms—such as 10x Genomics Visium, Stereoseq, and fluorescence in situ hybridization (FISH)—has generated large-scale datasets with single-cell or near-single-cell resolution [3–6]. These resources have catalyzed the development of sophisticated computational methods for spatial domain identification, which typically integrate spatial coordinates, gene expression profiles, and histological image information. Modern frameworks often employ a multi-stage approach, modeling cells as graph nodes connected by spatial proximity or transcriptional similarity before utilizing deep learning architectures like Graph Neural Networks (GNNs) or Transformers to learn low-dimensional feature representations [7–12]. To refine these embeddings, self-supervised strategies such as masked feature reconstruction and contrastive learning are frequently employed to capture both local neighborhood contexts and global relationships [13–16].

Despite their performance across various datasets, existing computational approaches often struggle to jointly model multi-level biological information or incorporate explicit prior knowledge. Many models rely strictly on data-driven metrics like Euclidean distance or gene co-expression, rarely accounting for established signaling pathways or functional constraints. Furthermore, feature modeling typically fluctuates between using only highly variable genes or full expression profiles, which can make it difficult to balance local variation with global regulatory patterns. This reliance on "flat" modeling structures often fails to capture the inherent hierarchy of biological systems, which naturally span from gene-level regulation to micro-scopic cellular interaction networks and macroscopic tissue-level functional regions.

To address these structural and functional gaps, this study introduces a multi-view contrastive learning framework that integrates multi-scale biological priors across gene, cellular, and tissue levels. We incorporate Hallmark signaling pathways and ligand-receptor-based communication signals into the spatial relationship modeling to ensure that node connections reflect both transcriptional consistency and functional interactions. By employing a prototype learning mechanism with hierarchical node fusion, the model softly aggregates fine-grained node representations into coarse-grained prototypes to capture high-level semantic structures. In summary, the contributions of this paper are as follows:

1. We propose a novel framework that transcends "flat" modeling by integrating multi-scale biological priors, enabling hierarchical representation across gene-level regulation, cellular interaction networks, and macroscopic tissue regions.
2. We incorporate signaling pathways and cell communication into spatial relationship modeling, ensuring node embeddings reflect functional biological mechanisms.
3. Validation on DLPFC and human breast cancer datasets demonstrates that our method significantly outperforms existing approaches, identifying spatially cohesive domains with higher biological accuracy.

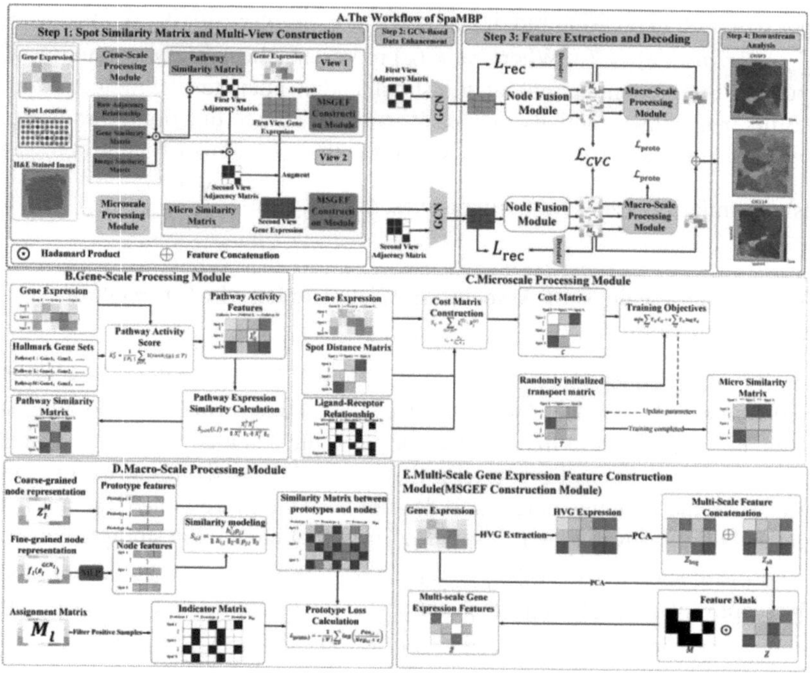

Fig. 1. The framework of the SpaMBP model.

2 Methods

Figure 1 illustrates that the SpaMBP framework identifies spatial domains through four integrated stages. Initially, the model constructs multi-view spot association matrices by fusing gene-level and microscopic-scale information, incorporating tissue images, gene expression, and spatial coordinates. Secondly, a single-layer GCN aggregates neighborhood information to enhance node feature representations. The third stage employs a hierarchical node fusion module with a sparse attention mechanism, generating fine-to-coarse assignment matrices alongside multi-scale node representations. A macroscopic-scale module subsequently learns prototypes to capture tissue-level functional characteristics, while a linear decoder reconstructs the expression matrix. SpaMBP is trained by jointly optimizing reconstruction, cross-view contrastive, and prototype learning losses. Finally, the Leiden algorithm is applied to the concatenated row vectors of the assignment matrices from the two views to delineate spatially distinct domains.

2.1 Gene-Scale Spot Association Matrix Construction

To construct the gene-scale spot association matrix, we utilize the Hallmark gene sets from MSigDB as a functional prior. Given spatial transcriptomics data $X \in \mathbb{R}^{N \times G}$ and a pathway set $P = \{P_1, P_2, \ldots, P_K\}$, where N and G denote the number of spots and genes, respectively, $K = 50$. We employ AUCell 17 to quantify pathway activity within each spot. This method calculates a relative activity score for the k-th pathway in the

i-th spot based on expression rankings, ensuring scale-insensitivity, defined as: $X_{ik}^P = \frac{1}{|P_k|}\sum_{g\in P_k}\mathbb{I}(rank_i(g) \leq T)$. Where $rank_i(g)$ represents the expression ranking of gene g in spot i, T is a predefined ranking threshold, and $\mathbb{I}(\cdot)$ denotes the indicator function. This results in a pathway activity matrix $X^P \in \mathbb{R}^{N\times K}$. Since functional similarity often aligns with shared pathway activation, we define the spot similarity matrix S_{path} using the cosine similarity of these activity profiles: $S_{path}(i,j) = \frac{X_i^P X_j^{P^\top}}{\|X_i^P\|_2 \cdot \|X_j^P\|_2}$.

2.2 Microscopic-Scale Spot Association Construction via Intercellular Communication

To quantify intercellular signaling, we adopt COMMOT 18, which utilizes an optimal transport framework to model ligand-receptor interactions while incorporating spatial proximity. For a given set of ligand–receptor pairs, the potential signaling capability of each cell as both a sender and a receiver is first calculated based on gene expression data. For each spot i, the signaling potential is derived from the expression of ligands L_i in the i-th spot and the receptor of the j-th spot R_j. The initial interaction strength between the spot i and j is defined as: $S_{ij} = \sum_{(l,r)\in\mathcal{P}} L_i^{(l)} \cdot R_j^{(r)}$. Where P denotes the set of known ligand–receptor pairs. COMMOT then solves for the optimal cell–cell transport matrix T by minimizing the following objective: $\underset{T}{min}\sum_{i,j} T_{ij}C_{ij} + \varepsilon\sum_{i,j} T_{ij}logT_{ij}$, $C_{ij} = \frac{d_{ij}}{S_{ij}+\epsilon}$. The cost matrix C_{ij} is constructed using spatial distances d_{ij} and the interaction strength, ε is the entropy regularization coefficient and ϵ is a small constant to prevent division by zero. The resulting matrix T is defined as the microscopic-scale association matrix S_{Micro}, representing the functional interaction between spots.

2.3 Multi-view Construction and Node Feature Enhancement

First View Construction and Node Feature Enhancement. The first view integrates transcriptomic, spatial, and histological data to construct a robust adjacency matrixa1. This process involves computing three similarity matrices.

The gene similarity matrix, S_{gene}, is constructed by computing the cosine similarity between spots using the top 50 principal components derived from the full expression profile. The histological similarity matrix, S_{image}, is constructed by calculating the cosine similarity between 128-dimensional image feature vectors. These features are extracted from spot-centered image patches using a pre-trained Vision Transformer (ViT) and subsequently refined via Principal Component Analysis (PCA) to retain the top 128 components. We construct the spatial neighborhood relationship matrix A based on the spot center coordinates. An element of A is set to 1, if the distance between two spots is less than a threshold $2r$, and 0 otherwise. The neighborhood radius, r, is determined by calculating the mean of the Euclidean distances to the six nearest neighbors for every spot across the entire dataset. Finally, the integrated similarity matrix, S_1, is defined via the Hadamard product of the aforementioned three similarity matrices and the pathway activity similarity, defined as: $S_1 = S_{gene} \odot S_{image} \odot A \odot S_{path}$.

We then select the 20 nearest neighbors for each spot to form the adjacency matrix A_1 of the first view. To enhance the signal, we compute an augmented gene expression matrix

X_1^{aug} by aggregating neighboring features: $X_1^{aug} = X + \sum_{i=1}^{k} X_{A_1}^i$. Where k denotes the number of neighboring nodes. To balance the local variation of highly variable genes (HVGs) with global expression patterns, we construct multi-scale feature representations for each spot. Using the Seurat-v3 method via the Scanpy package, we identify the top 3,000 HVGs from the original gene expression matrix X. The augmented matrix X_1^{aug} is log-transformed and normalized to obtain $X_1^{aug\_n}$, from which we extract the HVG expression matrix $X_{HVG1}^{aug\_n} \in R^{N\times 3000}$. To reduce noise and dimensionality, PCA is applied to both the full expression matrix Z_{all1} and the HVG matrix Z_{hvg1}: $Z_{all1} = PCA(X_1^{aug\_n}) \in R^{N\times d_1}$, $Z_{hvg1} = PCA(X_{HVG1}^{aug\_n}) \in R^{N\times d_2}$. Where the output dimensions d_1 and d_2 are both set to 500. These low-dimensional features are concatenated to form the multi-scale node features: $Z_1 = [Z_{all1} \| Z_{hvg1}] \in R^{N\times(d_1+d_2)}$.

Finally, to support self-supervised contrastive learning, we apply a random masking operation with a probability $p = 0.4$, where the mask is sampled from a Bernoulli distribution and applied via element-wise multiplication to obtain $\tilde{Z}_1$, which serves as the initial input for the encoder.

Second View Construction and Node Feature Enhancement. The second view focuses on functional clustering and intercellular interactions. We first apply the Leiden algorithm to the first view's augmented features X_1^{aug} to generate a clustering similarity matrix $S_{cluster}$, where $S_{cluster}^{i,j} = 1$ if spots i and j share a cluster. The second view's similarity matrix is constructed as: $S_2 = S_1 \odot S_{cluster} \odot S_{Micro}$. Where S_{Micro} represents the microscopic-scale spot association matrix. Following the same pipeline as the first view, based on the similarity matrix S_2, we construct a 20-nearest-neighbor adjacency matrix A_2 of the second view and produce the augmented gene expression X_2^{aug}.

$$A_2 = \begin{cases} 1, if \left(S_2^{ij}(i,j) \in max_{20}\left(S_2^i\right)\right) \\ 0, others \end{cases} \quad (1)$$

$$X_2^{aug} = X + \sum_{i=1}^{k} X_{A_2}^i \quad (2)$$

Following the same strategy as in the first view, we perform log-transformation and normalization on the augmented expression matrix X_2^{aug} to derive the multi-scale feature matrix Z_2. This integrates the top 500 principal components from both the full expression and the identified highly variable genes. Finally, a random masking operation is applied with a probability of $p = 0.2$ to generate the initial input feature matrix $\widetilde{Z}_2$ for the second view.

2.4 Neighborhood Feature Enhancement Based on GCN

To mitigate the inherent sparsity in the multi-view gene expression matrices, we employ a single-layer GCN to aggregate local neighborhood information and enhance node representations. For each view $l = \{1, 2\}$, the GCN transforms the multi-scale features $\widetilde{Z}_l$ into an enhanced feature space $Z_l^{GCN_l} \in \mathbb{R}^{N\times G_{GCN}}$, where N is the number of spots. The output dimension G_{GCN} is 512. The graph convolution operation is: $Z_l^{GCN_l} = \sigma\left(\tilde{A}_l \tilde{Z}_l W_l\right)$. Where $\tilde{A}_l$ denotes the normalized adjacency matrix in the l-th view. W_l denote learnable weight matrices, and σ represents a nonlinear activation function. This process effectively propagates information across the spatial and functional edges defined in our multi-view construction. The resulting embeddings, $Z_l^{GCN_l}$, $l = 1, 2$ serve as the input features for the subsequent Hierarchical Node Fusion Module.

2.5 Hierarchical Node Fusion Module (NFM)

Inspired by the SpaNFM method 19, the Hierarchical Node Fusion Module (NFM) models multi-scale relationships by adaptively pooling fine-grained nodes into coarse-grained representations. The module utilizes a dual-branch Transformer architecture designed for simultaneous feature extraction and node fusion. Given the input features $Z_l^{GCN_l} \in \mathbb{R}^{N \times G_{GCN}}$, $l = 1, 2$, the NFM generates three outputs: (1) Node assignment matrix $M_l \in \mathbb{R}^{N \times N_M}$, $l = 1, 2$, which maps N original nodes to N_M coarsened nodes; (2) Fine-grained node feature representation matrix $f_l\left(Z_l^{GCN_l}\right) \in \mathbb{R}^{N \times d_{fg}}$, where d_{fg} is the dimension of fine-grained node features; (3) Coarse-grained node feature matrix $Z_l^M \in \mathbb{R}^{N_M \times d_M}$, $l = 1, 2$, where N_M and d_M denote the number of fused nodes and the feature dimension after fusion, respectively.

Rotary Positional Encoding (RoPE). In spatial transcriptomics, functional regions depend on relative topology and long-range dependencies rather than absolute coordinates. To capture these relationships without adding learnable parameters, we integrate Rotary Positional Encoding (RoPE) into the self-attention. RoPE rotates the Query and Key vectors in the complex plane based on their spatial coordinates. Taking the Query vector $Q_j \in \mathbb{R}^d$ of node j with coordinate t_j as an example, the d-dimensional vector Q_j converted into a complex-valued representation by pairing adjacent dimensions as real and imaginary parts: $Q_{j,c}^{(k)} = Q_j^{(2k)} + i \cdot Q_j^{(2k+1)}$, $k = 0, 1, \ldots, \frac{d}{2} - 1$. Next, for each dimension pair $(2k, 2k+1)$, we define a rotational frequency ω_k and a positional angle $\phi_{j,k}$ based on a base hyperparameter $\theta = 10{,}000$: $\omega_k = \frac{1}{\theta^{2k/d}}$, $\phi_{j,k} = t_j \cdot \omega_k$. Subsequently, the complex vector is rotated by a positional angle $\phi_{j,k}$, effectively encoding the spatial coordinate into the phase: $\text{freqs\_cis}_{j,k} = \cos(\phi_{j,k}) + \mathrm{i} \cdot \sin(\phi_{j,k})$, $Q_{j,c}^{'(k)} = Q_{j,c}^{(k)} \cdot \text{freqs\_cis}_{j,k}$. Finally, the rotated complex values are mapped back to the real domain to produce the encoded query vector: $Q_j^{'(2k)} = Re\left(Q_{j,c}^{'(k)}\right)$, $Q_j^{'(2k+1)} = Im\left(Q_{j,c}^{'(k)}\right)$.

This operation is applied identically to the key vector K, and the entire encoding process is denoted as $Q' = \text{RoPE}(Q)$ and $K' = \text{RoPE}(K)$. This allows the subsequent attention mechanism to capture spatial dependencies based on the relative distance between nodes.

Node Feature Extraction Branch. The node feature extraction branch $f_l\left(Z_l^{GCN_l}\right)$ is based on the Transformer's self-attention mechanism, adapted to capture functional associations between spots. For input features $Z_l^{GCN_l}$ in view l, we first compute the query (Q), key (K), and value (V) matrices using learnable projection matrices W_{Q_1}, W_{K_1}, and W_{V_1}. After applying the RoPE positional encoding to Q and K, the feature extraction function is defined as: $f_l\left(Z_l^{GCN_l}\right) = \text{entmax}\left(\frac{Q_1 K_1^{\mathrm{T}}}{\sqrt{d_{fg}}}\right) V_1$. Where $entmax(\cdot)$ is a sparse attention mechanism (detailed in Section Sparse Attention Mechanism).

$$Q_1 = RoPE\left(Z_l^{GCN_l} W_{Q_1}\right);\ K_1 = RoPE\left(Z_l^{GCN_l} W_{K_1}\right);\ V_1 = Z_l^{GCN_l} W_{V_1} \tag{3}$$

To capture diverse relational patterns, we extend this to Multi-Head Attention (MHA) with H = 8 heads. For each head h, unique projection matrices produce an output $f_l^h\left(Z_l^{GCN_l}\right)$. The final output of the node feature extraction branch of all H heads:

$$f_l\left(Z_l^{GCN_l}\right) = \left[f_l^1\left(Z_l^{GCN_l}\right), f_l^2\left(Z_l^{GCN_l}\right), \ldots, f_l^H\left(Z_l^{GCN_l}\right)\right] \quad (4)$$

Node Fusion Branch. The node fusion branch adaptively learns the node assignment matrix $M_l \in \mathbb{R}^{N \times N_M}$, which maps N fine-grained spots to N_M coarse-grained nodes. In this study, we empirically set $N_M = 512$. Each element in M_l represents the probability from fine nodes to coarsened region. Given the feature matrix $Z_l^{GCN_l}$ of N input nodes, the assignment matrix M_l is learned through a sparse attention mechanism: $M_l = \text{entmax}\left(\frac{Q_2 K_2^{\mathrm{T}}}{\sqrt{N_M}}\right) V_2$. Where $Q_2 \in \mathbb{R}^{\mathrm{N} \times \mathrm{N_M}}$, $K_2 \in \mathbb{R}^{\mathrm{N} \times \mathrm{N_M}}$ and $V_2 \in \mathbb{R}^{\mathrm{N} \times \mathrm{N_M}}$ are computed as follows.

$$Q_2 = RoPE\left(Z_l^{GCN_l} W_{Q_2}\right); K_2 = RoPE\left(Z_l^{GCN_l} W_{K_2}\right); V_2 = Z_l^{GCN_l} W_{V_2} \quad (5)$$

Sparse Attention Mechanism. While the standard Transformer utilizes a softmax function to generate dense probability distributions, spatial transcriptomics data is inherently sparse, with limited gene expression information per spot. To better align with these biological characteristics and reduce model complexity, we incorporate a sparse attention mechanism in both the node feature extraction and node fusion branches. Specifically, we employ the entmax function, which generalizes softmax by solving the following optimization problem: $\text{entmax}(z) = \text{argmax}_{p \in \Delta^d} \boldsymbol{p}^{\mathsf{T}} z + H_\alpha^{\mathrm{T}}(\boldsymbol{p})$. Where $\Delta^d = \left\{\boldsymbol{p} \in \mathbb{R}^d : p_i \geq 0, \sum_i p_i = 1\right\}$ is the probability simplex, z is the input score vector, and H_α^{T} represents the Tsallis α-entropy. In this work, $\alpha = 1.5$. Hence, the above maximization problem can be characterized by a unique threshold τ: $\text{entmax}(z) = [(\alpha - 1)z - \tau 1]_+^{\frac{1}{\alpha} - 1}$. Where $[\cdot]_+$ denotes the positive part of the ReLU function and 1 represents an all-one vector. Under this formulation, when the score $z \leq \tau/(\alpha - 1)$, the output of $\text{entmax}(z)$ becomes zero.

2.6 Macro-scale Processing Module

Cells with similar physiological functions tend to aggregate spatially to form tissue regions through cell communication and signaling regulation. Based on gene-level and micro-level modeling, we further introduce a macro-scale module that models tissue regions via prototype learning. This module treats the coarse-grained representations from the NFM as region prototypes, where each prototype represents a functional tissue domain. For each view l, the NFM outputs coarse-grained node features Z_l^M and a soft assignment matrix M_l. Let $p_l = \left\{p_{1,l}, p_{2,l}, \ldots, p_{N_M,l}\right\}$ be the prototype set of l-th view. The fine-grained spot features output by the network $f_l(\cdot)$ are projected into the prototype space via a two-layer MLP: $h_{i,l} = MLP_l\left(f_l\left(Z_l^{\mathrm{GCN}_l}\right)\right), i = 1, \ldots, N$.

The relationship between spots and tissue regions in the l-th view ($l = \{1,2\}$) is then quantified using the cosine similarity matrix S_l, where$S_{ij,l} = \text{cosine}(h_{i,l}, p_{j,l})$. Unlike traditional spot-centric assignments, we determine positive spot-prototype pairs from the prototype perspective using the learned assignment matrix $M_l \in \mathbb{R}^{N_l \times N_M}$. We first apply row-normalization to M_l to eliminate scaling bias: $\tilde{M}_l(i,j) = \frac{M_l(i,j)}{\sum_{k=1}^{K_l} M_l(i,k)+\varepsilon}$. Where $\tilde{M}_l(i,j)$ is regarded as the weight that spot i is assigned to prototype j. For each prototype $p_{j,l}$, we select the top $r\%$ spots ($r\% = 1\%$) with the highest assignment weights as its positive samples (see Eq.6). This results in a binary indicator matrix I_l, where $I_{ij,l} = 1$ if spot i is a positive sample for prototype j in view l and 0 otherwise. This strategy filters out noisy spots and ensures the prototype maintains distinct semantic boundaries.

$$\mathcal{P}_{j,l} = \text{Top}-k\left(\tilde{M}_l(:,j)\right), k = \max(1, \lfloor r \cdot N_l \rfloor) \tag{6}$$

We employ a Noise Contrastive Estimation loss function to align spot representations with their corresponding tissue prototypes. After applying temperature scaling τ, the contrastive objective for a spot i in view l is: $\mathcal{L}_{\text{proto,l}} = -\frac{1}{|\mathcal{V}|}\sum_{i\in\mathcal{V}} \log\left(\frac{\text{Pos}_{\text{i,l}}}{\text{Neg}_{\text{i,l}}+\varepsilon}\right)$. Where V denotes the set of spots with valid positive samples, and ε is a constant introduced to avoid numerical instability. For each spot i, the positive and negative similarities are defined as: $\text{Pos}_{i,l} = \sum_j \tilde{S}_{ij,l} \cdot I_{ij,l}$, $\text{Neg}_{i,l} = \sum_j \tilde{S}_{ij,l} \cdot (1 - I_{ij,l})$, $\tilde{S}_{ij,l} = \exp\left(\frac{S_{ij,l}}{\tau}\right)$. The total macro-scale loss is: $\mathcal{L}_{\text{proto}} = \mathcal{L}_{\text{proto},1} + \mathcal{L}_{\text{proto},2}$.

2.7 Decoder

To reconstruct the spatial and functional relationships of the spots, we employ two identical decoders that process the hierarchical features (M_1 and M_2) learned from each view. Each decoder (a fully connected layer) transforms the coarsened node assignments back into the original spot space to validate the learned representations. The decoders are formulated as follows: $Z_1^{rec} = D(M_1)$, $Z_2^{rec} = D(M_2)$.

2.8 Loss Function

The model is trained by jointly optimizing a multi-task objective comprising reconstruction loss, cross-view contrastive loss, and prototype learning loss. The reconstruction loss L_{rec} is defined as the mean squared error between the input and reconstructed features: $\mathcal{L}_{rec} = \frac{1}{n}\sum_{i=1}^{n}\left(\|Z_{1,i} - Z_{1,i}^{rec}\|_2^2 + \|Z_{2,i} - Z_{2,i}^{rec}\|_2^2\right)$. Where n denotes the number of spots and $\|\cdot\|_2^2$ represents the squared Euclidean distance between two vectors.

The cross-view loss enforces consistency across the two views through three distinct components: first, we maximize the cosine similarity between the fine-grained node representations $f_1 = f_1\left(Z_1^{GCN_1}\right)$ and $f_2 = f_2\left(Z_2^{GCN_2}\right)$ under the two views to enhance feature robustness.

The contrastive loss is defined as: $\mathcal{L}_{con} = -\frac{1}{N}\sum_{i=1}^{N} \log\frac{\exp(\text{cosine}(f_{1,i},f_{2,i}))}{\sum_{j=1}^{N}\exp(\text{cosine}(f_{1,i},f_{2,j}))}$. Second, to align the views at a global level, we minimize the KL divergence between the probability distributions $P_1 = \text{softmax}\left(Z_1^M\right)$ and $P_2 = \text{softmax}\left(Z_2^M\right)$, obtained by applying softmax normalization to the coarse-grained node representations in two views, is defined as: $\mathcal{L}_{KL} = D_{KL}(P_1 \| P_2)$.

Third, we enforce fine-grained structural similarity by minimizing the KL divergence between the spot-to-spot cosine similarity matrices of the two views, ensuring consistent high-level topology: $\mathcal{L}_{sim} = D_{KL}(\mathrm{Sim}(M_1, M_1)\|\mathrm{Sim}(M_2, M_2))$.

The total cross-view loss is defined as: $\mathcal{L}_{CVC} = \mathcal{L}_{con}+\mathcal{L}_{KL}+\mathcal{L}_{sim}$. The final optimization objective integrates all loss terms to guide the model toward learning biologically meaningful and spatially consistent representations: $\mathcal{L} = \mathcal{L}_{rec} + \mathcal{L}_{\mathrm{CVC}} + \mathcal{L}_{\mathrm{proto}}$.

3 Experiments and Result

3.1 Datasets and Experimental Setup

The proposed SpaMBP model was evaluated on two representative spatial transcriptomics datasets: the human dorsolateral prefrontal cortex (DLPFC) dataset and the human breast cancer dataset (Block A Section 1). The DLPFC dataset contains 12 tissue sections from three individuals (3,498–4,789 spots per section) with annotated cortical layers (L1–L6) and white matter (WM) as ground truth, while the breast cancer dataset contains 3,798 spots with 20 pathology-annotated regions. For SpaMBP, the number of coarse-grained nodes was set to 512 with a feature dimension of 128 and 8 attention heads, and the model was optimized using Adam with a learning rate of 1e−5. In the DLPFC dataset, the number of clusters was set to 5 for Sections 151669–151672 and 7 for the remaining sections, while it was set to 20 for the breast cancer dataset. All models were trained for 3000 epochs, and results were reported as the average of 10 independent runs. Baseline methods were implemented using the default parameters from their original papers to ensure fair comparisons.

3.2 Comparative Analysis with Baseline Methods

To evaluate the effectiveness of the proposed SpaMBP framework, we adopt the Adjusted Rand Index (ARI) as the evaluation metric and compare it with nine representative state-of-the-art methods for spatial domain identification, including GraphST [14] (2023), SEDR [7] (2024), StLearn [9] (2023), STAGATE [8] (2022), SpaGCN [20] (2021), MVCLST [15] (2024), MCGAE [16] (2025), MAEST [13] (2025), and SpaNFM [19] (2024). As shown in Table 1, results on the human dorsolateral prefrontal cortex (DLPFC) dataset indicate that SpaMBP achieves the best ARI performance on 8 out of 12 slices. Specifically, on the 151507 dataset, SpaMBP attains an ARI of 0.5052, improving by approximately 7.2% over the second-best method SpaNFM (0.4713) ($p < 0.05$). To further validate its performance, experiments on the human breast cancer dataset (Table 2) show that SpaMBP achieves the highest ARI score of 0.6135, slightly outperforming SpaNFM (ARI = 0.6083). Overall, these results demonstrate that SpaMBP can stably and accurately identify spatial domain structures across different types of spatial transcriptomics data.

Table 1. Average ARI values of the baseline methods and SpaMBP on the DLPFC dataset.

Dataset	GraphST	SEDR	StLearn	STAGATE	SpaGCN	MVCLST	MCGAE	MAEST	SpaNFM	SpaMBP
151507	0.4653	0.4204	0.4480	0.4172	0.3679	0.3347	0.3592	0.3560	0.4713	**0.5052**
151508	0.3863	0.4204	0.4490	0.3560	0.3257	0.2772	0.3210	0.2760	0.4669	**0.4736**
151509	0.3967	0.4236	0.3650	0.3169	0.3595	0.3849	0.3102	0.3664	**0.4473**	0.4441
151510	0.3509	0.4000	0.3270	0.2736	0.3264	0.3240	0.2439	0.3124	0.4170	**0.4941**
151669	0.2526	0.2721	0.2100	0.3160	0.2650	0.5544	0.1942	0.2950	0.5584	**0.7183**
151670	0.2353	0.2738	0.2220	0.2859	0.2739	0.5436	0.1647	0.3197	0.5464	**0.5695**
151671	0.5316	0.3697	0.5760	0.2731	0.4309	0.5737	0.3764	0.4940	0.6081	**0.7177**
151672	0.5433	0.4004	0.4360	0.3208	0.3829	0.5792	0.4164	0.3900	0.5924	**0.6323**
151673	**0.4904**	0.3403	0.4330	0.2567	0.4146	0.3652	0.3357	0.3337	0.3693	0.4491
151674	**0.4911**	0.3416	0.2992	0.3779	0.3788	0.3073	0.3737	0.2814	0.3991	0.4338
151675	**0.4750**	0.3466	0.3270	0.2850	0.3386	0.2372	0.3457	0.3589	0.2648	0.4575
151676	0.3737	0.3258	0.3630	0.2887	0.3283	0.2436	0.2425	0.2392	0.3562	**0.5034**

Table 2. Average results of baseline methods and SpaMBP on the HBC dataset.

Methods	GraphST	SEDR	STAGATE	SpaGCN	StLearn	MVCLST	MAEST	MCGAE	SpaNFM	SpaMBP
ARI	0.5092	0.4897	0.5512	0.2480	0.5423	0.4591	0.3594	0.5478	0.6083	**0.6135**

3.3 Ablation Study

To systematically evaluate the impact of each core component in SpaMBP on model performance, ablation experiments were conducted on the 151507 dataset, comparing the full model with variants where specific modules were removed. The experimental settings include removing the reconstruction loss (w/o Rec), removing the cross-view contrastive loss (w/o Cross CL), removing the gene-level module (w/o Gene Level), removing the micro-level module (w/o Micro Level), and removing the macro-level module (w/o Macro Level), all compared against the full model (Full model). The results show that the full model achieves the best performance in terms of ARI, while removing any key module leads to a performance decline, indicating that each component plays an important role in the overall framework Table 3.

Table 3. The results of the ablation experiment.

	w/o Rec	w/o Cross CL	w/o Gene Level	w/o Micro Level	w/o Macro Level	Full model
ARI	0.2439	0.4811	0.4479	0.3625	0.4844	**0.4969**

4 Conclusion

This study proposes SpaMBP, a spatial domain identification method that integrates multi-scale biological information to model spatial transcriptomics data from the gene level, microscopic cellular interaction level, and macroscopic tissue structure level. The method constructs a hierarchical feature representation framework and incorporates multi-scale feature fusion with contrastive constraints to enable collabo-rative learning across different biological levels, thereby improving the accuracy and stability of spatial domain identification. Experimental results demonstrate that SpaMBP achieves superior overall performance compared with existing methods across multiple spatial transcriptomics datasets. Furthermore, ablation studies verify the importance of the gene-level, micro-level, and macro-level modules, indicating that multi-scale information integration is a key factor in improving spatial domain identification performance. Overall, SpaMBP effectively integrates multi-level bio-logical information and provides an efficient computational framework for the fine-grained analysis of complex tissue spatial structures.

Acknowledgments. This work was supported in part by the National Natural Science Foundation of China (No.62472202,No.U25A20449,No.62472108,No.U24A20256) and Nature Science Foundation of Yunnan Provice (202601AS070066).

Disclosure of Interests. The authors have no competing interests to declare that are relevant to the content of this article.

References

1. Qian, X., et al. Spatial transcriptomics reveals human cortical layer and area specification. Nature **644**(8075), 153–163 (2025)
2. Steele, L., et al.: A single-cell and spatial genomics atlas of human skin fibroblasts reveals shared disease-related fibroblast subtypes across tissues. Nat. Immunol. **26**(10), 1807–1820 (2025)
3. Shakoori, A.R.: Fluorescence in situ hybridization (FISH) and its applications. In: Chromosome Structure and Aberrations, pp. 343–367. Springer, New Delhi, India (2017)
4. Ståhl, P.L., et al.: Visualization and analysis of gene expression in tissue sections by spatial transcriptomics. Science **353**(6294), 78–82 (2016)
5. Nawy, T.: In situ sequencing. Nat. Methods **11**(1), 29 (2014)
6. Chen, A., et al.: Spatiotemporal transcriptomic atlas of mouse organogenesis using DNA nanoball-patterned arrays. Cell **185**(10), 1777–1792 (2022)
7. Xu, H., et al.: Unsupervised spatially embedded deep representation of spatial transcriptomics. Genome Med. **16**(1), 12 (2024)
8. Dong, K., Zhang, S.: Deciphering spatial domains from spatially resolved transcriptomics with an adaptive graph attention auto-encoder. Nat. Commun. **13**(1), 1739 (2022)
9. Pham, D., et al.: stLearn: integrating spatial location, tissue morphology and gene expression to find cell types, cell-cell interactions and spatial trajectories within undissociated tissues. Biorxiv (2020). 2020–05
10. Battaglia, P.W., et al.: Relational inductive biases, deep learning, and graph networks. arXiv preprint arXiv:1806.01261 (2018)

11. Kingma, D.P., Welling, M.: Auto-encoding variational Bayes. arXiv preprint arXiv:1312.6114 (2013)
12. Vaswani, A., et al.: Attention is all you need. In: Advances in Neural Information Processing Systems, vol. 30 (2017)
13. Zhu, P., et al.: MAEST: accurately spatial domain detection in spatial transcriptomics with graph masked autoencoder. Briefings Bioinf. **26**(2), bbaf086 (2025)
14. Long, Y., et al.: Spatially informed clustering, integration, and deconvolution of spatial transcriptomics with GraphST. Nat. Commun. **14**(1), 1155 (2023)
15. Peng, W., et al.: A multi-view comparative learning method for spatial transcriptomics data clustering. In: 2023 IEEE International Conference on Bioinformatics and Biomedicine (BIBM). IEEE (2023)
16. Yang, Y., et al.: MCGAE: unraveling tumor invasion through integrated multimodal spatial transcriptomics. Briefings Bioinf. **26**(1), bbae608 (2025)
17. Van de Sande, B., et al.: A scalable SCENIC workflow for single-cell gene regulatory network analysis. Nat. Protocols **15**(7), 2247–2276 (2020)
18. Cang, Z., et al.: Screening cell–cell communication in spatial transcriptomics via collective optimal transport. Nat. Methods **20**(2), 218–228 (2023)
19. Peng, W., et al.: Sparse attention-based hierarchical node representation for spatial domain identification. In: 2024 IEEE International Conference on Bioinformatics and Biomedicine (BIBM). IEEE (2024)
20. Hu, J., et al.: SpaGCN: integrating gene expression, spatial location and histology to identify spatial domains and spatially variable genes by graph convolutional network. Nature Methods **18**(11), 1342–1351 (2021)

scAQUA: A Quintuplet Constraint-Based Batch Effect Correction Method for Single-Cell Multi-omics Data

Tiezheng Qiao[1,2], Fei Teng[1,2], Huiyong Zhang[1,2], and Xiaoshu Zhu[1,2](✉)

[1] School of Computer Science and Information Security, Guilin University of Electronic Technology, Guilin, China
{tzqiao,23032201035}@mails.guet.edu.cn, zhanghuiyong@gxmu.edu.cn
[2] Guangxi Academy of Artificial Intelligence, Nanning, China
xszhu@guet.edu.cn

Abstract. Single-cell multi-omics datasets are often generated across multiple batches, introducing technical noise. However, existing batch effect correction methods frequently cause over-correction, erroneously mixing distinct cell subpopulations. We propose scAQUA, a novel batch effect correction method based on quintuplet constraint learning. The method employs a dual-stream architecture to extract complementary features from single-cell RNA sequencing (scRNA-seq) and single-cell assay for transposase-accessible chromatin sequencing (scATAC-seq) data. To prevent over-correction, a quintuplet loss function featuring a pseudo-neighbor repulsive force is applied as a topological constraint, explicitly penalizing the unnatural blending of different cell types. We evaluated scAQUA against four current scRNA-seq methods and two multi-omics methods on five diverse datasets. Experimental results show that scAQUA consistently achieved the highest performance in cell-type preservation metrics while effectively mitigating batch effects. These findings demonstrate that scAQUA offers an effective solution for constructing single-cell atlases across batches.

Keywords: single-cell multi-omics · batch effect · dual-stream coupled autoencoder · quintuplet constraint learning

1 Introduction

Recent advances in scRNA-seq and scATAC-seq multi-omics technologies provide unprecedented resolution for deciphering cellular heterogeneity [1–4]. However, technical variations from sequencing platforms and sample sources inevitably introduce severe batch effects, which not only reduce the accuracy of data integration but also obscure true biological signals [5,6]. Therefore, developing a batch correction method that can effectively mitigate cross-experiment batch effects while preserving cell-type boundaries is of critical importance [7–9].

X. Cui et al. (Eds.): ISBRA 2026, LNBI 16690, pp. 381–392, 2027.
https://doi.org/10.1007/978-981-92-3716-6_30

Although various batch correction algorithms have been proposed, they still exhibit limitations in balancing batch removal and cell-type separation [10–12]. Traditional graph-based and clustering-based methods, such as BBKNN [13], Scanorama [14], and Harmony [15], are prone to erroneously connecting distinct cell types or blurring the boundaries of similar subpopulations when processing highly heterogeneous multi-omics data [16]. Deep metric learning methods like scDML [17] are highly susceptible to over correction during forced alignment, causing the underlying cellular topological manifolds to fragment. Furthermore, integration methods specifically designed for multi-omics, such as Seurat v4 [18] and MultiVI [19], often struggle to achieve an ideal balance between effectively removing batch residuals and maintaining clear cell type specific resolution when dealing with complex nested batches [20,21].

To overcome these limitations, we propose scAQUA, a single-cell multi-omics batch correction framework based on quintuplet constraint learning. scAQUA utilizes a dual-stream coupled autoencoder to map RNA and ATAC data into a shared latent space and innovatively introduces a quintuplet constraint learning module. This module leverages positive samples to robustly fuse similar cells across batches while strictly pushing dissimilar cells apart using negative samples, such as pseudo neighbors. This mechanism effectively prevents over-correction and maintains clear biological boundaries. We benchmarked scAQUA against six state-of-the-art methods on five complex real multi-omics datasets using six evaluation metrics: ARI [22], NMI [23], ASW_celltype [24], ASW_batch [25], iLISI [26], kBET [27]. The results demonstrate that scAQUA achieves favorable performance in both mitigating batch effects and preserving cellular structures.

2 Methods

To effectively mitigate complex experimental batch effects while precisely preserving the high-resolution boundaries between different cell types, we propose scAQUA, a dual-stream deep learning framework based on quintuplet constraint learning. This framework aims to achieve unsupervised batch effect correction for single-cell multi-omics data and consists of four core modules, as illustrated in Fig. 1.

2.1 Data Preprocessing

The primary challenge in single-cell multi-omics integration is addressing the cross-modal feature space heterogeneity. First, we convert the scATAC-seq peak matrix into a Gene Activity Matrix (GAM). Subsequently, to mitigate systematic biases caused by sequencing depth, we apply library size normalization and log-transformation to the raw count matrices X of both modalities. Based on this, we separately calculate the highly variable genes (HVGs) for the RNA and ATAC matrices and take their intersection to form a shared feature space. The unified feature matrices after alignment and filtering, denoted as $X_{rna} \in \mathbb{R}^{N \times D_{rna}}$ and

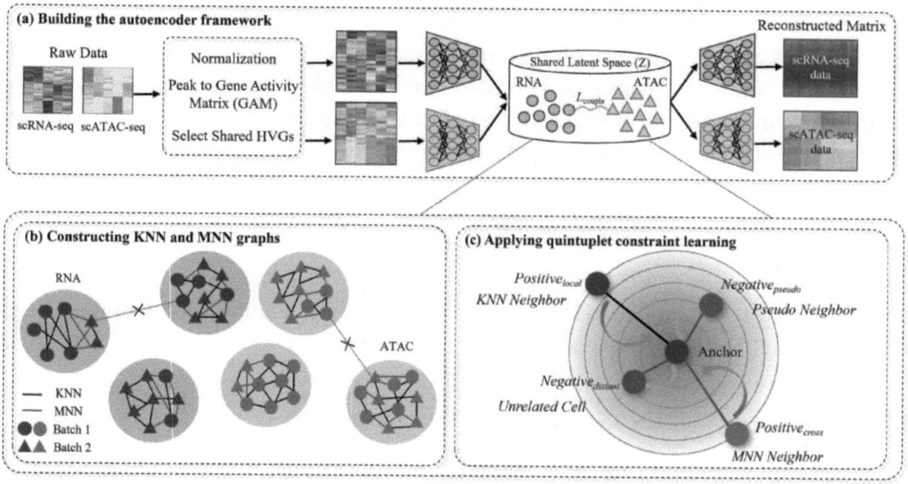

Fig. 1. The overview of scAQUA for single-cell multi-omics integration and batch effect correction. (a) The autoencoder framework extracts unified latent representations from multi-omics data via coupling alignment and matrix reconstruction. (b) The construction of intra-batch KNN and cross-batch MNN graphs identifies reliable anchor cells through structural consistency filtering. (c) The quintuplet constraint learning optimizes the latent space by pulling positive samples and pushing negative samples to balance batch fusion and boundary preservation.

$X_{atac} \in \mathbb{R}^{N \times D_{atac}}$, where N is the total number of cells, serve as the standardized inputs for the subsequent networks.

2.2 Dual-Stream Coupled Autoencoder

To extract consistent and robust low-dimensional manifold representations from heterogeneous multi-omics data, we design a dual-stream coupled autoencoder network. Let $f_{\theta_m}(\cdot)$ and $g_{\phi_m}(\cdot)$ denote the multi-layer perceptron encoder and decoder for modality $m \in \{rna, atac\}$, with learnable parameters θ_m and ϕ_m, respectively. The input features are non-linearly projected into a shared latent space of dimension d ($d \ll D_m$) to obtain the low-dimensional embeddings $Z_m = f_{\theta_m}(X_m) \in \mathbb{R}^{N \times d}$, which are then reconstructed by the corresponding decoders as $\hat{X}_m = g_{\phi_m}(Z_m)$. To ensure the dimensionality reduction process retains the key biological information of the original data, we employ the mean squared error as the reconstruction loss L_{recon}:

$$L_{recon} = \frac{1}{N} \sum_{i=1}^{N} \sum_{m \in \{rna, atac\}} \|x_m^{(i)} - \hat{x}_m^{(i)}\|_2^2 \tag{1}$$

where N is the total number of cells, and $x_m^{(i)}$ and $\hat{x}_m^{(i)}$ respectively represent the original input feature and the reconstructed output of the i-th cell for modality m.

More importantly, to bridge the modality gap and extract the intrinsic biological states of cells, we introduce a modality coupling loss L_{couple} for the dual-omics latent representations of the same cell i. This loss enforces cross-modal feature alignment by minimizing the Euclidean distance between the two modality representations in the shared latent space:

$$L_{couple} = \frac{1}{N} \sum_{i=1}^{N} \| z_{rna}^{(i)} - z_{atac}^{(i)} \|_2^2 \tag{2}$$

where $z_{rna}^{(i)}$ and $z_{atac}^{(i)}$ respectively denote the low-dimensional latent embeddings of the i-th cell for the RNA and ATAC modalities.

2.3 KNN and MNN Graph Construction

After obtaining unified low-dimensional representations, distribution shifts may still exist in the latent space due to experimental batch effects. To guide the subsequent cross-batch fusion, we construct high-dimensional topological graphs in the latent space to mine structurally consistent anchor cells.

2.3.1 Constructing Intra-batch Local Topological Graphs

For any independent experimental batch b, we construct a K-nearest neighbor (KNN) graph based on its latent representation. For cell i, we identify its K nearest neighbors based on Euclidean distance, denoted as the neighborhood set $\mathcal{N}_K(i)$. The edge weight between cell i and its neighbor j is defined using a Gaussian kernel function as $w_{i,j} = \exp(-\|z_i - z_j\|_2^2 / 2\sigma_i^2)$, where the adaptive bandwidth σ_i accommodates variations in local data density.

2.3.2 Extracting Cross-Batch Candidate MNNs

Let b_1 and b_2 be two independent subsets with batch effects. If cell i in b_1 is a neighbor of cell j in b_2, and vice versa, they are considered mutual nearest neighbors (MNNs). The candidate set is defined as:

$$\mathcal{M}_{b_1,b_2} = \{(i,j) \mid i \in \mathcal{N}_K(j, b_1) \wedge j \in \mathcal{N}_K(i, b_2)\} \tag{3}$$

where $\mathcal{N}_K(j, b_1)$ denotes the neighborhood set of the K nearest neighbors for cell j within batch b_1.

2.3.3 Structural Consistency Filtering and Confidence Scoring

Under severe batch effects, the initially extracted $\mathcal{M}_{b_1,b_2}$ often contains pseudo-matches due to distribution distortions. Therefore, we innovatively introduce a graph-topology-based structural consistency score $C(i,j)$ to evaluate the reliability of candidate anchor pairs:

$$C(i,j) = \exp\left(- \frac{\|z_i - z_j\|_2}{\text{median}_{(u,v)\in\mathcal{M}_{b_1,b_2}} \|z_u - z_v\|_2} \right) \tag{4}$$

where z_i and z_j are the latent representations of cell i and cell j.

The denominator which is the median distance of all candidate MNN pairs acts as a robust global scaling factor. If the latent distance of a cell pair is significantly smaller than the median inter-batch distance, its score $C(i,j)$ approaches 1; otherwise, it approaches 0. This scoring mechanism provides strong adaptive robustness to varying datasets and inter-batch distances. Finally, by setting a confidence threshold $\gamma \in (0,1)$, we retain only the cell pairs satisfying $C(i,j) \geq \gamma$ as the reliable anchor set $\mathcal{A}$, which is directly utilized for contrastive learning in the next module.

2.4 Quintuplet Constraint Learning

This module is the core innovation of our framework for balancing "batch removal" and "cell-type separation." Traditional unsupervised contrastive learning often leads to the erroneous fusion of distinct cell types. Therefore, based on the topological graphs and anchor set $\mathcal{A}$ from the previous module, for any anchor cell A in the shared latent space, we dynamically construct a quintuplet comprising two sets of positive samples $\mathcal{P}$ and two sets of negative samples $\mathcal{N}$:

Positive sample set $\mathcal{P} = \{P_{local}, P_{cross}\}$: Contains the same-modality local real neighbors P_{local}, preserves the underlying topology within a single modality and the cross-batch matched cells filtered by the confidence score P_{cross}, serves as a bridge for cross-batch fusion.

Negative sample set $\mathcal{N} = \{N_{pseudo}, N_{distant}\}$: Contains the pseudo-neighbors N_{pseudo} which cells are close in the latent space but not adjacent in the high-dimensional topology and distant background cells $N_{distant}$. Notably, N_{pseudo} can keenly identify distinct cell subpopulations that are erroneously squeezed together due to forced alignment, effectively sharpening the decision boundaries of cell types.

Building upon this, we adopt and extend the InfoNCE loss to define the quintuplet contrastive loss function:

$$L_{quintuplet} = -\frac{1}{|\mathcal{P}|} \sum_{z_p \in \mathcal{P}} \log \frac{\exp(sim(z_A, z_p)/\tau)}{\exp(sim(z_A, z_p)/\tau) + \sum_{z_n \in \mathcal{N}} \exp(sim(z_A, z_n)/\tau)} \tag{5}$$

where z_A, z_p, and z_n denote the latent embeddings of the anchor cell, positive samples, and negative samples. $|\mathcal{P}|$ is the cardinality of the positive sample set, and $sim(u,v) = (u^\top v)/(||u||||v||)$ represents the cosine similarity function. τ is the temperature scaling factor, which controls the model's sensitivity to hard negative samples. A properly tuned τ ensures that the model focuses on repelling N_{pseudo}, thereby sharpening the decision boundaries between erroneously mixed cell types.

By maximizing the similarity between the anchor and positive samples while strictly penalizing the similarity with negative samples especially the pseudo-neighbors N_{pseudo}, this objective function enables the model to effectively mitigate batch effects while maintaining high-resolution boundaries between cell types.

2.5 Overall Objective Function

In summary, the overall loss function of the scAQUA framework is formulated as a joint combination of the reconstruction loss, modality coupling loss, and quintuplet constraint loss:

$$L_{total} = L_{recon} + \lambda_1 L_{couple} + \lambda_2 L_{quintuplet} \tag{6}$$

where λ_1 and λ_2 are hyperparameters balancing the strengths of the respective constraints. Through end-to-end backpropagation optimization, the model ultimately learns a unified multi-omics representation space that fuses batches while preserving biological boundaries.

3 Results

The commonly used UMAP method was utilized to visualize the latent representations of scAQUA and all compared methods. To comprehensively evaluate the integration performance, we adopted three metrics (ARI, NMI, and ASW_celltype) to assess the clustering performance of biological cell types, while utilizing three other metrics (ASW_batch, iLISI, and kBET) to measure the ability to remove batch effects. We analyzed single-cell multi-omics datasets derived from various species and tissues. The performance of scAQUA was benchmarked against six state-of-the-art integration methods—Harmony, Scanorama, scDML, BBKNN, Seurat v4, and MultiVI—as well as the unintegrated raw data. Overall quantitative results demonstrate that scAQUA achieved the highest average scores across all three cell-type preservation metrics on the tested datasets. Furthermore, it exhibited favorable performance on batch correction metrics, confirming its robustness and effectiveness in balancing batch effect removal and biological boundary preservation.

3.1 Datasets

Five real single-cell multi-omics datasets were utilized in this study to comprehensively evaluate the performance of our method. These datasets encompass diverse species including human and mouse, and a wide range of tissues, including Bone Marrow, Thymus, Skin, Embryonic Brain, and Retina. All datasets were publicly obtained from the National Center for Biotechnology Information (NCBI) Gene Expression Omnibus (GEO) (https://www.ncbi.nlm.nih.gov/geo/). The selected datasets span varying scales and complexities, with the number of cells ranging from approximately 4,000 to over 90,000, and containing diverse numbers of experimental batches and cell types. Detailed statistical information for these datasets is summarized in Table 1, and their corresponding GEO accession codes are provided in the Data Availability statement.

Table 1. The details of the five multi-omics datasets

Dataset	#Cells	#RNA	#ATAC	#Celltypes	#Batches
Human Bone Marrow	69249	14087	129921	45	12
Mouse Thymus iNKT	4373	27998	77555	8	2
Mouse Skin	32321	21478	340341	22	3
Mouse Embryonic Brain	5081	28930	241757	14	12
Mouse Retina	9383	6275	59353	18	2

3.2 Benchmarking scAQUA on Real Multi-omics Datasets

To systematically evaluate the integration performance of scAQUA, we benchmarked it against six state-of-the-art methods on five real single-cell multi-omics datasets covering diverse tissues and species. These selected datasets include both small-scale and large-scale studies which ranging from approximately 4,000 to over 90,000 cells and present varying levels of batch effects, sequencing depths, and biological complexity.

As illustrated in Fig. 2, scAQUA consistently achieved the highest ARI and NMI scores across the tested datasets, indicating its superior ability to recover the true biological cell-type structure while aligning paired modalities. The boxplots in Fig. 2 summarize the clustering performance of all compared methods across the five datasets. Notably, scAQUA not only attained the highest median scores in these cell-type preservation metrics but also exhibited lower performance variance, reflecting its exceptional robustness regardless of data scale.

Furthermore, compared to conventional integration methods that often suffer from over-correction on complex tissues, our approach maintained high-resolution boundaries for distinct cell subpopulations. These quantitative results collectively demonstrate that scAQUA provides a highly favorable trade-off between batch effect removal and biological topology preservation, making it a reliable integration tool across a wide variety of multi-omics datasets.

3.3 Removing Batch Effects and Preserving Cell Type Structure with scAQUA

To evaluate the effectiveness of scAQUA in removing batch effects while strictly preserving underlying biological structures, we conducted detailed visual and quantitative experiments on the highly complex Human BMMC multi-omics dataset, which contains 12 batches and 45 fine-grained cell types. We compared scAQUA with six representative integration methods alongside the uncorrected Raw data.

As shown in the UMAP visualizations colored by batch (Fig. 3a), the unintegrated Raw data exhibited severe batch-specific separation. While conventional methods like Harmony, Scanorama, and MultiVI managed to mix the batches to some extent, scDML aggressively shattered the data into artificial and isolated islands, completely destroying the global manifold. In contrast, scAQUA

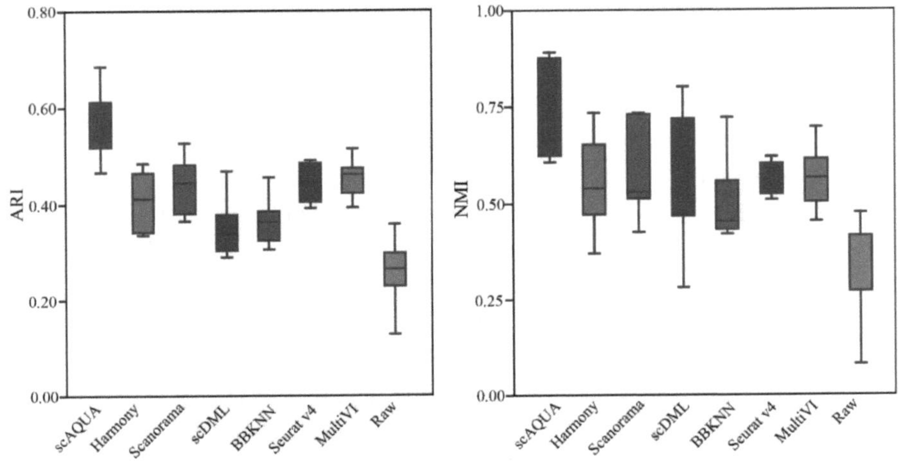

Fig. 2. Comparison of ARI and NMI scores between scAQUA, raw data, and six benchmark methods.

achieved highly uniform and natural batch alignment, seamlessly integrating the 12 batches without introducing artificial mixing artifacts.

Furthermore, the UMAP embeddings colored by cell type (Fig. 3b) explicitly demonstrate the superiority of scAQUA in preserving fine-grained biological topology. Baseline methods such as Harmony and Scanorama exhibited severe over-correction by heavily compressing complex cell populations, such as the densely packed central clusters, and blurring the boundaries between closely related subtypes. Conversely, guided by the repulsive force of pseudo-neighbors in the quintuplet constraint, scAQUA successfully maintained sharp and distinct boundaries for various cell types while keeping the overall developmental manifold continuous and biologically meaningful.

In summary, scAQUA consistently outperforms existing methods in qualitative UMAP visualizations, offering a highly robust balance between deep batch integration and the accurate preservation of fine-grained cell identities.

3.4 Ablation Study

To validate the effectiveness of the core components in our proposed method, we conducted a comprehensive ablation study on the highly complex Human BMMC dataset, which contains 45 fine-grained cell subtypes. We systematically compared the full scAQUA model, scAQUA-Quintuplet-R/A, with three degraded variants: (1) scAQUA-Triplet-R, using only RNA data and standard triplet loss; (2) scAQUA-Quintuplet-R, using only RNA data but equipped with our quintuplet loss; and (3) scAQUA-Triplet-R/A, which utilizes dual-omics data but removes the pseudo-neighbor repulsive force to assess its role in preventing over-correction. The quantitative results are summarized in Table 2.

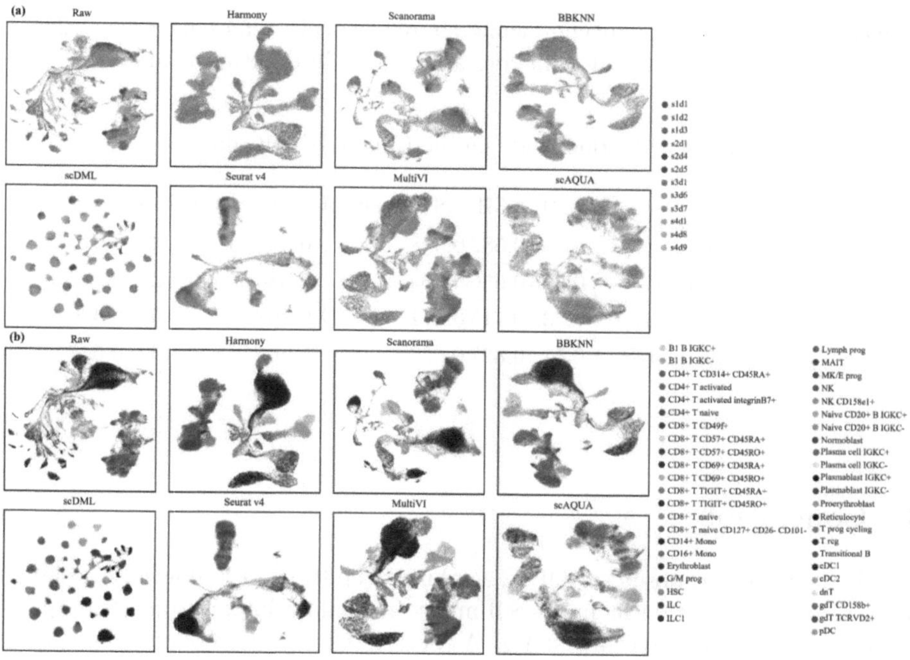

Fig. 3. Comparison of scAQUA and baseline methods on the Human BMMC dataset in terms of batch correction and cell type preservation. (a) UMAP visualizations colored by batch. (b) UMAP visualizations colored by cell type.

The results explicitly demonstrate that relying solely on transcriptomic data is fundamentally insufficient to distinguish the highly similar hematopoietic lineages in bone marrow. Regardless of the loss function used, the single-modality variants Triplet-R and Quintuplet-R exhibited significant performance degradation across all cell-type preservation metrics compared to their dual-omics counterparts. The dual-stream architecture of scAQUA successfully harnesses scATAC-seq data as crucial complementary information, significantly enhancing the resolution of cellular heterogeneity, ARI increased from 0.385 to 0.572 under the quintuplet constraint.

The comparisons between the Triplet and Quintuplet models across both single and dual modalities highlight the critical role of our custom loss function in preserving biological topology. Without the pseudo-neighbor repulsive constraints, the Triplet variants aggressively forced cells from different batches to mix, achieving slightly higher batch correction scores, scAQUA-Triplet-R/A yielded an ASW_batch of 0.968 and an iLISI of 6.050. However, similar to the phenomenon observed in the UMAP visualizations, this aggressive integration led to severe over-correction, causing a catastrophic drop in cell-type preservation, ASW_celltype plummeted from 0.562 to 0.471. By contrast, the models equipped with the quintuplet loss effectively maintained clear boundaries between closely related subtypes while simultaneously removing batch effects, with the full scAQUA model achieving an optimal integration trade-off.

Table 2. Ablation study on the Human BMMC dataset

Model	ARI	NMI	ASW_celltype	ASW_batch	iLISI	kBET
scAQUA-Triplet-R	0.315	0.582	0.398	0.912	4.85	0.615
scAQUA-Quintuplet-R	0.385	0.650	0.455	0.885	4.21	0.720
scAQUA-Triplet-R/A	0.432	0.715	0.471	0.968	6.05	0.490
scAQUA-Quintuplet-R/A	0.572	0.827	0.562	0.961	5.52	0.547

4 Conclusion

In this study, we proposed scAQUA, a robust deep learning framework designed to tackle over-correction in single-cell multi-omics data integration. By employing a dual-stream architecture, scAQUA effectively harnesses the complementary nature of scRNA-seq and scATAC-seq data to resolve complex cellular heterogeneity. Crucially, our innovative quintuplet loss function introduces a pseudo-neighbor repulsive force that acts as a strict topological constraint, successfully preventing the erroneous mixing of distinct but molecularly similar cell subpopulations.

Extensive benchmarking across five diverse datasets demonstrated that scAQUA achieves state-of-the-art performance in preserving intrinsic cellular identities while effectively eliminating batch variations. Furthermore, our ablation studies confirmed that scAQUA avoids the biological distortion inherent in traditional triplet-loss models, achieving an optimal integration trade-off.

Ultimately, scAQUA provides a highly reliable computational tool for constructing high-fidelity single-cell atlases and facilitating downstream biological discoveries. Future work will explore extending this framework to incorporate emerging spatial transcriptomics data.

Declarations

Funding. This research was supported by the National Natural Science Foundation of China (No. 62462020), and the Postgraduate Innovation Project of Guilin University of Electronic Technology and Guangxi Artificial Intelligence College (No. C25YJRGZSX07).

Data Availability. All data used in this study are from the public domain. The raw data are downloaded from the GEO database with the accession numbers for: Human Bone Marrow: GSE194122. Mouse Thymus iNKT: GSE130184. Mouse Skin: GSE140203. Mouse Embryonic Brain: GSE126074. Mouse Retina: GSE201402.

References

1. Le, J., Dian, Y., Zhao, D., et al.: Single-cell multi-omics in cancer immunotherapy: from tumor heterogeneity to personalized precision treatment. Mol. Cancer **24**(1), 221 (2025)
2. Cai, L., Ma, X., Ma, J.: Integrating scRNA-seq and scATAC-seq with inter-type attention heterogeneous graph neural networks. Brief. Bioinform. **26**(1), bbae711 (2025)
3. Baysoy, A., Bai, Z., Satija, R., et al.: The technological landscape and applications of single-cell multi-omics. Nat. Rev. Mol. Cell Biol. **24**(10), 695–713 (2023)
4. Hao, Y., Stuart, T., Kowalski, M.H., et al.: Dictionary learning for integrative, multimodal and scalable single-cell analysis. Nat. Biotechnol. **42**(2), 293–304 (2024)
5. Zhou, Y., Sheng, Q., Wang, G., et al.: Quantifying batch effects for individual genes in single-cell data. Nat. Comput. Sci. **5**(8), 612–620 (2025)
6. Tran, H.T.N., Ang, K.S., Chevrier, M., et al.: A benchmark of batch-effect correction methods for single-cell RNA sequencing data. Genome Biol. **21**(1), 12 (2020)
7. Li, S., Lücken, M., Marioni, J.C., et al.: Toward informed batch correction for single-cell transcriptome integration. Nat. Comput. Sci., 1–11 (2026)
8. Tan, Y., Xie, L., Yang, H., et al.: BioDSNN: a dual-stream neural network with hybrid biological knowledge integration for multi-gene perturbation response prediction. Brief. Bioinform. **26**(1), bbae617 (2025)
9. Argelaguet, R., Cuomo, A.S.E., Stegle, O., et al.: Computational principles and challenges in single-cell data integration. Nat. Biotechnol. **39**(10), 1202–1215 (2021)
10. Antonsson, S.E., Melsted, P.: Batch correction methods used in single-cell RNA sequencing analyses are often poorly calibrated. Genome Res. **35**(8), 1832–1841 (2025)
11. Hu, X., Li, H., Chen, M., et al.: Reference-informed evaluation of batch correction for single-cell omics data with overcorrection awareness. Commun. Biol. **8**(1), 521 (2025)
12. Baião, A.R., Cai, Z., Poulos, R.C., et al.: A technical review of multi-omics data integration methods: from classical statistical to deep generative approaches. Brief. Bioinform. **26**(4), bbaf355 (2025)
13. Polański, K., Young, M.D., Miao, Z., et al.: BBKNN: fast batch alignment of single cell transcriptomes. Bioinformatics **36**(3), 964–965 (2020)
14. Hie, B., Bryson, B., Berger, B.: Efficient integration of heterogeneous single-cell transcriptomes using Scanorama. Nat. Biotechnol. **37**(6), 685–691 (2019)
15. Korsunsky, I., Millard, N., Fan, J., et al.: Fast, sensitive and accurate integration of single-cell data with Harmony. Nat. Methods **16**(12), 1289–1296 (2019)
16. Wang, G., Zhao, J., Lin, Y., et al.: scMODAL: a general deep learning framework for comprehensive single-cell multi-omics data alignment with feature links. Nat. Commun. **16**(1), 4994 (2025)
17. Yu, X., Xu, X., Zhang, J., et al.: Batch alignment of single-cell transcriptomics data using deep metric learning. Nat. Commun. **14**(1), 960 (2023)
18. Hao, Y., Hao, S., Andersen-Nissen, E., et al.: Integrated analysis of multimodal single-cell data. Cell **184**(13), 3573–3587.e29 (2021)
19. Ashuach, T., Gabitto, M.I., Koodli, R.V., et al.: MultiVI: deep generative model for the integration of multimodal data. Nat. Methods **20**(8), 1222–1231 (2023)
20. Zhang, Z., Zhao, X., Bindra, M., et al.: scDisInFact: disentangled learning for integration and prediction of multi-batch multi-condition single-cell RNA-sequencing data. Nat. Commun. **15**(1), 912 (2024)

21. Hrovatin, K., Sikkema, L., Shitov, V.A., et al.: Considerations for building and using integrated single-cell atlases. Nat. Methods **22**(1), 41–57 (2025)
22. Xu, C., Cai, L., Gao, J.: An efficient scRNA-seq dropout imputation method using graph attention network. BMC Bioinform. **22**(1), 582 (2021)
23. Chang, L.Y., Hao, T.Y., Wang, W.J., et al.: Inference of single-cell network using mutual information for scRNA-seq data analysis. BMC Bioinform. **25**(suppl. 2), 292 (2024)
24. Peyvandipour, A., Shafi, A., Saberian, N., et al.: Identification of cell types from single cell data using stable clustering. Sci. Rep. **10**(1), 12349 (2020)
25. Li, J., Yu, C., Ma, L., et al.: Comparison of Scanpy-based algorithms to remove the batch effect from single-cell RNA-seq data. Cell Regen. **9**(1), 10 (2020)
26. Alavi, A., Bar-Joseph, Z.: Iterative point set registration for aligning scRNA-seq data. PLoS Comput. Biol. **16**(10), e1007939 (2020)
27. Büttner, M., Miao, Z., Wolf, F.A., et al.: A test metric for assessing single-cell RNA-seq batch correction. Nat. Methods **16**(1), 43–49 (2019)

Author Index

X. Cui et al. (Eds.): ISBRA 2026, LNBI 16690, pp. 393–394, 2027.
https://doi.org/10.1007/978-981-92-3716-6

MIX
Papier aus verantwortungsvollen Quellen
Paper from responsible sources
FSC® C105338
FSC
www.fsc.org

If you have any concerns about our products,
you can contact us on
ProductSafety@springernature.com

In case Publisher is established outside the EU,
the EU authorized representative is:
Springer Nature Customer Service Center GmbH
Europaplatz 3, 69115 Heidelberg, Germany

Printed by Libri Plureos GmbH
in Hamburg, Germany